American

Local

Government

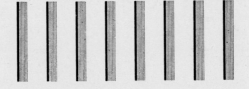

GEORGE S. BLAIR

Claremont Graduate School

Harper & Row, Publishers

New York, Evanston, and London

H-P

Contents

v

Four. *Processes of Local Government*

Five. *Local Finance*

Six. *Public Services*

Seven. *Metropolitan Areas*

Eight. *A Look Ahead*

Figures

Tables

Preface

By and large, American local government has been analyzed segmentally. There are a number of books devoted to some aspect rather than the whole design of our pattern of local government. Thus, we have books concerning city government, county government, rural government, urban government, or government in metropolitan areas. While the form and practice of city and county government will be emphasized, this book encompasses all major divisions of local government—counties, cities, townships, towns, school and other special districts—and includes three chapters on governmental patterns and problems in metropolitan areas.

In addition to this comparative treatment of the several types of local governmental units, there are other aspects of this book which differentiate it from currently available textbooks. One difference concerns the discussion of the major governmental processes at the local level. Several chapters are devoted to a comparative description of the legislative, executive, judicial, and administrative functions rather than giving them hasty analysis in discussing alternative patterns of government. Secondly, there has been an attempt to weave local government theory into the discussion throughout the book. Current literature in this field in both book and article form is surprisingly void of such discussion and a frame of reference is desirable in discussing problems of contemporary change and proposals for local government reorganization. A third difference relates to the internal treatment of the material. The writer has attempted to avoid overworked cliches and stereotypes in describing governmental structure, processes and services, and has drawn widely from materials and writings in other social sciences. Local government can be more meaningfully studied when it is viewed in its cultural context, and writings in related disciplines are quite helpful in this regard.

It is pertinent to assert that the writer holds certain value judgments about American local government. The first of these is a belief in the tradition and values of local self-government. In current times both the theoretical justification and practical significance of local government are often challenged. One purpose of this book is to rechallenge these challenges through an analysis of their content and implication to American local government. A second value judgment is a belief that institutions of local government currently need strengthening in our federal system. Intergovernmental cooperation is a fine thing and is on the increase at both federal-local and state-local levels. But cooperation implies voluntary relationships, not forced or mandatory administrative requirements. Further, there is a difference between local assistance in setting goals and establishing programs, and local administration of centrally determined goals and programs. A third belief is the premise that local governments and their institutions are too often resistant of reforms and change which are both needed and desirable. Local government can be effective government only if the local communities meet the needs of their citizens effectively.

I should like to acknowledge my appreciation and give proper credit to the many students and practitioners of local government who have helped me as critics and in supplying information. Unfortunately, I cannot even name them because of their number. Two persons, however, must be singled out for special appreciation. One, Charles S. Hyneman, my major teacher in graduate school, has remained a continuing teacher, friend and gadfly. The other, my wife Gloria, provided constant encouragement and understanding in addition to typing the original manuscript and its revision.

While it is conventional to do so, it is also quite proper to add that the responsibility for debatable conclusions—and errors of fact—are mine alone.

Claremont, California GEORGE S. BLAIR

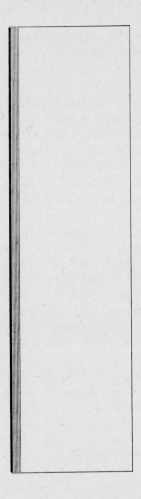

THE SETTING OF
LOCAL GOVERNMENT

One

Tradition and Values
of Local Government

1

In the present era of convenience and comfort, it is difficult to visualize the struggles of the early settlers in laying the foundations of our nation. Yet it is fitting that we remind ourselves of these heroic endeavors. The beginnings of popular government in the New World were early established in the small settlements along the Atlantic seaboard and spread upward, downward and in to the inland communities. Though the names now sound strange, local government had its beginnings in population clusters or land divisions variously known as manors, shires, hundreds, parishes, gores, plantations, tenths, liberties, and hamlets, as well as in the more familiar towns, townships, boroughs and counties.

The struggle to conquer the wilderness began successfully with the English settlement at Jamestown, Virginia, in 1607. Within three decades, communities appeared both up and down the Atlantic coast. The site of New Amsterdam on Manhattan Island was selected in 1625 for the trading center of the Dutch West India Company. By 1650, the future New York had achieved a population of 1,000 inhabitants. The city of Boston was founded in 1630. Located at the mouth of the Charles River, this site had the natural commercial advantage of a landlocked port open most of the year. Often called the first important city in American history, Boston attained a population of 1,200 by 1640 and about 2,000 in 1650. The point has been made that commercial advantage was the most important single factor in the location of early cities and towns, although some communities were founded for reasons of conscience or politics.[1]

The county as a unit of local government appeared first in Virginia where such units were established in 1634. The Virginia county served four essential purposes since it was entrusted with functions heretofore scattered in administrative areas, militia districts, election districts and judicial areas. A similar pattern of county government was adopted in Massachusetts in 1643. In that year, the Bay Colony created four counties or shires which were not only patterned after their English prototypes but bore the English names of Essex, Middlesex, Norfolk and Suffolk. Following the British victory over the Dutch in 1664, counties evolved from areas known as ridings which were laid out in the middle colonies under the Duke of York's laws. These three colonial experiences in establishing counties seem largely similar on the surface; however, the governmental ecology in the colonies differed markedly. The county was not too important as a unit in the New England area, since the people settled in small clusters with the town becoming the dominant local governing unit. In the southern colonies, settlements were more dispersed and the county became the more important unit. Both the town and county were important in the middle colonies, with the relative powers of the two varying among the four colonies of this geographic section.[2]

The actual chartering of municipal corporations did not begin until the early 1650s. The inhabitants of Boston petitioned the General Court of Massachusetts on four occasions between 1650 and 1677 that "they might become a corporation." While the General Court indicated a willingness to grant the charter, nothing came of

[1] The historical data in this paragraph and in those to follow in this section are adapted from information in Carl Bridenbaugh, *Cities in the Wilderness: The First Century of Urban Life in American, 1625–1742*, Ronald Press, 1938; Edward Channing, *Town and Country Government in the English Colonies of North America*, Johns Hopkins University Studies in Historical and Political Science, October, 1884; George E. Howard, *An Introduction to the Local Constitutional History of the United States*, Vol. I, Johns Hopkins University Studies in Historical and Political Science, 1889; H. L. Osgood, *The American Colonies in the Seventeenth Century*, Macmillan, 3 vols., 1904–1907; and Henry Cabot Lodge, *A Short History of English Colonies in America*, Harper, 1881.

[2] The reasons for the establishment of these three systems of local government in the colonies will be discussed in some detail in Chapter 2.

these requests and existing records do not offer a satisfactory explanation for their failure. The first municipal charter in America was granted to New Amsterdam in 1653 by the director of the Dutch West India Company. The charter was a rudimentary one but it did provide for a government of burgomasters and schepens and for some measure of home rule. In 1664, the Dutch charter was altered by the British by changing the titles of the local officials to mayor and common council, but the status of New York as a chartered municipality remained intact. The privilege of self-government there was further enlarged by a third charter granted in 1685. In the New England colonies, no boroughs or towns were granted charters but it is probable that these units enjoyed a greater freedom in practice than they would have been granted under the terms of specific charters.

The lack of corporate status, however, did not prevent colonial towns from assuming an important position. The towns of Hartford, Wethersfield, and Windsor were founded in the Connecticut Valley by a group of migrants led by the liberal-minded Thomas Hooker who fled eastern Massachusetts for religious reasons. In 1639, these three towns expressed their *de facto* independence and adopted the Fundamental Orders of Connecticut as a constitution for their joint governance. In regard to civil affairs, this document provided that the inhabitants, their successors and those who might join them there in the future should be "guided and governed according to such laws, rules, orders and decrees as shall be made, ordered and decreed."

This brief historical statement is presented here only to illustrate the point that units of local government have experienced a longevity significantly greater than that of the thirteen original states as states or of our national government. The tradition of local government was firmly embedded in the American colonies and the values of such units in the success of democratic government in the United States has never seriously been questioned.

The general acceptance of American local government in the late eighteenth century is implicit in the Constitution, which was ratified by the thirteen states starting in 1787. This document establishing our federal system recognizes only a two tier scheme of government in the United States, and thus does not consider the question of how power should be distributed between the states and their political subdivisions. This seeming oversight, however, reveals the

Framers' intent that the creation and supervision of local governments was and should remain entirely the concern of the states. Local governments had proven their necessity and desirability in colonial times for such purposes as judicial, militia, taxing and administrative centers. Thus, it was presumed that the states would not only utilize existing units of local government but would also establish additional units to serve state purposes as well as to supervise affairs in smaller communities.

The reasonableness of this interpretation of the intent of the Framers is borne out by policies advanced in the Northwest Ordinances of 1785 and 1787. These laws were enacted by the Continental Congress under the Articles of Confederation as a blueprint for the general pattern of government in the western territories. The Ordinance of 1785, commonly called the "Land Ordinance," provided for the survey and sale of these lands. The Ordinance of 1787 provided for governmental organization of the territory, including the creation of counties and townships as units of local government. This Act also guaranteed the sanctity of private contracts, abolished the age-old law of primogeniture, prohibited slavery and involuntary servitude, and contained a rudimentary statement of human rights.[3] Most of the humanitarian provisions of this Ordinance became part of the Constitution in the first amendments added to it, and subsequent Congresses traced the course of new states by the provisions prescribed in this basic Act.

■ Defense of Local Democracy

Democracy is not an easy concept to explain adequately. As defined in *Webster's Collegiate Dictionary*, it is "government by the people; government in which the supreme power is retained by the people and exercised either directly (absolute, or pure democracy), or indirectly (representative democracy) through a system of representation." Government by the people in the United States, however, means more than simply government by the majority. Certain basic rights are guaranteed to all the people whether they are members of the current majority or members of groups within the minority. Thus, our system of democracy reflects three basic principles—majority rule, minority rights, and political equality.

[3] R. H. Nelson and J. J. Wuest, *The Primary Sources of American Government*, Putnam, 1962, pp. 45–49.

According to MacIver, "Democracy is not the rule of 'the masses' nor is it something for 'the masses' only. Democracy is not the enthronement of mediocrity, to the disadvantage of the elite, the enlightened, the cultivated. Democracy is the political liberation of all men from the chains of power. . . . Democracy provides the way of liberation alike from mass intolerance and from the ruthlessness and corruption of power. . . . Democracy gives equal rights to all men. And in doing so it breaks all barriers of education, of culture, and of opportunity, that formerly set men hopelessly apart, as preordained inferiors and superiors."[4]

The rationalization of democracy in local government is largely the same as that for democracy in general and cannot be developed very adequately in only a few paragraphs. It is commonly accepted that the core concepts of democratic theory evolve around the nature of the individual citizen from which the concept of the state in which he lives is developed. This sequence of roles is in sharp contrast to other systems of government which explain the nature of the state first and then construct the concept of man around his life and duties as a citizen of the state. Two central threads of the democratic theory are the Greek contribution of the capacity of man to reason and the Christian concept of man as a creature of God. Embracing the doctrine of the rationality of man, Christianity developed the theory of equality, a basic tenet in democratic dogma.

Beginning with these concepts of the equality of man, the tenet of freedom developed logically. Within the limits of action not harmful to his fellowmen, democratic theory holds that man is free to will and determine his own public and private activities. The qualification on this freedom, that man's actions must not harm his fellowmen, is an important concept leading to the establishment of sanctions and communities to enforce them on errant members of society. Thus, the citizen became a member of a civil community and was a shareholder of its power in that he has the right and duty to participate in its political processes.

Democratic theory also embraces a preference for the method by which community decisions or will is registered. In terms of procedure, this method can be described in simple terms as a process of ratification by the electorate following discussion of the issues at hand. As principles for a machinery of government, Charles Wilson states that the spirit and methods of democracy imply three such

---

[4] Robert M. MacIver, *The Ramparts We Guard*, Macmillan, 1950, pp. 42–43.

guides: first, political decisions must be taken by a system in which all citizens can share; second, political decisions must be made only after discussion and vote; and third, political decisions must be made so that a process of continuing public political education is carried on.[5] Since universal discussion and consent are highly impracticable, if not impossible, in modern society, the concept of representative democracy rather than direct democracy is both desirable and acceptable as a meaningful adaptation of democratic theory in local as well as in central government.

Institutions of American local government are designed to meet these three fundamental requirements of functioning democracy—participation, discussion and education. Our local governments across the nation enable their citizens to share in political decision-making and in the administration or carrying out of policies so determined; they provide the media of discussion to inform the citizen, and the machinery to enable him to register his voice of consent or disapproval; and the governments and their agencies operate in the public eye to further the continuing political education of the voters. Since the citizen can truly share in the local political process, the democracy of local government in action is its own best justification and rationalization.

It would be theoretically possible to design a system of democratic central government without democratic local governments within the larger community. But such a plan would be extremely difficult to adapt into a community previously governed under an alternative system or to institute as a first experiment in self-government in a new nation. It is also possible that the theoretically perfect system would fail miserably in actual application. Thus, we can conclude that democratic local governments are not only a desirable counterpart of democratic national government but that they are necessary and vital partners in and to the larger community.

■ Values of Local Government

The case for the affirmative concerning the values of local self-government has been very convincingly made by two foreign observers of the American scene. Following his visit to the United

    [5] Charles H. Wilson (ed.), *Essays on Local Government*, Basil Blackwell, 1948, p. 16.

States, the French statesman, Alexis de Tocqueville, expressed his admiration of township government in New England in these words, "In the township, as well as everywhere else, the people are the source of power; but nowhere do they exercise their power more immediately. In America the people form a master who must be obeyed to the utmost limits of possibility." In commenting on local government more generally, de Tocqueville wrote, "Yet municipal institutions constitute the strength of free nations. Town meetings are to liberty what primary schools are to science; they bring it within the people's reach, they teach men how to use and how to enjoy it. A nation may establish a free government, but without municipal institutions it cannot have the spirit of liberty."[6]

The second foreign observer, James Bryce, an Englishman, based his arguments for local self-government largely upon his reflections of the American and Swiss systems which he had observed. He described small communities as the "tiny fountain-heads of democracy, rising among the rocks, sometimes lost altogether in their course, sometimes running underground to reappear at last in fuller volume. They suffice to show that popular government is not a new thing in the world, but was in many countries the earliest expression of man's political instincts." In commenting further on local government in the United States, Bryce stated; "These examples justify the maxim that the best school of democracy and the best guarantee of its success, is the practice of local self-government."[7]

Americans, however, are not immune from lauding the values of their local governments. A staff report to the President's Commission on Intergovernmental Relations in 1955 stated that "Local governments are to total government what basic tissues are to the human body. Without them, government would have no vitality." In a similar vein, the staff report added, "The counties, cities, towns, villages, and boroughs serve as training schools for the leaders of government and in the affairs of local government are tried those who aspire to State and National office."[8]

One of the positive virtues of local self-government accrues from

[6] Alexis de Tocqueville, *Democracy in America,* Vol. I, Vintage Books, 1954, pp. 63-64.

[7] James Bryce, *Modern Democracies,* Vol. I, Macmillan, 1921, pp. 131-3.

[8] Advisory Committee on Local Government, *Local Government,* a report to the Commission on Intergovernmental Relations, Government Printing Office, 1955, p. 9. While the Commission did not repeat this flowery phrasing in its *Report,* its general acceptance of this philosophy seems rather apparent.

the important services which these units provide through officials who are selected by, are close to, and who know the problems of the citizenry of the community. Through these processes of approving services to be rendered, choosing persons to administer them, and checking upon their performance in office, the vital democratic processes of participation, discussion and political education are in visible operation to both office-holder and constituent alike.

Evolving from the conditions described above, the positive concept of community becomes meaningful to the citizens within its boundaries. A sense of common interest in community affairs arises from the many opportunities for local service, and it becomes a common duty of the citizens to see that their representatives perform efficiently and honestly. Although a popular song would have us believe that "anywhere I hang my hat is home," studies of sociologists underscore the direct and indirect values if alienation from the local political process is to be avoided. Such alienation sometimes occurs among recent migrants to urban centers who fail to identify themselves with their new and larger communities. As a result, the responsibility for controlling the local government is abdicated to others.[9]

A third positive virtue in local government is the "schoolroom of democracy" concept. Service in local government not only trains men and women to work for others but to work with others since government at any level involves a large measure of compromise. Service in local institutions often serves as a springboard for service in branches of state and national government. In Pennsylvania, a former mayor of the largest city was elected to the United States Senate in 1956 and a former mayor of the state's second largest city won the office of governor in 1958. The same story is and has been repeated in a number of states across the nation. A second aspect of the "schoolroom of democracy" concept results from the wide citizen participation in government which is possible at the local level. The large number of boards, commissions, offices and committees provide opportunities for participation by a large num-

[9] Three informative and illuminating articles which elaborate upon this thesis are: Robert C. Angell, "The Moral Integration of American Cities" in Paul K. Hatt and Albert J. Reiss, Jr. (eds.), *Cities and Society,* rev. ed., The Free Press, 1957, pp. 617-30; Basil G. Zimmer, "Participation of Migrants in Urban Structures," *American Sociological Review, 20* (April, 1955), 218-24; and Morris Axelrod, "Urban Structure and Social Participation," *American Sociological Review, 21* (February, 1956), 14-18.

ber of citizens and helps generate a feeling of actual sharing in the processes of community self-government.

A fourth contribution of local governments is their role as administrative agencies of the state. Many of the programs and services provided by city and county governments result from the carrying out of policies prescribed by the state government, and in some cases even policies of the national government, as with county agricultural agents, welfare administrators and civil defense directors. Local application of centrally determined policies results in modification of these more general goals to local conditions, local social and economic needs, and local cultural patterns. The role of administrative unit of the state is important in another way in that state policies are often established after consultation with local administrators or upon recommendations of committees or commissions which include representatives from local governments.

A fifth positive benefit of local self-governing institutions is their contribution to the development of local centers of thought and action. According to Arthur E. Morgan, "for the preservation and transmission of the fundamentals of civilization, vigorous, wholesome community life is imperative. Unless many people live and work in the intimate relationships of community life, there can never emerge a truly unified nation or community of mankind. If I do not love my neighbor whom I know, how can I love the human race, which is but an abstraction? If I have not learned to work with a few people, how can I be effective with many?" He continues by stating, ". . . the small community has supplied the lifeblood of civilization, and neglect of it has been one of the primary reasons for the slowness and the interrupted course of human progress."[10] Many small units of local government would not be recognized as communities in the sense Morgan uses the term while some neighborhoods in large cities would be so identified. The key test of community, according to Morgan, is an attitude and action pattern of common attention to matters of common concern rather than a pattern of action in which citizens respond and act in highly individualistic ways.

While these general statements concerning the values of local self-government are commonly accepted, they have not gone unchallenged by writers and other observers of the American scene.

[10] Arthur E. Morgan, *The Small Community*, Harper, 1942, pp. 3, 19.

Some persons feel that democracy cannot effectively be served by outworn or outdated forms or units and that such obsolete institutions must be scrapped and replaced by new ones which are better fitted to our modern pattern of living. Arthur C. Millspaugh advanced this argument some 25 years ago when he wrote, "Few facts have been found and few principles have been established regarding the role of 'local self-government' in the drama of democracy. Here, indeed, is a rich and almost unpenetrated field awaiting exploration. Localized democracy has tremendous emotional support. Many impartial students give it their benedictions. It has been the subject of some obituaries. Its praises have been sung, but its values have not been scientifically determined. Until they are, it is doubtful whether the concept of local self-government deserves any large place in a realistic political science. The concept, once vitally related to facts, may at present be worse than irrelevant to the ideal of popular government. It may now be merely another example of 'the degradation of the democratic dogma.' "[11]

A second critical voice is that of William Anderson who has skillfully countered the major political arguments for small governmental units. Concerning the "school of self-government" concept, Anderson suggests that the school needs both a new teacher and a new curriculum and that many of its "classrooms" are merely experiences in parochialism, parsimony and extravagance. The principle of keeping government close to the people is not always complemented by the demands of these same people for new and improved public services. Anderson points out that the standards of efficient administration in terms of minimum population requirements, economic support, or accommodation to geographical features may run counter to the political tenets of "grass-roots" governments.[12] Anderson, however, is a staunch supporter and defender of local government and his plan for a "rationalized" system of local governments will be discussed in some detail in a subsequent chapter.

Other critics point out the wide gap between the theory and practice of American local government. While citizens, practitioners, and writers almost uniformly applaud the ideas of grass-roots gov-

[11] Arthur C. Millspaugh, *Local Democracy and Crime Control,* The Brookings Institution, 1936, p. 69.

[12] William Anderson, *The Units of Government in the United States,* Public Administration Service, 1945, pp. 40–41.

ernment, an apparently strong case can be made to show their failure to practice it. Voting statistics support this criticism since actual voter registrations seldom total more than three-fourths of the potential number and voter participation in local elections often measures less than half the registered total. However, even such substantiating evidence for this hypothesis might lead to the drawing of unwarranted conclusions. Perhaps the core of the local self-government concept is the psychological fact that the opportunity to participate exists, rather than the quantitative response to this opportunity as measured by the turnout on election day. Certainly, the odds of being heard are more favorable in a typical local government than in a government at a higher level, and the wide acceptance of the idea that "my voice is effective when I choose to use it" should not be too strictly measured against the frequency of its use as an indicator of its basic importance.

■ *Importance of Local Government*

Pluralism is a necessary feature of a citizen's interest in his government. There are many factors which determine an individual's interest in the several units of local government in which he is a citizen (almost every voter is a resident of at least three governmental units—a county, a school district, and either a city or a special district) as well as his interest in his state and national government. Particularly since World War II, the American citizen has seen the spotlight of public interest and attention focused increasingly on the serious problems of national and international affairs. The shift in popular interest from the local to the national and international scenes was not sudden or unwarranted. Certainly, the problems of national security and international peace are deserving of the serious consideration of all citizens as are the many attendant national problems arising from the interactions of big government, big business, big labor, and big interest groups.

However, it is much more than a nostalgic sentiment or romanticized yearning for the good old days that prompts the writer to believe in the present and continued importance of strong units of local government. Perhaps "atoms of democracy" is a better phrase than "pillars of democracy" to describe the place of local units in our federal system. The term atom represents a basic unit of matter;

in a political sense, the local community represents the basic unit of government. The Lincoln-coined "government of the people, by the people, for the people" can still accurately describe the citizen's role in the affairs of his local government, while his role in higher levels of government becomes more one of choice and ratification rather than of participation and consent.

Although we often hear much about the march of power from the city hall and county courthouse to the state capitol, the obligations of local governments continue to increase and the services they provide grow in both number and importance. Public education, public health, protection of person and property, recreation, water supply and sewage disposal facilities are truly vital services and each is still supplied principally by local governments. In 1950, the board of supervisors in Milwaukee County was responsible for more than 200 different services, compared to only 36 a century ago.[13] The functions of both city and county government have expanded markedly in recent years as new or increased services are offered in such diverse program areas as hospitals, recreation, housing, renewal, airports, libraries, planning, and zoning.

A further evidence of the importance of local governments is the increasing budgets to provide these services. There is a possible fallacy in equating quantity with quality, but certainly the continued growth of local governmental expenditures attests to the acceptability of these services by the citizens who demand and pay for them. In 1960 alone, the total expenditures of local governments reached an all-time high of $35.8 billion as compared to a new record total of state government expenditures of $25.3 billion.[14] Local government expenditures have increased over fivefold since 1929 and were three times as great in 1960 as they were in 1948.

The fact that local government is big business is also shown by the five and a half million full and part-time workers on its payrolls and the expenditure of $18.2 billion for their services in 1960. While this expenditure represents a new high and is truly a considerable amount, it should not be forgotten that many of the "citizen-politicians" at the local level receive little or no compensation other than the satisfaction that comes from serving one's neighbors and community. Many of these local employees are truly

[13] Citizens' Governmental Research Bureau, *Citizens at Work*, Milwaukee, 1950.
[14] Lillian P. Barnes, George M. Cobren, and Joseph Rosenthal, "State and Local Activity," *Survey of Current Business*, *41* (March, 1961), 16–24.

amateurs in governmental administration, but their service in a way gives some balance to the total picture of government service which must increasingly rely on the use of experts and career public servants at the higher levels. Since the concept of democracy implies the type of citizen interest and service which is found at the local level, local governments can still be described as the bulwark of American democracy.

Another argument for the importance of local government can be built around the nature of the problems they face currently and will be called upon to face in the future. While problems of water supply, public health, education, care for dependents, transportation, urban renewal, etc., cannot compete with international problems for the interest of the citizen, nevertheless it is essential that approaches which solve or ameliorate these and the myriad other local problems be determined—hopefully—within the framework of local democratic institutions. The single factor of population mobility raises problems which all three levels of government are attempting to meet, but it is in the day-by-day operations of the local governments that the problems must be met head-on. Whether the population base of a particular community is expanding or contracting, the problems of adjustment in increasing or curtailing services, in finding new revenue sources, in responding to citizen needs and demands, are truly tremendous ones which must be solved largely within the local area with the sympathetic understanding and assistance of higher levels of government.

The increasing concern of our state and national governments with programs to meet local problems and pressures is a further testimony to the importance of these communities in our governmental system. As local problems become common to many places, they become of considerable importance and pass from local to higher governmental levels for action. They become of state or national concern because of their importance to local communities, rather than because they are basically statewide or nationwide in scope.

In the immediate years ahead, citizens are almost certain to continue to focus their major attention on higher levels and to take their local governments for granted. Although the activities of local governments may remain somewhat obscured, their underlying importance will also remain. The reasons for this rather paradoxical condition have been aptly phrased in these words: "No incumbent mayor or city councilman will ever sign a treaty of peace ending all war; no city engineer will ever build a hydrogen bomb; no police chief will ever command a victorious United Nations army; but these local officials . . . will determine whether the several communities in which we live will remain relatively civilized and decent."[15]

SUGGESTED READINGS

Books

Adrian, Charles R., *Governing Urban America,* 2nd ed. (New York: McGraw-Hill, 1961).

Anderson, William, *The Units of Government in the United States* (Chicago: Public Administration Service) 1945.

Advisory Committee on Local Government, *Local Government, A Report to the Commission on Intergovernmental Relations* (Washington: Government Printing Office, 1955).

Bridenbaugh, Carl, *Cities in the Wilderness, The First Century of Urban Life in America, 1625–1742,* (New York, Ronald, 1938).

Commission on Intergovernmental Relations, *A Report to the President for Transmittal to Congress* (Washington: Government Printing Office, 1955), Chap. II.

de Tocqueville, Alexis, *Democracy in America,* Vol. I (New York: Vintage Books, 1954).

Gettell, Raymond G., *History of American Political Thought* (New York: Appleton-Century, 1928), Chap. XVIII.

Maass, Arthur (ed.), *Area and Power, A Theory of Local Government* (New York: The Free Press, 1959), Chaps. I, II, III.

Martin, Roscoe C., *Grass Roots* (University, Ala.: University of Alabama Press, 1957).

Millspaugh, Arthur C., *Local Democracy and Crime Control* (Washington: Brookings Institution, 1936).

Mumford, Lewis, *The City in History* (New York: Harcourt, Brace and World, 1961).

National Resources Committee, *Our Cities* (Washington: Government Printing Office, 1938).

Wilson, Charles H. (ed.), *Essays in Local Government* (Oxford: Basil Blackwell, 1948).

---

[15] Stephen K. Bailey, H. D. Samuel, and Sidney Baldwin, *Government in America,* Holt, Rinehart and Winston, 1957, p. 455.

Articles

Herson, Lawrence J. R., "The Lost World of Municipal Government," *American Political Science Review*, 51 (June, 1957), 330–44.

Langrod, Georges, "Local Government and Democracy," *Public Administration*, 31 (Spring, 1953), 25–34.

Long, Norton E., "Aristotle and the Study of Local Government," paper presented at American Political Science Association Meeting, Boulder, Colorado, September 8, 1955.

Snider, Clyde F., "American County Government: A Mid-Century Review," *American Political Science Review*, 46 (March, 1952), 66–80.

Historical Foundations
of American Local
Government

2

American local government has an ancient lineage reaching far back in history.[1] The system of local institutions in the colonies strikingly resembles the pattern of local government existing at that time in England. This should not be unexpected since most of the earliest settlers came from England and brought their homeland's ideas, concepts and institutions to the New World. Thus, the colonists transplanted the English pattern of local government in their new land. However, not all of these agencies and institutions survived and modifications were evolved by the practical colonists to fit the needs of their strange and undeveloped surroundings.

■ *Local Government in England*

Three types of local governing agencies existed in the ninth century when the several small kingdoms of the Anglo-Saxons were

[1] For an interesting study which traces these roots back to Rome in the time of Caesar and Tacitus, see George E. Howard, *Local Constitutional History of the United States*, Vol. I, Johns Hopkins University Studies in Historical and Political Science, 1889, esp. Chaps. I, V, and VI.

ments was not free land waiting to be claimed. Rather all such lan~~~ were considered to be the property of either the crown or of th~~ charter colony itself. By 1640, no one was permitted to settle in such lands without a grant. It was the policy of the Massachusetts General Court to award such grants only to groups of seven or more persons who desired to live and worship together. Thus, the grants were for the dual purposes of establishing towns and erecting churches.[7] A third cause was that the social philosophy of the ~~~ritans affected their economic, political, and religious institutions ~~~the extent that they wanted all to be centered in the small area ~~~he town.

~~~he New England town of this period can properly be defined as ~~~all territorial area the inhabitants of which belonged to a single ~~~h. Since the practice was to fine persons for absence from ~~~meetings and to censure them for non-attendance at church, it ~~~perative that these towns be small in area to permit all to ~~~both civic and religious meetings without undue incon~~~ ~~~e or personal danger. One astute observer has written that, ~~~w England Meeting House is the symbol of much that is ~~~istic of New England life. Its erection was the starting ~~~ every one of the earlier New England communities, and it ~~~he rallying point of everything that is distinctive in their

~~~ England town, as a unit of local government, combined ~~~s of the town, parish and manor of England. The con~~~ affairs was handled at the annual town meeting and ~~~meetings which were called from time to time. The ~~~ began as an assemblage of the persons who held the ~~~roprietors to decide such matters as the site for the ~~~out of the village green and the division of tillable ~~~ for themselves as individual proprietors. Just as the ~~~began as a means for settling questions of local ~~~ts main purpose continued to be for this same ~~~ider and pass upon such matters as extent of re~~~ch, the need and location for a new highway, the ~~~to be raised by taxation for the coming year.

~~~the town meeting still holds much charm for ~~~ince this was and is our closest experience to

~~~ 24.
~~~ President Porter.

united to form the kingdom of England. These were the shires, hundreds, and townships.[2] The shires were created in the areas of some of the older separate kingdoms and these districts retained certain limited features of self-government. The lineage of the office of sheriff in the American county can be traced to the position of shire-reeve who served as the chief representative of the crown in these local districts. Each shire at this time also served as a judicial area with a semiannual court to administer justice in both civil and criminal matters.

Below the shire was the district known as the hundred. These were of varying size but normally consisted of three or more townships. Their chief agency of government consisted of a monthly court composed of landlords and township representatives. These officials served as deputies of the shire-reeve who twice each year visited each of the hundred courts. The township served more as a social and economic rather than as a political unit and it was normally a small rural community. However, local civic affairs were managed by a town reeve and a constable who were chosen by the inhabitants of the township. The citizens also selected four representatives to serve as their agents along with the town reeve and local priest in the courts of the hundred and the shire.

Following the Norman Conquest of England in 1066, the role of the nobility in the shires declined and the powers of the sheriff were enhanced. The name of the area was changed from shire to county, and the sheriff became the chief agent of the central government. He became the king's representative in military affairs, was granted greater financial powers, and his duties as a police and judicial officer were strengthened. Another change was effected when feudal manorial courts developed to replace the courts of the old hundred. The chief officer in the manor was the lord's steward whose position locally was similar to that of the sheriff for the county as a whole. A new type of officer developed in the thirteenth century with the appointment of justices of the peace. Gradually, these justices gained in authority at the expense of the older offices of

[2] Excellent discussions of English local government from the ninth to the seventeenth century are found in: Charles A. Beard, *The Office of Justice of the Peace in England*, Columbia University Press, 1904; Edward Channing, *Town and Country Government in the English Colonies of North America*, Johns Hopkins University Studies in Historical and Political Science, 1884; John A. Fairlie and Charles M. Kneier, *County Government and Administration*, Century, 1930, Chap. I; and M. M. Knappen, *Constitutional and Legal History of England*, Harcourt, Brace, 1942.

sheriff, coroner, and constable and they became administrative as well as judicial officials.

During the five and a half centuries following the Norman Conquest and before the founding of the colonies in America, the system of local government and institutions developed into the system which was transplanted to the New World. The local units known as towns and parishes were often used as interchangeable terms by both the common and educated people at this time. The inhabitants of one town were the parishioners of one church and thus both terms were used for both a territorial division and its citizenry.[3] As a unit, the town or parish was responsible for the preservation of peace, maintenance of highways, care of the poor, and for the transaction of other town or parish business. The major town officers were the constable, churchwardens, swornmen and waymen who were usually elected at regular town meetings. However, there was considerable diversity among towns and parishes due to varying local traditions. The phrasing of a seventeenth-century writer is sufficiently quaint and descriptive to warrant quoting in full. Concerning the method of choosing local officials, he wrote, "where the custom of the place is for the jury in the leet to choose these officers, there they may and must be chosen still; for this is a good way and custom and the best way of choosing these officers; but where the custom is otherwise there it may be otherwise."[4]

During this same period the justices of the peace had emerged as the principal administrative officers in the counties. While the number varied from 20 to 60 in individual counties, they were commonly chosen from the rural gentry by the lord chancellor. Their powers and duties were many and varied, and legal textbooks of the time required over 500 pages just to enumerate their functions, which were both judicial and administrative. Other important county officers were the sheriff, the lord lieutenant who supervised the local militia, the coroner, the keeper of the records, and the clerk of the peace who was the prototype of the present county clerk.[5]

Other local units remained or had evolved during this period, but they were less important than the county and town or parish.

[3] Channing, op. cit., pp. 9–11.
[4] From James Spedding (ed.), Works of Francis Bacon, Vol. VIII, p. 70, as quoted in Channing, op. cit., p. 14.
[5] Howard, op. cit., p. 315.

The hundred still existed but served primarily as a district taxing and militia purposes. Manors were becoming fewer in number and the local nobility continued to lose the privileges they formerly enjoyed. Boroughs were organized in some urban and a few cities operated under royal charters. In most cases governments of the boroughs and cities were controlled by a number of persons. In some boroughs, the local officials operated as a closed corporation by filling vacancies in their membership, while in others aldermen were either elected by taxpayers or by a limited class of freemen.

Briefly, this was the pattern of local government in England the time the American colonies were founded and this was pattern which was introduced onto American soil by the settlers. Adaptations and modifications actually resulted in velopment of three basic patterns of local government colonies. These were the New England town system, system in the southern colonies, and the county-town in the middle colonies. While there were many similar the three, there were also important differences.

■ The New England Town System

Local government in New England started as among the first settlers. Thus, the unincorpora the basic governing unit in Massachusetts, necticut and Rhode Island. In part, this pa dictated by the geography of the area. founded along the coastline or inland or Neither the soil nor the climate encourag parcels of land or dwelling in scatt flourished because it served the econom

There were other reasons which e settlement in New England. First, forded a means of protection aga system of land ownership held tha

[6] For further discussion of the rise growth and development, see Channin VII; Herman G. James, Local Gov and Co., 1921, Chap. II; and John 1620–1930, Harvard University Pre

democracy in its purest form. However, it was not entirely practicable for even these small towns to govern themselves completely
by direct popular government. There was always the need for selected officials and representatives to look after the affairs of the
community between general meetings and to administer the functions ratified at them. The major functions of the town included the
care of the poor, maintenance of roads, support of public elementary
schools, preservation of peace, registration of land titles and regulation of business enterprises. The town also served as a unit for tax
assessment and collection, for judicial purposes, for militia organization, and for representation in colonial assemblies.

At the annual town meeting, the citizens chose a committee of
selectmen to exercise general supervision over the affairs of the
town and selected such other officers as constable, treasurer, surveyor, assessors, fence viewers, and clerks of the market. These
officers, however, were limited by the reserve authority of the
citizens to make major policy decisions at the town meeting. The
town meeting functioned as a day of reporting as well as a day of
policy-making. The citizens had their say at these meetings about
what had been done as well as in making clear what they wanted
done in the future and how it was to be accomplished.

The committee of citizens known as selectmen or townsmen was
the most important of the town officers. These committees ranged
in number from three to 13 and were all popularly elected for terms
of one year at the annual town meeting. The duties of the selectmen
were many and varied, depending in part upon the specific instructions given them by the citizens. They summoned the town meetings, served as election officers, supervised the common lands,
handled financial matters, administered the specific programs approved by the town meeting, and usually exercised some judicial
powers. Other important officers included a town clerk, who served
as the register of deeds and recorder of vital statistics; a constable,
who was responsible for the preservation of peace and law enforcement; surveyors of highways, who planned the routes of new roads,
reported on maintenance needs of existing roads and recommended
the days on which able-bodied male citizens would devote their
labors to the laying or improvement of roads; and overseers of the
poor.

There were a number of advantages in the town meeting method
of running the affairs of the community. For one thing, the powers

held in reserve by the citizens probably enhanced the concept that the elected officers of the town were the servants and not the masters of the people who chose them. Second, the people actually shared equally in the processes of government and were reassured that they could not only influence their government but also control its actions. And third, the citizen's appreciation of the oft-stated concept that government exists to do those things which the citizens cannot do individually was no doubt sharpened. Here the citizens themselves attempted to provide a responsible and acceptable government for a group of people all of whom did not always want the same things.

A major problem which arose under the town meeting system concerned the degree of distinction, if any, which should be made between the proprietors who founded the town and the later citizens who joined them there. Generally, the newer citizens were admitted as full inhabitants possessing all political rights except the right of sharing in the control of the common lands of the town. This custom lead to interesting and protracted struggles in some towns which usually ended in a compromise such as that agreed to at the town meeting in Boston in 1640. At that meeting, the citizens approved the concept of equal rights of commonage to all those who were currently inhabitants of Boston, while denying such rights to those who might become citizens at a later date.[9]

Founded in 1630, Boston grew from a population of 1,200 in 1640 to 12,000 in 1720. A list of town officials in 1690 is both interesting and informative as to the range of its economic activities. These officials were "ten constables, seven surveyors of highways, four clerks of the market, four sealers of leather, six hog reeves, three criers, sixteen corders of wood, eight overseers of wood-corders, four overseers of chimneys, and thirty-six tithingmen."[10] The town meetings of Boston fill a glorious page of American history since the people of this town under the leadership of Samuel Adams led the opposition to British control which led to the Revolutionary War.[11] Boston retained its town meeting form of government until 1822, when it had reached the sizeable population of 40,000 inhabitants.

[9] Howard, *op. cit.*, pp. 54–55.
[10] *Ibid.*, p. 99.
[11] James K. Hosmer, *Samuel Adams, The Man of the Town-Meeting*, Johns Hopkins University Studies in Historical and Political Science, 1884, pp. 5–60.

While the town developed as the basic unit of local government in New England, there were other local units including plantations, villages, townships, precincts, districts and counties. The term plantation there was used to connote a community in the making but one which had not yet acquired the dignity of a town. Villages were specific plantations made by a town, such as Charlestown Village. "Township" came to be used synonymously with "town," but at first the term meant tracts of land granted for the purpose of settling towns. Precincts and districts were terms used indiscriminately to describe subdivisions of towns and parishes for either civil or religious purposes, and there is no accepted definition for either term.

Counties were established at an early date in Massachusetts and such units were organized later in the neighboring colonies. As mentioned in Chapter 1, the Bay Colony was divided into the four counties of Essex, Middlesex, Norfolk and Suffolk in 1643. However, this division was little more than a formal recognition of what had existed in fact since 1636, when the judicial affairs of the colony were decentralized into four quarter courts. The principal functions of the county remained its judicial administration in both civil and criminal affairs. However, the role of the county court in civil administration increased in importance. Among its functions, the court approved town by-laws in some areas, equalized tax apportionments among the towns, licensed retailers of liquors and keepers of coffee houses, registered land titles, recorded deeds, counted votes for other elective county officers, audited the accounts of other county officers, and erected prisons.

The principal county officers were the commissioners or members of the county court who were originally appointed by the governor, but who later were chosen locally by the towns, subject to the approval of higher authorities. The system of town delegates to the county court which evolved in Massachusetts is actually quite similar to the board of supervisors system which exists today in a number of American counties and is certainly the forerunner of the supervisor system as it developed in the middle colonies. The commissioners were responsible for the administration of most of the functions listed above, but, particularly in financial administration, the county court exercised considerable authority. The court established the county tax rate, equalized assessments between towns and properties, and established standards and regulations for taxes payable in kind by setting prices for corn and other produce and for beaver skins, all of which were receivable in payment.[12]

Other officers of the county court included the marshal, who was later superseded by the sheriff; the clerk; the treasurer; and the chief militia officer. Methods of filling these four offices underwent a varied history. Sometimes they were appointed by the county court, at other times appointed by the royal governor, and later they were popularly elected by the qualified voters of the county.

The Massachusetts pattern of county government was adopted in its general form in New Hampshire, Maine and Connecticut. Counties were not organized in Rhode Island until 1703 and they served only as judicial districts in that colony. It can be generalized that the county played a relatively minor administrative role in the New England colonies. Its functions were not insignificant, but they did not match those of its counterpart in the southern colonies, and counties have never achieved many governmental functions in this portion of the United States, even to the present time. As a result, counties as governing units do not exist today in Connecticut and Rhode Island, and they have only limited functions other than judicial in Maine, Massachusetts, New Hampshire, and Vermont.[13]

■ The County System

The rise of the county as the dominant unit of local government in the southern colonies was a natural response to their prevailing economic and social conditions. Just as town government flourished in New England because it served the needs of the settlers, so did the county in the more southernly areas. And again, there are a number of reasons for the emergence of this unit over the alternate units of local government.[14]

The geography and climate of Virginia contrasted sharply with that of Massachusetts. Here the climate was suited to rural living

[12] Howard, op. cit., pp. 39–44.

[13] The five counties in Rhode Island continue to this day as judicial districts, but they have no county governing body for performing the usual functions of county governments. The eight Connecticut counties were formally disbanded as of October 1, 1960.

[14] For a fuller discussion of the system of county government as it developed in the southern colonies, see Channing, op. cit.; Howard, op. cit., Chap. IX; Fairlie and Kneier, op. cit.; and Clyde F. Snider, Local Government in Rural America, Appleton-Century-Crofts, 1957.

united to form the kingdom of England. These were the shires, hundreds, and townships.[2] The shires were created in the areas of some of the older separate kingdoms and these districts retained certain limited features of self-government. The lineage of the office of sheriff in the American county can be traced to the position of shire-reeve who served as the chief representative of the crown in these local districts. Each shire at this time also served as a judicial area with a semiannual court to administer justice in both civil and criminal matters.

Below the shire was the district known as the hundred. These were of varying size but normally consisted of three or more townships. Their chief agency of government consisted of a monthly court composed of landlords and township representatives. These officials served as deputies of the shire-reeve who twice each year visited each of the hundred courts. The township served more as a social and economic rather than as a political unit and it was normally a small rural community. However, local civic affairs were managed by a town reeve and a constable who were chosen by the inhabitants of the township. The citizens also selected four representatives to serve as their agents along with the town reeve and local priest in the courts of the hundred and the shire.

Following the Norman Conquest of England in 1066, the role of the nobility in the shires declined and the powers of the sheriff were enhanced. The name of the area was changed from shire to county, and the sheriff became the chief agent of the central government. He became the king's representative in military affairs, was granted greater financial powers, and his duties as a police and judicial officer were strengthened. Another change was effected when feudal manorial courts developed to replace the courts of the old hundred. The chief officer in the manor was the lord's steward whose position locally was similar to that of the sheriff for the county as a whole. A new type of officer developed in the thirteenth century with the appointment of justices of the peace. Gradually, these justices gained in authority at the expense of the older offices of

[2] Excellent discussions of English local government from the ninth to the seventeenth century are found in: Charles A. Beard, *The Office of Justice of the Peace in England,* Columbia University Press, 1904; Edward Channing, *Town and Country Government in the English Colonies of North America,* Johns Hopkins University Studies in Historical and Political Science, 1884; John A. Fairlie and Charles M. Kneier, *County Government and Administration,* Century, 1930, Chap. I; and M. M. Knappen, *Constitutional and Legal History of England,* Harcourt, Brace, 1942.

sheriff, coroner, and constable and they became administrative as well as judicial officials.

During the five and a half centuries following the Norman Conquest and before the founding of the colonies in America, the system of local government and institutions developed into the system which was transplanted to the New World. The local units known as towns and parishes were often used as interchangeable terms by both the common and educated people at this time. The inhabitants of one town were the parishioners of one church and thus both terms were used for both a territorial division and its citizenry.[3] As a unit, the town or parish was responsible for the preservation of peace, maintenance of highways, care of the poor, and for the transaction of other town or parish business. The major town officers were the constable, churchwardens, swornmen and waymen who were usually elected at regular town meetings. However, there was considerable diversity among towns and parishes due to varying local traditions. The phrasing of a seventeenth-century writer is sufficiently quaint and descriptive to warrant quoting in full. Concerning the method of choosing local officials, he wrote, "where the custom of the place is for the jury in the leet to choose these officers, there they may and must be chosen still; for this is a good way and custom and the best way of choosing these officers; but where the custom is otherwise there it may be otherwise."[4]

During this same period the justices of the peace had emerged as the principal administrative officers in the counties. While the number varied from 20 to 60 in individual counties, they were commonly chosen from the rural gentry by the lord chancellor. Their powers and duties were many and varied, and legal textbooks of the time required over 500 pages just to enumerate their functions, which were both judicial and administrative. Other important county officers were the sheriff, the lord lieutenant who supervised the local militia, the coroner, the keeper of the records, and the clerk of the peace who was the prototype of the present county clerk.[5]

Other local units remained or had evolved during this period, but they were less important than the county and town or parish.

[3] Channing, op. cit., pp. 9–11.
[4] From James Spedding (ed.), Works of Francis Bacon, Vol. VIII, p. 70, as quoted in Channing, op. cit., p. 14.
[5] Howard, op. cit., p. 315.

The hundred still existed but served primarily as a district for taxing and militia purposes. Manors were becoming fewer in number and the local nobility continued to lose the privileges they had formerly enjoyed. Boroughs were organized in some urban areas and a few cities operated under royal charters. In most cases, the governments of the boroughs and cities were controlled by a small number of persons. In some boroughs, the local officials actually operated as a closed corporation by filling vacancies in their own membership, while in others aldermen were either elected by local taxpayers or by a limited class of freemen.

Briefly, this was the pattern of local government in England at the time the American colonies were founded and this was the pattern which was introduced onto American soil by the early settlers. Adaptations and modifications actually resulted in the development of three basic patterns of local government in the colonies. These were the New England town system, the county system in the southern colonies, and the county-township system in the middle colonies. While there were many similarities among the three, there were also important differences.

■ The New England Town System

Local government in New England started as a community affair among the first settlers. Thus, the unincorporated town emerged as the basic governing unit in Massachusetts, New Hampshire, Connecticut and Rhode Island. In part, this pattern of settlement was dictated by the geography of the area. Early communities were founded along the coastline or inland on the banks of the rivers. Neither the soil nor the climate encouraged the cultivation of large parcels of land or dwelling in scattered homesites. The town flourished because it served the economic, social and political needs.[6]

There were other reasons which explained this pattern of town settlement in New England. First, such compact communities afforded a means of protection against Indian attacks. Second, the system of land ownership held that territory beyond the first settle-

[6] For further discussion of the rise of the town in New England and its growth and development, see Channing, *op. cit.*; Howard, *op. cit.*, Chaps. II and VII; Herman G. James, *Local Government in the United States*, D. Appleton and Co., 1921, Chap. II; and John F. Sly, *Town Government in Massachusetts, 1620-1930*, Harvard University Press, 1930.

ments was not free land waiting to be claimed. Rather all such lands were considered to be the property of either the crown or of the charter colony itself. By 1640, no one was permitted to settle in such lands without a grant. It was the policy of the Massachusetts General Court to award such grants only to groups of seven or more persons who desired to live and worship together. Thus, the grants were for the dual purposes of establishing towns and erecting churches.[7] A third cause was that the social philosophy of the Puritans affected their economic, political, and religious institutions to the extent that they wanted all to be centered in the small area of the town.

The New England town of this period can properly be defined as a small territorial area the inhabitants of which belonged to a single church. Since the practice was to fine persons for absence from town meetings and to censure them for non-attendance at church, it was imperative that these towns be small in area to permit all to attend both civic and religious meetings without undue inconvenience or personal danger. One astute observer has written that, "The New England Meeting House is the symbol of much that is characteristic of New England life. Its erection was the starting point of every one of the earlier New England communities, and it has been the rallying point of everything that is distinctive in their history."[8]

The New England town, as a unit of local government, combined the functions of the town, parish and manor of England. The control of town affairs was handled at the annual town meeting and the special meetings which were called from time to time. The town meeting began as an assemblage of the persons who held the land as joint proprietors to decide such matters as the site for the church, the layout of the village green and the division of tillable land into farms for themselves as individual proprietors. Just as the town meeting began as a means for settling questions of local public policy, its main purpose continued to be for this same function—to consider and pass upon such matters as extent of repairs for the church, the need and location for a new highway, the amount of money to be raised by taxation for the coming year.

The concept of the town meeting still holds much charm for many Americans since this was and is our closest experience to

[7] Channing, *op. cit.*, p. 24.
[8] *Ibid.*, p. 22, quoting a President Porter.

democracy in its purest form. However, it was not entirely practicable for even these small towns to govern themselves completely by direct popular government. There was always the need for selected officials and representatives to look after the affairs of the community between general meetings and to administer the functions ratified at them. The major functions of the town included the care of the poor, maintenance of roads, support of public elementary schools, preservation of peace, registration of land titles and regulation of business enterprises. The town also served as a unit for tax assessment and collection, for judicial purposes, for militia organization, and for representation in colonial assemblies.

At the annual town meeting, the citizens chose a committee of selectmen to exercise general supervision over the affairs of the town and selected such other officers as constable, treasurer, surveyor, assessors, fence viewers, and clerks of the market. These officers, however, were limited by the reserve authority of the citizens to make major policy decisions at the town meeting. The town meeting functioned as a day of reporting as well as a day of policy-making. The citizens had their say at these meetings about what had been done as well as in making clear what they wanted done in the future and how it was to be accomplished.

The committee of citizens known as selectmen or townsmen was the most important of the town officers. These committees ranged in number from three to 13 and were all popularly elected for terms of one year at the annual town meeting. The duties of the selectmen were many and varied, depending in part upon the specific instructions given them by the citizens. They summoned the town meetings, served as election officers, supervised the common lands, handled financial matters, administered the specific programs approved by the town meeting, and usually exercised some judicial powers. Other important officers included a town clerk, who served as the register of deeds and recorder of vital statistics; a constable, who was responsible for the preservation of peace and law enforcement; surveyors of highways, who planned the routes of new roads, reported on maintenance needs of existing roads and recommended the days on which able-bodied male citizens would devote their labors to the laying or improvement of roads; and overseers of the poor.

There were a number of advantages in the town meeting method of running the affairs of the community. For one thing, the powers

held in reserve by the citizens probably enhanced the concept that the elected officers of the town were the servants and not the masters of the people who chose them. Second, the people actually shared equally in the processes of government and were reassured that they could not only influence their government but also control its actions. And third, the citizen's appreciation of the oft-stated concept that government exists to do those things which the citizens cannot do individually was no doubt sharpened. Here the citizens themselves attempted to provide a responsible and acceptable government for a group of people all of whom did not always want the same things.

A major problem which arose under the town meeting system concerned the degree of distinction, if any, which should be made between the proprietors who founded the town and the later citizens who joined them there. Generally, the newer citizens were admitted as full inhabitants possessing all political rights except the right of sharing in the control of the common lands of the town. This custom lead to interesting and protracted struggles in some towns which usually ended in a compromise such as that agreed to at the town meeting in Boston in 1640. At that meeting, the citizens approved the concept of equal rights of commonage to all those who were currently inhabitants of Boston, while denying such rights to those who might become citizens at a later date.[9]

Founded in 1630, Boston grew from a population of 1,200 in 1640 to 12,000 in 1720. A list of town officials in 1690 is both interesting and informative as to the range of its economic activities. These officials were "ten constables, seven surveyors of highways, four clerks of the market, four sealers of leather, six hog reeves, three criers, sixteen corders of wood, eight overseers of wood-corders, four overseers of chimneys, and thirty-six tithingmen."[10] The town meetings of Boston fill a glorious page of American history since the people of this town under the leadership of Samuel Adams led the opposition to British control which led to the Revolutionary War.[11] Boston retained its town meeting form of government until 1822, when it had reached the sizeable population of 40,000 inhabitants.

[9] Howard, op. cit., pp. 54–55.
[10] Ibid., p. 99.
[11] James K. Hosmer, Samuel Adams, The Man of the Town-Meeting, Johns Hopkins University Studies in Historical and Political Science, 1884, pp. 5–60.

While the town developed as the basic unit of local government in New England, there were other local units including plantations, villages, townships, precincts, districts and counties. The term plantation there was used to connote a community in the making but one which had not yet acquired the dignity of a town. Villages were specific plantations made by a town, such as Charlestown Village. "Township" came to be used synonymously with "town," but at first the term meant tracts of land granted for the purpose of settling towns. Precincts and districts were terms used indiscriminately to describe subdivisions of towns and parishes for either civil or religious purposes, and there is no accepted definition for either term.

Counties were established at an early date in Massachusetts and such units were organized later in the neighboring colonies. As mentioned in Chapter 1, the Bay Colony was divided into the four counties of Essex, Middlesex, Norfolk and Suffolk in 1643. However, this division was little more than a formal recognition of what had existed in fact since 1636, when the judicial affairs of the colony were decentralized into four quarter courts. The principal functions of the county remained its judicial administration in both civil and criminal affairs. However, the role of the county court in civil administration increased in importance. Among its functions, the court approved town by-laws in some areas, equalized tax apportionments among the towns, licensed retailers of liquors and keepers of coffee houses, registered land titles, recorded deeds, counted votes for other elective county officers, audited the accounts of other county officers, and erected prisons.

The principal county officers were the commissioners or members of the county court who were originally appointed by the governor, but who later were chosen locally by the towns, subject to the approval of higher authorities. The system of town delegates to the county court which evolved in Massachusetts is actually quite similar to the board of supervisors system which exists today in a number of American counties and is certainly the forerunner of the supervisor system as it developed in the middle colonies. The commissioners were responsible for the administration of most of the functions listed above, but, particularly in financial administration, the county court exercised considerable authority. The court established the county tax rate, equalized assessments between towns and properties, and established standards and regulations for taxes

payable in kind by setting prices for corn and other produce and for beaver skins, all of which were receivable in payment.[12]

Other officers of the county court included the marshal, who was later superseded by the sheriff; the clerk; the treasurer; and the chief militia officer. Methods of filling these four offices underwent a varied history. Sometimes they were appointed by the county court, at other times appointed by the royal governor, and later they were popularly elected by the qualified voters of the county.

The Massachusetts pattern of county government was adopted in its general form in New Hampshire, Maine and Connecticut. Counties were not organized in Rhode Island until 1703 and they served only as judicial districts in that colony. It can be generalized that the county played a relatively minor administrative role in the New England colonies. Its functions were not insignificant, but they did not match those of its counterpart in the southern colonies, and counties have never achieved many governmental functions in this portion of the United States, even to the present time. As a result, counties as governing units do not exist today in Connecticut and Rhode Island, and they have only limited functions other than judicial in Maine, Massachusetts, New Hampshire, and Vermont.[13]

■ *The County System*

The rise of the county as the dominant unit of local government in the southern colonies was a natural response to their prevailing economic and social conditions. Just as town government flourished in New England because it served the needs of the settlers, so did the county in the more southernly areas. And again, there are a number of reasons for the emergence of this unit over the alternate units of local government.[14]

The geography and climate of Virginia contrasted sharply with that of Massachusetts. Here the climate was suited to rural living

[12] Howard, *op. cit.,* pp. 39–44.

[13] The five counties in Rhode Island continue to this day as judicial districts, but they have no county governing body for performing the usual functions of county governments. The eight Connecticut counties were formally disbanded as of October 1, 1960.

[14] For a fuller discussion of the system of county government as it developed in the southern colonies, see Channing, *op. cit.*; Howard, *op. cit.,* Chap. IX; Fairlie and Kneier, *op. cit.*; and Clyde F. Snider, *Local Government in Rural America,* Appleton-Century-Crofts, 1957.

and the rich native soil was favorable for the growth of tobacco. Its production was so profitable that it was grown in the streets of the only village which existed in the early years of settlement. Thus colonists were encouraged to locate on farms rather than to congregate in group settlements. The Virginia terrain was cut by large navigable rivers which made it possible to establish interior ports to rival the coastline cities as trading centers. The method of transferring land from the crown or colony to private ownership also differed fundamentally from the system used in New England. Since large plantations for farming were both possible and economically feasible, land was usually given or sold in large tracts to individuals or small companies. The pattern of settlement took the form of a manor with the owner surrounded by his tenants and servants rather than by others of equal economic status who would share in its management. The clusters of people on the plantation differed in this important respect from those settling a New England town. The land system in Virginia has been described as one which seemed to secure the largest amount of land to the smallest number of persons, and as such it was diametrically opposed to the system used in New England.[15]

Just as in New England, there was a close relationship between the church and local government. The parish, as a rule, was a division of the county primarily for religious purposes, but the governing body of the parish had considerable authority in civil affairs. The governing board was known as the vestry and it consisted of twelve persons. It elected churchwardens, provided the parson with a home and salary, presented ministers for induction, supervised the work of the churchwardens in poor relief administration, counted tobacco, arrested and sold negroes improperly freed, and recorded property limits within the parish. Originally, vestrymen were chosen by popular vote, but by 1675 each vestry had become a closed corporation and vacancies were filled by the remaining members. Thus, the office became almost hereditary and the vestry became a social class in itself.

The two churchwardens, chosen annually by the vestry from among its own membership, served as its executive agents. They were the fiscal officers of the parish, collecting and disbursing funds in support of the church. The churchwardens also served as

---

[15] Channing, *op. cit.*, p. 25.

moral protectors of the parish and they were required to make presentations in writing to the county court for such offenses as drunkenness, swearing, and fornication. Two other parish officers were the sexton and clerk, who were appointed either by the incumbent minister or by the vestry to assist the minister in his religious duties and record-keeping.

In addition to the plantation and parishes, the hundred was also an early land division in Virginia. The county and the parish absorbed the limited functions of the hundred, but early records indicate that it was originally a division of coordinate importance with the plantation and parish. When the first assembly of burgesses was called in 1619, two representatives from each of three hundreds appeared alongside the representatives from cities and plantations.[16] However, there was no revival of the old English hundred in Virginia and these early districts became *de facto* parishes. Occasionally the term guift is also found in early records of the dominion colony. Apparently this was a term used synonymously with plantation, or perhaps more technically, to describe a plantation which resulted from a gift of land rather than from its purchase. The term borough was sometimes used to designate an election district for the house of burgesses before the county became the constituent unit.

The sharp contrast between vestry government in Virginia and the town meeting in New England has been vividly pointed out by one writer in these words: "Town government satisfied the people of New England because the heads of families determined what government would do. The Virginia vestry, in contrast, became an organization by which one class of people got the kind of government they wanted while the rest of the people got the kind of government they were allowed to have."[17]

There was little opportunity for political activity on the large, scattered plantations, and the county or shire evolved as a unit better suited to care for the governmental as well as the judicial needs of parish citizens. Size of the unit had little relationship to its name since in some cases the county and parish were identical in area, while in others a single parish might include two or more counties. However, the most common pattern was for a county to be comprised of several parishes. Judicial functions prompted the

[16] Howard, *op. cit.*, p. 273.
[17] Charles S. Hyneman, "Our Systems of Local Government," p. 11 of Chap. XIV of an unpublished manuscript dated 1950.

rise of the county in Virginia. The colonial governor and council had been ordered to divide the colony into counties for judicial purposes in 1618, but instead the court of record was authorized to sit monthly in several sections of the colony. In 1634, however, the colony was divided into eight counties which were patterned after the English shire and were to be governed by county lieutenants, sheriffs, and sergeants and baliffs where the need required.[18]

The county was created in Virginia as a territorial division of the colony whose inhabitants normally belonged to one militia district, one election district, and one judicial and administrative area. The county court which was both the judicial and administrative agency consisted of eight or more justices who were appointed by the governor. After the initial appointments, however, the apparent practice was for the governor to appoint persons nominated by the justices themselves. Thus, the county court became a closed corporation composed of the leading gentry of the county and paralleling the form of the vestry in the parishes. This pattern of non-elective county government in the south was to continue throughout the colonial period and was not altered in any significant way until the fever of Jacksonian democracy swept the nation in the late 1820s and 1830s. The appeals of the Jackson-inspired movement for popular election, short terms, and an expanded suffrage base transformed the major county offices into elective positions.

The general administrative functions of the county court included the construction of bridges and highways, regulation of ferries, offering of bounties for killing wolves, appointment of tobacco viewers, licensing and regulation of occupations, regulation of relations between whites and Indians, and the admission of attorneys to legal practice. For fiscal purposes, the county court divided the county into taxing districts. After determining the monies needed for the year, assessments were apportioned among the several properties in each of the tax precincts. In addition, the county court was the collection agency for the state-imposed poll tax. The county also served as the unit of representation for the colonial assemblies of burgesses and as the sole unit of militia organization. The command of the county militia was under the office of county lieutenant who received his appointment from the governor.

In addition to the county court and county lieutenant, there were

[18] Channing, *op. cit.*, pp. 43–44.

other appointive county officers. The county court itself appointed a clerk who performed the usual duties of recorder, while the sheriff was the chief executive officer. Originally, he was a member of the court with the longest period of service, holding the office for one year and then yielding it to the next in line in point of continuous service. Later, however, he was appointed by the governor from a list of names of three justices nominated by the county court. The sheriff acted as tax collector and treasurer of the county and as election officer for selecting representatives for the house of burgesses. The coroner was also appointed by the governor and the county land surveyor was appointed by the surveyor general of the colony.

Although there were settlements which served as cities, no provision was made for incorporated cities in Virginia until early in the eighteenth century. The first charter of incorporation was granted to Williamsburg in 1722 and it was soon followed by similar grants to Norfolk and Richmond, with all three grants coming from the office of the colonial governor. The governing bodies of these early cities consisted of common councils made up of mayors, recorders, aldermen, and councilmen sitting as single administrative and legislative bodies. The council had authority to enact by-laws and ordinances which were not in conflict with colonial statutes and to administer such affairs as the establishment of market-places, public buildings, preservation of order, police and fire protection services, and street improvement.[19]

While the pattern of local government which evolved in Virginia became dominant in other southern colonies, two other systems developed and existed for a time in the Carolinas and Georgia. The proprietary colony of Carolina was governed from 1669 to 1691 under the Fundamental Constitutions generally attributed to John Locke and Anthony Ashley Cooper. These established a medieval, feudal political structure in which land ownership and social rank were synonymous. Sectionalism and unrest resulted in the division of the colony into North and South Carolina and their establishment as royal colonies in 1729. Georgia, originally a part of South Carolina, became a charter colony in 1732. James Oglethorpe and his associates were granted the right to settle this area and encouraged its settlement by paupers and imprisoned debtors. Little

[19] James, *op. cit.*, pp. 80–82.

local government developed in Georgia since the trustees were forced to the cynical conclusion that "many of the poor who had been useless in England were inclined to be useless likewise in Georgia."[20] Counties were not organized in Georgia until after the Revolutionary War.

In the course of the later colonial period and in the early years of statehood, differences in the patterns of county and city government did emerge in the southern states. However, it is generally correct to state that a common pattern of strong county-parish government developed in the south just as the single pattern of strong town-county government was dominant in the New England colonies.

The actual differences between the county-parish and the town-county systems are often overstated. Both sections were settled primarily by English peoples and both were settled in part by the ventures of commercial companies. And in both sections, the county was a later development growing out of needs arising from the town and plantation systems of local settlements. Here lies an important difference, however. The town remained the basis of social organization in New England while the municipal divisions in the southern counties weakened. Thus, the two patterns did differ in several important respects. First, town governments were less extensive in area and hence more numerous than were county governments. Second, because of the larger number and smaller area of the towns, there was a greater opportunity for the actual citizen participation in government than was provided in the county system. Third, the towns developed a large measure of local self-government with popularly elected officers while the county was administered by appointive officers. Finally, the town served less as an administrative area of the colonial government than did the county and hence it enjoyed a greater degree of autonomy than did the southern county.

■ The County-Township System

As with the town-county and county-parish systems, geographical, economic, social, religious, and political factors were important influences in the middle colonies of New York, Pennsylvania, New

[20] Warren Miller, *A New History of the United States*, George Braziller, 1958, p. 71.

Jersey, and Delaware. The system which developed in this section has often been called a compromise between the two patterns existing in the neighboring colonies to the north and south. Its distinguishing feature is the division or distribution of authority for local rural government between the county and its subdivision, the township, rather than its concentration in a single unit as in the New England town or in the southern county. Under this system of divided local authority, the county was stronger than in New England but somewhat weaker than its southern counterpart, and the township was stronger than the southern parish but had less authority than the New England town.[21]

The impact of geography is noticeable since the division of the county was and still is known as town rather than township in New York, while township was and remains the preferred name in the other three middle colonies. Economically, there appears to have been no system for land development in the middle colonies except for the short-lived Dutch system briefly described below. Also, two great commercial towns, New York and Philadelphia, grew early and dominated cultural and social life as well as economic life in this area. The religious background of the early settlers was considerably more heterogeneous than in the other two regions. Rather than a single dominant church as the Puritans in New England or the Anglicans in Virginia, there was a mixture of Puritanism, Anglicanism, Quakerism, and Catholicism in the middle colonies.

As for the political factor, the first settlements in both New York and Pennsylvania were made by the Dutch under the New Netherlands Company, which became the Dutch West India Company in 1629. A system of local government paralleling somewhat the feudal manors in Europe was the intended pattern of settlement by the Dutch. Large tracts of land, sixteen miles along a navigable river on one bank or eight miles along both banks and of indefinite width were to be granted to patroons who established colonies of 50 or more persons of over 15 years of age. The patroons were granted the land as a perpetual inheritance and were entitled to the "fruits, rights, mines, and fountains thereof," along with a monopoly of the "fishing, fowling, and grinding" rights.[22] The patroons were also

[21] General sources for the information relating to the county-township pattern in the middle colonies are as follows: Channing, *op. cit.*; Howard, *op. cit.*, Chaps. III, VIII; James, *op. cit.*, Chap. II; and John A. Fairlie, *Local Government in Counties, Towns and Villages,* Century, 1906, Chaps. I, II, III.

[22] Howard, *op. cit.*, p. 103.

to exercise all governmental powers over the settlers on their estates and no settlements were to be permitted outside these manors. While the system of patroonships was planned for general use, only five were actually granted by the Dutch. Of the three which made any attempt at settlement, only one survived for any length of time.

Thus, the Dutch settlers attempted to establish a system of settlement which allowed no rights of self-government to the colonists. Settlers were required to remain in the service of the patroon for the time which they had bound themselves for passage to the New World. Since these policies were not too attractive to prospective emigrants, a new charter was granted in 1640 modifying the privileges of the patroons, creating a new class of small proprietors, and authorizing the creation of municipal governments to consist of magistrates and justices of the peace. These officers were selected to handle the judicial and administrative affairs of the communities by higher authorities from three names submitted by the towns and villages. Following this change of policy, a number of hamlets and small villages were settled in New York and Pennsylvania.

After the defeat of the Dutch by the English in 1664, a system of local government was authorized by the Duke of York's laws. Combining features of both the English and the New England patterns of local development, this code provided for the establishment of both county and town governments. The governing body of the town consisted of a constable and eight overseers who possessed legislative, financial, executive, and judicial powers. The overseers served two-year terms of office, with four elected each year by the freeholders. The constable's term was for one year and he was chosen by the voters from among the four retiring overseers. In addition, two of the overseers served as churchwardens whose chief duty was to present in writing to the courts charges relating to misdemeanors such as "Swearing, prophaness, Sabbath breaking, Drunkenness, fornication, Adultery, and all such abominable Sinnes."[23] Annual town meetings were also provided for but these seemed to have been called for the sole purpose of electing town officers. Thus, town government in New York and Pennsylvania tended to be representative rather than pure democracy as in New England.

Foundations of county government in New York were also laid

[23] *Ibid.*, pp. 108-09.

by the Duke of York's laws with the establishment of ridings, which were judicial districts comprising several towns. These units were administered by a sheriff who received his appointment from the governor and by a court of sessions which was comprised of several justices. The territories of the twelve counties created in 1683 followed the boundaries of the old ridings in general and the county court corresponded in both function and jurisdiction to the riding court. At first the county in the middle colonies was governed by a county court and other officers common to county government generally in the colonies.

However, on June 19, 1703, a law of great importance to American local government was passed by the New York colonial Assembly.[24] This act created the essential features of county-township government as it exists today by establishing a county board of supervisors comprised of one supervisor from each township in the county to function as the civil administrative body of the county. Thus, non-judicial administration passed from the county court to the new board, resulting in a separation of administrative and judicial functions in county government. The county board was responsible for the levying and collection of taxes and for the appointment of the county treasurer. At this time, the county court still exercised some administrative duties in such areas as licensing, regulation of business, and approval of rules and regulations of other public bodies. However, this separation of administrative and judicial powers and the evolution of a county board to administer the non-judicial affairs were important steps which not only affected the form of local government in the middle colonies but also in all the states which were to be carved later from the western wilderness.

A significant modification in the plan for selecting the county board was initiated in Pennsylvania in 1724.[25] A law of that year provided that three commissioners would be elected at large in each county to manage the fiscal affairs of the county in place of the justices of the peace who had exercised this power until this time. Like the board of supervisors in New York, this body became the chief administrative authority of the county in Pennsylvania. Unlike the New York board, however, the Pennsylvania board was composed of three persons elected for the county as a whole rather than as a board composed of township representatives. From this law

[24] *Ibid.*, p. 111.
[25] James, *op. cit.*, p. 87.

and its administration developed the so-called commissioner system of elective county boards as distinguished from the supervisor system in which county members hold their office *ex officio* because of their positions in local units within the county.

There were also differences in the systems which developed in the four middle colonies. As indicated above, the town was the basic unit in New York since it served as the constituent unit of the county board as well as being a strong political unit in itself. A similar pattern of strong township government occurred in New Jersey. In Pennsylvania, on the other hand, strong county government evolved in place of strong township organization, and this general pattern was also true in Delaware. However, the generalization holds that the pattern of local government in the middle colonies falls into a somewhat common mold of a dual system of county and township government.

The subdivisions which lay within the counties in the four colonies were not always known as towns or townships. For instance, these smaller units had such interesting and varied names as tenth, city, town corporate, village, hamlet, and liberty in New Jersey. Gradually, however, the term township came to replace these more colorful names. In Delaware, local authority below the county was centered in a unit known as the hundred rather than the township. The relationship of the hundred to the Delaware county, however, was the same as the township-county relationship in Pennsylvania, and the hundred may be presumed to be a misnamed township in Delaware rather than a revival of the old English unit known as the hundred.

As mentioned earlier, New York and Philadelphia soon became the dominant economic and cultural centers of the middle colonies. In 1690, both had populations of roughly 4,000 people and were second only to Boston as urban centers in the New World. The patterns of government in the two cities were similar and the political institutions developed were similar to those in Boston. New York, which had received the first colonial borough charter under Dutch rule in 1653, received a similar charter under the Duke of York's laws in 1664. Local affairs were under the management of a mayor and common council. In Philadelphia, the county court and the provincial council of Pennsylvania controlled the local affairs until 1684 when it became a borough. Philadelphia received its first charter in 1691 providing for government by a mayor and common council, but there was limited participation by the freeholders since council vacancies were filled by the council itself as a closed corporation. The charter of 1701, granted by William Penn, differed little from the original charter except that councilmen were granted life tenure and the mayor was an appointee of the colonial governor. However, the city was endowed with the usual municipal powers of the time and exercised them in a manner quite similar to that in New York.[26]

There was one other feature of local government in the middle colonies that is worthy of discussion. Except for the specifically chartered borough corporations, the units of local government, including the counties, were considered to be subdivisions of the colony for administrative convenience. In this way, the relationship of local governments to the colonial government was more like that in the southern than in the New England colonies. Thus, the distinction between municipal and quasi-municipal governments arose to distinguish between those which were created primarily for the satisfaction of local needs (such as cities and boroughs), and those such as counties which were created principally as units of state administration. Although this distinction between cities and counties is gradually lessening, in many states the county is still legally regarded as only a quasi-municipal incorporation.[27]

■ A Territorial Plan of Local Governments

As noted in Chapter 1, the blueprint for the general pattern of local government in the western territories which were to be admitted as states in the nineteenth and twentieth centuries was established in two fundamental laws enacted by the Continental Congress. Known as the Northwest Ordinances of 1785 and 1787, these laws provided for territorial government and for the creation of local governmental units in the western lands.[28]

[26] Carl Bridenbaugh, *Cities in the Wilderness, the First Century of Urban Life in America, 1625–1742*, Ronald, 1938, pp. 7–8, 144–5.

[27] George S. Blair, "The Changing Legal Status of Counties," *The County Officer, 21* (May, 1956), 92–94.

[28] For a fuller discussion of these ordinances and the system of local governments which were established in the Northwest Territory, see Howard, *op. cit.*, Chaps. IV and X; and Northwest Territory Celebration Commission, *History of the Ordinance of 1787 and the Old Northwest Territory*, 1937.

The Ordinance of 1785 is important because it provided for the laying out of the area of the Northwest Territory into congressional townships by a corps of surveyors under the direction of the geographer of the United States.[29] The language of the Ordinance itself is clear and specific, stating that "The surveyors . . . shall proceed to divide the said territory into townships of six miles square, by lines running due north and south, and others crossing these at right angles, as near as may be." This system was used in the entire future settlement of the United States, and its benefits have been great in number. The congressional or survey township, though quite different from the township as it had developed earlier in the middle colonies, still remains a unit of government in most midwestern states.

The Ordinance of 1787 further outlined a system of territorial and local government for the western lands. During the first stage of territorial status, the general government of the area was placed in the hands of a governor, a secretary, and judges who were appointed by the President by and with the consent of the Senate.[30] The governor was authorized to create proper divisions for the administration of civil and criminal matters, and he was empowered to "appoint such magistrates and other civil officers, in each county and township, as he shall find necessary for the preservation of the peace and good order in the same."

The second stage of development in a territory was reached when its population numbered 5,000 free male inhabitants of full age. At that time, the powers of legislation were transferred to the general assembly which was composed of the governor, a legislative council, and a house of representatives. The representatives were chosen by the people with the counties and townships serving as the constituent units. The general assembly had the power to prescribe the duties of magistrates and other civil officers in the counties and townships. The third stage of governmental evolution was achieved upon the admittance of the territory as a state with full rights and privileges in the federal union.

The formal inauguration of civil authority in the Northwest Territory occurred on July 15, 1788, and the first county was created

[29] At the time of its organization, the Northwest Territory included all of the present states of Ohio, Indiana, Illinois, Michigan and Wisconsin, and a portion of Minnesota.

[30] The act originally provided for the election of these officers by Congress, but this provision was amended as indicated in 1789.

eleven days later. Known as Washington County, it comprised about half of the present state of Ohio. The local officers provided for the county included the sheriff, coroner, treasurer, recorder of deeds, probate judge and justices of the county court of quarter sessions and common pleas.[31] Actually, local self-government had been begun in the territory some three months before by the arrival of a group of veteran officers and soldiers of the Revolutionary War at the site of Adelphia on April 7, 1788. The settlers enacted laws for their own common governance and security and officially promulgated them by nailing them to an oak tree for public inspection and information. The community shortly afterwards rechristened itself as Marietta.[32]

In 1790, a law was enacted by the territorial legislature to provide for township government by requiring the court of quarter sessions to divide the territory of the county into civil townships. A rudimentary government was provided through the offices of a constable, clerk, and one or more overseers of the poor. A more popular plan of organization was provided by an act of the general assembly in 1802 instituting the annual town meeting for the purpose of selecting the following township officials: "a clerk, two or more overseers of the poor, three fence viewers, two appraisers of houses, one lister of taxable property, one or more constables, a sufficient number of supervisors of roads, and three or more trustees or 'managers.' "[33] The latter were to exercise the general supervisory powers of a town board. In this listing of officials, the sectional compromise between eastern and southern influences can be detected resulting in a pattern which was quite similar to that already developing in the states which had been the former middle colonies.

■ *Local Governments under Early State Constitutions*

With the organization of state governments and the adoption of constitutions by the former colonies, the basic pattern of American local government remained unchanged. The patterns of the three systems continued in the various states which replaced the colonial governments. As a rule, the first state constitutions had little to say

[31] Howard, *op. cit.*, p. 415.
[32] Northwest Territory Celebration Commission, *op. cit.*, pp. 30–44.
[33] Howard, *op. cit.*, p. 144.

THE SETTING OF LOCAL GOVERNMENT

in regard to municipal government. An important exception was the New Jersey constitution which gave the township a constitutional basis by requiring that constables be elected at the annual town meetings in such communities.[34] Some changes were made in the selection of county officials, with the sheriff becoming an elective official in several states and the Georgia constitution providing for the popular election of several minor county officials.

The history of American local government since 1789 has been a colorful and a varied development. However, it is not the purpose of this book to present a history of local government except as some understanding of its beginnings aids in the appreciation of current forms and practice. Flashes of historical development will be cited in many of the subsequent chapters, but there will be no attempt to develop their contents in a chronological ordering of events.

SUGGESTED READINGS

Books

Beard, Charles A., *The Office of Justice of the Peace in England* (New York: Columbia University Press, 1904).

Bridenbaugh, Carl, *Cities in Revolt, Urban Life in America, 1743–1776* (New York: Knopf, 1955).

Bridenbaugh, Carl, *Cities in the Wilderness, The First Century of Urban Life in America, 1625–1742* (New York: Ronald, 1938).

Channing, Edward, *Town and County Government in the English Colonies of North America* (Baltimore: Johns Hopkins University Studies in Historical and Political Science, 1884).

Fairlie, John A., *Local Government in Counties, Towns and Villages* (New York: Century, 1906).

Fairlie, John A. and Kneier, Charles M., *County Government and Administration* (New York: Century, 1930).

Griffith, Ernest S., *History of American City Government—The Colonial Period* (New York: Oxford University Press, 1938).

Howard, George E., *Local Constitutional History of the United States,* Vol. I (Baltimore: Johns Hopkins University Studies in Historical and Political Science, 1889).

James, Herman G., *Local Government in the United States* (New York: Appleton, 1921).

---

[34] The text of these early state constitutions can be found in Francis N. Thorpe, *The Federal and State Constitutions*, 7 vols., Government Printing Office, 1909.

Knappen, M. M., *Constitutional and Legal History of England* (New York: Harcourt, Brace, 1942).

Lancaster, Lane W., *Government in Rural America*, 2nd ed. (New York: Van Nostrand, 1952).

Lodge, Henry Cabot, *A Short History of the English Colonies in America*, rev. ed. (New York: Harper, 1881).

Mumford, Lewis, *The City in History* (New York: Harcourt, Brace and World, 1961).

Northwest Territory Celebration Commission, *History of the Ordinance of 1787 and the Old Northwest Territory* (Marietta, 1937).

Osgood, Herbert L., *The American Colonies in the Seventeenth Century*, Vol. I (New York: Macmillan, 1904).

Sly, John F., *Town Government in Massachusetts, 1620–1930* (Cambridge: Harvard University Press, 1930).

Snider, Clyde F., *Local Government in Rural America* (New York: Appleton-Century-Crofts, 1957).

Thorpe, Francis N., *The Federal and State Constitutions*, 7 Vols. (Washington: Government Printing Office, 1909).

Articles

Alderfer, Harold F., "Historical Foundations of the American County," *The County Officer*, 20 (December, 1955), 246–51.

Beard, Charles A., "Teutonic Origins of Representative Government," *American Political Science Review*, 26 (February, 1932), 28–44.

Fast, Richard E., "A Southern Experiment in Township Government," *Sewanee Review*, 10 (April, 1902), 134–42.

Goodman, A. Bristol, "Westward Movement of Local Government," *Journal of Land and Public Utility Economics*, 20 (February, 1944), 20–34.

Types and Numbers
of Local Governments

3

A team of interplanetary social science researchers investigating local government in the United States would find their study both fascinating and frustrating. Either through travel around the country or through perusal of Bureau of the Census data, they would discover that 51 cities had populations in 1960 which exceeded that of our least populous state. Even more surprising would be their discovery that our largest city and county, New York City and Los Angeles County respectively, each contained more people than all but seven of the states.

These same facts, however, are equally fascinating and frustrating to students and teachers of American local government. While the basic structure of local government in the 1960s reflects the forms which developed during colonial days, there have been extensive changes in numbers, functions and size of local units. In 1962, the Census Bureau reported that there were 91,236 units in the United States. While this total sounds large, the number for the nation as a whole has been declining in the past two decades. The decline is accounted for through the consolidation of school districts and to a small decrease in the number of townships. The number of counties has remained almost constant, while both municipalities and special districts have increased. This point will be elaborated upon in a later section in this Chapter.

■ What is a Local Government?

There is no commonly accepted definition of what a local governmental unit is in the United States. Roger H. Wells has suggested that while scholars have difficulty in defining a local government the matter is a simple one to the average citizen. The citizen knows that our government is like all Gaul—divided into three parts—federal, state and local.[1] Thus, it follows that a local government is the government of some particular local community. While area is a necessary characteristic of a local government, size is not in itself an acceptable identifying concept.

A more complete definition of a local governmental unit has been compiled by the Bureau of the Census. While this definition is usually not repeated in full, its application is accepted by all. It includes three general criteria which a local unit must meet to qualify as a unit of government. The first holds that a unit must have existence as an organized entity with such corporate powers as the right to sue and be sued, make contracts, and own property. Second, the unit must possess governmental character. Third, the unit must enjoy substantial autonomy as evidenced by fiscal and administrative independence subject only to requirements of state law and supervision.[2]

THE CRITERION OF AUTONOMY

The criterion of substantial autonomy is probably the most essential characteristic of a local government, since this implies a degree of independence from external control. As creatures of the state, all local governments are subject to state control in at least certain areas and in the exercise of certain powers. However, substantial autonomy exists if the unit has a reasonable degree of independence in administrative and fiscal affairs.

Administrative independence is related primarily to the method by which the members of the local governing body are selected

---

[1] Roger H. Wells, *American Local Government*, McGraw-Hill, 1939, p. 1.
[2] Bureau of the Census, *Census of Governments, 1962, Vol. I., Governmental Organization*, Government Printing Office, 1962, pp. 9–10.

and to the functions which they perform. Thus, an agency with a popularly elected governing body or one with a governing body composed of representatives from two or more state or local governments is considered to be an independent unit of government. Similarly, this status of independence is achieved if the unit has an appointed governing body which performs functions that differ from those exercised by and which are not minutely specified by the creating government or governments.

The status of fiscal independence for a unit is met by the existence of one or more of the following powers: (1) the right to determine its own budget without review or major modification by another unit; (2) the right to prescribe the taxes to be levied for its support; (3) the right to fix and collect charges for services rendered; and (4) the right to incur debt without review by another local government.[3]

THE CRITERION OF ENTITY EXISTENCE

To exist as a corporate entity, it is apparent that a local government must embrace both area and population—that is, it must be created to serve a citizenry which exists in a known location. Similarly, it must be identifiable in that its corporate name distinguishes it from other existing units. To serve its citizenry, it is obvious that the unit must have some form of organization and that it must be empowered to exercise certain essential governmental powers. These include the rights to a distinguishing name, to sue and be sued, make contracts, acquire and dispose of property, and to perpetual succession, subject to the possibility of deorganization by the state.[4] Commonly, local governments are identified by state law as municipal corporations, public corporations, or as bodies corporate and politic.

THE CRITERION OF GOVERNMENTAL CHARACTER

There are three essential characteristics of governmental character which identify a unit of local government. The first relates

[3] *Ibid.*, p. 15.
[4] According to William S. Carpenter, at least 36 states have provided for the deorganization of counties, townships, municipalities, or special districts through general law. Other states, especially those of New England, provide for such deorganization by special legislative act. See Carpenter, *Problems in Service Levels: The Readjustment of Services and Areas in Local Government,* Princeton University Press, 1940, pp. 96-97.

to its officeholders and requires that they either be elected by the citizenry of the unit or that they be appointed by other officials who are popularly elected. Second, the unit must bear a high degree of public responsibility and accountability. This requirement is met if it reports periodically to its citizenry or if its records are open to inspection by its public. The third characteristic implies the responsibility for performing one or more functions which are commonly regarded as governmental in nature.

A second and briefer definition of a local government has been advanced by William Anderson. He identifies as a local government any agency which has a "resident population occupying a defined area that has a legally authorized organization and governing body, a separate legal identity, the power to provide certain public or governmental services, and a substantial degree of autonomy including legal and actual power to raise at least a part of its own revenue."[5] Thus, the Anderson definition embodies a sevenfold test of essential characteristics.

It is obvious that both definitions exclude types of units which might better be described as special purpose organs of the state or federal government which service local geographical areas, and some special purpose local districts. Examples of the former would be judicial districts, highway maintenance districts, and federal reserve districts, while election districts and police precincts are illustrations of the latter type. Although these units encompass a territory, population, and have continuing organization, they do not have a separate legal identity, autonomy, or basic governmental powers and functions.

In summary, the term "local government" as it will hereafter be used in this book will mean simply a subordinate territorial unit of an American state which enjoys a reasonable degree of independence.

■ The Pattern of Government

Although American states vary widely in physical size and population, the types of local governmental units found within them follow a fairly common mold. The four major types of units en-

<hr/>

[5] William Anderson, *The Units of Government in the United States*, rev. ed., Public Administration Service, 1949, pp. 8-10.

trusted with public responsibilities at the local level are counties, municipalities, townships, and special districts. Many states create special districts for school purposes rather than entrust that function to some general purpose unit. These school districts are so significant that some treat them as distinct from other types of special districts. However, this distinction seems more one of traditional convenience than one of logic or meaningful difference. In citing numbers of local units below, the pattern of enumeration used by the Bureau of the Census will be followed but the textual material will discuss school districts as merely one form of a single-purpose special district.

While it is convenient to discuss local governments in a small number of categories, it must be remembered that the units within a single category may exhibit wide variations in both size and population as well as in functions performed. Townships are an interesting illustration. The term is used to embrace towns in the New England states, the rural township of midwestern states, and incorporated municipalities in such states as New Jersey and Pennsylvania. Thus the term identifies such differing communities as Warren, Maine (a small town), Homewood Township, Kansas (a rural township), and Upper Darby, Pennsylvania (a municipality of over 90,000 population). However, the differences in local governments in the 50 states are actually far less than might be expected in our federal system which permits each state to design its own system of local government.

COUNTIES

A map of the United States showing local governmental boundaries reveals that the county is the most inclusive local unit. Numbering more than 3,000, the county exists in every state but Alaska, Connecticut, and Rhode Island.[6] However, this land division is known as a parish in Louisiana. Since these units differ more in terminology than in purpose and function, the term county will be used to include the Louisiana parish.

There are only a limited number of areas in the United States, however, which have no organized county governments even though

6 Counties were never organized in Rhode Island, and the eight counties of Connecticut were abolished in 1960 after an existence of over 300 years. In Alaska, the plan to establish boroughs will result in a unit somewhat parallel to the county.

Table 1. *Number of Governmental Units, by State: 1962*

State	All Local Governmental Units	Counties[a]	Municipalities	Townships[b]	Special Districts	School Districts[c]
Alabama	732	67	349	—	202	114
Alaska	56	—	40	—	6	10
Arizona	378	14	61	—	52	251
Arkansas	1,208	75	417	—	299	417
California	4,022	57	373	—	1,962	1,630
Colorado	1,193	62	253	—	566	312
Connecticut	398	—	34	152	204	8
Delaware	207	3	51	—	63	90
Florida	764	67	366	—	264	67
Georgia	1,218	159	561	—	301	197
Hawaii	20	3	1	—	16	—
Idaho	834	44	200	—	469	121
Illinois	6,452	102	1,251	1,433	2,126	1,540
Indiana	3,091	92	546	1,009	560	884
Iowa	2,642	99	944	—	263	1,336
Kansas	5,410	105	618	1,546	880	2,261
Kentucky	872	120	365	—	179	208
Louisiana	628	62	258	—	241	67
Maine	658	16	21	470	125	26
Maryland	351	23	152	—	176	—
Massachusetts	586	12	39	312	194	29
Michigan	3,816	83	509	1,259	99	1,866
Minnesota	5,212	87	845	1,822	115	2,343
Mississippi	772	82	266	—	266	158
Missouri	3,726	114	892	329	742	1,649
Montana	1,387	56	124	—	192	1,015
Nebraska	5,124	93	537	478	752	3,264
Nevada	136	17	17	—	85	17
New Hampshire	550	10	13	221	85	221
New Jersey	1,395	21	334	233	295	512
New Mexico	305	32	80	—	102	91
New York	3,802	57	612	932	970	1,231
North Carolina	675	100	449	—	126	—
North Dakota	3,028	53	356	1,387	246	986
Ohio	3,358	88	932	1,328	177	833

Table 1. (*Continued*)

State	All Local Governmental Units	Counties[a]	Munici- palities	Town- ships[b]	Special Districts	School Districts[c]
Oklahoma	1,959	77	533	—	124	1,225
Oregon	1,469	36	222	—	727	484
Pennsylvania	6,201	66	1,003	1,555	1,398	2,179
Rhode Island	97	—	8	31	56	2
South Carolina	552	46	255	—	142	109
South Dakota	4,463	64	307	1,072	80	2,940
Tennessee	657	95	280	—	268	14
Texas	3,327	254	866	—	733	1,474
Utah	423	29	212	—	142	40
Vermont	424	14	68	238	72	32
Virginia	380	98	236	—	46	—
Washington	1,646	39	263	66	867	411
West Virginia	389	55	224	—	55	55
Wisconsin	3,726	72	563	1,271	68	1,752
Wyoming	464	23	90	—	144	207
Total	91,185	3,043	17,997	17,144	18,323	34,678

[a] Excludes areas corresponding to counties but having no organized county government.
[b] Includes town in six New England states, New York and Wisconsin.
[c] Excludes local school systems operated as part of state, county, municipal or township government.

the areas correspond to counties in other regards. Such areas include the consolidated city-counties of Denver, Philadelphia, and San Francisco; the independent cities of Baltimore, St. Louis and a number in Virginia which administer generally recognized county functions within their own areas; unorganized county areas in Rhode Island, Connecticut, and South Dakota; and federal areas embracing the nation's capitol at Washington, D.C. and Yellowstone National Park.[7]

As Table 1 shows, there is a wide range in the number of county governments among the states. Texas with 254 counties has the greatest number, while Delaware and Hawaii with three each have the fewest. The average number per state is 61, with 25 states

[7] Bureau of the Census, *op. cit.*, pp. 16–17. Unless otherwise specifically noted, data on numbers of units are based on this source.

exceeding this number. Generally speaking, this average is exceeded by midwestern and southern states while northeastern and western states have fewer than the average. In terms of population served in 1960, counties range from a low of 208 in Hinsdale County, Colorado, to 6,038,771 in Los Angeles County. The average population of counties in 1962 was 52,135. However, sixty-five counties—only 2.1 percent of the total number—accounted for 37 percent of the total population in 1960 while the smallest 294 counties, 9.3 percent of the total, embraced only 0.5 percent of the total population.[8]

MUNICIPALITIES

Called by a variety of names including cities, boroughs, and villages, municipalities are the most important general-purpose units of local government in the United States and exist in all 50 states. Although not as inclusive in territory as counties, municipalities exercise more powers and provide a greater variety of services than those rendered by county governments. As incorporated communities, municipalities operate under local charters which are either prescribed by or approved by state legislative action or prepared under a self-executing home rule provision.[9] Functionally, municipalities perform some operations as state instrumentalities and some because of the benefits to be derived primarily by the local residents.

While municipalities exist in all 50 states, the number of incorporated communities range from a high of 1,251 in Illinois to one, the city of Honolulu, in Hawaii. Three states—Pennsylvania, Iowa, and Ohio—have over 900 municipalities, and 11 others have over 500. On the other hand, eight states have fewer than 50 municipalities, with only eight, 13, and 17 existing in Rhode Island, New Hampshire, and Nevada respectively.

The spread in population of municipalities is also a wide one. In 1960, 130 municipalities in 37 states had populations of over 100,000, ranging from New York City with 7,781,984 down to Santa Ana, California, with a population of 100,350.[10] However, the majority

---

[8] Bureau of the Census, *United States Summary,* PC(1)1A, Government Printing Office, 1961, p. xxi.

[9] The process of municipal incorporation will be discussed in Chapter 10.

[10] Bureau of the Census, *United States Summary,* pp. 66–67.

of municipalities in the United States are still small and have populations of fewer than 1,000 inhabitants.

TOWNSHIPS AND TOWNS

Local governmental units classified as townships exist in 21 states, largely in the central, north central, and northeastern sections of the nation. In the six New England states and in some areas of New York and Wisconsin, these units are known more commonly as towns, while in 14 states in addition to most of New York and Wisconsin, the unit is identified usually as the township. Both units were primarily established to serve rural communities and most of them are still fulfilling this function. Of the 17,144 units of this category existing in 1962, 14,329, or 83.6 percent, had populations under 2,500. However, both in New England and in areas adjoining urban centers in other states, the township is becoming increasingly like municipalities, both in governmental form and in services provided.

For convenience, the three major types of units embraced in this category of local governments—the New England town, the rural township, and the urban township—will be briefly described to indicate their major differences.[11] As discussed in Chapter 2, the town is the traditional and most important unit of local government in New England. The term as now used includes rural areas known as plantations in Maine and locations in New Hampshire, as well as the more celebrated small town. In terms of numbers, Rhode Island with 31 has the smallest number while Maine with 470 has the greatest. In the less densely populated sections of New England, the town still operates as a unit of rural government and is organized simply and performs only a limited number of governmental services. In more urban sections, the town provides a greater number of services and has powers similar to those of municipalities.

The rural township as a unit of local government exists in 15 states and more than 1,000 of these entities are found in Illinois, Indiana, Kansas, Michigan, Minnesota, North Dakota, Ohio, Pennsylvania, South Dakota, and Wisconsin. Except around urban centers, these units are rural in nature and perform few functions and are simply organized. The influence of the congressional township

---

[11] This discussion will be elaborated upon in Chapter 11.

system used in surveying these states is evident in the size of townships in sections of several states. The congressional township was uniformly an area of 36 square miles, while the average area of townships in Kansas is 36.6 square miles and the average area of Indiana townships is 35.5.[12]

As mentioned previously, towns and townships adjacent to more urban areas are themselves increasingly becoming units of urban government. The necessity for this development is apparent from the size of some townships, since 213 had populations of 25,000 or more in 1962.[13] Such large townships are found especially in Pennsylvania, New Jersey, Indiana, Illinois and Michigan outside the New England states. In some states, all municipal territory is excluded from township jurisdiction while in others only larger cities are excluded. In a third group of states, such densely populated clusters, even though incorporated, remain within the township for certain governmental purposes.

SPECIAL DISTRICTS

Special district governments exist in all 50 states and are the most numerous of all types of local governments. In 1962, the Bureau of the Census reported a total of 53,001 special districts of which 34,678 were independent school districts with the other 18,323 serving a variety of single or multi-purposes ranging from air pollution control to water supply, storage, conservation or maintenance.[14] In terms of numbers, 15 states have over 1,000 school districts and three—California, Pennsylvania, and Illinois—have over 1,000 other types of special districts. The three major types of special districts other than school are those for fire protection, soil conservation, and drainage. These accounted for 43.2 percent of the over 18,000 special districts. In addition to the large number of independent school districts, the Bureau of the Census recognized 2,341 other school systems in 1962 which were operated as part of a state, county, municipal, or township government, or as an agency of a group of school districts.

The two basic types of special districts—school and non-school— have shown a contrasting pattern of development in recent years.

12 Clyde F. Snider, *Local Government in Rural America*, Appleton-Century-Crofts, 1957, p. 238.

13 Bureau of the Census, *Census of Governments, 1962, op. cit.*, p. 3.

14 *Ibid.*, pp. 5-6.

THE SETTING OF LOCAL GOVERNMENT

Since 1942, the number of independent school districts has declined significantly from 108,578 units to 34,678 in 1962 as school reorganization and consolidation increased. On the other hand, non-school districts have increased from 8,299 in 1942 to 18,323 in 1962. The problems generated, as well as the benefits resulting from the creation of special purpose districts will be discussed in detail in Chapter 12.

STANDARD METROPOLITAN AREAS

Although standard metropolitan areas are neither governmental units or legal entities, the importance of these large urban communities necessitates a brief mention of them at this point. As defined by the Bureau of the Census, a standard metropolitan area is a county or group of contiguous counties which contain at least one city of 50,000 or more. Other adjacent counties are included in the metropolitan area if they are densely populated, have a large number of non-agricultural workers, and are socially and economically integrated with the center city.[15]

In 1960, the Bureau of the Census recognized 212 standard metropolitan areas ranging in size from the New York area with a population of over 10.5 million to Meriden, Connecticut, with 51,850 residents.[16] In number of metropolitan areas, Texas leads with 21, Ohio has 13, Pennsylvania 12, and California, Massachusetts, and Michigan 10 each. Only four states—Alaska, Idaho, Vermont, and Wyoming—have no such urban population concentrations. More than three of every five Americans (63.07 percent) were living in these 212 urban communities in 1960 compared to 56.7 percent in 168 areas in 1950. The areas around the center cities are experiencing a rapid increase in population and this more than counteracts the decline in population of many of the center cities as the trend toward concentration in large urban communities continues at a rapid pace.

Since metropolitan areas are not units of government, they will not be discussed further in this chapter, which is concerned with numbers and types of local governmental units. However, three later chapters will explore the growth and increase of these areas,

[15] Bureau of the Census, *Local Governments in Standard Metropolitan Areas*, Government Printing Office, 1957, pp. 2–3.
[16] Bureau of the Budget, *Standard Metropolitan Statistical Areas*, Government Printing Office, 1961.

their resulting problems, and the governmental patterns which are evolving or have been advanced to meet their needs.

■ The Paradox of Numbers

The challenging and illuminating phrase, "too many local governments, not enough local government," was advanced by the President's Commission on Intergovernmental Relations to describe the basic problem facing state governments in their relationships with local government.[17] While the phrase at first glance may seem to be a better alliteration than a proper diagnosis of local government ills, it is a provocative statement in capsulized form embracing two of the major weaknesses of American local government. Though the phrase is largely self-explanatory, it is worthy of closer analysis.

THE CRITERION OF SIZE

Size is not in itself a satisfactory criterion to measure the meaningfulness of the unit. Certainly it must be admitted at the outset that some very small units are quite well governed while some large units are poorly governed—or have been at some point in their recent history. The concept of an ideal size for a unit of local government has been a topic of speculation and concern at least since the times of Plato and Aristotle and it remains a matter of discussion and research even today.

According to Plato, the "fairest" standard for the regulation of the size of a city by its guardians was that "the city may go on increasing so long as it can grow without losing its unity, but no further."[18] While the number of citizens in his ideal city-state was limited to 5,040, this would probably imply a total population of about 25,000 persons, since there were warriors, slaves, and workers to provide protection and other services for the guardian class. Aristotle went beyond the standard of a single ideal size for cities. He believed that the law of size limitation so apparent in nature was equally applicable to cities and that a city might be quite useless either because of smallness or largeness. In his words, "one that is too small has not in itself the power of self-defence, but this is

<hr>

[17] Commission on Intergovernmental Relations, *A Report to the President for Transmittal to Congress*, Government Printing Office, 1955, p. 47.
[18] Plato, *The Republic*, Book IV, p. 108, Everyman's Library Edition, 1948.

essential to a city; one that is too large is capable of self-defence in what is necessary; but then it is a nation and not a city; for it will be very difficult to accommodate a form of government to it; . . . The first thing therefore necessary is, that a city should consist of such numbers as will be sufficient to enable the inhabitants to live happily in their political community. . . ."[19]

The figure of 25,000 as a desirable population standard was advanced by three other writers. In describing their ideal cities, both Leonardo da Vinci and Ebenezer Howard envisioned a citizenry of this size.[20] Similarly Millspaugh selected 25,000 as the necessary population base of a local government if it were to have an adequate staff and perform enough functions to keep these persons meaningfully employed.[21] To Millspaugh this figure represented the minimum population base and he cautioned that the figure for some functions or in some regions of the country might be considerably higher.

In his *Representative Government*, John Stuart Mill presented a clear case against the very small municipality. He believes that small villages whose inhabitants or the wants of their inhabitants do not differ markedly from those of residents of rural districts surrounding them should not be municipalities. His reasoning holds, "Such small places have rarely a sufficient public to furnish a tolerable municipal council; if they contain any talent or knowledge applicable to public business, it is apt to be all concentrated in some one man, who thereby becomes the dominator of the place. It is better that such places should be merged in a larger circumscription."[22]

More recent writers searching for the ideal size of local governing units have emphasized the population base needed for the adequate provision of particular public service. Thus, in education the National Commission on School Reorganization has set the minimum school-age population of a district at 1,200 but prefers a base of 10,000 persons between the ages of 6 and 18.[23] Similarly, the American Public Health Association advocates that each public health unit contain at least 50,000 persons on the ground that an

---

[19] Aristotle, *A Treatise on Government*, Book VII, Chap. IV, pp. 209–10, Everyman's Library Edition, 1947.

[20] Lewis Mumford, *The City in History*, Harcourt, Brace & World, 1961, p. 180.

[21] Arthur Millspaugh, *Local Democracy and Crime Control*, Brookings Institution, 1936, p. 86.

[22] John Stuart Mill, *Utilitarianism, Liberty and Representative Government*, Everyman's Library Edition, 1948, p. 352.

[23] National Commission on School Reorganization, *Your School District*, Washington, 1948, p. 131.

adequate health program requires a minimum staff of qualified public health personnel.[24]

While other examples of desired population bases could be offered, these two illustrations suffice to show that the ideal size of a local government or service area varies according to the values of the criteria against which size is measured.[25] While such studies are valuable as long as their limitations are realized, it seems important to reiterate the findings of the British Local Government Boundary Commission concerning the appropriately-sized unit for specific functions. In its report, the Commission states, "It is not possible by any process of arithmetic or logic to arrive at an optimum size of a local government unit either in relation to local government as a whole or to any one function or group of functions. At best one can—to use an engineering term—arrive at a reasonable tolerance."[26]

THE CRITERION OF POWER

While we can agree that there is no ideal size for any particular category of local units, it might well be possible to develop some tests of "reasonableness" which a unit could be expected to meet— particularly if it were a community seeking the status of a municipal corporation. Since the power to create local governmental units is a responsibility of the states, it would seem desirable for state legislatures to enact minimum standards for incorporation. At the least, these requirements should aim to establish only new units which can provide essential services and which would maintain frequent and wide citizen participation in their governmental affairs.

The constitution of Alaska makes a significant breakthrough in this regard. The purpose of the local government article, according to the constitution, is "to provide for maximum local self-government with a minimum of local government units."[27] While authorizing the creation of boroughs in the state, the constitution specifies certain standards which were to be considered in establishing such entities including "population, geography, economy, transportation and other facts. Each borough shall embrace an area of population with com-

[24] American Public Health Association, *Local Health Units for the Nation,* The Commonwealth Fund, 1945, pp. 1–5.

[25] Otis D. Duncan, "Optimum Size of Cities" in Paul Hatt and Albert Reiss, Jr. (eds.), *Cities and Society,* rev. ed., The Free Press, 1957, pp. 757–72.

[26] Local Government Boundary Commission, *Local Government: Areas and Status of Local Authorities in England and Wales,* (cmd. 9831), H.M.S.O., 1956.

[27] Alaska Constitution, 1956, Art. X, Sec. 1.

mon interests to the maximum degree possible."[28] While these requirements are necessarily somewhat vague and general, they present some sort of standards other than that of mere legality in following prescribed procedures for incorporation.

The reason such standards appear desirable relates to the second part of the indictment of local government by the President's Commission on Intergovernmental Relations—the statement that "too little local government" now exists. There can be no serious doubt that the amount of local self-government that can be effectively exercised is directly related to the size of the unit practicing it. A unit too small to provide the essential functions of public safety and public health is not really a self-governing unit, since in communities too small to finance these two vital services they pass by default to a higher level of government.

At least a partial explanation for our large number of local governments is the wide application of the principle that government closest to the scrutiny and control of its citizenry is the best government. While there is much to be admired in this concept, it leaves out any real tests for the creation of a unit of government in terms of size, community served, or self-reliance as a service-rendering or self-financing unit. It would appear that small units actually thwart rather than abet citizen control since special arrangements which the citizens can control less directly must be made with agencies of state government or with other local units to provide these services. Local control of a unit can be effective only if that unit is an adequate one to meet the needs of its citizenry. Certainly the theory of local popular control is stretched out of its original intent by small units which make no effort to provide services but contract with larger units to provide such services at a negotiated cost. Such communities may be logical communities but illogical governmental units.

In addition to ineffective local self-government by many small units, local self-government is also often thwarted by the nature and number of state controls which guide the affairs of local communities. Home rule is a desirable objective of local government and a benefit to state government since it enables the state legislatures to concentrate more on matters of statewide rather than local concern. This point will be discussed in more detail in the following chapter, which is devoted to the topic of state-local relations.

[28] *Ibid.*, Sec. 3.

There have been numerous proposals advanced for the reduction in numbers or the elimination of certain classes of units of local government. The greatest progress in reduction of numbers has occurred from the consolidation of school districts, although there have been a small number of mergers of adjacent municipalities and small counties. Proposals for jointures other than school districts, however, have met but little success and there is no real reason for optimism concerning further reduction through this process.

Concrete proposals for the reduction of numbers of counties have been advanced in a number of states including California, Colorado, Georgia, Kentucky, Nevada, Tennessee, Virginia and Washington.[29] A study of county government in the states of the Tennessee Valley in 1940 concluded "that there is need for consolidation of counties in the seven Valley states goes without question."[30]

In contrast to county government in which reduction in numbers is the desired goal, it has often been proposed that townships be abolished in the 16 non-New England states where they still exist. The Commission on County Government of the National Municipal League in a 1934 report recommended that steps be taken for the elimination of the township since it was judged to be "no longer a satisfactory organization for the administration of local services."[31]

[29] In the order of alphabetical listing above, see: Winston Crouch and Dean McHenry, *California Government*, University of California Press, 1948, p. 203; S. R. Heckart and G. S. Klemmedson, *County Consolidation in Colorado*, Colorado Experiment Station, Fort Collins, 1933; M. C. Hughes, *County Government in Georgia*, University of Georgia Press, 1944, Chap. XI; J. W. Manning, "The Progress of County Consolidation," *National Municipal Review*, XXI, (August, 1932), 510-4; Nevada Legislative Counsel Bureau, *County Consolidation and Reorganization in Nevada*, Carson City, 1948; Carlton O. Sims, *County Government in Tennessee*, Murfreesboro, 1932, Chap. VIII; Virginia Commission on County Government, *A Further Report on Progress in County Government and Consolidation*, Richmond, 1936, pp. 42-45; and S. C. Menefree, *A Plan for Regional Administrative Districts in the State of Washington*, University of Washington, 1935.

[30] M. H. Satterfield, *County Government and Administration in the Tennessee Valley States*, Knoxville, 1940, p. 121.

[31] Arthur W. Bromage, "Recommendations on Township Government," *National Municipal Review*, 23 (suppl.), (February, 1934), 138-45. Other studies which also recommend the abolition of townships include: L. D. Melton, "The Elimination of Township Government in Oklahoma," *National Municipal Review*, 27 (August, 1938), 405-7; Frank G. Bates, "The Indiana Township—An Anachronism," *National Municipal Review*, 21 (August, 1932), 502-4; Clyde F. Snider, "The Twilight of the Township," *National Municipal Review*, 41 (September, 1952), 390-6; and R. C. Spencer, "Iowa Townships Still Here?", *National Municipal Review*, 41 (September, 1952), 397-9.

Since there are over 17,000 townships currently existing in these 16 states, it would be a truly significant reduction if townships were abolished and their functions transferred to city and county governments.

Although the number of independent school districts has already declined sharply through consolidation, some proposals for their abolition have been advanced. Anderson has advocated the abolition of school districts with school administration becoming a function of city and county governments.[32] This same proposal has also been advanced by Henry and Kerwin[33] and closer school district-local government coordination has been advocated by two respected scholars of local government.[34]

The most comprehensive proposal for the reorganization of American local government has been advanced by William Anderson. In concluding his well-known study of the units of local government, he proposed a plan which he termed, "A Rationalized Scheme of Local Government Units in the United States," which would reduce the number of such entities to only 17,800. This small number would be realized through (1) the elimination of all independent school districts, with school administration taken over by counties, cities and other incorporated places; (2) the abolition of most special districts through the transfer of their functions to other units; (3) the elimination of townships except for the larger New England towns; (4) the consolidation of small towns in New England; (5) the merger or deorganization of very small municipalities; (6) the consolidation of city and county government in metropolitan urban centers; and (7) the consolidation of small rural counties.[35]

As a result of the elimination and consolidation recommended by Anderson, there would be only four remaining categories of local governments. The nature and number of the remaining local units are given on the following page.

[32] Anderson, *op. cit.*, p. 45.

[33] N. B. Henry and J. G. Kerwin, *Schools and City Government,* University of Chicago Press, 1938, p. 92.

[34] See Robert L. Morlan, "Toward City—School District Rapprochement," *Public Administration Review, 18* (Spring, 1955), 113-7; and Ernest A. Engelbert, "Education – A Thing Apart?", *National Municipal Review, 42* (February, 1953), 78-82.

[35] Anderson, *op. cit.*, pp. 35–46.

NUMBER	TYPE OF UNIT
200	City-counties (each having a central city of not less than 50,000)
2,100	Counties for rural and semi-rural areas
15,000	Incorporated places
500	Miscellaneous units
17,800	Total units[36]

In addition to the proposals discussed above for the reduction in numbers of local governments, there have been a large number of other suggestions relating to structural reform, reallocation of functions, functional consolidation, state supervision, and improved administrative procedures. These proposals will be taken up in subsequent chapters discussing the specific organizations, procedures, or relationships for which these reform proposals have been advanced. It should be noted, however, that some elimination of counties and townships has occurred in recent years and that a number of functional transfers have occurred among local governments. While this movement has not reached the flood proportions of school district reorganization, its potential significance should not be lightly considered.

SUGGESTED READINGS

Books

Advisory Committee on Local Government, *Local Government, A Report to the Commission on Intergovernmental Relations* (Washington: Government Printing Office, 1955).

Anderson, William, *The Units of Government in the United States* (Chicago: Public Administration Service, 1945, 1949).

Bollens, John C., *Special District Governments in the United States* (Berkeley: University of California Press, 1957).

Bureau of the Census, *Local Government Structure in the United States* (Washington: Government Printing Office, 1954).

Carpenter, William S., *Problems in Service Levels: The Readjustment of Services and Areas in Local Government* (Princeton: Princeton University Press, 1940).

[36] *Ibid.*

Commission on Intergovernmental Relations, *A Report to the President for Transmittal to Congress* (Washington: Government Printing Office, 1955).

International Union of Local Authorities, *Local Government in the United States of America* (The Hague: Martinus Nijhoff, 1961).

Kneier, Charles, *City Government in the United States*, 3rd ed. (New York: Harper, 1957).

Lancaster, Lane, *Government in Rural America*, 2nd ed. (New York: Van Nostrand, 1952).

Maass, Arthur (ed.), *Area and Power: A Theory of Local Government* (New York: The Free Press, 1959).

Millspaugh, Arthur, *Local Democracy and Crime Control* (Brookings Institution, 1936).

Sly, John F., *Town Government in Massachusetts, 1620–1930* (Cambridge: Harvard University Press, 1930).

Snider, Clyde F., *Local Government in Rural America* (New York: Appleton-Century-Crofts, 1957).

Wells, Roger H., *American Local Government* (New York: McGraw-Hill, 1939).

Articles

Bates, Frank G., "Village Government in New England," *American Political Science Review*, VI (August, 1912), 367–85.

Cassella, William N., "County Government in Transition," *Public Administration Review*, XVI (Summer, 1956), 223–31.

Drury, James W., "Townships Lose Ground," *National Municipal Review*, XLIV (January, 1955), 10–13.

Duncan, Otis D., "Optimum Size of Cities" in Paul Hatt and Albert Reiss, Jr. (eds.), *Cities and Society*, 2nd ed. (New York: The Free Press, 1957), pp. 757–72.

Havard, W. C. and Diamant, Alfred, "The Need for Local Government Reform in the United States," *Western Political Quarterly*, IX (December, 1956), 967–95.

Manvel, Allen D., "Local Government in the United States," *The County Officer*, XVII (July, 1952), 192–3, 219.

Porter, K. H., "A Plague of Special Districts," *National Municipal Review*, XXII (November, 1933), 544–7.

Snider, Clyde F., "The Twilight of the Township," *National Municipal Review*, XLI (September, 1952), 390–6.

State-Local Relations

4

The American Revolution freed the thirteen colonies and resulted in their creation as states. It had an opposite effect on colonial local governments. Instead of gaining more freedom, the cities actually had less as they passed from the control of the colonial governors to that of the early state legislatures.

While the number of municipal charters granted during colonial times was not large, such charters were granted by the colonial governor in the name of the English crown or of the proprietor of the colony. Since these communities performed few service functions, they were more judicial than administrative organizations, but they enjoyed a degree of independence in their operations. After the colonies had gained their independence, the fear of strong executives resulted in the establishment of strong legislatures as the dominant organ of state government. Thus the power of colonial governors to grant charters passed to the state legislative assemblies rather than to state governors. The legislative articles of the new state constitutions clearly recognized this new power of making and amending city charters. Illustrative was the provision of the New York constitution of 1777 which provided that borough charters would remain in force "until otherwise directed by the legislature."[1] With this development, a municipal charter became similar

[1] Raymond G. Gettell, *History of American Political Thought*, Appleton-Century, 1928, p. 596.

to a statute and might be replaced or amended at the whim of the legislature.

Although extensive state control over local government was possible, legislatures generally did not intervene in local affairs except upon request by the municipality. As cities grew in importance, however, the attitude of state legislators underwent a decided change. Local offices provided a source for patronage and city franchises and contracts provided a tempting source of income in return for favors granted. Thus, about 1850 the state legislatures began to exercise more extensive controls over local governments not only for pecuniary and selfish benefits but also to correct certain local defects which were called to their attention by alarmed citizens and reformers.

Local government opposition to this exercise of state control was soon aroused and became quite vocal. However, there was really little to question about the legal power of the state legislature to control the sub-units it created in whatever ways and to what degree it desired. This legal relationship was well defined by Judge John F. Dillon of the Iowa Supreme Court in 1868 in these words: "Municipal corporations owe their origin to, and derive their powers from, the legislature. It breathes into them the breath of life, without which they cannot exist. As it created, so it may destroy. If it may destroy, it may abridge the control. Unless there is some constitutional limitation on the right, the legislature might, by a single act, if we can suppose it capable of so great a folly and so great a wrong, sweep from existence all of the municipal corporations of the state, and the corporations could not prevent it. We know of no limitation on this right so far as the corporations themselves are concerned. They are, so to phrase it, the mere tenants at will of the legislature."[2]

It is interesting to note that Judge Dillon clearly recognizes that there may be a significant difference between acts that are legal and acts that are politically practicable. Thus while the state could "destroy, abridge, and control," he warned that this would be a great folly and wrong if carried to excess. A counter-doctrine developed as a reaction to the acts of excessive legislative interference in local affairs. Known as the "inherent right of local self-government" theory, this doctrine held that as corporations local governments possessed the common-law rights and powers of other corporations. Similarly, since local governments existed before the

[2] *City of Clinton* v. *Cedar Rapids and Missouri Railroad Company*, 24 Iowa 455 (1868).

states were established, the right of local self-government was an inherent right that the state could not take away. This point of view received its highest form of expression in an opinion of Judge Charles Cooley in 1871. He stated, "The State may mould local institutions according to its views of policy or expediency; but local government is a matter of absolute right; and the State cannot take it away. It would be the boldest mockery to speak of a city as possessing municipal liberty where the State not only shaped its government, but at discretion sent in its own agents to administer it; or to call that system one of constitutional freedom under which it should be equally admissable to allow the people full control in their local affairs, or no control at all. . . . when the State reaches out and draws to itself and appropriates the powers which from time immemorial have been locally possessed and exercised, . . . we seemed forced back upon and compelled to take up and defend the plainest and most primary axioms of free government . . ."[3]

While this doctrine was followed for a time by some state courts, it was never widely recognized. For constitutional protection against the state, local governments must find some guarantee of home rule in their own constitution. It would be rare to encounter a situation where local government could successfully resist state action because of some provision of the national constitution. Mr. Justice Cardozo speaking for the United States Supreme Court in 1933 stated that a municipal corporation "has no privileges or immunities under the Federal Constitution which it may invoke in opposition to the will of its creator."[4] Thus, it seems clear that the doctrine of the Dartmouth College case holding that the state is not privileged to use its police power to impair the obligations of a contract does not apply to relations between the state and its local governments.[5]

The statement of Judge Dillon quoted above still remains the classic statement on the legal relationships between a state legislature and the sub-units of government it creates. While the state could legally control and even deorganize its local governments, it would be politically impracticable—if not impossible—to do so. The result then is a finely balanced relationship between the state and its local government in which state aid and assistance exists alongside state direction and supervision in an intricate pattern of cooperative

---

[3] *People ex rel. Le Roy* v. *Hurlbut*, 24 Michigan 44 (1871).
[4] *Williams* v. *Mayor and City Council of Baltimore*, 289 U. S. 36 (1933).
[5] *Dartmouth College* v. *Woodward*, 4 Wheaton 518 (1819).

relations.[6] In the last century, however, there has been a great growth of restrictive provisions in state constitutions which protect local governments from whims of the legislature which might be directed against a particular local unit.

■ Creation of Local Governments

Since units of local government are legally created by the state, the right of the state to provide a general framework for its subdivisions is unquestioned. The nature of and the specific provisions in the state-prescribed framework, however, are subjects on which uniform agreement does not exist. In the local government article of the Model State Constitution, prepared for the National Municipal League, the legislature is assigned a sixfold task in shaping its local governments. Specifically, it is provided that the legislature will (1) provide for the incorporation of local units; (2) determine the powers of local governments; (3) provide alternative forms for local governments through general law and home rule charters; (4) prescribe methods for the alteration of boundaries; (5) permit the consolidation of neighboring local units; and (6) enact provisions for the dissolution or deorganization of such civil divisions.[7] Each of these proposed state powers over local governments will be briefly discussed below.

TYPES OF MUNICIPAL CORPORATIONS

Local governmental units are usually accorded the status of municipal or public corporations or that of bodies corporate and politic in terms of the laws of the creating state. Following a practice that existed in England and was transplanted to the American colonies, American courts have distinguished between two types of such public corporations, designating them as municipal or quasi-municipal agencies. While the distinction between the two classes is blurring in a number of states, the distinction is still

---

[6] For an excellent discussion of current thinking concerning state-local relations see William N. Cassella, Jr., "State-Local Relations, Recent Trends and Fundamental Questions," *State Government*, 27 (December, 1954), 247-51, 258-9.

[7] National Municipal League, *Model State Constitution*, 6th ed., 1963, Art. VIII, Secs. 8.01, 8.02, and 8.03.

firmly embedded in law and will have practical significance in the years ahead.

The basis for the distinction between these two types of corporations lies in the nature of the created units. Concerning municipal corporations, it has generally been held that they are created upon the request of, or certainly with the consent of, the inhabitants and primarily for local benefit and advantage since such units provide services which are local in nature. Quasi-municipal corporations, on the other hand, are created without reference to local wishes, primarily as administrative subdivisions of the state for carrying out activities of statewide interest. As such, units of the latter type have a more limited corporate existence.

There are additional differences between the two types of corporations. Quasi-municipal corporations usually have a greater immunity from suit than do municipal corporations since the former are agencies for state as well as for local services. In many states municipal corporations have a more extensive liability for torts and have a broader power of eminent domain than do quasi-municipal corporations. Municipal corporations have broader law-making powers, and have greater freedom from state control and regulation than do quasi-municipal corporations in acquiring, holding and disposing of property.[8]

While allowance must be made for the frequent variations from the general rules which exist among the states, local governments can be classified in terms of their corporate status as follows:

Municipal Corporations

1. Cities.
2. Villages.
3. Boroughs.
4. Towns (other than in New England states).

Quasi-municipal Corporations

1. Counties.
2. Townships.
3. Towns (in New England states).
4. Special districts.

[8] The widely accepted authorities on this subject are John F. Dillon, *Commentaries on the Law of Municipal Corporations*, 5th ed., Vol. I, Little, Brown, 1911; and Eugene McQuillin, *The Laws of Municipal Corporations*, 3rd ed., Vol. I, Callaghan, 1949. See also Jefferson B. Fordham, *Local Government Law*, Foundation Press, 1949; and Roger W. Cooley, *Handbook of the Law of Municipal Corporations*, West, 1914.

Since local governments are created by the state, it follows that such units derive all their powers from their creator. It is also clear that local laws and administrative actions must not be in conflict with higher forms of law at either the state or national level. Beyond this clear limitation, however, are the restrictions inherent in the classic statement of municipal powers by Judge Dillon. Often referred to as "Dillon's Rule," the statement holds that, "It is a general and undisputed proposition of law that a municipal corporation possesses and can exercise the following powers, and no others: First, those granted in express words; second, those necessarily or fairly implied in or incident to the powers expressly granted; third, those essential to the accomplishment of the declared objects and purposes of the corporation—not simply convenient, but indispensable. Any fair, reasonable, substantial doubt concerning the existence of power is resolved by the courts against the corporation, and the power is denied."[9] The same conclusions were reached by McQuillin in a slight modification of the Dillon Rule. According to McQuillin, "Excluding the question as to the existence of so-called inherent powers of a municipal corporation, the powers of a municipal corporation include (1) powers expressly conferred by the constitution, statutes or charter; (2) powers necessarily or fairly implied in, or incident to, the powers expressly granted; and (3) powers essential to the declared objects and purposes of the municipality, the latter often being classified as among the implied powers. This enumeration of powers is exclusive and no other powers exist. . ."[10]

It has been inevitable that a large number of cases have arisen concerning the meaning of the "implied powers" recognized by both Dillon and McQuillin, and the intent of the "powers essential to the declared objects and purposes of the corporation." This relatively narrow grant of implied powers for local governments is in sharp contrast to the broad interpretation and effect of the "necessary and proper" clause regarding powers of the national government.

While judicial interpretations vary in strictness or liberality from state to state, some courts tend generally to adopt a more liberal interpretation of these restrictions when dealing with matters arising

9 Dillon, *op. cit.*, sec. 237.
10 McQuillin, *op. cit.*, Vol. II, sec. 10:09.

from the exercise of proprietary powers than they do in matters arising from powers strictly in the governmental field. Basically, the distinction between these two kinds of powers is that governmental functions are those exercised by the local unit as an agent of the state, while proprietary functions are exercised by the unit as a municipal corporation and are more private or corporate in nature. Some of the commonly recognized governmental functions are public safety, public health, education and welfare, while such functions as water supply, power production, gas supply and transit facilities are classified as proprietary. Many of the newer functions exercised by local governments exist in a so-called "twilight zone" or "no man's land" and are recognized as governmental powers in some states and as proprietary functions in others.[11]

PROVISION OF ALTERNATIVE FORMS

Two movements to decrease the burden on state legislatures while allowing maximum freedom for local discretion within a general range of state policy have resulted in the adoption of home rule and optional charter legislation or constitutional amendments in a number of states. In general harmony with this objective is a reviving effort to prohibit special legislation by state legislatures by requiring local approval of such legislative acts before they become operative in the community singled out for such prescription.

The home rule movement has often been heralded as the most satisfactory alternative to state controls over local affairs. While the term "home rule" has no exact and precise meaning, it is customarily used to denote the power of a local government to draft and control its own charter and to control its own "local" affairs. The end of such action confers more power of local self-government and self-determination on local governments, freeing them from legislative control and domination. The major objectives of home rule, according to the American Municipal Association, are to prevent legislative interference with local government, to enable local governments to adopt the kind of government they desire, and to provide local governments with sufficient powers to meet the increasing needs for local services.[12]

[11] J. C. Phillips, "'Active Wrongdoing' and the Sovereign-Immunity Principle in Municipal Tort Liability," *Oregon Law Review*, XXXVIII (February, 1959), 122–57.
[12] Rodney L. Mott, *Home Rule for American Cities*, American Municipal Association, 1949, pp. 11–12.

There are three principal methods by which the privileges of home rule have been extended to local governments. First, in some states home rule can be granted by statute by legislative action. Second, some states have self-executing constitutional provisions under which local governments may draft or change their charters. Third, home rule may be extended by constitutional provisions which require enabling legislation by the state legislature before they become operative.

Under statutory home rule, the legislature enacts a law by which in effect it abdicates its powers to intervene in the internal municipal affairs of its local governments and grants them the power to govern themselves. The earliest use of this type of home rule occurred in Iowa in 1858 and it now exists in the states of Connecticut, Florida, New Mexico, and North Carolina.[13] In addition, the states of Georgia and Nevada can be included in this group since constitutional amendments in these states authorize the state legislatures to grant home rule to cities rather than directly grant such power to the cities. While statutory home rule is generally not regarded as a satisfactory method of handling the relations between a state and its local governments, it undoubtedly is superior to detailed legislative supervision through the enactment of special legislation. Its chief weakness lies in the possibility of state repeal of the grant at a future time or the overriding of local provisions by subsequent state legislation.

Self-executing constitutional home rule is recognized as the most satisfactory method for extending the powers of local self-government by the state to its subdivisions. Under this type of grant, local governments may draft and change their charters according to procedures laid down in the home rule article of the constitution. In Ohio, which has such a home rule article, municipalities are authorized to exercise all powers of local self-government and to adopt and enforce local regulations not in conflict with other general laws.[14] Other states with self-executing home rule provisions are Arizona, California, Colorado, Missouri, Nebraska, Oklahoma, Oregon, Rhode Island, Tennessee, Utah, and Washington.[15]

Constitutional home rule provisions requiring enabling legislation

[13] Adapted from International City Managers' Association, *Municipal Year Book, 1956*, International City Managers' Association, 1956, p. 258; subsequent issues of the *Year Book;* and various issues of the *National Municipal Review.*

[14] Ohio Constitution, Art. XVIII, Secs. 2–3, 7–9.

[15] See footnote 12 *supra.*

are usually classified as mandatory or permissive.[16] Under either form, the legislature is free to enact in detail the manner in which such status is granted and the extent of the power to be enjoyed by such units. Mandatory home rule provisions require legislative action to implement the constitutional principle of home rule, while under permissive home rule provisions the legislature may fail to enact the necessary enabling legislation for a long period of time. The Pennsylvania experience is illustrative of the latter system. A constitutional amendment adopted in 1922 permitted the legislature of that state to grant home rule, but Philadelphia, its largest city, was not extended the privilege until 1949. Similarly a constitutional home rule article in the Nevada constitution has remained without implementation since its adoption in 1924. Although self-executing home rule is preferred by a majority of students and reformers of local government, one writer ascribes two advantages to provisions that require enabling legislation. First, such provisions can permit greater flexibility, and, second, if prudently classified the concept of what are "local affairs" can avert court litigation.[17]

The aim of the optional charter movement is to allow local governments the right to choose the preferred form from among several standard forms of local organization. Citizens of the local areas do not have the full freedom to determine their plan of government or to control their local affairs as they do under home rule since they are still subject to state legislative control. Optional charter systems represent a compromise between home rule and general charter systems and are often more acceptable to state legislatures which hesitate to end legislative control over local affairs or which fear home rule abuses. Beginning in Iowa in 1907 when an optional commission form charter was made available to Iowa cities, the optional charter movement has received acceptance in both home rule and non-home rule states. At the present time, 30 states allow their local governmental units to select from optional forms of governmental organization.

Heralded as a means for providing charters to meet the particular needs of particular local governments, the optional charter plan

---

[16] States having these provisions include Alaska, Kansas, Louisiana, Maryland, Michigan, Minnesota, New Jersey, New York, Pennsylvania, Texas, West Virginia and Wisconsin.

[17] J. C. Phillips, *State and Local Government in America*, American Book Company, 1954, p. 383. For a home-rule provision which attempts to avoid these legal problems, see American Municipal Association, *Model Constitutional Provisions for Municipal Home Rule*, New York, 1953.

adopted in New Jersey in 1950 provides the best example of the full possibilities of this device. Municipalities in that state may select one of three general alternative plans—mayor council, council-manager, or small municipalities plan. But within each of the three basic plans are a number of options so that the choice can be further refined to one of six kinds of the mayor council form, one of five council-manager options, and one of four varieties in the small municipalities plan.[18] Among the sub-options available are those relating to size of council, the partisan or non-partisan election of council members, and the election of councilmen at large or by wards. The citizens of a community may vote for one of the possible optional plans either following a report of an elected charter commission or by direct citizen petition and referendum. It appears that New Jersey's liberal optional charter plan is a satisfactory method of granting a local charter while retaining some state supervision over its chartered cities. Details of the various optional plans commonly available will be more thoroughly described in Chapters 9 and 10.

ALTERATION OF BOUNDARIES

Since local governmental units are not static creatures, it follows that some provision must be made for changing the boundaries designated at the time of their creation or incorporation. Guidelines for the expansion or contraction of local boundaries are usually spelled out in a constitutional provision or by general statute and specific changes may be made by procedures that may involve a local referendum in accordance with state law.

Legal boundaries of cities in particular have tended to lag behind the actual boundaries that result from the growth of the urbanized areas. This problem is most acute in metropolitan areas and will be discussed in detail in later chapters devoted to such areas. The most common method for the extension of boundaries is through annexation of territory by a city. Most states require that annexation can occur only after an election called for that purpose in which a majority of the voters both in the city and in the area to be annexed voice their approval. Some states, however, allow the courts to determine the desirability of an annexation proposal, and other states prescribe that only unilateral approval by the annexing city

[18] Benjamin Baker, *Municipal Charter Revision in New Jersey,* Bureau of Government Research, Rutgers University, 1953.

without the consent of the residents in the area to be annexed is necessary. Missouri and Texas are two states which allow the latter procedure, while the Virginia system of allowing court determination in such cases is well-known.[19]

Another method of altering local boundaries is to permit the consolidation of neighboring or contiguous local governments. Since the use of this method is most frequently discussed in terms of units of governments within metropolitan areas, the details of this method will also be discussed in a subsequent chapter.

DISSOLUTION OF LOCAL GOVERNMENTS

The 1950 census returns revealed the interesting statistic that there were five incorporated towns in the United States with zero populations. The communities had actually disappeared but remained as legal entities since the prescribed legal procedures necessary for their dissolution had not been completed before they ceased to operate.

Before a municipal corporation can be dissolved, it is usually necessary that a judicial decree or a legislative act acknowledge the unit's deorganization, although some states apparently provide for automatic dissolution. The three most common methods for dissolution of local units provide that a petition by a designated number of citizens of the community be presented to a named court which orders an election to be held on the question, that a similar petition be presented to the legislative body of the community in question with an election to be called on the matter, or that direct judicial or legislative action for dissolution can follow the presentation of the petition without the need of a popular vote on the question.[20]

■ Forms of State Control

Part of the control that a state has over its local governments is established in provisions of the state constitution. Several of these major controls as they relate to the creation and organization of

---

[19] For interesting descriptions of annexation procedures in these states, see J. M. Claunch, "Land Grabbing—Texas Style," *National Municipal Review, 42* (November, 1953), 494–6; and Chester W. Bain, "Annexation: Virginia's Not-so-Judicial System," *Public Administration Review, 15* (Autumn, 1955), 251–62.

[20] Charles M. Kneier, *City Government in the United States*, 3rd ed., Harper, 1957, p. 47.

local units have been discussed in the preceding section. However, in addition to these general provisions, state constitutions vary widely in the scope of constitutional directions pertaining to local governments. For instance, the Oklahoma constitution goes so far as to name the counties, specify their boundaries, and designate their county seats.[21] More commonly, constitutions merely state that a uniform system of county government will be provided by law and will exist throughout the state.

State constitutions may also contain varying specific directions and prohibitions for their local governments. Local debt and tax limitations are common and there may be others relating to the control of local financial abuses or transactions. Other constitutions will enumerate county or township officers and thus present a common mold for their governmental organization. Generally speaking, cities are freer of such elaborate controls regulating officers than are other local units, with the legislature being authorized to establish machinery for the organization and government of cities and other incorporated municipalities. Some of the more specific constitutional controls will be discussed briefly in subsequent chapters relating to particular types of local units, their finances, and their governmental processes.

LEGISLATIVE CONTROL

The more traditional and inclusive manner in which the state exercises control and direction over its local governments is through legislative prescription and supervision. Such legislative control is exercised largely through the enactment of statutes, through appropriations for subsidies or grants-in-aid, and through legislative investigations. Typically, there are standing state legislative committees on cities, counties, or local government, and there are frequently special committees or legislative commissions on the problems of local governments.

Initially, legislative supervision over local governments was exercised largely through the device of special legislation pertaining to a single local community named in the act. Special legislation is still an important feature in state-local relations but such direct supervision has declined in the twentieth century. There were a number of disadvantages in this system, and the task became too time-consuming and complicated for handling by legislative bodies

[21] Constitution of Oklahoma, Art. XVII, Sec. 8.

meeting only for a limited time once a year or biennially. Several disadvantages of continued legislative control through local or special legislation were advanced by the Committee on State-Local Relations in its 1946 report. The burden of local legislation makes undue demands on the time and energy of state legislators and brings local affairs into the arena of state politics. Special legislation encourages log-rolling among legislators, and causes instability and confusion in local government. Such legislation accentuates the feeling of localism in state legislatures and removes control of local government from the hands of local citizens where it belongs.[22]

The reaction against legislative control by special act resulted in prohibition of this practice in state constitutions adopted after the middle of the nineteenth century. Generally, the new constitutions held that laws regulating the affairs of cities or counties must have general application instead of singling out individual units. Thus, laws regulating the affairs of cities in a state must pertain to cities of over half a million as well as to those of 5,000 inhabitants. Obviously, it was difficult for legislators to draft such all-encompassing bills and it was even more difficult to enforce them uniformly. Out of this dilemma emerged the concept of classifying local units for legislative purposes. By this device, they could be divided into groups on the basis of population, providing a compromise between special and general legislation. Now legislation could be general for all cities and counties of a certain size, but it could also be special in that it would not apply to governmental units outside the populations limits designated in the act. While early classifications were often artificial and overlapping, order and common sense gradually prevailed and the concept of classification became an important feature of state legislation pertaining to local government.

According to McQuillin, lawful classification of local governments must be based on several criteria. First, classification must be based on substantial distinctions making one class different from another. Second, it must be germane to the purpose of the law. Third, established classes must be based on existing circumstances rather than on future possibilities. Fourth, the classifications must apply equally to each unit within the class. And, fifth, the classes must be based on characteristics sufficiently different from those of

[22] Council of State Governments, *State-Local Relations*, Council of State Governments, 1946, pp. 146-8.

THE SETTING OF LOCAL GOVERNMENT

other classes to suggest the appropriateness of establishing them as separate classes.[23] Thus it was easy to see why the Supreme Court of Pennsylvania in 1879 declared the following action of the state legislature as special legislation—even though it was passed under the guise of general legislation—since it applied to "all counties . . . where there is a population of more than 60,000 inhabitants, and in which there shall be any city incorporated at the time of the passage of this act with a population exceeding 8,000 inhabitants, situate at a distance from the county seat of more than 27 miles by the usually traveled public road."[24]

While it was mentioned above that legislative supervision has declined since the turn of this century, this does not mean that supervision by state government has declined. Rather much of the direction and control formerly exercised by the legislature has now been entrusted to agencies of the administrative branch of the state government.

ADMINISTRATIVE CONTROL

Supervision of local activities by state administrative agencies is largely a development of the twentieth century in the United States. European countries, however, have provided for such control for a much longer period of time. Such agencies as the Ministry of Local Government in England and the Ministry of the Interior in France have rather concentrated supervisory controls over their local governments. Not only did this develop later, but in the United States, the tendency has been to entrust such controls on a functional rather than on an agency basis. Thus, instead of a single agency of local government exercising general controls, local health activities are supervised by the state health department, local welfare programs and standards by the state welfare agency, local education by a state department of education, and so on.

As the functions of local governments have expanded, there has been a parallel growth in administrative regulation by state agencies.[25] The general purposes are to raise government services to higher levels of performance, to lessen the inequities of service levels among local governments, to improve the efficiency of ad-

[23] McQuillin, *op. cit.*, Vol. 1, p. 678.
[24] *Commonwealth* v. *Patton*, 88 Pa. St. 258, 260 (1879).
[25] Council of State Governments, *op. cit.*, pp. 11–12.

ministration of such services, and to distribute their costs more equitably among the governmental units.[26]

Administrative supervision is believed superior to legislative control since it offers more certain means for achieving efficiency in the administration of programs of statewide concern while granting local governments a larger measure of freedom in meeting their own day-to-day problems. Two specific advantages of administrative supervision include greater flexibility in application and more expedient exercise of supervision without the delay of time-consuming litigation. Administrative control is also more effective since it can be remedial rather than punitive in effect as legislative control must be.[27]

The methods of state administrative control are several in number and range from techniques of persuasion to those of coercion. In a pioneer but still widely used study of state administrative supervision of cities, Schuyler Wallace listed eleven devices in an "ascending order of their individual effectiveness." These were reports, inspection, advice, grants-in-aid, approval, review, orders, ordinances, removal, appointment, and substitute administration.[28] While the right of state agencies to utilize the more coercive devices, if they are authorized to do so, cannot be challenged, the long-term effectiveness of heavy-handed methods as against more persuasive techniques can be questioned. Thus, the Council of State Governments recommended that state advisory programs be based upon the following six principles. First, control devices be utilized only (a) to establish minimum standards of performance, and (b) to meet emergency situations, while persuasion, consultation and education be used in most situations. Second, that certification of employees by state agencies be limited to certifying the qualifications of teachers, while the prescription of minimum standards be used for other local employees. Third, states should increase their facilities for aiding and improving local personnel administration. Fourth, states should expand their facilities to assist in training local officials and employees. Fifth, states should increase and improve programs of technical assistance and initiate more cooperative undertakings with local governments. And sixth, state grant-in-aid programs should be administered and supervised

[26] *Ibid.*, pp. 12–13.
[27] *Ibid.*
[28] Schuyler Wallace, *State Administrative Supervision Over Cities in the United States,* Columbia University Press, 1928, p. 39.

to insure adequate standards of service performance by the receiving local governments.[29]

While state administrative supervision and control in the field of local finance is more pronounced than that exercised in many other areas, this field can serve as an example of such control. In a careful report prepared in 1953, T. E. McMillan itemized the following forms of state financial supervision: budget supervision in 32 states, auditing of municipal accounts in 30 states, supervision of municipal accounts in 25 states, financial reporting in 23 states, and debt supervision in 20 states.[30] The application of these and other administrative controls in local finance will be discussed more thoroughly in Chapter 17.

Generally speaking, state administrative supervision attempts to function in accord with the principles advanced by John Stuart Mill over a century ago. Mill wrote, "The principal business of the central authority should be to give instruction, of the local authority to apply it. Power may be localized, but knowledge, to be most useful, must be centralized; there must be somewhere a focus at which all scattered rays are collected, that the broken and coloured lights which exist elsewhere may find there what is necessary to complete and purify them. To every branch of local administration which affects the general interest there should be a corresponding central organ, either a minister, or some specially appointed functionary under him; . . . It (the central agency) ought to keep open a perpetual communication with the localities: informing itself by their experience, and them by its own; giving advice freely when asked, volunteering it when seen to be required; compelling publicity and recordation of proceedings, and enforcing obedience to every general law which the legislature has laid down on the subject of local management."[31]

JUDICIAL CONTROL

Because of the subordinate legal position of local governments, such units are continuously called upon to prove or defend their rights to exercise powers or to employ their powers to accomplish particular purposes. While judicial review is an important principle

---

[29] Council of State Governments, *op. cit.*, pp. 41-46.

[30] T. E. McMillan, Jr., *State Supervision of Municipal Finance*, Institute of Public Affairs, University of Texas, 1953.

[31] John Stuart Mill, *Representative Government*, 1860, Everyman's Library Edition, 1948, pp. 357-8.

in our system of American government, the principle has particular pertinence for local governments. This point is aptly emphasized by Jefferson B. Fordham in these words, "Judicial review of legislative, executive and administrative action is extensive and crucial at all levels of government, but we find it to be most detailed and most persuasive at the local level."[32]

Since local law is subordinate to both national and state enactments, it is necessary that local governments act within the recognized limits of these higher levels as they relate to both substantive powers to be exercised and the procedures to be followed. Through the issuance of a writ of *mandamus*, local governments or their officers may be compelled to act, while a writ of prohibition may be issued to stop their actions. Other judicial writs of *quo warranto* (asking by what power or right an action is being promulgated) or of *certiorari* (calling a lower court judgment up for full review by a higher level) may also be issued. In addition, courts may also issue judgments relating to civil liability for damages, criminal liability for action or inaction, and equitable relief by injunction which are binding on local governments. Thus, one writer has drawn a simile between the relationships of a baseball umpire looking over the shoulder of the catcher and the role of the judge overseeing the actions of local officials.[33]

In summary, judicial control over local government is basically no different from judicial control over the state itself. State administrative supervision, though increasing, should not be construed as meaning that the ordinary activities of local governments are under continuous state inspection. While quite extensive state supervision exists in some service areas, such as education and health, in other service fields, such as police and fire, the state often intervenes only upon request of the local government unit.

■ A State Department of Local Government

As indicated in the preceding discussion, administrative relations between states and their local governments have stressed aid and service rather than supervision and control. The increased number

---

[32] Fordham, *op. cit.*, p. 36.
[33] Charles R. Adrian, *State and Local Governments, A Study in the Political Process*, McGraw-Hill, 1960, p. 96.

and growing complexity of these relationships, however, have caused some concern among students who believe that the further fragmentation of state supervisory activities along existing functional lines may result in undesired problems of coordination for both state and local governments. Thus, there is a growing sentiment for the creation of a department or agency of local government in each state, in which the general responsibility for supervision of local activities could be centered. While no such agency currently exists in any of the American states, agencies with more than the usual responsibilities for aiding and supervising local governments and their activities now exist in the states of New Jersey, Pennsylvania and New York.

As viewed by students of government, the functions of such a local government agency would include the following major programs and services. First, they would assist the governor in coordinating information and action regarding local government problems and in developing appropriate legislative programs and administrative policies. Second, they would serve as the central point in the state government for information, study, and evaluation of proposals relating to local governments and their affairs. Third, they would serve as a collection point and clearing house for studies of local governments conducted by private and other public agencies. Fourth, they would act as a coordinating agency for local governments seeking assistance from other local, state or federal agencies. Fifth, they would carry out legislative requirements relating to local standards of performance or service. And sixth, they would initiate and recommend to local government useful state services which do not currently exist.[34]

Of the possible arguments which can be mustered in defense of creation of such an agency, the most convincing relates to the clear responsibility of the state to assume leadership in meeting the problems of its local governments. Thus, although many state agencies have somewhat specialized relationships with local units, there is no central point to coordinate these many programs into a unified

[34] For a fuller discussion of the functions or powers of such a state agency of local government, see James R. Bell, "The Desirability of a Special Unit for Local Government in State Administration," *Metropolitan California*, Report of Governor's Commission on Metropolitan Area Problems, 1961, pp. 149-51 ; Harold Alderfer, *American Local Government and Administration*, Macmillan, 1956, pp. 169-70 ; and John G. Grumm, "A State Agency for Local Affairs?" *Public Affairs Report*, 2 (October, 1961), pp. 3-4, Bureau of Public Administration, University of California, Berkeley.

approach to solve the problems faced by local governments. Since the idea of such an agency has received little firm support from either officials of state or local government, it can be assumed that the chief obstacle to its creation on both sides is the concern about the manner in which such an agency would actually operate and carry out its functions.

However, some steps—though considerably short of the single agency concept described above—have been taken in a few states, and this may signify greater interest in such agencies in the future. The Division of Local Government in the New Jersey Department of the Treasury has existed for over 40 years and has gradually assumed functions other than supervision over general fiscal affairs of local governments. Recent studies emanating from the Division have been devoted to such problems as conservation, health, housing, and borough consolidation as well as to fiscal problems. In Pennsylvania, a Bureau of Municipal Affairs in the Department of Internal Affairs, is responsible for a wide range of services to local governments and for limited supervisory functions in fiscal affairs. New York in 1959 established the Office of Local Government within the Executive Department to aid the governor in coordinating state activities relating to local government, informing him of local government problems, and assisting him in formulating appropriate policies for their solution.[35]

■ Interlocal Relations

Cooperative arrangements among local governments have long been utilized to meet common problems. The earliest recorded examples were in the form of mutual aid arrangements to defend towns against surprise Indian attacks in the New England colonies, and they have continued to exist and grow in number since those early times. Since state courts have generally tended to approve the principle of limited local powers as set forth in "Dillon's Rule," the power to enter into formal cooperative arrangements must be conferred upon local governments either through direct legislative grant or through reasonable indirect or implied legislative grant. Although these arrangements are known by a number of different

[35] Bell, *op. cit.*, pp. 149–50 and Grumm, *op. cit.*, pp. 1–2.

names, they might properly be identified as interjurisdictional agreements. This term could then be defined to include both formal or written compacts and informal or clearly understood unwritten agreements by which two or more local units voluntarily attempt to solve or ameliorate a mutual problem. A study completed in 1960 counted a total of 693 such agreeements among the local governments in a five-county area in southeastern Pennsylvania centering around Philadelphia. The four suburban counties, their 237 municipalities and 238 school districts, and the City-County of Philadelphia had a network of interlocking agreements which were almost areawide in such fields as police radio and fugitive search plans, but which were limited in such important service fields as health, zoning, water supply, and refuse disposal.[36]

Interjurisdictional agreements, however, represent only one of the several methods by which local governments can cooperate for mutual advantage. A statement prepared by the International City Managers' Association in 1942 listed conferences, exchange of services, temporary loans and joint use of equipment or personnel, performance of service by one governmental unit for another, joint performance of a service, and cooperative administration through state leagues as six common methods for cooperative undertakings.[37] Thus the term interlocal cooperation embraces cooperative arrangements between like units (e.g., two neighboring cities for sewage disposal), and between different types of units (e.g., a city and a township for fire protection), as well as those activities which a county government performs for some or all of the other local units within it.

While interlocal cooperative arrangements cannot solve the problems arising from the interrelationships between local governments, they are useful in achieving some degree of coordination of the efforts of local units to provide common services. Such arrangements allow joint action on problems of mutual concern without any loss of corporate identity on the part of any of the cooperating units. Thus, as an acceptable device to meet common problems, it is highly probable that the interjurisdictional agreement and the other means of interlocal cooperation will be increasingly called

[36] George S. Blair, *Interjurisdictional Agreements in Southeastern Pennsylvania,* Fels Institute, University of Pennsylvania, 1960.
[37] International City Managers' Association, "Relations with Other Local Governments," *Public Management, 24* (March, 1942), 73–79.

upon in the immediate future to meet the problems of small governments in metropolitan areas as well as those of governmental units across the nation as a whole.

SUGGESTED READINGS

Books

Adrian, Charles R., *State and Local Governments, A Study in the Political Process* (New York: McGraw-Hill, 1960).

Alderfer, Harold, *American Local Government and Administration* (New York: Macmillan, 1956).

Blair, George S., *Interjurisdictional Agreements in Southeastern Pennsylvania* (Philadelphia: Fels Institute, University of Pennsylvania, 1960).

Council of State Governments, *State-Local Relations* (Chicago: Council of State Governments, 1946).

Council of State Governments, *The Book of the States* (Chicago: Council of State Governments, Biennial).

Dillon, John F., *Commentaries on the Law of Municipal Corporations*, 5th ed. (Boston: Little, Brown, 1911), Vol. 1.

Fordham, Jefferson B., *Local Government Law* (New York: Foundation Press, 1949).

Graves, W. Brooke (ed.), *State Constitutional Revision* (Chicago: Public Administration Service, 1960). See especially Chap. XV.

Kneier, Charles M., *City Government in the United States,* 3rd ed. (New York: Harper, 1957).

Kresky, Edward M., "Local Government," in National Municipal League, *Salient Issues of Constitutional Revision* (New York: National Municipal League, 1961), pp. 150–62.

McMillan, T. E., Jr., *State Supervision of Municipal Finance* (Austin: Institute of Public Affairs, University of Texas, 1953).

McQuillin, Eugene, *The Laws of Municipal Corporations*, 3rd ed. (Chicago: Callaghan, 1949).

Phillips, J. C., *State and Local Government in America* (New York: American Book Co., 1954).

Wallace, Schuyler, *State Administrative Supervision over Cities in the United States* (New York: Columbia University Press, 1928).

Articles

Bain, Chester W., "Annexation: Virginia's Not-so-Judicial System," *Public Administration Review, 15* (Autumn, 1955), 251–62.

Cassella, William N., Jr., "State-Local Relations: Recent Trends and

Fundamental Questions," *State Government*, *27* (December, 1954), 247–51, 258.

Desmond, Thomas C., "The States Eclipse the Cities," *New York Times Magazine*, (April 24, 1955), pp. 14, 42, 44.

National Municipal League, "New Look at Home Rule," reprint of articles appearing in *National Municipal Review*, *44* (March and April), 1955.

Phillips, J. C., "'Active Wrongdoing' and the Sovereign-Immunity Principle in Municipal Tort Liability," *Oregon Law Review*, *38* (February, 1959), 122–57.

Federal-Local Relations

5

Although the federal government has never been isolated from certain types of contacts with units of local government, these contacts remained largely negative in character until the early 1930s. In upholding the Constitution, federal courts nullified local ordinances which were found contrary to the spirit or letter of the basic law of the land. The power of Congress over interstate commerce also resulted in a requirement of federal approval of local harbor improvements and the building of bridges over navigable rivers. In a more positive vein, Congress in 1914 passed the Smith-Lever Agricultural Extension Act under which the office of county agent developed in counties across the nation.

In a study of the relations of the federal government with cities, the National Resources Committee in 1939 traced the growth of national services affecting urban communities. As summarized in this report, there were only 11 such services up to 1850; between 1851 and 1875 four new services were added, and 16 services were initiated in the next 25 years; thus, there was a total of only 31 federal services affecting cities by 1900. In the next four decades, however, the number increased substantially with the addition of 12 by 1910, of 19 more by 1920, of 17 services by 1930, and of 41 new services in the seven-year period from 1930 to 1937.[1] Of the

---

[1] National Resources Committee, *Urban Government*, Vol. 1 of the Supplementary Report of the Urbanism Committee, Washington, 1939.

expansion in this last seven-year period, 19 existing agencies began rendering services affecting municipalities and 22 new agencies were established whose work involved relations with cities. While there has been no recent counting of federal agencies with services to local government, it seems logical to presume that few of the 120 services found by the National Resources Committee have been abandoned and that a sizable number have been added in the years since 1937.

Though federal-local relations existed prior to 1935, the traditional theory of American federalism asserted that the federal government had no direct concern with local governments. Thus, it was not unexpected, though it now sounds a bit dated, for President Coolidge to state in his message to Congress in December, 1925, that "The functions which the Congress are to discharge are not those of local government but of national government. The greatest solicitude should be exercised to prevent encroachment upon the rights of the states or their various political subdivisions. Local self-government is one of our most precious possessions. It is the greatest contributing factor to the stability, strength, liberty, and progress of the nation. It ought not to abdicate power through weakness or resign its authority through favor. It does not at all follow that because abuses exist it is the concern of the Federal Government to attempt their reform."[2] However, this traditional concept of federalism was already under challenge by a noted political scientist. In May, 1924, a year and a half before the Coolidge message, William Anderson in a perceptive article wrote, "The time has come in the United States for those interested in the progress of our institutions to consider the relations existing between the national and the municipal authorities."[3]

We have come a long way from the view expressed by President Coolidge less than 40 years ago. Perhaps the degree of this change is most vividly shown by contrasting that view, generally accepted at the time, with the tone of a message delivered to Congress by President Kennedy in 1961. In his special message on Housing and Community Development submitted March 9, 1961, President Kennedy said, "Our communities are what we make them. We as a nation have before us the opportunity—and the responsibility—

[2] As quoted in Roger H. Wells, *American Local Government*, McGraw-Hill, 1939, p. 137.

[3] William Anderson, "The Federal Government and the Cities," *National Municipal Review, 13* (May, 1924), 288-93.

to remold our cities, to improve our patterns of community development, and to provide for the housing needs of all segments of our population. . . . An equal challenge is the tremendous urban growth that lies ahead. . . . We must begin now to lay the foundation for livable, efficient and attractive communities of the future. . . . Urban renewal programs to date have been too narrow to cope effectively with the basic problems facing older cities. We must do more than concern ourselves with bad housing—we must reshape our cities into effective nerve centers for expanding metropolitan areas."[4] After touching upon transportation needs and problems of urban communities, Kennedy then recommended the establishment of a new Cabinet-rank Department of Housing and Urban Affairs to bring an awareness of urban problems to the Cabinet table and to provide coordinated leadership for the "functions related to urban affairs but appropriately performed by a variety of Departments and agencies."[5] The feasibility and possible functions of such an executive department will be discussed in a later section in this chapter.

■ *The Turning Point: 1932*

While it is usually difficult to pick a single point in time to signify a change in a continuing policy development, the year 1932 can serve as such a point in tracing the pattern of direct relationships of the federal government with units of local government. In initiating a broad program for combatting the economic depression, wide-ranging programs were adopted which matured into an entirely new role for the national government viz-à-viz the people, the states, and local governments.

A delegation from the United States at the International Congress of Cities held in London in 1932 reported that no direct administrative relationships then existed here between the local and federal governments. Also in that year, the word "municipalities" appeared for the first time in an act of Congress authorizing the Reconstruction Finance Corporation to make loans to cities for self-liquidating public works projects.[6] This specific act can be singled out as the

[4] *Congressional Quarterly Weekly Report,* XIX (March 10, 1961), 402–4.
[5] *Ibid.,* p. 404.
[6] Raymond S. Short, "Municipalities and the Federal Government," *The Annals of the American Academy of Political and Social Science,* 207 (January, 1940), 44–53.

beginning of a more positive approach by the federal government, since many of these newer problems had technological and economic causes beyond the control of local government. The development of a national system of transportation and communication and the welfare needs arising from the great depression prompted federal actions which affected local governments more directly.

Thus, the start of a basic change in our interpretation of the American federal system was initiated in 1932. Local governments now began to emerge as partners in a system of cooperative federalism instead of being viewed as the bottom layer of governments in a three-tier federal system. One writer has described this change as discarding a layer-cake for a marble-cake theory of federalism. In his words, "The American form of government is often, but erroneously, symbolized by a three-layer cake. A far more accurate image is the rainbow or marble cake, characterized by an inseparable mingling of differently colored ingredients, the colors appearing in vertical and diagonal strands and unexpected whirls. As colors are mixed in the marble cake, so functions are mixed in the American federal system."[7]

The extent of current federal-local relationships is clearly indicated in a publication issued annually by the American Municipal Association which attempts to provide a brief description of some of the more important federal programs of aid to local governments.[8] Thirty-one federal programs are outlined in the 1960 issue, including those in the important service fields of civil defense, housing, urban renewal, planning assistance, hospital construction, sewage treatment facilities construction, air pollution, flood control, watershed projects, major disaster relief, mental health, school lunch and milk programs, library services, airports, highways, training courses for local personnel, and health grants for cancer, heart disease, and veneral disease control. A few of these programs will be described in a subsequent section in this chapter discussing programmatic grants available to local governments.

Of all currently existing federal agencies, the Housing and Home Finance Agency is one of the most directly concerned with programs of services and grants to local governments. Six of its administrative units have major programs which are vitally important,

[7] Morton Grodzins, "The Federal System" in *Goals for Americans*, The Report of the President's Commission on National Goals, Prentice-Hall, 1960, p. 265.

[8] American Municipal Association, *Federal Technical Assistance and Grant Programs of Interest to Local Governments*, Washington, 1960, 28 pp.

particularly to urban communities. First, the Urban Renewal Administration helps cities eliminate blight, rehabilitate rundown areas and plan for their redevelopment; encourages comprehensive planning for metropolitan areas; and assists cities in the preservation of open space. Second, the Office of the Administrator assists communities in the development of mass transportation systems. Third, the Community Facilities Administration helps local governments plan and build public works and aids in financing housing for senior citizens. Fourth, the Public Housing Administration assists communities in clearing slums and in constructing homes for those who cannot afford decent private housing. Fifth, the Federal Housing Administration insures mortgages and in this way helps finance housing construction. Sixth, the Federal National Mortgage Association provides a secondary market for these mortgages and buys up certain special types of mortgages from the communities.[9]

In large measure the growth of direct federal-local relations has resulted from economic needs of local urban governments to meet the demands of their rapidly growing populations. Since state legislatures are constantly called upon to provide new statewide services, the needs of local governments cannot be fully met even by sympathetic lawmakers in state capitols because of state financial problems. Limitations on taxing powers and indebtedness plus the fear that increasing tax burdens may have an undesirable impact on business within the state create difficult financial hurdles in most states. Thus, urban communities have turned to Washington for financial aid to meet their ever-growing requirements.

While there is some loss of municipal autonomy from programs that have federal matching-money requirements or other conditions, the same is true of state grants. To harrassed local officials, it probably matters little whether this loss of autonomy depends on the purse strings of one level or the other until a more equitable reapportionment of tax resources can be realized. In 1929, local governments received 6.8 percent of their total receipts from state government payments and only 0.3 percent from federal grants-in-aid. By 1960, state payments had increased nearly four times and totaled 24.1 percent of local receipts; federal grants, however, had increased 15 times and now totaled 4.6 percent of all local govern-

---

[9] From "Opportunities for Our Cities," keynote address by Jack T. Conway, Deputy Administrator, Housing and Home Finance Agency, White House Regional Conference, Los Angeles, November 20, 1961.

ment receipts.[10] State sharing is commonly for such costly local programs as schools, health, and roads, while federal aid seems more readily available than state aid for some less traditional programs.

■ Selected Programmatic Grants

It is not feasible or necessary to attempt to catalog all the programs of federal grants which are available to local governments or all the relationships which now exist between these two levels. However, it is possible to classify these relationships into four types to facilitate a brief discussion. First, there are a number of indirect relations involving no coercion or real control by the federal government. Fact-finding and informational services of a number of federal agencies fall into this category as, for example, the series of studies prepared by the Bureau of the Census, the quarterly bulletin of uniform crime reporting by the Federal Bureau of Investigation, or the special studies of the Bureau of Standards. Second, there are direct relations involving no federal coercion or control, such as the preparation of position examinations by the United States Civil Service Commission, assistance in crime detection by the F. B. I., and services of the Department of Health, Education and Welfare. Third, there are direct relations involving contracts or other circumstances in which the federal government is permitted to exercise controls or coercion under prescribed conditions. Illustrative of this type are local airport development, radio broadcasting operations, and power projects involving navigable rivers. Fourth, there are direct relations involving grants-in-aid where the federal government exercises control under certain circumstances.[11] It is this latter type which is of most immediate interest at this point and a few selected examples of such programmatic grants will be briefly described below.

The avowed purposes of grants-in-aid were succinctly stated in a Senate subcommittee report in 1951. These were to stimulate states and local governments to act in fields of national interest but within state jurisdiction; to grant financial and administrative sup-

[10] Lillian P. Barnes, George M. Cobren and Joseph Rosenthal, "State and Local Government Activity, The Postwar Experience Related to the National Economy," *Survey of Current Business, 41* (March, 1961), 17.

[11] J. C. Phillips, *State and Local Government in America,* American Book Company, 1954, pp. 389-92.

port for such programs of national interest; to lessen disparity and inequality in service levels among the states; and to complement state and local revenues to finance these services.[12] Provisions of the specific program grants in the fields of urban renewal assistance, highways, and hospitals and other medical facilities discussed below will be checked to test conformity with these purposes of grants-in-aid generally.

URBAN RENEWAL PROGRAM

Urban renewal is the term used to describe the efforts of cities to accomplish the three major objectives of slum prevention through neighborhood conservation and housing code enforcement, rehabilitation of structures and neighborhoods, and clearance and redevelopment of structures and neighborhoods. Under provisions of the Housing Act of 1949, as subsequently amended, particularly in 1954 and 1960, Congress has provided a "kit of tools" including loans, grants, technical assistance, and special mortgage insurance for concentrated attention against slums and urban blight by the concerted actions of local government, citizens, private enterprise, and federal government.

The emphasis in urban renewal is upon neighborhood improvement and the installation of necessary public improvements by the city. Such projects are conceived, planned and executed by a local public agency which may be a separate urban renewal agency, a local housing authority, or a department of city government, depending on state law. Federal financial assistance is available for urban renewal projects and comes in a variety of grants, advances, and loans. Generally speaking, federal aid consists of reimbursement of two-thirds of the loss on a public project whether it is an action of slum clearance, redevelopment, or urban renewal. This grant is based on the valid assumption that the fair value of the cleared land for such a project does not equal the overall loss of public funds entailed in its clearance through the loss of taxable properties and other possible revenue producing land uses.

To qualify for federal assistance, communities must apply to the Housing and Home Finance Agency and present a workable plan

[12] Committee on Expenditures of the Executive Departments, *Intergovernmental Relationships between the United States and the States and Municipalities*, Report of the Subcommittee to Study Intergovernmental Relations, Senate Report No. 94, 82nd Congress, 1st Session, 1951.

to attain certain objectives of community improvement, to eliminate blight and to prevent its recurrence. The seven elements of the workable plan include (1) adequate and reasonable housing and building standards established in codes and ordinances, (2) a comprehensive plan for the community, (3) neighborhood analyses showing the extent, intensity and causes of blight, (4) adequate local machinery to enforce the plan and codes and carry out other renewal activities, (5) a plan for local financing of the community's role in the renewal program, (6) a relocation program for the families displaced by the project, and (7) methods for citizen participation throughout the project.[13] The project itself may involve (a) the acquisition and clearance of a slum or blighted area, either residential or nonresidential, and the disposition of the cleared area to private developers for redevelopment, (b) rehabilitation and conservation of structures in such an area by action of the property owners and accompanying action by the local government to improve facilities such as lights, parks, streets, playgrounds, etc., or (c) any combination of the above two programs.

Acceptance of the urban renewal program by local governments is shown by the fact that as of June 30, 1960, the Urban Renewal Administration had approved a total of 797 projects. These were spread among 455 communities in 44 states, the District of Columbia and Puerto Rico, and involved a total expenditure of $1.6 billion. While the largest number, a total of 284, was in cities with populations of less than 25,000, the value of such projects was $156 million as contrasted with a value of $742 million for the 139 projects in cities of over 500,000.[14]

Concerning the purposes of grants-in-aid in general, the urban renewal program advances three of the objectives. The federal financial and technical assistance available does stimulate activity in urban renewal by state and local governments, grant financial and administrative support to such undertakings, and complement state and local revenues in paying for renewal projects. Since the program of financial aid follows a common formula, the urban renewal program does not directly contribute to lessening the disparity among states and their local governments in ability to finance such projects on their own.

[13] Housing and Home Finance Agency, *The Urban Renewal Program*, Fact Sheet on Federal Assistance to Communities for Urban Renewal and Related Activities, Washington, September, 1961.
[14] American Municipal Association, *op. cit.*, pp. 5–6.

The Urban Planning Assistance Program is administered by the Urban Renewal Administration within the Housing and Home Finance Agency. Established by Section 701 of the Housing Act of 1954, this program is sometimes known as the "701" program and provides basically for federal grants to match state and local funds to finance comprehensive planning studies for small cities and counties as well as such studies for metropolitan areas and urban regions. The program encourages planning which embraces all the basic essentials of sound urban development, including land use studies to guide residential, commercial, and industrial expansion, and planning the general location of necessary public works such as transportation facilities, schools, sewers, water, and recreational facilities.

Nearly all types of communities may benefit from the "701" program. For metropolitan areas or urban regions of over 50,000 population, federal grants may be made directly to official metropolitan or regional planning agencies authorized to undertake area-wide planning, or to a state planning agency for use in such urbanized areas. Grants to smaller cities, counties, or groups of adjacent communities with total populations of less than 50,000 are made directly to an appropriate state planning agency which provides planning assistance to these localities. Applications for aid by smaller communities must be made through the state planning agency which forwards them to the HHFA Regional Office, while applications from larger cities or urban regions are made directly to the Regional Office.[15]

As of August 31, 1959, nearly 1,500 communities had secured federal assistance under this program. These included 98 metropolitan areas or regional planning units in 32 states and Guam, and 1,399 smaller cities, counties and groups of cities in 38 states.[16] The number of participating communities is probably considerably larger now since the Housing Act of 1961 increased the total appropriations authorized by the federal government from $20 to $75 million. This act also increased the share of the total cost which the federal government could contribute from one-half to two-thirds

[15] Housing and Home Finance Agency, *The Urban Planning Assistance Program,* Fact Sheet on Federal Assistance for Comprehensive Planning in Metropolitan and Other Urban Areas, Washington, September, 1961.
[16] American Municipal Association, *op. cit.,* pp. 6–7.

for urban planning projects and from one-half to three-fourths for project costs in areas designated as Redevelopment Areas.[17]

With the 1961 change in the share of the total costs for particular projects which the federal government could contribute, this programmatic grant advances all four of the general objectives of grant-in-aid programs. More specifically, the program stimulates comprehensive planning by state and local governments, grants financial support, complements state and local expenditures, and makes it possible for the federal government to contribute a greater portion of the costs in urban areas or smaller communities less able to match federal grants as was required prior to 1961.

HIGHWAY GRANTS

Federal grants to states for aiding local street and road construction began in 1916 with the primary objective that of improving rural roads. This program began with the prohibition against the use of any federal funds in cities with populations greater than 2,500. Federal money first became available to cities in 1933 and this program of aid has steadily increased during the last three decades. The present highway aid program is based upon the Federal Aid Highway Acts of 1944 and 1956 as both have been amended by succeeding sessions of Congress. The act of 1944 established a formula for the distribution of federal funds among the primary, secondary, and urban road systems on a 50-50 matching fund basis, and the act of 1956 established a "National System of Interstate and Defense Highways" with the federal government contributing 90 percent of the cost.

At present, federal aid is authorized for four road systems. The first is the primary system of major through highways selected by state highway departments and subject to approval by the Bureau of Public Roads. Second is the secondary system of feeder roads including farm-to-market roads and county roads. These routes are selected by state highway departments with the cooperation of local officials and approved by the Bureau of Public Roads. The third system is the secondary system of city arterial streets which are the urban extensions of the roads in the second system and which are chosen in the same manner as roads in that system. And, fourth, is the system of interstate highways which consists of 41,000

[17] Housing and Home Finance Agency, *The Urban Planning Assistance Program, loc. cit.*

miles of highways connecting the principal metropolitan areas, cities, and industrial centers of the nation. These interstate routes are a part of the primary system of major through highways and are selected in the same manner as other routes in this system of highways.

Financing arrangements for the first three road systems are identical in that the federal funds made available must be matched by the states on a dollar-for-dollar or 50-50 basis. In determining state apportionments of the money available for these systems, the three factors of area, population, and mileage of rural mail delivery and star routes are given equal weight. The share of any particular state is determined by the ratio of the three factors in that state to their total in all the states. The federal funds plus matching state funds must be divided for use as follows: (a) 45 percent for projects on the primary system of major through highways; (b) 30 percent for projects on the secondary system of feeder roads; and (c) 25 percent for projects on streets in the secondary system of city arterial streets.[18] As mentioned previously, the financing arrangement for the system of interstate highways calls for contributions of 90 percent from the federal government and 10 percent from the state governments.

The extent of federal highway funds apportioned to the states in the period from 1917 to 1962 shows the magnitude of this program. During this 45-year period, such federal grants totaled more than $26 billion with the six states of California, Illinois, New York, Ohio, Pennsylvania and Texas each receiving well over a billion dollars each and another twelve states each receiving more than a half-billion dollars in highway grants.[19]

The system of highway grants again advances three of the four overall objectives of grants-in-aid in general. However, because of the common formula for matching requirements on the part of the states receiving federal highway grants, this program does not operate to lessen the disparity of road systems within the states or the inequality in the ability of states to match federal funds.

GRANTS FOR HOSPITALS

Since 1946, local governments and communities have been eligible for federal grants to assist in the construction of needed general and mental hospitals and public health centers under the

[18] American Municipal Association, op. cit., pp. 22–23.
[19] Ibid., p. 24.

provisions of the Hill-Burton Act. This program was broadened in 1954 when Congress authorized additional grants for such facilities as nursing homes, chronic disease hospitals, diagnostic and treatment centers, and rehabilitation facilities.

The program of federal grants is administered by the surgeon general of the United States Public Health Service through appropriate state agencies. Individual projects must fit into a general state plan and be approved by both the state administering agency and the surgeon general. In determining the priority among proposed projects, the relative needs of the areas to be served are weighted heavily and special consideration is given to projects which would serve rural communities in low-income areas. There is no fixed formula for determining the federal contribution to individual projects and this ratio may vary from a maximum of two-thirds to a minimum of one-third of the construction cost plus the cost of initial equipment.

As of December 31, 1959, the Community Facilities Administration had approved some 4,800 projects in over 2,600 communities spread among all 50 states, the District of Columbia, Guam, Puerto Rico, and the Virgin Islands. That the purposes of the program are being achieved is evidenced by the fact that nearly 1,800 of the communities availing themselves of this assistance had populations of 10,000 or less while only 17 communities with populations greater than 500,000 had qualified for such assistance. In declining order, the ten states with the largest federal grants were Texas, Pennsylvania, New York, North Carolina, California, Ohio, Georgia, Illinois, Alabama and Tennessee.[20]

Because of the sliding scale of federal contributions available and the heavy emphasis placed on the need of communities for hospitals or other medical facilities, this program of federal assistance advances all four of the general objectives of grant-in-aid programs.

■ A Federal Agency of Local Government?

The recommendation of President Kennedy in March, 1961, that a Cabinet-rank Department of Housing and Urban Affairs be established was not without precedent. Recognizing the increasing national activities in interlevel relationships, the temporary President's Commission on Intergovernmental Relations in its report issued in 1955 recommended that two actions be taken to improve

[20] American Municipal Association, op. cit., pp. 8–9.

relationships among the federal, state, and local levels of government. First, it recommended that a special assistant be appointed in the Executive Office of the President to serve with a small staff as his chief aide and adviser on state and local relationships with the federal government. Second, it proposed that an Advisory Board on Intergovernmental Relations be appointed by the President to consider fiscal adjustments and other interlevel problems.[21]

President Eisenhower accepted both Commission proposals and appointed his special assistant in the spring of 1956 and assigned the assistant director of the Bureau of the Budget specific responsibilities in the field of metropolitan area problems. In 1959, the Permanent Advisory Commission on Intergovernmental Relations was established by action of Congress as a bi-partisan board of 26 members. The composition of the Commission was to include three United States senators appointed by the president of the senate, three United States representatives appointed by the speaker of the house, three officers of the executive branch appointd by the President, and three private citizens also appointed by the President. In addition, the President would appoint as members four governors from a panel of at least eight names submitted by the Governors' Conference, three state legislators from a panel of at least six submitted by the Board of Managers of the Council of State Governments, four mayors from a panel of at least eight submitted jointly by the American Municipal Association and the United States Conference of Mayors, and three elected county officials from a panel of at least six submitted by the National Association of Counties. The primary purpose of the Commission was to serve as a forum for discussing the administration and coordination of federal grants and other programs requiring intergovernmental cooperation.

In 1955, the first bill incorporating the idea of a central agency in the federal government to deal with municipal problems was introduced in Congress by a California representative. The new agency was proposed as a Department of Urbiculture to parallel the existing Department of Agriculture. The bill was received favorably by the Congressional Committee to which it was assigned but no action was taken that year.[22] In the next Congress,

[21] Commission on Intergovernmental Relations, *A Report to the President for Transmittal to Congress*, Government Printing Office, 1955, pp. 87–88.

[22] Hearings before a Subcommittee of the Committee on Government Operations, House of Representatives, 84th Congress, 1st Session, (1955), on H.R. 1864, "A Bill to Create a Department of Urbiculture and to Prescribe its Functions."

three separate bills were introduced calling for the creation of a department of urban affairs and similar bills were introduced again in 1959–1960 with one (the bill of Senator Clark) proposing a Department of Housing and Metropolitan Affairs. In late January, 1962, President Kennedy attempted to create a Department of Urban Affairs and Housing through his powers to reorganize agencies of the executive branch, but the proposal was defeated in a roll-call vote in the House of Representatives on February 21, 1962.[23]

The basic arguments of the proponents for the creation of such an executive agency are four in number. First, since the population of the country as a whole is now 65 percent urban, cities should be represented at the Cabinet level. Second, states cannot solve the many problems of metropolitan areas which are interstate in character. Third, state legislatures are often not responsive to needs of urban areas because of their domination by rural lawmakers. Fourth, planning for metropolitan areas is really national in character and properly a function of the federal government.[24] To these can be added a fifth supporting point. Such a federal agency now exists in embryonic form in the Housing and Home Finance Agency which already administers such diverse programs as grants for planning, urban renewal and slum clearance, public housing, and community facility loans. Elevating an agency with these and other functions to the Cabinet level would be only proper in terms of the importance of its activities and show the intensity of the interest of the federal government in problems of urban areas.

Opponents of such an executive department point out several major problems. First, they believe the federal government must determine a general philosophy of its role in urban affairs before creating a single organizational unit to administer the many programs currently existing. Second, a department of urban affairs would be geographical rather than functional in concept and would run into conflict with other executive departments and agencies which are now carrying out functions and services to local governments. Third, the creation of such a department might cause government officials at all three levels to relax, believing that something definite had finally been accomplished while in actuality only an agency for doing something had been established. Fourth, such an agency would be a line department to undertake what by their

[23] *Congressional Quarterly Weekly Report, 20* (February 23, 1962) 275–7.
[24] Robert F. Connery and Richard H. Leach, "U. S. Needs a Program," *National Municipal Review, 46* (September, 1957), 394–400.

very nature are primarily staff functions. And fifth, such a department would be politically inexpedient since it would arouse deep-rooted antagonisms between the city and farm and rural and urban interests.[25]

Connery and Leach have proposed that a Council on Metropolitan Areas, similar in function and purpose to the Council of Economic Advisers, be established in the Executive Office of the President to furnish him with continuous staff assistance in this important field and that committees on metropolitan problems be established in both houses of Congress.[26] They believe that such an agency is well within established precedent since similar agencies have been established in other areas of governmental affairs, that this arrangement would clearly establish the new agency as a staff rather than a line agency, and that this type of agency would be freer to "free-lance" in its activities and utilize *ad hoc* advisory groups, regular advisory committees, ask questions of operating agencies, collect data and make policy and program recommendations to the president.

Since an important problem concerning federal-state-local relationships seems to lie in the area of coordination of existing policies and programs, it seems probable that an executive department will be established in the near future. While such a department would not solve the problem of coordinating the service and grant programs which would remain in the departments now administering them, it is probable that greater coordination would result from the meetings of the head of this and the several other departments around the Cabinet table than would result from the pleading of a staff agency without any responsibility or authority for coordinating such programs and services.

■ *The Future of Federal-Local Relations*

This recent expansion of direct federal-local relationships has not gone without challenge by serious students of government nor been free of difficult problems many of which have not yet been answered satisfactorily. Writing in 1941, George C. S. Benson

[25] *Ibid.,* pp. 398–9, and Connery and Leach, "U. S. Council on Metro," *National Municipal Review, 48* (June, 1959), 292–6.

[26] Connery and Leach, "U. S. Council on Metro," *loc. cit.,* 295–6, and Connery and Leach, *The Federal Government and Metropolitan Areas,* Harvard University Press, 1960, pp. 228–9.

cautioned that "This hierarchical principle of federal-local contact only through the states has much logic to support it. Not only is it the implicit theory which underlies the Constitution, but the fact that the states are larger in size and fewer in number implements, by practical considerations, the logic of administrative feasibility."[27] He concluded that, "from a long-range view, it would be far better if all local units fell into their conventional subordination to reinvigorated state governments which were able and willing to engage in comprehensive and thoughtful planning for their entire jurisdiction and which were, for both political and administrative reasons, better fitted to be the agents of communication with Washington."[28]

In a recent reappraisal of his point of view, Benson continues his questioning of centralization in these words, "Those who support centralization will on the whole admit candidly that their programs tend to the derogation of state and local governments, but they will maintain that concentration of power is not dangerous while the national government is still subject to 'popular control' under free elections. Let us admit that a freely granted power is not 'usurpation'. But a power 'freely' granted under financial pressure or under an increasing political and economic lassitude on the part of individuals may very well result in a concentration which is dangerous to individual liberty of thought and action. Contrarily a mechanism which forces back onto individuals and onto state and local officials a sense of dignified responsibility seems to have inherent value."[29]

A similar questioning of the implications of direct federal relations with local governments was made by Estes Kefauver in 1947. He stated that "Wise and strong local governments go far toward assuring a sound national government. People of a democracy are made more capable of carrying on their duties if they participate actively at the local levels. They can, if they will, handle most problems better than some bureau of the central government, and they will be stronger for having found their own solution. Therefore, let us hope that when a job can be done at home or at Washington that it will be done at home."[30]

[27] George C. S. Benson, *The New Centralization,* Farrar and Rinehart, 1941, p. 88.
[28] *Ibid,* p. 103.
[29] George C. S. Benson et. al., *Essays in Federalism,* The Institute for Studies in Federalism, Claremont Men's College, 1961, p. 7.
[30] Estes Kefauver, "Cities and Congress," *Proceedings of the Seventh Annual Southern Institute of Local Government,* Knoxville, 1948, p. 33.

However, the crucial questions in the future of federal-local relations are not closely tied in with past concepts of our federal structure or with efforts to strengthen local governments as the bottom tier of independent units in our tri-level system. Rather these questions seek to determine whether or not there are certain governmental functions which can be performed better or governmental problems which can be solved more effectively by cooperative federal-local relations than by state-local actions or by local actions alone. It seems apparent that our large cities have accepted an affirmative answer to these queries and are working toward more effective federal-local relationships. This acceptance is evidenced by making Washington the headquarters of the United States Conference of Mayors, which services cities of over 50,000, and the site of an office of the American Municipal Association, an organization of state municipal leagues with headquarters in Chicago. In addition, the National Association of Counties has its headquarters in the nation's capital, and these three large organizations comprise an effective lobby in Washington to advance and protect their interests.

Two serious students of the problems of and possibilities for intergovernmental cooperation make a strong case that future state constitutions incorporate express provisions authorizing interlevel cooperative actions and undertakings. They suggest the following statement as one which provides a broad permissive base authorizing a variety of forms of such cooperation: "The state, or any one or more of its municipal corporations and other subdivisions, may exercise any of their respective powers, or undertake any function jointly or in cooperation with any one or more states, or municipal corporations, or other subdivisions of such states, or the United States, or with a foreign power, and may participate in the financing of any such joint or cooperative projects or undertakings; provided that any municipality or other subdivision of this state does not exercise or perform, or bind itself to exercise or perform any power or function not conferred upon it by its constitution or by statute; and provided further that the joint or cooperative exercise of such power or performance of such function is not contrary to statute."[31]

The developments in federal-local relations in the last three decades represented a sharp departure from the traditional concept of the relationships of these two levels of government. However,

[31] Frederick L. Zimmermann and Mitchell Wendell, "No Positive Barriers," *National Civic Review*, 47 (November, 1959), 525, 554.

it seems reasonable to predict that this recent concept of cooperative federalism will not only remain but will continue to expand in the years ahead. Joseph S. Clark, a United States Senator from Pennsylvania, looks forward to the development of what he calls a new "national federalism" in which the financial relationships of the federal and local levels would be significantly increased. Under this new federalism, revenues would be collected preponderantly at the federal level since a national tax system could best tap an economy that is national in character. Decision-making concerning the use of this money, however, would be decentralized to the states and local communities when local decision-making could be effective or when national uniformity is not essential.[32] This would mean block grants to states or their local governments which, within reasonable limits, could be used for whatever purposes seem necessary. As the reader will recall, federal grants and most state grants to local governments up to now are for particular purposes. In view of recent developments, the concept of national federalism as envisioned by Senator Clark seems a probable future extension of the current path of federal-local relations.

SUGGESTED READINGS

Books

American Municipal Association, *Federal Technical Assistance and Grant Programs of Interest to Local Governments* (Washington: American Municipal Association, 1960).

Anderson, William, *The Nation and the States, Rivals or Partners?* (Minneapolis: University of Minnesota Press, 1955), Chap. IX.

Benson, George C. S., *The New Centralization* (New York: Farrar and Rinehart, 1941).

Clark, Jane Perry, *The Rise of A New Federalism* (New York: Columbia University Press, 1938).

Commission on Intergovernmental Relations, *A Report to the President for Transmittal to Congress* (Washington: Government Printing Office, 1955).

Connery, Robert H. and Leach, Richard H., *The Federal Government and Metropolitan Areas* (Cambridge: Harvard University Press, 1960).

Council of State Governments, *Federal Grants-in-Aid* (Chicago: Council of State Governments, 1949).

[32] Joseph S. Clark, "Toward National Federalism," speech at George Washington University, Washington, March 28, 1960, in George Washington University, *The Federal Government and the Cities,* The School of Government, Business, and International Affairs, 1961, pp. 39–49.

George Washington University, *The Federal Government and the Cities* (Washington: The School of Government, Business and International Affairs, 1961).

Goldwin, Robert A. (ed.), *A Nation of States* (Chicago: Rand McNally, 1963).

Grodzins, Morton, "The Federal System" in *Goals for Americans*, Report of the President's Commission on National Goals, (Englewood Cliffs: Prentice-Hall, 1960).

National Resources Committee, *Urban Government*, Vol. 1 of the Supplementary Report of the Urbanism Committee (Washington: Government Printing Office, 1939).

Phillips, J. C., *State and Local Government in America* (New York: American Book Company, 1954).

Kneier, Charles M., *City Government in the United States*, 3rd ed. (New York: Harper, 1957), Chap. VIII.

Wells, Roger H., "General Analysis," *The Impact of Federal Grants-in-Aid on the Structure and Functions of State and Local Governments*, A Survey Report submitted to the Commission on Intergovernmental Relations (Washington: Government Printing Office, 1955).

Articles

Anderson, William, "The Federal Government and the Cities," *National Municipal Review*, 13 (May, 1924), 288–93.

Bromage, Arthur W., "Federal-State-Local Relations," *American Political Science Review*, 37 (February, 1943), 35–48.

Connery, Robert H. and Leach, Richard H., "U. S. Needs a Program," *National Municipal Review*, 46 (September, 1957), 394–400.

Connery, Robert H. and Leach, Richard H., "U. S. Council on Metro," *National Municipal Review*, 47 (June, 1959), 292–6.

Conway, Jack T., "Opportunities for our Cities," Keynote address, White House Regional Conference, Los Angeles, November 20, 1961.

Hanks, D. W., Jr., "Neglected Cities Turn to U. S.," *National Municipal Review*, 35 (April, 1946), 172–3.

Merriam, Robert E., "Partners or Rivals? The Role of the National Government in Intergovernmental Relations," speech at National Conference on Government, Memphis, November 12, 1956.

Satterfield, M. H., "T.V.A.-State-Local Relationships," *American Political Science Review*, 40 (October, 1946), 935–49.

Short, Raymond S., "Municipalities and the Federal Government," *The Annals of the American Academy of Political and Social Science*, 207 (January, 1940), 44–53.

Zimmermann, F. L. and Wendell, Mitchell, "No Positive Barriers," *National Civic Review*, 47 (November, 1959), 522–5, 554.

CITIZENS AND THEIR POLITICS

Two

The Citizen and
Local Government

6

In Chapter 3 a local government was defined as a "subordinate territorial unit of an American state which enjoys a reasonable degree of independence from external control and which is accountable to its citizenry." The degree of external control exercised by states and the federal government in their relations with local governments has been examined in the past two chapters, and we are now ready to look at the role of the citizen in determining, conducting, and controlling the public affairs of his own community. In this chapter, the role of the citizen will be described both in theoretical and practical terms, while in the subsequent two chapters the organizations through which he associates and the types of actions he can take will be discussed.

■ *Democracy in Local Government*

Since the essence of democracy is respect for the individual, a democratic community is one which is devoted to the principle that everybody counts and in which the government is controlled by its whole citizenry rather than by a particular group or fraction of the whole. A number of recent studies of local communities have concluded that they are actually oligarchic rather than democratic in form since there is a community power structure or an elitist group or groups which really make the important decisions which are merely ratified by the other members of the community.[1]

At one time, the notion that there was a dispersed inequality of power among the members of a community was considered a conspiracy of the power holders against the common people. This view is now rather outdated since the term "political power" has lost much of its sinister connotation and increasingly represents a relationship necessary to achieve the desired goals of government. As defined by Harold Lasswell, political power is "an interpersonal situation; those who hold power are empowered. They depend upon and continue only so long as there is a continuing stream of empowering responses."[2]

If we accept the Lasswell definition, three important propositions concerning political power become evident. The first is that political power is never unlimited. Since the elements or resources that comprise political power—office, position, status, money, influence, land, manpower, etc. are limited in both quantity and quality, it follows that political power itself is not without limits. The second proposition is that political power is never perfectly concentrated in any one person or group. Even more important in a democratic society, no person or group is completely devoid of political power. Such a perfect concentration of power as the power of punishment envisioned by George Orwell in his frightening novel 1984 or the power of rewards as foreseen by Aldous Huxley in his Brave New World is indeed a hideous concept, but fortunately both societies

[1] The number of these studies has increased annually since the pioneering work of Floyd Hunter in his *Community Power Structure: A Study of Decision-makers*, University of North Carolina Press, 1953. Among the best of these studies are: Robert Dahl, *Who Governs? Democracy and Power in an American City*, Yale University Press, 1961; Martin Meyerson and E. C. Banfield, *Politics, Planning and the Public Interest*, The Free Press, 1955; C. Wright Mills, *The Power Elite*, Oxford University Press, 1956; Arthur J. Vidich and Joseph Bensman, *Small Town in Mass Society*, Princeton University Press, 1958; Robert C. Wood, *Suburbia: Its People and Their Politics*, Houghton Mifflin, 1959; Scott Greer, "Individual Participation in a Mass Society" in Roland Young (ed.), *Approaches to the Study of Politics*, Northwestern University Press, 1958; R. E. Agger and Vincent Ostrom, "The Political Structure of a Small Community," *Public Opinion Quarterly, 20* (Spring, 1956), 81–89; George Belknap and Ralph Smuckler, "Political Power Relations in a Midwest City," *Public Opinion Quarterly, 20* (Spring, 1956), 73–80; and Norton Long, "The Local Community as an Ecology of Games," *American Journal of Sociology, 64* (November, 1958), 251–61.

[2] Harold Lasswell, *Power and Personality*, Norton, 1948, p. 10.

are figments of the imagination rather than realities. The third proposition holds that political power is a competitive rather than a monopolistic concept and that there are eager competitors and competing forces struggling to win the favor and support of the mass of citizens.

This concept of political power is quite different from that described by C. Wright Mills in his study *The Power Elite*. Concerning power in local communities, Mills had this to say: "In every town and small city of America, an upper set of families stands above the middle classes and towers over the underlying population of clerks and wage workers. The members of this set possess more than do others of whatever there is locally to possess; they hold the keys to local decision; their names and faces are often printed in the local paper; in fact, they own the newspaper as well as the radio station; they also own the three important local plants and most of the commercial properties along the main street; they direct the banks. Mingling closely with one another, they are quite conscious of the fact that they belong to the leading class of the leading families. All their sons and daughters go to college, often after private school; then they marry one another, or other boys and girls from similar families in similar towns. After they are well married, they come to possess, to occupy, to decide. . . . So it has traditionally been, and so it is today in the small towns of America."[3]

While not enough is yet known about the distribution and use of political power in American communities, it is quite possible that some unwarranted conclusions have been drawn about their oligarchic power structure. It would appear that the ideal of democracy against which the community is measured remains that described by Lincoln as "government of, by and for the people." Any defection from this theoretical ideal implies a miscarriage in the practice of democracy in that community. It is possible that the ideal concept of democracy is more at fault than the citizenry which does not always participate in large numbers, which may sometimes exercise poor judgment, or which may place its trust in its elected leaders and follow their direction. At the local level, it is possible that the real key to democratic government lies in the ability of the voters to say "no" and to throw the "rascals" out occasionally, rather than to give positive guidance to the elected officials on many inconsequential issues.

Before writing off a local community with a recognized pattern

[3] Mills, *op. cit.*, p. 30.

of leadership and a voter turnout of less than 50 percent as an undemocratic place to live, it might be better to see if the institutions of democracy exist and function with reasonable adequacy rather than with perfection. While there have been a number of efforts to define the essential elements of a democracy, the list of necessary attributes as defined by Charles S. Hyneman is an inclusive and encompassing one. In his view, a local community would be a democratic one if the following six principles existed: (1) an inclusive electorate; (2) ways for the people to get informed; (3) ways for the people to get together; (4) means for recording the will of the people; (5) a structure of government that enables the elected representatives of the people really to run the government; and (6) a state of mind that causes government officials either to exercise their authority in keeping with the instructions given them by the voters or to give up their positions.[4]

Accepting this view of a democratic community and the point that no member of it is completely devoid of political power, the old concept that a democracy exists only if the government is controlled by all the people is still a basic and valuable one. For what a local government is and what it does is ultimately determined by its total citizenry. The theory of local representative democracy has never held that all decisions must be made by the whole body of citizens; rather such theory holds that the decisions made by their chosen representatives must be acceptable by—or at least not unacceptable to—a majority of the citizens.

▪ The Right to Vote

A commonly accepted definition of a citizen is a person who owes allegiance to a government and is entitled to protection by it. However, this definition is so broad that it embraces a number of persons who are unable or unfit to participate in community affairs. It is obvious that very young children, the mentally incompetent, and certain other groups should not share in community decision-making. Thus, certain standards are prescribed, and only those who meet these qualifications are entitled to take part in running the affairs of their community. The common term for this portion of the total citizenry is the electorate, and it is this group which

---

[4] Charles S. Hyneman, *Bureaucracy in a Democracy*, Harper, 1950, pp. 12–15.

selects the government officials and guides their actions in determining the nature, character, and services of their government.

There has been a long-running controversy among some persons as to the status of the power of a citizen to cast his ballot. To some, the opportunity of the qualified citizen to vote is an inalienable "right" as are the rights to free speech, freedom of assembly, freedom of religious choice, and the right to trial by jury. To others, voting is a privilege extended by government to all citizens who meet its qualifications. Actually the controversy is more one of semantics than logic. There can be no real argument that voting is a right since there is no such constitutional guarantee as exists concerning the recognized rights of free press, speech, and assembly. Thus, voting is a privilege to all persons who meet the conditions prescribed for its exercise, just as are such other legally regulated activities as driving an automobile, selling real estate, engaging in certain professions or licensed occupations, or operating certain kinds of business undertakings. Just as permits to engage in such undertakings or licenses to operate an automobile cannot be withdrawn by government except under prescribed conditions, so the privilege to vote and the conditions which authorize its withdrawal must apply equally to all. Thus, a person may be said to have the right to cast his ballot after the privilege of voting has been extended to him.

■ *Voter Qualifications*

The power to establish suffrage qualifications for voters is one of the powers reserved to the states in our federal system. Instead of prescribing specific voter qualifications, the framers of the Constitution provided that persons eligible to vote for members of the House of Representatives (originally the only federal officers elected directly by the voters) would be those who "have the qualifications requisite for electors of the most numerous branch of the State legislature."[5] The same qualification was required for electors of United States Senators when the seventeenth amendment was added in 1913. Restrictions on this general power of the states, however, have resulted with the adoptions of the fifteenth and nineteenth amendments. The former prohibits states from discriminating

[5] Art. I, Sec. 2.

against persons because of their "race, color, or previous condition of servitude" and guarantees equal protection of the laws in relation hereto. The latter prohibits such discrimination on "account of sex." Thus, the states still retain the power to determine voter qualifications subject to these limitations.

In most states, the qualifications for voting in state and local elections are identical and are set by the state. However, the constitutions of some states do authorize the establishment of local suffrage qualifications which differ from those of electors in state elections. In addition, state supreme courts have upheld property ownership as a reasonable qualification in elections on issues involving the proprietary functions of cities.[6] In Virginia, the legislature may establish by special act a property qualification not exceeding $250 for voters in any county, city, or town; and the Mississippi constitution provides in Section 245 that "Electors in municipal elections shall possess all the qualifications herein prescribed, and such additional qualifications as may be provided by law."[7] The general rule, however, is that the qualifications for state elections apply equally to local electorates.

Since Americans generally subscribe to the ideal of universal suffrage, the specific qualifications which are prescribed are basically not intended to disenfranchise groups of potential voters but to assure that the enfranchised electors will have the capacity to participate meaningfully in the selection of local officials and in shaping local government policies. In general, the qualifications for suffrage fall into two groups: first, those that exist commonly in all states, and, second, those that are not uniformly prescribed and do not exist in all states. The three general requirements relate to age, residence, and citizenship, while other qualifications pertain to registration, literacy requirements, property ownership and other miscellaneous qualifications.

AGE

Since 21 is the generally recognized age in both English and American law at which a person becomes an adult of legal competence or has reached his majority, it was quite logical to fix this also as the age requirement for voting. This was the common mini-

---

[6] See *Carville* v. *McBride,* 45 Nev. 305 (1922) and *Mayor* v. *Shattuck,* 19 Colo. 104 (1893).

[7] Charles M. Kneier and Guy Fox, *Readings in Municipal Government and Administration,* Rinehart, 1953, p. 204.

mum age requirement in all states until 1943, when the minimum age was lowered to 18 in Georgia. Kentucky followed Georgia's lead in 1955. The number of states not accepting the age of majority as the minimum voting age was increased to four with the admission of Alaska and Hawaii in 1959. Alaska prescribes 19 as the minimum voting age and it is set at 20 in Hawaii.

It seems fairly certain that there will be a trend in the future to lower the voting age to 18 in other states. While specific action to implement this trend has been defeated in some states, the general movement received an endorsement from President Eisenhower in his State of the Union message to Congress in 1954 and by the Presidential candidates of both major parties in the 1956 election. Similarly, the *Model State Constitution* prepared by the Committee on State Government of the National Municipal League has recommended a minimum voting age of 18 since its fourth edition in 1946. There have been a number of arguments advanced by both the proponents and opponents of lowering the age requirement to 18, but it seems reasonable to conclude that even its sudden and uniform adoption would not result in either the marked improvement in public officials foreseen by its supporters or in the dire consequences predicted by its foes.

Even without lowering the voting age, however, the electorate of American local communities is becoming a younger one. As the bumper crop of children born since World War II matures, the electorate will become increasingly one dominated by voters under 50 years of age. Dickinson predicts that the peak year and peak percentage of voters over 50 in the United States will be reached in 1970 when such voters will equal 40 percent of the electorate but the decline of percentage of older voters thereafter will be quite rapid.[8]

CITIZENSHIP

Citizenship is now a suffrage qualification in all 50 states. Formerly, a number of states permitted aliens to vote and nine states continued this practice up to the outbreak of World War I. However, in 1926, Arkansas, the last state to permit alien voting, abandoned this principle, making citizenship a uniform prerequisite for over 35 years. United States citizenship is a specific requirement

[8] Frank G. Dickinson, "The 'Younging' of Electorates," *The Journal of the American Medical Association, 166* (March, 1958), 1051-7.

in 46 state constitutions while state citizenship is prescribed in two states. One state constitution grants suffrage to "every citizen," and the constitution of New Hampshire does not specify citizenship as a suffrage qualification.[9] Legislation in that state, however, prescribes citizenship as a prerequisite for voting.

The uniform requirement of citizenship probably resulted from two factors. The first is the generally held belief that only citizens should participate in the political process in states and local communities, and the second resulted from our participation in World War I and the new tide of immigrants coming to our shores in the early years of the twentieth century. Most states do not impose a specific time period of citizenship for naturalized citizens to be eligible to vote, but five states do have such requirements. These range from one month in Pennsylvania, to three months in Minnesota and 90 days in California, New York, and Utah.[10]

RESIDENCE

While all states require a definite period of residence as a requirement for voting, the length of the period varies considerably, whether it pertains to length of time in the state, in a county, or in a ward or precinct within the county. The actual variation in these requirements is shown in the table below. The basic residence requirements, however, are modified in a number of states for such persons as returning residents, teachers, clergymen, students, members of the armed forces, and other special cases.

In general, residency as a suffrage qualification has been adopted for two primary reasons. The first is to assure that voters will have resided in the community long enough to know the candidates seeking election and to be aware of the general issues involved. The second is to protect the community against fraudulent voting by assuring that no voter casts a ballot in more than one election district. This is now actually achieved in most communities through the registration requirement which is discussed below, and the long time periods of residency are being increasingly challenged. Thus, it is probable that the length of the residency requirements within the county and particularly within the ward or precinct will be shortened in the years ahead.

[9] Paul J. Piccard, "Citizen Control of Government" in National Municipal League, *Salient Issues of Constitutional Revision,* 1961, p. 26.
[10] Russell W. Maddox, Jr. and Robert F. Fuquay, *State and Local Governments,* Van Nostrand, 1962, pp. 244-5.

Table 2. *Residence Requirements for Voting in Fifty States*

Length of Period	In State	In County	In Ward or Precinct
2 Years	3	—	—
1 Year	35	3	1
6 Months	12	8	6
4 Months	—	2	1
3 Months	—	3	5
90 Days	—	7	—
2 Months	—	—	—
60 Days	—	6	4
54 Days	—	—	1
40 Days	—	2	1
1 Month	—	—	1
30 Days	—	5	16
15 Days	—	—	1
10 Days	—	—	5
None stated	—	14	8
Total	50	50	50

SOURCE: Council of State Governments, *The Book of the States, 1962-63*, Chicago, 1962, p. 20.

In a study published in 1956, a political scientist estimated that about five million persons are deprived of their vote in presidential elections because of their inability to meet specific residency requirements. He estimated further that about one million of these disfranchised voters have merely moved from one residence to another within the same ward, precinct or county.[11] Certainly, such results are not intended, and some states have now shortened the residency for voting in presidential elections to 60 days and election boards in some states will permit the voter who has moved within the same jurisdiction, to vote, even though he has not fulfilled the local residency requirement in full in his latest precinct.

REGISTRATION

The growth of registration of voters as a suffrage qualification has paralleled somewhat the growth of cities in the United States. In the early years of our nation, it was the practice for the would-be voter to present himself at the polling place on election day and cast his ballot. If his right to exercise this privilege were chal-

[11] Ralph M. Goldman, "Move—Lose Your Vote," *National Municipal Review*, 45 (January, 1956), 6-9, 46.

lenged, the issue would be settled by his identification by friends or acquaintances. However, this system was not sufficient as rural towns became urban communities. Thus, the system of registration to prevent fraudulent voting was initiated in Massachusetts in 1800 and gradually spread to other New England states and then to the rest of the nation. Today registration as a suffrage requirement exists in all but four states—Arkansas, North Dakota, Texas, and Virginia. In Arkansas, Texas, and Virginia, however, a form of registration may be said to exist since only those persons who can show a poll tax receipt are permitted to vote.

There are two basic types of registration systems—permanent and periodic—although eight states permit the use of both. Under the permanent system, which is used in all areas of 32 states and some areas of 11 others, a voter's name remains on the list of voters as long as he resides in the same precinct. Thus, he need not reregister unless he moves, changes his name or party, or fails to vote with the frequency specified in his state. Under the periodic registration as used in South Carolina, Vermont, and Wyoming, all voters must reregister periodically since a new list of voters is prepared at specific intervals, usually of one, two, or four years. The major disadvantages of periodic registration are the inconvenience to voters and the expensiveness of the procedure, while its major advantage is assuring the relative purity of the registration lists. Much of this advantage is gained in states using permanent registration by providing that a voter's name is removed from the voter lists if he does not participate in either the primary or the general election in any election year. As an example, the names of 344,668 persons were removed from the voter lists in Los Angeles County alone in early 1961 because of their failure to vote in either election in 1960.[12] To have their names placed again on the rolls, it would be necessary for these persons to reregister even though California uses the permanent registration system.

LITERACY

Of all suffrage qualifications, the greatest controversy centers around the literacy requirement, since this is the one test which relates to the quality of voters. In fairness to much of the opposition to a literacy requirement, it should be noted that they are much more concerned about its administration than about the principle

[12] James Bassett, "344,668 Lose Ballot Registration for Failing to Vote in November," *Los Angeles Times,* January 12, 1961.

underlying it, although some are opposed to the principle, believing it to be undemocratic in intent.

The concept of a quality test for voters is not a recent development in our country. Connecticut voters in 1855 approved a constitutional amendment providing that "every person shall be able to read any section of the constitution or any section of the statutes of this state before being admitted as an elector," and a similar amendment adopted two years later in Massachusetts stipulated that "no person shall have the right to vote, or be eligible for office under the Constitution of this Commonwealth, who shall not be able to read the Constitution in the English language, and write his name."[13] Today such educational tests for voters are prescribed by the constitutions of 19 states and the constitutions of two other states authorize the state legislatures to establish such tests.

The severity of the literacy tests actually imposed varies considerably among the 20 states imposing them. In Virginia, a voter must merely be able to complete a written registration application to demonstrate literacy, while ownership of $300 worth of property and payment of all taxes is an alternative to literacy in South Carolina. In Alaska, the literacy requirement is satisfied by the ability of the voter to read or speak English, but Mississippi requires the voter to give a reasonable interpretation of the section of the state constitution he reads to the registrar of voters. Under the New York system, literacy tests are administered through the public school system to persons who have not completed eight grades of education in a school in which English is the language of instruction. This system has been highly praised as achieving both fair testing and the ends sought by the constitutional amendment establishing it.[14] Election officials in other states, however, have misused the literacy requirement as a ruse to discriminate against groups of people who would otherwise be entitled to vote.[15] This has been particularly true of Negro voters in several southern states.

PROPERTY OWNERSHIP

In the early history of our country, property ownership was a uniform requirement for voting in state and local elections. The

[13] Charles M. Kneier, *City Government in the United States,* 3rd ed., Harper, 1957, p. 325.
[14] F. G. Crawford, "Operation of Literacy Tests for Voters in New York," *American Political Science Review,* 25 (May, 1931), 342-5. The system is now a bit more controversial because of the influx of Puerto Ricans in recent years.
[15] Kirk Porter, *History of the Suffrage in the United States,* University of Chicago Press, 1918, p. 218.

defense of this qualification centered around the belief that property owners would comprise a broad and yet intelligent and well-meaning class of persons. Particularly with the rise of Jacksonian democracy, the property qualification was attacked as an aristocratic concept and it had disappeared as an absolute voting requirement in all states by the end of the Civil War.

A new interest in property ownership as a qualification for voting arose during the depression of the 1930s and took two forms. The first was the re-institution of a property ownership requirement for voting in a number of states and the second was a denial of the right to vote to paupers. More generally property ownership as a qualification was limited to questions concerning the expenditure of public money or the issue of bonds, and the requirement still exists in a number of states and is widely used by local communities. A Michigan constitutional amendment adopted in 1932 is illustrative of this movement. It provided that "Whenever any question is submitted to a vote of the electors which involves the direct expenditure of public money or the issue of bonds, only such persons having the qualifications of electors who have property assessed for taxes in any part of the district or territory to be affected by the result of such election or the lawful husband or wife of such persons shall be entitled to vote thereon." As a result of this amendment, a 1938 study revealed that from 50 to 60 percent of the citizens of Detroit were denied the right to vote on such issues.[16]

There are other cases in which the property tax remains a qualification for suffrage. It serves as an alternative to the literacy test in South Carolina, and the test is waived for owners of $500 worth of taxable property in Georgia. It remains a qualification on all questions creating a levy, debt or liability in Montana, and on similar questions affecting local communities in Alaska, New York, Rhode Island, Texas, and Virginia. Legally, the right to vote can still be denied to paupers in 13 states, but apparently this provision is not strenuously enforced.

PAYMENT OF TAXES

Closely related to the property qualification is the requirement of a receipt showing that payment of certain taxes has been made.

[16] D. S. Hecock and H. A. Trevelyan, *Detroit Voters and Recent Elections,* Detroit Bureau of Governmental Research, 1938, p. 10.

The best known of such taxes are the poll taxes of several southern states, where their payment remains a prerequisite for voting. The actual amount of these taxes is not heavy, ranging from $1.00 in Arkansas and Texas to $1.50 in Alabama and Virginia, and to $2.00 (subject to an extra $1.00 at the discretion of the county supervisors) in Mississippi.[17] The taxes have a cumulative feature in Alabama and Virginia where they must be paid for two and three years respectively immediately preceding an election. An arrangement similar to a poll tax still exists in New Hampshire where any person excused from paying town taxes at his own request is denied the right to vote.

At the present time, poll taxes are still levied in 12 states but they are used primarily to raise revenue in the seven states not specifically mentioned above. The restrictiveness of the poll tax has gradually been lessened as exceptions are granted to certain groups of voters. It is now quite common to find such groups as veterans, members of the armed forces, the aged, and the disabled exempted from the requirement.

Congress in 1962 approved a constitutional amendment barring the requirement of a poll tax as a qualification for voting in federal elections and primaries. The proposal was ratified by legislatures in the required 38 states, and in January, 1964, became the Twenty-fourth Amendment to the Constitution. While this proposal will not affect purely state and local elections, poll taxes will probably be abandoned or enforced less severely in the years ahead and the literacy requirement may be more abused as a means to keep certain groups from the polls.

MISCELLANEOUS REQUIREMENTS

Since the seven important suffrage qualifications have been discussed in some detail above, it will suffice here to note merely that there are additional qualifications for voting in almost every state. In large part, these relate more to the disqualification of voters than to their qualification and typically deny suffrage to those persons who are institutionalized in state or local facilities, whether the detention is for mental deficiency or for crime. In addition, three states—Alabama, Connecticut, and Louisiana—require that a voter must be of "good character," and voters in four states are

[17] Piccard, op. cit., p. 29.

required to take an oath that they are qualified electors. Since enforcement of the "good character" qualification would be difficult, it is probable that it is not strictly—or uniformly—administered.

■ Special Voting Problems

The preceding discussion of suffrage qualifications has indicated the variations in specific requirements possible within our federal system. It has also shown that there has been a definite trend since earlier days to broaden the electoral base by extending the privilege of voting to new groups of people and by abandoning the most restrictive qualifications. At the present time, the principle of universal suffrage has been pretty generally realized in many communities. However, there are still a number of problems facing the individual voter and the broader community of voters.

THE ABSENTEE VOTER

The mobility of Americans presents a special problem to many voters who find that they will be away from home on election day. The problem is not a new one since there have been persons in the military and other government services, as well as persons pursuing their private interests away from their homes since the beginning of our nation. However, the number seems to be increasing because of increased travel, college enrollments, and employment in service-type industries which involve travel.

Recognizing the special problem of servicemen, several northern states provided for them to vote during the Civil War. In 1896 Vermont became the first state to broaden the absentee voting regulations to include civilians as well as military personnel. By 1960, all 50 states had provisions permitting servicemen to vote by absentee ballot and all but the four states of Maryland, New Mexico, Pennsylvania, and South Carolina permitted other citizens who were out of state or out of town to vote in this manner.

The argument is sometimes raised that a voter away from home may not be sufficiently aware of issues or knowledgable of candidates to cast an informed vote. As a reason for limiting absentee voting, however, it seems to have little validity. Casting an absentee ballot is not an easy or convenient process and a voter who takes the time and bears the inconvenience to do so should certainly be allowed this privilege. In a number of states, absentee voting regulations also enable persons who are ill or physically disabled to cast a ballot without physical presence at the polls.

While the details of absentee voting provisions vary among the states, there are two principal types which can be identified. The more widely used plan requires that the absentee ballot be secured from the voter's local voting district prior to election day. Application for the ballot must be made a specified number of days preceding election day and the ballot must be marked in the presence of a notary and returned in a sealed envelope along with the notary's affidavit that the ballot was cast in secret and by the voter intended. Upon its receipt by the precinct election officials, again within a specified time period, it is counted as any other ballot. The other major type of absentee voting law pertains only to voters who are in their home states but away from their home districts. Such voters secure a ballot from the local election board in the community where they are on election day, mark them and return them to their home county which in turn delivers them to the proper election district for counting. The major difficulty with this type is that the voter who uses it is required to write in the names of the candidates of his choice for his home district and county if he is in another county. This often results in such electors voting only for national and state officers or for a small number of lesser officials since it is difficult for them to remember the names of all local candidates.

While the actual use of absentee voting has been somewhat disappointing to the supporters of the movement, the problems involved in extending this privilege to persons away from home and in their exercise of this privilege are important enough to warrant further concern and action by state legislatures. The belief that means should be available to enable the temporarily dislocated voter to cast his ballot in elections is widely accepted and it is likely that less stringent requirements will be provided in a number of states in the near future.

THE MINORITY VOTER

Because of unfortunate antipathies and prejudices between groups of Americans in local communities, the problem of the minority voter poses peculiar and difficult questions across the nation. While the problem is often limited to that of Negro suffrage, it becomes significantly broader when it includes the tensions which still exist concerning Oriental-American voters in west coast communities, Mexican-American voters in southwestern areas, immigrant voters in eastern cities, and poor white voters in southern communities. In most cases these minorities have been extended the privilege of voting but their participation is not encouraged, while the peculiar problem of the Negro voters relates to attempts to restrict their vote in some southern communities.[18]

There are those who argue that the problems of the minority voter are social and economic rather than legal and therefore that civil rights legislation is not needed or, at best, is premature. However, this point of view cannot be comfortably defended since the absence of legal sanctions would seem to endorse such pressures. It is true that the southern Negro now has the legal right to register and vote,[19] and yet many do not because of increased social and economic pressures—particularly in rural areas—which are still beyond the scope of federal legislation. In more urban areas, however, the Negro voters have registered and voted in increasing numbers since 1944. The appearance of new Negro leadership in these areas is becoming evident and their general philosophy appears to be that which was expressed by a Negro spokesman in a Georgia county who said, "If we don't register and vote, we can't get the benefits which are comparable to those received by whites—or comparable to our needs."[20]

While prejudice and discrimination at the polls are to be condoned in no community, it is highly probable that with the passage of time racial prejudice will become less serious, resulting in less marked discrimination. With our present deep concern for the problem, it is possible that we are a little too impatient with the rate of progress now being made in southern communities. One writer advances the interesting observation that the most remarkable aspect

[18] Margaret Price, *The Negro Voter in the South,* Southern Education Reporting Service, 1957.

[19] In 1944, the United States Supreme Court in the case *Smith* v. *Allwright,* 321 U. S. 649, declared that the primary election was an integral part of the election process and thus Negro voters could not be barred on the basis that the primary was a private affair of a political party, which in itself was a private association.

[20] Price, *op. cit.,* p. 3.

CITIZENS AND THEIR POLITICS

of the "political revolution taking place in the South since 1944 is not the white resistance to Negro voting in a few areas but the widespread acceptance of Negro voting by Southern whites. Although many regard it as a 'necessary evil,' they see it as an inevitable fact and accept it."[21]

THE NON-VOTER

While no general studies of non-voting in local governments exist, a growing number of case studies of particular communities confirm the point that large numbers of citizens do not participate directly in the electoral process.[22] In a major study of voter turnout in elections in Los Angeles County for the 17-year period 1935–1952, O'Rourke found that voter apathy was higher in municipal and county than in state or national elections. During this period, the voter participation was 77.2 percent of those registered in national and state elections with a range from 68 to 87 percent. For municipal and county elections, however, the voter turnout averaged only 41.1 percent of the registered voters and the range varied from 10 to 61 percent.[23]

As a result of the pioneer voting studies in this field, it was often concluded that grass-roots democracy was in jeopardy because so many citizens failed to perform their civic duties and responsibilities. This conclusion has been tempered somewhat by depth studies of political awareness which typically find that non-voting is most prevalent among citizens who are less informed than among those with a higher level of awareness. This finding raises the important question of the desirability of uninformed votes in local elections. William B. Munro asked this question in 1928 in this manner: ". . . is there anything to be gained by having them certify their

[21] H. D. Price, "The Negro and Florida Politics," *Journal of Politics, 17* (May, 1955), 198–220.

[22] Among the many studies which might be cited are: Dahl, *op. cit.*; Arthur Kornhauser, *Attitudes of Detroit People Toward Detroit*, Wayne University Press, 1952; Charles E. Merriam and H. F. Gosnell, *Non-voting, Causes and Methods of Control*, University of Chicago Press, 1924; Morris Rosenberg, "Some Determinants of Voter Apathy," *Public Opinion Quarterly, 181* (Winter, 1954–1955), 349–66; and Charles H. Titus, "Rural Voting in California, 1900–1926," *Southwestern Social Science Quarterly, 9* (September, 1928), 198–215.

[23] Lawrence W. O'Rourke, *Voting Behavior in the Forty-Five Cities of Los Angeles County*, Bureau of Governmental Research, University of California, Los Angeles, 1953.

bewilderment and lack of knowledge at the ballot box?" Munro answered his own query by replying, "It is hard to see what real service can be rendered to the cause of enlightened government by the mere expedient of herding to the polls, with some sort of militant propaganda, reluctant people who go because they are shamed into it by clarion calls to the performance of their duty as citizens."[24]

There can be no question that continued small turnout of voters can have undesirable results to the voter, public officials and community alike. However, the most common reason given for not voting is apathy or lack of interest. Thus, it would seem that "get-out-the-vote" drives might be more successful if they were re-oriented to become "inform-and-interest-the-voters" campaigns. The chances that an informed and interested voter will cast a ballot are relatively high; the fact that an apathetic voter is transported to the polls and casts an uninformed vote is not a boon in itself to enlightened self-government. Several recent studies reveal that a large number of voters have a sense of futility and believe that even casting their vote will have no effect on the outcome of the election and that city affairs will be handled in the same way regardless of which candidates or party wins.[25]

It has sometimes been suggested that one way to encourage the voter to fulfill his civic obligations and responsibilities would be to adopt a compulsory voting system. As such systems usually function, a voter who fails to cast a ballot is subject to a fine. While compulsory voting apparently operates with some degree of success in Australia and some European countries,[26] the weight of opinion in the United States is opposed to such a system. It is interesting to note that the legislatures of Massachusetts and North Dakota have been authorized to provide for compulsory voting at their discretion, but neither has made any attempt to enact such measures. Simply put, the case against compulsory voting in the United States is that it is not consistent with our concept of democracy or conducive to informed voting.

As indicated earlier, it is highly significant that the voter has the privilege of exercising his voting right if he chooses to. It is less

[24] William B. Munro, "Is the Slacker Vote a Menace?" *National Municipal Review, 17* (February, 1928), 80-86.
[25] See Kornhauser, *op. cit.,* p. 28 ; and Elmo Roper, "New York Elects O'Dwyer," *Public Opinion Quarterly, 10* (Spring, 1956), 53-56.
[26] Henry J. Abraham, *Compulsory Voting,* Public Affairs Press, 1955.

important that he exercise this privilege with any high degree of consistency. It is probable that more responsive local government will result when a larger number of citizens become interested and participate in the choice of their elected representatives and in deciding questions of public policy. But the means to this end must be largely through education rather than compulsion or regulatory legislation.

■ Characteristics of the Local Voter

While it is always risky to generalize, it is possible to advance probabilities concerning groups within the community electorate. On the basis of completed studies, it is possible to predict that men will vote more than women, older persons more than young, property owners more than non-owners, conservatives more than liberals, and white voters more than Negro voters. In an interesting study of voting patterns in New Haven, Connecticut, Dahl discovered that participation in local political affairs was greater among citizens with (1) high income than among those with lower income, (2) high social standing than among those with lower standing, (3) more formal education than among citizens with little, (4) occupations in the professional, business or white collar classes than among those with working-class occupations, and (5) homes in better residential areas than among citizens living in poorer areas.[27]

The correlations indicated above seem to bear out the general theory that people will vote more often if they feel they have a stake in or can influence the outcome of elections. This is not meant to imply that such voters are not also responding to the civic impulse of exercising their privilege of voting. This is undoubtedly an important factor, but its reinforcement by a feeling that the outcome of the election is important to themselves is particularly significant. Apathy among some groups of the electorate enhance the political importance of other groups, and in a democracy it is essential that we have an increasingly alert public. This will result also in a citizenry increasingly active in the community's electoral and governmental processes.

[27] Dahl, *op. cit.*, pp. 282-3.

SUGGESTED READINGS

Books

Abraham, Henry J., *Compulsory Voting* (Washington: Public Affairs Press, 1955).

Adrian, Charles R., *Governing Urban America*, 2nd ed. (New York: McGraw-Hill, 1961).

Campbell, Angus, Guerin, Gerald and Miller, Warren E., *The Voter Decides* (New York: Harper, 1954).

Childs, Richard S., *Civic Victories* (New York: Harper, 1952).

Council of State Governments, *The Book of the States, 1962–63* (Chicago: Council of State Governments, 1962).

Dahl, Robert, *Who Governs? Democracy and Power in an American City* (New Haven: Yale University Press, 1961).

Johnson, J. B. and Lewis, I. J., *Registration for Voting in the United States*, rev. ed. (Chicago: Council of State Governments, 1946).

Kneier, Charles M., *City Government in the United States*, 3rd ed. (New York: Harper, 1957).

Kneier, Charles M. and Fox, Guy, *Readings in Municipal Government and Administration* (New York: Rinehart, 1953).

McGovney, Dudley O., *The American Suffrage Medley* (Chicago: University of Chicago Press, 1949).

Merriam, C. E. and Gosnell, H. F., *Non-voting, Causes and Methods of Control* (Chicago: University of Chicago Press, 1924).

O'Rourke, Lawrence W., *Voting Behavior in the Forty-Five Cities of Los Angeles County* (Los Angeles: Bureau of Governmental Research, University of California, 1953).

Piccard, Paul J., "Citizen Control of Government" in National Municipal League, *Salient Issues of Constitutional Revision* (New York: National Municipal League, 1961).

Price, Margaret, *The Negro Voter in the South* (Nashville: Southern Education Reporting Service, 1957).

Articles

Crawford, F. J., "Operation of Literacy Tests for Voters in New York," *American Political Science Review*, 25 (May, 1931), 342–5.

Goldman, Ralph M., "Move—Lose Your Vote," *National Municipal Review*, 45 (January, 1956), 6–9, 46.

Munro, W. B., "Is the Slacker Vote a Menace?" *National Municipal Review*, 17 (February, 1928), 80–86.

Ogul, Morris S., "Residence Requirements a Barrier to Voting in Presidential Elections," *Midwest Journal of Political Science*, 3 (August, 1959), 254–62.

Price, H. D., "The Negro and Florida Politics," *Journal of Politics, 14* (May, 1955), 198–220.

Roper, Elmo, "New York Elects O'Dwyer," *Public Opinion Quarterly, 10* (Spring, 1956), 53–56.

Rosenberg, Morris, "Some Determinants of Voter Apathy," *Public Opinion Quarterly, 181* (Winter, 1954–55), 349–66.

Sherbenou, Edgar L. "Class, Participation and the Council-Manager Plan," *Public Administration Review, 20,* (Summer, 1961), 131–5.

Weeks, O. Douglas, "Permanent Registration of Voters in the United States," *Temple University Law Quarterly, 14* (November, 1939), 74–88.

Political Process
in Local Government

7

Periodically voters in communities across the nation face the task of selecting over 500,000 men and women to fill policy-making and executive positions in our local governments. For the citizen whose participation in local politics is limited to casting a ballot on election day, the electoral process seems to operate smoothly and he may be a bit chagrined about his few friends and neighbors who become deeply involved in such a simple process. While performing his quadrennial act of civic responsibility, this voter may also wish that he were choosing among better candidates for fewer offices. This brief description of the local voter is an inadequate one and even unfair to many citizens; however, it is indeed unfortunate that for too many citizens the local political process begins with the opening of the polls on election day and ends when the ballots have been tallied.

By its very nature, the electoral process in local government is a political process. There must be some form of organization to recruit candidates for less popular offices, screen those willing to run for the top positions, advance positions on matters of public policy, and work for the election of candidates to implement those policies when in office. It is true that anyone legally eligible to do so can seek local office, but some minor offices go unfilled and candidates for other positions are recruited only with urging and persuasion. Thus, without local political organizations to set the wheels of the political process in motion, local representative government would be both less representative of and responsive to the community of voters.

This point was aptly phrased by President Truman in answer to the question, "Can a man be a non-partisan in politics?" He replied, "There never was a non-partisan in politics. A man cannot be a non-partisan and be effective in a political party. When he's in any party he's partisan—he's got to be. The only way a man can act as a non-partisan is when he's in office, either as President or head of a state or county or city. Then he should recognize the fact that there are people on both sides whom he is responsible for and must act for. But when it comes to politics, a man's either one thing or the other."[1]

It is the purpose of this chapter to examine the local political process by identifying local political parties and organizations, examining their functions and operation, and reviewing the major proposals for improving their performance. While there are many definitions of the political process, the one which has most relevance at the local level is that it is the process that "changes citizens into public officials and individual wishes into public policy."[2] So defined, the political process is essential to local democratic government and is deserving of more sympathetic and unprejudicial acceptance and involvement. Although non-partisan elections are becoming a more common means of selecting local officials, machinery for partisan election will be examined first, since this system can serve as a base for discussing the merits and weaknesses of non-partisan systems.

■ *What is a Political Party?*

Since political parties play a vital role in the political process, it is essential to begin with a common agreement on what a party is. There is no lack of acceptable definition of what a political party

---

[1] Harry S Truman, *Mr. Citizen,* Popular Library Edition, 1961, p. 126.
[2] Charles Adrian, *State and Local Governments, A Study in the Political Process,* McGraw-Hill, 1960, p. 158.

is or what its functions are, but one without the other too often presents an inaccurate view of this political institution. In terms of our American experience with parties, an acceptable definition is that such an organization consists of a group of persons banded together to gain control of the machinery of government through elective processes in order to promote a program of interests.

This definition standing alone, however, leaves much to be desired. But since parties are justified in large part because of the functions they perform, a cataloguing of these major activities might be helpful in distinguishing why such organizations are considered basic to our democratic form of government. According to Rossiter, the functions of parties are to: (1) control and direct the struggle for power as openly as possible; (2) serve as personnel agencies by setting up and operating the machinery that places men and women in public office; (3) serve as important sources of public policy by converting hopes and frustrations into proposals for action by the voters; (4) organize the legislative and executive branches of government if they are the majority party and run these branches with the aid of the appeals and disciplines of party loyalty; (5) make concrete promises to the electorate and follow through on them if elected; and (6) serve as the 'loyal opposition' if unsuccessful in the last election.[3]

In addition to the political functions of parties listed above, Rossiter assigns three social and one psychological function to parties. The social functions are to instruct citizens in the practices of democracy and inform them on current issues, to serve as buffers and adjusters between individuals and society, and to dispense legitimate aids, favors, and immunities to persons in need. The final function—the psychological one—is to serve as an institution to which citizens can extend their allegiance and feel, in return, some sense of belonging.[4]

■ Local Party Organization

The opening sentences of Frank Kent's interesting and rewarding book, *The Great Game of Politics*, dramatically underscores the importance of local party organization. In his words, "No clear idea

[3] Clinton Rossiter, *Parties and Politics in America*, Cornell University Press, 1960, pp. 39–47.
[4] *Ibid.*, pp. 48–50.

of a party organization can be had unless you start from the bottom. To discuss Presidential politics without understanding precinct politics is an absurdity. It is like trying to solve a problem in trigonometry without having studied arithmetic."[5] The same general philosophy is expressed in a recent party workers' manual which opened with these words, "The success of a Party Organization rests primarily on the precinct committeeman, the precinct committeewoman and the auxiliary workers. They are the roots of the 'Official Organization.' Their ultimate job is to see that every Republican voter in the precinct or voting district is registered, eligible to vote and actually casts his ballot on election day. They must also work with all 'independent' voters who can be influenced to vote the Republican ticket."[6]

Party organization charts typically take the form of a hierarchy of committees arranged in descending order from the national party committee to the precinct committees. Each committee layer has jurisdiction over specified geographical areas ranging from the nation as a whole to an area of a few city blocks. While there are increasing interrelationships between local committees and state and national committees, our concern will be with organization at the precinct, ward, and city or county levels, in that order.

PRECINCT ORGANIZATION

The precinct is the unit cell in the organization of a political party and the term is used throughout the nation to connote a voting district of from 200 to 2,000 voters with an average voting strength of 600. There are some 130,000 precincts in the United States with as many as 3,000 existing in several of the largest cities. While precinct organization varies among the states, two common patterns emerge. One is to have two co-equal officers—a committeeman and a committeewoman—to guide the affairs of the party in that area. The second is to have party matters in the hands of a committee of three or more members with one member serving in a dominant capacity.

In a majority of states, precinct committeemen or committee members are elected at the primary election, usually for a term of two years. However, in a number of large cities these local

---

[5] Frank R. Kent, *The Great Game of Politics,* Doubleday, 1923, p. 1.
[6] Republican National Committee, "How to Organize the Precinct," from *Republican Workers' Manual,* Washington, 1952.

officials are appointed by the ward leaders, and in other cities precinct officers are selected at party caucuses. While election is the common means of securing precinct leaders, there is usually little competition for the offices since candidates without the blessing of high party officials rarely challenge such endorsed office-seekers. The average voter knows very little about the duties of the precinct officers and many ignore the position when casting primary ballots. Such non-voting for the office by disinterested citizens makes it almost certain that the core of the party faithful can vote in their candidate.

Precinct workers are in charge of the affairs of their party in their area.[7] Their one major function is to get out a big vote and carry their precinct by as large a margin as possible. To accomplish this, precinct leaders are encouraged to set up a card file of persons of voting age in their precinct and to organize committees of precinct workers to contact these potential voters and to secure their support. Near election day, precinct activity picks up considerably as auxiliary party workers are rounded up to man important election day committees. In a well-organized precinct these committees will include a poll committee to remain at the polls to see who votes, a checking committee to prepare lists of persons who have not yet voted, a telephone committee to call and remind voters to go to the polls, a transportation committee to carry voters to and from the polls (if this is legal), a baby-sitter committee to allow mothers to get to the polls, a challenge committee to watch for possible irregularities at the polls, and a headquarters committee to take care of physical arrangements at the polling site itself.[8]

It is apparent that the fortunes of a party locally are largely in the hands of precinct leaders and workers. The type of person elected or appointed to these positions varies with the nature of the precinct itself, and the methods used to gain support also varies widely from precinct to precinct. Obviously the problems of a precinct committeeman in an exclusive residential section differ from those in a section with homes of unskilled laborers. Usually

[7] For an informative and interesting discussion of precinct organization and politics see Don P. Cass, *How To Win Votes and Influence Elections,* Public Administration Service, 1962.

[8] For an interesting account of the activities of a precinct worker in large cities, see Kent, *op. cit.,* Chap. IV, and Sonya Forthal-Spiesman, "The Precinct Worker," *The Annals of the American Academy of Poltical and Social Science,* 259 (September, 1948), 30-45.

all precinct officers have one thing in common, however. They recognize that a job well done in the precinct can serve as a spring-board to a higher party or even an elective public position. This message of hope and reward is held out to precinct workers in a recent party publication which assured these persons that "Being a Precinct Worker is a hard job but it has its own rewards. You're helping people to understand the issues that affect us all. You're making the machinery of government work. You're doing your job as a citizen in a working democracy. You're working to keep America free through the ballot box. You're proud to be a Precinct Worker. You're stepping up as a Party Leader."[9]

While number of voters is the basis for laying out precincts in urban communities, area is the primary determinant in sparsely populated rural areas. Precincts large enough to embrace hundreds of voters would require rural voters to travel inconvenient distances to the polls. Where township organization exists, this unit often serves as a rural election precinct. Ordinarily, both major parties will maintain an organization at the township level, headed by a precinct or township committeeman. However, the strength of the dominant party in some townships is so overriding that the minority party maintains no formal organization at all.

WARD ORGANIZATION

The next rung in the ladder of party hierarchy is the organization at the ward level which typically embraces several precincts. Two patterns are found at this level—the ward committee and the ward president or executive systems. The ward committee, which is the more common of the two, is normally composed of the committee-man and committeewoman from the constituent precincts. The committee selects a chairman to manage its affairs, but it remains an approval body and directs the actions and policies of the chair-man. Under the ward president or executive system, this person typically appoints the precinct officers in his area. Usually he will have begun as a precinct worker and gained the higher position be-cause of his loyal and active work at that lower level.

The party organization at the ward level is becoming increasingly important since this election unit is often one at which the party

[9] Women's Division, Democratic National Committee, *The Key to Democratic Victory, A Guidebook for County and Precinct Workers,* Washington, 1952.

begins to nominate candidates for public office. Wards are sometimes laid out to correspond with city councilmanic or state representative districts and in such cases the word of the ward committee or executive carries considerable weight in selecting candidates. In addition, the campaigning for office tends to be increasingly geared to the ward rather than the precinct level.

Because of its strategic position in the party organization, the ward committee or executive has real importance in determining the fortune of his party. Through this committee will be funneled the patronage and campaign funds to the precincts and the money from the precincts will be channeled through the ward organization on its way to party coffers at higher levels. Thus, increasingly strong party organization at the ward level seems to be necessary, particularly in larger cities. In describing the power of the ward executive, Frank Kent estimated that the average party cog at this level had about 1,300 sure votes which he could swing and that this represented about one-fourth of all persons entitled to vote in primary elections and approximately three-fourths of the persons who would actually cast primary ballots.[10]

CITY OR COUNTY ORGANIZATION

The city and county are important political units throughout the nation since both serve as the election area for a number of local officers and state legislative districts for one house typically follow county lines. The party organizations at this level reflect the importance of these units for the fortunes of the party at both the local and higher levels. Since the merit system has made little headway in county government and there is both national and state patronage to be dispensed on the county level, county committees—or their chairmen—are usually influential links in the chain of party command.[11]

In cities, the ward committeemen normally serve as the city committee, but in some states the city committee members are elected at the primary election. The organization of county committees take one of three forms in various parts of the nation. Often

[10] Kent, op. cit., p. 37.

[11] For an entertaining and enlightening discussion of national and local politics at the county level in a presidential year, see James A. Michener, Report of the County Chairman, Random House, 1961.

CITIZENS AND THEIR POLITICS

the county committee is made up of all the precinct committeemen in the county; sometimes its members are elected in party primaries; and in some areas committee members are chosen in county party conventions. The chairmen of both city and county committees are usually chosen by the committee they serve and normally are the most powerful member of that committee. In counties with large cities, the county committee, though important, does not tend to dominate the political affairs of the city. This is sometimes the case because the party alignment in the city differs from that in the outlying area of the county.

The responsibilities and functions of the city and county committees are the same for their larger jurisdictions as are those of the precinct leaders in their much smaller areas. Simply put, this means that candidates who have a chance to win must be supported and efforts must be made to make the margin of victory as decisive as possible. It is at this level of party machinery that "bossism" once ran rampant and is probably still quite important.[12] However, most of the new city and county chairmen are leaders rather than bosses and they head organizations instead of machines.[13] The difference between the two is much more than a semantic one and this becomes quite evident in contrasting present techniques of leadership with those of the old-style bosses.

■ Partisanship in Local Government

The question of the desirability of partisanship in local government has been a continuing controversy during the twentieth century. Students and practitioners of local government align themselves on both sides of the question with about equal fervor and intensity. However, partisan elections remain the most common basis for selecting local officials at the county, city and township levels. Partisanship is much less a factor in school district and other special district elections.

[12] Hamilton Owens, "The County Boss," *American Mercury, 17* (May, 1929), 70-74; J. N. Feldman, "How Tammany Holds Power," *National Municipal Review, 39* (July, 1950), 330-4; L. P. Cookingham, "Inside the Story of Kansas City," *National Municipal Review, 37* (December, 1948), 596-9; and Roy V. Peel, "The Political Machine of New York City," *American Political Science Review, 27* (August, 1933), 611-8.
[13] Warren Moscow, "Exit the Boss; Enter the Leader," *New York Times Magazine,* June 22, 1947, pp. 16-17, 47-48.

Much of this controversy has stemmed from a bad choice of words by those opposed to deciding local issues on the basis of national and state party labels. In choosing "non-partisan" as the adjective for elections decided locally without Republican or Democratic labels, the reformers were placed in a paradoxical position. "Non-partisan" elections imply the absence of party or group activity to advance particular candidates and policies, and this is antithetic to the political process. While many might agree that there is no "Republican or Democratic way to pave a street or lay a sewer," there might well be policy differences over the needs for such public works programs as against the needs for expanded health and welfare activities.

Earlier in our history, local matters were pretty well isolated from state and national concerns. However, this is now much less true because of the growing interrelationships of our three levels of government. While it is true that partisan-determined issues can be administered objectively at the local level by officials wearing either no label or the label of the opposite party, it is also probably true that state and national issues will become an increasingly important factor in local elections—particularly in large cities and in heavily populated counties. This point was advanced by Charles A. Beard in 1917 when he wrote, "Not a single one of our really serious municipal questions—poverty, high cost of living, over-crowding, unemployment, low standards of life, physical degeneracy —can be solved, can be even approached without the cooperation of the state and national government and the solution of these problems calls for state and national parties."[14]

It is possible that the proponents of non-partisan elections in local government are still fighting the city bosses, machines, and corruption of the late nineteenth and early twentieth century and are still blaming the political party almost solely for those conditions. As described by Steffens, Zink, and others,[15] these conditions were deplorable and shameful, but it is quite unfair to continue to project this image of the American city and of its political parties. In 1946 Luther Gulick wrote that, "Graft and corruption and the dominance of bosses are not the shame of the cities today as they

[14] Charles A. Beard, "Political Parties in City Government: A Reconsideration of Old Viewpoints," *National Municipal Review, 6* (March, 1917), 201-6.

[15] Lincoln Steffens, *The Shame of the Cities,* McClure, Phillips and Co., 1904; Harold Zink, *City Bosses in the United States,* Duke University Press, 1930; J. T. Salter, *Boss Rule: Portraits in City Politics,* McGraw-Hill, 1935; and W. B. Munro, *The Invisible Government,* Macmillan, 1925.

were 40 years ago. The shame of the American city today is found in three things: first, lazy citizenship with low standards; second, lack of city pride; and third, failure to look ahead and make great plans for the future."[16] A more recent analysis of big city governments advanced the opinion that, "Where the problems are the toughest—in the big, crowded, noisy city—government has vitally transformed itself. Today the big city must rank as one of the most skillfully managed of American organizations—indeed considering the problems it has to face, it is better managed than many U. S. corporations."[17]

In describing the current crop of big city mayors, Freedgood writes of the conditions and problems they face and how they meet them. In his words, "Above all the mayor is a politician. True, he may have risen to office on the back of a reform movement. But he is not, as happened too often in the past, a 'non-political' civic leader who rallies the do-gooders, drives the rascals out of City Hall, serves for an undistinguished term or two, and then withdraws—or gets driven out—leaving the city to another cycle of corruption. Instead, he fits the qualifications of the mayors whom Lincoln Steffens called on the public to elect: 'politicians working for the reform of the city with the methods of politics.' His main interest is in government, not abstract virtue, and he knows that the art of government is politics."[18]

In a fascinating study of the government and politics of Chicago, Meyerson and Banfield describe its governmental pattern in these words, "In Chicago, political power was highly decentralized formally but highly centralized informally. The city had what textbooks in municipal government called a 'weak-mayor' form of government to be sure, but it also had a powerful mayor, a powerful leader of the Council. This paradox of a 'weak' government that was strong was to be explained by the presence of the Democratic machine, an organization parallel to the city government but outside of it, in which power sufficient to run the city was centralized. The weakness of the city government was offset by the strength of the party."[19] These authors concluded that, "If overnight the bosses

[16] Luther Gulick, "The Shame of the Cities—1946," *National Municipal Review*, *36* (January, 1947), 18-25.
[17] Seymour Freedgood, "New Strength in City Hall," in Fortune Magazine, *The Exploding Metropolis*, Doubleday, 1958, pp. 62-63.
[18] *Ibid.*, pp. 67-68.
[19] Martin Meyerson and Edward C. Banfield, *Politics, Planning and the Public Interest*, The Free Press, 1955, pp. 286-7.

became model administrators—if they put all of the city jobs on the merit system, destroyed the syndicate and put an end to petty grafting, then the city government would really be . . . weak and ineffective . . ."[20]

While the supply and influence of "city bosses" seems definitely on the wane, Roscoe Martin writes that this is not so of "the supply of rural bosses, who continue in full production—and often in full command of tightly organized, highly disciplined machines. There must be, and there must always have been, a hundred nameless grass-roots bosses for every big city boss who found his way into the headlines."[21] He continued his analysis of local rural politics by stating, "It is clear that the traditional concept of intimate, tranquil, personal, 'non-political' little government by friends and neighbors, while an idyllic one, is not always or necessarily in accord with fact. . . . There are relatively few trammels on political activity at the grass roots, where the lack of formal restraints is matched by the absence of personal inhibitions. The difference between politics in big government and politics in little government is largely quantitative in character: in kind, politics in rural government is pretty much like politics everywhere else. It may not be any worse in its consequences for democracy, generally speaking, but almost certainly it is no better."[22]

Writing in 1908, Woodrow Wilson stated that it was "ideally desirable that the voter should be left free to choose the candidates of one party in local elections and the candidates of the other party in national elections," but he believed this to be an unattainable ideal.[23] Carrying this point of view further, some writers have advocated the creation of dual two-party systems—one for the state and national level and the second for the local level. On the surface, this proposal appears to have merit, but it would be very difficult to create and maintain these two separate party systems. We have shown earlier that the state and national parties depend on local committees to carry their programs and candidates to the people. Thus, there would be parallel committees in local communities, both making appeals to the same citizens—and often in separate elections that occur on the same day. The biggest prob-

[20] *Ibid.*, p. 287.
[21] Roscoe C. Martin, *Grass Roots*, University of Alabama Press, 1957, p. 65.
[22] *Ibid.*, pp. 67–68.
[23] Woodrow Wilson, *Constitutional Government in the United States*, Columbia University Press, 1908, pp. 207-8.

lem in this proposal, however, would result from its lumping of all local governments together as the arena of contest for the local parties. There is often very little relationship between the problems and issues in a city with those of the county in which it is located, or with the school district and other special districts providing essential services to its citizens. While a slogan calling for "national parties for national issues, state parties for state issues, and local parties for local issues" may appear attractive, one has only to consider the nature of our federal system to write this proposal off as another "unattainable goal."

A directly opposite view to the separate party systems concept was advanced by the Committee on Political Parties of the American Political Science Association in its Report issued in 1950. The central thesis of its challenging report was summarized by the Committee members as follows:

> Historical and other factors have caused the American two-party system to operate as two loose associations of state and local organizations, with very little national machinery and very little national cohesion. As a result, either major party, when in power, is ill-equipped to organize its members in the legislative and the executive branches into a government held together and guided by the party program. Party responsibility at the polls thus tends to vanish. This is a very serious matter, for it affects the very heartbeat of American democracy. It also poses grave problems of domestic and foreign policy in an era when it is no longer safe for the nation to deal piecemeal with issues that can be disposed of only on the basis of coherent programs.[24]

At the core of the Committee's proposals for change was the establishment of a Party Council of 50 members for each party. One of the important functions of the Council would be to prepare the initial draft of party platforms and to interpret them. Such policy statements would be prepared every two years as a guide in biennial elections. The platform in presidential election years would deal generally with party principles and national issues, while the off-year statements would emphasize state and local issues while conforming to the national platform.[25] A second function of the Council would be to recommend action to appropriate party organs

---

[24] The Committee on Political Parties of the American Political Science Association, "Toward a More Responsible Two-party System," *American Political Science Review, 44,* pt. 2 Suppl. (September, 1950), v.

[25] *Ibid.,* p. 56.

"with respect to conspicuous departures from general party decisions by state and local party organizations."[26]

The rationalization of the Committee for its general recommendations of greater party integration at all levels is summed up in the following statement from its Report:

It is necessary for both parties to reexamine their purposes and functions in the light of the present-day environment, state and local, in which they operate. Modernization of local party machinery in the interest of effective performance in this environment is long overdue. A reorientation of the leaders is needed from preoccupation with patronage and control of offices to interest in local, state, regional and national policies. Many county chairmen have failed to understand the reasons for the creation of competitive party associations and for the activities of organized labor's political action committees and such groups as the local units of Americans for Democratic Action. One of the main reasons is the dissatisfaction with the attitudes, purposes and operation of the official party organization.[27]

Two methods for possible change in local party organization and operation have been discussed. One would create a separate system of local parties as a means to keep national politics out of local elections. The second would integrate the actions and policies of local party committees more closely with principles and policies of parties at the state and national levels. A third method would be the elimination of local parties or non-partisanship.

■ *Non-Partisan Elections*

One of the innovations in local government resulting from the "efficiency and economy movement" in the early years of the twentieth century was the concept of non-partisan elections or election of local officials without party designation. Grounded in the theory that local governments were corporations rather than political bodies and that questions in local government were administrative rather than political in nature, it followed that local officials should be more like businessmen than politicians. To recruit such candidates, it seemed essential to do away with party labels

[26] *Ibid.,* p. 43.
[27] *Ibid.,* p. 45.

CITIZENS AND THEIR POLITICS

and to let local contests be waged around the qualifications of the candidates for the positions they were seeking. This point of view was expressed well by Brand Whitlock, former mayor of Toledo, who said the man responsible for the ills of our cities was "not the boss, not the politician, not the lobbyist for the streetcar company, but instead the man who in municipal elections always votes the straight party ticket."[28]

Theoretically, there is much justification of the non-partisan system. When local candidates run as Republicans or Democratics, the party affiliation rather than qualifications or stands on local issues is often the determining factor on the side of the winner. This result is more likely to occur when local and state and national elections fall on the same day and a landslide for a party nationally carries over into state and local contests. However, the same principle of party faithfulness carries over to a lesser degree even when local elections are held on different dates. There is no question but that the ardent supporters of non-partisanship continue to support it because they sincerely believe that it is best for local governments if local contests are decided strictly on the basis of local issues.

Non-partisan elections are dependent on the use of the non-partisan primary or nomination by petition as the means for nominating candidates. While the features of this type of primary vary in some details among the states using it, names of candidates in the primary election are placed on the ballot by petition and appear with no party label after their names. Often the occupation of the candidate is placed on the ballot to give the voter some indication of his experience and qualification for the position. Typically, the two persons gaining the highest vote totals in the primary are nominated for that office and their names appear on the general election ballot—again without party designation. If a candidate receives a majority of the votes cast for the office in the primary election, he is usually declared elected and the run-off feature of the general election is then eliminated.

Until recently, non-partisan elections were pretty much accepted on faith. Supporters argued that such elections would weaken national political parties at the local level, that better candidates

[28] Brand Whitlock, "The Evil Influence of National Parties and Issues in Municipal Elections," *Proceedings of the National Conference for Good City Government*, 1907, p. 193.

would be willing to seek local office if party labels were abandoned, and that local elections would be decided strictly on local issues. Recent studies, however, have cast some doubt as to the non-partisan nature of non-partisan elections.[29] In a study of non-partisan elections, Adrian concluded that such elections do serve to weaken political parties because the number of offices to be filled is reduced and the incentive to recruit new members is lessened. He also found that fewer new channels for the recruitment of candidates to fill local offices are opened by non-partisanship. He cautioned, however, that non-partisanship did not insure that local offices would be filled by successful persons since the "perennial office-seeker" was a familiar figure in many communities utilizing non-partisan elections.[30]

Adrian advanced several other propositions concerning non-partisan elections, however, which are not so commendable. First, non-partisan elections tend to segregate political leaders into strictly partisan or non-partisan paths as a general rule. As a result, a successful mayor in a non-partisan city may make an unsuccessful candidate for higher partisan office. Second, non-partisanship encourages the avoidance of issues of policy in local campaigns. Candidates prefer to take an ambiguous or no stand on issues to avoid the possible loss of potential electoral support. Third, non-partisanship tends to frustrate protest voting since there are no identifiable "in" and "out" groups. Fourth, non-partisanship tends to advance conservatism by the re-election of officeholders. And fifth, there is no collective responsibility in a non-partisan body since the members are elected as individuals rather than as members of a slate of nominees.[31]

In a study of non-partisan elections in four cities with populations between 50,000 and 75,000, Adrian and Williams discovered that there was a similarity of voting patterns between local support for slates of non-partisan candidates and political support for partisan candidates for higher office. This finding mitigates somewhat the assumption that local voting will be based upon local issues. A

[29] Some of this "surprise" over finding that non-partisan elections are not totally non-partisan is unwarranted since we have known for a long time that partisan elections are not totally partisan. It is a rare local election when one of the two candidates does not catch the public eye and win considerable support from members of the opposite party.
[30] Charles R. Adrian, "Some General Characteristics of Nonpartisan Elections," *American Political Science Review, 46* (September, 1952), 766–76
[31] *Ibid.*

CITIZENS AND THEIR POLITICS

second finding showed that a non-partisan election or an election-at-large in these cities tended to increase the relative voice of persons who normally vote Republican. The authors warn, however, that the non-partisan ballot is not a device favoring Republicans since the system does permit the recruitment of Democrats for elective posts in cities with strong Republican majorities.[32]

Writing in 1917, Charles A. Beard criticized American political parties in these words, "If I were to make an excursion into utopian politics and sketch a new 'City of the Sun,' assigning to political parties their proper place in my dream-made republic, I should start out by saying with the great chief justice, John Marshall, that nothing more debases and pollutes the human mind than partisan politics. When we see men otherwise just and fair in their judgments vilifying, maligning, and slandering their opponents, even in unimportant political campaigns, those of us who are not enamoured of billingsgate are moved to exclaim that political parties have no place at all in a rational society. But this would be a vain flying in the face of the hard and unpleasant facts of life and a vain longing for the impossible." Beard concluded that corrective and cleansing action could come only by working through parties rather than around them and declared he was prepared to defend the thesis that "non-partisanship has not worked, does not work, and will not work in any major city in the United States."[33]

It is interesting to note that Beard limited his thesis to "major" cities. It cannot be denied that non-partisanship can work because it has worked and is working in a number of American communities. Generally, these communities tend to be under 50,000 in population and their citizens tend to be relatively like-minded. In such governmental units, the lack of controversial issues keeps partisan activity to a minimum and greatly enhances the success of the non-partisan concept. Where no important policy differences exist, contests can be waged on the basis of candidate qualifications; and in such communities non-partisan elections can be an ideal solution.

A serious questioning of the nature of and desirability of non-partisanship as it operates in suburban communities has been raised by Robert Wood.

[32] Oliver P. Williams and Charles R. Adrian, "The Insulation of Local Politics Under the Nonpartisan Ballot," *American Political Science Review, 53* (December, 1959), 1052-63.
[33] Beard, *op. cit.*, p. 205.

More completely non-partisan than one-party small towns in rural areas, and with the activities of the party leader more severely limited, the suburban municipalities represent the principle of direct popular political participation in a mode theoretically workable under modern circumstances. Paradoxically, although the tenets of modern municipal reform have been rejected as an adequate basis for city or metropolitan government, they have been embraced as a political creed for suburban communities. Each suburbanite is expected to undertake the responsibilities of citizenship on his own initiative and determine the common good by himself. . . . Under these circumstances, the importance of the professional public servant—the expert and the bureaucrat—obviously increases. The new positive role of local government makes his existence necessary. The non-partisan vacuum places him in a strategic position to assume a role as community leader, especially since political leaders are suspect. . . . Under modern conditions, the power of the expert is the price the suburbanite pays for maintaining order in his home town.[34]

■ Methods of Nomination

Whether a unit of local government uses a system of partisan or non-partisan elections, there must be some means for determining the names of candidates to appear on the primary and general election ballots. Since selecting candidates and then supporting them for office are the major political activities at the local level, it is important to understand the process by which citizens are converted into public officials. Most nominees for local offices are selected by either partisan or non-partisan primaries, but several other methods can also be utilized in many states.

The first and oldest method can be called simply an act of self-announcement. Under this method, a person aspiring for local office merely indicates his intention to seek the office and informs persons around him. Such announcements may take the form of a public address, newspaper story, or wide mailing of a form letter. This method is most common now for candidates who offer themselves to the voters as write-in candidates for local office. Self-announcement is also often the first step in the process of nomination by petition, a method which will be described later.

A second method of nomination is the caucus, or meeting of political leaders. Widely used in our early history, the system consisted of a meeting of acknowledged party leaders who met to

[34] Robert C. Wood, *Suburbia, Its People and Their Politics*, Houghton Mifflin, 1958, pp. 195-6.

discuss and agree upon candidates for public office at all levels. The efforts of Andrew Jackson to destroy the "King Caucus" are well known and since the middle of the nineteenth century it has been used solely to nominate candidates for local office. The party caucus is still used in some small New England, midwestern, and western communities as the means for nominating candidates to stand for office in the general election.[35]

Nomination by party convention is a third method of selecting candidates. This system came into wide use following the abuses of the caucus system and it proved a more democratic device since the convention was composed of delegates representing all communities or electoral units in its district. However, the convention system was prone to the same abuses as the party caucus until state laws regulating its composition and operation were passed. Today the convention system is not in use at the local level, but is still utilized at both the state and national levels. However, a form of convention action still exists in some states in which pre-primary endorsements are given candidates by meetings of delegates from local political organs or clubs.[36]

Nomination by petition is another means by which a candidate can get his name on either the primary or general election ballot. The petition for a spot on the primary ballot is the means which must be used in non-partisan primaries. For the general election ballot, the petition provides a means by which independent candidates can have their names placed on the ballot alongside those nominated by other means. This method is also used sometimes by hopeful candidates of minor parties who are prohibited by state law from selecting candidates in primary elections because they do not formally qualify as a political party in the state. Some states do not permit nomination by petition but do permit such aspirants to become candidates by depositing a stipulated filing fee. The purpose of the filing fee is to eliminate non-serious candidates; however, its success in doing so is doubtful. In Detroit, a filing fee of $100 is required for salaried offices and $50 for non-salaried positions. In a special primary to fill one vacancy in 1953, 29 persons deposited the $100 fee and 26 were required to forfeit the fee because of lack of voter support in the election. In the primary

[35] Charles M. Kneier, *City Government in the United States*, 3rd ed., Harper, 1957, p. 356.
[36] For an account of pre-primary endorsements by the Republican Assembly and the Democratic Council in California, see Henry A. Turner and John A. Vieg, *The Government and Politics of California*, McGraw-Hill, 1960, pp. 37–38.

elections for council candidates in Detroit in 1949 and 1951, 110 of the 176 candidates similarly forfeited their filing fees.[37]

One method which in effect combines the primary and general election processes is the system of preferential voting. Under this arrangement, the voter is asked to indicate the order of his choices rather than merely his first choice. Such an election assures that a majority candidate will be elected since second choice votes (and if needed third and fourth choice votes and so on) are counted until one candidate has a clear majority. There are several varieties of preferential voting schemes known as the Bucklin or Grand Junction system, the Nanson system, and the Ware system.[38] None of the preferential voting systems is widely used today. Proportional representation, which is sometimes considered a method of preferential voting, will be discussed in Chapter 8 since it is used exclusively for the election of council members in local government. However, it is another plan which combines the nomination and election processes.

The direct primary is the most common means for selecting candidates. This system was devised as an effort to overcome the abuses of the caucus and convention methods and sought to return the nomination process to the voters. The first statewide primary law was enacted in Wisconsin in 1903, and the method is now in use or may be used in all 50 states.[39] The partisan primary is an intra-party affair in which party members select their candidates from among their aspirants to public office. The winning candidates in this partisan primary then face the winners of the primary election of the other party or parties in the general election.

During its use in the twentieth century, there have been a number of innovations in the primary election system. The most common plan is to classify the primary as an open or closed election. The open primary, as the term implies, is an election in which any qualified voter may participate but its use is limited to eight states.[40] In some states the voter is given ballots of all parties and instructed to select the ballot of his party preference and to return unused ballots. In Alaska, a consolidated primary ballot is used with can-

---

[37] Harold M. Dorr, "Nomination by Money Deposit," *National Municipal Review, 43* (June, 1954), 288.

[38] Kneier, *op. cit.,* pp. 365–70.

[39] In Connecticut, primary elections are called only upon challenge of nominations made by the state convention or by town committees.

[40] These are Alaska, Hawaii, Michigan, Minnesota, Montana, Utah, Washington, and Wisconsin.

didates listed in party columns. The voter, however, is restricted to marking on one column only. Washington has a still more wide-open primary ballot listing all candidates for nomination. Thus, the voter there is free to switch freely from one party to another in indicating his choices. Open primaries are commonly criticized since they enable members of other parties to raid a party and select its candidates—even to the extent of selecting weak candidates as opponents of the nominees of their party in the general election.

By far the more common system is the closed or partisan primary in which only members of the party can participate. Each of the major parties will hold closed primaries, which usually are state-conducted, to determine their candidates to appear on the general election ballot. The test of party affiliation varies from community to community and can be nominal or quite rigidly applied.

A further refinement of the partisan or closed primary is the "run-off" primary which is used most commonly in ten southern states.[41] Under this adaptation, if no candidate receives a majority of the primary votes cast, then the two highest candidates face each other in the special or "run-off" primary. This system is used in those states in which nomination in the Democratic primary almost assures election to office in the general election. The run-off feature makes sure that the eventual winner secures a majority of the votes in his own partisan primary.

The last common method of nomination occurs through the use of the non-partisan primary. This device has already been described in the section on non-partisanship above. As is true of the other means of nomination, this method is an elimination process so that the choice of general election voters is usually limited to one of two candidates unless other names appear on the ballot through nomination by petition or as a write-in candidate.

While the direct primary is the most common and probably the best of the alternative systems of nomination, it is not without its disadvantages. It is an expensive system for both the public and the candidates, and it increases the burden on the voters by resulting in two separate elections. The system results in a long ballot since most positions—particularly in county and townships—are elective ones. In states not using the run-off election, it is possible to have candidates nominated by a plurality rather than by a majority of voters. Primary elections are often held too far in advance

---

[41] These are Alabama, Arkansas, Florida, Georgia, Louisiana, Mississippi, Oklahoma, North Carolina, South Carolina, and Texas.

of general elections, resulting in unnecessarily long and expensive campaigns. Primary elections discourage independent candidates and independent voters who choose not to align themselves with either major party, and tend to weaken party responsibility by making the appeal of the candidates voter-oriented rather than party-oriented. And finally, despite the ease of getting one's name on the primary ballot, voters are often given little if any choice of candidates for a number of elective offices.

While the following quotation may be more a tribute to the unattractiveness of county office in Iowa a few years back than to a shortcoming of the direct primary system, it at least illustrates the last point made above of limited voter choice. Porter found that, "In thirty-four counties, there were no Democratic candidates for nomination for any county office; and in nineteen of these the Republicans presented only one candidate for each office. In fifty-four counties, there was only one candidate for nomination for each office on either the Democratic or the Republican ticket. Thus in more than one-third of the counties of the state [Iowa has 99], there was no contest for any county office, either in the primary or in the general election. And in well over half of the counties, there was no contest in the primary for any county office. In many of the remaining counties, there were contests for only one or two of the offices available."[42]

Despite the shortcomings of the direct primary, it has worked reasonably well and certainly better than its opponents predicted. It is doubtful that better candidates are nominated by this system, but it does provide the citizenry of a community with a potential weapon of real importance. One writer concludes that, "The direct primary is in a sense a shotgun over the door of the municipal electorate. Such a weapon need seldom be used. As long as the party organization presents satisfactory candidates, there is no serious objection to the fact that they are 'organization candidates.' If the organization falls to the level that it did in some cases under the convention, then the voters have an effective weapon in the direct primary."[43]

It is obvious that the political process in local government does not end with the nomination of candidates for public office or that

---

[42] Kirk H. Porter, "The Deserted Primary in Iowa," *American Political Science Review, 39* (August, 1945), 732–40.
[43] Kneier, *op. cit.*, p. 363.

it is without activity by pressure or interest groups. However, the methods of citizen control over their local governments are to be discussed in the following chapter. Thus, it seems appropriate to begin that discussion by an examination of the election process, since this is the vehicle which gives the citizen his greatest control over his government and the devices of direct democracy—the initiative, referendum, and recall. That will be followed by a discussion of pressure groups since these provide another important means whereby the citizen can give direction to and exercise a degree of control over his government.

SUGGESTED READINGS

Books

Banfield, Edward C., *Urban Government, A Reader in Administration and Politics* (New York: Free Press, 1961).

Bone, Hugh A., *American Politics and the Party System*, 2nd ed. (New York: McGraw-Hill, 1955).

Cass, Don P., *How To Win Votes and Influence Elections* (Chicago: Public Administration Service, 1962).

Freedgood, Seymour, "New Strength in City Hall" in Fortune Magazine, *The Exploding Metropolis* (New York: Doubleday, 1958).

Hinderaker, Ivan, *Party Politics* (New York: Holt, Rinehart and Winston, 1956).

Kent, Frank R., *The Great Game of Politics* (New York: Doubleday, 1933).

Key, V. O., Jr., *Politics, Parties and Pressure Groups*, 4th ed. (New York: Crowell, 1958).

Kneier, Charles M., *City Government in the United States*, 3rd ed. (New York: Harper, 1957).

Martin, Roscoe C., *Grass Roots* (University, Ala.: University of Alabama Press, 1957).

Meyerson, Martin and Banfield, Edward C., *Politics, Planning and the Public Interest* (New York: Free Press, 1955).

Michener, James A., *Report of the County Chairman* (New York: Random House, 1961).

Rossiter, Clinton, *Parties and Politics in America* (Ithaca, New York: Cornell University Press, 1960).

Salter, J. T., *Boss Rule: Portraits in City Politics* (New York: McGraw-Hill, 1935).

Steffens, Lincoln, *The Shame of the Cities* (New York: McClure, Phillips & Co., 1904).

Williams, Oliver P and Press, Charles, *Democracy in Urban America, Readings in Government and Politics* (Chicago: Rand, McNally, 1961).

Wood, Robert C., *Suburbia, Its People and Their Politics* (Boston: Houghton Mifflin, 1959).

Zink, Harold, *City Bosses in the United States* (Durham, N. C.: Duke University Press, 1930).

Articles

Adrian, Charles R., "A Typology for Nonpartisan Elections," *Western Political Quarterly, 12* (June, 1959), 449–58.

Adrian, Charles R., "Some General Characteristics of Nonpartisan Elections," *American Political Science Review, 46* (September, 1952), 766–76.

Beard, Charles, "Political Parties in City Government: A Reconsideration of Old Viewpoints," *National Municipal Review, 6* (March, 1917), 20–26.

Brown, Seyom, "Fun Can be Politics," *The Reporter, 21* (November 12, 1959), 27–28.

Committee on Political Parties of the American Political Science Association, "Toward a More Responsible Two-Party System," *American Political Science Review*, Vol. 44, Part 2, Supplement (September, 1950).

Forthal-Spiesman, Sonya, "The Precinct Worker," *The Annals of the American Academy of Political and Social Science, 259* (September, 1948), 30–45.

Freeman, J. L., "Local Party Systems: Theoretical Consideration and a Case Analysis," *American Journal of Sociology, 64* (November, 1959), 282–9.

Gulick, Luther, "The Shame of the Cities—1946," *National Municipal Review, 36* (January, 1947), 18–25.

Keefe, William J. and Seyler, William C., "Precinct Politicians in Pittsburgh," *Social Science, 35* (January, 1960), 26–32.

Moscow, Warren, "Exit the Boss; Enter the Leader," *The New York Times Magazine,* June 22, 1947, pp. 16–17, 47–48.

Owens, Hamilton, "The County Boss," *American Mercury, 17* (May, 1929), 70–74.

Peel, Roy V., "The Political Machine of New York City," *American Political Science Review, 27* (August, 1933), 611–18.

Porter, Kirk H., "The Deserted Primary in Iowa," *American Political Science Review, 39* (August, 1945), 732–40.

Williams, Oliver P. and Adrian, Charles R., "The Insulation of Local Politics Under the Nonpartisan Ballot," *American Political Science Review, 53* (December, 1959), 1052–63.

Citizen Action
and Control

8

The foundation of the democratic process in local government lies in open and free elections at reasonably frequent intervals. At such periods of public accounting by the "in's" and their challenge by other contestants, it is vital that the individual voters act as independent citizens rather than as ciphers of election statistics. When the voters enter the voting booth on election day, they hold its outcome in their hands. Regardless of how thorough the work of the local party, group, or organization has been, the individual voter in the secrecy of the private booth is free to re-examine his predilections and is capable of doing unexpected things. The importance of the voter to the cause of good government in his community is clearly indicated in this brief quotation, "The word idiot is derived from the classical Greek idiōtēs, which meant 'those citizens who did not take part in public voting'. In ancient Greece it was because they could not; in the United States today it is because they do not—and the word idiot is still appropriate."[1]

---

[1] From *The Ladies' Home Journal* as cited in Joseph E. McLean, "Politics is What You Make It," Public Affairs Pamphlet No. 181, New York, 1954, p. 1.

■ Local Election Administration

The conduct of both primary and general elections is governed by state law, but most local electoral functions are performed by citizens of the local community. At the state level, the office of secretary of state usually oversees elections to the extent of checking compliance with state laws, and a state election board canvasses and certifies the results. However, the responsibility for local election administration is entrusted to the election board of the governmental community. At the county level, this board is normally the board of county commissioners, while the city council sitting as an *ex officio* board or a special election board serves this capacity in cities. This local election board has ballots printed as prescribed by state law, designates and makes provisions for polling places, sets up the election machinery, and reports the results to the state election board.

In the actual conduct of elections, the local governmental unit, except when it is very small, is divided into precincts or election districts ranging from 200 to 2,000 voters. A polling place is established in each precinct or district with public buildings such as schools, fire, or police stations usually so designated. Rented buildings or portable structures are sometimes used, but this practice is less frequent than in earlier days when there were more partisan favors passed out to party workers on election day. A board consisting of judges or inspectors to conduct the election is established in each precinct. These normally consist of two or more judges or inspectors from each major party and a small number of clerks to assist them. The bi-partisan nature of the board is aimed to promote honest elections by having workers of one party checking those of the other party. In non-partisan elections, of course, the board may also be non-partisan in its composition. Normally, these local election officials are appointed by the election boards of the governmental unit, but sometimes they are elected or selected by a merit system procedure.

Typically the polls are open for a ten- or twelve-hour period with the day beginning at seven or eight o'clock in the morning. The precinct or district election board must see that the voter is properly identified, is given a ballot, and that the ballot is deposited in the ballot box after it has been marked. If the district has voting machines, these must be manned by workers to see that they are kept in proper working condition and that the elector gets his vote duly recorded on the machine. Then when the polls close, the election board tabulates the votes and certifies the results to the city or county election board. To relieve the burden of the long day on the election board, several states now authorize two election boards. One board performs the functions outlined above except for counting ballots and certifying the results. These two functions are performed by the second election board which comes on duty a few hours before the polls close and begins the tally of the ballots in a room adjacent to the election room itself. In an effort to prevent fraud in counting ballots in the election districts, some cities and counties require that all votes be tabulated at a central headquarters, but this is not the common practice.[2]

BALLOT FORMS

The ballot form in common use in all 50 states is known as the "Australian ballot," named for the country of its origin. As defined by one author, this ballot is "an official ballot, printed at public expense, by public officers, containing the names of all candidates duly nominated, and distributed at the polls by the election officers."[3] This ballot is so widely used and accepted that it is hard to realize that voting was once done by public oral announcement by individual electors or by utilizing ballots printed by the individual parties or candidates.

The original form of the Australian ballot carried no party designation to identify the candidates, but today two basic forms of ballots are used. The office-block type originated in Massachusetts in 1888 and groups candidates by office. Under the heading of "treasurer," for example, the names of the several candidates with their party affiliations are listed in a block on the ballot. This block is followed by similar groupings of candidates for the other offices to be filled. The other common form, the party-column ballot, originated in Indiana in 1889. Under this form, all candidates of one party are placed in a single column headed by the name of the

[2] An Indiana law requires that votes in counties having first or second class cities within their borders must be tabulated centrally. See J. K. Eads, "Indiana Experiments with Central Ballot Count," *National Municipal Review*, 29 (August, 1940), 545.

[3] Joseph P. Harris, *Election Administration in the United States*, Brookings Institution, 1934, p. 154.

party. It is possible under this form to vote a straight party ticket by placing a single mark in the spot provided by the name of the party. Party leaders favor this form since it makes it simpler to vote a straight party ticket. This form is now used a little more commonly than the office-block type which tends to make straight ticket voting more difficult. It is difficult to generalize about this point since some states using the office-block ballot have special provisions for straight ticket voting and not all states using the party-column form have such a provision.

Voting machines make the use of paper ballots unnecessary, since the decisions of the individual voter in no way deface the ballot form set up on the machine. The machine enables the office titles, names of candidates, and party affiliations to be arranged in either the party-column or office-block type of ballot, and space is provided for write-in candidates. When the party-column ballot is used, a party lever makes it possible to vote a straight ticket. In addition, there is a lever above the name of each candidate which the voter pulls down to indicate his choice if he does not pull the party lever or when the machine is using the office-block ballot. It is not possible to vote for more than one candidate for each office on the machine or to spoil the ballot in any other manner. Before the voter leaves the booth, he can change any part of his vote since the votes are recorded only when he opens the curtains to leave the booth.

The voting machine offers a number of advantages over the printed paper ballot. First, the voter can select his choices on the machine and have his vote recorded in less time than it takes to mark and deposit a paper ballot. Second, it is impossible to spoil a machine vote. Third, the votes are automatically tallied by the machine as the individual votes are recorded. Fourth, the results are tallied more accurately since it is almost impossible to tamper with the voting machine. And fifth, machines result in more economical elections since precincts can be larger, fewer election officials are neded, and much less time is required to tally the votes. It is probable that continuing wider use of voting machines will occur in the future. However, there are two aspects of machine use which present serious problems to local governments. The first is the necessary outlay of funds to purchase the machines and the second relates to the size of the face of the machine. A machine adequate for general election purposes may be too small to provide the space necessary for listing the names of all the contestants in the primary election.

The development of a new form of ballot which is equivalent to a specially marked card is being considered in at least two states, Ohio and California. Once marked, the ballots could be machine totaled for speed and accuracy.

Whether the voter is asked to mark a paper ballot or pull the levers on a voting machine, the very form of the means by which he indicates his choice gives him an essential control over his local government and its officers. By recording his will secretly, the voter is free to express his convictions by splitting his ballot, voting for a change, or electing to maintain the present officers or their party in control of the affairs of his community.

THE SHORT BALLOT

The control that the voter has through the secret ballot is considerably strengthened if the job facing him on election day is to choose a limited number of officers to fill important positions rather than to select a large number of officers, many for minor offices. This principle of greater voter control if the ballot is short may seem contrary to logic at first glance. It would seem to follow that the influence of the voter would increase with the number of positions he is asked to fill. But the long ballot listing a large number of minor offices can be more than a little frustrating when the voter is asked to choose between candidates he doesn't know to fulfill the duties of an office with which the voter is unfamiliar. In such cases, the voter's control passes from his hands by the process vividly described by Richard S. Childs, since the voter begins "to accept ready-made tickets of candidates tied up in bunches like asparagus, and power thereby leaves the hands of the voter and gravitates to the politicians and ticket makers. The persons who get elected on long ballots are frequently under more obligation to the ticket makers than to the rank and file of voters."[4]

To combat the evils of the long ballot and the tendency to lengthen it even more, the Short Ballot Organization was founded in 1911. The two basic principles of this reform movement were (1) that voters should be asked to elect candidates to only those offices which were important enough to attract and deserve public attention, and (2) that only a limited number of offices should be

[4] Richard S. Childs, "Theories of Responsive Government Prove Practical," *Public Management*, 29 (December, 1947), 353–5.

filled at any one election so that the voters could know the merits of the candidates.[5] In implementing the second principle, it was hoped that local elections would be held on different dates than those on which national and state elections occurred.

Progress in realizing the objectives of the short ballot movement has been steady but unspectacular in the half-century since its initial efforts. The greatest progress has been achieved in municipal government, and cities of all sizes, especially those with strong mayor-chief administrative officer, council-manager, or commission forms of government, have adopted the principles of the short ballot. In rural government, the short ballot has received little acceptance and most county ballots are still long and list a number of minor elective offices. However, in counties which have modified their structure to permit county executive or administrative officers the concepts of the short ballot principle have been generally embraced.

To date the short ballot principles have not received the wide acceptance they deserve on the basis of their merits. However, the short ballot is only another of the essential tools in the citizen's arsenal of weapons to control his government. It does not in itself improve local government or increase its representativeness, but it can result in more careful and informed voter participation in the local electoral process, a goal worthy of pursuit and implementation.

■ Methods of Direct Popular Control

While direct legislation techniques were used in Switzerland a number of years before their introduction into American local government, the devices of initiative, referendum, and recall found fertile soil in the minds of American reformers. Soon they were widely heralded as the means to end boss rule and to restore government to the people. The spirit behind the drive to put these devices into the hands of the citizens was well phrased by Brand Whitlock, a former mayor of Toledo. In his words, "the cure for the ills from which cities suffer is not, as many suppose, less democracy, but more democracy."[6] And the initiative and referendum—as the

[5] Richard S. Childs, *Civic Victories*, Harper, 1952, pp. 83–84.

[6] Brand Whitlock, "The Evil Influence of National Parties and Issues in Municipal Elections," *Proceedings of National Conference for Good City Government*, New York, 1907, p. 193.

two methods of direct legislative action—were intended to give the voter "more democracy" by letting him take remedial actions when his elected representatives failed to act or made a decision which he did not endorse.

A similar logic was advanced for placing the device of recall in the voter's hands. While it is not directly concerned with the determination of policies as are the initiative and referendum, it seeks to insure honesty and good behavior on the part of public officers. The case for the use of the recall has been aptly phrased by W. B. Munro who stated, "Just when the people have elected a man burning with patriotic zeal, he suffers some sort of intracerebral accident. He is no longer able to interpret *vox populi*. His memory fails him. His formerly clear-cut views upon public questions become confused and incoherent. . . . The recall proposes to aid the officeholder in retaining a candidate's state of mind."[7] The recall was first formally adopted by the city of Los Angeles in 1903, and it was first applied to elective state officers in Oregon by a constitutional amendment approved in 1908. The recall is now applicable to elective officials in 13 states and it has spread much more widely on the local level.

The first state to formally adopt the initiative and referendum for law-making purposes was South Dakota, which did so in 1898 while under the control of the Populists. These devices were adopted in the California cities of San Francisco and Vallejo in the same year. A number of other states followed during the next few years and 20 states now provide for the initiative and 22 authorize the use of the referendum on statewide proposals. The use of these devices, however, is much wider at the local level and in all but three states[8] at least some local governmental units have one or both of these means of direct legislation available. Direct legislation provisions are more common in local governments with strong legislative councils than in those with weaker law-making bodies. Thus they are found more often in cities with newer and stronger forms of government such as the council-manager, commission, or strong mayor-chief administrative officer forms and in counties with executives serving at the pleasure of an elected board. Citizens have seemed willing to accept the stronger governing bodies inherent in

[7] W. B. Munro, (ed.), *The Initiative, Referendum and Recall*, D. Appleton & Co., 1912, pp. 299–300.
[8] These are Delaware, Indiana, and Rhode Island.

these plans if they are provided the safeguards of the initiative, referendum, and recall.

THE INITIATIVE

Simply defined, the initiative is a device whereby a prescribed number or percent of qualified voters, through the use of a petition, may have a charter amendment or local ordinance placed on the ballot for adoption or rejection by the electorate. Such petitions for ordinances are normally submitted to the local legislative body. If that body adopts the proposed ordinance, the matter is not placed before the electorate since the aim sought by the petitioners has been gained. If the legislative body fails to approve the proposal, it is placed on the ballot at the next general or at a special election and if approved by a majority of the voters it becomes a statement of local policy with the same force as an ordinance approved by the council or commission.

There are seven basic steps in the direct initiative process. The first consists of drafting the proposal. This may be done by any group of interested citizens but commonly such groups request legal assistance to assure acceptable wording. In the second phase, the proposal is given a preliminary filing with the proper local official who prescribes the form and outlines the procedures to be followed in its circulation for signatures, which is the third step. The actual percentage or number of signatures required varies among governmental units but generally it is prescribed as either a fixed percent of qualified voters or of votes cast in the last preceding election. At the fourth stage, the petitions are filed with the proper official and the signatures thereon are checked for irregularities and unqualified signers. The fifth step is actually a continuing one and it began simultaneously with the first phase. This concerns the education of the electorate about the nature and purpose of the proposal. However, the educational campaign steps up in intensity at this stage and is worthy of listing as a separate and distinct step. The sixth step is the actual election in which the proposal is submitted to the voters. If rejected by the voters, the matter ends, at least temporarily; but if approved by a majority, then the seventh step or the promulgation of the proposal in ordinance form is made and it becomes a part of the law of the community.

Under indirect initiative proceedings, the same first four steps are followed except that a larger percentage of signatures may be required. At this point, however, the proposal goes to the local law-making body for consideration. If the local legislature approves the proposal without amendment, the fifth and sixth steps outlined above are eliminated and the proposal becomes law upon passage of the implementing ordinance by the legislative body.

THE REFERENDUM

The referendum is a means by which decisions of local law-making bodies do not become public policies until the electorate of the community votes its concurrence with the policies and accepts them by majority vote. The concept of the referendum as a means to secure public approval of proposals is not a recent development. It was used as early as 1641 in Massachusetts and the 1780 constitution of that state was ratified by a popular vote of its citizens.

There are now three distinct forms which the referendum vote can take. The eldest is usually identified as the compulsory referendum and it pertains to the mandatory referral to the voters of such issues as charter amendments, bond issues, extraordinary tax levies, and boundary changes. Referenda on such issues are stipulated in local charters, state constitutions, or by state laws; since they are mandatory they are examples of the compulsory referendum. Thus, some measures must always be submitted to voters for approval, even in states where the initiative and referendum systems herein described do not prevail.

A second form is known as the optional referendum since the decision to put the proposal to a popular vote lies with the legislative body. This means of learning public sentiment is sometimes used on matters which are controversial and on which local lawmakers may be hesitant to take a stand. Examples might be approval of certain types of activities such as horseracing or the prohibition of beer parlors or to key policy questions such as a master plan for the community's development. There is some difference of opinion as to the nature of the electorate's decision on optional referendum questions. In most communities, the vote is considered a binding one on the law-making body, but in some areas the vote is considered to be advisory only and members of the local legislative body can either implement or ignore the results as they see fit. In a few states, action by a local governing body referring a measure, in the absence of state permission, is deemed an act of improper delegation.

The third type of referendum is known as the protest or petition form. This procedure enables the voters to pass upon measures already approved by their law-making body. In communities authorizing this form of popular referendum, the charter stipulates (or state law may prescribe) that ordinances will not become effective for a period of 30, 60, or 90 days after their passage. During this interim, citizens may file a protest petition by securing a prescribed number of signatures asking that the ordinance be submitted to the electorate. If the petitions are in order and a sufficient number of signatures are obtained, the legislative body must submit the ordinance to the voters at either a special or at the next general election. If the vote by the electorate is an unfavorable one, then it has been popularly vetoed and does not become effective. Certain types of actions by the law-making body are exempt from this type of protest referendum because of their importance and controversial nature. These normally include such matters as tax rates and appropriations, location of public buildings, major public works programs, and emergency measures.

The procedural steps in the referendum process, if petitions are required, are very similar to those in the initiative. The basic difference between the two devices is clear, however; the referendum is negative in character since it seeks to check actions which have or might be taken while the initiative is used to initiate policies when the lawmakers refuse to act. Thus, Kneier concludes that the referendum is a tool to combat errors of commission while the initiative is used to correct errors of omission.[9]

THE RECALL

While methods have always existed for the removal of public officers from their positions by the judicial process, by impeachment, or by legislative or executive action, a new method for removing such officers first appeared in the Los Angeles city charter of 1903. This was the device of recall, which provides a means for voters to remove an unsatisfactory official before the expiration of the term for which he was elected. Thus, the recall was designed for a specific purpose and differs from the devices of initiative and referendum. It is similar, however, in that it is set in motion and executed by citizen action and is another weapon in their hands to make their control of their government more effective.

[9] Charles M. Kneier, *City Government in the United States*, 3rd ed., Harper, 1957, p. 389.

CITIZENS AND THEIR POLITICS

The procedural steps in initiating recall proceedings are similar to those in other direct legislation actions, but there are several significant differences. While the process is begun by petitions, the petitions must state the precise grounds for the removal of the official and the percent of signatures required is usually from two to three times higher than that for initiative proceedings. The petitions must be filed and, if found valid upon checking by the appropriate official, the election must be called for within a specified time limit.

The recall ballot may take one of three general forms. Under the first, the name of the official in question is placed on the ballot and the voters are asked to decide whether he should or should not be removed. If a majority vote for his removal, then a second election must be held to select his successor. While this method has the disadvantage of two elections, it usually assures that the successor will be a majority rather than a plurality choice of the voters. More important is the fair consideration it gives the incumbent, since he is running against his record in office rather than engaging in a popularity contest with the other candidates.

A second ballot form combines the questions of removal and the selection of a successor. The question of removal is at the top of the ballot and those who vote "yes" are asked to vote for their choice of successors listed below. The successor is almost certain to be a plurality choice since several candidates may be seeking the office in question.

The third type of recall ballot requires the official in question to run against other candidates to determine who, the incumbent or someone else, shall serve the balance of the term. This is the least desirable form since the voters favoring recall may split their votes among several candidates to succeed the incumbent, while his supporters will vote solidly for his retention. Thus, the officer may be kept in office although a majority of the voters favor his removal. This type of election also amounts to a new popularity contest rather than an evaluation of whether the incumbent's performance violates his original mandate.

EVALUATION

The democratic devices of initiative, referendum, and recall were widely adopted at a time when reformers were demanding that government be returned to the control of the people from whom it had been wrested by bosses and machines. However, a word of caution was sounded even at the time these reforms were being widely championed. Writing in 1909, Charles Beard stated that, "We have apparently assumed that it (the electorate) can do everything from deciding who among ten thousand should be the clerk of a municipal court to prescribing what should be done with the surface dirt removed from a street by a public contractor."[10] As with all reforms, the results have not lived up to the expectations of their proponents or caused the sad consequences predicted by their opponents. And, again as with all reforms, there are both merits and shortcomings to the direct legislation devices.

Concerning the initiative and referendum, the case for their use can cite the following merits: (1) popular sovereignty is strengthened because these devices can be used by the people to enact desired proposals and to defeat objectionable legislation; (2) the devices can be used by the people as a counterbalancing force to the efforts of special interest groups to secure favorable legislation; (3) their use stimulates the interest of many persons in issues of public policy and helps in the education of voters; (4) their availability lessens citizens' fear in authorizing strong local legislatures, and results in fewer charter restrictions on legislative action; (5) their possible use has a salutary effect on law-making bodies, stimulating them to take action in cases when they might otherwise take no action if such direct citizen controls did not exist; and (6) the devices function as an essential check on legislative action (except for emergency and other excepted measures) and thus give the voters the opportunity to participate in the enactment of much important legislation—if they desire to do so. This feature of direct legislation has been singled out by one writer as the "most important and effective argument in its favor."[11]

The major arguments on the other side are largely reverse statements of the merits of direct legislative devices making shortcomings of their merits through excessive use. Briefly outlined, these are as follows: (1) while popular sovereignty may be strengthened, representative government is impaired since popular distrust of elected representatives is encouraged and some lawmakers may refuse to take stands, leaving too many decisions in the hands of the

[10] Charles A. Beard, "The Ballot's Burden," *Political Science Quarterly*, 24 (December, 1909), 589-614.

[11] J. G. LaPalombara, *The Initiative and Referendum in Oregon, 1938-1948*, Oregon State College Press, 1950, p. 118.

voters; (2) use of these devices assumes that the voters are informed on the many issues which they are called upon to support or defeat, but in practice they operate to further the interests of special and minority groups; (3) their use runs counter to the principle of the short ballot movement since the ballot is lengthened by these proposals; (4) many important decisions of public policy are decided by a mere plurality since many voters will not vote in special elections on such issues, or on all the issues at any single election; (5) their use adds significantly to the costs of elections and campaigns and often results in special elections; and (6) their use ignores the fact that government is becoming more technical and complex and that it is not politically feasible to frame many issues of policy so that a simple "yes" or "no" vote by the electors can result in a satisfactory decision.

Similarly a case both for and against the use of the recall can be made by listing its advantages and disadvantages. And its practice has revealed that it is a weapon which can be used either in behalf of the public interest or to serve the selfish or partisan interests of a strong and vocal minority. On the positive side, the availability of the recall may have (1) a salutary effect on the conduct of public officials who recognize the possible force of this "gun" behind the door; (2) encouraged citizens to grant their officers a longer term in office since this means for their removal, if deemed desirable, exists; and (3) increased voter confidence in his government since the unfaithful officeholder can be removed before the end of his scheduled term. Certainly, it can be demonstrated that the device has been used to remove some local officials who betrayed the trust placed in them or who lost the confidence of the voters.

As in the case of the initiative and referendum, the use of the recall can result in a longer ballot, increase the public costs when special elections are called, and impose a greater burden on the voter by asking him to make a further public decision. In addition, the threat of recall may serve as a restraining influence on public officers to tread softly and take no controversial stands. And lastly, a case can be made that the recall is not necessary since other means for the removal of unfaithful officeholders exist, and that the device is sometimes used more for political recrimination than for the purposes intended.

As a summary evaluative statement concerning citizen use of the initiative, referendum, and recall, the devices should not be condemned because they have been misused occasionally. Certainly some poor choices for elective offices have won the support of the people and yet we would not seriously consider doing away with elections even though some demagogues have been chosen over more public-spirited candidates. The three devices are useful and effective means of citizen control and they should be recognized as such rather than as cure-alls for the ills of local government. When the devices are so conceived, they can be used to achieve their purposes and citizen control will be appreciably enhanced.

■ Open Meetings

In an effort to achieve the goal of "open decisions arrived at openly," the device of public hearings has long been in wide use in local government. Meetings of local governing bodies are open to the public, and the meeting chambers of city councils, county commissions, and township officials are designed to accommodate interested citizens and to enable them to participate in the proceedings. When controversial matters are under consideration, it is common practice for the governing body to hold public hearings. Normally, these proceedings are run rather informally and interested citizens who desire to do so are afforded an opportunity to speak for or against the matter which is pending. Such hearings serve the double purpose of letting citizens air their grievances and informing the public body of citizen opinion.

While it is generally agreed that public business should be open to the public, this has not always occurred in practice. Often the public meetings of public bodies were held after private sessions prior to the open meeting. Decisions were actually arrived at in discussion behind closed doors and the formal meeting became a "rubber stamp" session to legalize the decisions reached in the closed session. In such cases, the public was denied the opportunity to listen to the discussion on the matter or to participate effectively in decisions affecting local public policy.

In several states in recent years, legislation has been enacted forbidding closed meetings on the part of local governing bodies. Such a law was passed in California in 1953, and it is typical of similar laws in other states.[12] The key words of the California law state

---

[12] *California Code,* Sections 54950–54958.

that, "All meetings of the legislative body of a local agency shall be open and public, and all persons shall be permitted to attend any meeting of the legislative body of a local agency, except as provided in this chapter." The exception refers to personnel matters, but all other deliberations of such agencies as planning commissions, library boards, or recreation commissions must be held in open sessions. The California act even extends this requirement to the meetings of private agencies if they are supported in part by public funds and have a public official as an *ex officio* member of their board. Violation of the act is a misdemeanor, and a citizen can obtain a court order to prevent secret or closed sessions.

While the right and ability of the people to have free and open access to meetings of public bodies is vital, it can also be carried to an excess. Suppose the acquisition of sites for public purposes is being discussed "openly." This could pave the way for "honest graft" as the term was defined by George Washington Plunkitt of Tammany Hall. He said "There's an honest graft, and I'm an example of how it works. I might sum up the whole thing by sayin': 'I seen my opportunities and I took 'em.'"[13] In his case, it was the matter of buying up properties and selling them to the city at a considerable personal profit. Another possible shortcoming of open meetings is that excessive discretion may be vested in an administrative officer when it seems necessary to short-circuit the open hearing requirement.

■ Pressure Groups

While pressure groups have been variously defined, an acceptable and working concept is that a pressure group is any organized group which attempts to influence some phase of public policy. This brief definition points out the two principal differences between political parties and pressure groups. The latter are more interested in controlling or affecting specific policies of governmental agencies than in controlling their principal officers, and they are more homogeneous groups than political parties can be. Pressure groups are composed of persons who share the same basic interests and point

[13] W. L. Riordon, *Plunkitt of Tammany Hall*, Doubleday, 1905, p. 3.

of view while a political party has to be considerably broader in interests and policy viewpoints if it is to gain sufficient support to fulfill its basic purpose of winning public office.[14]

However, parties and pressure groups have much in common in the arena of the local political process since both seek the implementation of policies. Only in recent years have pressure groups been accorded the dignity of being recognized as "necessary evils" rather than merely as evils. One writer has suggested that public policy might well be defined as the "end result of the interaction of the various interested pressure groups upon one another. It is the sum of the vector forces, where each vector represents the total force and direction of each group as determined by its age, respectability, size of membership, wealth, ability of leadership, skill at lobbying, inside connections, intensity of interests, and other pertinent factors."[15]

The factors affecting pressure groups identified by Adrian result in a large variety of pressure groups in local government. In rural areas the agricultural interests will often predominate, while labor groups will normally wield considerable influence in industrial cities. The business community is always an active interest group and so are many citizen organizations such as taxpayers' associations, home-owners' leagues, roadside councils and other groups. In fact, it is difficult to think of any organized group which does not attempt to influence policy at some time or another; in this sense all function as interest groups. Churches, women's clubs, Kiwanis, Rotary, Boy Scouts, P.T.A.'s, etc., take formal stands in support of or in opposition to particular policies, and when they do they become pressure groups the same as chambers of commerce, labor leagues, farm groups, and other organizations more generally identified with special interests.

Since the basic objective of all pressure groups is to influence ac-

[14] For further analysis of pressure groups, their activities and role in shaping policies, see V. O. Key, Jr., *Politics, Parties and Pressure Groups*, 4th ed., Crowell, 1958; E. E. Schattschneider, *The Semisovereign People*, Holt, Rinehart and Winston, 1960; David B. Truman, *The Governmental Process*, Knopf, 1951; Arthur Bentley, *The Process of Government*, University of Chicago Press, 1908; *Annals of the American Academy of Political and Social Science*, "Unofficial Government: Pressure Groups and Lobbies," Vol. 319, entire issue, September, 1958; Donald C. Blaisdell, *American Democracy Under Pressure*, Ronald, 1957; and Earl Latham, "The Group Basis of Politics: Notes for a Theory," *American Political Science Review*, 26 (June, 1952), 376-9.

[15] Charles R. Adrian, *State and Local Government, A Study in the Political Process*, McGraw-Hill, 1960, p. 160.

tion favorable to their own interests, there are a number of techniques or methods of action which are engaged in commonly. These include: (1) appearing at public meetings of local legislative bodies or at public hearings to present the views of their members; (2) initiating favorable legislation and working to defeat legislation deemed harmful to their interests; (3) exerting influence on lawmakers by direct and/or indirect means; (4) issuing news stories, reports, or other forms of publicity; (5) spearheading letter-writing or telephone campaigns to disseminate their views; (6) engaging in research to prepare reports and uncover evidence in support of their views; and (7) attempting to influence the selection of candidates within local political parties and then working to secure their nomination and election. Many other methods might be used by particular groups at specific times, but the above list catalogs the general activities which are common to most pressure groups.

Since these groups are now recognized as vital to the democratic process, or at least as evils necessary for its proper functioning, it follows that there must be some useful functions which they fulfill. First, pressure groups do help inform the citizenry on policy issues and stimulate open discussion. Second, they often supply public officials with useful information which enables the persons in office to make more informed decisions. Third, they gather, organize and present individual opinions on specific issues in a more effective way than if the voices remained unmarshaled. Fourth, they provide a form of functional representation for their members since it is extremely difficult for a city councilman or county commissioner to know and reflect the views of the several different groups within his constituency. And, fifth, they serve in large part to fill the political vacuum resulting from weak political parties at the local level.

The activities of pressure groups, however, are not always commendable and there are a number of criticisms directed at them and their actions. Chief among these are (1) the use of certain methods or techniques which are inimical to the proper functioning of local democratic government—such as inordinate pressure or the offer of bribes; (2) the inequality of groups because of their wide differences in membership, financial resources, and cohesion; (3) the lack of interest groups to represent certain points of view, placing such unorganized groups at a disadvantage; (4) the inability to determine the real purpose of some organized groups with impressive but unrepresentative names; and (5) the absence of internal checks within the machinery of local government to counterbalance the influence of pressure groups.

Although such internal checks may be missing, there are a number of external checks which operate to hold pressure groups in line. First is the rise of new interest groups to espouse other points of view than those championed by existing groups. Second, local lawmakers must usually rely on the support of a number of interest groups rather than on a single organized interest and the groups keep each other in balance. Third, there are standards of conduct which no pressure group can flaunt too often or too deliberately. Fourth, the quality of leadership in local government is improving so that the public interest is more effectively represented as a countervailing force to special interests. While the system of checks and balances in local government operates somewhat imperfectly to limit the effectiveness of such groups, their influence will not normally embrace all three branches of government, and officials of the legislative, executive, and judicial branches do serve as brakes or checks on the actions of each other.

While there are still insufficient studies of the operation of interest groups in local government, it is possible that their effectiveness and role has been overemphasized at this level. In a careful and systematic study of 90 major pieces of federal legislation in the fields in which pressure groups have been highly active—business, tariff, labor, national defense, agriculture, immigration, conservation, and others, Lawrence H. Chamberlain concluded, "Of the ninety major laws studied, approximately twenty per cent fall to the credit of the President; roughly forty per cent were chiefly the product of Congress; about thirty per cent fall into the joint presidential-congressional category; and slightly less than ten per cent are identified as primarily the handiwork of external pressure groups."[16] This study did not analyze legislation which failed to pass (and perhaps because of the activities of pressure groups). It is significant that the effect of such groups was less influential than the efforts of the President, the Congress, or of their joint efforts. The importance of this finding on the national level should not be overlooked when analyzing the efforts of pressure groups in local communities. On the other hand, most local communities will not represent the intermixture of competitive and actually opposing interests

[16] Lawrence H. Chamberlain, *The President, Congress and Legislation,* Columbia University Press, 1946, p. 453.

that operate in the national arena so that such groups might be considerably more effective at the local level.

■ Information for Citizens

If the citizen is to carry out his responsibilities to and for controlling his local government, he needs to give considerable time to the study of politics in his community or have a number of resources which can assist him in assembling the necessary information. The important relationship of available knowledge to the exercise of responsible citizenship by a voter is drawn by one writer in these words, "a lack of information about city government usually results in a paucity of interest in government."[17] This section will be devoted to a brief discussion of several of the important sources of information which are helpful in aiding the citizen to be informed about his community and its government.

Among community resources for informing citizens and shaping their opinions, special mention must be made of the local newspaper or the local section of a larger newspaper serving that community. While few of us would go so far as to agree with Walter Lippman that the newspaper is the "Bible of democracy," its influence as a constructive—or obstructive—force in the community cannot be denied. The influence of the local press extends both to the voter and to the public officials. The fear of adverse newspaper publicity in the local press is one of the factors that help keep public officers toeing the mark in the performance of their duties. While the power of the press can be misused, this suspicion is rightly or wrongly largely reserved for newspapers with large circulations and big advertising accounts such as metropolitan dailies. A recent study of community papers in Chicago revealed that their readers thought them to be (1) agents of community welfare and progress rather than political or partisan organs, (2) a medium relatively free of "commercialized" aspects, and (3) a device for democratizing prestige within the community.[18] Numerous studies have shown a declining role for the newspaper in the shaping of public policies and

[17] Murdock Martin, *The Annual City Report: Why and How*, Bureau of Governmental Research and Service, Florida State University, 1955, p. 1.

[18] Morris Janowitz, "The Imagery of the Urban Community Press" from his book, *The Community Press in an Urban Setting*, Free Press, 1952, as exerpted and adapted in Paul K. Hatt and Albert J. Reiss, Jr., *Cities in Society*, rev. ed., Free Press, 1957, pp. 597-606.

in the success of press-supported candidates in elections, but the newspaper remains an important source of information whether or not its recommendations win public acceptance at the polls.

Local election campaigns are another important means for informing citizens about their government and their local officials. Too many local campaigns are still devoted to "mud-slinging" tactics and the outcome of local elections is still too frequently determined by inconsequential factors. However, most campaigns are filled with public appearances of the candidates, and citizens are afforded a number of opportunities to direct questions to such aspirants for public office. While the primary purpose of campaigns is to win votes rather than to inform the voters, there is reason to hope that local campaigns can be and are being conducted on a higher level than they were in earlier years. This is the responsibility of the citizen himself, since candidates and their parties will conduct the type of campaign necessary to win voter support. If buffoonery, appeal to prejudices, and mud-slinging prove successful, then these methods will be used. As one writer has stated, "The Madison Avenue experts in public taste and public demand demonstrated that logic and pertinent facts often were second in effectiveness to oft-repeated emotional stimuli. Campaign managers discovered that portraits of a good-looking candidate, accompanied by a catchy slogan, influenced more votes than did treatment of the real issue."[19] On the other hand, if voters support candidates because of their personal qualifications, stand on public issues, and promises of performance in office, these factors will become increasingly important campaign issues. In general, there is room for optimism since the belief that "good government is good politics" seems to be gaining wider acceptance at the local level.

Citizen organizations form a third important source of information. As used here, the term "citizen organization" is limited to citizen research and fact-finding agencies with a broad interest in local government and to community councils. These agencies bear such labels as bureaus of municipal or governmental research, voter leagues, leagues of women voters, citizen unions or leagues, civic council or leagues, and citizen committees. Regardless of their specific names, such agencies share the common features of being nonpartisan in composition and of working for the improvement of the

[19] John Anson Ford, *Thirty Explosive Years in Los Angeles County*, Huntington Library, 1961, p. 209.

government of their community. Such agencies can be quite effective in arousing and sustaining citizen interest in government and in centering voter attention on community problems.

Community councils, or coordinating councils as they are often called, are usually composed of representatives of the several agencies which are interested in the health and welfare services and activities in the community. As of 1954, there were such councils in 600 American communities, functioning as clearing houses and to coordinate citizen activity in attacking problems of general concern.[20]

In addition to the citizen agencies and organizations which serve to inform the citizenry, there are other agencies or avenues to provide information within the government structure itself. At the local level, extensive use is made of citizen advisory commissions or councils to work with government agencies and programs. Park commissions, library boards, planning commissions, recreation commissions, welfare boards, and health boards, to name only a few, are adjunct agencies of local governments in communities all across the nation. In addition to such standing boards and commissions, a number of special or *ad hoc* citizen committees are appointed as the need for their services arises.

The annual report to its citizens is becoming an increasingly common practice in communities across the nation. By giving the citizen the facts about his government, the purpose such reports are aimed to serve, it is hoped that the citizens can reach a more informed judgment in selecting the officers to serve them and in shaping the policies of their government. In earlier years, annual reports were too often tabulations of uninterpreted statistics and columns of figures or "publicity statements" in praise of current officials. Modern reports, however, are often attractive and readable accounts of the progress, projects and problems of the community prepared in pamphlet form or as supplements to the local newspaper. While some citizens object to the expenditure of tax monies for the preparation and distribution of annual reports, this is an unwarranted attitude. It is only fitting that taxpayers be given an accounting of the use of their money and the annual report is a good device to accomplish this purpose.[21]

[20] United Community Funds and Councils of America, Inc., *Teamwork in Our Town Through a Community Council*, New York, 1954, pp. 1–2.
[21] Pan Dodd Wheeler, *A Municipal Public Relations Program That Works for Small and Medium Sized Cities*, Government Public Affairs Association, 1955.

In addition to the public hearings discussed earlier, budget hearings provide another means for the citizen to inform himself about the operations and programs of his local government. Such hearings open to the public are required by law in most states, but few citizens normally attend. Too often those who do attend do so in protest against some proposed tax increase or expenditure rather than to gain information about their government. Such hearings, however, can be a valuable source of information to citizens and provide the local legislative body with insight into the sentiments of the community.

Democratic local government is based on the premise of informed citizen interest and participation in the affairs of his community. Thus, educational programs to interest citizens and to inform them about their government are to be encouraged. Although local governments are now faced with a number of grave problems in finding adequate sources of financial support, improving levels of particular services, providing new services, etc., the greatest problem lies in arousing their citizens to take an active interest in and to participate in the affairs of their community. Democracy functions most adequately when each citizen contributes his best to the community and this can be achieved only if citizens are informed. Informed citizens are active citizens and these are two of the surest safeguards against corrupt and uncontrolled local government.

The possible unfortunate result of continuing citizen abdication of their responsibilities and obligations is pointed out by Robert C. Wood. In his concluding paragraph describing the politics of suburban communities, he writes:

In the final analysis, the suburban man may become apolitical altogether. He has escaped from the divisive conflicts and hostilities of the great city in search of peace and fellowship among his own kind. The theory is that he has created a democratic haven in which a consensus of right-thinking men replaces a compromise among partisan-thinking men. This theory wraps him in a cloak of nonpartisanship and no politics, which makes active expression of political views socially unacceptable, if not immoral. If faithfully followed, the theory would demand so much of his time, so great a communion with his neighbors, so high a competence in public affairs, as to be nearly all-consuming. For most suburbanites, the feasible way out is indifference, as revealed by apathy in local elections. If the expert is entrusted with the really tough problems, the suburbanite has the best of all possible worlds: grassroots government run by automation. Under these circumstances, the purest theory of democracy requires no democratic action or responsibility at all.[22]

SUGGESTED READINGS

Books

Aronfreed, Eva, *Public Relations as a Function of City Government: A Study of Municipal Public Relations in the City of Philadelphia,* unpublished doctoral dissertation (Philadelphia: University of Pennsylvania, 1958).

Bird, F. F. and Ryan, F. M., *The Recall of Public Officers* (New York: Macmillan, 1930).

Childs, Richard S., *Civic Victories* (New York: Harper, 1952).

Crouch, Winston W., *The Initiative and Referendum in California* (Los Angeles: The Haynes Foundation, 1950).

Gallup, George, *Public Opinion in a Democracy* (Princeton: Princeton University Press, 1939).

Key, V. O., Jr., *Politics, Parties and Pressure Groups,* 4th ed. (New York: Crowell, 1958).

Kneier, Charles M., *City Government in the United States,* 3rd ed. (New York: Harper, 1957).

La Palombara, J. G., *The Initiative and Referendum in Oregon, 1938–1948* (Corvallis: Oregon State College Press, 1950).

Lundberg, Louis B., *Public Relations in the Local Community* (New York: Harper, 1950).

Martin, Murdock, *The Annual City Report: Why and How* (Tallahassee: Bureau of Governmental Research and Service, Florida State University, 1955).

Munro, W. B. (ed.), *The Initiative, Referendum and Recall* (New York: D. Appleton & Co., 1912).

Schattschneider, E. E., *The Semisovereign People* (New York: Holt, Rinehart and Winston, 1960).

Stewart, Frank M., *A Half-Century of Municipal Reform* (Los Angeles: University of California Press, 1950).

Truman, David, *The Governmental Process* (New York: Knopf, 1951).

Wheeler, Pan Dodd, *A Municipal Public Relations Program That Works for Small and Medium Sized Cities* (Chicago: Government Public Affairs Association, 1955).

Wood, Robert C., *Suburbia, Its People and Their Politics* (Boston: Houghton Mifflin, 1958).

[22] Robert C. Wood, *Suburbia, Its People and Their Politics,* Houghton Mifflin, 1958, p. 197.

Articles

Annals of the American Academy of Political and Social Science, "Unofficial Government: Pressure Groups and Lobbies," Vol. 319, entire issue (September, 1958).

Beard, Charles A., "The Ballot's Burden," *Political Science Quarterly, 24* (December, 1909), 589–614.

Childs, Richard S., "Theories of Responsible Government Prove Practical," *Public Management, 29* (December, 1947), 353–5.

Frank, Forest, "Know-How of Civic Action," *National Municipal Review, 36* (January, 1947), 43–44.

La Palombara, J. G. and Hagen, C. B., "Direct Legislation: An Appraisal and a Suggestion," *American Political Science Review, 45* (June, 1951), 400–21.

Latham, Earl, "The Group Basis of Politics: Notes for a Theory," *American Political Science Review, 46* (June, 1952), 376–9.

McLean, Joseph E., "Politics is What You Make It," Public Affairs Pamphlet No. 181, Public Affairs Committee, New York, 1954.

Whitlock, Brand, "The Evil Influence of National Parties and Issues in Municipal Elections," *Proceedings of the National Conference for Good City Government*, New York, 1907.

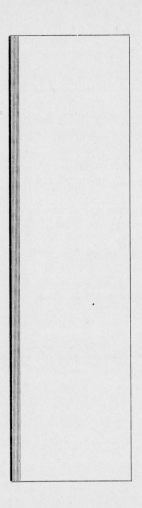

LOCAL GOVERNMENT STRUCTURE

Three

County Government

9

The term "county" is of little value in connoting a standard unit of American local government. The 3,043 counties in the United States are unevenly distributed among 47 states, varying in number from three in Delaware and Hawaii to 254 in Texas.[1] While technically no counties exist in Louisiana, the parishes there differ more in name than in form and function and are treated as counties in the figures given above and in the discussion that follows. Counties were never organized in Rhode Island except as judicial districts, and the eight counties of Connecticut were abolished in 1960 after an existence of over 300 years. Alaska has no counties as such but its proposed boroughs are units somewhat like counties and their basic functions will largely parallel those of the county.[2]

■ Types of American Counties

The variance among counties within a single state is considerably less than the difference between the extremes mentioned above. However, in one section of a state, counties will typically present a

[1] In January, 1963, two Virginia counties were terminated by the merger of Norfolk County and the City of South Norfolk, and of Princess Anne County and the City of Virginia Beach.
[2] Bureau of the Census, *Census of Governments, 1962, Vol. I, Governmental Organization*, Government Printing Office, 1962, pp. 16-17.

rural governmental problem, while in another section, they may be primarily urban in character. As a reflection of such differences, counties have been the object of classification in a number of states. The purpose of classification is to provide greater freedom and variation of treatment than would be possible under uniform legislation, with less state interference and direction than is customary under special legislation. Thus, classification is sometimes described as a compromise between the prohibition of special legislation for an individual county and the enactment of uniform legislation binding on all counties.

Classification by legislative enactment is the most common method of realizing this objective, although the constitutions of some states set up classification devices for local governmental units. The general legality of classification has been tested and upheld in a number of state court systems. The test most commonly applied by the courts is that of "reasonableness" and "fairness" in that the units within each class are to be treated similarly.[3] Classification by population is now generally accepted and followed as best meeting the requirements prescribed by the courts.

Classification by population alone, however, is somewhat inadequate since a number of factors may tend to distort the basic plan. An unusually large rural county may be grouped with counties which are essentially urban if total population is the only base, or a county more densely populated may be so small in area that its total population is low enough to classify it with more rural counties. Although not now used, population density is a more realistic base for differentiating among the several classes of counties. Under this plan, the area of a county becomes an important adjunct of its population since the two are combined for determining average population density. In 1960, the population density of the over 3,000 American counties showed a wide range varying from a high of 77,195 persons per square mile in New York County, New York, to a low of less than one-half person per square mile in 11 counties scattered throughout the United States.[4]

Although the number of classes of counties in any particular state should be determined by the density range of the counties

[3] See, for example, the cases of *Christoph* v. *City of Chilton*, 205 Wisc. 418, 237 N.W. 134 (1931) and *Commonwealth ex rel. Fertig* v. *Patton*, 88 Pa. St. 258 (1878).

[4] These density figures and others to follow are from the Bureau of the Census, *County and City Data Book*, Government Printing Office, 1962.

in that state, a four-fold division or classification of counties is suggested.[5] The classification of *rural* would be reserved for counties with a population density of 100 or fewer persons per square mile. Citizens in such areas receive only a minimum of governmental services and usually are not too vocal in demanding the newer, so-called "urban type" services. The second classification, *semi-rural*, would embrace counties with densities ranging from 101 to 250 persons per square mile. The third classification is *semi-urban*, a grouping to include counties with densities ranging from 251 persons per square mile to a maximum of 1,000 persons. Counties in this group discharge a number of services and functions not provided by their more rural counterparts. The fourth classification, *urban*, is reserved for counties with population densities of 1,001 or more persons per square mile. These counties are truly units of urban government and are called upon to perform all of the urban type services.

Table 3 illustrates the application of this proposed classification plan in selected states. The states were chosen to represent geographic sections of the nation as well as to include states which are primarily urban or rural in character. A meaningful classification

Table 3. *Proposed Classification of Counties in Selected States*

State	Number of Counties	Average Density	NUMBER OF COUNTIES BY CLASSIFICATION			
			Rural	Semi-Rural	Semi-Urban	Urban
New Jersey	21	807	1	6	6	8
Massachusetts	14	655	3	3	4	4
Pennsylvania	67	252	33	13	17	4
California	58	100	43	6	6	3
Florida	67	91	52	8	6	1
Missouri[a]	114	63	107	5	2	2
Mississippi	82	46	78	4	0	0
Kansas	105	27	100	1	2	2
Oregon	36	18	33	2	0	1
Nevada	17	2	17	0	0	0

[a] St. Louis City is separated from St. Louis County and is not shown in this table.

[5] For an expansion of this suggestion, see George S. Blair, "Population Density as a Basis for Classifying Counties," *The County Officer*, 23 (June, 1958), 121, 127.

system, however, is only the first part of a two-phase program for making counties more effective governmental units. The other part relates to a system of optional charters under which citizens of any country can select, by popular vote, one from among several alternative plans of organization. General legislation by class is more beneficial if the substance of the laws can be implemented through a governmental organization selected by the citizens in any particular county. Laws providing optional forms of county government are still the exception rather than the rule, but progress in this area has been realized in recent years. The typical alternatives open to counties in those few states which grant county home rule privileges will be discussed in a subsequent section in this chapter.

Although the classification system based on population density outlined above does not yet exist in any state, the four-fold classification of counties as rural, semi-rural, semi-urban, or urban will be followed for discussion purposes in this chapter. This will avoid a stereotyped approach to counties, their organization, problems and prospects. The four-fold classification system also enables us to differentiate more meaningfully among the three major roles that counties undertake. In its first role as an administrative district of the state, the county performs a number of functions including those of an elections and judicial district. In its second role, as a unit of local government, the county is recognized increasingly as a municipal rather than a quasi-municipal entity and performs both governmental and proprietary functions. In its third role, the county is becoming a coordinating agency for certain programs and functions of the local governments within it in such areas as planning, zoning, centralized purchasing, personnel administration, library services, air pollution control, etc. While the first role is common to all counties, the second and third roles are limited to the more urban counties.

THE RURAL COUNTY

Rural counties in America by and large assume only the first of the three suggested roles of county government—that as an administrative district of the state. As such, there are a number of traditional functions which are performed, but direct services to citizens are quite limited. Typically the county renders such required functions as law enforcement and judicial administration,

LOCAL GOVERNMENT STRUCTURE

elections administration, road construction and maintenance, public welfare, and recording of legal documents. Health is another function normally assigned to counties, but in rural counties this ends up as the part time services of one doctor. While this might meet the legal requirement for filling this county office, it fails to provide even the minimum health services expected of such an office.

Another important function of rural counties is agricultural extension work through the office of the county agent. While the program is financed jointly by national, state, and county governments, actual administration of the program rests with the county agent working in close cooperation with the state agricultural college. In many counties, services to farm wives are provided by a home demonstration agent, and a 4-H Club agent works with the boys and girls in Club activities.

The structure of government in rural counties is usually as simple as the constitution of the state and its statutes permit it to be. Normally none of the optional offices are created, but the required elective offices are filled. The incumbents provide minimum services required by law but these are not full-time positions and the officers usually pursue other means of livelihood. Such counties provide the intimate and personal government of friends and neighbors that is often stoutly defended as a bastion of local democracy in action— or sharply criticized as inadequate and unresponsive.

THE SEMI-RURAL COUNTY

The semi-rural county differs from the rural county in degree rather than in kind. It probably has a few more and slightly larger cities and towns which combine to pull the average density of its population above 100 per square mile. Usually the largest of these towns will be the county seat and its citizens will receive urban-type services from their own city government. As counties approach the upper limit of the suggested density range of this classification (250), their governmental problems change both in kind and size from those in counties at the lower end of the density scale, and citizen demands will begin to mount for expanded county services in such areas as health, welfare, libraries, and law enforcement.

Such counties present really two patterns of living—rural and small town. However, the county will have a uniform pattern of limited services except within the town of the county seat. Here often a bit of rivalry may actually develop between city law enforcement officers and those of the county, between the city health officer and his county counterpart, etc. What county parks exist are usually found in or near the county seat, but these are provided for the use of all its citizens.

Again the pattern of government will be fairly simple and provide few of the optional offices permitted by state law. Normally, the elective offices will be full-time positions and the county courthouse serves as the real center of county government. The county board will continue to perform most of the functions that might be lodged in special-function boards for such purposes as welfare, assessment, elections, etc.

THE SEMI-URBAN COUNTY

The semi-urban county will still have sections which are agricultural in character, but the number and size of its urban centers are greater than are those in the semi-rural counties. A portion of the county's area will be quite urban in character as a number of its cities and towns will probably cluster around each other. Often the clustering of people extends beyond the incorporated limits of the cities and towns into county areas surrounding them. In such unincorporated but urban areas, the citizens will require organized police and fire protection services, garbage and refuse collection, and sewer services. If these are not provided by the county, then special districts will be established, since the citizens need these services and will secure them by one means or another.

In counties of this class, it is increasingly common for the county to establish service districts in which only the citizens who benefit from the special services provided are taxed to support them. Such services include street lighting and paving, garbage and refuse collection, sewers, and recreational facilities. The county will provide expanded and more adequate services in such fields as health, welfare, and libraries for all its citizens. Here the county begins to assume the second and third roles—as a unit of local government providing direct services and as a unit to coordinate certain activities of cities and towns, particularly in the areas of planning, zoning, and subdivision control.

The governmental structure in semi-urban counties becomes more complex. Deputies or assistants are needed for the several row offices, and citizen advisory boards are established to work with the government agencies. In addition, several special-function boards will exist to lighten the work load of the county governing board.

THE URBAN COUNTY

Counties with population densities of 1,001 or more persons per square mile are likely to be truly urban in character and render urban-type services for their citizens in unincorporated areas. Such counties will have at least one large city and will be identified as a metropolitan area or as a constituent part of such an area by the Bureau of the Census. Among the services such counties will probably provide, in addition to those offered by the other classes of counties, are one or more public utilities, public housing, airports, and an expanded program in recreational and cultural activities.

Since the urban county will be discussed at some length in the chapters dealing with metropolitan areas, it will not be further described at this point. Although the number of urban counties across the nation is small, such counties fulfill all three of the important roles of counties identified above and are major units of local government worthy of careful study.

■ *Forms of County Government*

As indicated in Chapter 2, three general patterns of county government developed in the United States to meet the local values and needs of people in different sections of the county. However, with the admission of new states and the rapid population growth, counties began to develop a great organizational variety across the country and sometimes even within a single state because of classification and home rule charters. This variety is particularly apparent in discussing county governing bodies which are known by some 27 different titles in American counties.[6] While we need not agree with Roger Wells that if any principle of county organization can be distinguished, it is the principle of confusion,[7] we must admit that there is considerable diversity among the organizational pat-

---

[6] Edward W. Weidner, *The American County—Patchwork of Boards*, National Municipal League, New York, 1946, p. 1.

[7] Roger H. Wells, *American Local Government*, McGraw-Hill, 1939, p. 80.

terns. At any rate, in a general way, three major forms of county government can be identified.[8]

THE COMMISSIONER FORM

From its beginning in Pennsylvania in 1724, the commission form of county government spread rapidly and it is now the basic pattern in nearly two-thirds of the counties. The distinguishing feature of this form is that the members of the county governing board are elected specifically for this purpose and fulfill both the executive and legislative functions in county government. Governing bodies under this form are usually small in number, with three or five members chosen by district or at large. In some counties where members are elected at large, they stand for election as representatives from one of the districts laid out within the county.

In addition to their legislative and executive functions, county commissioners (called supervisors in some states such as Iowa and California) still exercise judicial powers in some states. This is not the common practice, however, since the county judiciary is usually separate. Normally, the members of the county board will hold no other county office, but as board members they will be called upon to wear a number of different "hats." They may also serve as the elections board, the assessment board, the tax appeals board, the planning board, etc., in addition to their basic roles as members of the county governing board.

An adaptation of the commission form exists in some 350 counties in which the chairman of the board is a judicial officer, usually a judge of probate. The other members of the board, however, are commissioners and function solely in this role. The common size of these boards is again small, with three or five members as a rule.

THE SUPERVISOR FORM

The second most common pattern of county government evolved in New York in 1703, and is known as the supervisor form. The distinguishing feature of this plan is that the composition of its governing body is made up of persons who were first elected as

---

[8] For a fuller discussion of forms of county government, see Bureau of the Census, *County Boards and Commissions,* Government Printing Office, 1947.

LOCAL GOVERNMENT STRUCTURE

township supervisors and who sit on the county board in an *ex officio* capacity. This plan is now used in nearly one-third of the American counties. The size of the governing body in such counties varies widely, depending on the number of townships and cities (which are usually given representation based on population) lying within it. While the more typical size of such boards is about 20 supervisors, 21 counties have boards of over 50 members and the Wayne County (Detroit), Michigan, board has a membership of over 100.

Because of the nature and size of the governing board in these counties, much of its actual work is done through committees. This practice tends to make county government more obscure to its citizens since they will often know few of the committee members by name and even fewer of the members of the whole board. It also makes "buck-passing" easier since there is safety for inaction in large numbers.

An adaptation of the supervisor form exists in most Kentucky and Tennessee counties. In these states, the members of the county board are justices of the peace within the county and the chairman is a county judge, usually the judge of probate. Thus, the members of these county governing boards serve judicial as well as administrative and legislative functions.

COUNTY EXECUTIVE FORMS

Since 1930, when Durham County, North Carolina, adopted a county manager form of government, there has been a slow but continuing trend to correct a major weakness of county government in general—the absence of a single executive officer as a counterpart of the mayor or manager in American cities. Elected county executives have existed in counties since 1893 when Cook County, Illinois, established the position of President of the Board.[9] Plans calling for an elective chief executive officer have been adopted in recent years in several large counties.

The county-manager plan of county government is patterned after the council-manager plan of city government and has the same two essential features. The first is a relatively small elective county board which serves as the policy-making body, and the

[9] Samuel K. Gove, "A County Executive Office," *The County Officer, 19* (September, 1954), 190-3.

second is an appointive manager who is selected by and serves at the pleasure of the county board. Thus, this plan separates the determination of policy from its administration, with the latter the function of the manager within the limits prescribed by the board. The principal functions of the board are to adopt ordinances expressing policy decisions, approve appropriations and tax levies, and to appoint the manager. The manager's major duties, in turn, are to enforce the ordinances established by the board, appoint and supervise his principal subordinates, prepare the budget for board review, and give recommendations to the board on those matters on which his advice is sought.

At the present time, 26 counties in 10 states have adopted the manager form of government, and unsuccessful efforts have been made in several other counties. In population as of 1960, the counties with this form range from a low of 894 in Petroleum County, Montana, to 935,047 in Dade County, Florida. County manager forms also exist in 10 counties in North Carolina, four in Virginia, three in California, two each in Georgia and Maryland, and single counties in Nevada, New York, and Tennessee. While most manager plans are in counties with relatively large populations, its successful operation in Petroleum County, Montana, shows that the plan can work effectively in small counties. The plan has been implemented under a variety of methods. Five plans have been adopted through home-rule charters, four by local approval of special legislative acts for specific counties, 16 under optional statute laws, with local approval in nine counties, and one by special charter passed by state legislature.[10]

County chief administrative officer plans are more common than are county manager plans. The former is similar to the manager plan in that the chief administration officer (hereafter referred to as CAO) is appointed by and is responsible to the county governing board. The major differences pertain to the lesser powers of this officer in budget and personnel matters and his fewer "functional" powers, since other elective officers are more likely to exist than under the manager form. While the manager is expected to "prepare" the annual budget for submission to the board, the CAO "collects" annual departmental requests and "transmits" them with

[10] International City Managers' Association, *Recent Council-Manager Developments and Directory of Council-Manager Cities,* International City Managers' Association, 1963.

LOCAL GOVERNMENT STRUCTURE

recommendations to the board. In personnel matters, the manager's power is broader and he appoints his subordinates while the CAO "makes recommendations" on which the board takes action.

The office of CAO was first created in the City and County of San Francisco in its new charter of 1932. However, since San Francisco is counted as a city rather than as a county for most purposes, the first bonafide CAO's office was created in Los Angeles County in 1938. As of 1963, there were 46 counties with such administrators, including 33 in California, six in New Mexico, two each in Ohio and Virginia, and one each in Georgia, North Carolina, and South Carolina.[11] The plan seems to have worked with a considerable degree of success where it has been adopted, and there have been but few abandonments. It seems to provide a reasonable compromise for counties desiring to achieve a substantial degree of administrative integration but not wishing to adopt the manager plan.

Administrative leadership has been provided in a small number of American counties through the creation of an elective position somewhat similar to the office of mayor in city government. First adopted in Cook County (Chicago), Illinois, in 1893, the office of President of the Board was established to provide a presiding officer and chief executive for the county board. His powers include the power of appointment of a number of non-elective county officers, usually with the advice and consent of the board. He also has the power to exercise a veto or an item veto of appropriation measures which can be overridden only by a four-fifths majority vote by the board. Elected county executives known as county supervisors were created in Hudson and Essex Counties, New Jersey, in 1900, and in St. Louis County, Missouri, in 1950. A similar office, known as the county executive, exists in Nassau and Westchester Counties, New York, and in Baltimore County, Maryland, Jefferson Parish, Louisiana, and Milwaukee County, Wisconsin. The last three offices have been established since 1956, so the interest in this method of providing county administrative leadership seems to be growing. While the specific powers of the elected county executive vary among the counties in which it exists, in general they parallel those of the Cook County office.

A form of quasi-executive leadership exists in a number of counties through the assignment of administrative functions to one

[11] *Ibid.*, p. 42.

of the existing elective officials. A study of Wisconsin counties in 1942 revealed that the county clerk in seven counties "performed all the functions of a full county executive" and clerks in 23 additional counties were "the key general administrators of their counties."[12] Other studies have shown that such roles are assigned to or assumed, for instance, by the county judge in Arkansas; the "ordinary" or commissioner of roads and revenues in Georgia; the probate judge in Tennessee, Alabama, and Kentucky; the chairman of the county board in Wisconsin and North Carolina; the auditor in Indiana; and the chancery clerk in Mississippi. In many of these counties, however, the leadership exercised was in large part dependent on the incumbent of the office and his ability to get along with other county officials. While almost any arrangement to provide executive leadership in county government is a worthwhile one, the informal strengthening of an existing office seems hardly to meet the need adequately.

■ The Structure of County Government

Since the infinite variety among American counties has been pointed out, it may seem a bit unrealistic to describe the structure of a "typical" county government. However, except for the nature of the composition of the governing board under the so-called commissioner and supervisor forms, the remaining structure of government in these counties is strikingly parallel. Since these plans are used in over 97 percent of all American counties, it is reasonable to discuss the structure of county government in general terms.

THE COUNTY BOARD

Except in a few instances in which a single judge or non-judicial officer serves as the central governing agency, county government is organized around a plural member governing body. Although known by a variety of names and consisting of a varied number of members serving differing terms of office, the administrative and legislative functions of county boards are quite uniform. As a quasi-municipal corporation serving primarily as an agent of

[12] L. H. Adolfson, "The County Clerk as Manager," *National Municipal Review, 34* (March, 1945), 125-8.

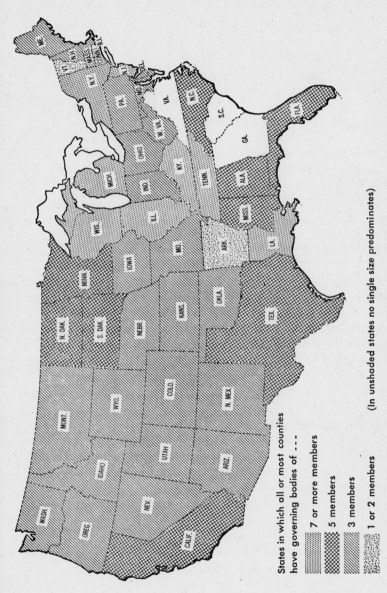

Figure 1. *Size of County Governing Bodies.* (U.S. Bureau of the Census, *County Boards and Commissions,* Washington, 1947, p. 1.)

States in which all or most counties have governing bodies of ---

- 7 or more members
- 5 members
- 3 members
- 1 or 2 members

(In unshaded states no single size predominates)

state government, the primary legislative powers of the county board are fiscal and regulatory. In exercising its fiscal powers, the board levies county taxes, appropriates funds for public purposes, and incurs indebtedness. County regulatory powers embrace such actions as local health ordinances, zoning ordinances, licensing businesses and amusements, regulating the sale of fireworks, etc.

Table 4. *Titles of County Governing Bodies*

Title of Governing Body	Number of Counties
Board of Commissioners	1,271
Board of Supervisors	673
County Court	369
Commissioners Court	254
Fiscal Court	120
Board of Commissioners of Roads and Revenue	118
Police Jury	63
Court Commissioners	37
Commissioners of Roads and Revenue	30
Board of Freeholders	21
Board of Revenue	20
County Commissioners	15
Assistant Judges	14
Ordinary	11
All Others (13 different titles)	34
Total	3,050

SOURCE: Bureau of the Census, *County Boards and Commissions*, Washington, D.C., 1947, p. 2.

Among the administrative powers of county boards are their responsibility for such county activities as the courthouse, jail, poor farm, and other county property; appointment of some officials; negotiation of contracts on behalf of the settlement of claims against the county; administration of elections, etc.[13]

Except in a very small number of counties, members of county governing boards are popularly elected. Within the general framework of popular choice, however, there are five general methods for comprising county boards, as shown in Figure 2. Both election

[13] Since the legislative and executive processes in local government are described more fully in subsequent chapters, these roles of the county board will not be elaborated upon at this point.

of members at large and by district have some advantages. If the board is small and terms are staggered, election at large assures that the members will feel a loyalty to the whole county and gives the voters a greater voice in choosing members of this board. Election by district is defended as assuring that board membership will be spread geographically throughout the county and that local interests will be more adequately represented. In counties with larger boards, the plan combining election of some at large and district election of others has considerable merit.

Terms of county board members also show considerable diversity from state to state. Township supervisors serving on county boards

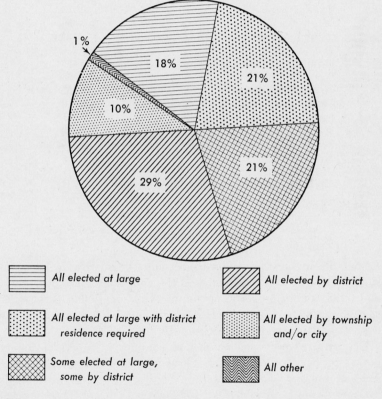

Figure 2. *Percent Distribution of County Governing Bodies by Method of Membership Selection.* (U.S. Bureau of the Census, *County Boards and Commissions,* Washington, 1947, p. 6.)

in Michigan have only one-year terms, while county judges who serve as board chairmen in Tennessee have eight-year terms. Two- and four-year terms are by far the most common, although other boards serve terms of three and six years. In slightly over half the counties, terms of board members are staggered so that the terms of only a part of the membership expire in any election year. Four-year terms are most common, followed by two-year terms, three-year terms, and six-year terms in that order. Most commonly all members have terms of the same length, but this is not true in some 175 counties in which the chairman has a term longer than other members and in another 240 counties in which the terms of some members exceed that of others.

ELECTIVE OFFICERS

Elective county officers in American county government can be divided into two groups—those who are general administrative officers and those who are law enforcement or court officials. In the first group are the offices of treasurer, surveyor or engineer, assessor, superintendent of schools, recorder or register of deeds, and county clerk. In the "judicial group" are the positions of sheriff, attorney or solicitor, court clerk, and coroner. While there are other elective county officers in a number of states, the ten listed above are the only ones found in over half of the states. These ten, then, qualify as fitting into the structure of the "typical" county government. The duties of each of the ten are presented in outline form below.

TREASURER. Where it exists, this office usually has both tax collection and funds custody powers. The treasurer receives all moneys paid to the county and holds them in safekeeping until ordered to pay them out by warrants. In some counties, the office has been abolished or consolidated with another office such as tax collector which performs these functions.

SURVEYOR OR ENGINEER. Although a county office of long standing, the office is of declining importance today and sometimes goes unfilled. Principal duties include location, design and construction of roads and bridges; making land surveys; and determining boundary lines.

ASSESSOR. As the title of the office implies, his principal responsibilities are to locate, identify, and appraise the value of all property—both real and personal—which is subject to county taxation. Since county revenues come largely from the property tax, the importance of impartial and qualified administration of this office is apparent.

SUPERINTENDENT OF SCHOOLS. While the duties of this office vary considerably among the states, in general they include assisting in curricula development, checking the physical condition of schools, preparing reports for the state department of education, and advising local school district boards. Sometimes the superintendent actually manages the affairs of local districts which default on their responsibilities.

RECORDER OR REGISTER OF DEEDS. The duties of this office relate almost exclusively to the recording of documents. Among the items which are recorded are real estate title deeds, mortgages, leases, articles of incorporation, real estate subdivisions, livestock marks and brands, wills, and decrees of bankruptcy.

COUNTY CLERK. This officer is the chief record-keeper for the county governing board and usually serves as the registrar of voters and performs other functions regarding election administration. Such records as births and deaths, marriages and divorces, election returns, etc., are commonly kept by this officer. He often serves as chief financial officer of the county and issues such licenses as those for hunting and fishing, amusement permits, and marriage licenses.

SHERIFF. This is the most common of all county offices and historically the sheriff has served both as a law enforcement officer and as a court official. His major functions include keeping the peace, operating the county jail, regulating traffic, etc. As a court official, he issues writs and subpoenas, conducts foreclosures, and confiscates abandoned property.

ATTORNEY OR SOLICITOR. This officer prosecutes all persons accused of crime, advises the county on legal matters, and represents the county in court cases. Although variously known as the prosecuting attorney, district attorney, state's attorney, or solicitor, the duties of the office are fairly uniform throughout the states.

CLERK OF COURT. As the title implies, this officer is attached to the general trial court of the county to issue the processes of the court and to keep its records. Typically, he records all actions and writs of the court and keeps records of all court proceedings.

CORONER. The principal remaining function of this officer is to make inquests on the bodies of persons who have died by violence or under suspicious circumstances. While the duties of the office would require a knowledge of both law and medicine, incumbents are usually trained in neither and the office has given way to a medical examiner in a number of counties. In many states, the coroner succeeds to the office of the sheriff if the latter is removed or is unable to perform his duties for any reason.

Among the other elective county offices which exist in some, but not a majority of states, are the auditor or controller, county judge, probate judge, register of wills, prothonotary, revenue commissioner,

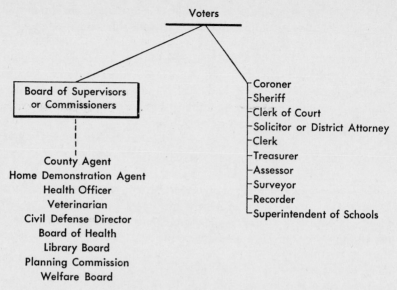

Voters

Board of Supervisors
or Commissioners

County Agent
Home Demonstration Agent
Health Officer
Veterinarian
Civil Defense Director
Board of Health
Library Board
Planning Commission
Welfare Board

Coroner
Sheriff
Clerk of Court
Solicitor or District Attorney
Clerk
Treasurer
Assessor
Surveyor
Recorder
Superintendent of Schools

Figure 3.   *Organization of a Typical County Government.*

welfare commissioner, bailiff, public weigher and public administrator.

APPOINTIVE OFFICIALS

While considerably less standardized among American counties than are the elective offices, there are a few county officials who usually obtain their offices through appointment by the county board. Principal among these are the health director, public welfare commissioner, and road commissioners. County offices which are elective in some states are appointive in others, with each of the ten officers listed above being appointive in one or more American states. Other county officers which are usually appointive, if they exist, are the county veterinarian, inspector of weights and measures, horticultural inspector, public defender, and probation officer.

The county agent and home demonstration agent are also appointed by the county board, but these are not purely local officials since they are also representatives of and approved by the state agricultural extension service. In some states, certain county officers are appointed by the governor of the state, but these again would not qualify as strictly local officials.

In a number of states, it is possible to consolidate one or more county offices. For example, there are 20 possible combinations of county offices for general law counties in California. (California has two classes of counties, charter and general law. Other states might classify these as home rule and non-home rule counties.) As of 1960, every one of the 47 general law counties in that state had at least one combination in operation, and one county had five combinations of offices in its organization.[14]

SPECIAL FUNCTION BOARDS AND COMMISSIONS

A practice has long existed in American county governments to superimpose upon the general structure of government a number of special purpose boards and commissions with prescribed administrative functions.[15] Counties vary widely in their implementation of optional legislation for establishing such boards and commissions. In general, New England counties and small rural counties have the fewest, and heavily populated urban counties have the largest number. While no count of such agencies has ever been undertaken, Snider reasons that the total would run "far into the thousands."[16]

Among the common activities in which such boards and commissions are utilized are welfare, health, libraries, elections, hospitals, property assessment, planning, zoning, personnel, recreation, airports, school finance, penal institutions and agriculture.[17] The picture of this part of county government structure is even further complicated by the presence of two or more boards responsible for different aspects of the same basic function, e.g., two welfare boards—one to supervise such county institutions as the orphanage and poor farm and a second to administer the program of welfare grants for dependent children, old-age assistance, and aid to the blind.

[14] Winston W. Crouch, Dean E. McHenry, et al., California Government and Politics, Prentice-Hall, 2nd ed., 1960, pp. 228-9.
[15] In 1944, the Bureau of the Census reported a total of 761 authorizations in the general laws of the states for the mandatory or optional creation of such bodies for 72 different functions. See Bureau of the Census, op. cit., pp. 9-16, 39-91.
[16] Clyde F. Snider, Local Government in Rural America, Appleton-Century-Crofts, 1957, p. 147.
[17] Edward W. Weidner, "The Confused County Picture," National Municipal Review, 35 (May, 1946), 228-32, 239.

While such boards and commissions are often useful and enable a number of citizens to participate in county government through their service on such agencies, they also tend to fragment even further the already diffused structure of county government. Some boards and commissions are wholly or partially integrated into the general governmental structure, but others—particularly those whose members are not appointed by the county board—enjoy a degree of independence and separateness which makes overall integration of county government an impossibility. Fragmented governments are generally weak governments and this is true of many county governments even in the 1960s.

■ *County Home Rule*

Traditionally, counties have not enjoyed freedom to alter their structures or to run their own affairs. As administrative units of the state, both constitutional and legislative controls specify their structure, powers and functions. The movement toward constitutional county home rule began in California in 1911 by the adoption of a constitutional amendment, and such home rule provisions are now available to some or all the counties of eight other states.[18] In addition, single counties in a few states have been granted home rule charters through constitutional amendments, as in the cases of Dade County, Florida, and Jefferson Parish, Louisiana. While nearly 400 counties in these nine states are entitled to frame and adopt their own charters, only 14 had done so by 1960. Of these 14 charters, 10 were for California counties, two in Maryland, and one each in Missouri and New York. Charters have been drafted in a number of other counties but they failed to secure citizen approval and did not become operative.

While the 14 home rule charters vary considerably in length and content, there are several points of general similarity among them. First, the basic governing board is an elective board with five or seven members. Second, most of the charters provide for a chief executive officer, either to be elected or to be appointed by the board. Third, structure of government has generally been simplified through a reduction of elective offices. And, fourth, administrative

[18] These states are Maryland, 1915; Ohio, 1933; Texas, 1933; Missouri, 1945; Washington, 1948; Minnesota, 1958; New York, 1958; and Oregon, 1958.

procedures have been improved through the installation of budget procedures and the merit system.

However, counties with home rule charters are not completely free to shape their governmental structure because of superior legislative and constitutional requirements. Neither does county home rule appreciably increase the power and functions of counties, since these also are regulated by state provisions. However, it does give the county some discretion that might not otherwise exist so far as its structure and powers are concerned. Home rule may also be a means of working out more satisfactory arrangements for the relative sharing of power with other units of local government. It is probable that the number of counties enjoying this privilege will increase in the years just ahead.

A degree of county self-determination has also been achieved through the enactment of optional charters which counties can adopt. Four such options are now available to counties in New York and Virginia, three in North Dakota, and one alternate form to the traditional pattern exists for counties in Montana, North Carolina, and Oregon. The four basic options in New York are: the county-manager form; the modified manager plan known as the county-director form; the county-administrator form; and the county president form in which the executive is elected.[19] As indicated in Chapter 4, optional charter legislation enables counties to adopt types of governmental organization most to their liking while retaining state legislative control over the counties.

■ Trends in County Government

Nearly a half-century ago a revealing study of American counties was written with the provocative title, *The County, The Dark Continent of American Politics*.[20] The author presented a clear indictment against county government as it then existed by enumerating the basic problems confronting counties in the hope that his study would stimulate further research on this unit of local government. His hope has been realized, at least in part, since the county

[19] Richard A. Atkins, "New County Plans Offered," *National Municipal Review*, *41* (June, 1952), 288-93.
[20] H. S. Gilbertson, *The County, The Dark Continent of American Politics*, National Short Ballot Organization, 1917.

now appears to be increasingly accepted as a legitimate rather than as merely a traditional unit of local government. A few years ago many people were happily predicting its early demise, but county units now appear to be enjoying a revitalization.

Among the several discernible trends affecting county government are the following:

1. The county continues to increase in importance. One reason for this is the use of the county as a base for a number of federal grant-in-aid programs in such areas as agriculture, health, and welfare. A second reason is the expansion of population in suburban counties surrounding our major cities. As suburban communities increase in both size and number, the role of the county in coordinating some services and in providing others is enhanced.

2. The services rendered by counties are increasing in number and importance. The traditional functions are improved through programs of federal and state grants, and new functions are encouraged by such programs. Citizen demands for new and improved services are also falling on more receptive ears at the county level.

3. County reorganization, while advancing slowly to be sure, continues to move ahead. County executives continue to grow in number, and county boards seem increasingly aware of their opportunities and responsibilities.

4. The problem of state-county relations seems to be emerging as a cooperative relationship rather than one primarily of state control and supervision. State legislatures appear more willing to permit flexibility among counties and to enact permissive rather than mandatory legislation in many fields.

5. The role of the county governing body is becoming increasingly important. As the county becomes a more important unit, the new strength is reflected in the powers and functions of the county board. With this expanded role of the board, it will become more obvious that many of the presently elective positions should be appointive, and this power will be gradually transferred to the county board.

6. The cost of county government is increasing to meet the costs of the expanded and added services rendered. As the property taxes increase and additional taxes are levied, citizens become more aware of their county government and may keep a closer watch on its operations.

7. The county is less a stereotype than it was formerly as it becomes increasingly recognized that there are several types of counties. The rural county (which once was the form of all counties) has been joined by its more urban counterparts serving densely populated counties. Cities were never expected to fit into a common mold, but counties for much too long were so treated by state control and supervision. The greater flexibility among counties will enable some to become outstanding units of local government and will erase the popular stereotype of the county as an inefficient unit of government.

But the county continues to face an uphill struggle. The typical rural county has insufficient resources to finance efficiently the modern service programs that its limited population should enjoy in such areas as health, education, and roads. The urban county, although increasingly useful for suburbanites in unincorporated communities, is less emphasized than formerly as the core unit in metropolitan government because such areas tend increasingly to cross county lines. Thus, it is probable that the future role of the county—whether rural or urban—depends in large part on its willingness to join in cooperative programs with neighboring counties. The number of bi-county and multi-county activities is encouraging, and these may point the way to an expanding and more useful role for the American county.

SUGGESTED READINGS

Books

Adrian, Charles R., *State and Local Governments, A Study in the Political Process* (New York: McGraw-Hill, 1960).

Bollens, John C., *Appointed Executive Local Government* (Los Angeles: Haynes Foundation, 1952).

Bureau of the Census, *County Boards and Commissions* (Washington: Government Printing Office, 1947).

Ford, John A., *Thirty Explosive Years in Los Angeles County* (San Marino: The Huntington Library, 1961).

Gilbertson, H. F., *The County, The Dark Continent of American Politics* (New York: National Short Ballot Organization, 1917).

Kammerer, Gladys, *County Home Rule* (Gainesville: Public Administration Clearing House, University of Florida, 1959).

Lancaster, Lane W., *Government in Rural America*, 2nd ed. (Princeton: Van Nostrand, 1952).

Maddox, Russell W., Jr. and Fuquay, Robert F., *State and Local Government* (Princeton: Van Nostrand, 1962).

Martin, Roscoe C., *Grass Roots* (University, Ala.: University of Alabama Press, 1957).

National Municipal League, *Model County Charter* (New York: National Municipal League, 1956).

Snider, Clyde F., *Local Government in Rural America* (New York: Appleton-Century-Crofts, 1957).

Spicer, George W., *Fifteen Years of County Manager Government in Virginia* (Charlottesville: University of Virginia, 1951).

Wager, Paul W. (ed.), *County Government Across the Nation* (Chapel Hill: University of North Carolina Press, 1950).

Weidner, Edward W., *The American County—Patchword of Boards* (New York: National Municipal League, 1946).

Wells, Roger H., *American Local Government* (New York: McGraw-Hill, 1939).

Articles

Adolfson, L. H., "The County Clerk as Manager," *National Municipal Review*, 34 (March, 1945), 125–8.

Annals of the American Academy of Political and Social Science, "County Government," Vol. 47, entire issue (May, 1913).

Atkins, Richard A., "New County Plans Offered," *National Municipal Review*, 41 (June, 1952), 288–93.

Atkinson, R. C., "Principles of a Model County Government," *National Municipal Review*, Supplement to Vol. 22 (September, 1933).

Blair, George S., "A New Look at the 'Dark Continent' of American Politics," *The County Officer*, 19 (September, 1954), 182–4.

Cassella, W. N., "County Government in Transition," *Public Administration Review*, 16 (Summer, 1956), 223–31.

Gove, Samuel K., "A County Executive Office," *The County Officer*, 19 (September, 1954), 190–3.

Overman, Edward S., "New Forms of County Government in Virginia," *The County Officer*, 17 (December, 1952), 357–9.

Pate, James E., "Virginia Counties Turn Cities," *National Municipal Review*, 41 (September, 1952), 387–9.

Snider, Clyde F., "American County Government: A Mid-Century Review," *American Political Science Review*, 46 (March, 1952), 66–80.

Weidner, Edward W., "The Confused County Picture," *National Municipal Review*, 35 (May, 1946), 228–32, 239.

City Government

10

Urbanization is one of the outstanding and continuing social developments in the United States. The first federal census taken in 1790 revealed an urban population of only 5.1 percent, or a ratio of one urbanite to 20 rural dwellers. This ratio was halved and the percentage doubled by 1840 when 10.8 percent of the nation's people lived in urban communities. By 1870, one out of every four persons in the United States lived in cities, and the ratio was one in every three by 1890. Urban dwellers became a majority in 1920 when the federal census revealed that 51.2 percent of the population lived in communities of 2,500 or greater. The ratio is now roughly seven out of ten citizens as urban dwellers, since the 1960 census showed that 69.9 percent of the people in the United States lived in such communities.[1]

That our society is becoming an urban one is an uncontestable fact. However, there is considerable disagreement concerning whether this development is a forward step or one that should be viewed with alarm and distrust. The "case" for cities has been well stated by a number of able writers in a variety of points of view. The following statements present two of the main lines of reasoning

[1] Bureau of the Census, *United States Summary*, PC(1), 1A, Government Printing Office, 1961, Table XX, pp. 1-29.

developed in support of continued urbanization. To Luther Gulick, "The cities that we have today around the world have grown where they are and the way they have to meet human needs. There is nothing quite so functional as an urban center where men have come together, living in congested areas, rearing those great buildings, and establishing the great centers, and the functions that are served by the city are primarily trade, industry, and then, third, a way of life, a place to live, a method of existence. Those are the three chief purposes that cities have served."[2] L. S. Rowe develops the case for cities in these words: "Throughout the history of civilization we can readily trace the close relation between the concentration of population and the development of the arts and sciences. The close association of city life first makes possible division of labor, and with division of labor comes increased productive power. . . . We speak of the country as the best place for meditation and reflection, but constantly lose sight of the fact that it is 'the crowd, the hum, the shock of men' that sharpens the intellect, develops inventive genius, stirs commercial activity, and arouses the spirit of cooperation."[3]

Students of American government and history are familiar with the distrust of cities held by Thomas Jefferson and his oft quoted phrase that cities were "sores on the body politic." However, this same general distrust of cities was apparent in the recent work of Elmer T. Petersen when he wrote, "The city today is not merely an aggregation of men and women with highly specialized functions. In addition, by virtue of modern technology, it represents an engulfing process of standardizing multiplication. . . . Within the city, intensity of conflict, the dangers of pestilence and of economic disaster have been multiplied. Human mutual relationships and valid, well-rounded personal development become more difficult."[4]

However we view the congregation of people in cities, there is no question that urbanism has given rise to social, economic, and political problems which are unprecedented in both number and complexity. Problems which do not exist or are relatively minor in rural communities become of major importance in cities, and many of these needs can be met only by cooperative action rather than by cultural progress of man as reflected in our social, economic and

[2] Luther Gulick, *Our Cities Today and Tomorrow*, The Municipal Forum of New York, February 19, 1947, p. 5.

[3] L. S. Rowe, *Problems of City Government*, D. Appleton & Co., 1908, pp. 2-3.

[4] Elmer T. Petersen (ed.), *Cities Are Abnormal*, University of Oklahoma Press, 1946, pp. vi-vii.

individual effort. Thus, whether cities have contributed most to the political systems, or have risen as a result of this progress, their growth presents new and challenging problems which must be faced.

■ Factors in Urbanization

While a distinction can be made between the conditions which have made urbanization possible and the factors which have caused it, there is an overlapping which can be avoided if growth is discussed in terms of factors promoting it rather than in terms of necessary preconditions and causes.[5] While any listing of such contributing factors is an arbitrary one, at least four major factors can be identified. These are the agricultural surplus resulting from increased efficiency of farm production, the industrial revolution and mass-production techniques, advances in public health and sanitation, and the development of public works engineering.

With the advance and adoption of the methods of scientific farming, the farmer became a quantity producer. As the number of persons who could be sustained by the labors of a single farmer increased, larger numbers of persons were freed from agricultural work and migrated to cities. In 1961, a study released by the Department of Agriculture revealed that the productivity of a single farmer could produce enough to feed himself and 25 other persons.[6] Thus the surplus of farm products are released to feed and clothe urban dwellers, making it possible for ever-growing numbers to reside in such communities.

The application of power and the development of labor-saving machinery removed industry from the home and resulted in the rise of factories. The growth of cities is closely related to the development of power-driven machinery which lead to mass-production techniques. As industries grew in size, city populations reflected this growth as farm migrants and emigrants from other countries came to the city for their livelihood.

[5] For two excellent discussions of this general topic, see National Resources Committee, *Our Cities: Their Role in the National Economy,* Government Printing Office, 1937, esp. pp. 29-41; and Lewis Mumford, *The City in History,* Harcourt, Brace and World, 1961.

[6] Department of Agriculture, "The Food We Eat," pamphlet, Government Printing Office, 1961.

Before the advent of modern sanitation and enhanced knowledge of germs and their control, it was impossible for cities to approach the size they have now attained. The problems of supplying pure water, removing human wastes, and controlling epidemics were so enormous that few cities achieved populations greater than 100,000. With the beginning of public health programs to control diseases, improve community sanitation and environment, and to insure a safe food and water supply, city populations grew and conditions of urban living greatly improved. Also as a result of expanding health knowledge, a natural increase in population bolstered urban populations as a result of the excess of births over deaths and longer life expectancy.

Closely related to the improvements in health and sanitation and to the industrial revolution was the gradual growth of technology in the field of municipal public works engineering. The term is used broadly here to include the whole range of public works programs, including water, other utilities, sewers, streets and bridges, etc., and the development of systems of transportation and communication. As these facilities and systems were developed, conveniences and comforts of urban living were greatly enhanced, while recreational and cultural activities also provided additional lures for city dwelling.

■ *Number and Size of Cities*

While the term municipality is in general usage to connote an incorporated community in an American state, it is almost impossible to ascribe any precise physical characteristics to the 17,997 municipalities existing in the United States in 1962. In size of population, the range varies from seven and three-fourths million in New York to zero population in a small number of places which had not completed prescribed procedures necessary for dissolution. In number of cities within the states, the range is from one in Hawaii, eight in Rhode Island and 13 in New Hampshire to 944 in Iowa, 1,003 in Pennsylvania, and 1,251 in Illinois. The average number of cities per state in 1962 was 360, but this number was exceeded in 20 states while 14 states had fewer than 100.

In terms of area, Los Angeles is the biggest American city, extending over an area of 454.8 square miles compared to areas of 315 and 224 square miles respectively for New York and Chicago,

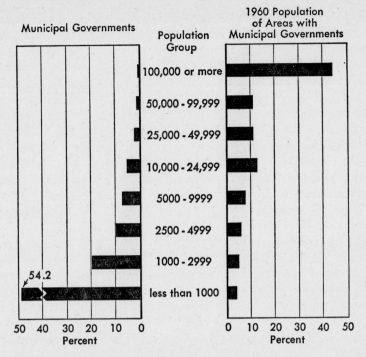

Figure 4. *Municipal Governments and Their Populations, by Population Size: 1962.* (U.S. Bureau of the Census, *Census of Governments, 1962,* Vol. I: *Governmental Organization,* Washington, 1962, p. 19.)

both of which precede Los Angeles in population. Philadelphia is the smallest of the five major cities in the United States with a land area of 127.2 square miles. Among cities with populations between 500,000 and 1,000,000, the land area varies from a high of 328.1 square miles in Houston to a compact 39.4 square miles in Buffalo. For cities in the 100,000 to 500,000 population category, the size ranges from 321.5 square miles in Oklahoma City to only 6.3 square miles in Cambridge, Massachusetts. At the other end of the population scale, Old Town, Maine, has the largest area of cities in the 5,000 to 10,000 size grouping with 44.2 square miles while Buttenberg, New Jersey, embraces only 0.2 square miles.[7]

[7] From the table entitled, "Governmental Data for All Cities Over 5,000: 1961," in International City Managers' Association, *Municipal Year Book, 1961,* Chicago, 1961, pp. 84–140.

Because of the great diversity in the problems of cities, legisla· tures in nearly half the states have established classification systems. While these systems are usually meaningful within a single state, when they are viewed comparatively they show quite a diversity. In Arkansas and Wyoming, the population requirement for first class cities is 4,000, while in Pennsylvania, first class cities must have 1,000,000 or more. The first, second, and second class A classifications in Pennsylvania are established so that only one city falls into each of these three groupings. This is not the usual pattern, however, and the population-based classification systems are used to group cities of fairly comparable size in most states for legislative purposes. The Pennsylvania pattern, in fact, resembles in part a classification system once used in Ohio in which eight of the 11 classes each contained only one city. The Ohio Supreme Court declared this system unconstitutional in 1902 and Ohio remains one of the states in which classification is generally invalid. Generally speaking, classification is more prevalent for cities than it is for counties.

◼ Process of Incorporation

While the creation of a new city should be a serious civic business, it is relatively easy for an area to be incorporated as a city. Several legal requirements must be met but these are not major obstacles if there is sufficient interest and support in the community. Although the specific steps to be followed differ among the states, the procedures outlined for incorporation in the *Government Code* of California are fairly typical of those in other states. In California, incorporation proceedings can be initiated in any unincorporated community containing at least 500 inhabitants or 500 registered voters in counties with a population of two million or more.[8] The essential procedural steps in incorporating are as follows:

1. A notice of intention to circulate a petition for incorporation must be filed with the county board of supervisors. The notice must specify the boundaries of the proposed city and must be signed by at least 25 voters in the area seeking incorporation.

2. This notice of intent must also be filed with the governing board of all cities with territorial limits lying within three miles of any of the territory in the proposed incorporation.

[8] California Government Code, *Government of Cities*, State Printing Office, Sacramento, 1955, plus supplements.

3. Within 90 days after the filing of the notice of intent, a petition must be filed with the county board asking that an election be called on the issue of incorporation. This petition must contain the signatures of at least 25 percent of the voters in the area and this number must also include the owners of at least 25 percent of the total value of the land lying within the proposed city.

4. The county board examines the petition to determine its validity in terms of number of signatures, their qualification as voters and property owners, and the reasonableness of the proposed boundaries.

5. A map showing the area of the proposed city must be submitted to the county boundaries commission which has 30 days to examine the proposal and to prepare its recommendation concerning it.

6. The county board must hold a hearing on the proposal at least two weeks after publication of the date of the proposed hearing in a newspaper serving the area. Following the hearing, which might be somewhat extended in time, the board may alter the proposed boundaries of the city by decreasing its size, but the board cannot increase the area by changing the proposed boundaries. At this point, the proceedings can be nullified if written protests are prepared by owners of 51 percent of the property lying within the area.

7. The county board sets the date of the election by giving at least two weeks' notice of the date in advance. At this election, the voters in the area are asked to vote for or against the incorporation and to select officers from among the nominees seeking the prescribed elective offices.

8. After the election and canvassing of returns, the county board must declare the results. If the proposal received a majority of the votes cast at the special election, the board declares the establishment of the new city. If the proposal is defeated by the voters, no further move for incorporation of the community can be initiated for a period of two years.

While the requirements for incorporation are simple and fairly easy to meet in most cases, the process sometimes becomes a heated affair with violent argument and debate within the particular community. This has been especially true of some of the recent incorporation proposals, particularly in Los Angeles County in which the number of cities has increased from 45 in 1953 to 74 by the end of 1962.

Across the country as a whole, there were 1,190 more municipalities in 1962 than there were in 1952 because of new incorporations. This trend will probably continue in the years ahead, particularly in areas surrounding the core cities in large metropolitan areas. In many instances, such communities incorporate as a defensive move to prevent being annexed to an existing governmental unit. In other cases, incorporation is undertaken to secure the power of local zoning to preserve existing land-use patterns or to prevent proposed changes. Such city names as Industry and Dairy Valley within Los Angeles County reflect the basic purposes for their incorporation. A third reason for incorporation may be basically financial—either to qualify for aid in the form of state-collected but locally-shared taxes or to take advantage of the fortuitous location of a particular industry, large manufacturing concern, or major shopping center. A fourth motivation may be a felt need for basic governmental services combined with a desire to control them locally. Since police, fire, and other services can normally be obtained only by annexation to an existing municipality or by establishing a new one, the concern for local control—particularly of the police function—may encourage a community of citizens to seek incorporation.

As large counties perform more urban-type services and sell such services to cities lying within them, a further inducement for incorporation arises. The sale of services by the county enables "a city to be born without the normal pains and labor attendent upon birth. Founding a city becomes largely a paper transaction, rather artificial or synthetic in nature."[9] This latter inducement has apparently encouraged a number of communities to change from an unincorporated status in California counties since they can begin receiving county services for their citizens immediately upon establishment as a city. This plan, now commonly referred to as the "Lakewood Plan," will be examined more thoroughly in our discussion of metropolitan areas.

■ Forms of City Government

Probably the best known "fact" about forms of city government is the fact that Alexander Pope, the famous British poet, once wrote a couplet in which he stated:

9 Henry A. Turner and John A. Vieg, *The Government and Politics of California*, McGraw-Hill, 1960, p. 208.

> For forms of government let fools contest;
> Whate'er is best administered is best.

But there are few who would currently agree with Pope unless there were added such qualifications as self-government and a democratic environment. However, it must be readily admitted that there is a close and direct relationship between form of government and its performance. While form determines what can be done and prescribes how it can be done, the persons who fill the offices are the force behind the form and set and guide its operations. Thus, a form which permits an officeholder to do his job well should result in better government than a form which unduly binds the officeholder and restricts his actions. If this is so, then form does become important; but this should not lead us to conclude that there is one best form which should be universally adopted.

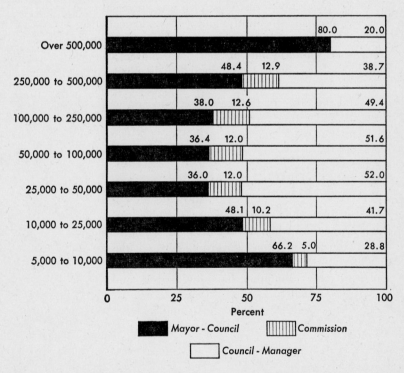

Figure 5. *Forms of Government in Cities over 5,000 Population.* (International City Managers' Association, *The Municipal Year Book, 1963,* Chicago, 1963, p. 160.)

There are three basic forms of city government in American cities. These are commonly identified as the mayor-council, commission, and council-manager plans. While each of these has its identifying characteristics, the varieties in the application of the basic plans are numerous. The number of cities with each form is shown in Figure 5, but it is possible that no two cities have exactly the same governmental structure because of local variations or state required deviations from the theoretical ideal or model.

MAYOR-COUNCIL FORM

The mayor-council form of government is the oldest and most common type in operation in American cities. While Figure 5 is limited to cities of over 5,000, a large majority of cities under this size also employ this form. This form was universal until the beginning of the twentieth century, and it was a logical outgrowth of the "council government" pattern in our early cities. Under council government, as the term implies, most local powers were vested in the plural-member council. In the course of the nineteenth century, the power and prestige of the council declined for a number of reasons, and the office of the mayor evolved and gradually gained in strength. Today there are three major variations of the mayor-council form—the weak mayor-council plan, the strong mayor-council plan, and the strong mayor-council plan with a chief administrative officer.

The Weak Mayor-Council Plan. The weak mayor-council plan still reflects the spirit of Jacksonian democracy and is a product of local government in colonial days. It evolved in the colonies from English practices when the functions of city governments were few and citizen fear of strong government was widespread. The structural form of this pattern still reflects the ideology that officeholders should be many in number, have few powers, and that there should be checks upon their exercise of these powers.

There are a number of distinguishing features or characteristics of this plan. First, the council has and exercises both legislative and executive powers. In addition to its policy-determining function, the council possesses the power to appoint certain administrative officers and to supervise some areas of administrative activity. Second, the council is usually a fairly large body ranging from five in small cities to over 50 in large cities, and its members are elected by

LOCAL GOVERNMENT STRUCTURE

wards. Third, the mayor is an elective office with quite limited controls over administration. Normally, the office has a limited veto power and a restricted appointive power, but the real weakness of the office lies in its lack of authority in administrative affairs. Fourth, this is so because there are several other popularly elected administrative officers, often including the city treasurer, attorney, clerk, and assessor. In addition, members of important administrative boards are also elected. Fifth, the ballot used is usually partisan in character and long in form. Sixth, the several departments and boards are quite independent of each other and there is no real coordination of their efforts possible since no single office is entrusted with this responsibility.

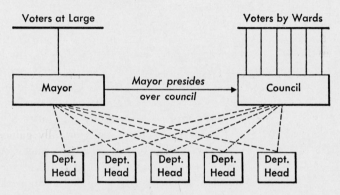

Figure 6. *Weak Mayor–Council Form.* (By permission of the National Municipal League, New York.)

These characteristics are rather vividly illustrated in the above figure diagramming the weak mayor-council form of government. The voters are shown in ward organization choosing the members of the council and choosing the mayor and four other citywide elective offices. The divided appointive power shared by the council, mayor, and other officials is shown by the lines leading from their respective blocks on the chart. This figure also reveals the bases for the several major criticisms of the weak mayor-council plan. First is the lack of administrative control in the office of the mayor. He is unable to coordinate the activities of the several departments or agencies and often does not even have a voice in selecting the persons who head these agencies. A second criticism, really a by-product of the first, results when the leadership is provided by a person or persons outside the government and beyond the popular control of the people. Thus, this form lends itself to political manipulation or boss control more readily than do better integrated forms of city government. Thirdly, the long ballot places an unnecessary burden on the voter and tends to confuse rather than enhance voter control.[10]

A recent study of Chicago's government in action found much to praise about the operation of the weak mayor-council form of government in that city.[11] Meyerson and Banfield found that political power was "highly decentralized formally but highly centralized informally." As the system worked, power over some matters was located in the city administration while power over others was left in the hands of neighborhood and ward leaders. The weakness of the city government was offset by the strength of the leading party which possessed sufficient power to run the city and passed out enough favors, protection, and patronage to keep itself in power. As the machine functioned in Chicago, the authors believe the mass of the people were given the kind of government they wanted—or objected to least—while traditional democratic values and institutions (the city government in particular) were insulated from misuse by unscrupulous demagogues. While such a happy wedding of a weak government and a strong majority party may exist in Chicago for the citizens benefit, it seems a dubious arrangement to encourage in other cities; it may succeed more in spite of the combination of government and party rather than because of it.

The Strong Mayor-Council Form. Just as there was a discernible trend to strengthen the powers of the chief executive at the state and federal levels near the end of the nineteenth century, a similar development occurred at the municipal level. The new plan was a logical development in city government and its similarity to the pattern at the federal level was stressed by its supporters. The weak mayor plan with its fragmented administrative structure seemed a replica in miniature of the pattern of state government, while the integrated administrative structure provided by a strong mayor more nearly paralleled the operation of our federal government. The growth of powers for the mayor was a gradual development as

---

[10] For two examples of the actual operation of the weak mayor-council plan, see Arthur Bromage, *Councilmen at Work*, George Wahr Publishing Co., 1954, pp. 72-80; and William N. Kinnard, Jr., *Appointed by the Mayor*, ICP Case Series No. 36, University of Alabama Press, December, 1956.

[11] Martin Meyerson and Edward C. Banfield, *Politics, Planning and the Public Interest*, The Free Press, 1950, esp. pp. 285-302.

the need for strong and active municipal administrative leadership became increasingly recognized, particularly in the larger cities.

The principal characteristics of this form of government show the increased role of the mayor. First, virtually complete control for administrative responsibility is concentrated in the office of an elective mayor. The mayor has the power to appoint and remove most department heads, is responsible for the preparation of the budget for consideration by the council, and is entrusted with a veto power over council actions which can be overridden only by an extraordinary majority in the council. Second, the mayor shares in the policy-making function of the council, although the ultimate responsibility for policy determination lies with the council. Third, the legal position of the mayor is such that he exercises strong political leadership, both within the city administration and within the community. Fourth, the council is usually a small body of seven or nine members who may be elected either at large or by wards and by a partisan or non-partisan ballot. Fifth, terms of both the mayor and councilmen are longer than in the weak mayor form and typically are four years in duration.

The advantages of the strong mayor-council form in relation to the weak mayor form are illustrated in Figure 7 which depicts its

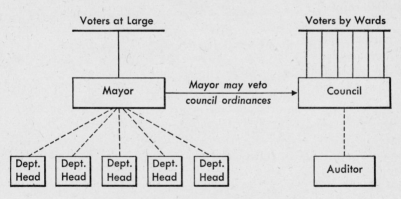

Figure 7. *Strong Mayor–Council Form.*

structure. Most apparent is the clear location of administrative authority and responsibility in the office of the mayor. The other elective offices are apt to be ministerial rather than policy-making and consist of such positions as treasurer, clerk, and controller. Second, the limited number of elective offices makes the short ballot a reality in most cities using this form. Third, the office of the mayor is the center for political as well as administrative leadership in the community.

The problems or disadvantages inherent in this form are also revealed in the diagram. The first is the possibility for friction between the mayor and the council, since they share in the policy-making function. Strong councilmen may resist the mayor's leadership and attempt to restrict his role in policy matters. The eras of such friction between a president and congress at the federal level are well known and fights between mayors and councilmen are certainly more frequent and hardly less intense in cities across the nation. A second major problem arises because of the dual nature of the mayor's office—he is both the political and administrative leader of the community. This combination of leadership qualities is not easy to find, since a mayor with strong political leadership may not be an expert administrator and a mayor who is an able administrator may be a rank amateur at playing politics with political leaders. Because so much is expected of the mayor, it is often difficult to get persons with the dual qualifications to seek this elective office. It is even more difficult to emphasize both sides of the office so that the voters can judge candidates for their abilities in both areas rather than support a popular political figure. A third problem arises if the council is able to compete effectively with the mayor, resulting in a virtual deadlock between the two branches in their efforts to check one another. In such cases, the necessary political leadership may be provided by a person outside the government in the form of a boss who is beyond citizen control and has no responsibility to the citizenry.

While the strong mayor-council form of city government does possess a number of problems or potential weaknesses, it is superior to the weak mayor form. It has provided good results in a number of cities and remains the pattern in a large number of cities, including both large metropolitan centers and smaller communities across the nation.[12]

Strong Mayor-Council with Chief Administrative Officer. To offset the weakness resulting from combining political and administrative leadership in the office of the mayor, a number of large cities in recent years have established the office of chief administrative officer (CAO) to assist the mayor in his administrative duties. This

12 Richard S. Childs, *Civic Victories,* Harper, 1952, p. 131.

plan has now become common enough in practice and described sufficiently in literature to be considered a third form of mayor-council government.[13] The concept of the CAO's office as an integral part of the mayor-council form of government had its origins in San Francisco in 1931. A charter revision movement there established the office of CAO to work with the mayor as a compromise arrangement between the supporters of the existing mayor-council form and the advocates of changing to the council-manager form. While the San Francisco plan did not receive wide notice nor early transplantation to other cities, it has served as a guide for other cities in recent years.

One of the points of least conformity among cities adopting this form of government is the title of the office to assist the mayor. Instead of chief administrative office, the office is known as city consultant-administrator in Louisville (1948), managing director in Philadelphia (1951), director of administrative services in Boston (1953), business administrator in Newark (1953), and city administrator in New York (1954). Los Angeles in 1951 and New Orleans in 1953 created the position of chief administrative officer and a similar office has been created in a number of smaller cities. In some cities, this officer is appointed by the mayor and serves at his pleasure. In others, his appointment and removal must be approved by the council, while councils in other cities must approve removal but have no voice in his appointment.

While the actual powers of the office vary slightly from city to city, the general powers of CAO's can be grouped into three major categories. First, such officers have the power to appoint and remove heads of certain departments and agencies. Normally, this power will be exercised with the approval of the mayor but the power is specifically placed in the office of the CAO. Second, CAO's have the power to supervise the operations of the departments and agencies under their office. Usually, these include only those for which he has appointive power but in some cities his office gives

[13] See John C. Bollens, *Appointed Executive Local Government: The California Experience*, Haynes Foundation, 1952; Gladys Kammerer and Ruth McQuown, *The City Consultant: Plan or Expedient?*, Bureau of Government Research, University of Kentucky, 1958; Wallace S. Sayre, "The General Manager Idea for Large Cities," *Public Administration Review, 14* (Autumn, 1954) 253-8; John M. Selig, "The San Francisco Story," *National Municipal Review, 46* (June, 1957), 290-5; and Charles R. Adrian, "Recent Concepts in Large City Administration," paper (mimeo) presented at annual meeting of American Political Science Association, Washington, D.C., 1956.

"general oversight" to other city agencies. Third, the office has the power to provide general advice and assistance to the mayor in many and varied matters, in preparing reports, and in recommending courses of action.[14]

The basic purpose of the CAO adaptation of the strong mayor-council plan is to free the mayor from administrative duties so he can provide political and policy leadership and give the city effective administrative leadership through the employment of a professionally competent administrator. Support for this purpose is largely responsible for the successful development of the CAO plan. According to Sayre, the plan is desirable because (1) it is a feasible and acceptable pattern of government for large cities which find the council-manager form unattractive; (2) it preserves the office of the mayor as the center of public leadership and government responsibility; and (3) it fits more comfortably into the traditions of the American political system by implementing the strong executive with administrative competence.[15]

While the strong mayor-council with CAO plan appears quite acceptable in large cities and seems to be operating well in both large and small cities in which it has been adopted, it is not without possible operating defects. An obvious source of potential conflict lies in the relations between the CAO and the mayor. An uncooperative mayor or an uncompromising CAO could find numerous occasions for disagreement. A second problem is the continued possibility of a deadlock between the mayor and the council in policy matters or in the exercise of policy leadership. While it is probable that both of these problems have arisen in each of the cities with this form, the plan of government has survived, indicating its adaptability to meet such problems when they do emerge.

THE COMMISSION FORM

The pattern of municipal government known as the commission form is an American invention of the twentieth century resulting more from a historical accident than as a planned reform. The plan was first adopted in Galveston, Texas, in 1901 following in the wake

[14] Sayre, op. cit., pp. 256-7.

[15] Ibid., pp. 257-8. For two rejoinders to the Sayre thesis, see John E. Bebout, "Management for Large Cities," Public Administration Review, 15 (Summer, 1955), 188-95; and William A. Sommers, "Council Manager Government: A Review," Western Political Quarterly, 11 (March, 1958), 144-7.

of a devastating hurricane the previous year which virtually destroyed the city and took some 6,000 lives.[16] During the period of rebuilding, the state legislature suspended the weak mayor-council local government and substituted a commission consisting of five local businessmen. Because the five Galveston commissioners were able men and attacked their job with great zeal, the plan was widely heralded as bringing the principles of business into the governing of cities and the form was retained there following its successful beginning and initial operation.

As the plan developed in Galveston, the five commissioners were elective officers with four becoming heads of city operating departments and the fifth serving as mayor-president of the city with general supervisory powers. While the mayor had no veto power, he had the full powers of a councilman and served somewhat as "first among equals." The plan was an immediate success in Galveston in spite of combining legislative and executive powers and it attracted wide attention as a "businessman's government." By 1910 the plan had been adopted in 108 cities, and the number rose to some 500 by 1917. The plan was looked upon so favorably in some states that it was made mandatory for certain classes of cities. For example, this was true for third class cities in Pennsylvania until the passage of an optional charter law there in 1957. Since World War I, however, there have been few new adoptions, and the number of abandonments of the plan have been many.

The main characteristic of the commission form of government is the complete lack of separation of powers, with the commission members performing both legislative and executive functions. While this pattern has sometimes been compared to parliamentary government because of this feature, the similarity between the two forms is difficult to accept for two major reasons. In the first place, the cabinet or executive branch in parliamentary government is composed of only a small portion of the members of the legislative body, so a large degree of separation of powers still exists. In the commission form, all members are participants in both the legislative and executive functions with no separation of powers at all. Secondly, parliamentary government depends upon party machinery to provide majorities and discipline, while commission members are usually selected through a non-partisan election. A second characteristic of the commission form is the small size of the board. Five is

[16] Childs, *op. cit.*, pp. 319–21.

the most common number of commissioners and normally they are selected at large for staggered terms of four years. Thirdly, administrative powers are normally exercised jointly with the power of appointment and removal as a common prerogative of the commission rather than of any individual member. Fourth, the commission plan incorporated the principle of the short ballot movement by having no elective offices other than commission members. These features of the plan are highlighted in Figure 8 depicting the structure of government in commission-governed cities. A fifth feature of the plan was the general provision for citizen use of the direct democratic devices of initiative, referendum, and recall. It was considered essential to place these tools in the hands of the citizenry since governmental powers were concentrated solely in the commission itself.

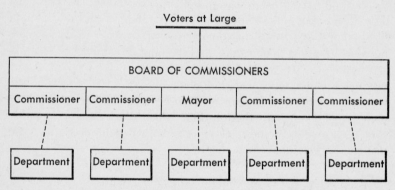

Figure 8. *Commission Form.* (By permission of the National Municipal League, New York.)

The advantages claimed for the commission form largely reflected its structure which is simple and easily understood by citizens. Second, full responsibility was concentrated in the commission so that "buck-passing" would be eliminated. Third, the plan resembled the organization of business corporations and would result in good, honest and efficient government. Fourth, the standard of officeholders would be raised since leading citizens would be willing to serve as commission members. And fifth, citizen control of government would be strengthened because of the short ballot and the provisions of direct democracy devices. In general, many of these advantages were realized in cities immediately following the adoption of the commission plan but it soon became apparent that these results accrued more from the spirit of citizen interest in reform and in government than from the plan itself. And when citizen interest waned, disadvantages of the plan were readily recognized.

What was heralded as its major strength soon became the outstanding weakness of the commission plan. In providing no organizational distinction between the policy-making and the executive function, diversity rather than unity became the operating pattern. Instead of exercising joint control over each of the major departments, criticism or oversight became a lost art as a mutual "hands-off" policy, for departmental operations became the common practice. A second difficulty arose because of the dual qualifications of legislator and administrator which each commissioner was expected to possess. Since these qualifications are not necessarily complementary, the expertise expected did not materialize. The failure to provide executive leadership for the city was a third weakness. While one of the commission members was a mayor-commissioner, he did not have powers over the other members and could not provide common leadership. The election of competent business and professional persons to the commission also failed too often to materialize. Since the combined position of lawmaker and law-enforcer required a considerable expenditure of time, the most frequent and willing candidates were amateurs rather than persons with proven administrative competence. Lastly, citizen control became somewhat thwarted since responsibility could be pinned only upon the commission as a whole rather than upon individual commission members.

In its operation, the commission form of government in its actions paralleled somewhat the actions of a motorcar with an accelerator but no brake.[17] Like the brakeless car which gains in speed, the costs of government are likely to accelerate when the persons who spend funds are identical with those who raise the monies. The ambitious commissioner is apt to be something of an "empire builder" in his arena of city affairs and such a tendency is highly contagious among fellow commissioners. The end result sometimes proved to be a "pork barrel" operation at the citizen's expense and sometimes without his full approval.

While the number of commission-governed cities continues to de-

17 This analogy is taken from Institute of Public Affairs, *Forms of City Government,* 4th ed., University of Texas, 1956, p. 19.

cline, this pattern of government still exists in nearly nine percent of American cities with populations of 5,000 or more and in 16 cities of over 100,000 population. Continuing abandonments of the plan are expected to occur, and the commission form has few current advocates. In discussing this form of city government, one writer has stated, "Outmoded structures of government live beyond the time when they are needed, as do all human institutions which suffer the rigidity of being organized on a formal basis. There is no future for the commission structure of government. Those commission cities that remain do so as a result of apathy or because officeholders have a vested interest in the *status quo*."[18]

THE COUNCIL-MANAGER FORM

In the first two decades of the twentieth century, a new form of government—the council-manager form—developed in American cities. While the origin of the council-manager concept is not known for certain, one of its earliest advocates was Haven A. Mason, editor of the magazine *California Municipalities*. In an editorial appearing in the August, 1899, issue, Mason advocated a "distinct profession of municipal managers."[19] Such persons should have some knowledge in such diverse fields as engineering, street construction, sewers, building construction, water, lighting systems, personnel, accounting, municipal law, police and fire services, and library management. Origins of the form are also claimed as an adaptation of the organization of a business corporation to the governing of a city. In this analogy, the voters represent the stockholders, the council serves as the board of directors of the company, and the manager has the role of the general manager. The council-manager form has also been described as an adaptation of school district government to the municipal arena. Here a parallel is drawn between the council and the popularly elected school board, and between the manager and the appointed and professionally trained superintendent of schools.

The practical application of the council-manager form occurred first in Staunton, Virginia, in 1908. In an effort to achieve some administrative supervision and integration in a town with a weak mayor and bicameral council form of government, the Staunton

---

[18] Charles R. Adrian, *Governing Urban America*, 2nd ed., McGraw-Hill, p. 218.
[19] This editorial is reprinted in Bollens, *op. cit.*, Appendix III.

LOCAL GOVERNMENT STRUCTURE

council passed an ordinance creating the position of "general manager." He was to be a full-time employee with substantial control over administration. Although this office lacked control over such departments as police and fire and did not have the full power to hire and dismiss subordinates, it was a clear first step in the development of the council-manager form. In a charter proposed for the city of Lockport, New York, in 1911, the concept of a manager for the city was more clearly developed. Although this specific charter was denied, it served as a model for a charter which was adopted by Sumter, South Carolina, the following year.[20]

Several small towns adopted the council-manager form in 1913, and it achieved national acclaim in 1914 upon its adoption in Dayton, Ohio, a city of over 100,000. Since that time, it has grown rapidly in terms of number of adoptions. In 1921, the plan was in use in 162 cities; by 1941, the number had increased to 548. As of January, 1961, there were 1,796 council-manager plans in operation in the United States.

The fundamental feature of the council-manager form of government is its unification of powers in an elective council, combined with the separation of legislative and executive functions through the employment of a manager to serve as the city's chief administrator. The council is a small board of from five to nine members, commonly elected at large on a non-partisan basis, for staggered terms of four years. The council is responsible for all legislative and policy-making functions and ultimately for the character of administration provided by the manager. The council employs a professionally trained city manager, who is subject to dismissal by the council at any time. The manager has the power to appoint and remove his subordinates subject to civil service rules and regulations and to prepare the budget for consideration by the council.

The essential characteristics of the council-manager form may be stated briefly to be as follows: (1) a small council elected at large on a non-partisan basis; (2) the unification of all legislative and policy-making functions in the hands of the council; (3) the employment of a competent administrator to serve as city manager; (4) the location of administrative responsibility in the office of the manager; (5) the application of the short ballot since only the council members are elected by the voters; (6) the absence of a formal

[20] Harold A. Stone, Don K. Price and Kathryn H. Stone, *City Manager Government in the United States*, Public Administration Service, 1940, p. 12.

separation of powers and a system of checks and balances. Most of these features are evident from the governmental structure of the council-manager form illustrated in Figure 9.

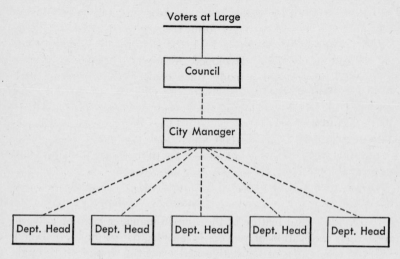

Figure 9. *Council–Manager Form.* (By permission of the National Municipal League, New York.)

The structural pattern of organization also shows that many of the weaknesses of the commission form of government are eliminated by the council-manager form. The fragmented administrative responsibility of the commission form is replaced by integrated responsibility in the office of the manager. Similarly, the combination of legislative and administrative powers in the commission is replaced by a system in which the legislative function is in the hands of the council and the administrative function is concentrated in the hands of the manager. These are two of the strongest advantages claimed for the plan. Other advantages claimed by its supporters include: (1) the simplicity of its structure makes it comprehensible to the citizen and facilitates his control over his elected representatives; (2) the presence of competent administrative leadership is assured through the appointment of a professionally trained manager; (3) the separation of politics and administration is achieved through the division of these functions between the council and the manager; and (4) the manager is a full-time employee who gives constant attention to the problems and needs of the city and its citizens.

Other extravagant claims have been made by the ardent advocates of the form, including reduced costs, better executives, elimination of the spoils system, removal of all politics from administration, more public spirited leadership, and enhanced prestige of the council. While such benefits are to be hoped for in any city, they can hardly be credited to the operation of any pattern of government. In a similar vein, a number of irrelevant disadvantages have been credited to the form by its opponents. It is sometimes described as being undemocratic because the manager is not elected by the people. Other charges levied against the plan are that it "results in one-man rule," it is "socialistic" in character, it results in "carpetbagger" rule, it is "anti-labor" in philosophy, and that it is government "for" but not "by and of" the people.

However, there are realistic criticisms which can be directed at the plan. It is often difficult to make a distinction between the policy-making and administrative functions. Yet the theory of the plan sets up this separation in very simple terms. The unrealistic nature of this oversimplification has been recognized by the International City Managers' Association and by students of government, but it has not yet been grasped by many citizens and, indeed, by some council members in council-manager cities.[21] A second potential weakness of the plan lies in its provision for a council of equals. Although one of the council members serves as mayor, he has no stronger powers than do other members in the functioning of the council. Thus, there is no plan for encouraging leadership in the council. As a result, the council may rely too heavily on the leadership of the manager or react unfavorably to his leadership. A third potential weakness of the plan is its stress on non-partisanship in regard to decisions of public policy. The plan seems to function best in communities which are not too heterogeneous in character and in which there is a fairly high degree of community consensus.

[21] See, for example, the three editions of the Manager's Code of Ethics prepared by the International City Managers' Association in 1924, 1938, and 1952. Also see Charles R. Adrian, "Leadership and Decision-Making in Manager Cities: A Study of Three Communities," *Public Administration Review*, 18 (Summer, 1958), 208–13; Karl A. Bosworth, "The Manager is a Politician," *ibid.*, 216–22; C. A. Harrell and D. G. Weiford, "The City Manager and the Policy Process," *ibid.*, 19 (Spring, 1959), 101–7; and Orin F. Nolting, "Changing Role of the City Manager," address delivered at National Conference on Government, Cleveland, November 18, 1957.

Thus, the plan may not operate too effectively in communities in which the citizenry is divided into two fairly equal groups and in which there is lack of consensus concerning the role of government. A possibility also exists that there will be conflict between a strong-willed mayor and the manager. In the event of such rivalry, the council members and the citizenry may be forced into the uncomfortable position of choosing to support one or the other in an internal struggle for power. It is largely for these reasons that the combination of a strong-mayor and CAO is often preferred for large cities where continued election of a chief executive is deemed desirable.

The success of the plan can be measured in part by its rapid and continuing growth and the small number of abandonments. A 1959 study listed only 90 cities which had dropped the plan subsequent to its adoption. However, in 18 of these communities, the plan was later re-adopted so that only 72 cities had actually abandoned the plan during its first half-century.[22] As of 1963, the council-manager form of government was found in two or more communities in 46 states, with only Hawaii and Indiana having no plans in operation. The form was most popular among California cities with 226 adoptions, and Texas, Maine, Michigan, and Pennsylvania each had over 100 council-manager cities.[23] In addition to its success in the United States, the plan has been widely adopted in cities in Canada, Finland, Germany, Norway, and Sweden.

While much has been written about forms of municipal government and the strengths and weaknesses of these alternative plans of organization, there is little to be concluded from these statements. Increasingly in recent years, it has been emphasized that structure is a means rather than an end in itself. This point has been vividly made by Adrian who writes, "Structures of government are tools. They make a difference as to how a community is governed and as to which groups and interests in the community are most influential. Local cultural circumstances will determine the type of structure that is wanted by the politically dominant, and the type of government that will be produced under any chosen form. Structure is significant, but it is only one of the factors that makes up the par-

[22] Arthur W. Bromage, *Manager Plan Abandonments,* 5th ed., National Municipal League, 1959.
[23] International City Managers' Association, *Recent Council-Manager Developments and Directory of Council-Manager Cities,* International City Managers' Association, January, 1963.

ticular characteristics of politics and community decision making in a city."[24]

SUGGESTED READINGS

Books

Adrian, Charles R., *Governing Urban America,* 2nd ed. (New York: McGraw-Hill, 1961).

Alderfer, Harold F., *American Local Government and Administration* (New York: Macmillan, 1956).

Baker, Benjamin, *Urban Government* (Princeton: Van Nostrand, 1957).

Bollens, John C., *Appointed Executive Local Government: The California Experience* (Los Angeles: Haynes Foundation, 1952).

Bradford, E. S., *Commission Government in American Cities* (New York: Macmillan, 1911).

Bromage, Arthur W., *Manager Plan Abandonments,* 5th ed. (New York: National Municipal League, 1959).

Childs, Richard S., *Civic Victories* (New York: Harper, 1952).

International City Managers' Association, *Municipal Year Book, 1963* (Chicago: International City Managers' Association, 1963).

Institute of Public Affairs, *Forms of City Government,* 4th ed. (Austin: Institute of Public Affairs, University of Texas, 1956).

Kneier, Charles M., *City Government in the United States,* 3rd ed. (New York: Harper, 1957).

Kneier, Charles M. and Fox, Guy, *Readings in Municipal Government and Administration* (New York: Rinehart, 1953).

National Municipal League, *The Story of the Council-Manager Plan,* 28th ed. (New York: National Municipal League, 1962).

Stone, Harold A., Price, Don K. and Stone, Kathryn H., *Council-Manager Government in the United States* (Chicago: Public Administrative Service, 1940).

Williams, Oliver P. and Press, Charles, *Democracy in Urban America* (Chicago: Rand McNally, 1961).

Articles

Adrian, Charles R., "Leadership and Decision-Making in Manager Cities: A Story of Three Communities," *Public Administration Review,* 18 (Summer, 1958), 208–13.

Adrian, Charles R., "Recent Concepts in Large City Administration," paper (mimeo) presented at annual meeting of American Political Science Association, Washington, D. C., 1956.

[24] Adrian, *Governing Urban America,* p. 231.

Bebout, John E., "Management for Large Cities," *Public Administration Review*, 15 (Summer, 1955), 188–95.

Bosworth, Karl A., "The Manager is a Politician," *Public Administration Review*, 18 (Summer, 1958), 216–22.

Sayre, Wallace S., "The General Manager Idea for Large Cities," *Public Administration Review*, 14 (Autumn, 1954), 253–8.

Sommers, William A., "Council-Manager Government: A Review," *Western Political Quarterly*, 11 (March, 1958), 144–7.

Town, Village, and Township Government

11

The three terms in the title of this chapter are used to identify for discussion purposes those units of local government that can be considered as small municipalities or their equivalent. Although there are variations in terminology among the 50 states, these small units are commonly known by one of the three terms. Some municipalities called by these specific terms might be so urbanized that they are no longer small municipalities. Others, on the other hand, might still be so rural that they would not approach municipal status in power.

The word "town" will be used in this chapter to describe units of government which are governed by the town meeting form of government rather than the diverse small communities which are called towns but do not operate under this plan. The term "village" is a general term and will be used to identify incorporated communities of under 2,500. Thus, it embraces units known variously as cities, towns, hamlets, and villages among the several states. Townships are of two classes—rural and urban—and both will be described herein. However, the rural township will be given more extensive discussion since the urban township is becoming increasingly like cities in structure, operation, and services.

■ The New England Town

Few governmental concepts are imbued with the nostalgic charm and reverence ascribed to the town meeting form of direct democracy in New England. Some of the spirit and contagious appeal of the town meeting has been captured by a number of writers describing its operation—usually in glowing and picturesque terms. In the words of one writer, "In these smallest units of American government, these 'cells' of pure democracy, the citizens rule directly. Here the lowliest inhabitant has a personal part in his town government, and if he has a good cause and a good speaking voice to go with it, his part is a leading one. For his will may become the will of the town meeting, and the will of the meeting regarding town affairs is the law within the town's boundaries—at least until the next meeting rolls around. Here the citizen is sovereign, and well he knows it, and so do the town officers whom he elects to perform the town chores for him."[1]

Since the town as a unit of government is limited to those communities with the town meeting form of government, local units known as towns in New York and Wisconsin are excluded, as are municipalities in a number of states which are known as towns because of their small population.[2] While not all of the 1,424 towns in the six New England states retain the pure form of town meeting, it remains the most common governmental pattern in these northeastern states. The number of towns in each state was shown in Table 1 (pp. 46–47), with the number ranging from 31 in Rhode Island to 470 in Maine.

THE TOWN MEETING

The pattern of town government is that of a direct democracy rather than indirect through elected representatives. The annual town meeting is the principal governing authority of the town and every qualified voter is eligible to attend and participate in this

[1] L. H. Robbins, "Democracy, Town Meeting Style," *The New York Times Magazine*, March 23, 1947, pp. 24, 35, 38.

[2] A municipality of 500 or fewer persons is known as a town in South Dakota and Virginia; 800 or fewer in Utah; 1,000 or fewer in Kentucky and Montana; and 2,000 or less in Colorado, Indiana, Iowa, and Oklahoma. Population is also a basis for calling municipalities towns in Mississippi and New Mexico. See Charles M. Kneier, *City Government in the United States*, 3rd ed., Harper, 1957, pp. 283-4.

deliberation. When assembled, the voters constitute the legislative body of the town and are called upon to make a number of major policy decisions as well as an even larger number of minor ones.

Except in Connecticut where the meeting is usually in the fall, the annual town meeting is usually held during the spring months. Well in advance of the annual meeting, a warrant is prepared by the selectmen, or signed by a majority of them, showing a notice of the time and place of the meeting and its agenda. These warrants or notices are either published or posted. Only the items or articles included in the call of the meeting can be considered and such items are placed on the agenda by action of the selectmen or in response to a request by a prescribed number of voters. The meeting is normally held in the town hall but may be held in a larger building if necessary to accommodate the voters. Town meetings usually convene about mid-morning, recess for a noon meal which is often served by a local women's organization, and continue through much of the afternoon. At some meetings, the business to be conducted is so heavy that one or more adjourned sessions must be held to dispose of all the items on the agenda.

The annual meetings are presided over by a moderator who might be elected for a definite term of office, appointed by the registrar of voters, or selected by the voters in assembly. It is common practice for the moderator, however first chosen, to retain this position for a number of years. The town clerk serves as the secretary of the meeting and keeps records of its proceedings. While the number of specific items on the agenda vary greatly from town to town and from year to year within a town, the principal functions of town meetings are the same.[3] In the order in which they are normally considered, these are:

1. To receive the reports of the several town officers and committees named at the last meeting.
2. To elect town officers for the coming year.
3. To levy taxes and vote appropriations for the functions and services to be provided in the ensuing year.
4. To authorize necessary temporary borrowing or bonded indebtedness.

[3] For a more detailed discussion see Clyde F. Snider, *Local Government in Rural America*, Appleton-Century-Crofts, 1957, Chap. VIII; John F. Sly, *Town Government in Massachusetts*, Harvard University Press, 1930, Chap. VI; and John M. Fairlie and Charles M. Kneier, *County Government and Administration*, Appleton-Century, 1930, Chap. XX.

5. To enact bylaws and/or ordinances and policies to be administered by the elected officers during the coming year.
6. To take appropriate action on the several other and lesser important items on the agenda.

As the specific items on the agenda are taken up for deliberation and action, any eligible voter may speak for or against the proposal under consideration. Some issues are hotly debated, while other issues are voted upon with little or no discussion.[4] First votes are usually taken *viva voce*, or by voice, and in case of doubt by a show of hands. Voting for officers is more formal, however, and is usually done by writing the names of preferred candidates on slips of paper or by the use of a printed ballot. Special meetings may be called at the discretion of the selectmen to transact town business or upon the petition of a specified number of town voters. Such meetings must be called by a warrant similar to that for the annual meeting and their conduct parallels that of the yearly session.

BOARD OF SELECTMEN

The plural-member board of selectmen elected at the town meeting serves as the principal administrative agency of the town. As a rule, there are three members of this board, but some communities choose a greater number of five, seven or nine. The term of office ranges from one to three years with re-election a custom of long standing.[5] Local boards of selectmen in Connecticut are required to have members of at least two political parties, but there is no such requirement in other New England states. Compensation is set by town bylaws and is usually rather low.

As elected representatives of the voters, the selectmen are empowered to carry on the business of the town between annual meetings and to make policy decisions necessary to implement broader policies. During their terms, they have charge of town property and manage elections. Among their other major duties are appointment and removal of various minor town officers and

[4] For an interesting and entertaining description of town meetings in session, see John Gould, *New England Town Meeting, Safeguard of Democracy*, Stephen Daye Press, 1940.

[5] A recent study of selectmen in a Maine town revealed that one member had held office for 41 years with only a one-year break in continuity, and two former members had served for periods of 32 and 18 years respectively. See Lincoln Smith, "Leadership in Local Government—The New England Town," *Social Science*, 29 (June, 1954), 147–57.

administrative subordinates;[6] granting of licenses and permits; preparation of warrants for special and annual town meetings; construction and maintenance of roads; settlement of claims against the town; and preparation of the budget for presentation at the town meeting. Selectmen, particularly in smaller towns, often serve in various other capacities such as assessors, overseers of the poor, health officers, or highway commissioners.

Generally speaking, the powers of the board of selectmen are collective powers and must be exercised in joint action. However, Connecticut towns select one member as first selectman and his role has become predominant in practice if not in legalized custom. One important power denied selectmen is the power to levy taxes. This power remains and is zealously guarded as a function of the annual town meeting.

OTHER TOWN OFFICERS

In towns not employing managers, most of the day-to-day administrative work is handled by the town clerk. Normally elected for a one-year term but traditionally re-elected year after year, the clerk is a key official and ranks only after the selectmen in importance. His duties are many and varied, including the registration of births, marriages, and deaths; recording of deeds, mortgages and other legal documents; keeping records of town meeting proceedings; acting as custodian of town archives; and maintaining and revising voter lists. One writer describes the town clerk not only as a "general factotum but often an encyclopedia of local information."[7]

While the selectmen and the clerk are the principal town officers, there are usually a number of other officials—some of whom are chosen by the voters at the annual meeting and others who are appointed by the board of selectmen. The other commonly elected officers include a treasurer, who receives revenues and honors claims against the town; town assessors, who set value on real estate and personal property for taxing purposes; constables, who serve as local peace officers; overseers of the poor, who dispense monies and aid to the indigent and needy; auditors, who check the financial records and make public reports; and a highway supervisor or

[6] A 1951 study of Connecticut towns enumerated 30 such appointments. See Max R. White, *Handbook for Connecticut Selectmen,* University of Connecticut Institute of Public Service, 1951, p. 31.

[7] Roger H. Wells, *American Local Government,* McGraw-Hill, 1939, p. 84.

road commissioner, who is responsible for the maintenance of local roads. In addition, there is an elective school board which is responsible for the management of the town schools.

There are a number of other officials found in some but not all towns, and which are elective in some and appointive in other towns. These include such descriptive officeholders as fence viewers who settle disputes over the location of fences between properties; sextons, who care for cemeteries; tree wardens; coal weighers; poundkeepers; and inspectors of lumber.[8] Usually a number of boards or commissions also exist, including a water commission, library board, park board, civil service commission, planning board, and aviation commission.

As mentioned previously, the actual form of town government varies considerably in its detail from town to town. A generalized picture of its common pattern is presented in Figure 10. It is quite

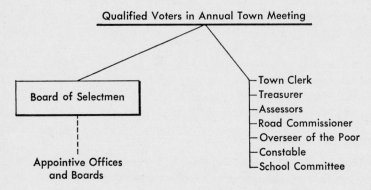

Figure 10. *New England Town Meeting Plan.*

evident that there are a number of offices to be filled and that there is no real single officer with overall administrative responsibility for supervising town affairs.

MODIFICATIONS OF THE TOWN MEETING

As the New England towns continued to grow in population and local problems became more complex, certain weaknesses in the

---

[8] Many of these offices are becoming obsolete, but incumbents are sometimes appointed or elected as a means of honoring deserving citizens or of pulling a practical joke on them. See Snider, *op. cit.,* p. 203.

town meeting form became apparent. While the basic pattern of the town meeting system has remained as the common form of town government, three significant modifications have developed. The first relates primarily to the size of the town and is known as the representative or limited town meeting form. The second grew out of the need for improved town financial planning and resulted in the creation of a town finance committee. The third modification, the introduction of the town-manager plan, evolved as the need for centralized and trained administrative leadership was recognized.

Representative Town Meeting. The concept of the representative town meeting first developed in Massachusetts where the state general court (legislature) passed special enabling legislation for the town of Brookline in 1915.[9] Since that time, other towns in Massachusetts as well as towns in Connecticut and Maine have adopted this modification. As the plan operates, the town is divided by the selectmen into precincts ranging in number from four to nine depending on its size. The voters in each precinct choose an equal number of delegates (usually 30 to 40) by popular vote. These delegates rather than the entire electorate then serve as town meeting members. Meeting with the town officers at the annual and special town meetings, these delegates and the town officers exercise essentially the same powers formerly exercised by the old town meeting. Any voter of the town is entitled to speak at the representative town meeting, but voting is restricted to the delegates. In effect, the representative town meeting is a compromise between the pure town meeting form and the smaller councils elected in New England cities. Experience with this modification appears quite satisfactory in the some 40 New England towns in which it is in operation.[10]

The Finance Committee. Although known by a number of names, the concept of the town finance committee is now operating in a number of towns in Connecticut, Maine, Massachusetts, and New Hampshire. As the need for financial planning was recognized, state enabling legislation was enacted permitting citizens of towns to create a finance committee of from three to 30 members to study town and school finances and to prepare the budget for submission at the town meeting. Members of the finance committee

[9] Alexander Lincoln, "Some Notes on Representative Town Meetings," *Massachusetts Law Quarterly, 33* (April, 1948), 30-46.
[10] Snider, *op. cit.,* pp. 206-7.

are often elected at the annual meeting, but in some towns the members are appointed by the moderator. Since the school budget is also prepared by the committee, school board members are usually given some committee memberships, but as a rule the committees are non-political in composition, with business and professional people comprising most of the membership. The function of the committee is chiefly advisory, since the budget must be submitted at the town meeting for approval. However, the committee recommendations carry considerable weight with the citizens and the budget as presented is usually approved without major change. Again this modification seems to be working well in New England towns, with the finance committee evolving as an important and effective factor in the formulation and adoption of town policies.[11]

The Town-Manager Plan. The adoption of the manager plan in some New England towns resulted from the same need as existed in other council-manager communities—the need for a single, responsible administrative officer. As the town-manager plan operates, the selectmen appoint a qualified person to the position of town manager to supervise administrative activities under the board's general supervision. The position and powers of the town-manager are similar to those of the manager in council-manager cities except that the policy-determining body is the town meeting rather than the board of selectmen. The manager, however, is directly responsible to the board rather than to the town meeting. Another unusual feature of the town-manager plan is that in some cases one manager serves more than one town. Such joint appointments occur when two or more small towns near each other want a trained administrative officer and combine their limited resources to hire a joint manager. The effectiveness of this modification of the town meeting form is borne out by the increasing number of New England towns which are adopting it. The town-manager plan is no longer in its experimental stage in New England since it has been in operation for 25 years in some towns. In general, the experience with this adaptation has resulted in the same typically good results produced by the council-manager plan in cities.[12]

[11] Richard A. Atkins and Lyman H. Ziegler, "Citizen Budgeting in Massachusetts," *National Municipal Review, 30* (October, 1941), 568-73.
[12] Lawrence Pelletier, "New England Pioneers Again," *National Municipal Review, 37* (February, 1949), 79-84.

LOCAL GOVERNMENT STRUCTURE

The concept of the pure town meeting form of local government has not been confined to the small towns of New England. Township meetings which parallel the town meeting are common in the northern tier of our central states, including Illinois, Michigan, Minnesota, Nebraska, North and South Dakota, Washington, and Wisconsin.[13] The authority of the voters assembled in a township meeting, in general, is usually less extensive than that in the New England town. Township functions tend to be fewer in number and this may account for the lesser voter interest and participation in township meetings.

Because the pure form of the town meeting represented democracy at its "best" and represented the closest compatibility of the theory of local democracy with its practice, it has not been fashionable to criticize the plan in operation. As recently as 1940, one enthusiastic town meeting supporter wrote, "In a world where Democracy perishes, and in a country where self-government occupies every thinking mind, it is startling and refreshing to find (the) New England Town Meeting alive and able and in the hands of a tightfisted people who keep their heritage well."[14] In our hope to make this picture a reality, we have too often tended to take the theory of the town meeting at its full face value without considering its actual performance.

In a study which included the observation of three New England town meetings in session, Alexander and Berger concluded that the "town meeting is a sacred cow that deserves to be laid to rest."[15] A town meeting in a town of 2,600 registered voters attracted fewer than 200 citizens and the "meeting produced fewer than a half a dozen questions and no hot arguments; it proceeded rather perfunctorily to its close an hour and fifteen minutes after it had begun."[16]

[13] Snider, *op. cit.*, p. 220; John A. Fairlie, *Local Government in Counties, Towns, and Villages,* Century, 1914, pp. 168-9. The township meeting form was also used in New York until the early 1930s.

[14] Gould, *op. cit.*, p. 10.

[15] John W. Alexander and Morroe Berger, "Is the Town Meeting Finished?" *American Mercury,* (August, 1949), pp. 144-51.

[16] *Ibid.*, pp. 144-5. For other accounts of poor citizen turnout and lack of participation in town meetings, see Roscoe C. Martin, *Grass Roots,* University of Alabama Press, 1957, pp. 60-61; and Robert C. Wood, *Suburbia, Its People and Their Politics,* Houghton Mifflin, 1959, pp. 282-5.

If citizen participation weakens but the town meeting form is retained, then the role of the elected and appointed town officials becomes more important. A detailed study of Winchester, Massachusetts, reported that the 69 public officials accounted for over 36 percent of the actual attendance at town meetings during the period studied.[17] The logical outcome of this trend is the growth of a "sort of untitled squirearchy recognized as the solid, permanent, and benevolent element of the community, though now increasingly composed in the larger places of energetic citizens from less distinguished ranks."[18] Lancaster believes that the general tendency to retain the town meeting has resulted in the trend to assign administrative functions to larger units and to strengthen state supervision over town functions of more than purely local interest.[19]

However, the town meeting form continues to work well in a number of small New England towns. Since the plan permits a town to retain "its identity, its vitality, its community consciousness, and the loyalty of its inhabitants,"[20] there is much to commend it. By adapting to one or more of the modifications of pure town meeting government as the need for change is recognized, the town meeting will remain the major characteristic of New England town government in the foreseeable future.

■ Village Government

While the term "village" is variously defined in population limits among the states, the definitions agree that the village is a small community. In Ohio, all municipalities below 5,000 in population are called villages; the population range is between 100 and 300 in Mississippi, and from 100 to 10,000 in Minnesota. Four states—Idaho, Iowa, Louisiana, and Nebraska—set 1,000 as the upper population limit for villages.[21] Since there is no common criterion among the states for determining the size of a village, the arbitrary figure of 2,500 or less will be used to identify the incorporated

[17] Charles Ball, "Metropolitan Boston: A Critique of Pure Integration," unpublished senior's thesis, Harvard University, 1956.
[18] From John F. Sly in *New England's Prospects*, p. 419, as quoted in Lancaster, *Government in Rural America*, 2nd ed., Van Nostrand, 1952, p. 45.
[19] Lancaster, *op. cit.*, p. 46.
[20] *Ibid.*
[21] Harold F. Alderfer, *American Local Government and Administration*, Macmillan, 1956, pp. 41-48.

places herein described as villages. Thus, this term will be used to embrace communities otherwise called towns, boroughs, and certain classes of cities ranging from 2nd class in Colorado to 6th class in Kentucky.

According to the 1962 census reports, there were 13,284 incorporated places in the United States with populations of 2,500 or less. Since the total number of incorporated places was 17,997, 73.8 percent of all municipalities are of the size herein described as villages.[22] But while there is a great number of such places, their total population comprised less than 5.4 percent of the national population in 1960.

STRUCTURE OF GOVERNMENT

Governmental organization in villages is comparatively simple. However, the variation in organization between villages and cities differs more in degree than in kind, since the differences relate more to the complexity of organization required for functions performed than to structural principles. Just as for cities, there are the three basic forms of village government—the mayor-council, commission, and council-manager plans. Of the three, the mayor-council form is used most extensively and it will be the only form which will be discussed. The commission and council-manager plans in villages parallel the operation of these plans in larger cities.[23]

The principal authority in villages lies in the plural-member legislative body commonly called the village council or board of trustees.[24] The council is normally small, consisting of three, five, seven, or nine members. Because of the small size of the community, election is usually at large but in some villages election is by wards. In general, village councils have power to pass ordinances on many subject matters which are typically enumerated in some detail in the statutes of the state. Their basic power lies in their control of the appropriation and expenditure of village funds, although unusually large expenditures sometimes must be approved by village voters. Village councils generally have limited taxing powers and

[22] This number includes, of course, incorporated places known as cities, boroughs, villages and towns (except for those in New England, New York, and Wisconsin).

[23] For a fuller discussion of village government, see Kneier, *op. cit.*, Chap. XV; and Fairlie, *op. cit.*, Chap. XI.

[24] This council is also known as burgesses in Connecticut and as commissioners in Maryland.

the right to levy special assessments for street improvements. Normally they are also empowered to borrow a limited amount on their own authority and greater amounts upon approval by the voters.

Non-financial powers of village councils normally include the control of village property; the right to own cemeteries, public pounds, public buildings and parks; the power to prescribe the terms and conditions for licensing certain establishments and occupations; and authority to construct and regulate the use of public works enterprises including roads, bridges, sewers, drains, and water. They may provide public health and safety services. In addition, village councils usually have more effective control over administrative officers than do their city counterparts by having appointive and removal powers concerning these officers.

The chief executive officer is generally called a mayor if there is a council and a president of the village board if the legislative body is composed of trustees.[25] If called mayor, the office is normally filled by popular election, while village presidents are typically selected by village boards of trustees from among their own membership. Mayors preside over the meetings of the village council and have the full rights of a member in most states. In some states, however, village mayors can vote only in the case of a tie vote in council. If a veto power exists, it is a limited one and can be overridden by a three-fifths or two-thirds vote in the council. Mayors also have a limited supervision over other village officers and usually a more fixed responsibility for the enforcement of local police ordinances. If a trend is discernible in village government, it seems to be toward strengthening the office of the mayor, but this varies so widely among states that it is hazardous to risk a generalization.

The remainder of the governmental organization in villages is usually simple and consists of few officers and employees. It is common for marshals to exist as local law enforcement officers, and the part-time services of a treasurer or collector and of a clerk or recorder are required. The three offices are usually filled by popular election. Most villages also have an officer known as street or road commissioner and may have an assessor and solicitor. In addition, village governments may have an assortment of local boards and

25 Other titles include intendant in Alabama, warden in Connecticut, and chairman of the board of trustees in Indiana and Missouri.

LOCAL GOVERNMENT STRUCTURE

commissions including health boards, cemetery commissions, and boards for public utilities services such as water, sewers, and lighting if such facilities exist.[26]

In a recent detailed study of Springdale, a rural village in upstate New York, two sociologists described the governmental structure and the decision-making process in this community. Concerning the government and its officials, they wrote,

> The elected officials of village government (three trustees, a mayor and a clerk) are with but few exceptions local businessmen, primarily owners and operators of retail stores. However, not all businessmen qualify for public office and not all officials are businessmen. As a primary qualification for election an individual must have been a resident of the community for at least ten years; preferably and most frequently he has been a life-long resident of the village. Hence his personal "character" and his ideology are well known to the community at large. To be selected as a candidate for public office he must subscribe to a low-tax, low-expenditure ideology and be relatively unsophisticated in the techniques of political analysis and public administration. These qualifications tend to reside in the business community.[27]

The authors proceed to show that most of the important decisions affecting Springdale are made outside the community and that the village adapts to necessary changes rather than initiate them.

AN EVALUATION OF VILLAGE GOVERNMENT

It is difficult to evaluate village government in general terms since the villages range in population from only a few persons to 2,500. They can be a part of the satellite system of a larger municipality or be a small independent community in the center of a rural area. Similarly, the number and level of services rendered by village governments range from only limited police protection to a number of efficiently operated urban-type services. Generally, however, the services provided are few and inadequate when measured against any standards for determining satisfactory levels of service. Since the governmental structure is simple in organization and part-time in nature, it is difficult to praise or condemn its operation. The needs of citizens in villages are not great in terms

---

[26] See Kneier, op. cit., pp. 288–90 ; and Fairlie, op. cit., pp. 210–1.
[27] Arthur J. Vidich and Joseph Bensman, Small Town in Mass Society, Princeton University Press, 1958, pp. 114–5.

of services, and village government seems reasonably responsive to the demands ordinarily made on it.

However, village government tends toward conservatism in both politics and actions and often presents a front of singlemindedness or unanimity. The authors of the Springdale study concluded that "Although the principle of unanimity of decision is almost a requirement in Springdale politics, few items of business outside of routine and legally required action ever reach the decision-making stage. It is an outstanding characteristic of village government that it does not initiate new undertakings and new projects. . . . It is a common complaint among all groups in the community that the village board does nothing."[28] Such forced one-mindedness and stand-pattism has interesting implications for our cherished concepts of "grass-roots" democracy which have not been adequately studied.

Perhaps one change is essential in state statutes relating to the incorporation of future villages. The minimum population required in a number of states is still as low as 100 persons. Since it is impossible for a village of this size to function with any real meaning as a municipality, it would seem wise to raise the minimum population requirement and to require that any new incorporated village provide at least a minimum level of services in important functional areas, or present plans for the purchase of these services from a neighboring city, or for providing them through joint action with other incorporated places.

Village government has received scant attention from political scientists in recent years. Both the number of these units and the number of citizens served by them make future consideration of methods of improving their structure and services a worthy objective in the years ahead. Since roughly one of every 20 Americans lives in units of 2,500 or less population, small government is still big business and is deserving of careful and concentrated concern and study.

■ *Township Government*

Communities known as townships exist in 15 states stretching across the nation but generally concentrated in the Midwest. In 1962, there were 15,720 such incorporated places, with ten states

[28] *Ibid.*, p. 113.

LOCAL GOVERNMENT STRUCTURE

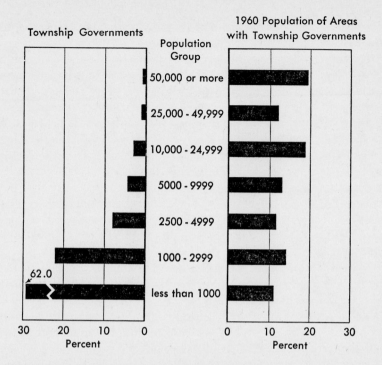

Figure 11. *Township Governments and Their Populations, by Population Size: 1962.* (U.S. Bureau of Census, *Census of Governments, 1962.* Vol. I: *Governmental Organization,* Washington, 1962, p. 20.)

each having more than 1,000 township units. A distribution of townships was shown in Table 1 (pp. 46–47). Township organization encompasses the whole area of the state in nine of the 15 states, but it is limited to only two counties in Washington. Establishment of township government is optional with each county in some states, and in a number of counties only a part of the total area is formally organized into townships.

In their pattern of government, townships in the United States fall into two main groupings. In eight states, township meetings patterned after the New England town meeting are prescribed by state legislation.[29] Since the meetings are open to all qualified voters of the township and their conduct parallel to the town

[29] These are Illinois, Michigan, Minnesota, Nebraska, North Dakota, South Dakota, Washington, and Wisconsin.

meeting, their structure and operation need be discussed only briefly. Township organization in the other seven states reflects a miniature of county government and consists of several offices elected by the voters as well as the members of the township board.

A second meaningful classification of township government is a division of townships into rural and urban groupings. This distinction is clearly drawn between provisions for charter and first class townships in Michigan, New York, and Pennsylvania. A 1947 law in Michigan enables townships of 5,000 or more population and those of 2,000 or more bordering a city of at least 25,000, to organize as charter townships and exercise considerably broader powers than their more rural counterparts. First class townships in New York are those with a population of 10,000 or more, while in Pennsylvania they must have a population density of 300 or more persons per square mile. In addition, the more urban townships in Minnesota, New Jersey, Ohio, and Wisconsin are authorized to undertake urban-type services for their citizens.

STRUCTURE OF GOVERNMENT

In townships with the township meeting form of government, the board is known as a board of trustees or supervisors. One member serves as the chairman and is known either as the board supervisor or chairman. Other common elective officers include a clerk, assessors, a treasurer, and constables or justices of the peace.[30] While a limited number of other elective or appointive township officers may exist, the number is far fewer than in New England towns.

As the principal governing authority of the township, the township meeting has four primary powers. These are (1) the election of township officers, (2) levying taxes and appropriating funds for township functions, (3) authorizing the borrowing of money or bond issue, and (4) enacting bylaws for the management of local affairs. The parallel between the town and township meeting can be drawn more meaningfully in terms of their legal composition than in their functioning. In a study of township government in Illinois, Snider concluded that, "Many citizens, some of them

[30] Snider, *op. cit.*, pp. 221–2.

otherwise well-informed, seem to be completely unaware of the meeting's very existence to say nothing of its importance."[31]

As mentioned above, the township in the other eight states assumes a governmental pattern quite like the structure of county government in miniature. The township governing board, whose title varies from state to state, is the principal governing agency, but there are also some elective officers. The governing board is known as the advisory board in Indiana; board of trustees in Kansas and Ohio; board of directors in Missouri; township committee in New Jersey; board of supervisors and board of commissioners in Pennsylvania second- and first-class townships respectively. The board consists of three or more members who are either elected as board members or who sit as *ex officio* members because of their other township offices. The term of office is usually for two or four years. As the general governing authority in the township, the board possesses general, but normally limited, taxing powers. It commonly has a limited appointive power and may exercise some licensing and regulating authority.

Other township officers vary from state to state, but where the offices exist their duties are quite parallel. The structure of township government in Kansas is not atypical. There the elective township officers are a clerk, treasurer, two justices of the peace, and two constables, in addition to the trustees. The township board is composed of the trustees, clerk, and treasurer, who also sit as the audit board to supervise township finances and as the board of highway commissioners in townships still caring for local roads.[32] The offices of clerk, treasurer, and justice of the peace are common in many townships across the nation. The number of justices of the peace varies from one to two per township and he may handle local police functions on his own or share them with the constable, as in Kansas. The assessor is another elective office in some townships, while in others he is appointed by the township board; in some areas the office has been abolished with assessment becoming a function of county government. Two other common appointive township officers are the highway commissioner or commissioners and the overseer of the poor, sometimes known as the welfare administrator.

[31] Clyde F. Snider, "The Illinois Town Meeting," *Illinois County and Township Official,* 8 (February, 1949), 5–7.

[32] James W. Drury, *Township Government in Kansas,* Governmental Research Bureau, University of Kansas, 1954.

The basic structure of rural township government is shown in Figure 12. The functions performed by this unit are on the decline in a number of states, with the county assuming functions formerly performed at the township level.[33] The principal local function remaining at the township level is the maintenance of local roads and bridges in Kansas, Missouri, and Ohio, and the administration of poor relief in Indiana. Other township activities in some areas include cemeteries, libraries, fire protection, parks, and health.

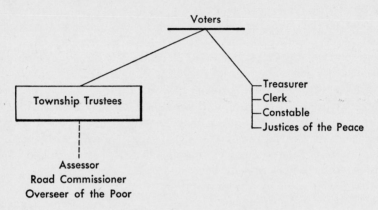

Figure 12. *Rural Township Government.*

In charter, first-class, or urban townships, the structure of government becomes a bit more formal and the services provided increase in number. The township board is usually increased in size and there is a larger number of appointive officers. In contrast to their rural counterparts, functions have been expanded in these townships in recent years in several states. The functions of first class townships in Pennsylvania are now quite extensive and in general parallel those of most cities of similar size.[34] A number of larger townships have adopted the township manager plan by local ordinance to obtain the benefit of the full-time services of a trained administrator. In such communities, the township manager functions in a capacity parallel to that of the town manager, although

[33] See Clyde F. Snider, "The Twilight of the Township," *National Municipal Review*, *41* (September, 1952), 390-6; and James W. Drury, "Townships Lose Ground," *National Municipal Review*, *44* (January, 1955), 10-13.

[34] For a distinction between first- and second-class townships in Pennsylvania see, Jacob Tanger, Harold F. Alderfer and Nelson McGeary, *Pennsylvania Government*, Penns Valley Publisher, 1950, pp. 197-201.

LOCAL GOVERNMENT STRUCTURE

his powers may be more limited since the office is established by local ordinance rather than through adoption of an optional charter.

AN EVALUATION OF TOWNSHIP GOVERNMENT

It might be noted that most present-day townships have changed somewhat from the units which were once described by Jefferson as "pure and elementary republics." However, townships continue to serve three important functions: (1) as units of local government; (2) as units of representation for some county governing bodies; and (3) as constituent units of party machinery in some states. In spite of these functions, however, there are few strong supporters to township government as it now exists in rural areas.[35]

Snider advances three primary reasons for the decline of the rural township. These are: (1) improvements in communications and transportation no longer make subdivisions of the county necessary for easy citizen access; (2) township operations often are duplications of county services or are inefficiently rendered; and (3) rising costs of government have intensified tax consciousness of citizens who often see the township as an unessential and expendable unit of local government. He concludes that "available evidence points to the conclusion that the midwestern township as a governmental institution is on the way out and, furthermore, that this fact is not to be regretted."[36]

An even stronger indictment of township government is presented by Lancaster. He states that "What we are doing is keeping alive mere shells of government, staffed by do-nothing officials whose titles are empty ones and whose salaries are gifts. If, as seems clear, the most hopeful way of attacking the problem of administrative inadequacy of local areas is through the reallocation of functions, the persistence of the township as a legal entity simply delays this attack or compels illogical subterfuges. The elimination of this area, either through its outright abolition or through the process of attrition, might be expected to reduce the overhead cost of local government, bring about greater uniformity in the quality of governmental services, and equalize the burden of taxation."[37]

[35] One of the few recent defenses is found in William B. Guitteau, *Ohio's Townships: The Grassroots of Democracy*, Toledo Printing Co., 1949.
[36] Snider, "The Twilight of the Township," *op. cit.*
[37] Lancaster, *op. cit.*, p. 70.

Thus, in the years ahead it is to be expected that the rural township will continue to decline in importance while urban townships will increasingly assume the status of cities. The county will assume more functions of the rural townships—some by default and others for reasons of efficiency and economy. The formal abolition of townships, however, faces a number of difficult obstacles and their demise will probably result more from attrition of functions than through abolition.

SUGGESTED READINGS

Books
Alderfer, Harold F., *American Local Government and Administration* (New York: Macmillan, 1956).

Drury, James W., *Township Government in Kansas* (Lawrence: Governmental Research Bureau, University of Kansas, 1954).

Fairlie, John M., *Local Government in Counties, Towns and Villages* (New York: Century, 1914).

Fairlie, John A. and Kneier, Charles M., *County Government and Administration* (New York: Appleton-Century, 1930).

Gould, John, *New England Town Meeting, Safeguard of Democracy* (Brattleboro, Vt.: Stephen Daye Press, 1940).

Kneier, Charles M., *City Government in the United States*, 3rd ed. (New York: Harper, 1957).

Lancaster, Lane, *Government in Rural America*, 2nd ed. (Princeton: Van Nostrand, 1952).

Martin, Roscoe C., *Grass Roots* (University, Ala.: University of Alabama Press, 1957).

Snider, Clyde F., *Local Government in Rural America* (New York: Appleton-Century-Crofts, 1957).

Vidich, Arthur J. and Bensman, Joseph, *Small Town in Mass Society* (Princeton: Princeton University Press, 1958).

Wells, Roger H., *American Local Government* (New York: McGraw-Hill, 1939).

Articles
Alexander, John W. and Berger, Morroe, "Is the Town Meeting Finished?" *American Mercury*, (August, 1949), pp. 144–51.

Drury, James W., "Townships Lose Ground," *National Municipal Review*, 44 (January, 1955), 10–13.

Lincoln, Alexander, "Some Notes on Representative Town Meetings," *Massachusetts Law Quarterly*, 33 (April, 1948), 30–46.

Pelletier, Lawrence, "New England Pioneers Again," *National Municipal Review*, 37 (February, 1949), 79–84.

Robbins, L. H., "Democracy Town Meeting Style," *The New York Times Magazine*, (March 23, 1947).

Smith, Lincoln, "Leadership in Local Government—The New England Town," *Social Science*, 29 (June, 1954), 147–57.

Snider, Clyde F., "The Illinois Town Meeting," *Illinois County and Township Official*, 8 (February, 1949), 5–7.

Snider, Clyde F., "The Twilight of the Township," *National Municipal Review*, 41 (September, 1952), 390–6.

Government of
Special Districts

12

In numbers and variety, special districts exceed all other types of local governments in the United States. Such units are found in every state and exist in both rural and urban sections throughout the states. In 1962, the Bureau of the Census reported a total of 53,001 special districts, 34,678 of which were school districts.[1] The other 18,323 districts represent such a variety in terms of size, function, and character that general description is very difficult. However, this class of unit is deserving of careful study since it has become a significant part in the patchwork design of American local government. As of 1962, school districts alone accounted for 38 percent and other types of special districts represented 20 percent of the aggregate number of local governments. One careful student of special districts has stated that such non-school units "constitute the 'new dark continent of American politics,' a phrase applied earlier in the century to counties."[2]

As organized units of local government, special districts have the essential characteristics common to other local units. They

[1] Bureau of the Census, *Census of Governments, 1962, Vol. I, Governmental Organization,* Washington, 1962, p. 1.

[2] John C. Bollens, *Special District Government in the United States,* University of California Press, Los Angeles, 1957, p. 1.

have substantial autonomy from other units, including fiscal and administrative independence.[3] Special districts also have official and identifying names and perpetual succession. In addition, they enjoy the three basic rights of municipal corporations to sue and be sued, make contracts, and to obtain and dispose of property.[4] As indicated in Chapter 3, the two basic types of special districts—school and non-school—have shown a contrasting pattern of development in recent years.[5]

■ School Districts

The general pattern for providing public education in the United States is through local school districts. Such independent districts have full responsibility for the operation of public schools in 23 states, the predominant responsibility in 16 other states,[6] and partial responsibility in seven additional states.[7] In the five states of Hawaii, Maryland, North Carolina, Rhode Island, and Virginia, there are no independent school districts and public schools are administered by local county, city, or town governments, as is true in some parts of 16 other states.

To distinguish between the two basic types of organizations for public education, the Bureau of the Census classifies the latter type as "dependent" school systems.[8] In 1962, there were 2,341 such school systems operating in the 27 states which operate solely or in part through this kind of organization. Since dependent school systems are not separate governmental units, they will not be treated further at this time, but will be discussed more fully in Chapter 21.

The number of independent school districts varies greatly among the states. Among the states entirely organized into independent school districts, Nebraska with 3,264 has the largest number while Nevada with only 17 has the fewest. The five states of Kansas, Minnesota, Nebraska, Pennsylvania, and South Dakota each has over 3,000 independent school districts. The distribution of the

[3] Bureau of the Census, *op. cit.*, pp. 4–5.
[4] Bollens, *loc. cit.*
[5] See p. 51 above.
[6] These are Arizona, California, Delaware, Indiana, Kentucky, Louisiana, Minnesota, New Hampshire, New Jersey, New York, North Dakota, Ohio, Pennsylvania, South Carolina, Texas, and Wisconsin.
[7] These are Alaska, Connecticut, Maine, Massachusetts, Rhode Island, Tennessee, and Vermont.
[8] Bureau of the Census, *op. cit.*, pp. 3–8.

number of independent school districts was shown in Table 1 (pp. 46–47). The diversity in the area characteristics of school districts also shows wide variation. Many districts have the same boundaries as other general units of local government such as counties, cities, townships or towns. Many other districts, however, have boundaries which do not conform to those of any other governmental unit, resulting in districts extending over a very small area to those embracing more than 5,000 square miles.[9] The national average area for school districts in 1948 was about 18 square miles.

THE SCHOOL BOARD

Paralleling the pattern of government in general purpose local units, the governing authority of school districts is exercised by a plural member board commonly known as the board of education or board of school trustees. In about four of every five independent districts, the board members are chosen by direct election by the voters of the school district. In the other districts, board members are appointed rather than popularly elected. The appointing authorities range from the county board, the city council, the mayor, the mayor and council jointly to the grand jury, the district judge and the governor.[10] In the township school districts of Indiana, a single school trustee is elected, but the size of the board varies from three to 21 members in other states. Boards most commonly consist of three, five, or seven members who are elected for terms of from three to seven years.

School boards have been described by one writer in these words: "Typically they are chosen without regard to party preference. Each is a member of an unpaid group of from three to nine people, who meet together at least monthly and often more frequently in committees. Each serves for a specified term—three years, in most cases—and is eligible for re-election. The board member is usually not a person whose own career is directly concerned with education; more likely, he is a businessman or lawyer or farmer. In some cities, labor union officials have in recent years won an increasing share of school board posts, and the same is true of women."[11]

[9] National Commission on School District Reorganization, *Your School District,* National Education Association, 1948, p. 15.

[10] Bollens, *op. cit.,* p. 185.

[11] Thomas P. Eliot, *State and Local Supplement to Governing America,* Dodd, Mead, 1961, p. 158. For the results of a careful sample survey concerning school board composition, see Robert H. Brown, "The Composition of School Boards," *American School Board Journal,* 129 (August, 1954), 23-24.

Within the legal framework of state constitutional and legislative requirements, the local school board has wide discretion in exercising its responsibilities for the scope and quality of educational services. Its financial powers include the preparation and adoption of an annual budget, determination of the tax rate of the district, and the issuance of bonds after approval by the voters. Its appointive functions include selection of the school superintendent and the teaching and administrative staffs of the schools. Its educational policy powers range from determining what should be taught, the extent of extracurricular activities, the nature of the educational pattern in terms of grade divisions, or cooperation with other governmental units for school or recreational purposes, to choosing sites and approving construction plans for new school buildings. One writer has noted that, "The legal powers given to school boards include authority to make all reasonable rules and regulations for the government and management of the schools, for the discipline of pupils and teachers, and for the admission and even exclusion of children for sufficient legal cause."[12] These powers, however, are not inherent, and in accord with Dillon's rule, exist only when quite specifically granted by the legislature.

The internal organization of the school board is usually fairly simple. The common officers consist of a chairman or president, a clerk, and a treasurer. In many districts, these three board offices are filled by direct election by the voters while in others the board selects its own officers from among or outside the membership of the board. The three officers have the functions which would normally be associated with their offices. The chairman presides at board meetings and serves as the general spokesman of the board. The clerk keeps minutes of board meetings and has custody of district records, while the treasurer receives revenues and pays out monies on orders signed by the other two board members.

THE SCHOOL SUPERINTENDENT

To assist the school board in discharging its educational responsibilities, the board appoints a trained educator and school administrator to serve as the superintendent of schools. Unlike his counterpart in council-manager cities, the school superintendent is typically appointed to serve for a fixed term. This is often for

[12] G. T. Contalonia, "Some Powers and Duties of School Boards," *American School Board Journal, 129* (October, 1954), 28.

one year, but renewal is almost automatic subject only to mutual satisfaction. Like the city manager, the career pattern of the superintendent is to move from smaller to larger districts.

The responsibility for developing educational policy is largely delegated by the board to the superintendent. This officer normally plans the school curriculum for the board's approval; hires teachers to teach in the school system; purchases supplies for the school; plans the bus routes and schedules for transporting pupils to and from school; employs necessary administrative, clerical, and custodial employees, and suggests innovations to be implemented within the school's educational program. In such matters the superintendent's relations with the board parallel those of the manager with the council in council-manager governed cities. The superintendent also serves as the chief policy advisor to the board, and his success in directing the educational policies of the district depends in large part on his relations with the board.

The degree of delegation of responsibility by the board to the superintendent varies widely among school districts. As school administrators become a more professional group, the tendency has been for the school board to rely more heavily upon their superintendent not only for developing educational policy but for recommendations in other aspects of school administration as well.[13] Thus, the most important decision that some boards make in the course of their deliberations is their choice of superintendent. If the choice is a good one, the district's educational program moves ahead smoothly; if the choice is less fortunate, there may be considerable friction and bickering between the superintendent, the board, and the parents in the community.

ANNUAL SCHOOL MEETINGS

A number of states still make provision for an annual school meeting which is somewhat comparable to the annual town and township meetings discussed in Chapter 11. Such meetings are open to all voters residing in the district and the citizens in attendance give general instructions to the board members and ratify board policy recommendations. Notices of the pending meeting must be placed at conspicuous spots, normally including the schoolhouse door. Often telephone poles at busier intersections serve as other posting points.

[13] This is less true in large school districts which have other executive officers, often including an attorney, a finance chief, and a head of the physical plant.

The agenda of the annual school meeting follows a fairly uniform pattern. The first order of business is the election of board members. Since such meetings are more frequent in rural districts which tend to have three-member boards, there is usually just one member to be selected at any particular meeting. Following the election, the board presents its policy relating to the district tax levy for the coming year. This is normally the item which sparks the most discussion; if the meeting is well attended, it is often to oppose a rumored tax increase for school purposes. With the two major pieces of business taken care of, the meeting then discusses such topics as the beginning of the school term, who will clean up the buildings and yards prior to the opening of the term, and other district policies relating to the district's educational program.

In general, school meetings attract a level of citizen interest far less than that evidenced in New England town meetings. As the small districts are reorganized and become parts of larger districts, the tradition of the annual school meeting is a passing one in many areas. However, it remains a feature of school government in a number of rural and small town areas with highly varying degrees of voter interest and participation.

SCHOOL REORGANIZATION

School districts were originally established in Connecticut in 1766 and grew steadily in both number and area covered up to the early decades of the present century. The common school pattern up to the early 1930s in rural areas was one-teacher schools within walking distance of all homes in the district. In 1934, the Bureau of the Census reported a total of 125,627 independent school districts. The sharp decline in number of school districts in the past quarter century is clearly revealed in Figure 13.

The movement toward school consolidation has resulted largely from state action to encourage the merger of small districts. In some states, such action took the form of economic incentives with local districts qualifying for financial awards under voluntary compliance. In other states, consolidation was forced on small districts by legislation affecting districts failing to meet certain conditions or standards, or with too few pupils. In spite of the fine record of continuing school mergers across the nation, the Bureau of the Census reported in 1962 that nearly one-sixth of the existing public school systems did not actually operate schools but paid tuition

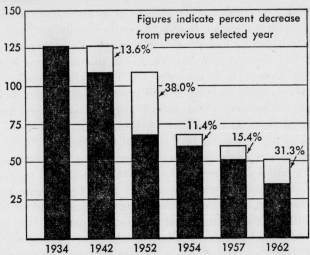

Thousands of School Districts

Figures indicate percent decrease from previous selected year

13.6%

38.0%

11.4%

15.4%

31.3%

1934 1942 1952 1954 1957 1962

Figure 13. *Number of Independent School Districts in Selected Years.*

to other districts for the education of their pupils. Another one-eighth of the districts had fewer than 15 pupils and an additional one-sixth had enrollments of between 15 and 49 pupils.[14] Thus nearly 47 percent of the public school systems had no schools or operated schools with fewer than 50 pupils.

In the years ahead, it is highly probable that reduction in school districts will continue. While it is difficult to establish meaningful school district population criteria, two recent studies have both advanced the standard of 1,200 pupils as a desirable school enrollment. A careful study of New York schools concluded that, "the school population of any district should be sufficiently large that an educational program designed to meet the abilities, needs, interests, and activities of all children from the kindergarten to the twelfth grade inclusive may be provided. The minimum total population to insure this program should be approximately 6,000 with a school population of approximately 1,200 pupils."[15] A decade later the National Commission on School Reorganization advanced the

[14] Bureau of the Census, *op. cit.,* p. 4.
[15] A. G. Grace and G. A. Moe, *State Aid and School Costs,* McGraw-Hill, 1938, p. 67.

same standard that each administrative school unit should have at least 1,200 pupils between the ages of 6 and 18. The Commission went on to state that no elementary school should have fewer than 175 pupils with seven teachers and that no junior or senior high school should have fewer than 300 pupils and 12 teachers.[16]

Of the school systems existing in 1962, 58 of every 100 had fewer than 150 pupils. However, the enrollment in these districts comprised only 1.6 percent of the total school population. These figures are evidence that further consolidations are in order. On the other hand, some alarm has been expressed in recent years over the loss of citizen and parental interest in the public schools when the district becomes too large and the members of the school board are not widely known. On the basis of the 1962 figures, only 2.9 percent of the over 37,000 public school systems had enrollments of 6,000 or more pupils; however, these schools concentrated in large cities, accounted for 52.4 percent of the total pupil enrollment in schools operated by independent school districts.[17] The problem of citizen interest in schools will be commented on more fully in Chapter 21.

A continuing controversy rages concerning the status of the independent school district in our local governmental system. The core of the conflict lies in the question of whether the district should continue as an independent governmental unit or become a "dependent" school system operating as a part of the program of a general purpose local government. The question is certainly not an academic one since schools have the latter status wholly in five states, predominately in seven others, and partially in nine. In large part, the argument is between educators, who support the continued independent status of school districts, and political scientists, who favor the integration of education into the machinery of general units of local government.[18]

In recent years there appears to be a mellowing by both sides in the controversy. Instead of exchanging verbal brickbats in pro-

---

[16] National Commission on School District Reorganization, op. cit., p. 131.

[17] Bureau of the Census, op. cit., pp. 6–7.

[18] For a fuller presentation of these two points of view, see Ernest A. Engelbert, "Education Administration and Responsible Government," School and Society, 75 (January 19, 1952), 33–36; Frederick C. McLaughlin, "Local Government and School Control," ibid, (April 5, 1952), 211–4; W. F. Fordyce, "Independent School Board," ibid. 214–6; Robert L. Morlan, "Toward City-School District Rapprochement," Public Administration Review, 18 (Spring, 1958), 113–7; and Thomas H. Eliot, "Toward an Understanding of Public School Politics," American Political Science Review, 53 (December, 1959), 1032–51.

fessional journals, both see some merits in the arguments of the other and seem to be supporting a policy of closer cooperation between school districts and other local governments. In a number of communities there is continuing and close cooperation between the school and the municipal government in such areas as recreation, parks, libraries, use of public buildings, and adult education programs. This is a hopeful development since such cooperation in programs can result in better and more economical services to the taxpayers supporting both governmental units.

■ Non-School Special Districts

The nature and variety of non-school special districts makes a general description of them quite difficult. However, an attempt at such a description is necessary because of their growing numbers and importance. The Bureau of the Census reported in 1962 that the 18,323 non-school special districts were quite unevenly distributed among the states. Alaska with 6, Hawaii with 16 and West Virginia with 46 had the fewest, while Illinois and California with 2,126 and 1,962 respectively made the greatest use of them. Ten other states each had over 500, while only 10 additional states each had fewer than 100.[19]

An essential first step in discussing special districts is to classify them into managable groupings. One scheme for classification is by function and divides special districts into groups according to the services rendered. Such a division is given in Figure 14. Three types of districts—fire protection, soil conservation, and drainage—accounted for over 43 percent of all special districts in 1962. However, 310 or nearly 2 percent of the districts were concerned with more than one function. The services most frequently rendered by such multi-functional districts involve urban water supply in combination with sanitation, fire protection, irrigation, or flood control.

A second basis for classifying special districts is by the area served. Under this scheme, four such groupings emerge. First, metropolitan or regional districts are created to solve or ameliorate areawide problems encompassing a number of separate govern-

[19] Bureau of the Census, *op. cit.*, p. 8.

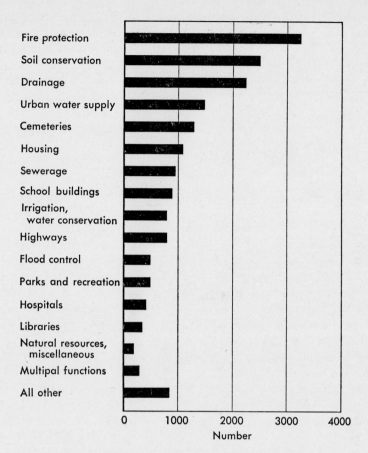

Figure 14. *Number of Special Districts, by Function: 1962.*
(U.S. Bureau of Census, *Census of Governments, 1962*, Vol. I:
Governmental Organization, Washington, 1962, p. 20.)

mental units. An example is the Metropolitan Water District of
Southern California which supplies water to municipalities in six
counties, or the Metropolitan Sanitary District of Greater Chicago.
Second, there are coterminous special districts which have boundaries identical to those of an existing general purpose local government. Such districts are often created for such functions as housing
or parks. Third, special districts are often established in urban
fringe areas bordering on cities to provide municipal-type services
for the residents of these unincorporated areas. Such districts are

created for such varied purposes as water, sewerage, sanitation, street lighting, and fire protection. Fourth, in rural areas special districts are established to meet agricultural needs and provide such functions as soil conservation, drainage and irrigation.[20] In addition to these four basic types, there are a number of other governmental entities bearing some of the characteristics of special districts. These are variably known as dependent districts, quasi-districts, or authorities. Since they are not recognized as independent units of government, being classed as departments of some recognized unit of local government, this type of district will not be discussed further in this chapter, but it is essential to recognize that such entities exist in large numbers in some states and are in addition to those identified as special districts.[21]

THE INCREASE IN SPECIAL DISTRICTS

Since the 1940s, the increase in numbers of special districts has been rapid, showing an increase of 123 percent. Because of their growing importance, the reasons underlying their rapid growth are of considerable consequence to both students and practitioners of local government. Rather than a single all-inclusive cause of growth, there have been a series of factors.

Seven of the major reasons have been identified by Bollens in his thorough study of special districts. He lists: (1) the unsuitability of other existing local units because of the area to be serviced; (2) the unsuitability of other local units because of limitations on their powers to perform and finance needed services; (3) the lack of suitable administrative machinery and willingness to assume new responsibilities by existing local units; (4) the desire for independence by the persons or groups supporting the creation of the special district; (5) the advocacy of special districts by existing units

[20] This classification is adapted from the scheme used in Bollens, *op. cit.*, Chaps. 2–5. His fifth classification is reserved for school districts which have been discussed above.

[21] This number was decreased appreciably in 1962 when the Bureau of the Census included nearly 1,700 of them in its count of special districts. For a fuller discussion of these agencies, see Bollens, *op. cit.*, Chap. 7; Charles F. LeeDecker, "Special Districts in Pennsylvania," *Municipal Finance, 24* (February, 1952), 107–10; and Harold F. Alderfer, "Is 'Authority' Financing the Answer?", *American City, 79* (February, 1955), 115–6; Lennox L. Moak, "Authorities : Boon, Panacea or Menace?", address at a meeting of Philadelphia Regional Chapter, American Society for Public Administration, Philadelphia, April 1, 1958.

to serve a common need; (6) expediency in obtaining a service and the need for only certain types of services in areas not requiring typical services of general-purpose local governments; and (7) the unadorned self-interest or selfishness of some groups and individuals in creating special districts.[22] To these reasons might be added at least two others. One might be called the psychological attraction, since a specific tax is applied for a specific purpose in a prescribed area. The taxpayer is aware of the use to which his money has been put and is sometimes quite willing to support such services.[23] A second reason relates to the general efforts of the reform movement in local government to "keep politics out of government." The special purpose district with its governing board appears to be less subject to partisan influence than a department or commission existing within a general purpose local government. Certainly this belief has been a factor in the continuing separate status of school districts and it has probably been influential in seeking this independence for other special purpose districts as well.

Of the nine reasons which have been advanced for their creation, it is probable that the area and financing needs have been most important. The area factor would be quite important in establishing the two types classified as metropolitan and urban fringe districts. Since both of these types provide services to citizens living in several different jurisdictions, the special district device provides a means whereby the existing governmental units are least affected and yet no one of them assumes the new function, which might arouse jurisdictional jealousy and discontent. The need to circumvent restrictions on the taxing and borrowing powers of existing units is also a highly important factor. As a new unit, the special district has taxing and borrowing powers of its own and this provides a means for obtaining the needed moneys or borrowing potential to finance the essential capital improvements to render the needed services.

In most instances, it is a combination of the specific reasons listed above rather than a single one which results in the creation of any particular special district. It is evident that a number of the underlying causes are not independent but are intertwined to a

[22] Bollens, *op. cit.*, pp. 6–15.
[23] This factor is discussed more fully in Emmett Asseff, *Special Districts in Louisiana*, Louisiana State University Bureau of Government Research, Baton Rouge, 1951, p. 3.

considerable degree. The reasons underlying their creation also point out some of the potential problems of maintaining democratic local control over the districts once they have been created. These problems will be discussed in the concluding section of this chapter which evaluates the strengths and weaknesses of special districts as they now function.

CREATION AND ORGANIZATION

Since special districts are established under state rather than local authority, the state legislature holds the key position in initiating them. In most cases, the pertinent legal base is statutory in form, whether the authorization is by special legislative enactments or general enabling legislation. Sometimes, however, the legal basis to create such districts lies in a constitutional provision. The process of establishment usually begins with action by local residents, either in following procedures detailed in general statutes or in asking the legislature for a special legislative act authorizing the district for the affected area, or to authorize the type of district desired and setting up procedures to be followed by individual communities in creating them.

The procedural steps required to create a special district under general authorization are fairly simple and uniform, although there is considerable variation in the details of such enabling legislation among the states. The first step is initiated with the circulation of petitions requesting the creation of a special district. The petitions must specify the type of district to be created, define the area to be serviced, and be signed by a specified number of qualified voters residing in the area or by owners of a determined percentage of the property within the area. Second, the petition is filed with a designated governmental agency which is normally the governing board of the county or the judge of a court serving the area. The power of the approving agency varies considerably. In some states, the petition is checked merely to confirm its compliance with provisions of the enabling law. In other states, the agency conducts hearings on the proposal and is empowered to determine the desirability and suitability of the proposed district. If approval by the reviewing agency is obtained, the third step consists of a local referendum on the proposal. Normally the election is open to all qualified voters in the area but it may be limited to property owners only. If the popular vote is favorable, the special district is established by a resolution or order of the county board or court as the final step in the process.[24]

The organizational pattern for the governing of special districts also reflects considerable variety. The general governing body is ordinarily a plural-member board which is made up in one of four ways. First, the board may be made up of independently elected members chosen by the voters at large or from subdivisions of the district. Second, the board members may be appointed by some other governmental agency—generally the agency which supervised and proclaimed its establishment. Third, the board may be composed of *ex officio* members holding their positions on the district board because of their positions in other local governments. Fourth, the board may consist of members selected by the governing bodies of local governments within the district. In a few districts, a single district administrator rather than a board is entrusted with the general management. The size of the governing boards vary, but the most common numbers are three, five, or seven members who are known as commissioners, supervisors, directors, or trustees. In boards of the fourth type, the number of members depends on the number of participating local governments and their populations, since additional representation is often granted to larger constituent units. Terms of office of members range from two to six years, with three- or four-year terms most common.

The governing board of the special district is vested with two general classes of power. As a unit of local government, the district possesses the general powers common to other local governments, e.g., the power to sue, hold property, and make contracts. In addition, the district has the more specific authority to discharge the service or services for which it was created.[25] This district's board has the authority to select its employees, to authorize expenditures, to tax and borrow, and to establish policies concerning its operations. As is true of other local governments, the special district possesses and can exercise only those powers conferred upon it and these are subject to whatever statutory or constitutional limitations exist. Their sources of revenue are usually quite narrow but

[24] Stanley Scott and John C. Bollens, *Special Districts in California Local Government*, Berkeley, University of California, Bureau of Public Administration, 1949, pp. 4-5.
[25] *Ibid.*, pp. 3-4.

include local taxes, special assessments, service charges, and inter-governmental grants. These will be discussed more fully in Chapter 18, which concerns tax structures of local governments.

The administrative practices of special district boards also vary from state to state. Board meetings range in frequency from once a year to monthly or even weekly meetings. Some boards handle many of the administrative details in their districts, but if the services of the district are such that full-time supervision is required, the board members usually select the person or persons so needed rather than engage in the actual operation themselves. The meetings of the board are usually attended only by board members even though they are open to interested citizens and to coverage by the local press. This lack of citizen interest in the affairs of special districts is unfortunate since the same disinterestedness is too often characteristic of the governing bodies which create or are represented on the district's governing board.

■ An Evaluation of Special Districts

As a form of local government of increasing numbers and importance, the special district has both ardent supporters and vocal critics. In a statement which recognizes that the use of special districts has both advantageous and disadvantageous results, Bollens writes "Not all of their deviations from widely known governmental molds and practices are beneficial, and in total their characteristics are a mixed blessing."[26] The nature of the "mixed blessing" will be quite apparent in the discussion of particular characteristics which follows since most of the advantages can be reworded into disadvantages, depending upon their application in particular districts.

From the list of reasons for their creation enumerated above, it is evident that special districts do make possible the provision of governmental services to meet the need of citizens in areas whose boundaries are not coterminous with those of existing general purpose local governments. This device enables existing governments to cooperate on an acceptable basis which keeps the separate units in control of all services except those entrusted to the special district. It also avoids the jurisdictional jealousies which would arise if one existing unit attempted to render the same service on

[26] Bollens, *op. cit.,* p. 251.

an areawide basis. While the provision of services is advantageous, the divisive effects of the functional approach has inherent disadvantages. As noted by Roscoe Martin, "Interest and concern tends to become program-centered rather than county-city-state centered, and loyalties tend to follow interest and concern. In short, program (or administrative) loyalties tend to supplant the geographic loyalties of other days."[27]

The use of the special district to expand the taxing and borrowing power of local units is another heralded advantage which can be overdone. By creating this new unit, a community on its own or in cooperation with adjoining units may be able to finance some needed public service which it could not otherwise provide because of taxing and debt limitations. However, it is obvious that the revenue must come from the pockets of the same citizens. If the financial limitations on the existing local governments are reasonable ones, then their circumvention through the creation of a new unit is not commendable.

Allied with the total financial picture is the question of the desirability of earmarking revenues for particular services at the local level. This problem has been succinctly presented by Asseff in these words. "The use of the special district destroys, to a large extent, the necessary flexibility of financial policy which all governments must have today in order to handle most effectively and efficiently the changing and complex problems with which they are faced. The dedication of any revenue to a particular function, and this results when a special district is credited, means that that revenue must be spent for that particular purpose even though at a later date there is a greater need for it elsewhere."[28] It would be quite possible for a local government which participated in several special districts to be sadly in need of revenues at a time when some of the single-purpose districts (including the independent school district) might have a surplus of funds on hand.

A fourth feature concerns the "out of politics" operation by boards of special districts. It may be quite desirable to have services provided by employees chosen primarily on the basis of merit rather than on partisan influence or loyalty. However, too often special districts do not exhibit any features of standard merit

---

[27] Roscoe Martin, "Therefore is the Name—Babel," *National Municipal Review*, *40* (February, 1951), 70-74.

[28] Asseff, *op. cit.*, p. 61.

systems in their employment practices. Partisan loyalty is tossed aside in favor of personal loyalty and the citizen is not afforded the safety of party responsibility as a screening device. The "out of politics" feature also indirectly implies a lack of direct citizen control, since this, too, would be political. In districts where board members are appointed by other officials, such persons are removed from the direct control of the voters and are seldom subject to removal by recall through citizen action. Thus, the lack of effective and continuing citizen control over special districts is a serious problem which needs careful attention if such units are to continue as agencies of local democratic government.

Special districts are also often defended as devices whereby already overburdened general-purpose local governments are relieved of the responsibility of providing one or more additional services. But in practice, special districts have tended to be detrimental rather than helpful to general local governments. Local governments are not strengthened by by-passing them in providing certain services or in removing part of the community's taxing resources from their control and placing these in single-purpose districts. Rather this process weakens these general units, so it appears desirable to lighten their responsibilities even further by creating new special districts to perform other specific functions more "efficiently." The rapid growth of special districts can only contribute to a general weakening of other units of local government, making them less responsive and responsible; this would not be so unfortunate if it were not for the fact that special districts were not designed to be responsive or responsible to the citizens they serve.

There can be no denial of the fact that the special district represents a political response to the needs of citizens for services. As such, it represents an attempt to innovate within the American system in a way that meets specific needs but does not seriously alter the structure of local government. As such units operate, they achieve the first half of their general goal quite effectively (though often not very economically in terms of duplication, overlapping, small-scale operations, etc.), but fail on the second count. Special districts weaken other local governments and further fragment citizen responsibility and control. This is a serious price to pay for a single service or a limited number of services, and this core issue must be clearly faced up to in the near future.

SUGGESTED READINGS

Books

Asseff, Emmett, *Special Districts in Louisiana* (Baton Rouge: Bureau of Government Research, Louisiana State University, 1951).

Bollens, John C., *Special District Governments in the United States* (Berkeley: University of California Press, 1957).

Henry, Nelson B. and Kerwin, J. G., *Schools and City Government* (Chicago: University of Chicago Press, 1938).

National Commission on School District Reorganization, *Your School District* (Washington: National Education Association, 1948).

Scott, Stanley and Bollens, John C., *Special Districts in California Local Government* (Berkeley: Bureau of Public Administration, University of California, 1949).

Snider, Clyde F., *Local Government in Rural America* (New York: Appleton-Century-Crofts, 1957).

U. S. Bureau of the Census, *1957 Census of Government,* Vol. 1, No. 1, Washington, 1957.

Articles

Alderfer, Harold F., "Is 'Authority' Financing the Answer?" *American City,* 79 (February, 1955), 115–6.

Brown, Robert H., "The Composition of School Boards," *American School Board Journal, 129* (August, 1954), 23–24.

Contalonis, G. T., "Some Powers and Duties of School Boards," *American School Board Journal, 129* (October, 1954), 27–28.

Eliot, Thomas H., "Toward an Understanding of Public School Politics," *American Political Science Review, 53* (December, 1959), 1032–51.

Engelbert, Ernest A., "Education Administration and Responsible Government," *School and Society, 75* (January 19, 1952), 33–36.

LeeDecker, Charles F., "Special Districts in Pennsylvania," *Municipal Finance, 24* (February, 1952), 107–10.

Martin, Roscoe, "Therefore is the Name—Babel," *National Municipal Review, 40* (February, 1951), 70–74.

McLaughlin, F. C., "Local Government and School Control," *School and Society, 75* (April 5, 1952), 211–4.

Morlan, Robert L., "Toward City-School District Rapprochement," *Public Administration Review, 18* (Spring, 1958), 113–7.

Porter, Kirk H., "A Plague of Special Districts," *National Municipal Review, 22,* (November, 1933), 544–7, 574.

Scott, Stanley and Bollens, John C., "Special Districts in California Local Government," *Western Political Quarterly, 3* (June, 1950), 233–43.

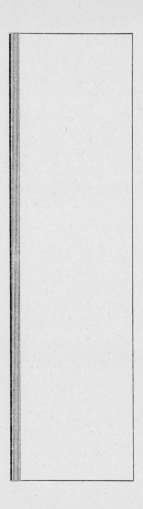

PROCESSES OF
LOCAL GOVERNMENT

Four

The Legislative Process

13

Anyone who is presently serving or has served as a member of a local legislative body can appreciate the definition of democracy once advanced by William James. He observed that democracy is a system in which the government does something and waits to see who "hollers"; then it does something else to relieve the "hollering" as best it can and waits to see who reacts by "hollering" at the adjustment so it can take further action.[1] Since the agency of local government most empowered to "do something" is the local lawmaking body, this description of democracy is also fairly accurate for the legislative process in local government. In addition to their function of establishing major policy decisions for their community, local legislatures hold the key position in the exercise of the general powers granted by the state to the several types of local governmental units. Unless such powers are specifically conferred upon a particular officer or agency, courts have held that such general powers reside in the local law-making body.

[1] T. V. Smith, *The Promise of American Politics,* University of Chicago Press, 1936, pp. 199–200.

■ Local Legislative Authorities

As noted in Chapters 9 through 12, the policy-determining authority in local government is normally vested in a plural-membered, popularly elected board variously known as a board, council, commission or committee. In counties, the governing board which is entrusted with the ordinance-making power is most frequently called the board of commissioners or board of supervisors. However, the titles of county court, commissioners court, fiscal court, and board of commissioners of roads and revenues are each found in over 100 counties. To the extent that legislative power is conferred on county governments by state legislatures, it is exercised by the county board, whatever its specific title.

In most cities in the United States, the city council is vested with policy-determining and ordinance-making powers. In commission-governed cities, this power lies in the board of commissioners; and in other cities, this council may be known as a board of aldermen. The law-making body in villages and boroughs is the local council or board of trustees, burgesses, or commissioners. And in townships, the local legislative body is known as the board of supervisors, commissioners, or trustees. In New England towns with the town meeting form of government, the legislative power is still vested, in large part, in the whole citizenry meeting in annual session. However, the board of selectmen exercise some functions of legislative bodies and the chosen delegates fulfill the role of the whole citizenry in towns with the representative town meeting form of government.

The general pattern of a plural-member governing board is also found in both school and non-school special districts. While special districts, in general, have a very restricted legislative or ordinance-making power, they do have discretion in matters of policy-determination and function as other local legislative bodies in this regard.

■ The Legislative Function

The principle of separation of powers so basic in our national and state governments is not a feature common to all types of local units. However, the vital function known as the legislative process is fulfilled in all units of local government. Except in communities retaining the pure town meeting form of government, the law-making body consists of chosen representatives rather than an assembly of all the citizens. However, the functions of local legislative bodies are the same, whether they consist of all the citizens or of their selected representatives.

Broadly described, the legislative process in local government has five major aspects. These are policy leadership, enactment of ordinances and resolutions, debate, criticism, and investigation. The latter four are historic prerogatives of legislative bodies throughout all of western civilization while the first—policy leadership—is primarily a result of American experience.[2] The distrust of strong executives in colonial America encouraged legislative bodies to exercise a greater voice in community decision making and this tradition was carried over after independence from England was won. The frontier influence of egalitarianism also encouraged the development of legislative rather than executive power.

Local government theory still holds to the traditional concept of legislative supremacy through its policy-making powers, but in actual practice the local governing board's role is often one of policy ratification rather than policy innovation. There is agreement, however, that the local governing board "determines" all municipal policies which are not set forth in the charter itself or specifically granted to some other officer or agency of local government. By using the verb "determine" to connote the local legislature's role, the possible conflict between theory and practice can be avoided, since this more neutral verb can cover both innovating and ratifying actions. While law-making bodies are called upon to make a large number of policy decisions, the biggest single policy determination faced by local legislators is the adoption of the community's budget. This one decision allocates relative emphases among the several programs and services carried on within the community and apportions the community's resources to carry them out.

After agreement on questions of policy or other matters has been reached by the local legislators, the decision is implemented through the enactment of a local law. Such enactments are variously known as ordinances or resolutions. The several rather clearly defined procedural steps which are followed by the law-making body in passing a local law or rule will be described in a subsequent section of this chapter.

[2] Charles R. Adrian, *State and Local Government*, McGraw-Hill, New York, 1960, pp. 286-7.

The functions of debate and criticism are traditional functions of legislative bodies at all levels of government. Debate or discussion is essential in reaching a consensus so that a policy can be announced or an ordinance enacted. John Stuart Mill assigned two important functions to national legislatures which are also highly relevant to local bodies. These are the functions of serving as a Committee of Grievances and as a Congress of Opinions.[3] In fulfilling these functions, local legislative bodies find frequent opportunities for debate and criticism as well as a chance to provide citizens with a means to express their opinions and make known their wishes. In Mill's words, "I know not how a representative assembly can more usefully employ itself than in talk, when the subject of the talk is the great public interests of the country [community], and every sentence of it represents the opinion either of some important body of persons . . ., or of an individual in whom some such body have reposed their confidence."[4]

The investigative function of local legislative bodies has assumed increased importance in recent years. For one reason, citizen interest in local government has risen as local tax levies have increased. Thus, citizens often request more extensive hearings and investigations before new functions are assumed or older services expanded. The legislative investigation has also grown in importance as a legislative check or threat of check into the activities of local executive officers. A third reason for the increasing importance of the investigative function results from the delegation of certain types of policy formulation to administrative officers or to more specialized boards or commissions. Mill's words on this point are also worth consideration. He states that, "The business of the elective body (in local government) is not to do the work, but to see that it is properly done, and that nothing necessary is left undone. This function can be fulfilled for all departments by the same superintending body; and by a collective and comprehensive far better than by a minute and microscopic view."[5]

In addition to the several aspects of the legislative function discussed above, a number of local legislative bodies have administrative functions to perform. This is especially true of county governing boards and of commissions in commission-governed cities. A number of legislative bodies, however, exercise administrative

[3] John Stuart Mill, *Representative Government,* Everyman's Edition, 1948, pp. 239–40.
[4] *Ibid.,* p. 240.
[5] *Ibid.,* p. 351.

functions beyond those specifically required of them. This is one function which Mill believed the legislative body should not undertake. In his words, "But a popular assembly is still less fitted to administer, or to dictate in detail to those who have the charge of administration. . . . The proper duty of a representative assembly in regard to matters of administration is not to decide them by its own vote, but to take care that the persons who have to decide them shall be the proper persons."[6]

■ The Role of the Legislator

Representation occurs when a person is chosen to stand in place of another person or group of people. While there are a number of methods by which representatives or agents can be selected, direct election is the means most commonly used at the local level. Only the members of governing boards of some school and other special districts are chosen by other means, and popular vote is the most common method of selecting school board members. The concept of representation is basic to representative government since it is founded on the principle that certain individuals will be chosen to act for the community on matters of policy for a fixed period of time.

Although there is general agreement concerning the concept of representation, there is no unanimity of opinion concerning the proper function or role of the representative. Yet the relationship between the chosen agent of the people and his constituency is at the very core of representational theory. Basically, there are two conflicting theories. The first holds that the representative is a free agent and is to use his own judgment as to the particular decisions he arrives at, within the general concept of advancing the public interest. The second holds that the representative is merely an agent of those who elect him and that he is bound to act in accordance with definite instructions from his electors.

These two basic role concepts are well-defined and distinguished in a careful study of state legislators.[7] The first type identified above is labeled a "trustee" and the second a "delegate." The trustee has

---

[6] *Ibid.*, pp. 231, 233.

[7] Heinz Eulau, John C. Wahlke, William Buchanan and Leroy C. Ferguson, "The Role of the Representative: Some Empirical Observations on the Theory of Edmund Burke," *American Political Science Review,* 53 (September, 1959), 742-56.

two major characteristics: "First, a moralistic interpretation: the representative is a free agent, he follows what he considers right or just—his convictions or principles, the dictates of his conscience. Second, a rational conception: he follows his own judgments based on an assessment of the facts in each case, his understanding of the problems involved, his thoughtful appraisal of the sides at issue."[8] The characteristics of the delegate's concept of his role are as follows: "All Delegates are, of course, agreed that they should not use their independent judgment or convictions as criteria of decision-making. But this does not mean that they feel equally committed to follow instructions, from whatever clientele. Some merely speak of consulting their constituents, though implying that such consultation will have a mandatory effect on their behavior. Others frankly acknowledge their direct dependence on instructions and accept them as a necessary or desirable premise for their decisions. Some may even follow instructions counter to their own judgment or principles."[9]

Obviously, the two roles described above are not always mutually exclusive. Recognizing the need for a third category, the role of "politico" was also described. This type of representative differs from the other two types because, "Depending on circumstances, a representative may hold the Trustee orientation at one time, and the Delegate orientation at another time. . . . The Politico as a representational role type differs from both the Trustee and the Delegate in that he is more sensitive to conflicting alternatives in role assumption, more flexible in the way he resolves the conflict of alternatives, and less dogmatic in his representational style as it is relevant to his decision-making behavior."[10]

The contrast between the roles of a trustee-oriented and a delegate-oriented legislator in a small community is noted by Vidich and Bensman. In their study, local councilmen held one of two self-perceived roles:

". . . Some drew an analogy between the functions of the councilmen and the member of the corporation board of directors. Others viewed themselves as a vehicle through which the wishes of the public could be translated into public action.

The first view implies that the public interest is both ascertainable

[8] *Ibid.*, p. 749.
[9] *Ibid.*, p. 750.
[10] *Ibid.*

and indivisible. The good of the city, like the good of the corporation, must be stated in all-encompassing terms. This requires the councilman to view himself not as a delegate, but as a person possessing a mandate to use his own judgment in solving the problems presented to him. This judgment is shaped not only by his personal values, but by the exchange of views on the council. Thus the councilman is a participant in a dialogue which "serves the interest of all the people."

The second view asserts instead that the job of the legislator is to do what the people, both individually and collectively, want. The councilman is a public servant who should entertain the requests and grievances of citizens and attempt to accommodate their desires, if it is possible within the framework of the law. The public interest is articulated by the adjustment of individual claims expressed through the representatives. Each councilman is an advocate of what he believes to be his constituents' desires.[11]

The actual functions and responsibilities of local legislators have been described by a number of writers. According to F. N. Mac-Millin, the job of a local alderman consists of five basic principal commitments. First, it must be his policy to serve all citizens rather than special interests or groups. Second, as a member of the governing board, he should concentrate on broad policy matters rather than on administrative and minor details. Third, he should strive to maintain a balance among the several services provided for the citizens and apply the same standards of efficiency and adequacy in measuring particular services. Fourth, it is his function to anticipate problems and needs rather than to react to them. And, fifth, an alderman must have the courage of his convictions once he has made up his mind.[12] It is obvious that these are sane principles for all local lawmakers to adopt and follow.

Arthur W. Bromage advances a tenfold classification of traits of city councilmen which also have relevance to all local legislators.[13] These are: (1) a willingness to serve which for most comes from a sense of duty and a desire to serve the public interest; (2) an ability to recognize names and faces to give government a personal touch; (3) a desire to be re-elected; (4) a desire to sit tight without tipping their hand until they estimate how to vote on a particular

[11] A. J. Vidich and Joseph Bensman, *Small Town in Mass Society,* Princeton University Press, 1958, p. 110.

[12] F. N. MacMillin, "The Job of an Alderman," *The Municipality, 45* (June, 1950), 117.

[13] Arthur W. Bromage, "Ten Traits of City Councilmen," *Public Management, 33* (April, 1951), 74–77.

question; (5) a personality not adverse to publicity; (6) a talent for taking administrators with a grain of salt; (7) a talent for taking experts with two grains of salt; (8) a generalist approach except in handling fellow-citizens and taxpayers; (9) physical stamina; and (10) a willingness to compromise.

In all fairness to local legislators, it is important to state that many of them have no conception of themselves in any particular "role" nor do they have a preconceived concept of how they are to function except to "serve the community." The nature of their service, however, may depend in large part on whether they assume that their function is to reflect the views of their constituents or to represent them for the period of their term in office.

■ Methods of Selection

The problem of electoral areas in local government is essentially similar to that existing at other levels—how to make a fair division of territory so that the elected representatives have approximately equal numbers of citizens as constituents. Many units of local government avoid this problem by electing all their legislators in at-large elections. This pattern is particularly common among cities as indicated in Table 5, which shows that 60 percent of all cities of over 5,000 population use this system. The frequency of at-large elections varies considerably with the type of governmental structure in cities. In 1963, at-large election of councilmen occurred in 94 percent of commission cities, 93 percent of town meeting governed cities, 83 percent of representative town meeting cities, 78 percent of council-manager cities, and 46 percent of mayor-council governed cities.[14]

At-large elections of local lawmakers normally operate in one of two ways. First, the election might really be an at-large one in that all the voters may vote for the number of candidates to be elected, with the candidates residing anywhere within the boundaries of the local governing unit. This system is the most common. Second, while all voters may vote for the number of candidates to be selected, there are district residence areas within the unit and candidates must come from these internal election areas. This pattern is found

[14] International City Managers' Association, *Municipal Year Book, 1963*, p. 163.

Table 5. *Type and Method of Councilman Election in Cities Over 5,000*

	Cities Reporting	TYPE OF ELECTION		Cities Reporting	METHOD OF ELECTION		
		Partisan	Non-Partisan		At-Large	Ward	Combination
Form of Government:							
Mayor–Council	1,551	51%	49%	1,551	46%	31%	23%
Commission	246	37	63	242	94	5	1
Council–Manager	1,142	15	85	1,155	78	12	10
Town Meeting	14	50	50	14	93	0	7
Representative Town Meeting	17	24	76	18	83	17	0
Population Group:							
Over 500,000	20	35	65	20	45	20	35
250,000–500,000	31	23	77	31	64	10	26
100,000–250,000	78	38	62	77	66	13	21
50,000–100,000	194	31	69	192	57	23	19
25,000– 50,000	400	29	71	398	62	19	19
10,000– 25,000	1,010	37	63	1,001	62	20	18
5,000– 10,000	1,237	38	62	1,245	60	25	15
All Cities over 5,000	2,970	37%	63%	2,964	60%	22%	17%

SOURCE: International City Managers' Association, *The Municipal Year Book,* 1963, Chicago, 1963, p. 163.

in over 50 cities and in many counties; the three or five county commissioners or supervisors are elected by all the voters but the board members are required to be residents of particular areas within the county.

The advantages of at-large election of local legislators are several in number. First, it enables the election of the best of the willing candidates without regard to their area of residence. Second, it makes it possible to place the interests of the whole community above district or ward interests. Third, it eliminates the possibility of gerrymandering and the frequent need to redraw district boundaries to keep up with population shifts. Fourth, this plan generally results in smaller governing bodies than is true of ward or district plans. At-large elections, however, are not without their disadvantages. The council may be so small that it is not adequately representative of a diversified citizenry. Second, a reasonably strong and disciplined minority may receive no actual representation on the council or board. Third, at-large elections lengthen the ballot and increase the voter's responsibility to inform himself about several candidates rather than one. Fourth, at-large elections increase the campaign costs of some candidates while other potential candidates without adequate financial backing may not seek election. Requiring local legislators to live in the wards or districts they represent but be voted on by the whole community combines some of the good features while eliminating some of the possible disadvantages. This plan results in representation of the various geographical sections of the community while still encouraging the elected representatives to work for the interests of the whole community as well as for those of the areas of their own residence.

The second most common electoral pattern is to elect all local legislators by wards within cities or townships within counties. This system exists in 22 percent of the cities over 5,000 population and in nearly one-third of all American counties. The advantages of the ward system may be stated briefly as follows: (1) the chosen representative serves as the voice of his district or ward and as the point of citizen access for his constituency; (2) the representative understands the special needs of his district and can represent those interests more knowingly than an at-large legislator; (3) the system provides a better opportunity for minority representation on the governing council or board; and (4) the voter has fewer representatives to choose and can be better informed on their relative merits. Disadvantages of the plan include these points: (1) district needs are placed above community needs by some legislators; (2) such legislators may become "errand boys" of special interests; (3) the districts become unequal in size, resulting in unfair representation or gerrymandering; and (4) better qualified candidates may be residents of the same ward or few wards, but only one from each ward can be elected. As a result, successful candidates in some wards may be less able than unsuccessful contestants in other wards.

A third pattern, combining election of some legislators at large and some by ward, is becoming increasingly common in American cities. This system now exists in 17 percent of the cities of over 5,000 in population and in 35 percent of cities of over 500,000 population. The home-rule charter of Philadelphia adopted in 1951 provides for the election of 10 councilmen from districts and seven from the city at large, while in Buffalo nine of 15 councilmen are selected from wards with six elected at large, and in Houston three are elected at large with five from wards. It is obvious that this plan seeks to maximize the potential merits of both systems while minimizing their potential weaknesses. Results to date are encouraging, since voters in cities using this plan seem quite pleased with the results of their mixed systems.

A fourth electoral system of local legislators utilizes the principle of limited voting or the system of proportional representation. Both devices are essentially means to achieve minority representation in local law-making bodies. The limited vote system provides that each voter may vote for a number of candidates which is smaller than the total number of representatives to be elected. In a number of American counties with three-member boards, each voter is permitted to vote for only two candidates. Thus a reasonably large and disciplined minority party can elect one of the three members of the county board. This same principle is incorporated in the Philadelphia charter of 1951 by providing that each elector can vote for only five of the seven councilmen to be elected at large.

While there are several plans of proportional representation, the Hare System is the best known and is in most common use, although it is still not very prevalent. Essentially all such plans provide for representation of parties or groups in proportion to their voting strengths. As the Hare System operates, the voter indicates his numerical preference among the several candidates by placing a "1" behind the candidate of his first choice, a "2" behind his second choice, and so on. To be elected, a candidate must receive a "quota" of votes which is determined by dividing the total number of votes cast by the number of places to be filled and then adding one. The quotient stated in terms of the next highest whole number then becomes the "quota." For example, if 14,000 votes are cast with seven councilmen to be elected, the quota is 2,001 votes. The process of vote tabulation is a time-consuming one since it involves the elimination of candidates with the lowest vote totals and the transfer of their votes to the other candidates until the number to be elected have all received totals equal to or greater than the "quota" required for election.

Proportional representation is still the method recommended by the National Municipal League in its model city and county charters. The advantages claimed for this system include: (1) it provides for the fair representation of local parties and groups in proportion to their relative voting strengths; (2) it makes boss or machine control of the local board more difficult because of the board's more varied composition; (3) it eliminates primary elections and saves both the taxpayer and candidate money; (4) it encourages able independents to run since the system is conducive to cleaner campaigns; emphasis is on achieving the necessary "quota" rather than in defeating other candidates; and (5) it eliminates gerrymandering and unfair districting since candidates run at large or from a small number of plural-membered districts. Opponents of proportional representation advance the following arguments against the system: (1) it weakens our conventional two-party system and the concept of party responsibility; (2) it is too complicated in its mechanics, resulting in many spoiled ballots; (3) there is a long delay in ascertaining the outcome of elections because of the time necessary to count and transfer votes; (4) it makes the development of an effective local leadership within the council very difficult, and such direction may come from an outside source; and (5) it is a divisive force which splits local governing councils into factions, necessitating coalitions which often give small groups too great a bargaining power with a larger group trying to obtain their support.[15]

As indicated in Table 5 above, the members of the local governing boards are elected on a ballot without party designation in nearly two out of every three cities of over 5,000 population. This number includes 13 of the 20 cities of over 500,000 and 24 of the 31 cities with populations between 250,000 and 500,000. Members of school boards and other special districts are also usually selected without party designation, but most county and township elections are still conducted on a partisan base. In California and Minnesota all county elections are of the non-partisan type and specific county offices in other states are also non-partisan. The offices of county superintendent of schools and judge are often filled in this manner. Ohio law specifies that all township elections are to be non-partisan. However, these are exceptions to the more general pattern of partisan elections in county and township governments. As discussed in

[15] For a more thorough study of proportional representation see George H. Hallett, Jr., *Proportional Representation: The Key to Democracy*, National Municipal League, New York, 1940. It might be inferred from the title that the objectivity of this study could be questioned.

Chapter 7, one or all the local parties in many communities bear labels which have no counterparts among the national parties.

■ Structure of Local Councils

The basic structure of local governing bodies was discussed in pertinent sections in Chapters 9 to 12. While county boards vary in size from one to over 100 members, by far the most common size was boards of three or five commissioners or supervisors. The number of councilmen in cities of over 5,000 population is shown in Table 6. While the range in number is from two to 50, the median

Table 6. *Number of Councilmen in Cities over 5,000*

Population Group	Mayor–Council Range	Mayor–Council Median	Commission Range	Commission Median	Council–Manager Range	Council–Manager Median
Over 500,000	7–50	15	–	–	–	–
250,000–500,000	4–41	9	4–7	5	5–13	9
100,000–250,000	5–33	9	3–9	5	5–12	7
50,000–100,000	4–40	9	3–13	5	4–18	7
25,000– 50,000	3–25	9	3–7	5	3–20	5
10,000– 25,000	3–20	7	3–9	5	3–18	5
5,000– 10,000	3–19	6	2–9	4	2–15	5
All Cities over 5,000	3–50	6	2–13	5	2–20	5

SOURCE: International City Managers' Association, *The Municipal Year Book, 1963,* Chicago, 1963, p. 162.

numbers were seven councilmen in mayor-council cities and five members in both commission and council-manager cities. Boards of selectmen in New England towns with town meeting government ranged from three to nine, with three the most common number. Village boards parallel those of New England towns in size, with three or five the most common numbers of members. Three is also the most common number of members found on governing boards of townships, school districts, and special districts, although the range in each case included some boards of five, seven, and nine members.

As this table reveals, there is a tendency for councils to increase in size of membership as the population of cities increases. Thus, with the mayor-council form of government the median number of councilmen in cities of over 500,000 is 15 in contrast to seven for all cities of over 5,000. This same generalization holds true for counties in which the board is composed of township representatives and for New England towns. A second variable concerning size of local councils is the form of government in the community. For instance, county boards composed of supervisors are larger than those with commissioners as the two types were distinguished in Chapter 9. Table 6 reveals the same phenomenon in city government. Councils in mayor-council cities are larger than those in council-manager cities which in turn have more members than boards in commission-governed cities when cities are 50,000 or larger.

Terms of office of local legislators range from one to six years. One-year terms are found in cities with the town meeting form while six-year terms are found in some counties and in a few commission and council-manager cities. By far the most common lengths of terms are two and four years, with four-year terms becoming more general in recent years. With four-year terms, it is common to have staggered terms of office so that half of the positions on the local governing board are filled at each biennial election. In cities of over 100,000 the more common pattern is not to provide overlapping terms, so that the entire council membership is elected at four-year intervals. Pertinent data relating to terms of councilmen in cities are given in Figure 15.

The bicameral council which was a common feature of city governments in the eighteenth and nineteenth centuries has now virtually disappeared. As of 1961, only four New England cities retained the two-chamber legislature, and the Board of Estimate functioned largely as an upper chamber for New York City. Waterville, Maine, and Danbury, Connecticut, both under 25,000, have boards of councilmen and smaller boards of aldermen. In Everett and Springfield, Massachusetts, cities of 43,000 and 174,000 respectively, the larger chamber is composed of councilmen elected by wards and the smaller body consists of aldermen elected at large. The City Council of New York is composed of members elected by wards, while the Board of Estimate has an *ex officio* membership consisting of the mayor, controller, and president of the council, and the president of each of the five boroughs of the city. The powers of the

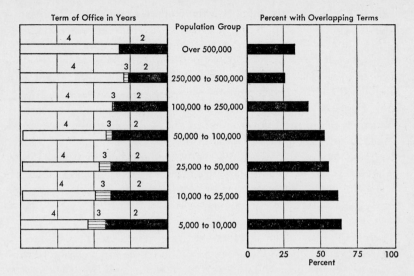

Term of Office in Years	Population Group	Percent with Overlapping Terms

Figure 15. *Percentage Distribution of Length of Councilmanic Terms by Population Groups, Cities over 5,000.* (International City Managers' Association, *Municipal Year Book, 1963*, Chicago, 1963, p. 163).

Board are both financial and ordinance-making. It receives the city's budget, holds hearings and is free to alter the proposed budget as it sees fit. After approval by the Board, the budget goes to the city council which has more limited financial powers and can only reduce or delete items from the budget. According to a recent study of New York City government, the city council has "no important power in adopting local laws which the Board does not share on equal terms; the Board is, in effect, the upper chamber in a bicameral city legislature."[16]

■ *Council Organization and Operation*

While the internal organization and procedures of local legislative bodies varies considerably among the several types of local units and among various sizes of units, there are several general

[16] Wallace S. Sayre and Herbert Kaufman, *Governing New York City*, Russell Sage Foundation, New York, 1960, p. 627. The five borough presidents each have two votes, while the mayor, controller and council president each have four votes.

principles which can be identified. The first is the need for and functions of a presiding officer. This person may be elected to the position of chairman of the board as in the case of the supervisor in townships, the mayor in commission cities, and the board chairman in some counties. More typically, the chairman or presiding officer is elected by the members of the legislative body itself. The functions of this officer are to conduct the meetings of the council, appoint members of committees, and serve as the general spokesman for the governing board. In "weak executive" forms, the chief executive is likely also to be the presiding officer of the council.

Generally speaking, little use is made of committees in councils consisting of five or fewer members since the board is small enough to handle the affairs of the community as a group. However, as the size of the local council increases and as the population of the community rises, council committees become important agencies for transacting the work of the legislative body. In counties with boards composed of township supervisors and in mayor-council governed cities, an elaborate system of standing committees exists. For example, the governing board of Ford County, Illinois, consists of 12 supervisors and two assistant supervisors; the board membership is divided to embrace 23 standing committees to oversee such various activities as finance, police, fire, civil defense, and thistle control.[17]

Where the committee system prevails in local government, the local council as a whole becomes chiefly a ratifying body for approving the actions of its committees. Before matters are considered by the whole body, they are referred to the appropriate committees for consideration and recommendation; it is rare that the council votes to override a recommendation of one of its committees. In some communities, and particularly on some matters, neither the committee nor the governing group as a whole would ordinarily act contrary to the views of the representative from the area most substantially affected.

Meetings of local legislative bodies may be classified into four basic types. The first is the regular session which is held at intervals prescribed by statute or council rule. Meetings of county, township, and school district boards are usually held monthly as is true of small towns and villages. As the size of cities increases, the meetings occur more frequently. In large cities, councilmen may meet at least

[17] Robert Nelson, "Rural Areas Hold on to Counties," *The Christian Science Monitor*, April 25, 1962.

weekly and sometimes almost daily for committee work. The city council of Los Angeles meets in formal session each weekday throughout the year—a distinction believed unique among legislative bodies around the world. The second type of meeting is the adjourned session which is used to convene the council at some date following a regular meeting and before the next regular session. This type of session is most often used when regular meetings are held at more lengthy intervals. County boards in Illinois, for example, are limited to two regular sessions per year, so other meetings are known as adjourned sessions of one of these two regular meetings. The third type is special sessions which may be called in various ways and for a number of purposes. Usually such meetings are called by the presiding officer at his discretion, in response to a request by a certain number of board members, or in response to a request by a prescribed number of citizens within the community. The fourth type might be called the "conference session," and it is an informal executive session called before regular meetings at which time the members consider many of the matters to come up for discussion at the regular meeting.

One writer observed that, "Meetings of small boards are perfunctory, because it is possible for three or five men to determine policies beforehand in a very informal manner. Important matters can be decided on the courthouse steps, in a hotel lobby, or on the street corner . . . and they go into formal session merely to legalize decisions which in effect have already been made."[18] As indicated in Chapter 8, this technique has been banned in a number of states by legislation requiring that local policy-determining bodies hold "open meetings to arrive at decisions openly."

Forms of board or council decisions are normally taken in one of three types of actions—motions, resolutions, or ordinances. Motions are largely internal actions pertaining to such substantive matters in the conduct of council business as adopting reports, instructing officers, and authorizing council proposals for future actions. Resolutions are less important and less authoritative in form than ordinances and are commonly used to accomplish an administrative action. Examples would be an expression of sentiment by the local board on a matter beyond its authority such as a bill before the state legislature, an expression of appreciation for the services of an in-

[18] Kirk H. Porter, *County and Township Government in the United States,* Macmillan, 1922, p. 115.

dividual or group, or the expression of sympathy upon the passing of a local official or long-time employee. Ordinances are the form of action used in laying down a rule that applies generally throughout the community. Typical uses include ordinances setting tax levies, approving appropriation requests, changing the rules or regulations pertaining to some community project or service, and all the more important acts of the local council.[19]

The legislative procedure involved in the enactment of a local ordinance follows a fairly common pattern in all types of local government units. Proposals are introduced in writing by a council member and copies are filed with the clerk or secretary or presented on the floor to each member. This step is known as the first reading of the bill. At this time, the bill is referred to the appropriate committee, if the council operates with a committee system, and also to pertinent administrative officers for the information necessary to weigh the merits of the proposal. During its study of the bill, the committee may hold public hearings or study the bill on its own. Upon the reporting out of the bill, the committee's recommendations will include any amendments to the original bill that it deems desirable. At this point, the bill is given its second reading. Final or third reading of the bill is normally listed on the council agenda so that interested citizens will be aware that the measure is coming up for discussion and can appear before the council to endorse or oppose it. At this third reading, debate on or amendment of the bill are possible before final council action is taken. Upon passage of the bill, it becomes an ordinance and is published in local newspapers and made a part of the codified ordinances of the governmental unit, thus becoming a local law. The process can be speeded up considerably by the local council with a motion to suspend the rules. Approval of such a motion dispenses with the three-reading rule, but this is normally done only for "emergency" bills.[20]

In the conduct of a meeting of a local legislative board or council, there are eight steps in the normal order of business. First, the

[19] In general practice, the title of "resolution" applies to action of most sorts in quasi-municipal corporations such as counties, school districts, and special districts, while the term "ordinance" is used when municipal-type functions (e.g., planning) are involved. Thus, even such important action as adoption of the budget by these units would be by resolution.

[20] For a clear and detailed discussion of the local legislative process see, Emmett L. Bennett, "Legislative Procedures in City Councils," *Public Management*, 17 (July, 1935), 199-205; and Clyde F. Snider, "The Organization and Functions of County Boards in Indiana," *Indiana Law Journal*, 12 (April, 1937), 281-315.

council is called to order and the presence of a quorum of members is determined. The names of those present are recorded in the minutes by the clerk or secretary. Second, minutes of the previous meeting are read, corrected or amended if necessary, and then approved. Third, the presentation of petitions, memorials and remonstrances is called for. Such matters are usually presented by the clerk or secretary unless there is a delegation of citizens present who wish to present matters before the council. Fourth, the reports of officers, standing committees and special committees are received. Following each report, motions are made to adopt them if they contain a recommendation. If they do not, the reports are merely filed without action. Fifth, unfinished business not settled when the last meeting adjourned, if any, is taken up for action. Sixth, the call for new business is made. The order of new business is usually taken up in this sequence: (1) introduction of ordinances and resolutions; (2) first reading of ordinances usually by caption only with the introducers briefly explaining their content; (3) second reading of ordinances by caption only; (4) third reading of ordinances with reading in full. Any changes or amendments are offered at this time; (5) council action on ordinances. Seventh, announcements are called for following the completion of business. Eighth, the adjournment of the meeting. If the business of the meeting has been completed, no motion for adjournment is necessary. If the body wishes to adjourn before the completion of its business for the evening, a motion to adjourn must be made and receive a favorable vote.[21] The procedural steps in the disposition of usual items of business coming before a local council are shown in Table 7 (p. 284).

■ Powers of Local Councils

As mentioned previously, the local legislative body holds a key position in the exercise of the general powers granted to local governments. If these powers have not been conferred upon a particular officer or agency, then they reside in the local legislative body. Thus, the actual authority of any local council depends upon the distribution of powers within the local units organization. However,

[21] This outline of a meeting's order of business is adapted from Henry M. Roberts, *Robert's Rules of Order*, Scott, Foresman, 1951, which is normally used as a guide by all local legislative bodies.

Table 7. Steps in the Disposition of Usual Items of Business Coming Before the Council

Item	Source	Initial Action	Intermediate Action — Refer and Report: Officer	Intermediate Action — Refer and Report: Committee	Intermediate Action — Debate	Intermediate Action — Readings	Final Action — Accept or Approve	Final Action — File	Final Action — Refer with Power	Final Action — Summary Disposal[a]	Final Action — Adopt or Reject by Direct Vote
Unofficial communications	Any	Receive	X	X	X		X	X	X	X	
	Officers and committees	Receive	X	X	X		X	X	X	X	
Reports, Motions, etc.	Members	Receive	X	X	X					X	X
Resolutions, ordinances	Members	Read	X	X	X	X				X	X
	Members	Read	X	X	X	X				X	X

[a] As by indefinite postponement, tabling, or other parliamentary expedient.

SOURCE: E. L. Bennett, "Legislative Procedure of City Councils," *Public Management*, 17 (July, 1935), 199–200. Reprinted by permission of the International City Managers' Association.

there are several broad categories of power which all local councils retain and exercise to some degree.

The first category of powers is those which are legislative in character and involve the determination of public policy for the community. While legislative powers include both fiscal and regulatory actions, the fiscal powers will be discussed as a part of the council's financial powers rather than its legislative. In this more limited context, the legislative powers include those relating to public improvements and to the regulation of the health, safety, and morals of the community.

Financial powers comprise the second category of general powers of local councils. These include the power to approve the local budget, levy taxes, raise revenues, appropriate monies, and incur indebtedness. Other financial powers are buying and selling government property, passing upon local contracts involving major expenditures, and in many communities serving as the board of tax equalization. While there are many state-imposed limitations concerning financial transactions of local governments, including rate of tax levy, types of taxes which can be levied, and the extent of indebtedness, no money can be raised or spent without council authorization. In addition to being a financial document, the budget is the most important public policy decision the council makes since it allocates relative emphases among the programs and services of the community.

The third category consists of the administrative powers of local councils. These powers vary widely among the several types of local units and their forms of government. In local units without a central executive officer, as in the case of most counties, the council exercises broad administrative powers. In units with central executive leadership as provided by city and county managers, school superintendents, and strong mayors, the council exercises fewer administrative functions. However, such bodies give general supervision to their executive officers, receive financial reports, receive the reports of auditors, and have their powers of investigation to use when the occasion demands even as do the councils which exercise broad administrative functions. Thus the careful exercise of its administrative powers consumes a considerable amount of the council's time whatever the form of government.

Judicial powers, broadly interpreted, constitute a fourth broad type of council function. Many county boards, particularly those composed partly or wholly of judges or justices of the peace, still exercise judicial duties. Local councils are typically empowered to punish contempt actions and to enforce obedience of their orders by attachment or other compulsory process. A council exercises quasi-judicial functions when it sits as a board of tax equalization or tax appeal board. The investigatory powers of a local body also have some characteristics of a quasi-judicial function since in addition to serving the end of producing a better legislative product, they also serve to keep administrators honest and to uncover any wrongdoing. While the investigatory power of local boards has been misused on occasion, it is a desirable part of the process in local government. One writer has pointed out that, "The greatest protection in the future, as it has been in the past, is the election of council members who are interested in the furtherance of the general welfare by the determination of wise public policy."[22]

The final category of council powers relates to its activities in the field of public relations. The council as a whole and its individual members serve both as "middlemen" or "brokers" between the individual and his local government. As middleman between the individual and the city, the council has public relations functions which neither it nor its members can fail to provide. One writer describes the council member in these graphic words, "If he tries to evade his former friends and neighbors, he is high-hat; if he says he will try to fix things up and does not deliver, he is incompetent; if he makes promises that are not fulfilled, he is a liar."[23] As a representative of the city, he is a salesman of the community's needs to the citizenry and plays a major role in securing popular acceptance of necessary changes in local regulations and policies and in voter approval of bond issues. Such a role for the elected legislators assumes an intermixture of politics and administration which is abhorred by some writers. However, as Bromage points out in writing about his city of Ann Arbor, "Politics and administration come in one package in small and large matters. Every alderman has a constituency, and voters have their demands. In theory, it may be wrong, in practice, it appears to keep the voters reasonably well-satisfied. I suspect that in many cities, the impact of politics on ad-

[22] Alice L. Ebel, "Investigatory Powers of City Councils," *Marquette Law Review*, *38* (Spring, 1955), 223–36.
[23] Harold F. Alderfer, *American Local Government and Administration*, Macmillan, 1956, p. 333. For a more detailed discussion of the brokerage role of a city councilman, see Arthur W. Bromage, *On the City Council*, George Wahr Publishing Co., 1950, pp. 51–57.

ministration is very profound, whenever one probes beneath the surface of charts, reports, and statistics."[24]

In general, the public relations function of the local legislative body may be described as those activities which result in a community consensus evolving from conflicting points of view. Failure to accept this role and to work to achieve this goal can result in both community factionalism and factionalism on the governing board itself. A recent study of local city councils within Los Angeles County revealed that in 18 of 51 cities surveyed, the existence of factions on the council was reported.[25] This study also revealed that councils divided on a number of basic policy issues including zoning, personnel matters and capital improvement projects. Agreement or harmony for its own sake is not necessarily a good thing, but united council action after careful study of a problem or course of action can assist greatly in achieving community support for that undertaking.

■ Problems of a Local Legislator

The task of the conscientious local legislator is not an easy one. Five major problems facing the council or board member were identified by a political scientist at the midpoint of his first four-year council term in a community of 20,000. These were: (1) trying to determine the public's real opinion on a controversial issue; (2) learning to roll with the inevitable verbal punches and criticisms of his stand on issues; (3) ascertaining what things are to be taken on faith and which "expert" advisers to trust; (4) informing the public on what the council is doing and why; and (5) not taking a position too quickly on a major issue.[26] McGeary concluded, however, that "serving on council is a headache. But democracy is based on the supposition that some citizens will be willing to endure headaches. Actually the travail is not unbearable. And sometimes, for brief periods, it is forgotten—believe it or not—in the knowledge that some little service is being offered."[27]

[24] Bromage, op. cit., p. 57.

[25] R. J. Huckshorn and C. E. Young, "A Study of Voting Splits on City Councils in Los Angeles County," Western Political Quarterly, 13 (June, 1960), 479-97.

[26] M. Nelson McGeary, "The Councilman Learns His Job," National Municipal Review, 43 (June, 1954), 284-7.

[27] Ibid., p. 287.

A second writer has noted that, "At its best, the job of councilman takes up hundreds of hours and raises havoc with the nervous
system. At its worst, it becomes so intolerable that under no conditions will the councilman run for reelection, at least not until he
smells the smoke of the coming primary."[28] But the problems confronting local communities and the prospects for actions in meeting
them continue to attract public-spirited men and women to seek
positions on the local governing boards. On the shoulders of such
persons rest the future of democratic local government.

SUGGESTED READINGS

Books
Adrian, Charles R., *Governing Urban America* (New York: McGraw-Hill,
1960).
Alderfer, Harold F., *American Local Government and Administration*
(New York: Macmillan, 1956).
Bromage, Arthur W., *On the City Council* (Ann Arbor: George Wahr
Publishing Co., 1950).
Bromage, Arthur W., *A Councilman Speaks* (Ann Arbor: George Wahr
Publishing Co., 1951).
Bromage, Arthur W., *Councilmen at Work* (Ann Arbor: George Wahr
Publishing Co., 1954).
Childs, Richard, *Civic Victories* (New York: Harper, 1952).
Freeman, J. Lieper, "A Case Study of the Legislative Process in Municipal
Government," in J. C. Wahlke and Heinz Eulau, *Legislative Behavior*
(New York: Free Press, 1959), pp. 228–37.
Hallett, George H., Jr., *Proportional Representation, the Key to Democ-
racy* (New York: National Municipal League, 1940).
International City Managers' Association, *Municipal Year Book, 1961*
(Chicago, 1961).
Kneier, Charles M., *City Government in the United States*, 3rd ed. (New
York: Harper, 1957).
Merriam, C. E., *Chicago: A More Intimate View of Urban Politics* (New
York: Macmillan, 1929).
Vidich, A. J. and Bensman, Joseph, *Small Town in Mass Society* (Prince-
ton: Princeton University Press, 1958).

Articles
Adrian, Charles R., "The Role of the City Council in Community Policy-
Making," paper delivered at annual meeting of American Political
Science Association, Washington, September 11, 1959.

[28] Alderfer, *op. cit.,* p. 333.

Bennett, Emmett L., "Legislative Procedures in City Councils," *Public Management, 17* (July, 1935), 199–205.

Bromage, Arthur W., "Ten Traits of City Councilmen," *Public Management, 33* (April, 1951), 74–77.

Bromage, Arthur W., "Reducing the City Council's Work Load," *Public Management, 34* (April, 1952), 74–76.

Crane, W. W., Jr., "Reflections of a County Board Member," *The County Officer, 21* (September, 1956), 202, 204.

Ebel, Alice L., "Investigatory Powers of City Council," *Marquette Law Review, 38* (Spring, 1955), 223–36.

Eulau, Heinz, Wahlke, J. C., Buchanan, William and Ferguson, L. C., "The Role of the Representative: Some Empirical Observations on the Theory of Edmund Burke," *American Political Science Review, 53* (September, 1959), 742–56.

Huckshorn, R. J. and Young, C. E., "A Study of Voting Splits on City Councils in Los Angeles County," *Western Political Quarterly, 13* (June, 1960), 479–97.

McGreary, M. Nelson, "The Councilman Learns His Job," *National Municipal Review, 43* (June, 1954), 284–7.

The Executive Function

14

The characteristic features of the local executive office vary widely among types of governmental units and among various size units of a single type. In authority, these officers vary from mere figureheads to powerful chief executives with wide variation in specific powers and functions. Such diversity exists because four basic patterns of the executive role in local government evolved in the United States and remain a feature of our contemporary local government scene.

Two of the fundamental executive patterns in local government developed in colonial America. In some classes of local units, no one official served as the chief executive in any real sense, nor was all administrative authority vested in the local governing board. This fragmented executive authority developed in county, township, and town governments and may be described as the divided executive form. In cities, the general pattern was a mayor-council form of government patterned after the English system. The mayor was usually appointed by the governor although he was selected by the council in a few communities. While his term was normally for one year, reappointments were quite common. Early colonial charters conferred few executive or administrative powers upon the mayor. While he had neither the veto nor appointing power, he did preside over council meetings. He was usually a man experienced in municipal affairs, and because of his position and status he "became something more than a dignified figurehead, and was a real force in municipal government."[1] This pattern of executive leadership is labeled the weak executive form, because of the limited legal authority of the office.

With the establishment of state governments following the Revolutionary War, most states provided for the selection of the mayor by the city council, although this office continued as an appointment of the state executive council in New York until 1821. By 1825, however, the pattern of locally chosen mayors was common throughout the existing American states. In the early 1820s, the mayor became an elective office in Boston, St. Louis, and Detroit, and this was the common practice by the end of the next decade. There was also a steady increase in the powers of the mayor during this period. As presiding officer of the council, his power to appoint committees became increasingly important. A new charter in New York City adopted in 1830 gave the mayor the veto power, and by 1850 the mayor was generally granted the power to appoint administrative officers with council approval and confirmation.[2]

In addition to the plural executive and weak executive patterns of executive leadership, two other forms have developed. During the last half of the nineteenth century, the strong-mayor plan emerged, gradually becoming the accepted form for larger cities where active and forceful administration was needed. Then in the first decade of the present century, the concept of appointed local executives developed. This form of appointed executives has resulted in the creation of the positions of manager and chief administrative officer in cities, counties, towns, and townships across the nation. These four patterns form the basic character of the executive function in local government today. How the executive fulfills his functions in each of the four will be examined following a discussion of the essential features of the executive process in local government.

---

[1] John A. Fairlie, *Municipal Administration*, Macmillan, 1901, p. 74.
[2] Charles M. Kneier, *City Government in the United States*, 3rd ed., Harper, 1957.

■ Defining the Executive Function

The executive function in local government in recent years has been increasingly described as a role of leadership rather than a role of specific functions. Where once it was assumed that the activities of the executive in any organizational setting conformed to a fairly well-defined pattern, now greater emphasis is placed on the personal qualifications of the effective leader and his ability to guide and direct the operations of the governmental organization toward agreed upon objectives.

Illustrative of the pattern of duties concept was the work of Luther Gulick in 1937 in coining the word "POSDCORB."[3] The letters in this term designate the different elements of the executive's seven fold task—planning, organizing, staffing, directing, coordinating, reporting, and budgeting. The expansion of the executive's role is evidenced by the coinage of a new word—POSIDDOCEM—by Ordway Tead in 1959.[4] Here again, each letter represents a component of the administrator's functions which, in order, are planning, organizing, staffing, initiating, delegating, directing, overseeing, coordinating, evaluating and motivating. The change in executive emphasis from doing things to getting things done is apparent from the addition of new and substitution of words for those comprising the Gulick concept.[5]

In a study completed in 1958, the leadership role of administrative policy-making officers, their responsibilities, and the prerequisite attitudes or skills needed were analyzed in some detail.[6] The leadership role was viewed as a function with both external and internal responsibilities.

External leadership refers to an administrator's responsibilities toward organizations and groups (such as legislatures, clientele groups, and the general public) which are physically outside the agency he directs. . . . The exercise of internal leadership refers to the administrator's responsi-

[3] Luther Gulick and L. Urwick, *Papers on the Science of Administration*, Institute of Public Administration, 1937, p. 13.

[4] Ordway Tead, *Administration, Its Purpose and Performance*, Harper, 1959, p. 31.

[5] For an interesting statement concerning the changing concept of the role of the executive, see John M. Pfiffner, "What Has Happened to POSDCORB?" keynote address, Western Governmental Research Association, Disneyland, October 10, 1960.

[6] Stephen B. Sweeney and Thomas J. Davy (eds.), *Education for Administrative Careers in Government Service*, University of Pennsylvania Press, 1958.

bilities within the agency he directs. Although by definition this is a more narrow area of activity, it makes up in depth and intensity what it may lack (particularly in small agencies) in breadth and dimension. Neither the external nor the internal aspects of leadership exercise are mutually exclusive since one clearly impinges upon the other. Administrative leadership in its fullest dimension demands both, and success or failure in one may qualify success or failure in the other.[7]

The fundamental responsibility of the local executive is "to achieve the results desired by, and attain the goals set by, the person or persons to whom they are accountable. (This includes, as well, responsibility for developing facts and recommendations for changing goals and results desired.)"[8] To achieve this general accountability, four major categories of responsibilities were identified. The first consists of responsiveness to superiors and clientele and embraces (a) assisting superiors to enable them to discharge their responsibilities efficiently and effectively; and (b) seeking maximum understanding of, compliance with, and support for the policies and programs of the governmental unit on the part of the general public and people especially served or regulated. Articulation of objectives and programs comprises the second category. Among the specific responsibilities embraced in this grouping are (a) the formulation and presentation of policy and program proposals that are professionally sound and likely to be politically acceptable; and (b) anticipation of community trends and needs through appropriate plans and programs. The third category of responsibilities includes those relating to the procurement, organization, and control of resources. Two sub-responsibilities in this grouping are (a) recruiting and placing the most competent people available and promoting such persons according to merit and potential; and (b) procuring, distributing, utilizing, and maintaining the physical resources of the community economically, expeditiously, and with the maximum degree of organizational harmony. Responsibilities for direction, communication, and supervision are grouped to form the fourth major division of administrative responsibilities. These include (a) establishing and maintaining effective communication channels; (b) assuming direct leadership and supervision in major emergencies and politically sensitive situations which threaten the breakdown of a vital function or the stability

[7] Frederick T. Bent, "The Administrator's Leadership Role," *ibid.*, p. 247.
[8] Thomas J. Davy, "The Administrator's Responsibilities," *ibid.*, p. 272.

of the government; and (c) evaluating the adequacy and efficiency of the services under his direction.[9]

There have been a number of good statements concerning the major attitudes, skills or qualifications essential to administrative leadership. Four such prerequisites have been identified by Stephen Bailey. These are: (1) a sense of organizational relevance by which the administrator gets the feel of his precise role in the common purpose of the enterprise. In Bailey's words, "The successful administrative leader, like the successful pilot, is the one who always takes account of what's above him, what's below him, and what's on both sides of him, in relation to what is in front of him";[10] (2) a capacity for human warmth and understanding; (3) a spirit of enthusiasm coupled with courage—a person who exudes contagious excitement about his work and who is never entirely satisfied with the way things are going and has the courage to say so; and (4) a technical proficiency in the procedural and substantive aspects of his job.[11]

In viewing the administrator's role, Ordway Tead advances a fivefold classification of personal qualities which appear to be almost universal prerequisites. These are: (1) sheer physical and nervous vitality and drive; (2) ability to think logically, rationally, with problem-solving skills that "get the point" quickly; (3) willingness to take the burdens of responsibility for executive decisions and actions; (4) ability to get along with people in a sincerely friendly, affable, yet firm way; and (5) ability to communicate effectively by voice and pen.[12] While the attributes of effective leadership are situational, certainly a person with the personal qualities listed above would be able to exercise discretion to achieve concrete action in any given administrative situation.

A more politically-oriented way of looking at the local executive's many roles has been advanced by Paul Ylvisaker. His baker's dozen of executive functions is as follows:

1. Winning elections.
2. Leading—or deciding when not to lead.
3. Persuading.
4. Developing ideas of what to do and strategy for doing it.

[9] *Ibid.*, pp. 289–91.

[10] Stephen Bailey, "Administrative Leadership in Local and State Government: Its Meaning and Educational Implications," *ibid.*, p. 330.

[11] *Ibid.*, pp. 329–32.

[12] Tead, *op. cit.*, p. 59.

5. Performing and getting performance.
6. Trouble-shooting, making peace, and raising hell.
7. Winning elections.
8. Surviving friends and enemies.
9. Getting informed and being challenged and needled.
10. Keeping intact family and sense of humor.
11. Finding good people to help.
12. Realizing his ambitions.
13. Winning elections.[13]

It is obvious that the local executive is expected to play a positive role in the formulation of as well as in the execution of local government policies. This expanded role was in large part responsible for the development of the strong executive form in local government.

The notion of a policy-neutral type of business manager is inconsistent with new views concerning local executives—both appointive and elective. This change in philosophy is vividly apparent in statements contained in the Code of Ethics formulated by the International City Managers' Association. In the 1924 edition of the Code, Section 5 stated "Loyalty to his employment recognizes that it is the council, the elected representatives of the people, who primarily determine the municipal policies, and are entitled to the credit for their fulfillment." This relationship in the 1952 Code had been restated in Section 4 to read, "The city manager as a community leader submits policy proposals to the council and provides the council with facts and advice on matters of policy to give the council a basis for making decisions on community goals. The city manager defends municipal policies publicly only after consideration and adoption of such policies by the council."[14] Such a leadership role is, of course, even more expected of elected executives.

In spite of the increasingly important responsibilities of the local executive in the formulation and initiation of policies, however, the primary responsibility for determining the direction of action and the policies to attain the accepted goals remains a function of local legislative bodies. The degree and type of controls exercised over the local executive varies considerably among legislative bodies. The discretion and powers of the local executive obviously vary

[13] Paul Ylvisaker, "Administrative Assistance for Mayors," address presented at National Municipal League Conference on Government, Cleveland, November 20, 1957.

[14] International City Managers' Association, "The City Manager's Code of Ethics," 1924 and 1952.

with the type, nature and intimacy of legislative councils. This relationship is worth examining in some detail in the following discussion of the four basic patterns of executive leadership in local government.

■ Divided Executive Forms

The pattern of divided executive leadership in local government is often referred to as the no-executive form. This does not infer that the executive function is not performed—only that it is not centered in any one office or single agency. Thus, in county government the administrative function is performed in part by the county governing board, but this power is shared with the separately elected row officers—sheriff, treasurer, clerk, recorder, surveyor, assessor, solicitor, superintendent of schools, clerk of court, and coroner. Since the duties of these several officers were briefly noted in Chapter 9, they will not be repeated at this point. The excessive use of popular election in county government has prompted one writer to describe county administration as a "hydra-headed monstrosity."[15]

The fragmented nature of the executive function in the government of most counties is clear. Since the row officers listed above are popularly elected and derive their authority from state constitutional or statutory provisions rather than from county ordinances, the county board exercises only limited control, if any, over them. The treasurer runs his office as he interprets his powers and the same is true of the other county administrative officials. The administrative powers of the county board itself are numerous and varied. On the fiscal side, they prepare and administer the county budget. But the board often exercises budgetary discretion only over its own activities and accepts the statement of needs of the other officers and agencies without question. They have responsibility for and exercise control over a number of functions and services including the courthouse, jail, poor farm, and children's home and other county programs. The board appoints certain county officers and employees and gives general supervision to their conduct and performance. However, most officers and other agencies are responsible for their own employees, including hiring, firing, and salary policies. The board makes contracts for the county and cares for all county prop-

---

15 Roger Wells, *American Local Government*, McGraw-Hill, 1939, p. 81.

erty. Snider concludes that "All in all, the administrative work of the board constitutes by far its greatest task."[16]

This same pattern of fragmented executive leadership exists in most townships and is less of a problem only because there are fewer township officers and they undertake fewer services and activities. Divided executive leadership is also a characteristic of government in town meeting governed communities where the administrative responsibilities are divided among the board of selectmen and the several separately chosen town administrative officers.

The divided executive pattern is also a feature of the commission form of city government. Under this form, each of the members of the governing board also serves as the head of an administrative department. Since there are usually five commissioners, the administrative function is divided among five persons with no overall guidance and direction except that offered by the five administrators when they change hats and sit as members of the governing board. The fragmentation of the administrative function is less in commission governed cities than in the types of local governments discussed above since specific city activities are generally centered in one of the five departments headed by a commissioner. However, no single commissioner exercises authority over his fellow board members in their administrative capacities unless he assumes this responsibility or the others default to his leadership. The common tendency of the individual commissioners is not to interfere in the provinces of their colleagues because reciprocal "independence" is then more likely. However, often one commissioner is in charge of finance and accounts and this could give an energetic and forceful commissioner a vehicle for exercising a degree of control in fiscal affairs. A second source of leadership in commission governed cities can come from the commissioner who serves as mayor. In some commission cities, the office of mayor exists largely to give the municipality a ceremonial head. A forceful leader in this position can exercise the functions of his office in a manner to overcome the inherent structural weaknesses of the plan. He does so, however, because of his personality rather than the powers of his office.[17]

[16] Clyde F. Snider, *Local Government in Rural America*, Appleton-Century-Crofts, 1957, p. 134. Snider, of course, was referring to rural counties and a different conclusion might well be drawn in urban counties where the range and number of policy questions is greater.

[17] For an interesting case study of the activities of such a strong mayor in a commission governed city, see John H. Vanderzell, "Mayor Joseph T. Moriarty" in Richard T. Frost (ed.), *Cases in State and Local Government*, Prentice-Hall, 1961, pp. 28-38.

Along with the issue of the divided executive, local government faces the dilemma of finding among its executives the proper balance between the generalist with a broad understanding of government but with little technical skill and the specialist with technical knowledge but only a limited appreciation of the broader problems and procedures. As Roscoe C. Martin has put it, with special reference to rural government:

The student of public affairs distinguishes broadly between government, politics, and administration; but in little government these distinctions are not valid, or if valid in principle, are not overly useful in practice. The smaller the unit or area is, the closer the government is to the grass roots, the less meaningful is the distinction between politics, government, and administration; the larger the unit or area, the sharper the distinction. Grass-roots government is therefore pre-eminently the domain of the generalist, big government that of the specialist. Big government needs the generalist, of course, and it is, indeed, one of the prime problems of public administration to develop managers with a general sense of government and administration. Little government by contrast has generalists in plenty; for there the lines separating politics from government and both from administration blur and grow dim, with the result that nothing more than a general impression of government remains. The differentiations in process common in big government are hardly known at the grass roots.[18]

◼ Weak Executive Forms

The weak executive form is the oldest of the main types of city government in the United States. Although it has been losing ground in larger cities since the turn of the present century, it is still the predominant pattern of municipal government among smaller cities, villages, and towns, and is a feature of government in a small number of counties with an elective executive. The distinguishing features of the executive function in this form are (1) the limited role of the elected executive in the administrative process because of the restrictions on his appointive and financial powers and the absence of a veto; (2) the existence of several popularly elected administrative officers, often including a treasurer, attorney, clerk, and assessor; (3) the independence of these elective officers from direction

[18] Roscoe C. Martin, *Grass Roots,* University of Alabama Press, 1957, p. 40.

and control by the executive; and (4) a relatively strong council with administrative functions as well as its policy-determining authority.

At this point, it seems necessary to point out how this form differs from the divided or no-executive forms discussed above, since many of the administrative problems are commonly shared. In those forms, there was no single officer to whom the executive functions could be entrusted; in the weak-executive form, the office of mayor or county supervisor does exist but the administrative function is still shared with the governing board and with other elected administrative officers, a product of colonial fear and distrust of concentrated executive power. In addition, weak executives in both city and county governments have certain legislative powers. They have the right to recommend policy actions to the governing board, attend meetings of the council, and in some communities to preside over council meetings. In some communities, they vote in the event of an even split by the governing board and in some policy areas they have a veto power which can be overridden by the council. These legislative powers, even though sometimes quite limited, give the so-called weak executive an opening to exercise influence in matters of administration which is not a feature of the no- or plural-executive forms.

To have effective power over administration and to coordinate administrative activities, the mayor or county supervisor, at a minimum, should have general powers to shape fiscal policies and to appont his key officials and hold them accountable. The mayor in the weak executive plan has neither of these basic powers. The budget in such cities is normally prepared by a committee of the council, and the controller, if the office exists, is either a council appointee or is popularly elected. The financial powers of the weak mayor are so restricted that they provide no means of real influence in determining either fiscal policy or in controlling municipal expenditures. The appointive power of the weak mayor is similarly restricted with the popular election of some administrative officers and council appointment of others. A general rule of thumb in such cities gives the mayor the right to nominate for unpaid positions while nominations of paid administrative officials is lodged in the council or other city boards or commissions. An interesting study of the role of a "weak" mayor in selected appointments in a small city on the northeastern seaboard concludes, "There were 199 appointments made during the two years of Jackson's administration. Of these, 100 were formally initiated by the Mayor, 70 by the various Boards and Commissions, and 29 were Council Committee assignments. Speaking very generally, the Mayor nominated to non-renumerative policy posts, the Boards and Commissions nominated the paid officers of administration . . . the weak Mayor form of government does not restrict the influence of the Mayor to the appointments that are formally within his jurisdiction."[19]

The weak executive plan in county government is well illustrated by the office of elective county supervisor in Hudson and Essex Counties, New Jersey. Elected for a three-year term, the supervisor is nominally responsible for supervising subordinate officers and employees. He may remove county employees for neglect of duty or insubordination, but he lacks the power of appointment. In practice, few employees have been removed by the supervisor in either county since the employee so removed may appeal to the state civil service commission or to the courts. The fiscal powers of the county supervisor are similarly restricted since he neither prepares the budget nor controls expenditures.[20] Thus, the administrative powers exercised by the elective county supervisor in Hudson and Essex Counties—or the lack of them—parallels to a large degree those of his counterpart in city governments with the weak-mayor form.

Chicago is one of the last large cities with the weak-mayor form of government. A careful study of Chicago in 1955 stated, along the lines of an analysis noted previously, that "The city has what textbooks in municipal government called a 'weak-mayor' form of government to be sure, but it also had a powerful mayor, or, if not a powerful mayor, a powerful leader of the Council. The paradox of a 'weak' government that was strong was to be explained by the presence of the Democratic machine, an organization parallel to the city government but outside of it, in which power sufficient to run the city was centralized. The weakness of the city government was offset by the strength of the party."[21] As mentioned in Chapter 10, one shortcoming of the weak mayor-strong council form of government was that the policy leadership essential for the welfare of the

[19] William N. Kinnard, Jr., *Appointed by the Mayor*, Inter-University Case Program, No. 36, 1956, p. 14.
[20] James M. Collier, *County Government in New Jersey*, Rutgers University Press, 1952, pp. 16-17.
[21] Martin Meyerson and Edward C. Banfield, *Politics, Planning and the Public Interest*, Free Press, 1955, p. 287.

citizen sometimes fell by default to some person or group outside the formal machinery of government since there was often no person within the framework of the government who could provide it.

This structural weakness can often produce less happy results than those which Meyerson and Banfield found to exist in Chicago. In their words:

The "Big Boys"[22] could get and keep power enough to run the city only by giving the favors, protection, and patronage which were essential for the maintenance of the machine. It is quite possible, of course, that they preferred to operate the city government in this way. But whether they preferred it or not, the "spoils system" and even to some extent the alliance between crime and politics were the price that had to be paid to overcome the extreme decentralization of formal power. If overnight the bosses became model administrators—if they put all of the city jobs on the merit system, destroyed the syndicate, and put an end to petty grafting, then the city government would really be . . . weak and ineffective. . . . Indeed, under Kennelly the government of Chicago became a great deal cleaner and a great deal weaker than it had been for many years.

The people of Chicago probably did not fully realize the price that was being paid to assemble power enough to govern the city. But although it had never calculated the costs in deliberate ways, the public, it seems safe to say, had some awareness both that these costs were there and that there were some benefits in return—in fact, the disadvantages of a formal centralization of power, although different in kind, might possibly be even greater.[23]

The weak executive form of local government has few supporters among students of government. Its inherent structural disadvantages far outweigh the possible advantages of keeping government close to the people through popular election of a number of officials and protection against the "abuses" which can result from the concentration of too much power in one office. In 1948, the New Jersey Commission on Municipal Government evaluated the weak mayor-strong council form of local government in these words, "The characteristics of the plan—the long ballot of elected administrative officers, and the futile position that the mayor must occupy as the responsible head of the municipality—has long been outmoded in municipal thinking and is wholly inadequate to modern municipal

---

[22] This term refers to the members of the city council which represented the centers of the powerful, Democratic leadership clique.

[23] *Ibid.*, pp. 287–8.

THE EXECUTIVE FUNCTION   *301*

requirements."[24] However, no one seriously questions that the form will continue to exist, especially in smaller cities, for the foreseeable future.

■ Strong Executive Forms

Governments in large cities in recent decades have followed the general trend in American government of strengthening the powers of the chief executive officer. The same development has occurred in a small number of counties where an elected executive serves as the real head of county administration. Four characteristics distinguish the strong executive form from the plural- and weak-executive types. In the first place, much stronger controls over administration are vested in the chief executive office. Secondly, this officer is empowered to appoint and remove his department and agency heads. Third, the strong executive officer prepares the budget, or it is prepared by a budget officer responsible to and appointed by him. And fourth, the executive has both the general and item veto power. In communities with this form, the council exercises its policy-determining power, but is expected to leave administration to the executive and his subordinates within the general policy guides it determines.

While the strong executive form is not limited to large cities, their need for forceful, imaginative, executive leadership has made its growth and development there particularly striking. This need was graphically described a few years ago by a perceptive journalist as follows:

The suburbanization of the countryside has plunged America's big cities—specifically the twenty-three cities with population of 500,000 and over—into a time of crisis. Hemmed in by their hostile, booming suburbs, worried about the flight of their middle class, and hard pressed to maintain essential services for their own population, they need, if they are to hold their own, let alone grow, top-notch leadership.

They have it. Since the 1930's, and at an accelerating rate after the second world war, the electorate in city after city has put into office as competent, hard-driving, and skillful a chief executive as ever sat in the

[24] New Jersey Commission on Municipal Government, *Preliminary Statement of the Commission on Municipal Government*, 1948, p. 14.

PROCESSES OF LOCAL GOVERNMENT

high-backed chair behind the broad mahogany desk. At the same time they have strengthened the power of the office.[25]

The coordinative, appointive, and fiscal powers of the strong mayor give him a significant influence over and important sanctions which he can bring to bear upon the administrative process in his city. His coordinative powers include general supervision over the activities of the departments and agencies, while his powers in the preparation and administration of the budget give him influence over their activities. His appointive powers extend to department heads and in many cities even to the major subdivisions within the departments. While approval of the council is necessary in most cities, the mayor definitely exercises the leadership in the selection of his subordinates and "consults" with the council rather than shares this important responsibility. The basic fiscal power of the mayor relates to the preparation of the budget, but its administration also gives him important powers not only over his subordinates but also over agencies independent of his general control.

This same pattern of strong executive powers and sanctions is found in the office of an elective executive in a small number of counties. The position of President of the Cook County (Illinois) Board and the county executive's office in Nassau and Westchester Counties, New York, were noted previously. In St. Louis (Missouri) County, which adjoins but does not include the city of St. Louis, the position of an elective county supervisor was created by a home-rule charter of 1950. Elected for a four-year term, the officer has the same powers as those of the county executive in the New York counties. A county executive post was also established by the home-rule charter adopted by Baltimore County, Maryland, in 1956, with general powers to serve as the "chief executive officer of the county and the official head of the county government."[26]

Points of general information concerning the office of mayor in cities of over 5,000 population with the three common forms of city government are presented in Tables 8, 9, and 10. The term of office ranges from one to six years, with two-year terms the most common in both mayor-council and council-manager governed cities. Four year terms occur in nearly two out of every three commission-governed cities. One-year terms are still surprisingly common in

[25] Seymour Freedgood, "New Strength in City Hall," in Fortune Magazine (ed.), *The Exploding Metropolis,* Doubleday, 1958, p. 63.
[26] Snider, *op. cit.,* pp. 185–8.

THE EXECUTIVE FUNCTION

Table 8. *Term of Office of Mayors in Cities over 5,000*

Form of Government	Number of Cities Reporting	Percent of Reporting Cities					
		1 yr.	2 yr.	3 yr.	4 yr.	5 yr.	6 yr.
Mayor–Council	1,464	2.9	54.2	1.0	41.7	x	x
Commission	233	3.9	19.3	6.4	67.0	3.0	x
Council–Manager	1,101	21.3	54.6	2.3	21.7	x	x
All Cities over 5,000	2,798	10.3	51.4	2.0	35.9	x	x

x=Less than 0.5 percent.
SOURCE: International City Managers' Association, *The Municipal Year Book, 1963*, Chicago, 1963, p. 162.

Table 9. *Method of Selection and Voting Power of Mayors in Cities over 5,000*

Form of Government	Number of Cities Reporting	Percent of Reporting Cities			Percent of Directly Elected Mayors Voting	
		Directly Elected	Selected by Council	Highest Vote in Election	All Issues	Tie Vote
Mayor–Council	1,563	95.3	4.1	0.6	12.9	65.8
Commission	243	76.6	22.6	0.8	94.2	4.1
Council–Manager	1,137	49.4	49.4	1.2	47.8	47.6
All Cities over 5,000	2,943	76.0	23.2	0.8	28.7	56.0

SOURCE: International City Managers' Association, *The Municipal Year Book, 1963*, Chicago, 1963, p. 160.

council-manager cities with one in every five cities having such an abbreviated term.

Table 9 shows the wide variations in the methods by which the mayor is selected and the extent of the voting powers of mayors when the office is filled by direct election of the people. Methods of selection vary considerably among the three major forms of city

Table 10. *Veto Power of Directly Elected Mayors in Cities over 5,000*

Form of Government	Total Number of Cities	Number of Cities Reporting	Percent of Reporting Cities		
			Veto All Measures	Veto Selected Items	No Veto
Mayor–Council	1,489	1,289	33.5	32.9	33.6
Commission	186	158	4.4	3.8	91.8
Council–Manager	562	537	11.4	18.2	70.4
All Cities over 5,000	2,237	1,984	25.2	26.6	48.2

SOURCE: International City Managers' Association, *The Municipal Year Book, 1963,* Chicago, 1963, p. 161.

government. The mayor is elected directly by the voters in most mayor-council cities, in three out of four commission-governed cities, but in less than half of the cities with the council-manager form of government.

The veto power of mayors as shown in Table 10 is most prevalent in mayor-council cities and least common in commission-governed cities.

The problem of securing able and effective leaders to serve as strong executives in city and county governments is a continuing one. In commenting on the enhanced position and power of big city mayors, Freedgood states:

This has not been a victory for "good government." To most people, good government is primarily honest and efficient administration, and they believe that the sure way for the city to get it is to tighten civil service, eliminate patronage, and accept all the other artifacts of "scientific" government, including the council-city-manager plan. But today's big-city mayor is not a good-government man, at least in these terms, and if he ever was, he got over it a long time ago. He is a tough-minded, soft-spoken politician who often outrages good-government people, or, as the politicians have called them, the Goo-Goos.

One of the biggest threats to his leadership, indeed, is too much "good government." The big problem at City Hall is no longer honesty, or even simple efficiency. The fight for these virtues is a continuous one, of course, and Lucifer is always lurking in the hall, but most big-city governments have become reasonably honest and efficient. Today, the big problem is not good housekeeping; it is whether the mayor can provide the aggressive leadership and the positive programs without which no big city has a prayer. What is to get priority? Industrial redeveloment? More housing? (And for whom?) There is only so much money, and if hard policy decisions are not made, the city's energies will be diffused in programs "broad" but not bold.[27]

Freedgood also identifies the four major challenges facing the big city mayor as he strives to exercise his powers of policy leadership. These are the staff experts and the civil-service bureaucrats who attempt to increase their own authority at his expense; the growing "external bureaucracy" in the form of public corporations and authorities; the state legislature which has a controlling voice in the fiscal affairs of his city; and the continuing struggle between the mayor and the suburbs which surround his city.[28] Freedgood believes that the omens are promising that the mayors can meet these challenges and enable the city to reassert itself as a vital center in American life.

■ Appointed Executive Forms

In the strong executive form discussed above, the control over administration is vested in an elective official. In other local units, this power is entrusted to an appointive administrator who is generally known as a manager or chief administrative officer. Both plans are more common in cities than in counties, but the number of county adoptions of strong appointive executive plans is an encouraging development.

The two basic features of the manager plan in both city and county government are the unification of authority and political responsibility in an elected governing board, and the centralization of administrative responsibility in the manager who is appointed by and is responsible to the council. A corollary characteristic of the centralized administrative responsibility in the manager is the understanding that the governing board normally deals with administration only through the manager, that the manager has power to select and direct the department heads, and that neither individual councilmen nor council committees will undertake administrative functions.

[27] Freedgood, *op. cit.,* pp. 63–64.
[28] *Ibid.,* pp. 64–65.

While city and county charters vary widely in their prescription of the duties of the manager, there is rather common agreement that these duties are to include: enforcing all laws and ordinances; appointing and removing department heads and employees on the basis of merit; exercising control and supervision over all departments; making such recommendations to the council concerning the affairs of the city as he may deem desirable; keeping the council informed of the financial condition of and the future needs of the city; preparing and submitting the annual budget to the council; preparing and submitting such other reports as may be required by the council; informing the public, through reports to the council, regarding the operations of the city government; and performing such other duties as may be prescribed by the charter or required by ordinance or resolution of the council.[29]

In addition to the manager, cities with this form have a mayor with legislative, political, and ceremonial functions. He presides at council meetings and is a leader in the development and determination of municipal policies. With the other council members, he interprets municipal policy to the people and shares the responsibilities of local political leadership. He represents the city in ceremonial functions and maintains contact with civic groups. He also appoints citizen advisory committees and commissions and coordinates their efforts in studying problems of the community. In counties these functions are provided, in a more limited way, by the president of the board.

When the manager plan first developed, there was a sharp distinction between the policy functions of the manager and those of the mayor in mayor-council cities. The changing concept of the manager's function in this regard was noted earlier in this chapter. In a study published in 1958, it was stated that 75 to 90 percent of all policies adopted by city councils originated outside of the council with the manager and his staff the source of many such proposals.[30] A recent defense of this heavy reliance of the council on the manager in policy matters stated, "In his relationship to the council, the manager's key role is that of fact finder. It is his duty to assemble all of the pertinent facts on any policy matter which involves the operation of the city as a municipal corporation and to

[29] International City Managers' Association, "Questions and Answers About the Council-Manager Plan and the City Manager Profession," pamphlet, January, 1961, p. 7.
[30] Clarence E. Ridley, *The Role of the City Manager in Policy Formulation,* International City Managers' Association, 1958, p. 4.

submit them to the council for review. Stated another way, it is the duty of the manager to assimilate the growing body of municipal knowledge as it relates to policy matters and to pass on to the council the results of his analysis and research. It is necessary for this to be done for the simple reason that the city council as a lay body is unable to obtain much of this information in any other way."[31]

The chief administrative officer or general manager idea for cities and counties began in the consolidated City and County of San Francisco with the adoption of a new charter in November, 1931. The office represented a compromise between the members of the charter revision committee who supported the manager plan and those who endorsed the strong mayor-council form.[32] There are two distinguishing differences between the chief administrative officer (hereafter referred to as CAO) and manager plans. Instead of acting directly as does the manager, the CAO makes recommendations which are reviewed by the governing board before implementation. This supports the basic theory of the plan that the CAO is the agent of the board, acts for it and in its name in carrying out his assigned duties. Secondly, the assignment of duties of the CAO are generally more limited than those entrusted to the manager.

While the specific duties assigned CAO's vary considerably, the following list of assigned duties are farily common. It includes: supervising, coordinating, and reporting on designated activities and operations; carrying out administrative policies and rules adopted by the governing board; making suggestions on departmental activities to increase overall efficiency; recommending changes in annual departmental budget estimates; administering the adopted budget; supervising expenditures; controlling expenditures; developing and assisting in carrying out public improvement programs; serving as public relations officer; cooperating with community organizations; itemizing all property owned by the local governmental unit; recommending purchase, transfer, and disposal of equipment and supplies; suggesting abolition or consolidation of positions; handling routine administrative business, such as mail, occurring between governing board meetings; and performing other duties assigned by the governing board, including recommendations on personnel.[33] While this is a more lengthy list of duties than those

[31] C. A. Harrell and D. G. Weiford, "The City Manager and the Policy Process," *Public Administration Review, 19* (Spring, 1959), 105.

[32] John C. Bollens, *Appointed Executive Local Government,* Haynes Foundation, 1952, pp. 12-13.

[33] *Ibid.,* pp. 117-8.

comprising the core functions of managers, they are more confined in scope thus bearing out an essential difference between the two plans of appointed local executive government. While the manager plan establishes a professional administrator who is free from control by the mayor, the CAO plan creates such a position but makes it responsible to the mayor. The success of the plan depends in large part upon the relationship between the mayor and the CAO. The key problem concerning the successful operation of the CAO plan has been pointed out by Adrian as, "The problem today for large cities is . . . one of finding a mayor who is willing to delegate responsibility for administrative detail to a cao and of finding a cao who can secure the confidence of the mayor."[34]

Concerning the future of the CAO plan, Adrian writes, "It is too early to predict with confidence that the cao plan will succeed. It is certainly possible that too much depends upon the personality of the mayor and his willingness to delegate appropriate authority. It is also possible that too few powers will be assigned by the charter to the cao to permit full use of his capabilities. It is possible that department heads cannot be persuaded to report to the cao rather than to the mayor, or that the mayor will not deal with department heads [only] through the cao. But if such dangers as these do not prove to be insurmountable barriers, it may be that the long-outstanding problem of finding an appropriate form of government for our largest cities has been resolved."[35]

■ *Other Executive Officers*

The existence of a large number of executive officers in the plural- and weak-executive forms has already been noted. However, the discussion of the strong and appointed executive forms has been limited to the role and responsibilities of the chief executive officer and the mayor in appointed executive forms. In cities and counties governed by these two forms, there are usually one or more other administrative officers either elected by the voters or appointed by the governing board and thus somewhat independent of the chief executive officer's control. In cities, the officers most likely to be elected are one or more of the following: clerk, city attorney, treas-

---

[34] Charles R. Adrian, "Recent Concepts in Large City Administration," paper presented at annual conference of American Political Science Association, Washington, 1956.

[35] *Ibid.*

urer or controller. In counties, the positions of attorney, clerk, and assessor are most often elective. Since the basic responsibilities of these officers have been discussed in an earlier chapter, it will not be necessary to repeat them here.

The importance of these lesser executive officers has been aptly pointed out by one writer in these words, "The lesser executive officers of the city, whether elected or appointed, are important to citizens because, despite their low visibility level, they significantly affect policy making. Though the citizen may not know it, when the headlines proclaim 'Mayor Zilch Announces New Bonding Program' or 'Councilman Announces Tax-free Parking Scheme,' the men given the credit are only acting out their roles in the play. The playwright probably will not even be mentioned in the news story. His is merely one of those 'unimportant routine' offices of the city."[36]

Many people still believe that strong local executive forms— whether the administrative head is elected or appointed—are a serious threat to democracy in local government because too much power is concentrated in the hands of one man. While many of these persons are sincere in their belief, the evidence of strong executive plans in practice is hardly on their side. The role of the governing board in holding the executive responsible has been pointed out in several sections of this chapter as well as in the previous one. When the local executive is responsible to the elected representatives of the people or directly to the people as are the managers, mayors, CAO's, county presidents, and county executives, there is no real danger to democracy. Such forms are not only compatible and reconcilable with effective democracy; they are conducive to it.

SUGGESTED READINGS

Books

Adrian, Charles R., *Governing Urban America*, 2nd ed. (New York: McGraw-Hill, 1961).

Bollens, John C., *Appointed Executive Local Government* (Los Angeles: Haynes Foundation, 1952).

Freedgood, Seymour, "New Strength in City Hall," in Fortune Magazine (ed.), *The Exploding Metropolis* (New York: Doubleday, 1958).

Frost, Richard T. (ed.), *Cases in State and Local Government* (Englewood Cliffs: Prentice Hall, 1961).

[36] Charles R. Adrian, *Governing Urban America*, 2nd ed., McGraw-Hill, 1961, p. 254.

Kneier, Charles M., *City Government in the United States*, 3rd ed. (New York: Harper, 1957).

Ridley, Clarence E., *The Role of the City Manager in Policy Formulation* (Chicago: International City Managers' Association, 1958).

Snider, Clyde F., *Local Government in Rural America* (New York, Appleton-Century-Crofts, 1957).

Sweeney, Stephen B. and Davy, Thomas J. (eds.), *Education for Administrative Careers in Government Service* (Philadelphia: University of Pennsylvania Press, 1958).

Tead, Ordway, *Administration, Its Purpose and Performance* (New York: Harper, 1959).

Articles

Adrian, Charles R., "Recent Concepts in Large City Administration," paper presented at meeting of American Political Science Association, Washington, 1956.

Bailey, Stephen K., "A Structured Interaction Pattern for Harpsichord and Kazoo," *Public Administration Review, 14* (Summer, 1954), 202–4.

Bebout, John E., "Management for Large Cities," *Public Administration Review, 15* (Summer, 1955), 188–95.

Bollens, John C., "Administrative Integration in California Counties," *Public Administration Review, 11* (Winter, 1951), 26–34.

Bosworth, Karl A., "The Manager is a Politician," *Public Administration Review, 18* (Summer, 1958), 216–22.

Collier, James M., "Elected County Chief Executives in New Jersey," *The County Officer, 20* (February, 1955), 47–48.

Gove, Samuel K., "A County Executive Officer," *The County Officer, 19* (September, 1954), 190–3.

Harrell, C. A. and Weiford, D. G., "The City Manager and the Policy Process," *Public Administration Review, 19* (Spring, 1959), 101–7.

Mathewson, Kent, "Democracy in Council-Manager Government," *Public Administration Review, 19* (Summer, 1959), 183–5.

Nolting, Orin F., "Changing Role of the City Manager," address presented at National Municipal League, Conference on Government, Cleveland, November 20, 1957.

Pealy, Dorothee S., "The Need for Elected Leadership," *Public Administration Review, 18* (Summer, 1958), 214–6.

Sayre, Wallace S., "The General Manager Idea for Large Cities," *Public Administration Review, 14* (Autumn, 1954), 253–8.

Ylvisaker, Paul, "Administrative Assistance for Mayors," address presented at National Municipal League, Conference on Government, Cleveland, November 20, 1957.

The Judicial Process

15

The problem of the administration of justice—like every other problem of government in a democracy—begins and ends with people. While millions of people year after year have no occasion to use the services of local courts, others are not so fortunate. Some may be stopped by policemen for exceeding posted legal speed limits; others may be victimized by or be accused of victimizing a fellow citizen; still others may fail to conduct their places of business in keeping with established norms of cleanliness, safety, or decency. For these and other purposes, our machinery of justice exists to regulate the relationships between individuals and between citizens and their government when a need arises. The judicial process, in brief, consists of the hearing and deciding of legal controversies, whether they involve the violation of a law or questions in the application of a law. Since the goal of the process is justice, the process itself, the machinery within which it is realized, and the persons who make the machinery operate are all important items for study and will be dealt with in this chapter.

There are no local courts in the sense that there are local legislative bodies and local executives. All courts within a state are a part of the state court system rather than purely local bodies. Thus the court serving a local community is the lowest rung on the state judicial ladder rather than an organ of local government. However, lower courts function as integral parts of the machinery of local government in several respects. It has been previously noted that the governing board in some counties is comprised of local judges and that justices of the peace are members of the township board in several states. In addition, most local judges are elected by the people within the geographical area under the jurisdiction of the court. But while it is essential to discuss local courts in a study of local government, it should be remembered that this level of the judiciary really comprises the base in the pyramidal structure of the state court system.

■ *The Role of the Courts*

As mentioned briefly above, the essential role of the courts is to interpret and apply the laws regulating relationships between individuals and between citizens and their government in such a manner as to approximate justice. More briefly, the courts are to administer justice. Since justice is a relative concept, it has not been possible to define its substance or essence very satisfactorily. Thus, a procedure has been established by which a person involved in a dispute receives a fair hearing and the benefit of a judgment by an impartial judge or a jury of his fellow citizens. The spirit of this process is well illustrated by our symbol of justice which depicts a blindfolded woman holding a balance scale in her hands. As the three main features of this symbol, according to one writer, the woman represents gentle protectiveness, the blindfold insures impartiality, and the scale reflects the desire to determine the merits of a case objectively.[1]

In a typical judicial proceeding, the court performs three basic functions. First, it must determine the facts in the case before it. Second, it must determine which rules of law are relevant. And third, it must apply the pertinent law or laws to the relevant facts to arrive at a judgment. Broadly speaking, law represents the community's rules of conduct which are backed up by the organized force of that community. It is one of the important and necessary

---

[1] Charles R. Adrian, *State and Local Governments*, McGraw-Hill, 1960, p. 351.

devices for social control which complements but also goes beyond the mores and folkways of the community.

The two main types of law that have evolved in our society are statutory law and common law. The former is law established by lawyers or legislators and is written and codified. Common law, on the other hand, is decreed by judges, appears first as case law, and is based upon custom.[2] In one of his well-known decisions, Mr. Justice Holmes defined common law in these words, "The common law is not a brooding omnipresence in the sky, but the articulate voice of some sovereign or quasi-sovereign that can be identified."[3] Case precedents in common law, while not codified, exist as a matter of record in courts of record, and previous judgments are not ignored by judges in cases coming before them. Most law today is statutory, whether civil or criminal in nature, but much of it has evolved as a codification and revision of common law. Thus, our system is really a "mixed system" consisting of both common law and statutory law.

In addition to interpreting the law, courts have an important role to play in the whole local governmental process. The wording of a local ordinance may be somewhat ambiguous and the court will need to clarify its meaning and intent. Another local ordinance may be contrary to a state law, and the court may declare it null and void because of its conflict with the higher law. Courts also have an effective role in protecting the rights of a citizen against unwarranted actions by local officials or other citizens. Thus, the role of the courts is much broader than that of applying and interpreting the law. Courts may also clarify local law, overrule it, and check its overenforcement or unreasonable application.

In 1929, W. F. Willoughby enumerated nine main functions of courts. While he did not have local courts in mind, lower courts do engage in each of the functions which he identified. These were to: (1) investigate and determine facts; (2) apply law to the facts thus determined; (3) determine and construe law; (4) prevent the infraction of law and the violation of rights; (5) advise the legislative and executive branches with respect to law; (6) act as public administrative agencies; (7) administer property; (8) act as agencies to enforce decisions; and (9) determine rules of judicial pro-

---

[2] Henry J. Abraham, *Courts and Judges, An Introduction to the Judicial Process*, Oxford University Press, 1959, pp. 1-2. Our concept of equity, as well as common law, is a part of our heritage from Great Britain.

[3] *Southern Pacific Co.* v. *Jensen*, 244 U.S. 205 (1916), p. 222.

cedure.[4] The first three functions have been touched upon above, but each of the others is worthy of brief discussion.

The aphorism "An ounce of prevention is worth a pound of cure" has high validity as courts attempt to fulfill their fourth function—preventing the infraction of laws and the violation of rights. Preventive relief is often provided by a local court through the granting of an injunction which restrains officials or persons from committing certain acts. This type of protection is more satisfactory than a monetary award following the occurrence of irreparable damages. Illustrative of this use would be the issuance of such a writ to prevent the county from hastily constructing a dam which would result in the flooding of privately owned property. Another form of relief can be obtained through a writ of mandamus compelling the proper official to issue a license to a qualified applicant.

The fifth judicial function—its advisory role—has been increasingly assumed by non-court officials such as the city solicitor or attorney, or the county attorney. The local governing board will almost always ask its legal advisor to judge the legality of a proposed ordinance before it is enacted, or of a possible course of action before it is undertaken. However, in rendering a local ordinance null and void, the court may on occasion point out specifically how the local law is in conflict with a higher law and how it might be brought into harmony with the superior statute. In most states, however, the concept of separation of powers prevents courts from giving legal advice except as this may result from actual litigation.

While administration of the law is the primary function of courts, a number of county courts serve varying administrative functions. In some counties, the governing board is comprised of judges who render both administrative and judicial services. In other states, as in Missouri and West Virginia, the county court is purely an administrative body. Lower court judges in other states have more specific administrative functions. For instance, judges of the probate court in Michigan serve as members of the board of election commissioners and of the county plat board (which supervises and approves land-use plans) and have jurisdiction in county drain proceedings. In Arkansas, the county judge performs most of the non-fiscal functions normally exercised by a county governing board.

In administering property, a number of special courts have been

[4] W. F. Willoughby, *Principles of Judicial Administration*, Brookings Institution, 1929, Chap. XVI.

established. Orphans' courts often exist to manage and settle the estates of homeless minors. Probate or surrogate courts exist to handle the probate of decedents' wills, the settlement of estates, or to serve as guardians in the case of insane persons, drunkards, or others incapable of self-management. These functions are more administrative than judicial and the courts exercise a close supervision over the persons named as administrators or executors in such cases. It might be noted that adherence to the theory of separation of powers has not substantially interfered with the practice of vesting some administrative powers in local courts, a carry-over from English practice.

In acting as agencies to enforce decisions, courts issue bench warrants for the arrest of persons accused of crimes and summons and subpoenas to insure the presence of persons in court at the proper time. Examples of other writs and processes available to the court are *habeas corpus*, to direct that a person being detained for any reason be produced in court to establish a legal basis for his retention or release; *mandamus*, to compel an official, person, or agency to perform certain duties; and mandatory injunction, to compel persons or officials to continue to do things they had previously been doing but had threatened to stop.

The last enumerated function of the courts—their rule-making power—is somewhat limited among lower courts since this is a function normally performed by a judicial council or conference within a state, or by higher courts. However, judges of lower courts are usually among the members of such organizations and thus do have a voice in the determination of procedural rules for the courts. Local courts must also determine the rule to apply in situations which arise locally and which are not covered by existing rules. In states where rules of practice and procedure are still prescribed by the state legislature, such rules are enacted commonly only after advice and testimony have been heard from judges of courts that would be affected.

■ *Types of Local Cases*

Before examining the structure of the local court system, it is advisable to differentiate among the several common types of cases which are heard by the lower courts. The jurisdiction of particular courts is often limited to civil or criminal cases or to cases in equity.

By defining each of these types, we should make the discussion of court authority clearer.

A civil case is normally one between private persons and/or private organizations; it deals with actions concerning the rights and duties of individuals in their relationships with each other. Proceedings, as a general rule, are initiated by a party or organization known as the plaintiff, while the party against whom the action is brought is the defendant. Civil cases include such actions as defamation of character, divorce, trespassing on private property, personal injury resulting from being struck by a bicycle or automobile, breach of contract, and suits to collect unpaid bills or overdue payments. While most civil cases do not involve governmental units, cities as municipal corporations may sue and be sued in much the same manner as persons or private corporations.

The most common type of offense which may involve a local government is a civil suit known as a tort. A tort has been defined as a civil wrong not arising out of a breach of contract. The majority of tort cases, as in civil cases generally, involve government only as an umpire providing facilities for settling disputes. On occasion, governmental bodies may be liable in damages for injuries to individuals or their property. There is also, of course, the possibility that the official committing the injury may be personally liable. While it is difficult to generalize, the tendency is to modify by statute or court decision the old rules which created a broad immunity from suit.

A criminal case is usually brought in the name of the "people" with the governmental unit serving as the prosecutor. The case involves an accusation stating that the defendant has violated some specific law regulating the conduct of individuals the infraction of which is punishable by penalties provided in the law. Criminal acts fall into one of three major categories—treason, felonies, or misdemeanors. Treason is the most serious offense against the state and is carefully defined. As found in the national constitution and in most state constitutions, treason consists of "levying war against them (the United States), or in adhering to their enemies, giving them aid and comfort." As such, treason is a federal or state crime and will not be given further consideration.

While the concept of felony is used to connote a major or serious crime, it is not uniformly defined by statutes in the fifty states. It typically includes such acts as murder, manslaughter, arson, larceny, burglary, rape, and aggravated assault. Misdemeanors again are not uniformly defined, but the term is reserved for less serious offenses such as public drunkenness, traffic violations, disturbance of the peace, rowdiness, and violation of local health ordinances. Sometimes the term misdemeanor is limited to lesser indictable offenses while non-indictable actions are known as petty offenses. There are, however, two useful distinctions which can be made between the two types of crimes. Felonies in most instances would be breaches of a major crime defined by state law while violations of local ordinances would ordinarily be only misdemeanors. The possibility of prison confinement is a further distinguishing characteristic of a major criminal action in contrast to an award of money damages in a civil suit and a monetary fine in minor criminal cases.

Cases in equity involve the application of rules and principles which supplement common law and provide a remedy to prevent an injustice in cases where common law fails to do so. It enables a judge to hand down an order that will prevent an injustice and is remedial in character. The decision of the judge in such cases is known as a decree rather than a judgment and it usually is in the form of a writ such as a writ of injunction, mandamus, or prohibition.

A common illustration of an equity case involves the actions of a man to keep a lovely old tree on the edge of his property from being pulled down even though it lies in the direct path of a future state highway. While he would receive just compensation for his property under this use of the eminent domain power of the state, he prefers the beauty and shade of the tree and the sentimental attachments that go with it (he proposed to his wife under it, he watched his children climb in it, etc.) to the monetary grant and so he appeals to the court for equity.[5] While he would probably lose this particular plea, many readers will recall seeing sudden jogs in streets or sidewalks around a tree—indications that such cases are not always lost in a court of equity. Over the years, the rules of equity have become quite rigid in contrast to its origin as a concept of preventative justice where the common law failed to provide an adequate remedy.

■ Court Organization and Jurisdiction

Generally speaking, there is a rather simple hierarchy of four levels of courts in most state judicial systems. The bottom level is

[5] Abraham, *op. cit.*, p. 3.

known as the minor judiciary and includes such courts as those headed by justices of the peace, magistrates, recorders, or aldermen. A number of specialized municipal courts (such as police courts or traffic courts) are also a part of the minor judiciary. The second rung of the judicial ladder is comprised of general trial courts known variously as county, district, or circuit courts. Next in line comes the court of appeals which serves as an intermediate court. At the top of the pyramid is the state supreme court. In the discussion below, only the first two levels will be treated, since these are the only two which can be described as local courts.

THE MINOR JUDICIARY

The best known and the traditional court for rendering community justice are the courts of the justices of the peace. In some rural sections of the country, these are headed by squires and in cities by magistrates or aldermen. As courts of limited jurisdiction, they exercise three main types of authority. First, they have the authority to hear and determine minor criminal cases. While their precise jurisdiction varies among the states and is prescribed by state law, their authority normally extends over such matters as traffic violations, violation of local ordinances, breaches of the peace including drunkenness and disorderly conduct, and other criminal actions in which the verdict of guilt entails a fine not exceeding $500 or a jail sentence of six months.

Second, these courts are generally empowered to hold preliminary hearings where persons are accused of more serious crimes. Following the hearing, the judge may release the defendant for lack of evidence, release him under bail pending a future trial or grand jury investigation, or hold him in jail custody to await his trial. Third, the minor judiciary also has jurisdiction in civil cases involving limited amounts of money including small claims, torts, and common law suits. Judges of these courts are generally authorized to render other services such as performing marriage ceremonies and attesting certain documents.

Generally speaking, these courts of the minor judiciary—often called inferior courts—are not courts of record and their judges are not trained in law. As courts not of record, no permanent records of proceedings, which are usually quite informal and without jury, are kept. The judges are elected by the voters of the township, borough, village, or city ward which serves as the jurisdictional area of the court. By and large, they serve only part-time in this capacity and in many areas are paid from fees derived from the cases they hear. This fact probably explains in large part their penchant for verdicts for plaintiffs which has averaged some 96 percent in civil cases and 80 percent in criminal cases.[6] In larger cities, these inferior court judges are commonly on a salary basis, are usually trained in the law, and work full-time at their judicial duties. Thus, they present a sharp contrast to their rural counterparts.

Increasingly in recent years, the justice of the peace courts have been widely criticized and in some states the character of the office has been changing. In many small communities, the positions go unfilled and in others the justices, though elected, are inactive. Ohio in 1957 abolished the office of justice of the peace, establishing a system of county and municipal courts with trained judges. One of the biggest criticisms concerns the lack of qualifications for the judges who preside over these minor courts in many states. They are not required to have legal training and most of them do not. A 1942 survey of nearly 300 justices in Pennsylvania revealed that 47 percent had received only an elementary school education or less, and less than 15 percent were college graduates. Only 71 percent of the justices were actually commissioned and their average term in office was slightly over six years, which is the length of a term in that state. Their occupational background was quite varied with these occupations listed in declining order of frequency: laborer and unskilled workers, farmers, skilled laborers, merchants, clerks, real estate and insurance. Other occupations included retired persons, housewives, and salesmen.[7] These figures are probably fairly representative of the qualifications—or lack of them—of justices of the peace in other states still using the system.

A second criticism concerns the court facilities of the minor judiciary. While some justices are provided with courtrooms, many hold court in their homes or in the place of their other and primary occupations. Their "law library" may consist of a copy of the state constitution or perhaps a copy of the revised statutes of their state—sometimes an outdated edition. The records maintained by

[6] *Ibid.*, p. 21.
[7] Pennsylvania Bar Association and Institute of Local Government, Pennsylvania State College, *Survey of the Minor Judiciary in Pennsylvania*, Pennsylvania Municipal Publications Service, 1942.

these justices are often scanty and inaccurate and sometimes even non-existent. But the greatest criticism of justice of the peace courts concerns the fee system of compensation. The penchant of these judges to decide in the plaintiff's favor has already been noted and Snider suggests that "J.P." (the usual abbreviation for justice of the peace) means "judgment for the plaintiff."[8] In many states, these justices are paid through the fees assessed against the defendant and thus they profit from each case coming before them. Some enterprising justices have engaged in fee-sharing arrangements with local peace officers and fared quite generously through over-zealous enforcement of a low speed limit zone which in effect was a speed trap.

These present weaknesses of the justice of the peace system are not recent innovations although the lack of training in law is a problem of increasing magnitude. After examining the system in 1927, Chester H. Smith wrote, "The justices of the peace as a class are wholly unqualified for the positions they occupy. The pernicious fee system and local politics break down their integrity and lead to corruption. They are often ignorant and wholly uncontrolled by statute or constitution. Their decisions are purely personal. The administration of justice by these lay magistrates is uncertain, unequal and unstable, and in truth, the system as such, is a denial of justice according to our highest concept of that term."[9]

As mentioned previously, the urban counterparts of the justice of the peace are quite unlike their more rural associates. But neither they nor their courts are shining lights in the overall judicial structure in too many cities. While salaried, the judges are not paid enough to attract many high quality candidates, and the courtroom facilities are often shabby and overcrowded. There appears to be a definite trend, however, for cities to establish under state enabling legislation special courts designed to improve administration of justice in minor cases. Such courts have various names, including magistrates courts, courts of common pleas, traffic, and police courts. A further trend is in evidence in large cities with the segregation of cases according to the nature of the question involved. Types of cases are assigned to a particular judge or judges

[8] Clyde F. Snider, *Local Government in Rural America*, Appleton-Century-Crofts, 1957, p. 309.
[9] Chester H. Smith, "The Justice of the Peace System in the United States," *California Law Review, 15* (January, 1927), 140.

resulting in specialized branches or divisions of the court. The municipal court of Philadelphia has five divisions—civil, criminal, juvenile, domestic relations, and misdemeanants. In the Chicago municipal court, the court of domestic relations, the speeders' court, the morals court, the boys' court, and the small claims court exist as five specialized branches.

In some cities municipal courts occupy a middle ground between the lower magistrate or justice of the peace courts and the general trial courts. More commonly their jurisdiction parallels that of other inferior courts but the limits in regard to amounts of money involved and the length of terms which can be meted out are less confining. For instance, justice courts in California exist in counties and townships with populations of less than 40,000. Their jurisdiction in civil cases is limited to cases involving $500 or less and in criminal suits to misdemeanors involving a maximum penalty of six months in jail or a fine of $1,000. Municipal courts have been established in cities of over 40,000 with jurisdiction in civil cases up to $3,000 and in criminal cases involving maximum penalties of a year in jail or a fine of $1,000 and preliminary felony hearings. The municipal courts are also courts of record while the justice courts are not.

GENERAL TRIAL COURTS

The next higher level in the state court system is the county court, which might aptly be called the workhorse of the judicial system.[10] Known in some states as the district, superior, circuit courts, or the court of common pleas, the term county court will be used to embrace these as well since in large part they have parallel jurisdiction. The jurisdiction of this court extends to four types of controversy: ordinary civil cases, cases in equity, criminal cases, and probate or inheritance cases. Typically, this general trial court is a one-judge court and the judge is chosen by popular election on a partisan ballot. In about one-fourth of the states, this judge is appointed by the governor or selected by the state legislature, and about an equal number of states provide for his election by non-

[10] Since terminology varies so among the states, there may be a "county" court with relatively limited jurisdiction intermediate between the minor judiciary and the general trial court. In urban areas, there would often be more than one judge for the general trial court, while the boundaries of the court may include several counties in less populated areas.

partisan ballot. His term of office ranges from two to 15 years with four- or six-year terms most common.

As indicated by the types of cases heard by general trial courts, their jurisdiction is quite extensive and normally include both original and appellate authority. Known as superior courts in California, this level has original jurisdiction in civil cases involving sums of over $3,000; probate of wills and guardianships; divorce, separate maintenance and annulment; juvenile delinquency and abandonment; insanity and other infirmities; naturalization; and criminal cases. Their appellate power extends to appeals from municipal and justice courts on which they have the authority to make final decision.[11] This pattern of authority is quite common for general trial courts. In addition, many such courts are authorized to review, on appeal, the actions of certain local administrative agencies.

In view of their broad jurisdiction, general trial courts are aptly called the "backbone" of our judicial system. The importance and heavy responsibilities of the general trial judge have been well summarized by a former trial court judge in these words:

> To the vast majority of the people he is the judiciary; the court of last resort. He is without question the keystone of the whole judicial edifice, the most important official in the entire judicial system. . . .
> To the people, the judge of the circuit court is the personification of all courts. To the extent that they respect him as a man; to the extent that they have confidence in his ability and integrity; to the extent that he metes out justice to those who appear before him; to that extent do they respect and repose confidence in all courts.
> The power he wields is almost beyond comprehension; and the responsibility of that power rests heavily on the shoulders of the judge who undertakes to perform his duties with a vision of justice before him as his pole-star.[12]

While general trial courts try many non-jury cases, they also make extensive use of the jury in both civil and criminal cases to serve as a fact determining agency. The essential duty of the trial or petit jury is to decide, on the basis of the evidence presented before it, the arguments of counsel, and the instructions of the court, whether the accused in a criminal case is guilty or innocent of the

[11] Henry Turner and John A. Vieg, *The Government and Politics of California,* McGraw-Hill, 1960, p. 243.

[12] Frank Hollingsworth, "That Beleagured Gentleman: The Trial Judge," *Journal of the Missouri Bar,* 7 (June, 1953), 83.

offense charged and in civil actions whether judgment should be in favor of the plaintiff or the defendant. State constitutions almost universally contain broad guarantees to citizens of a right to trial by jury, and even though the use of the jury is voluntarily waived by the parties involved in some cases, the trial jury continues to play an important role in judicial administration.

While many states now provide for the trial of misdemeanor offenses and some civil cases by juries of less than 12 members, the jury of 12 is still almost universally required in trials of more serious criminal cases and is widely used in other cases as well. The list of jurors is usually chosen at random from either local tax assessment rolls or voter registration lists. When a jury panel is needed, the court clerk draws a designated number of names from a box and these persons are summoned to appear for service. The jury hears the case and then retires to arrive at its verdict.

An application of the common-law rule holds that a valid verdict in either a civil or criminal case must be one of unanimous agreement of the 12 jurists. About half the states have now modified this unanimity rule in civil cases and in trials of lesser crimes by requiring a vote of two-thirds, three-fourths, or five-sixths of the jurists. This action has resulted in many fewer "hung" juries—the term used when the jury fails to agree, resulting in a new trial or the dropping of the case.

The jury system has long been criticized on two main counts. The first relates to the qualifications of persons comprising the jury and the second to the unanimity requirement in jury decisions. Because of the ease of obtaining an excuse from jury service, many persons qualified by education, experience, and temperament avoid this service. The legal qualifications for jury duty are fairly uniform and consist of lower and upper age limits, citizenship, and residence requirements. The Illinois law, which is typical of those in other states, prescribes further that juriors shall be "in the possession of their natural faculties and not infirm or decrepit. . . . Free from all legal exceptions of fair character, of approved integrity, of sound judgment, well informed, and who understand the English language." These qualifications are not very demanding but their careful application is not an easy undertaking because of their vagueness. The question of the unanimous verdict makes it 12 times as difficult to secure a conviction as it does to prevent one, since every member of the jury must be convinced, beyond a reasonable doubt, of the guilt of the defendant. Few would disagree with our principle that an accused person is presumed innocent until proven guilty and that the burden of proof lies with the state. However, it is probable that the unanimous verdict will continue to decline except in cases of capital offenses.[13]

Although it has fallen into partial disuse in some states, the grand jury remains a judicial device in wide use. A grand jury differs from the petit or trial jury both in size and function. In size, it varies from 12 to 23 members and its function is to determine whether or not sufficient evidence exists to bring a person to trial. The defense does not have an opportunity to present its side to the grand jury. Thus, it does not return a "verdict" but decides whether or not the evidence presented warrants an indictment of the accused so that he must stand trial.

While the return of indictments was historically the primary function of the grand jury, this is no longer the common procedure in some states for bringing a person to trial. An alternative procedure involves a preliminary hearing in an inferior court, followed by the filing of an "information," a sworn statement, by the district attroney in a general trial court. One of the chief advantages of the grand jury proceeding is its secrecy. Thus, it is still commonly used when a case is weak or doubtful to protect the accused against unfounded public accusations, or in cases that are sensational in nature.

As the percentage of time spent by grand juries in considering criminal indictments lessens, they have more time to devote to "watchdog" activities. In California, a grand jury of 19 citizens is impaneled annually in each county in the state. A considerable portion of its time is spent in looking into the conduct of public officials, the expenditure of public funds, and the functioning of local government. While grand juries have been accused of unwarranted harassment of public officials and of being cumbersome, amateurish, and time-consuming in their performance, they do seem to serve as a potentially powerful arm of direct democracy and many have rendered valuable service through studies and investigations.

[13] For further discussion of the jury system, its weaknesses and proposed reforms, see Jerome Frank, *Courts on Trial: Myth and Reality in American Justice*, Princeton University Press, 1949, Chaps. 8 and 9; and J. H. Miner, "The Jury Problem," *Journal of Criminal Law and Criminology*, 37 (May–June, 1946), 1–15.

■ Due Process of Law

The deeply cherished safeguards secured for American citizens by the Fifth and Fourteenth Amendments to our Constitution are also guaranteed by our state constitutions. As a result, we are twice assured that no person shall be deprived of life, liberty or property "without due process of law." This is not an easy concept to define and perhaps it becomes most meaningful in seeing the several procedural steps which occur in the trial of a person charged with an offense. These steps represent the procedural safeguards which must be followed and when taken together they comprise the major elements of the due process principle.

Since the major procedural steps differ in civil and criminal suits, these are listed in outline form in Table 11. A legal officer of the state serves as the prosecuting attorney since the state is the plaintiff in criminal cases while in civil cases the plaintiff is the person bringing the suit. Defendants in criminal cases have a number of general rights which include: a preliminary hearing in the case of a felony charge, the right to legal counsel, the right to know the charges against him, the right to trial by jury, the right to confront witnesses against him, and the right to summon witnesses on his own behalf.

■ Essentials of a Sound Judicial System

Observers, critics, and experts who have examined the organization and operation of our lower courts have commented on many imperfections in their structure and practice. Since court systems vary widely among the states and between sections within a single state, it would not be very meaningful to enumerate a number of specific and needed reforms. It is possible, however, to present a checklist of the essentials of a sound judicial system, and the lower courts in any particular state can be measured in terms of meeting the prescribed essentials. The following checklist of 13 essentials is adapted from an article by Arthur T. Vanderbilt, a respected writer and a judge of high repute.[14]

[14] Arthur T. Vanderbilt, "The Essentials of a Sound Judicial System," *Northwestern University Law Review, 48* (March–April, 1953), 1-15.

Table 11. *Major Procedural Steps in Civil and Criminal Cases*

CIVIL	CRIMINAL
1. Plaintiff, or his attorney, files complaint with court stating facts upon which claim against defendant is based.	1. Defendant commits an action which violates a specific law that makes such action a crime.
2. Court issues summons for defendant allowing him a period of ten days in which to answer complaint. At this point, defendant has one of three options: decide not to contest suit and thus allow plaintiff to win by default, seek to settle dispute out of court, or decide to contest action and file formal answer to stated charges; in some cases he may file a countersuit.	2. Defendant is properly arrested with or without a warrant.
	3. The accused person is "booked" at police station or sheriff's office and is informed of specific charges against him.
	4. Accused is brought before judge of an inferior court for preliminary hearing to determine if evidence against him is sufficient to hold him for trial or to require posting of a bond for release.
3. Assuming defendant takes the third course of action, judge reviews statements to decide whether or not there is sufficient cause for action. If he determines there is, a time is set for the trial.	5. Accused is held for trial either upon basis of an information signed by district attorney or indictment voted by grand jury.
4. Both parties and their attorneys appear in court. (Evolution of "pre-trial procedures" in civil cases has tended to expedite administration of justice by wide departures from common-law practice of trial by surprise, debate, etc. Essence of these procedures is conferences with judge in which issues are narrowed, some facts admitted, and the precise matter in dispute is clarified.) Trial begins before a judge, or if either party prefers a jury trial, before judge and jury.	6. Trial begins in general trial court. Accused has right to counsel of his own choosing or is assigned counsel by court. At this point, accused pleads either innocent or guilty. If he pleads guilty, he is sentenced without trial. If he pleads not guilty, trial commences, and, unless waived by accused, a jury of 12 is impaneled to hear proceedings.
	7. Next comes the trial proper with presentation of evidence both for and against accused, examination of witnesses, and arguments and counterarguments by prosecutor and counsel for accused.
5. Both sides present cases with witnesses appearing and attorneys for the plaintiff and defendant present arguments before court.	8. With submission of evidence and argument completed, judge instructs jury in questions of law and it retires for deliberation.

Table 11. (*Continued*)

CIVIL	CRIMINAL
6. If jury has been waived, judge takes case under consideration for decision. If it is a jury trial, judge instructs jury which then leaves courtroom for its deliberations.	9. Jury presents its findings to court. Its decision for conviction must be unanimous vote of jury panel. If verdict is guilty, judge pronounces sentence upon accused. If verdict is not guilty, accused is released and he may not be tried again on the same charge. If jury cannot reach a unanimous decision within a reasonable period of time, it is dismissed and new trial is ordered or accused is freed by virtue of a "hung" jury.
7. Judgment is rendered by court as a decision of the judge in a non-jury case or in a judgment by judge based on findings of the jury in favor of plaintiff or defendant.	
8. Either party may appeal to a higher court on grounds of a procedural error, misdirection of jury, or other errors which might result in miscarriage of justice.	10. Defendant has right to appeal to higher court if he believes he has been deprived of justice because of a mishandling of laws or evidence.
9. If appeal is accepted, case is tried again in a higher court with steps of trial repeated in the court of appeal.	11. If appeal is not granted, judgment of the general trial court is carried out. Following completion of his sentence, the person may not be tried a second time for the same offense.

1. A simple system of courts embracing (a) a local court of limited civil and criminal jurisdiction; (b) a trial court of general statewide jurisdiction; and (c) an appellate court or courts depending on the needs of the particular state. There should be considerable specialization by judges in the trial courts rather than courts with special jurisdictions.

2. A corps of independent judges beholden only to the law and constitution who are knowledgeable in the field of law, experienced at the bar, industrious, and believed to be honest.

3. Juries that represent a cross-section of the honest and intelligent citizenry.

4. Honorable and well educated lawyers and an effective bar organization.

5. Competent court clerks, stenographic reporters, and bailiffs, and an administrative judge to give general supervision to the judicial system.

6. Elimination of unnecessary delays in bringing cases to court and in the procedure of the courtroom.

7. Decisions based on merit rather than legal shenanigans. This involves restoration of power to preside effectively in the trial judge, careful review of judicial rules, and the use of pretrial procedures.

8. Elimination of judicial discourtesy by increasing the decorum of courtrooms and dignifying the role of the judge.

9. Fair division of work among judges by assigning judges of courts without backlogs to assist those who have work overloads.

10. Compilation of weekly and monthly reports by the administrative director of the courts from statistics supplied by court clerks and in the weekly reports from judges.

11. The use of these reports in assigning judges, supervising their work, and investigating complaints from individuals or bar associations.

12. The selection of an administrative director to assist the administrative judge in the many details of running the court system efficiently.

13. An abiding conviction that the law and the courts exist for the benefit of the litigants and the state rather than for the benefit of judges, lawyers, and court officers.

Vanderbilt concludes that,

There is nothing esoteric about these essentials of a sound judicial system. They are all quite obvious. They are not difficult to put into effect once there is the will to do so. They must be achieved in every state if we are to have an administration of justice worthy of the name. There can be no doubt as to the importance to us all of attaining such a goal if our kind of government is to function as it should. The only question is whether the judges and lawyers in each state will take the leadership in fulfilling the foremost obligation of the profession to society or whether they will abdicate to laymen.[15]

[15] *Ibid.,* p. 15.

SUGGESTED READINGS

Books

Abraham, Henry J., *Courts and Judges, An Introduction to the Judicial Process* (New York: Oxford University Press, 1959).

Adrian, Charles R., *State and Local Governments* (New York: McGraw-Hill, 1960).

Council of State Governments, *Trial Courts of General Jurisdiction in the Forty-Eight States* (Chicago: Council of State Governments, 1951).

Curran, H. H., *Magistrates Courts* (New York: Scribner, 1942).

Frank, Jerome, *Courts on Trial: Myth and Reality in American Justice* (Princeton: Princeton University Press, 1949).

Morlan, Robert L., *Capitol, Courthouse and City Hall*, 2nd ed. (Boston: Houghton Mifflin, 1960).

Pound, Roscoe, *Organization of the Courts* (Boston: Little, Brown, 1940).

Snider, Clyde F., *Local Government in Rural America* (New York: Appleton-Century-Crofts, 1957).

Vanderbilt, Arthur T., *Judges and Jurors* (Boston: Boston University Press, 1956).

Willoughby, W. F., *Principles of Judicial Administration* (Washington: Brookings Institution, 1929).

Articles

Annals of the American Academy of Political and Social Science, "Judicial Administration and the Common Man," Vol. 287 (May, 1953), entire issue.

Hollingsworth, Frank, "That Beleagured Gentleman: The Trial Judge," *Journal of the Missouri Bar,* 7 (June, 1951), 83–84.

Keefe, William J., "Judges and Politics," *University of Pittsburgh Law Review,* 20 (March, 1959), 621–31.

Miner, J. H., "The Jury Problem," *Journal of Criminal Law and Criminology,* 37 (May–June, 1946), 1–15.

Smith, Chester H., "The Justice of the Peace System in the United States," *California Law Review,* 15 (January, 1927), 118–41.

Vanderbilt, Arthur T., "The Essentials of a Sound Judicial System," *Northwestern University Law Review,* 48 (March–April, 1953), 1–15.

The Administrative
Process

16

The administrative process is both an extension and a part of the local political process which has been described in two preceding chapters. While the distinction commonly made between the two processes—that policies are formulated through the political process and executed through the administrative process—is valid in part, overlapping between the two is inevitable, and their complete separation is impossible. In determining local policies, the local legislative body and the executive delineate in varying degrees how they are to be carried out and the policies are modified somewhat in their execution by the administrative officers who shape the general policies to specific cases.

The intermixture of the political and administrative processes has been vividly described by Arthur W. Bromage in the terms of America's favorite sport—baseball.

Once the people have elected mayors and councilmen, these officials, together with the administrators, take the field in the municipal ball park. The municipal team plays against crime, fire, disease, poor housing, inadequate public parks, insufficient water supplies, inadequate recreational programs, pollution of our water resources, problems of planning and zoning, and many other heavy hitters. The citizens, if they are alert, fill the bleachers from week to week to see how the local team is doing. On the municipal ball team we have both councilmen and administrators, including clerks, attorneys, fiscal officers, public officers, police and fire chiefs, public works superintendents, planning officials, and many others. The administrators do the infield work, handling the hot grounders, and the councilmen patrol the outfield, handling anything that gets by the infielders. When something gets by the outfielders on this municipal team, there will be jeering from the bleachers, and there is likely to be a change in administration of the ball club.[1]

There are numerous definitions of the term "public administration." Two typical and common definitions are: (1) public administration is the organization and management of men and materials to achieve the purposes of government; and (2) public administration is the art and science of management as applied to the affairs of state. Neither of these, however, is very useful in explaining what public administration is. A more meaningful definition holds, "The central idea of public administration is rational action, defined as action correctly calculated to realize given desired goals."[2] Briefly stated, public administration in local government may be defined as the management of services rendered by that unit.

The process to achieve the "rational action" called for in the definition above may be described as the administrative process. Two key elements in this process are the structural or organizational pattern in local government to realize the desired courses of action, and the techniques of management utilized to guide and control these actions. The first part of this chapter will discuss the organizational aspects, and it will be followed by a description of the basic management techniques practiced in the local administrative process.

■ Local Administrative Organization

According to Waldo, "Organization is the structure of authoritative and habitual personal interrelations in an administrative sys-

[1] Arthur W. Bromage, "The Art of Governing American Cities," *Horizons for Modern Pennsylvania Local Government*, 3 (March, 1956), 3–4.
[2] Dwight Waldo, *The Study of Public Administration*, Random House, 1955, p. 11.

tem."[3] Our discussion of types of local governmental units and their organizational structure in Chapters 9 through 12 revealed that local agencies may be organized in a wide number of different ways. Agencies identified as independent offices in county and city government have a single elective officer at their head. Other agencies have a single administrator appointed by the local executive or the local legislative body. A third common pattern is for a plural-member board or commission to head particular agencies. In a small number of cases, the head of a local agency is appointed by the governor, as is true of the chief of police in some cities. There are infinite varieties in the arrangements for the appointment and removal of local administrative officers by other local officers, and plural-member boards also function in several different possible patterns. The board can act as a unit in administering its programs; the work can be divided equally or unequally among the members; one member of the board can serve as the operating head of it; or the board may appoint a person to serve as its director, executive secretary, or administrative officer.

While there is considerable disagreement concerning the existence and utility of principles of administrative organization,[4] there are several general rules for local governments which can be advanced with some certainty. First, administrative responsibility should be centralized in a single chief administrator who is armed with sufficient authority to perform his responsibilities and aided by an adequate staff. Second, the number of departmental units and governmental agencies reporting to the chief administrator should not be so numerous that he is unable to exercise effective direction over them. Third, related functions should be logically grouped into departments and agencies. This is essential since the number of functions and activities will be more numerous than the number of departments and agencies. Fourth, the factor of public convenience should be given careful attention in determining local administrative structure. Fifth, the use of boards and commissions for administrative purposes should be carefully considered.[5] The more proper uses for plural-member boards will be discussed in a later section.

[3] *Ibid.*, p. 12.
[4] See Herbert A. Simon, "The Proverbs of Administration," *Public Administration Review, 6* (Winter, 1946), 53-67.
[5] For an elaboration of these proposals, see Lennox L. Moak, "Realigning the Departments: Some Basic Factors," in Bureau of Municipal Research, *Citizens' Business, No. 1901* (November 8, 1949).

Of the several schemes for classifying administrative agencies, one of the most meaningful is a threefold division into line, staff, and auxiliary agencies, based on the primary purpose for which they exist. Line agencies are those which are concerned with the primary purposes for which the governmental unit exists and thus serve citizens directly by providing basic services or by regulating their conduct. Typical local government activities which are classified as "line" include police and fire, health, welfare, utilities and public works, education, and recreation. It is apparent that agencies carrying on these activities have operating responsibilities for providing these services.

Staff agencies, on the other hand, carry on those activities which are of service to other agencies of the government rather than directly for citizens. Their function is to advise but not act, to plan but not implement, and to inform but not enact. Thus, they are thinking, planning, and advisory—but not operating—agencies. Among local government activities which are properly labeled staff are those of planning commissions, budget officers, accountants, legal officers, zoning boards, research agencies, bill-drafting agencies, and public relations personnel.

The third type of agency—an auxiliary agency—combines one aspect of each of the other two. Like a line unit, the auxiliary agency has operating responsibilities, but these are performed for other governmental agencies rather than for the citizens. Thus, their clientele is like that of a staff rather than a line agency. The basic function of an auxiliary agency is to maintain other existing agencies. It does this by fulfilling specialized functions common to a number of operating agencies but removed from those agencies for reasons of economy, coordination, and specialization. Typical examples are central personnel agencies, central purchasing and disbursing agencies, central fiscal control agencies, and central custodial services. In large jurisdictions, there will often be a subordinate office in each major agency which carries on these activities within that agency under the general direction of the head of the auxiliary agency.

While this threefold division of administrative agencies seems clean-cut, the distinctions are certainly not uniformly accepted. Actually, there is good reason for this uncertainty as reflected in this statement by Albert Lepawsky: "Administrators must recognize that staff and line are coordinates, operating not in a hierarchical relation of staff over line, but on a horizontal plane of authority and responsibility under the chief executive. A staff man who does not give [what amounts to] commands to the line is ineffectual, and a line man who does not understand and exercise a modicum of staff functions is a failure."[6]

ADMINISTRATIVE DEPARTMENTS

The major administrative agencies in local government are the operating and service departments differentiated above. It is generally recognized that it is desirable to keep the number of departments reasonably small to permit their effective control and supervision. This desire leads to a problem in the grouping of functions and activities within departments, since it is also recognized that only similar functions should be grouped together in a single agency. Since the objective sought through administrative agencies is the efficient and economical execution of policies determined by the local executive and legislature, it is apparent that their organization should be planned with this goal in mind.

There are four principal bases for the organization of departments and the assignment of functions within them. These are the concepts of organization by purpose, process, clientele, and area. Organization by purpose is based on what is to be done; by process, how it is to be done; by clientele, the persons to be served; and by area, where it is to be done. The four bases are not exclusive and divisions within a single agency may be variously organized to reflect two or more. A health department is an example of a purpose agency—to protect health and prevent the spread of disease. A licensing bureau or a legal department is based on process. A department of assistance, dealing with persons who need relief aid, is organized on the clientele basis. Precinct stations of a police department and station houses of a fire department both represent area organization since each serves a distinct geographic area. Each of these examples is an agency with a purpose and all utilize certain processes in carrying out their functions. However, they do illustrate both the non-exclusiveness of the four basic concepts and the

---

[6] Albert Lepawsky, *Administration,* Knopf, 1949, p. 321.

fact that local agencies have varying organizational patterns which reflect the nature of their assignments.

While it is not possible to give a specific numerical answer to the question of the number of departments most desirable in a local government, there are certain rules which can be helpful. A recent study of the government of New York City advised, "Make certain that there is one main function for every major department, and one department for every major function." To place all activities in a few departments, the report stated, "would turn many departments into bushel baskets, each with various functions actually unrelated, and would produce within these multifunctional departments many orphan activities."[7] The number of departments will tend to vary directly with the size of the community. This is logical since the larger the unit, the more functions and activities it will provide for its citizens. Effective coordination can be achieved in part through executive supervision as well as through organization. Thus some local governments with effectively functioning staff and managerial aids for their executives may have more departments than communities in which the executive is weaker in powers of supervision and coordination. However, this is far from a universal practice and some of the strongest local executives have very few administrative departments operating under them.

The head of the local department plays an important role in policy formulation. He advises the chief executive of his needs and problems and testifies before the local legislative body when it is considering the budgetary needs of his department. He is also an important agent of his government in his relations with citizens and citizen groups and as a representative of his community in meetings with heads of similar departments of other units. Thus, he is important in both the internal and external affairs of his government.

While most departments have a single head, there are still some which are directed by a plural-member board or commission. If the department is empowered to determine policy, issue rules and regulations, or to exercise quasi-judicial or quasi-legislative functions, then there is merit in having a plural head. Policies should be the result of deliberation and rules are normally more readily accepted if issued by a board rather than by an individual. Thus, the board is still used in some health and personnel departments as well as

<hr/>

[7] Mayor's Committee on Management Survey, *Modern Management for the City of New York,* Vol. 1, 1953, p. 17.

PROCESSES OF LOCAL GOVERNMENT

for library and school administration. However, unless the department has these functions, a single head is preferable since executive supervision is simplified, the head can act with greater speed, and there is no opportunity for "buck-passing."

BOARDS AND COMMISSIONS

Although boards and commissions do not normally function effectively in operating a department, they are useful in an advisory capacity and are widely used by local governments. They provide an opportunity for a number of citizens to participate directly in their government and are valuable in selling governmental proposals for action to the citizenry. Usually service is uncompensated, so the members are persons interested in serving the community. Thus, their opinions and recommendations are usually accepted more readily than are those coming directly from governmental employees who have a more recognizable stake in the success of the incumbent officials or party.

There are no general rules concerning the use and existence of local advisory boards. They exist in all types and sizes of units. Normally, the number is greater in larger communities than in small ones and more use is made of them in strong- than in weak-executive forms. On the other hand, weak-executive forms are more likely to have some boards and commissions with formal policy-setting powers, while few, if any, will exist under stronger executive plans.

A recent evaluation of the use of citizen boards in local government concluded that: (1) they study complex problems which the local legislative body does not have time to study in depth; (2) they serve as a buffer to protect the local executive and legislature from certain types of political pressures; (3) they provide a considerable amount of staff work at little cost; and (4) they offer effective and useful aid to the local officials and the community. On the negative side, such boards (1) do not remove important problems from the arena of politics; (2) often perceive their functions quite narrowly; and (3) sometimes feel that they are not consulted often enough, that their advice is too freely ignored, and that they are not sufficiently informed of the outcome of or the use made of their recommendations.[8]

[8] Associated Institutes of Government of Pennsylvania Universities, *Horizons for Modern Pennsylvania Governments,* 5 (April, 1958), p. 1.

Los Angeles is one city that still makes wide use of citizen commissions for administrative purposes. Each administrative department has a five-member board which directly supervises and establishes rules for that department. The board members serve only part-time and are appointed for staggered terms so that no incoming mayor can name a majority of the board members during a single term of office. His power over the boards is further limited by the requirement that he receive the approval of the council for his appointments to or removals from those commissions. The general power of these boards is to supervise, regulate, manage, and control the departments they serve and to make and enforce internal rules and regulations. In addition, the commissions have the power to appoint and remove general managers of the departments. While the commissions vary in their effectiveness in terms of their own composition and the willingness of the mayor to retain the appointees of his predecessor, they do function as valuable adjuncts in a city with a mayor-CAO-council form of government.[9]

SUMMARY

As indicated in the brief discussion above the varieties of organizational structures in local government are many. While there are few general principles which have general validity for local governments regardless of size, type, or form of government, it is clear that wide use of independent administrative agencies and boards is not conducive to the smooth functioning of local administrative machinery. One astute student of administration has defined organization as "the relating of efforts and capacities of individuals and groups engaged upon a common task in such a way as to secure the desired objective with the least friction and the most satisfaction to those for whom the task is done and those engaged in the enterprise."[10] These realistic and worthwhile objectives can be attained more satisfactorily by an integrated plan of organization than by one characterized by the independence of some officers and agencies from the control of the local executive.

[9] "Should We Abolish Citizen Commissions in Our City Government?" *Town Hall*, 23, no. 30 (August 8, 1961), 3-4.
[10] John M. Gaus, "The Theory of Organization in Administration," in John M. Gaus, L. D. White and M. E. Dimock, *The Frontiers of Public Administration*, University of Chicago Press, 1936, pp. 66-67.

■ *Administrative Management*

As defined by Waldo, "Management is action intended to achieve rational cooperation in an administrative system."[11] Thus, it is the kinetic force in administration while structure represents a somewhat more static element. While such a distinction between administrative organization and management (often referred to as "O" and "M") is valuable as a means of analysis, they are not independent aspects in practical situations. The close relationship between "O" and "M" at the operating level can be seen in agencies combining the purpose and process bases of organization. The methods used in rendering the processes may directly influence the organizational structure of that agency. Similarly, the assignment of duties may directly determine the specific methods to be utilized within that agency.

A second definition of management holds that it "concerns the leadership and direction of groups of individuals to the accomplishment of desired objectives. The art of management is therefore simply the administrative means of getting the 'job done.' "[12] Since the entire leadership and direction of these groups cannot be unified and provided by a single executive, he has a number of aides depending on the size of the community and the number, variety, and level of services provided.

Administrative organization may be quite complex in large local governments but it is usually rather simple in small communities. Administrative leadership in small cities is sometimes described in terms of two key persons—a "Mr. Inside" and a "Mr. Outside." The "inside" man is responsible for many of the housekeeping operations, including finance, personnel, purchasing, and records. The "outside" man is often a major line official such as director of public works. He may handle such matters as street maintenance, parks, water supply, and planning.

LEADERSHIP

While proper organization is important, leadership is a prime essential of effective management. Successful administrative leadership is an elusive quality which cannot be adequately defined in

[11] Waldo, *op. cit.*, p. 12.
[12] John H. Ames, "The Art of Management," *Public Management, 32* (January, 1950), 2-6.

listings of duties to be performed or described in terms of personal character traits. Leadership clearly is not autocratic rule but the solution of problems and accomplishment of results. Thus, leadership may be more properly described as direction "based on knowledge and experience with the application of known facts to the proper attainment of desired objectives."[13]

As identified by Pope, the essential elements of effective administrative leadership are: (1) an intelligent and effective handling of personnel transactions and regularized patterns for doing so; (2) an adequate organization so that each member knows his job, authority, and responsibility; (3) a general understanding and appreciation of specialized programs and problems; (4) an opportunity for participation by subordinates in deciding how things are to be done; (5) an ability to time administrative decision and action so that many problems can be anticipated and avoided. Pope concludes that an "administrative leader is more like his subordinates than different from them. In this age of specialists he too is a specialist. His specialty is the art of furnishing leadership and coordinated purpose to other specialists."[14]

RESPONSIBILITIES OF THE ADMINISTRATOR

The responsibilities of an administrator may be broadly defined as embracing those activities for which he may be held accountable by superior executive or legislative officials. While specific responsibilities are established by law, regulation, and delegation from superiors, they may vary widely among jurisdictions with passage of time and even from position to position within the same community. However, three responsibilities are so basic that they are shared commonly by all administrators. These are (1) faithful execution of the laws pertaining to and regulating their jurisdictions; (2) efficient use of available resources in achieving goals; and (3) prompt reporting to superiors of changes in goals, laws, or resources which appear necessary or desirable.

These basic responsibilities are too broad and general to be of much help for administrators in specific agencies and jurisdictions. A recent listing of more carefully defined responsibilities advances

[13] *Ibid.*, p. 2.
[14] Herman G. Pope, "The City Manager as a Leader in the Administrative Organization," *Public Management, 30* (October, 1949), 294-7.

four major categories and suggests several specific examples under each.[15] The first general responsibility of the administrator pertains to his responsiveness to superiors and clientele. This requires him to help superiors to discharge their responsibilities, and to seek public understanding and support for the policies and programs of his own agency. The second responsibility calls for articulation of objectives and program proposals that are both professionally sound and politically acceptable, and for cooperating and working closely with other agencies. Third, his responsibilities in procurement, organization, and control of resources include organization and control of the resources of his agency for optimum efficiency. Fourth, responsibilities in the area of direction, communication, and supervision require systematic evaluation of the services under his direction, the maintenance of effective communication channels, and the stimulation of subordinates for self-improvement.

THE PUBLIC INTEREST

The concept of the public interest figures prominently in discussions of the leadership and responsibilities of an administrator. There is general agreement that it is the duty of government, at whatever level, to serve the interest of the public rather than any small portion of it, but there is no real consensus as to what constitutes the public interest, either among administrative theorists or practitioners.[16]

According to Charles Adrian, who qualifies as both a theorist and practitioner, there are four basic assumptions concerning the nature of the public interest shared by most administrators. These are: (1) the public interest is identified with the expectations of the professional peers of the administrator. The local recreation director is quite likely to consider the standards of his professional association as right and in the public interest of the community he serves; (2) the public interest is interpreted by the administrator as reflecting the expectations of his administrative superiors; (3) the public interest is rationalized by the administrator as the extension of his own personal value system; and (4) the public interest is identified

---

[15] Stephen B. Sweeney and Thomas J. Davy (eds.), *Education for Administrative Careers in Government Service*, University of Pennsylvania Press, 1958. pp. 289–91.

[16] Glendon A. Schubert, Jr., " 'The Public Interest' in Administrative Decision-Making," *American Political Science Review, 51* (June, 1957), 346–68.

by the administrator with the wishes of the interested public or publics.[17]

The commonality of the above views, however, does not make them necessarily sound. By injecting the necessity for ethical or moral considerations, it is possible to arrive at a process for determining the public interest more easily than it is to define the concept itself. Thus, the public interest may be considered as that which results when an ethical administrator follows good procedures, since decisions should reflect his highest ethical judgment based on an examination of facts and a careful analysis of them. Although the public interest is sometimes considered only a useful myth, decisions based on it are a goal worthy of the conscientious efforts of every administrator.

ACCOUNTABILITY

In the words of Arthur Bromage, "Democracy is not a matter of push buttons and gadgets. It calls for consistent hard effort by councilmen, administrators, and citizens who seek improved policies, techniques, and services. It is like pushing a big cart up the long hill of progress. You have to dig your toes in and push all the way. For this reason, councilmen and administrators should encourage the co-operation of civic-action groups that are willing to work."[18]

Keeping citizens intelligently informed is one of the chief problems of local government. Information is necessary if the citizenry is to have a legitimate and knowledgable basis for holding its governmental officials accountable to the mandates recorded in local elections. Reporting to the public, however, should spring from the desire to inform the citizenry so intelligent decisions can be made, rather than from the desire to advance the political fortunes of certain local officers or a political party.

Government officials, whether elected or appointed, are subject to a number of restraints. Chief among these checks are the periodic expressions of the citizens in local elections and on questions of policy submitted to them for decision. Other restraints exist in the structure of the local government. The division of powers and func-

---

[17] Charles R. Adrian, *Governing Urban America*, 2nd ed., McGraw-Hill, 1961, p. 321.
[18] Bromage, *op. cit.*, p. 4.

tions among a number of officials and agencies serves as a check on the actions of any single one. A third major check lies in the division of the citizenry into a number of small publics rather than its grouping into a single monolithic public. For example, the basic interest of a citizen in his government may come from his occupation, his area of residence, his tax bill, the level of services received, personal friendships with public officials, or from a number of other reasons. It is rare for the entire citizenry to hold a single point of view on any question of policy, and the divergent interests of its several divisions serve as brakes on the wishes of any single group in settling that question.

Citizen groups perform important functions as intermediaries between citizens and government and often perform "watchdog" functions on the government's operations. Since the typical citizen is a member of one or more such organizations, he is directly concerned in holding his officials accountable. As Bromage clearly states, effective citizenship calls for a consistent hard effort, but there is no better method for assuring effective and responsive local government.

THE CONCEPT OF STANDARDS

Administration cannot be wholly scientific or neutral. The interrelationships of the political process and the administrative process have been noted previously, and it need only be mentioned here that it is not yet possible (and probably never will be) to completely replace political considerations with objective criteria and administrative standards. But while there is no one "best way" to administer programs or organize local governments, certain guides have been developed which can be of assistance to local officials.

Perhaps the first administrative standard developed was the concept of official honesty. Reaction to the exposure of local corruption and inefficiency at the turn of the century resulted in a number of techniques to insure honesty of local officials. Among these were legal restraints on actions of local officials and such procedures as the annual audit, accounting systems, operating and capital improvement budgets, purchasing systems, and regularized personnel practices.

Today citizens expect their local governments to be both honest and reasonably efficient. Administrative efficiency has been described as measurable "by the ratio of the effects actually obtained with the available resources to the maximum effects possible with the available resources."[19] As this definition implies, efficiency is difficult to evaluate since, in the last analysis, it is largely a matter of point of view. What seems to be the best way to one official may seem to be a poor way to another.

In recent years, there have been increasing efforts to establish criteria for appraising governmental activities at all levels. According to Ridley and Simon, "The appraisal of administration can take place only after the objectives of administration have been defined in measurable comparable terms."[20] Thus, a comparison of gross expenditures by comparable units of local governments is no longer a meaningful method for determining very much about these communities or the efficiency of their services. When expenditures are broken down into more specific categories, such as personal services, equipment and materials, police and health services, etc., they become more helpful.

A recent measurement technique which is meaningful for a number of activities of local government is cost accounting.[21] One good definition of cost accounting describes it as "the process of searching out and recording all the elements of expense incurred to attain a purpose, to carry on an activity or operation, to complete a unit of work, or to do a specific job."[22] If costs for work units in specific service areas can be determined, e.g., mile of streets cleaned, ton of refuse collected, gallon of sewage treated, etc., then more meaningful data will exist for measuring the comparative performance of local governments.

A number of professional organizations set standards for appropriate areas of governmental activity. For example, the National Recreation Association advances standards for numbers, types, and sizes of needed recreational facilities, and the American Public Health Association suggests standards in terms of types of services and personnel needed and minimum citizen financial support.[23] In general, standards of such organizations should be considered as

[19] Clarence E. Ridley and Herbert A. Simon, *Measuring Municipal Activities*, 2nd ed., International City Managers' Association, 1943, p. 3.

[20] *Ibid.*, pp. 2–3.

[21] For a discussion of cost accounting, see pp. 367–69 below.

[22] International City Managers' Association, *Municipal Finance Administration*, 3rd ed., International City Managers Association, 1948, p. 142.

[23] Some of these specific standards of these and other professional organizations will be discussed in Chapters 19–22.

"optimum" since they are usually set so high that few governmental units can meet them. However, they do serve as stimuli in communities in which officials and citizens alike are interested in improving particular services. Nevertheless, it would be helpful if the limitations of such "standards" were more widely appreciated and if they were less frequently interpreted as being the "minimum acceptable" instead of the "desirable optimum."

■ Personnel Administration

In addition to the various elected officials and their top appointees, local governments require large numbers of employees. As of October, 1961, there were 4,990,000 public employees in local governments across the United States. In the first six decades of this century, the number of local employees (excluding school districts) rose from 317,000 to the present 2,943,000—a ninefold increase. The comparative sizes of the number of employees and monthly payrolls of the several types of local governments, along with data concerning state and federal government employment, are shown in Table 12. Probably the most significant fact is that the number of persons employed in local governments is a little more than twice the number employed by the federal government—this in spite of the common impression that most position-holders are in or near Washington, D.C.

Table 12. *Government Employment and Payrolls: October, 1961*

Governmental Level	Number of Employees (1,000)	Monthly Payroll (millions of dollars)
Federal (civilian)	2,484	$1,214
State	1,627	587
Counties	802	264
Municipalities	1,714	638
School Districts	2,047	811
Other (townships and special districts)	427	120
Local	4,990	1,833
Total	9,101	$3,634

SOURCE: Bureau of the Census, *Statistical Abstract of the United States, 1962,* Tables 560, 564, pp. 431, 433.

There are a number of acceptable definitions for the term personnel administration. One author defines it in these words: "Personnel administration is that phase of public administration which is concerned with the 'handling of persons' . . . that is, the employment, placement, and motivation of people within an organization, to the end that the objectives of that organization can be achieved most effectively and economically and with the maximum utilization of all employees."[24] Personnel administration, so defined, covers all aspects of employment, including recruitment, selection, placement, training, promotion, tenure, and separation.

EXTENT OF FORMAL PERSONNEL SYSTEMS

Every unit of local government has some employees and hence has some type of arrangement or process for hiring and firing employees. In communities without a formal system, the regularly elected officials are free to employ and dismiss employees without restrictions. Formal systems are identified as civil service or merit systems. While some writers make a distinction between the two, both imply selection on the basis of merit through competitive examination, the retention and promotion of employees on the basis of performance, and the absence of political affiliation as a major test for fitness for a position. Thus, the terms will be used interchangeably in this section.

There is little uniformity in the legal basis for local personnel systems. In some states, mandatory state laws apply to local employees. More commonly, states enact general "civil service" provisions applicable to various classes of local governments, often depending upon their size; and in some communities, the local personnel systems are provided by special acts of the state legislature. Home rule charters, where authorized, normally include authorization for local merit systems. Although less binding than the above legal bases, personnel arrangements may be governed by local ordinance or by local executive or administrative orders.[25]

There is no known compilation which accurately indicates the number of local employees covered by formal personnel systems.

[24] Kenneth O. Warner, "A Common Sense Personnel Program," *Tennessee Town and City*, 2 (April, 1951), 13.
[25] Kenneth O. Warner, "Municipal Personnel Administration in the United States," in *Local Government in the United States of America*, International Union of Local Authorities, 1961, p. 93.

In a 1958 study, Kaplan estimated that somewhere over 200 of the 3,050 counties in the United States operated under locally- or state-administered formal merit systems, and that not more than 800,000 non-school municipal employees were so covered.[26] Kaplan noted that, "All cities of more than 500,000, all but one of between 250,000 and 500,000, most cities between 100,000 and 250,000, and many smaller ones are under civil service laws." Few counties have merit systems, and this also seems true in the case of most special districts. Special tenure systems for academic employees are quite prevalent among school districts, but often there is no such system for their other employees. Thus, municipalities constitute the unit of local government in which something analogous to the state and federal merit systems is encountered.

CHARACTERISTICS OF LOCAL PERSONNEL ADMINISTRATION

Personnel administration in local government has a number of identifiable features. The first is organizational and pertains to the independent status of the agency administering the personnel system. Developed historically to keep "politics" out of the merit system, the independent civil service commission is still the most common type of administering agency. Appointed by the local legislative body or the chief executive officer, the board normally consists of three or five members who serve overlapping terms of office. The commission and its staff recruits and tests applicants and certifies lists of eligibles to the authorities who appoint employees to fill vacancies. In recent years, some governmental units have replaced the plural-member commission with a single-headed personnel agency responsible to the chief executive, but the older organizational pattern still prevails in most local governments. Most commissions are composed of laymen who serve on a part-time basis. Technical functions are performed by a personnel director and his staff, while the commission serves to represent the public interest in the administration of the local civil service law.

The "position" concept is a second important characteristic of local personnel administration. A position consists of a group of duties and responsibilties which are assigned to one employee. By describing positions in terms of duties and responsibilities, jobs can

[26] H. Eliot Kaplan, *The Law of Civil Service*, Matthew Bender & Co., 1958, p. 27.

be grouped into classes because of their similarities, and pay schedules can be established, resulting in equal pay for equal work. The concept of the position as the unit for recruitment distinguishes the American from the British system under which persons are recruited to broad classes of positions on the basis of educational attainments. In sharp contrast to the British system, a number of American local governments specify that no educational requirements can be established for some positions. This practice is especially common for the recruitment of police and firemen.

A third feature is the generally accepted principle of open competition for positions in local government service. Any person meeting the minimum qualifications established for a given position is eligible to compete for that position by taking the examination. Announcements of available positions must be posted, stating the time and place of the examination, and interested persons meeting the qualifications are eligible for the examination whether they are currently employees of that local government or not. Such open examinations are less frequent at higher levels and occasionally promotional examinations are held with only current employees of prescribed grades, qualifications, and experience eligible to seek the position.

A fourth characteristic also pertains to the nature of the examination. Testing for fitness of the candidates is for a specific position. This feature follows logically from the position concept described above and is emphasized by the common requirement of local civil service laws that examinations must be practical in character and based upon the nature of the work or duties to be performed. Thus, an examination for typists will consist, at least in part, of a speed and accuracy test of typing skills.

The "rule-of-three" is still a common feature of local personnel systems. This pertains to the certification of eligible candidates after the examinations have been scored. Usually the names of the top three candidates are certified to the appointing officer and he is free to select any one of the three for the opening. If for some reason none of the three persons is eligible or acceptable, the appointing officer can return the list and request three other names. Some local governments use the concept of the eligible list rather than the rule-of-three. Under this arrangement, the names of all persons passing the examination are certified to the appointing officer and he is free to select any person on the list. Other communities use the rule-of-one or the rule-of-five, both of which operate in the same manner as the rule-of-three.

The probationary period is a sixth common characteristic. Once appointed to a particular job, the employee is on probation for a period of six months. This is a trial period and the agency can reject, with reason, any employee who does not perform satisfactorily. In actual practice, the probationary period weeds out few employees, but it is an important safety valve for removing misfits, idlers, and persons with unacceptable personality traits from the local public service.

Professionalization of employees is a seventh important feature of local personnel systems. While the association of persons engaging in similar duties is more likely among high-level than low-level employees, organizations now exist for most employees if they wish to join with employees engaged in similar tasks in other jurisdictions. Thus, there are associations for city managers, recreation leaders, engineers, clerks, housing officials, public works employees, etc. One of the values of such associations is that the person who belongs usually feels an obligation to do his best because of his dual loyalty to his community and to his professional association.[27]

An eighth characteristic is the parallel existence of career and political services. The features described above pertain to the former group which consists of persons appointed through a competitive merit system. The political service, on the other hand, embraces elective officials and the persons appointed by them on a non-competitive base. Even the most inclusive systems exclude most department heads and their immediate assistants as well as private secretaries. Other systems find it impractical to include laborers in a formal merit system and exclude such employees. Employees in the political service serve at the pleasure of their appointers since they are responsible to them and are not covered by the same restrictions on removal as are members of the career service.

The recognition of distinctive differences between the rights of employees in the public service and workers in private industry is a ninth characteristic feature. The rights of public employees to join unions and bargain collectively are coming to be accepted, but public employees are denied the ultimate weapon of their counterparts

---

[27] For an analysis of the pros and cons of professionalization, see York Willbern, "Professionalization in the Public Service: Too Little or Too Much?" *Public Administration Review, 14* (Winter, 1954), 13.

in private industry—the right to strike. This right has been expressly renounced in the constitutions of some public employee organizations, and similar prohibitions are expressed in many state laws and local ordinances. There are two principal arguments against striking by public employees. First, a strike against the government would be a disloyal act since the government is the entire people and its interests must be placed above those of any part of it. Second, the public service is so closely connected to the health and welfare of society that continuity of these services is paramount in the interest of all citizens.[28]

BUREAUCRACY AND THE PUBLIC

While advocates of the merit system have won victories in most large cities and the larger counties as well as in many smaller cities in the past 75 years, the argument between them and the defenders of a purely amateur class of public employees continues to rage. Proponents of the latter insist that the best interests of democracy cannot be served by a professionalized public service. In this regard, they re-echo the fears of Andrew Jackson, often called the father of the spoils system. In warning about persons who "feed at the public trough," Jackson stated in his first annual message to Congress that,

There are, perhaps, few men who can for any great length of time enjoy office and power without being more or less under the influence of feelings unfavorable to the faithful discharge of their public duties. Their integrity may be proof against improper considerations immediately addressed to themselves, but they are apt to acquire a habit of looking with indifference upon the public interests and of tolerating conduct from which an unpracticed man would revolt. . . . Corruption in some and in others a perversion of correct feelings and principles divert government from its legitimate ends, and make it an engine for the support of the few at the expense of the many. The duties of all public officers are, or at least admit of being made, so plain and simple that men of intelligence may readily qualify themselves for their performance; and I cannot but believe that more is lost by the mere continuance of men in office than is generally gained by their experience.[29]

[28] For an interesting and balanced discussion of this problem, see the articles by Roger N. Baldwin, H. Eliot Kaplan, and Sterling D. Spero in Robert L. Morlan (ed.) *Capitol, Courthouse and City Hall*, 2nd ed., Houghton Mifflin, 1960, pp. 322-9.
[29] Quoted in Leonard D. White, *Introduction to the Study of Public Administration*, rev. ed., Macmillan, 1939, p. 280.

PROCESSES OF LOCAL GOVERNMENT

The problem of bureaucracy in contemporary local government is somewhat of a paradox. Many citizens want additional or expanded services from their governments, but they fear a loss of control over that government if the non-elective segment of the public service grows. This fear is not entirely ungrounded since most new positions are technical ones and require specialists rather than persons who can be appointed from the ranks of the citizenry. Adrian describes this paradox in these words, "People like the product of government; they do not like the means that seem necessary in order to deliver the product." He concludes that "Americans probably have reason to be on guard against an irresponsible, autocratic, muscle-bound bureaucracy. But there is no evidence to indicate that the danger from this direction is any greater than is the danger from an irresponsible legislative body, an autocratic chief executive, or a muscle-bound court system. Each contains its dangers; each must in turn be watched."[30]

Some of the methods for watching the local bureaucracy were briefly discussed in the section on accountability earlier in this chapter. But too constant and too critical citizen control is not a complete good. As Woodrow Wilson pointed out in his pioneering essay on administration in 1887, "The problem is to make public opinion efficient without suffering it to be meddlesome. Directly exercised, in the oversight of the daily details and in the choice of the daily means of government, public criticism is of course a clumsy nuisance, a rustic handling delicate machinery. But as superintending the greater forces of formative policy alike in politics and administration, public criticism is altogether safe and beneficial, altogether indispensable."[31]

SUGGESTED READINGS

Books

Adrian, Charles R., *Governing Urban America,* 2nd ed. (New York: McGraw-Hill, 1961).

Alderfer, Harold F., *Local Government and Administration* (New York: Macmillan, 1956).

International City Managers' Association, *Municipal Personnel Administration,* 6th ed. (Chicago: 1960).

[30] Adrian, *op. cit.,* p. 324, 326.
[31] Woodrow Wilson, "The Study of Administration," *Political Science Quarterly, 56* (December, 1941), 499.

International City Managers' Association, *The Techniques of Municipal Administration*, 4th ed. (Chicago: 1958).

Kaplan, H. Eliot, *The Law of Civil Service* (Albany, N.Y.: Matthew Bender and Co., 1958).

Morlan, Robert L. (ed.), *Capitol, Courthouse and City Hall*, 2nd ed. (Boston: Houghton Mifflin, 1960).

Stahl, O. Glenn, *Public Personnel Administration*, 4th ed. (New York: Harper, 1956).

Sweeney, Stephen B. and Davy, Thomas J. (eds.), *Education for Administrative Careers in Government Service* (Philadelphia: University of Pennsylvania Press, 1958).

Waldo, Dwight, *The Study of Public Administration* (New York: Random House, 1955).

Warner, Kenneth O., "Municipal Personnel Administration in the United States," in *Local Government in the United States of America* (The Hague: International Union of Local Authorities, 1961), pp. 91–113.

White, Leonard D., *Introduction to the Study of Public Administration*, 4th ed. (New York: Macmillan, 1955).

Articles

Bromage, Arthur W., "The Art of Governing American Cities," *Horizons for Modern Pennsylvania Local Government, 3* (March, 1956), 3–4.

Janowitz, Morris and Wright, Deil, "The Prestige of Public Employment: 1929 and 1954," *Public Administration Review, 16* (Winter, 1956), 15–21.

Kaplan, H. Eliot, "A Personnel Program for the County Service," *National Municipal Review, 16* (October, 1936), 596–600, 616.

Reining, Henry, "Recent Advances in Public Administration," *The County Officer, 21* (July–August, 1956), 147–52, 184–5.

Schubert, Glendon A., " 'The Public Interest' in Administrative Decision-Making," *American Political Science Review, 51* (June, 1957), 346–68.

Simon, Herbert A., "The Proverbs of Administration," *Public Administration Review, 6* (Winter, 1946), 53–67.

Willbern, York, "Professionalization in the Public Service: Too Little or Too Much?" *Public Administration Review 14* (Winter, 1954), 13–21.

Wilson, Woodrow, "The Study of Administration," *Political Science Quarterly, 56* (December, 1941), 481–506.

LOCAL FINANCE

Five

Local Fiscal Management

17

Faced with the contradictory demands of citizens for new and improved services at present or lower costs, local governments find monetary problems difficult ones indeed. Thus, while fiscal management is a part of the administrative process, it is treated in a separate chapter because of its importance.

As defined by White, "Fiscal management includes those operations designed to make funds available to officials and to ensure their lawful and efficient use."[1] It is beyond the scope of this chapter to examine all aspects of fiscal management, but emphasis will be placed on local fiscal organization, the budgetary process, custody of funds, accounting, purchasing, reporting, and financial planning. Since successful administration of local finance is dependent upon sound fiscal organization, this aspect will be examined first.

■ Organization for Fiscal Management

Existing patterns of fiscal organization vary widely among size and types of local governments. It can readily be appreciated that

[1] Leonard D. White, *Introduction to the Study of Public Administration,* 4th ed., Macmillan, 1955, p. 224.

the fiscal machinery of a city of over 7,000,000 would be more complex than that in a city of a few hundred persons. Similarly, the machinery for fiscal management in a large urban county differs from that in a small rural county. However, every unit of government has some form of organization and some type of process involved in its fiscal management—with both ranging from the highly integrated and complex to the highly decentralized and simple.

In most units of local government, fiscal functions and responsibilities are shared by a number of officials and agencies. Such a condition is known as decentralized administration, in contrast to the centralized pattern in which all fiscal officers are subject to the direct supervision of the chief executive officer. The integrated pattern is found in a number of cities with the strong mayor-council or council-manager forms of government. While the actual number of fiscal officers and agencies varies, four types are usually found. These are (1) the local legislative body; (2) the local chief executive; (3) other administrative officers; and (4) overseers or checkers on the fidelity and legality of expenditures after the transactions have been carried through.

The fiscal responsibilities of local legislative bodies have been discussed in earlier chapters. However, it bears repeating that the governing board in any unit is the supreme fiscal authority because it adopts the basic financial policies for that unit. While the budget is often presented by the local executive, the council or governing board must ratify it on behalf of the people. In addition, the local legislature determines the local tax rate, demands an accounting of funds spent by agencies and officers of the government, and may conduct investigations into the handling of public monies.

Except in cases where the governing board serves both as the chief legislative and administrative agency, the chief executive is also the chief fiscal officer and usually plays a major role in the fiscal process. Increasingly, the executive takes a leading part in establishing policies for raising and spending money through his preparation of the local budget. Even in communities where his budget role is limited, the executive is responsible for its administration. He assists in allocating funds, oversees their spending, and supervises their accounting.

In the third category of fiscal officers are such officials as the treasurer, who serves as custodian of public monies; the controller, who performs fiscal control functions; the assessor, who values property for determining the general tax rate; the purchasing agent, who procures materials and supplies; and the board of tax appeals to whom aggrieved citizens can carry their complaints concerning the taxes levied upon their property.

As an agent of the legislative body, the auditor is charged to determine the fidelity and legality of the manner in which money has been spent. It is important that the auditor be independent of the chief executive since he is checking the expenditures of that branch to determine if they have been made according to appropriations and are otherwise legal. In part, the relations of the auditor to the legislature parallel those existing between the controller and the executive. The controller exercises his checks before the money has been spent and is more concerned with the adequacy of the amount to be spent than with the legality of the expenditure.

The loose, decentralized organization for fiscal management described above is pictured in Figure 16. While the chart represents

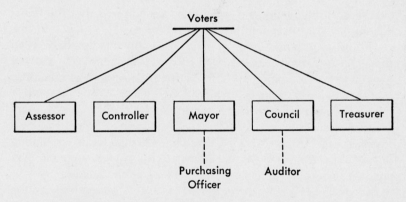

Figure 16. *Decentralized Fiscal Organization.*

fiscal organization in cities, it would also represent county fiscal organization by substituting the county board for the city council and deleting the office of mayor. If good fiscal management exists in local communities with such a decentralized system, it exists in spite of rather than because of the organization. With only the electorate to hold the several independently elected fiscal officers accountable, it is often difficult to achieve the kind of close cooperation necessary to plan, formulate, adopt, implement and

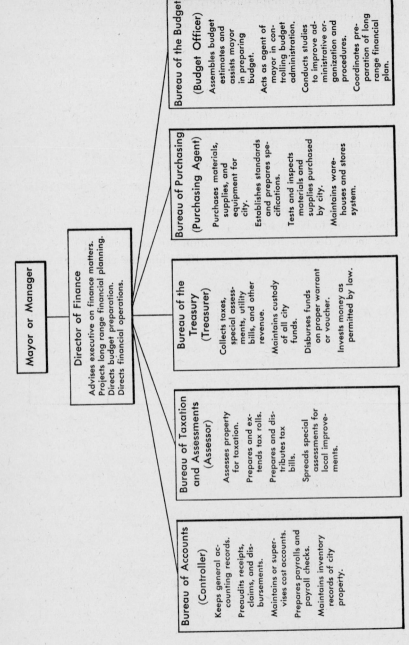

Figure 17. *Integrated Fiscal Organization.*

execute a sound financial program. Division of responsibility makes public responsiveness and accountability difficult to maintain.

In the past 35 years, there has been a clear trend toward a more centralized or integrated pattern of fiscal management. As strong executive plans for cities and counties have developed, fiscal officers have been placed in subordinate positions and are responsible to the chief executive officer. While there is considerable variation among the patterns of integrated fiscal organization, one plan is outlined in Figure 17. Here the lines of responsibility clearly center in the office of the local director of finance who is appointed by and is responsible to the chief executive. The sharp contrast between this and the decentralized organization in Figure 16 is evident even from a cursory examination.

■ *The Budget Process*

It is almost a truism that no local government will ever have sufficient money to satisfy all the needs of its citizens. Thus, the adoption of a budget serves as a guide to the community in estimating its needs and planning to raise the necessary funds to meet these needs. More technically, a budget has been defined as "A comprehensive plan, expressed in financial terms, by which an operating program is effective for a given period of time. It includes estimates of: (a) the services, activities, and projects comprising the program; (b) the resultant expenditure requirements; and (c) the resources usable for their support."[2]

Perhaps no other field of local management has experienced as many important technical advances in recent years as has the budget process. Budgeting developed first in municipal government at the turn of the present century and the 60 intervening years has witnessed a series of improved budgetary processes and techniques. It is no longer feasible to speak of a "local budget" since it may be an executive or legislative budget, an operating or a capital budget, a line-item or a program budget. Each of these types will be briefly discussed, but the basic budget is the operating budget which represents a financial plan for the operation of a local government for a fixed period of time known as a fiscal year.

[2] International City Managers' Association, *Municipal Finance Administration,* 1955, p. 61.

Originally, the local budget was a legislative document. The legislature proposed expenditures with the executive forced to accept this financial plan except in communities where he had the veto power or the item veto power. As one outgrowth of the general efficiency and economy movement the budgetary roles have been interchanged in a number of local governments. Now the executive proposes the financial plan and the legislature disposes by accepting, amending, or rejecting it. A budget so prepared is known as an executive budget in contrast to the legislative budget of earlier years. The legislative budget, however, is still the most common form in county and township governments.

A capital budget is a long-term financial plan embracing a program of capital improvement projects rather than the day-to-day expenditures in the operating budget. A line-item budget places emphasis upon the things to be acquired—typewriters, fire trucks, paper, police radios, etc. Such a budget specifies the exact amount to be spent for each item. A performance or program budget, on the other hand, emphasizes the services to be rendered by stressing what is to be accomplished rather than the specific items to be purchased. For example, a program budget might contain "snow removal" as an activity to be accomplished and show an amount of money for this program. A line-item budget would not itemize such an activity as such. It would show that so much money would be spent for salaries of workers, purchase of shovels, depreciation of trucks, etc., but it would not indicate whether the materials would be used for snow removal, cleaning of storm sewers, street repair, or any other particular activity.[3]

The object of the operating budget is to merge the plans for expenditures with the expected revenues so that there is enough money to accomplish the programs that the local legislative body has determined should be carried out. While this objective seems straightforward, it is often difficult to realize. The budget itself results from a budget cycle which involves its preparation, adoption, and execution.

The process of budget preparation begins in the office of the responsible local officer or agency. This office may be the governing

[3] For a fuller discussion of program budgeting, see John A. Donaho, "The Performance Budget," *Municipal Finance*, 22 (February, 1950), 103-6; Eugene R. Elkins, *Program Budgeting, A Method for Improving Fiscal Management*, Bureau of Government Research, University of West Virginia, 1955; and Jesse Burkhead, *Government Budgeting*, Wiley, 1956, Chap. 6.

board as in most counties and townships, a legislative committee as in some counties and cities, or the chief executive as in many cities and special districts and in a small number of counties. The first step should be a general request for the several operating agencies of the government to prepare their expenditure estimates for the coming year. This request comes from the responsible agency and should contain a general statement of policy as a guide in the development of these estimates. If no increases are to be approved, an order to "hold the line" should accompany this request. If a general cut-back or increase in programs is anticipated, this information similarly should be given the operating officials. When no such general guide is given, each agency is free to request what it deems necessary to meet its anticipated programs. While the preparation of the estimates is a responsibility of the head of each agency, the process of assembling the estimates is normally decentralized within the agency—at least in the early stages.

The second phase of the budget-making process begins with the collection of the several separate agency budget requests in the appropriate agency. This may be a legislative committee, a budget office, or the office of the chief executive. The major task of the budget officer is to shape the individual requests into a preliminary budget and to measure the requests against the revenues expected. Since the total amount of the former are almost certain to exceed the expected revenues, either a plan for increasing revenues or one for cutting back proposed expenditures must be made at this stage. At this point of the process, close cooperation between the officials heading the several agencies and the budget officer is most essential. Each operating official whose agency request is pared will feel some pain, but it is essential to note the difference between the roles of the agency head and the budget officer in preparing the budget document. The agency head estimates the needs of his agency only; typically, he has little trouble proposing programs for new or expanded services. The budget officer must have an overall view of the needs of his governmental unit and balance expenditure requests with anticipated revenues. He must also be prepared to establish priorities among the program proposals and to determine where cutbacks will be least painful to the community.

Since the budget officer will be the chief executive or responsible to him, the budget plan emanating from his office may be assumed to be in form for transmittal to the legislative body. With its submittal, the second stage of the budget cycle—adoption—begins. The form of the budget document presented to the council varies considerably among governmental units. A national organization states that "it is essential that the document include information of the appropriation and revenue policies. This means that the budget document must necessarily contain more than just the bare estimates of expenditures and revenues."[4] The budget document of the executive is usually accompanied by a budget message which explains the general policies followed in its preparation, points out and explains significant changes from the previous budget, and estimates the tax rate and revenue program necessary to support the expenditures proposed.

If the local legislature operates with committees, the usual practice is to refer the budget to the finance committee, or appropriate sections of it are parceled out among various "subject-matter" committees and subcommittees. During its deliberations, the committee holds hearings at which interested persons and groups may appear and department or agency heads attend to answer questions. Individual citizens rarely attend these hearings, except in small communities or in instances where the budget includes some controversial proposal, but representatives of citizen organizations often appear to give support to or to oppose certain proposals. Although the legislators will seldom acquire new information from these sessions, they are an important part of the democratic process and let groups and individuals express points of view and criticize existing or proposed programs.

Generally speaking, the legislative body is free to change the budget submitted to it as it sees fit. It may add to, reduce, delete, or modify any part of the budget. It is also free to accept, modify, or reject proposed new sources of revenue and to increase or decrease suggested tax rates. There is one general limitation on the council's budgetary powers—the budget it approves must be a balanced one with a revenue program sufficient to meet approved expenditures. In many communities other limitations exist, such as requiring an extraordinary vote of the council to approve changes, or limiting the board's power to reduction only. The council normally has freer reins in budgetary matters in council-manager cities than it does in mayor-council governed communities. The legisla-

---

[4] Municipal Finance Officers Association, *Municipal Budget Procedures and Budgetary Accounting*, Accounting Publication No. 9, 1942, p. 30.

LOCAL FINANCE

tive body's final action is taken when it votes approval of the budget either as transmitted or as amended. Approval takes the form of an ordinance or ordinances relating to appropriation measures, revenue proposals, and borrowing—if necessary—to carry out the budget.

The degree of state control over local budgeting varies widely. In some states, local governments are required to prepare their budgets on forms provided by the state. In other states review of local budgets by a state agency is provided to check their legality and compliance with state regulations.[5]

The third phase of the budget cycle—execution—begins following legislative approval of the budget document. The first step in the actual administration is a device for controlling expenditures and involves the submittal of work programs by agency heads to the chief executive for approval. Work programs are usually on a monthly or quarterly basis and show how much of the total appropriation of an agency is desired for each period of the fiscal year. This device is known as the "allotment system" which has been defined as the "determination by the budget officer of the amount of obligation which may be incurred under an appropriation or contract authorization during a specified period."[6] The purpose of an allotment system is to provide a means for keeping expenditure programs under constant review to prevent the disbursement of funds at a pace which will result in deficits later in the fiscal year.

After approval of the allotment schedule, the schedule is turned over to the controller or his counterpart, if one exists. In most small governmental units, there will be no officer to perform this essential pre-audit function to determine the propriety of a proposed expenditure. However, the governing board itself may perform this function by passing directly on all individual bills presented for payment. Two major considerations are involved in the pre-audit control function: the legality of the proposed expenditure, and the adequacy of funds to meet the obligation. This control is also an executive one and aims to achieve the double objective of realization of program goals and preservation of legislative intent.

[5] T. E. McMillan, Jr., *State Supervision of Municipal Finance,* Institute of Public Affairs, University of Texas, 1953.

[6] W. Brooke Graves, *Public Administration in a Democratic Society,* Heath, 1950, p. 331.

While there are many available techniques for budget execution, the following seven have been advanced as "tried and proven" and forming a series of comprehensive steps.

(1) a system of periodic allotments geared to anticipated revenues, (2) budgetary accounting and internal auditing, (3) a system of periodic departmental reports designed to show work done as well as dollars spent, (4) a hard-hitting, bargain basement purchasing and salvage system, (5) a personnel system that determines not merely that a position is open and that money is available but that there is a job to be done, (6) a comprehensive inventory system for both capital items and current supplies, and (7) a continuous and personal "nosiness" into departmental operations and expenditures on the part of the executive, the budget officer, and other members of the staff.[7]

The third step in the process of budget administration is the post audit, which comes at the close of the fiscal period. After the monies have been spent, the auditor is concerned with the honesty and legality of the completed transactions and the accuracy of accounts. One statement of the auditor's functions holds that it is his duty "to verify and check the financial transactions and records with respect to legality, mathematical accuracy, accountability and the application of accepted accounting principles."[8] The auditor may be a public officer or a private person or firm hired to perform the auditing function. He normally reports his findings to the local legislative body and frequently also to the state auditor. In some states, the auditing function is performed through a state bureau of supervision of public offices. Although the annual audit is widely implemented, some units of local government have never had a meaningful audit.

The responsibilities of the auditor and the local government in their relationships with each other have been clearly stated in the following words:

The auditor has numerous specific responsibilities attendant upon his assignment. He must be completely qualified and experienced in municipal accounting and auditing or he must not accept the assignment. He must be sure that the status of his work load and the adequacy of his staff are such that he can properly handle the work. He must see that the work is started and completed expeditiously and with the least pos-

---

[7] A. E. Buck, Jr., "Techniques of Budget Execution," *Municipal Finance, 21* (August, 1948), 8–11.

[8] International City Managers' Association, *op. cit.*, p. 29.

sible disruption of normal functioning of the municipality's operations. Staff accountants assigned to the job must be adequately trained and experienced and must be properly supervised by either a principal or supervising senior of the auditor's firm. . . . It is the local government's responsibility to make sure that all records are in order and readily available to the auditor. The municipality should not expect the auditor to do clerical work or bookkeeping necessary to bring the records into a state of completion. All too frequently the attitude when clerical discrepancies have developed in the records is to "wait and let the auditors clean it up." It must be emphasized that the function of the auditor is to "examine the balance sheets and statements of revenue and expenditures," not to prepare the records.[9]

As described above, the budget cycle may appear to consist of a series of interrelated but not overlapping steps. But this is not so in practice. As monies are being spent, checks are operating and plans are being laid for possible changes in the next budget. New programs are under study and methods for shaving costs are also under consideration. Thus, the budget process is a continuing and unending operation rather than a short interval of heavy pressure coming once a year.

■ Custody of Funds

The custodian of funds in local governments is the treasurer, often an elective officer. As custodian, the treasurer is responsible for depositing funds other than small amounts needed for daily operations in banks known as depositories. The most common practice for selecting depositories is for the council or an *ex officio* board of which the treasurer is a member to select the bank or banks in which local funds are to be deposited. In some communities, local banks bid competitively by offering varying interest rates to secure the deposit of the funds of the local governmental unit. It is obvious that safety should be the prime consideration in selecting banks as depositories. It is a common practice to divide funds between two or more local banks and to require security for the deposits.

To protect the public against loss of funds through dishonesty, negligence, or mistake on the part of the treasurer, he is usually un-

[9] Associated Institutes of Government of Pennsylvania Universities, "Relationship Between the Independent Auditor and a Governmental Unit," *Horizons for Modern Pennsylvania Governments*, 7 (March, 1960), 3.

der an indemnity bond. The two basic purposes of such bonds are (1) to protect the local government against monetary loss by such officials, and (2) to guarantee faithful performance of duty on the part of such bonded officials. Not many local officials misuse public monies today, but the requirement of the indemnity bond was enacted in some states only under pressure from local governments following experiences of official dishonesty.

The treasurer's office is still a widely coveted elective office in many counties. In some states, county treasurers are prohibited from succeeding themselves in office or from holding the office for longer than two successive terms. Such provisions concerning reeligibility are less needed now than in earlier years when regulations providing for checks on the custodian of county funds were few and poorly enforced. For example, it was common at one time to permit treasurers to keep any interest paid by banks on county funds deposited in them. Today the duties of the treasurer as custodian of public monies are ministerial only and are primarily bookkeeping in nature. There is little or no discretion now entrusted to this officer concerning the custody of or the deposit of local funds. Thus, there is little justification for its retention as an elective office in any type of local government.

■ Accounting

Accounting has been described as the heart of fiscal management since it records financial information and makes it available to administrators, legislators, pertinent employees, and interested citizens. Accounting activities are usually placed in the office of the controller, often an elective position. As "watchdog of the treasury," it is hoped that his election will make him independent of both the tax levying and spending authorities and that he can serve as a true representative of the public.

There are four main purposes for the maintenance of government accounts. These are (1) to provide information about past operations and present conditions; (2) to serve as a basis for future operations; (3) to establish controls over the acts of public bodies and officers in the use of public funds; and (4) to publicize the financial operations and conditions of government for the benefit of interested citizens.[10]

[10] Lloyd Morey and Robert Hackett, *Fundamentals of Governmental Accounting*, Wiley, 1942, pp. 10–11.

There are two principal bases for the maintenance of local accounts, known as cash and accrual accounting. Under the cash system, revenues are recorded only upon receipt and expenditures only when paid. In the accrual system of accounting, revenues are accounted for when earned or billed, as in the case of taxes, while expenditures are recorded when the liability has been incurred. The accrual system places emphasis on a fiscal period and gives a more accurate picture of the local financial condition for the period but may give quite a misleading picture at any one time. The cash system, on the other hand, gives a day-to-day picture but is not very helpful in seeing conditions over a longer period.

Since both systems have advantages and disadvantages, small units in particular may find it best to use the cash basis for revenues and the accrual basis for expenditures. Such a combined system would make it impossible to incur more liabilities than revenues could cover. By accruing revenues, property tax receipts would be recorded at the time the bills were sent out since they represent an asset to be received. Unfortunately, taxes on some pieces of property may not be received and yet these amounts are also shown as assets under this system. By recording expenditures only when paid, the local government may seem to have more assets than it actually has and it may overextend its funds.

A simple illustration will reflect the general operation of the two systems. If the property tax bills total $200,000 in each of two communities, community A using accrual accounting would record the total amount as a receipt on the day the bills were sent out. If $15,000 in taxes were not received, this community's accounts would show a non-existent asset of that amount. Community B, using the cash system, would show only the $185,000 actually collected as a ready asset and the other $15,000 would be shown in an accounts receivable fund. On the expenditure side, community A would record liabilities when the order is placed so that daily balance would give a true picture of remaining funds which can be spent. Thus, if on a day when the asset accounts show a $150,000 balance an order is placed for $60,000 in heavy machinery, the balance at the end of the day would be $90,000. If the same transaction occurred in community B with the same $150,000 balance, the balance at the end of that day would still show $150,000 since the $60,000 expenditure would be recorded only when that amount is actually paid out.

As the concept of the performance budget has gained wider usage in local government, a third basis of accounting—cost accounting—has developed. This method has been defined as the "recording of all expenditures incurred in the performance of some unit of work which can be enumerated."[11] The essential difference between cost accounting and other accounting systems has been described in these words. "In any cost determination all elements of expense must be considered. Yet appropriation accounting for many activities of government records only the direct items of cost: the personal services and the supplies of other items directly consumed."[12]

Cost accounting seeks to achieve a distribution of direct and indirect expenses to arrive at an accurate total cost. There are normally four basic types of costs—labor, equipment, materials and supplies, and overhead charges. As far as possible, standard work units are established for the various activities to which the cost accounting system applies. Examples of such standard units would be the mile of streets cleaned, patient days in a hospital, ton of refuse collected, gallon of sewage treated, square yard of street patched, etc. By establishing these standard work measures, unit costs can be determined and future work programs can be based upon these unit costs.

The greatest value of cost accounting is that it provides data for policy determination. By knowing what the cost of garbage collection is on a once-a-week schedule, cost for collection twice a week can be quite accurately determined and serve as a basis for the decision of the local governing board to continue the old schedule or to change to a twice-a-week collection. Cost accounting also protects against loss, waste, and inefficiency and provides a means of reporting to the public on the activities of local government in more understandable terms. A report that indicates that so much money was expended for such programs as street cleaning, snow removal, garbage collection, etc., is more meaningful than one by agencies of government showing that the streets department spent so much without a breakdown by particular programs carried on by that agency.

While cost accounting is valuable in program budgeting, it is not a necessity.[13] The term cost analysis has been used to describe an alternative to cost accounting. This method relies on measurement

[11] John D. Millett, *Management in the Public Service*, McGraw-Hill, 1954, p. 250.

[12] *Ibid.*

[13] Frank Sherwood, "Some Non-Cost Accounting Approaches to Performance Budgeting," *Public Management, 36* (January, 1954), 9-12.

LOCAL FINANCE

of direct costs of a program and does not require as elaborate an accounting system as does cost accounting. It is a periodic operation and may be done on a sampling rather than on a complete basis. It also emphasizes the manhour approach since the cost of personnel is the major cost in most service programs of local government.

If local accounts are to serve their purpose fully, they must be kept accurately in an intelligible system and be audited thoroughly at appropriate intervals. Both the pre-audit and the post-audit functions were described above in the section on the budget process. State auditing of local accounts is a common practice and represents one of the most important of state inspectional activities. In some states, this auditing of local accounts is performed by the office of the state auditor and in others this function is vested in a special agency that has a number of relations with local units.

▪ Reporting

Financial reports of one type or another are prepared by all units of local government. Such reports may be defined as statements which set forth the government's financial condition. Internal reports are made to the chief executive by his financial aides and he in turn makes periodic financial reports to the local board or council. Such reports are made primarily to assure that budget administration is proceeding legally and in accordance with the general directions prescribed by the local legislative body.

The most important of the local financial reports is the annual financial report, of which there are two common types. The first is a complete financial report with detailed data. Such reports have been described by one writer as containing "pages of columns of figures in fine print, unrelieved by textual interpretation, and altogether unintelligible to the layman. These volumes are more useful as paperweights or doorstops than as sources of information about the state of the government."[14] The second type is more usable in that it attempts to show what the citizenry is getting for its money as well as the general condition of local finances. In addition to essential data on the sources of revenues and the costs of local services, this report typically gives a brief description of functions

[14] James C. Charlesworth, *Governmental Administration,* Harper, 1951, p. 373.

performed, a chart or charts showing the organization of the local government, information on current, past and projected costs, a directory of local officials, and a statement of plans for the year ahead.

It may be argued that the annual report to the citizen and the annual financial report are separate and should not be confused. But the citizen should be given basic financial information about his government and spared the long and cumbersome financial report that may be required by state law or that must be submitted to a state agency for review. Generally, this will mean that the local government will prepare more than one financial report. It is better to have the format of each report relate to the purpose it is supposed to serve than to use a single report for several purposes. This is the reason for the two types of financial reports mentioned above. A report useful to the auditor would be of little value to the citizens and the annual report to the citizenry would be inadequate for the purposes of the auditor.

Great strides have been made in the format of local reports in recent years. Many are now short and readable and are quite informative as well. Instead of straight textual reporting or columns of financial figures, the report contains a readable text supplemented by charts, graphs, and pictures to attract and hold the attention of the reader as well as to tell the story of the local government to the citizen. The citizen in local government today is not unlike the citizen described in 1931 when the National Committee on Municipal Reporting suggested that "the things a voter is 'down on' are usually the ones he is not 'up on.' "[15] This more general financial and public report is prepared and distributed in a number of ways. It may appear as a feature in the local newspaper, be a separately prepared report, or appear as a leaflet or small brochure. While mailing of such reports is most frequent, it may be distributed by local employees, be available upon request at the city hall or county building, or be enclosed with local tax or utility bills.

■ Purchasing

It is common today for local governments to have purchasing or procurement officers or to establish this function as the basic purpose of a division or bureau within the local finance agency. This is

[15] National Committee on Municipal Reporting, *Public Reporting*, 1931.

in sharp contrast to the earlier practice under which purchasing was largely individual and decentralized, with each officer permitted to do the official buying for his agency in his own way and from supply sources of his own choosing. Since the turn of the century, many local governments have introduced centralized purchasing systems as a means to greater economy and efficient administration. This is an appropriate development since it has been shown that from 20 to 30 percent of the total operating budget is expended for supplies, materials and equipment.[16]

Forbes defines central purchasing as "the delegation to one office of the authority to purchase supplies, materials, and equipment needed for use by all the several operating branches of the organization."[17] Among the advantages claimed for centralized procurement are: (1) lower prices resulting from purchasing in larger quantities and from increased competition among suppliers; (2) additional savings accruing from expedited payments, fewer purchase orders and vouchers and simplified accounting procedures and controls; (3) purchases are made only from qualified vendors, preventing the acquisition of inferior supplies or equipment; (4) the development of standard specifications for items bought in large quantities facilitates bidding by competing suppliers; (5) the removal of vendors whose records of service are poor from the list of qualified vendors; and (6) centralized inspection of materials and supplies helps to prevent the purchase of inferior items.[18]

In the eyes of the heads of operating departments and agencies, centralized purchasing is not an unmixed blessing. Among the objections which have some validity are the "red tape" and delay involved in securing supplies, the dictatorial nature of some purchasing officers, the time consumed in developing adequate specifications for items used by a number of departments and agencies, and the stockpiling of certain items which may result from bargain buying. In addition, many agency heads feel that they are better able to determine the nature and quality of the items most suitable to their own needs. It is imperative that purchasing officers not lose sight of the fact that they are to assist and serve operating officials, and the latter should recognize the special competence involved in

[16] Russell Forbes, *Centralized Purchasing: A Sentry at the Tax Exit Gate,* National Association of Purchasing Agents, rev. ed., 1941, p. 5.

[17] *Ibid.*

[18] Adapted from advantages suggested in International City Managers' Association, *op. cit.,* p. 367.

purchasing the large number of items used by local governments today and the resulting economies which can accrue. Experience has demonstrated that in communities in which both the line officials and the purchasing officer remember that they are serving the public the economies resulting from centralized purchasing more than justify the creation of such an office. In some instances "centralization" of purchasing goes so far as to involve joint action by several units or the utilization of state government facilities.

The purchasing procedure typically begins with the preparation of a requisition which is sent to the purchasing agent by the using department. The purchasing officer attempts to get competitive bids on most items by advertizing to secure bids, by letters to suppliers requesting quotations of cost, or by telephone calls to prospective suppliers. After bids have been received, the purchase is awarded to the "lowest responsible bidder." Upon receipt of the goods, the purchasing agent records its receipt and notifies the using department. Many local governments give preference to local vendors but this practice is being increasingly limited to instances where the price, quality, and services offered locally are equal to those which can be realized from outside sources.

■ *Financial Planning*

If local fiscal plans are limited to each annual budgetary period, the result is often a somewhat haphazard allocation of the financial resources of that unit. Since revenues are seldom sufficient to meet all needs, funds are apportioned annually on an "emergency" basis since no serious effort has been made to foresee either operating or capital needs beyond the current year. Pressures both inside and outside the official government circle may result in unwise and stop-gap expenditure plans since no orderly pattern or plan of priorities has been established.

An important step to prevent such short-term developments is the careful preparation of a long-range comprehensive fiscal plan. Such a plan might be developed for a period of 16 to 20 years, with four-year installments or sub-plans of the total plan. In the development of such a plan, estimates should be prepared in four major areas. These are: (1) needs for local services in such functions as education, health, safety, transportation, water, sanitation, etc.; (2) capi-

LOCAL FINANCE

tal improvement needs in major public buildings and service facilities such as freeways, sewage disposal plans, water system, etc.; (3) schedule of priority of needs in terms of timing since all the programs and projects cannot be instituted or built at any one time; and (4) methods of financing the services and facilities to be developed.[19] Without a plan for getting the financial support needed to carry the specific projects and services to fruition, the plan is not worth the time and effort devoted to its preparation.

It might be objected by some that such a long-range plan is more properly an activity for the local planning commission than for the local finance agency. It is certainly true that much of local planning today is directly related to capital programming. Thus, the question does arise concerning where the responsibility for the development of such a plan should lie—in the local planning commission or in an administrative agency. In the latter case, such responsibility might be placed in the local finance agency or in the office of the chief executive. It has been suggested that such a plan be called a "long-term operating program" to indicate its similarity to a long-term capital program, and that it consist of a continuation of the annual budget "as part of a moving, long-range set of budgeting plans which will make more meaningful the decisions of today and the actions of tomorrow."[20]

In a study of capital programming in Philadelphia, Brown and Gilbert discovered that, "Generally speaking, the time horizons of the planners outrun those of the administrators; administrators take a somewhat longer view than the mayor's; and the time horizons of Council are the shortest of all. For many planners, of course, such a statement simply amounts to an implicit definition of 'planning,' 'administration,' and 'politics.' The use of the comprehensive plan as a guide to capital budgeting, or the emphasis upon spending today for site acquisition rather than on immediate improvements, are both commonplace evidences of the planner's concern with the long-run."[21]

The central point, regardless of where the responsibility for preparing the long-range plan lies, is the need for close cooperation

[19] Russell W. Maddox and Robert F. Fuquay, *State and Local Government,* Van Nostrand, 1962, pp. 412-3.

[20] Lennox L. Moak and Emma L. Bowman, "A Long-Range Operating Program," *Public Administration Review, 20* (Winter, 1960), 38.

[21] William H. Brown, Jr., and Charles E. Gilbert, "Capital Programming in Philadelphia," *American Political Science Review, 54* (September, 1960), 665-6.

between the planning commission and the administrative agency or agencies concerned. Evidence gained from the Philadelphia study would support placing this function where it exists, in the finance agency, since administrative agencies took a middle-range point of view—one longer than the council's or mayor's and one shorter than that of the planning commission.

As in the case of the operating budget, the preparation of the long-range fiscal plan would be decentralized at first, with departments and agencies submitting estimates of programs to be expanded or developed and capital facility requirements. These would be combined in the overall plan, and then the council or governing board would establish priorities of programs to be embraced in the four-year installments. It is essential that all aspects of the long-range plan be characterized by flexibility. It would also be desirable to prepare a number of alternative approaches so that unforeseen events would not effect the total plan too adversely.

SUGGESTED READINGS

Books

Alderfer, Harold F., *American Local Government and Administration* (New York: Macmillan, 1956).

Burkhead, Jesse, *Government Budgeting* (New York: Wiley, 1956).

Elkins, Eugene R., *Program Budgeting, A Method for Improving Fiscal Management* (Morgantown, W. Va.: Bureau of Government Research, West Virginia University, 1956).

Forbes, Russell, *Centralized Purchasing: A Sentry at the Tax Exit Gate* (New York: National Association of Purchasing Agents, 1941).

International City Managers' Association, *Municipal Finance Administration* (Chicago, 1955).

McMillan, T. E., Jr., *State Supervision of Municipal Finance* (Austin: Institute of Public Affairs, University of Texas, 1953).

Morey, Lloyd and Hackett, Robert, *Fundamentals of Governmental Accounting* (New York: Wiley, 1942).

Mosher, Frederick C., *Program Budgeting: Theory and Practice* (Chicago: Public Administration Service, 1954).

Articles

Appleby, Paul, "The Role of the Budget Division," *Public Administration Review, 17* (Summer, 1951), 156–8.

Brown, William H., Jr., and Gilbert, Charles E., "Capital Programming in Philadelphia," *American Political Science Review,* 54 (September, 1960), 659–68.

Buck, A. E., Jr., "Technique of Budget Execution," *Municipal Finance,* 21 (August, 1948), 8–11.

Donaho, John A., "The Performance Budget," *Municipal Finance, 22* (February, 1950), 103–6.

Moak, Lennox L. and Bowman, Emma L., "A Long-Range Operating Program," *Public Administration Review, 20* (Winter, 1960), 38–42.

Perkins, John A., "Preparation of the Local Budget," *American Political Science Review, 40* (October, 1946), 949–58.

Sherwood, Frank, "Some Non-Cost Accounting Approaches to Performance Budgeting," *Public Management, 36* (January, 1954), 9–12.

Local Revenues, Expenditure, and Debt Administration

18

Since this book is devoted to the study of local government, this chapter will discuss revenue, expenditure, and debt in local government only. However, the separation of local from state programs of taxation and spending is a particularly artificial one. The financial well-being of a state and its local governments is closely interdependent and interrelated at many points. There can be no real understanding of either level unless it is recognized that the state and its localities are partners in providing services and in assessing citizens to support such programs.

Illustrative of this point is a comparison of per capita state and local taxes and per capita general expenditures of state and local governments in selected states in 1957. The comparative roles of the two governmental levels varies appreciably among these ten states. In some, as in California and Ohio, the per capita taxes are fairly evenly divided between the state and its localities. In others, as in Pennsylvania and Michigan, the state's proportion is relatively higher, while in others, such as New Jersey and New York, the state's share is quite low. The same patterns of diversity are also shown in the per capita general expenditure figures for these states.

Such expenditures in Texas and Massachusetts are quite evenly divided, while Michigan shows an unusually high state expenditure and New Jersey a much higher local expenditure pattern.

The close interrelationships of a state and its local governments in financial matters can be shown in a number of other ways. For example, local governmental units serve as collection agencies for some state taxes and states collect some local taxes. Many states

Table 13. *Per Capita Data on Taxes and General Expenditures in Selected States*

State	Taxes		General Expenditures	
	State	Local	State	Local
California	49.6	50.4	53.9	46.1
Illinois	39.7	60.3	40.4	59.6
Indiana	46.7	53.3	53.0	47.0
Massachusetts	40.8	59.2	51.2	48.8
Michigan	55.3	44.7	60.1	39.9
New Jersey	28.7	71.3	35.1	64.9
New York	38.9	61.1	41.6	58.4
Ohio	48.1	51.9	47.7	52.3
Pennsylvania	55.6	44.4	54.8	45.2
Texas	52.4	47.6	50.6	49.4

SOURCE: Adapted from Governor's Office, *5 Fiscal Facts About Pennsylvania,* Harrisburg, September 28, 1959, pp. 19, 37.

levy taxes of one kind or another which they share with their local units and state grants-in-aid are an increasingly important source of financial support for local activities. Another pattern of relationships occurs in the field of state supervision and control over aspects of local revenue and expenditure programs, and debt size and administration. Some of these relationships will be described in subsequent sections in this chapter, but it is important to recognize their existence and nature throughout the discussion which follows.

■ *Local Revenue Patterns*

Local government costs have risen sharply in recent years, increasing over fivefold in the three decades between 1930 and 1960. In large part, the reasons for this increase parallel those for similar increases in state and national expenditures. These include the rise in the general price level, the decline in the purchasing power of the dollar, the increase in population, population concentration in urban areas, citizen demands for new and expanded services, and the high cost of capital facilities to provide many of the newer services. The changing pattern of these receipts is shown in Figure 18.

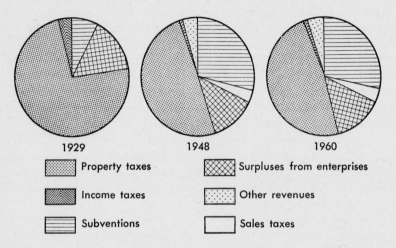

Figure 18. *Patterns of Local Receipts in Selected Years. Clockwise from the largest area, which represents property tax receipts, the shaded areas in order represent income tax, all other receipts, intergovernmental payments, sales tax, and non-taxes and government enterprises surplus.* (Lillian P. Barnes, G. M. Cobren, and Joseph Rosenthal, "State and Local Government Activity, The Postwar Experience Related to the National Economy," *Survey of Current Business, 41,* March, 1961, 20.)

While revenues from federal grants-in-aid and state government subsidies and grants have increased markedly in the past 30 years, the bulk of local revenue still comes from local taxes and charges which may be described as non-taxes. A tax may be defined as a compulsory contribution for the support of government based upon some criterion of ability to pay or benefit received. Commonly, "ability" is measured in terms of property ownership and income. The principle of the benefit theory has taken on increasing importance in local government as service charges have become a common method for financing certain services. For example, charges for most utility-type services—water, gas, and electricity—are determined on the principle that use implies benefit. The same theory is applied in cases of special assessments to finance such improvements as streets, sidewalks, and street lighting.

As creatures of the state, local governments have no inherent powers to tax and possess only such authority as the state confers upon them. For the most part, the local taxing power is granted by the state legislature; however, some local governments in strong home-rule states may have certain constitutionally granted taxing authority.

Limitations on local taxing powers are both statutory and constitutional and vary considerably among the states. Constitutional limitations commonly concern the exemption of certain classes of property from taxation (such as property used for educational, religious and charitable purposes); require uniform and equal tax rates; impose rate limitations on some kinds of taxes. Legislative limitations largely parallel constitutional ones and also relate to rate limitations, withholding or granting specific taxing powers to certain types of local units, and preventing taxing by local units of items also taxed by the state.

The changing nature of the tax structure in local governments is quite pronounced. While the yield from local property taxes in the past 30 years has increased some three and three-fourths times, the ratio of local revenue produced by this tax has declined from five of every six dollars to slightly more than three of every four. However, the general property tax remains the dominant revenue source for local governments with the ratio of revenue produced varying significantly among types of local governments. It is almost the sole source of revenue in many townships and in special districts not providing services for which direct charges can be assessed. It contributes in declining ratios in school districts, counties, and cities in that order.

LOCAL PROPERTY TAXES

Since the property tax still serves as the financial backbone of local government, it is deserving of some discussion. In the early years of our nation, the property tax was a fairly good measure of ability to pay, since there was a close relationship between property owned and income received. Now property is commonly divided

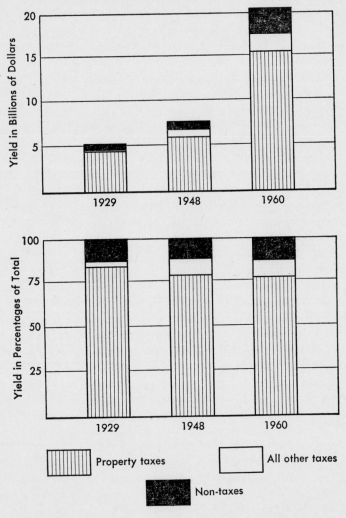

Figure 19. *Local Tax Yield in Selected Years.* (Lillian P. Barnes, G. M. Cobren, and Joseph Rosenthal, "State and Local Government Activity, The Postwar Experience Related to the National Economy," *Survey of Current Business, 41,* March, 1961, Table 3.)

into two kinds for local taxing purposes: real and personal. Real property includes land, buildings and permanent improvements, while personal property embraces all other kinds—clothes, furniture, automobiles, stocks, bonds, jewelry, etc. Because of its varied nature, personal property is further divided into tangible and intangible properties. The term tangible is used to describe such belongings as furniture, cars, and jewelry, while stocks and bonds are examples of the intangible type.

It is obvious from even this brief description of property that it is no longer a measure of one's ability to pay taxes. Some properties produce income for their owners; others do not. Many Americans own no tangible and perhaps little intangible property and yet have sizeable incomes. Thus, even while the property tax is the most productive source of local revenues, several serious criticisms have been raised against it. In the words of one writer, the general property tax "cannot be defended satisfactorily on the basis of ability to pay or the benefits received from government, because property is a suitable measure of neither."[1]

In addition to the unsoundness of the property tax in principle, there are other serious objections that manifest themselves in its administration. It has proven difficult to administer, resulting in inequities among taxpayers. Determining the value of property is not an easy task because of the great variation in its types and worth. A third major objection relates to the ease of hiding intangible personal property. Here the problem of valuation is one largely of uncovering stocks, bonds and other securities. A further problem is raised by the persons who serve as assessors. In many local governments, assessors are still elected and have no special competence for their positions. As the National Association of Assessing Officers has pointed out, there is "no necessary correlation between ability to secure votes and ability to run an assessment department."[2] A fifth problem is the large numbers of properties which are tax exempt. When property is so exempted, the owners of other properties must pay added taxes to furnish municipal services on the exempt property.

In light of these objections, the question might be asked as to why the property tax is retained. Five reasons for its retention have been

[1] Alfred Buehler, *Public Finance*, 3rd ed., McGraw-Hill, 1948, p. 341.
[2] National Association of Assessing Officers, *Assessment Organization and Personnel*, 1941, p. 185.

advanced by Adrian. These are: (1) inertia of taxpayers and government officials; (2) the belief that any old tax is a good tax and any new tax is a bad one; (3) the fact that real property tends to "stay put" and gives a degree of certainty to the local revenue base; (4) the high yield that the tax produces; and (5) the great need for revenues and the failure to find a satisfactory substitute.[3]

In addition, the property tax can be defended on the basis that many benefits of local government do go to people who live on property in the area. In most places, the idea of a general property tax has been attenuated in a number of major respects. Under these changes, personalty not used to produce income may be exempt and intangibles may be taxed through some form of income tax.

OTHER LOCAL TAXES

The recognition of the shortcomings of the property tax plus the need for additional revenues have prompted local governments to turn to widening use of non-property taxes. Such taxes contributed only 3.0 percent of the tax monies of local governments in 1929 but had increased to 10.3 percent by 1960. In looking for additional sources of local taxation, the principles of a tax system advanced by Adam Smith in 1776 are still quite pertinent. According to Smith, the tax program should be based on and reflect several "canons"—it should be based on ability to pay, provide diversity of sources, be economical to administer, be easy to understand and as convenient to pay as possible, provide certainty of collection, and yield an amount sufficient for the needs of the community.[4]

Although of recent vintage on the local level, local income taxes may be one of the major local taxes in the future. First assessed in Philadelphia and Washington, D. C., in 1939, local income taxes are now levied by over 650 local governments including cities, townships, and school districts. Unlike income taxes levied by higher levels of government, local income taxes are commonly assessed at a uniform low rate rather than on a graduated scale, and usually do not allow exemptions. Because of their uniform rates, local income taxes are not based strictly on the principle of ability to pay. However, they have three characteristics which contribute to their in-

[3] Charles R. Adrian, *Governing Urban America*, 2nd ed., McGraw-Hill, 1961, p. 359.
[4] Adam Smith, *Wealth of Nations*, Vol. II, Methuen & Co., 1904, pp. 310–12.

creasing use. First, they provide much needed revenue. Second, they are relatively easy and economical to administer. Third, they are assessed in the community where they are earned rather than in the community where the earner resides. Hence they enable a local government to exact contributions from non-residents as well as from residents.[5] Local income taxes are particularly prevalent in the states of Kentucky, Missouri, Ohio, and Pennsylvania.

The first local sales tax was adopted in New York City in 1934 as a "temporary" expedient to produce badly needed revenues. The tax served its purpose well, but New York has never outgrown the need for its revenues and this temporary tax appears to have become a permanent revenue source. By 1960, the sales tax had been adopted by some 60 counties and 1,300 municipalities and was in wide use among local governments in California and Illinois. One of the most serious objections to a local sales tax is the ease of avoidance and the shifting of purchasing to jurisdictions without a similar levy. Local sales taxes are also difficult and expensive to administer. Many of the administrative problems have been satisfactorily solved in California, which authorizes counties to levy a one percent sales tax to be collected by the state agency collecting the state sales tax. Cities within a county with a sales tax may levy a sales tax up to one percent and have it credited against the county tax, with the revenue coming to the city. If the city levies a sales tax of one-half percent, it receives half the revenues collected within its boundaries with the other half going to the county. All proceeds of sales in cities not levying a sales tax or in unincorporated areas go to the county. In counties not levying a sales tax, cities are free to impose and administer a municipal sales tax if they choose to do so.[6] Illinois communities use the device of having the state collect the local sales tax while collecting its own similar levy.

It has long been common for local governments to secure some revenue from business taxes and licenses. These may be sufficient only to pay the cost of supervising a business, or they may produce excess revenue. An example of the first type might be a restaurant license fee to finance health inspections of such businesses. License taxes upon retail liquor establishments and commercial amusements are illustrative of revenue-producing licenses. Among the variety of

---

[5] Robert A. Sigafoos, *The Municipal Income Tax; Its History and Problems,* Public Administration Service, 1955.

[6] John Vieg, H. C. Armstrong, Frank Farner, G. N. Rostvold, J. P. Shelton and Proctor Thompson, *California Local Finance,* Stanford University Press, 1960.

business and commercial enterprises which are licensed in one form or another are hotels, apartment houses, food and department stores, beauty and barber shops, pawnshops, taxicabs, and vending machines. Local taxes on privately owned public utilities are also quite common.

Local taxes on admissions to various types of entertainment and sports events have grown more common in recent years. Resort areas expand this concept a bit, since tourists and vacationers are favorite objects of taxation. Such areas commonly enact taxes on accommodations for their visitors as well as on the attractions pulling them there, either in the form of admission or use taxes.

NON-TAX REVENUES

Fees for direct services to citizens have declined but not disappeared in local governmental units. Once a means for paying the officeholder without burdening taxpayers directly for his services, fees were paid directly by those receiving services, especially in county, township, and town governments. Fees now collected usually are placed in the community's general fund rather than as salary for its collector. Fines are another source of local revenues and some local governments have abetted this source of revenue by unduly harsh traffic regulations and unusually strict enforcement, particularly in regard to non-residents.

Service charges are often imposed by local governments for certain services. These are particularly common in the field of utility services such as water supply and sewage disposal. In recent years, however, the service charge concept has been extended to such fields as street lighting, parking, and garbage and refuse collection. Various bases or formulae are used to determine the amount of these charges. For example, the charge for sewage disposal is computed on such varied bases as water consumption, number of water outlets, assessed valuation, and front footage. However, in general, service charges are based primarily upon the principle of benefits received.

While service charges are often described as a means of avoiding tax increases and making the tax level appear lower than it actually is, a case can be made for the argument that such charges serve to promote greater equity in local taxation. Putting some services on a service charge basis makes it possible to assess these charges against properties which are exempt from the local property tax. Similarly, they are a useful device to obtain revenues other than the property tax from properties which consume large amounts of water or contribute a disproportionate amount of sewage or other waste to the local sewerage system. Two types of commercial enterprises may be assessed at the same valuation for property tax purposes and yet one may consume a far greater amount of some public services, such as water, or contribute more waste into the sewerage system than the other. Whether a charge can be enough to more than cover out-of-pocket costs may depend upon the nature of the grant of power from the state.

SPECIAL ASSESSMENTS

A special assessment may be defined as an extra levy against pieces of real property made in rough proportion to benefits received by that property. It is assessed to defray the costs of services or conveniences of particular value to those properties. Common uses of special assessments include the financing in full or in part of the costs of new street paving, building sidewalks, installing water or sewage lines, street lighting, constructing off-street parking, and establishing parks and playgrounds.

The theory behind special assessments holds that improvements financed in this way make benefitting properties more desirable to own and are of greater value to these property owners than to the citizenry at large. The determination of benefits, however, presents a difficult problem. Certainly such improvements are not of benefit only to the nearby property owners. The citizenry at large profits and will utilize the improvements to some degree. Recognizing this principle of general as well as of specific benefit, most local governments establish a formula for assessing the properties immediately abutting the improvement. The comparative ratios of the cost borne by the citizenry at large and the nearby property owners varies considerably from community to community and may well vary from service to service within a single community. Ratios of cost supported by general fund contributions range from 25 to 80 percent of the total cost. Residents in older parts of the community are likely to support special assessments to pay for the extension of services to newer sections, while citizens in the newer section will support the use of general funds for such purposes.

Four principal methods of financing special assessments are now used in local governments. First, they may demand the advance payment of such assessments by the benefitting property owners. Second, local governments may make temporary loans to property owners from a revolving fund with repayment necessary within a relatively short period of time. Third, property liens may be issued by the local government against the property owners. They are given to the contractor doing the improvement works who typically sells the liens at a discount to a local bank. The bank, in turn, demands payment with interest within a period of from one to three years. Fourth and probably most common, the local government issues special assessment term bonds to obtain funds to pay for the improvement. Such bonds, with interest, must be paid within a period of from 5 to 15 years.

INTERGOVERNMENTAL REVENUES

In 1960, roughly two-sevenths of the revenues of all local governments came from grants by higher levels. State government payments to local governments totaled $7,700 million representing 24.1 percent of local receipts, while federal grants, totaling $1,500 million, equalled 4.6 percent. The drastic increase of intergovernmental revenues in the past 60 years is clearly evident in the contrast of the value of these grants in 1902 to those in 1960. In 1902, state and federal payments to local governments totaled some $56 million and equalled eight percent of locally-collected taxes.[7] The 1960 grants equalled 45 percent of the total received from locally-collected taxes. The increasing tendency for large urban units of government to turn directly to the federal government for financial assistance is an important development which will probably lead to expanding federal grants. This development, according to Alderfer, "has been encouraged, since the depression, by the federal government itself in such fields as housing, airports, assistance in federally impacted areas, and civil defense and bids fair to make federal-local channels deeper and more permanent each year."[8]

State financial assistance to local governments takes two major forms—grants-in-aid and shared taxes. Grants-in-aid are payments

[7] Municipal Finance Officers Association, *Municipal Nonproperty Taxes,* 1956 Supplement to *Where Cities Get Their Money,* Chicago, 1956, p. 1.

[8] Harold F. Alderfer, *American Local Government and Administration,* Macmillan, 1956, p. 412.

from one level of government to another; like federal grants-in-aid to states, state grants to local governments are allocated according to some formula and are normally made with conditions attached. The basic elements in the formula will vary with the end purpose of the appropriation. Thus, a formula for aid for highways will normally include mileage as one of its components and number of pupils will figure in the formula for aid to education. Conditions attached to the grant will normally include matching of funds in some ratio, the use of trained personnel in administering them, the right of the state to audit local accounts relating to expenditure of the funds, and the use of the money only for certain stated and specific purposes.

Shared taxes are collected by the state and apportioned among local governments according to a formula which is commonly a fixed percentage of the yield. The amount received by each local government is usually in direct ratio to the amount of the tax collected within its area or is a per capita grant with local receipts determined by population. Examples of the two common bases for state sharing of these taxes is as follows. Revenues returned to a county or city from a state-imposed liquor tax may depend on the income collected by the state from liquor sales in that community. Revenues returned to a local government from a state gasoline tax is more likely to be on a population basis than on a local sales basis. Among the taxes which are most often shared by the state with its local governments are those on motor fuel, motor vehicles, liquor, income, and general sales. Local governments are usually more free in using revenues from shared taxes than they are from grants-in-aid; but such revenues are often earmarked for specific purposes. While patterns of state aid vary from state to state, most state payments to local governments are in the four areas of education, welfare, highways, and health.

In a study released in 1949, six important trends in the use of grants and shared taxes were noted.[9] Since these trends are still evolving, their listing seems a good way to summarize important developments in the field of intergovernmental revenues. These are: (1) a tremendous growth in the dollar amounts of both grants and shared taxes; (2) an increase in use of tax sharing; (3) a recognition of the cyclical nature of shared taxes and attempts to alleviate

[9] John R. McKinley, *Local Revenue Problems and Trends,* Bureau of Public Administration, University of California, Berkeley, 1949, pp. 22-27.

this condition in some states; (4) a recognition that grants have been distributed inequitably in some states, with attempts to remedy the condition; (5) the realization that grants and shared taxes have now become permanent parts of the state-local fiscal structures and that they are an important means by which the state-local fiscal systems may be further integrated; and (6) a greater emphasis upon local government financial reporting as a means of assisting both local and state units to carry out their functions more effectively.

PATTERNS OF REVENUE

While the major types of local governments utilize essentially the same sources for their revenues, their relative dependence on any single source varies widely. As Table 14 shows, the property tax

Table 14. *Sources of Income of Local Governments: 1957*

Revenue Source	Counties	Munici- palities	School Districts	Special Districts
Property Tax	43.3	35.8	50.6	19.0
Other Taxes	3.3	13.3	—	—
Intergovernmental Grants	35.0	15.0	38.0	—
Utility Revenues and Charges	—	20.0	—	32.9
Charges and Miscellaneous General Revenues	11.7	13.3	—	32.4
All Other	1.7	2.6	11.4	15.7
Total	100.0	100.0	100.0	100.0

SOURCE: Bureau of the Census, *Graphic Summary of the 1957 Census of Governments,* vol. IV, no. 4 (August, 1959).

produces a little over half the total revenues of all school districts but less than one-fifth of special district revenues. Similarly, intergovernmental grants contribute 38 percent of school district revenues but only 15 percent of municipal revenues. Charges for services rendered comprise over 65 percent of the revenues of special districts in contrast to 33 percent for cities and less than 12 percent for counties. However, the "big three" revenue sources for all types of local government remain the property tax, intergovernmental grants, and service charges.

■ Local Expenditures

Just as the revenues of local governments have risen enormously in the past three decades, there has been a similar growth in local expenditures. In a satirical vein, Parkinson would say the latter is inevitable since his second "law" states that expenditures rise to meet revenues—whether personal or governmental. In Parkinson's words, "It is widely recognized that what is true of individuals is also true of governments. Whatever the revenue may be, there will always be a pressing need to spend it."[10] His solution is to "Put an absolute limit to the revenue, and let expenditures rise to meet it. These are the profits of experience and from these profits we should derive our law."[11]

This solution, however, is not a very practicable one for local officials on the receiving end of citizen demands for new and improved services and state-issued directives for higher standards for services. While there are many reasons for expanding local costs and rising expenditures, three in particular have been singled out by Kendrick. He stresses, first, the changes in our social and economic order resulting from our population growth and its concentration in urban areas; second, our changing theory of the proper role of government as it moves from a limited and protective role to one as a positive force in promoting the general welfare; and third, a changing conception of democracy which now recognizes social and economic needs of citizens as well as the goal for political equality.[12] Strayer advances a supporting reason for increased governmental activity arising "out of the changing valuation placed upon health, welfare, and security in a society that can afford for the first time the luxury of systematically making some provision for these areas of concern."[13]

While comparing expenditures of local governments over a period of years has limited value, it does point out the marked expansion of expenditures at this level. At the turn of the century, expenditures of local governments totaled one billion dollars. By 1929, this amount had risen sixfold to a little over six billion dollars. In the next 24 years, expenditures trebled to a little over 19 billion dollars

---

[10] C. Northcote Parkinson, *The Law and the Profits,* Houghton Mifflin, 1960, p. 5.

[11] *Ibid.,* p. 246.

[12] M. Slade Kendrick, *Public Finance,* Houghton Mifflin, 1951, pp. 46–59.

[13] Paul J. Strayer, *Fiscal Policy and Politics,* Harper, 1958, p. 170.

in 1953. In the next seven years, these costs doubled again, soaring to over 38 billion dollars. Shown another way, per capita expenditures of local governments were $10.70 in 1902 compared to $187.05 in 1960.

CLASSIFYING LOCAL EXPENDITURES

Of the several methods for classifying expenditures, the three most common are groupings by type, by character and object, and by function. There are four major subclassifications under "type" expenditures. These are: (1) general expenditure, a term embracing all expenditures other than those specifically enumerated in the other subclassifications; (2) utility expenditure, designating expenditures for construction or acquisition of utility facilities or equipment, for production and distribution of utility commodities and services, and for interest on utility debt; (3) liquor store expenditures, comprising all spending involved in provision and conduct of these undertakings; and (4) insurance trust expenditure, including only benefit payments and withdrawals of contributions from insurance trust funds.[14]

The five major subclassifications of expenditures by character and object are (1) current operation, (2) capital outlay, (3) assistance and subsidies, (4) interest on debt, and (5) insurance benefits and repayments.[15] Current operation spending includes amounts for compensation of officers and employees and for supplies, materials, and contractual services other than for capital items. Capital outlays are funds spent for construction of buildings, roads, and other improvements, and for purchase of equipment, land, and existing structures. Assistance and subsidies include payments to private individuals and organizations which are not subject to repayment, nor in return for goods and services, nor in repayment of claims against the government. Interest on debt involves amounts paid for use of borrowed money. Insurance benefits include payments to retired employees, unemployment compensation, workmen's compensation, sickness and other social insurance programs.

Expenditures according to function involve a number of groupings. As classified by the Bureau of the Census, major functions of

---

[14] Bureau of the Census, *Governmental Finances in 1961*, October, 1962, pp. 9–10.

[15] *Ibid.*, pp. 4–5.

local governments are (1) education, (2) natural resources, (3) highways, (4) interest on general debt, (5) health and hospitals, (6) public welfare, (7) police protection, (8) sanitation, (9) local fire protection, and (10) all others.[16] Functional classification is the most familiar, since local governments exist to render services and maintain functions that citizens in their individual capacities cannot provide effectively.

PATTERNS OF LOCAL EXPENDITURES

While comparative expenditures by types of local governments for four major services are presented in Table 15, the data provided are not very revealing as to the total spending patterns of types of local units. In every case except for school districts, the amounts shown for "all other expenditures" comprise a large percentage of the total.

Table 15. *Expenditures of Major Functions in Local Governments: 1961*
(millions of dollars)

Item	Counties	Munici-palities	Town-ships	School Districts	Special Districts
Education	$ 863	$ 1,926	$ 446	$13,470	$ 76
Highways	1,468	1,686	330	—	129
Public Welfare	1,659	643	107	—	—
Health and Hospitals	942	830	22	—	234
All Other	2,471	7,660	491	399	1,345
Total Direct General Expenditure	$7,403	$12,745	$1,396	$13,869	$1,784

SOURCE: Bureau of the Census, *Governmental Finances in 1961* (October, 1962), Table 13, p. 27.

A detailed analysis of general revenue expenditure of local governments was prepared by the Bureau of the Census in 1959.[17] Based on 1957 expenditures, highways and public welfare services each accounted for about one-fifth of the general expenditures of

[16] *Ibid.*, pp. 6–9.
[17] Bureau of the Census, *Graphic Summary of the 1957 Census of Governments,* August, 1959, pp. 30–38.

county governments. In order, the next three ranking county functions were health and hospitals (13.3 percent), education (13.3 percent), and general control (10 percent). Other major county expenditures, in order, were police, general public buildings, corrections, natural resources, sanitation, interest on general debt, parks and recreation, libraries, and fire protection. Such general revenue expenditures accounted for nearly 98 percent of all county spending that year.

General expenditures represented three-fourths of all municipal spending in 1957. The six major functions, in order, were education (15.6 percent), highways (13.5 percent), sanitation (12.5 percent), police (10.9 percent), fire protection (7.8 percent), and health and hospitals (7.4 percent). Items of other municipal spending, in order, were general control, public welfare, parks and recreation, interest on general debt, housing, non-highway transportation, and libraries.

Expenditures of school districts and special districts in 1957 were broken down by character and object rather than by function. School district expenditures were for personal services (58.3 percent), capital outlay (22.5 percent), and all other (19.5 percent). Expenditures of special districts in order of size were current operation, construction, interest on debt, land and existing structures, and equipment. Functionally, housing, electric power, water supply, and transit systems accounted for nearly half of all special district expenditures in 1957.

THE ROLE OF INTERGOVERNMENTAL ASSISTANCE

The major role of intergovernmental assistance in financing services of local governments has been mentioned previously. In 1959, such funds covered about one-fourth of all local outlays ranging from one percent of general government expenditures to three-fifths of the funds for public assistance. The comparative importance of intergovernmental grants in 1929 and 1959 for major programs is presented in Table 16.

State aid for education has existed for a long time and it is interesting to note that this remains a major emphasis of state aid, exceeded only by state assistance for highways. Federal grants to local governments are largest for public assistance; but as the table shows, federal grants in a number of important areas now represent sizable proportions of local spending. In addition to these specific

Table 16. *Intergovernmental Assistance for Programs of Local Governments:*

1929 and 1959

(percent)

Expenditure Item	1929 Federal	State	Local	1959 Federal	State	Local
General Government	1	—	99	1	—	99
Health, Education, and Welfare	—	10	90	6	25	69
Public Assistance	—	—	100	37	24	39
Education	—	16	84	2	33	65
Commerce and Housing	—	2	98	1	22	77
Highways	—	2	98	1	38	61
Agricultural and Natural Resources	—	—	100	5	2	93
Total	—	6	94	4	22	74

SOURCE: Lillian P. Barnes *et al.*, "State and Local Government Activity, The Postwar Experience Related to the National Economy," *Survey of Current Business, 41* (March, 1961), p. 19, Table 4.

programs, both federal and state governments extend assistance for a wide array of other activities, but individually each is rather small. However, their importance is an increasing one and commonly spurs additional spending in these activities on the part of local communities.

MANDATORY LOCAL EXPENDITURES

As creatures of the state, local governments can exercise only those functions specifically delegated to them by state law or constitution and those which are fairly implied therefrom. In addition, local governments must make many expenditures which state laws or constitutions require of them. When the local governing bodies which raise the money have no discretion in the matter, these are known as mandatory expenditures.

The New York State Commission for the Revision of Tax Laws identified five classes of such mandatory expenditures. First, where a state law fixes the amount of an appropriation required by a local unit, as in the case of a specified salary for a judge of the state court system serving a local community. Second, where the state confers the power to determine the amount of the appropriation upon some authority other than the agency or unit which adopts the local budget, as in cities where school boards determine expenses of the schools which must be borne by the city. Third, where a state law prescribes the service to be rendered but does not specify the amount to be expended, as in the case of aid to certain types of dependents. Fourth, where a state law specifies the salaries of local officers, as is sometimes true for teachers, policemen, and firemen. And, fifth, expenditures which become obligatory after voluntary action under general law, as interest payments on debt incurred or pension payments to employees.[18]

While the problem of mandatory local expenditures was particularly acute in the years of the Great Depression, it is still one of real concern to local governments. The American Municipal Association has recommended in its model home rule amendment that such authorizations by the state legislature for new activities or functions of local governments will not be carried on until either the local government has accepted the new responsibility by an affirmative vote of the governing board or until the legislature provides the local government with the money necessary to finance the new or expanded activity.

■ Local Debt Administration

Every local government theoretically enjoys the choice of paying for its capital improvement projects by increasing taxes and paying cash, or by issuing bonds to be paid off in future years. This statement assumes the acceptance of the principle that borrowing should not be used to meet current operating expenses, although this has often been done in the past, either in times of depression or as a means of keeping current taxes low—particularly in years of local elections.

Operating a local government on a strict pay-as-you-go or cash basis is impossible in most communities. Since capital expenditures would vary greatly from year to year, the local tax levies would have to show a similar wide variation. A solution would be to build up reserve funds in anticipation of future capital improvements. For example, if the construction of a new city hall is planned in 20 years, that city would set its tax rates to yield amounts over and

---

[18] As listed in Alderfer, *op. cit.*, p. 354.

above operating costs and adequate to meet the costs of the new building. Such stockpiling of reserve funds is prevented by political pressures in most local units, making the issuance of bonds both a practical and political necessity.

Borrowing to finance permanent or capital improvements is quite different from issuing bonds to pay for current and continuing governmental operations. If the life of the bonds is such that they will be paid off before the improvement or facility becomes obsolete or unusable, a good case can be made for financing such undertakings by this method. In addition to borrowing to finance major public improvements, local governments often incur debts for two other reasons. These are to meet unanticipated emergencies or to obtain funds in anticipation of revenues to be received a short time later. Borrowing for the latter reason is sometimes necessary because taxes and other revenues do not come into the treasury early enough in the fiscal year to meet current expenses. This type of borrowing is known as "short-term indebtedness" since it is normally repaid within a matter of months.

Once a community has decided to float a bond issue, the governing board enacts an ordinance outlining the general scope of the improvement to be undertaken and requesting the preparation of plans and specifications for its construction. Either engineers in the local government service or an outside firm is given the contract to draw up these plans. When these are ready, the governing board reviews them and makes necessary changes in the plans and estimates of the cost. A second ordinance is passed at this stage asking for bids to construct the improvement. Detailed plans are made available to companies interested in submitting bids. The bids are considered at a formal meeting of the board at which the contract is let to the "lowest responsible" bidder.

To obtain the money to finance the construction, the local governing board passes another ordinance providing for the bond issue. The ordinance prescribes the length of time the bonds will run, the kind of bonds to be issued, and other conditions affecting the bid. Financial companies and investment houses are invited to submit bids to float the bond issue, and the issue is awarded to the "lowest responsible" bidder. In this case, this will be the bidder offering the lowest rate of interest and the highest premium for the bonds. Often state review and approval is necessary at this point to determine the legality of the issue and the correctness of the procedures of the transaction. Upon state approval, the successful bidder sells the bonds to banks, estates, and investment houses at a premium sufficiently high to return a profit for him. The market for local bonds is considerably more complicated than this brief outline of procedure might imply, but these steps do give some idea of the mechanics of floating local bond issues.

TYPES OF LOCAL BONDS

Local bonds may be classified in a number of ways. One common classification is based on the method for paying off the indebtedness and divides issues into sinking fund and serial bonds. Sinking fund bonds normally all mature at the end of a definite time period and money is set aside in a sinking fund to retire the bonds when they come due. Serial bonds, on the other hand, have staggered maturity dates and money is appropriated directly for their payment. In recent years, serial bonds have gained in favor and are now the more commonly used. One of the major reasons for the decreasing use of sinking funds is the frequent mismanagement of these funds, resulting in past failures to have the funds to pay off the bonds at the time of their retirement.

A second classification of bonds relates to time of maturity and includes callable and non-callable bonds. If the bonds have a "call" feature, they can be paid off at any time prior to the date of maturity at the option of the debtor, subject to whatever time restrictions are placed on the issue. For example, an issue for 25 years might include the condition that none would be redeemable before a period of 10 years. Non-callable bonds, as the name implies, would be bonds which had a definite maturity date and could not be paid off before that time.

A third classification relates to the four major types of local bonds. These are (1) general obligation, (2) limited obligation or special assessment, (3) revenue, and (4) mortgage bonds. General obligation bonds are guaranteed by the taxing capacity of the issuing local government and are often called full faith and credit bonds. A community issuing this type promises to use any and all of its revenue sources to pay the interest on and to retire these bonds. Limited obligation or special assessment bonds are backed by income from one or more specific sources rather than by the full faith and credit of the community. As discussed briefly under revenue sources, these bonds are often issued to pay for public improvements directly benefiting only a part of the community. Revenue bonds are secured by the pledge of revenues from self-liquidating projects such as toll roads or bridges, water works, or public transit systems. Mortgage bonds are normally used in connection with the acquisition or construction of utilities and are in essence mortgages on the utilities, with the plant and the revenues to be realized from the sale of services as the security. When such bonds are issued, they usually require a higher rate of interest than general obligation bonds and therefore have been less popular. A pledge of full faith and credit is also used to back some mortgage bond issues and some revenue bonds to reduce interest rates.

As it is apparent from this summarization, some types of local bonds are not clearly distinguishable from others. It is possible to consider bonds as classifiable into two major groups rather than the four enumerated above—namely general obligation, and revenue or other limited obligation bonds.

THE SIZE OF LOCAL GOVERNMENT DEBT

At the end of fiscal 1961, total government debt in the United States amounted to $364 billion, of which nearly $20 billion represented state government debt and a little over $55 billion local government indebtedness. The size of debt by type of local government is shown in Figure 20. It is interesting to note that long-term debt is used in most instances by county, township and school districts and that most of the debt of these types of units is backed by the full faith and credit of the community. Municipalities also use long-term debt to finance most of their capital undertakings, but a little over one-third of the bond issues are not backed by the city's full faith and credit. Special districts, on the other hand, utilize full faith and credit bonds rather sparingly and generally issue revenue bonds.

The increasing size of local government debt is a problem of real concern. Since 1940 the total amount of local debt has increased three and one-third times, while the amount of per capita debt has risen by two and three-eighths. A bit of comfort may be found in the fact that while the absolute debt has risen substantially the relative debt per capita has not risen as sharply.

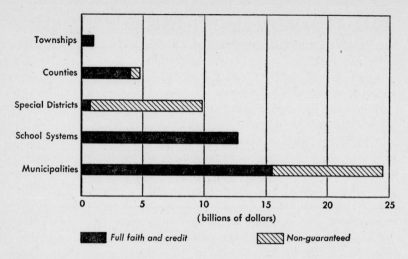

Figure 20. *Outstanding Debt, by Type of Local Government: 1961.* (U.S. Bureau of the Census, *Government Finances, 1961*, Washington, 1961, p. 27.)

LIMITATIONS ON LOCAL INDEBTEDNESS AND DEFAULTS

When the principal of or interest on a bond issue cannot be paid in accordance with the conditions prescribed in the bond contract, the bond issue is considered to be in default. The first municipal default on record in the United States occurred in Mobile, Alabama, in 1839; however, such defaults have an ancient history going back to the Greek cities in the fifth century B.C.[19] In the 100 years following the Mobile experience, at least one thousand additional defaults by local governments occurred. These defaults have been variously attributed to such causes as carpetbagger rule in southern cities following the Civil War, the issuance of local railroad aid bonds, real estate booms, irrigation bonds in the West, and the Great Depression in the 1930s.

The experience of local governments prompted the passage of permanent measures to minimize future defaults. Hillhouse identifies five types of restrictions which have become quite common. These are: (1) prohibiting public aid to private enterprise; (2) fixing debt limitations as a percentage of assessed value of taxable property; (3) prescribing maximum periods beyond which debt

[19] A. M. Hillhouse, *Municipal Bonds: A Century of Experience*, Prentice-Hall, 1936, p. 37.

LOCAL FINANCE

could not run; (4) requiring a public referendum on all bond issues; and (5) mandating that a direct tax be levied at the time the debt is incurred and annually thereafter to pay the interest on and principal of the debt.[20] Following the defaults of the 1930s, state supervision over local debt was established in a number of states.

In general, there are three major types of local debt limitations—those dealing with the purposes of local debt issues, amounts of local debt, and kinds of bonds which can be issued. These limitations have three primary sources—state constitutions, state statutes, and local charters. The first four specific limitations listed in the preceding paragraph are found in most state constitutions and the requirement concerning the direct tax levy is a common statutory requirement. In addition, statutory requirements often prescribe maximum interest rates, length of bond periods, and other limitations. Local charters often reiterate the state-imposed limitations, but sometimes contain additional limitations. Most often these concern the debt limitation of the unit prescribing it in terms of a fixed percentage of the assessed valuation of taxable property, a fixed sum, or prohibiting an amount in excess of the current revenues of the unit.

Six strong criticisms have been raised against rigid constitutional or statutory debt limitations. These are: (1) inadequate allowance for variation in the capacity of communities to carry debt; (2) unsatisfactory adjustment to the business cycle; (3) failure to curb injudicious use of local credit; (4) failure to consider the overlapping debts of local governments within the same physical area and with the same citizenry; (5) lack of uniformity because of wide variation of ratios of assessed valuation; and (6) consolidation or merger of local units is difficult because of the precise requirements of these limitations.[21]

In an effort to overcome some of the shortcomings of a system of such rigid controls, a number of states have established administrative agencies to pass upon debt proposals of local governments. State administrative control should not displace local discretion entirely, but it can prevent local abuses of borrowing power and provide aid to local governments by developing a borrowing policy which will avoid the recurrence of the financial disasters that have occurred at the local level in the past.

[20] *Ibid.*, pp. 438–40.
[21] Council of State Governments, *State-Local Relations,* 1946, p. 118.

SUGGESTED READINGS

Books

Adrian, Charles R., *Governing Urban America,* 2nd ed. (New York: McGraw-Hill, 1961).

Alderfer, Harold F., *American Local Government and Administration* (New York: Macmillan, 1956).

Bureau of the Census, *Governmental Finances, 1961* (Washington: Government Printing Office, 1962).

Chatters, Carl H. and Hillhouse, Albert M., *Local Government Debt Administration* (New York: Prentice-Hall, 1939).

Groves, Harold M., *Financing Government,* 5th ed. (New York: Holt, 1958).

Hillhouse, Albert M., *Municipal Bonds: A Century of Experience* (New York: Prentice-Hall, 1936).

International City Managers' Association, *Municipal Finance,* 5th ed. (Chicago: International City Managers' Association, 1955).

Kendrick, M. Slade, *Public Finance* (Boston: Houghton Mifflin, 1951).

Kneier, Charles M. and Fox, Guy, *Readings in Municipal Government and Administration* (New York: Rinehart, 1953), Readings 136–45.

McKinley, John R., *Local Revenue Problems and Trends* (Berkeley: Bureau of Public Administration, University of California, 1949).

McMillan, T. E., Jr., *State Supervision of Municipal Finance* (Austin: Institute of Public Affairs, University of Texas, 1953).

Municipal Finance Officers Association, *Municipal Nonproperty Taxes,* Supplement to *Where Cities Get Their Money* (Chicago: Municipal Finance Officers Association, 1956).

Sigafoos, Robert A., *The Municipal Income Tax: Its History and Problems* (Chicago: Public Administration Service, 1955).

Vieg, John A., Armstrong, Hubert C., Farner, Frank, Rostvold, Gerhard N., Shelton, John P. and Thompson, Proctor, *California Local Finance* (Stanford: Stanford University Press, 1960).

Winter, William O., *The Special Assessment Today with Emphasis on the Michigan Experience* (Ann Arbor: University of Michigan, 1952).

Articles

Anderson, Lynn F., "The Search for Money," *National Municipal Review,* 44 (February, 1955), 76–80.

Barnes, Lillian P., Cobren, George M. and Rosenthal, Joseph, "State and Local Government Activity, The Postwar Experience Related to the National Economy," *Survey of Current Business,* 41 (March, 1961), 16–24.

Egger, Rowland, "Nature Over Art: No More Local Finance," *American Political Science Review, 47* (June, 1953), 461–77.

Freeman, Roger A., "Grants Without Strings," *National Municipal Review, 48* (June, 1959), 298–302.

Harrell, C. A., "How Cities Can Adopt Pay-as-you-go Financing," *Public Management, 30* (March, 1948), 66–68.

Manvel, Allen D., "County Government Finances, Recent Levels and Trends," *The County Officer, 19* (April, 1954), 76–79.

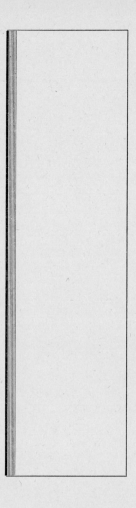

PUBLIC SERVICES

Six

Public Safety

19

Probably the oldest and most basic services provided by local communities are those encompassed under the term public safety. General purpose local governments are authorized to protect persons and property under the grant of general police power from the state. This grant of powers, however, is coupled with the responsibility to perform the services required. The contemporary trend is for local governments to emphasize preventive rather than remedial efforts, but this is a recent development. For too many years most of the efforts and resources in this field were largely remedial and attempts to keep abreast of social opportunities or to employ modern techniques are developments of the twentieth century.

Public safety activities by American local governments were begun in colonial days. The early "night watches" were to prevent fires in colonial settlements, but these soon changed to "patrols" with police functions added. Early patrolmen were armed with a special rattle which they could shake to give the signal for assistance. In these communities patrol service was a compulsory, non-paid duty of citizens, with rotation of duty among able-bodied males. It was permitted to hire substitutes to perform this duty and this became a common practice in many communities. As a result, the patrol function passed frequently to less able citizens and the function itself was held in low esteem. A number of cities actually passed ordinances to protect the members of patrols from public insult.

Conditions in Philadelphia in the 1730s were described by Benjamin Franklin in these colorful words:

The city watch was one of the first things I conceived to want regulation. It was managed by the constables of the respective wards in turns; the constable warned a number of housekeepers to attend him for the night. Those who chose never to attend, paid him six shillings yearly to be excused, which was supposed to be for hiring substitutes, but was in reality, much more than was necessary for that purpose, and made the constableship a place of profit; and the constable for a little drink, often got such ragamuffins about him as a watch, that respectable housekeepers did not choose to mix with. Walking the rounds, too, was often neglected, and most of the nights spent in tippling.[1]

Daytime police functions were not started until the 1820s even in older, established cities. The Peel Act in England pertaining to local police was imitated in American states, resulting in the provision that tax funds would be used to pay for the services of those on police duty, but conditions did not improve substantially even with this policy. One writer has stated that, "For the next fifty years, if mayors and police chiefs changed fast enough, everyone who 'deserved' it had his chance at a civic double-header—the public trough and the police racket against the underworld."[2] Uniforms for policemen were only slowly and hesitatingly approved in cities because many citizens feared the military consequences of uniforms and others objected to this outward display of patronage by the local political party in office.

As mentioned above, the original duty of colonial night watches was to be on the lookout for fires. In general, males between the ages of 16 and 50 were bound to aid in fighting fires and local ordinances prohibited wooden chimneys, regulated the stacking of grains and wooden materials, and dealt harshly with those found guilty of turning in false fire alarms. Freeholders were compelled to keep a leather bucket or ladder ready for use in the event of a

---

[1] Benjamin Franklin, *Autobiography of Benjamin Franklin*, William Macdonald, 1905, p. 123.
[2] Henry G. Hodges, *City Management, Theory and Practice of Municipal Administration*, Crofts, 1939, p. 417.

fire. One of the first recorded official acts by a local government to provide fire protection occurred in New York City in 1659, when 250 leather buckets and a supply of hooks and ladders were purchased by the city and paid by a revenue realized from a chimney tax.

Our first local fire "departments" were volunteer organizations, the one organized by Benjamin Franklin in Philadelphia in the 1730s being the best known. According to Franklin, the volunteer company was formed "for the more ready extinguishing of fires, and the mutual assistance in removing and securing goods when in danger." The company's articles also carried an agreement to meet "once a month and spend a social evening together."[3] Both the social and political activities of volunteer fire companies are better chronicled than are their fire fighting activities, but they provided this basic service until they were gradually replaced in large cities with organized, professional firemen. Volunteer fire companies remain a fixture in many communities across the nation, but the wooden ladder and leather bucket have been replaced with modern fire fighting apparatus. However, the "social evening together" remains a function of both importance and emphasis for many of these companies.

Public safety activities of local governments today are many and varied and differ markedly in degree, if not in kind, from those in our colonial communities. One writer recently wrote that, "Protection of cities is a big business, a technical challenge, and a work of art; it also is police service, fire fighting, fire prevention, and many other things. Basically, however, it is meeting hazards in such a way as to minimize loss, whatever those hazards may be."[4] Of the many functions of local government which are related to public safety, four will be discussed in this chapter. These are the activities of police protection, fire fighting and prevention, air pollution control, and civil defense.

■ *The Police Function*

The police function in local government can perhaps be best defined in terms of police objectives since the organization varies

---

[3] Franklin, *op. cit.*, pp. 124-5.
[4] Charles S. James, *A Frontier of Municipal Safety*, Public Administration Service, 1955, p. 1.

from the constable system in small towns and townships to the elaborate and complex organization of a big city police department. In general, however, police objectives are the same and include the maintenance of peace and order, control and prevention of crime and vice, traffic control, and police duties include a number of regulatory responsibilities.[5] As identified by the Institute for Training in Municipal Administration, the five major police activities are (1) prevention of criminality, (2) repression of crime, (3) apprehension of offenders, (4) recovery of lost and stolen property, and (5) regulation of non-criminal conduct.[6] The last is a growing one, embracing such varied activities as traffic control, enforcement of health and sanitary regulations, and compliance with safety precautions.

THE INCIDENCE OF CRIME

Crime is a social problem of major importance in the United States in both rural and urban areas. No one actually knows how much crime costs the nation in either money or misery, but estimates of the financial cost have been placed as high as $15 billion. While the rate of crimes in all major categories has increased in recent years, it is not clear whether this has resulted from increased criminality or better enforcement and reporting. The basic and primary source of data concerning crimes are the *Uniform Crime Reports* issued by the Federal Bureau of Investigation from statistics submitted by local police departments throughout the nation.

While urban crime rates are considerably higher in most categories than are those in rural areas, urban police facilities for detection and apprehension are also much better. Comparative arrest rates of urban and rural areas for 1960 are shown in Table 17. Except in the cases of manslaughter by negligence and offenses against family and children, in which the rate for rural areas exceeds that in urban areas, and in forgery and counterfeiting in which the rate is the same, the urban rate is higher in all categories.

The crime rate in the United States is considerably higher than that in European nations. Yet, in terms of technical equipment, our police are the best equipped in the world. The fact that police

[5] V. A. Leonard, *Police Organization and Management,* Foundation Press, 1951, p. 2.

[6] International City Managers' Association, *Municipal Police Administration,* 3rd ed., International City Managers' Association, 1950, p. 3.

Table 17. *Urban and Rural Arrest Rates: 1960*

Offense Charged	2,460 Cities Population 81,661,000 Number	Rate per 100,000	983 Rural Agencies Population 27,118,000 Number	Rate per 100,000
Criminal Homicide:				
Murder and nonnegligent manslaughter	4,506	5.5	1,027	3.8
Murder by negligence	1,766	2.2	656	2.4
Robbery	29,326	35.9	3,465	12.8
Aggravated assault	52,277	64.0	7,684	28.3
Other assaults	134,538	164.8	18,684	68.9
Burglary—breaking or entering	110,047	134.8	27,753	102.3
Larceny—theft	207,548	254.2	29,645	109.3
Auto theft	54,024	66.2	9,658	35.6
Embezzlement and fraud	32,550	39.9	9,639	35.5
Stolen property—buying, receiving, etc.	10,049	12.3	1,743	6.4
Forgery and counterfeiting	18,958	23.2	6,286	23.2
Forcible rape	6,068	7.4	1,651	6.1
Prostitution and commercialized vice	25,851	31.7	631	2.3
Other sex offenses	44,532	54.4	5,569	20.5
Narcotic drug laws	23,430	28.7	4,305	15.9
Weapons—carrying, possessing, etc.	34,520	42.3	3,600	13.3
Offenses against family and children	34,203	41.9	16,354	60.3
Liquor laws	86,818	106.3	19,529	72.0
Driving while intoxicated	146,381	179.3	37,562	138.5
Disorderly conduct	449,444	550.4	26,058	96.1
Drunkenness	1,326,407	1,624.3	85,760	316.2
Vagrancy	146,105	178.9	7,096	26.2
Gambling	119,243	146.0	3,703	13.7
All other offenses	453,462	555.3	79,447	293.0
Total	3,552,054	4,349.8	407,505	1,502.7

SOURCE: Department of Justice, Federal Bureau of Investigation, *Uniform Crime Reports for the United States,* annual report, 1960, as reproduced in *Statistical Abstract of the United States,* 1962, Table 196, p. 152.

technology, like Alice in Wonderland, must run fast to stand still has been aptly phrased by the police chief of Los Angeles. In his words, "Despite the technology that has been acquired through no small effort and expense, the police service today fulfills its task with no greater success than it did a quarter- or half-century ago."[7]

RURAL POLICE ORGANIZATION

The responsibility for keeping peace in rural areas lies primarily in the offices of county sheriff and local officers known as marshals, justices of the peace and constables. All have three principal categories of duties. First, they are conservators of the peace within the county and its civil subdivisions. Second, they are officers of the county court and justices of the peace court respectively, and serve summonses, warrants and subpoenas, and execute court judgments. Third, they are keepers of the jails of the county and its divisions. The last function is one of declining importance for constables since many communities now use county jail facilities rather than maintain their own detention facilities.

Both agencies of rural law enforcement have been subject to severe and continuing criticism in recent years. Concerning the county sheriff, one careful student of American local government has written, "As matters now stand, the sheriff is a formidable roadblock to the effective law enforcement in most American counties. He neither does his job well nor cooperates willingly and effectively with qualified police officers. Logically, the office of sheriff should be abolished, but logic does not always prevail in politics."[8] It has been suggested that reorganization of the sheriff's office should take one of two directions. First, his law enforcement position should be strengthened and qualified personnel provided for the office, or second, the responsibility for law enforcement should be shifted to other agencies such as the regional station of state police systems. This transfer of functions would leave the sheriff primarily as a process-serving officer. Both courses of action are now in evidence with the former occurring in more urban counties and the latter in rural counties.

The constable system has been even more sharply criticized. In the words of Bruce Smith, an outstanding American police authority, "So in state after state the evidence accumulates that the constable has outlived his usefulness, that his law enforcement

[7] W. H. Parker, "The Police Challenge in Our Great Cities," *The Annals of the American Academy of Political and Social Science, 291* (January, 1954), 5-13.

[8] J. C. Phillips, *State and Local Government in America,* American Book Co., 1954, p. 461.

activities have lapsed, and that the time has come when he can be abolished without any concern about the effect such action would have upon the administration of justice. . . . Thus, if the office is to be retained it can only be on the ground that it has become a symbol of local self-government, and as such should not be disturbed under any circumstances."[9]

Since the sheriff-constable system has proved inadequate for law enforcement in some rural areas, several alternative systems have been proposed. The use of centralized state police systems have been recommended in small and sparsely-populated states. This would require the placing of state police barracks at locations throughout the state so that law enforcement officers would be available to answer calls for assistance without delay. A second proposal is for the creation of a county police force as an alternative to the sheriff system. This force would consist of qualified personnel and be organized to function in a manner similar to that of a city police department. A third proposal suggests the establishment of specialized arms of a county police force to be used for such purposes as highway patrol or crime detection, with other rural law enforcement activities remaining with the sheriff and constables.

URBAN POLICE ORGANIZATION

The problem of police organization in urban areas varies from the simple arrangements in small cities with a one- to three-man police force to the complex and intricate law enforcement organizations in large cities with several thousands of employees. As the size of the police force increases, both specialization of functions and subdivision of levels of activity become essential. The first characteristic implies that not all duties are performed by all members of the department. Some will perform traffic control duties, others detective functions, others will work primarily with juveniles, etc. The second characteristic means that higher ranks will direct the performance of those of lower ranks. Thus, a large police department is organized along quasi-military lines.

As mentioned previously, the basic purposes of police are to prevent crime, suppress criminal activity, apprehend criminals, preserve the peace, regulate conduct, and protect life and property. To carry out these functions, the department is organized in several

[9] Bruce Smith, *Police Systems in the United States,* rev. ed., Harper, 1949, p. 99.

divisions, all of which are responsible to the head of the department, usually called the chief. The chief will normally be a professional officer, but in large cities the chief may be subordinate to a lay department head known as the police commissioner.

The core of police operations is centered in a patrol division which is usually the largest subdivision of the department. Its functions broadly consist of crime prevention, juvenile delinquency control, crime repression, protection of life and property, and providing advice, information and assistance to the public. Patrol activities are carried on by uniformed police who serve both as "cops" on the beat and in patrol cars. Among their specific duties are observing conditions while patrolling, controlling public gatherings, checking locks on commercial buildings after closing hours, settling minor complaints, answering emergency calls, and testifying in courts.

The second largest unit in an urban police department is often the detective division. Primary functions of this division include the investigation of crimes, recovery of property, and the identification and apprehension of offenders. Because of the nature of their work, detectives are not in uniform. This division is normally equipped with scientific and technical aids including equipment for microscopy, photography, fingerprinting, lie detectors, and impression casts. At least some of the members will be knowledgeable in such fields as chemistry, medicine, narcotics, and psychiatry.

Another large unit is the traffic division or bureau. As the name implies, men of this unit enforce traffic regulations, man busy traffic intersections, enforce parking laws, give first aid at accidents, furnish accident records, and help in the trial of traffic violators. Since this is the police activity which most directly affects the largest number of citizens, the personnel of this unit greatly influences the typical citizen's concept of his police department. Recognizing the importance of the public relations aspect of this unit, many police departments now demand high standards of appearance, conduct and impartial performance of duties by the men of its traffic division. School crossing guards, where not provided by schools, are usually civilians who are attached to the traffic division because their activities fall naturally into the operations of this unit.

The enforcement of laws relating to such activities as gambling, prostitution, narcotics, and liquor is known as vice control. In most cities, these laws are enforced either by a vice division or by vice squads in the patrol and detective divisions. Since vice operations are sometimes highly organized in cities, this function involves problems and techniques which differ from those of normal patrol and investigation. Because of occasional revelations of collusion between vice ring leaders and some policemen, the public often has a rather low regard of vice squads and their work. Police in most cities, however, are willing and able to suppress organized vice if the public demands and supports their efforts to do so.

Curbing juvenile delinquency is another major task of police departments carried on by specialized officers of the patrol division or by officers of a separate juvenile division. The work of these officers is largely preventive and seeks to prevent and correct conditions inducing criminality by teen-age boys and girls. Since delinquency is a broad social problem rather than just a police problem, members of this unit work closely with schools, recreation departments, health and welfare agencies, and probation officers. A well rounded program of a juvenile division, according to O. W. Wilson, would include: (1) the eradication of conditions that promote criminal activities, of elements that induce criminal activities, and of elements that induce criminal tendencies in youth; (2) the discovery and treatment of the delinquent, the near-delinquent, and those exposed to high-risk situations; and (3) the planning, promotion and direction of activities that provide wholesome influences on youth.[10]

In addition to the major divisions described above, large police departments also have staff services which serve all the operating divisions of the department. These might include such units as a personnel and training unit, technical service units, and administrative or headquarters units.

The organization, manpower, and activities of the Los Angeles City Police Department in 1960 can serve as an illustration of a large city's police department in action. In 1960, this department was organized in seven bureaus with a manpower complement as follows: (1) administration bureau with 167 officers and 102 civilian personnel; (2) detective bureau with 700 officers and 68 civilians; (3) traffic bureau with a complement of 621 officers and 36 civilian employees; (4) personnel and training bureau with a

---

[10] O. W. Wilson, *Police Administration,* McGraw-Hill, 1950, pp. 210–1.

force of 149 officers and 31 civilians; (5) bureau of corrections with 353 and 151 officers and civilian personnel respectively; (6) patrol bureau with 2,501 officers and 591 civilian employees; and (7) technical services bureau with 143 officers and 608 civilians. The number of employees for the whole department totaled 4,634 officers and 1,587 civilians. The cost of police activities totaled $44,332,385, of which nearly $41 million was for salaries. Among the activities performed during the year were the general policing of the Democratic National Convention which met in Los Angeles; the presentation of 163 recruitment talks at high schools, colleges, and service clubs; delivery of Christmas boxes to the blind and the repair of broken toys for needy children; investigation of 53,706 traffic accidents and citation of 595,820 moving traffic violations; making 31,975 major felony arrests and 233,571 other arrests; supervising 1,392,859 man-days by inmates in the city jail system; handling 26 strikes and 14 labor disturbances without incident; and identification of 157 juvenile gangs comprised of 3,200 youths between the ages of 13 and 20.[11]

The extent of local police employment by counties, municipalities, and townships in the United States in 1962 is shown in Table 18. The magnitude and importance of police activity is partially re-

Table 18. *Summary of Local Police Employment: 1962*

Item	Total	Counties	Municipalities	Townships
Police Employees (in thousands)	324	52.4	254.3	17.3
Full-time	279			
Part-time	45			
Full-time equivalent	4			
Total on full-time basis	283			
Payroll (in millions of dollars)	130.9	20.5	105.8	4.6
Police Employment as Percent of Total Public Employment	11.4	5.9	14.8	7.4
Police Pay Roll as Percent of Total Public Payroll	12.8	6.9	15.9	7.8

SOURCE: Bureau of Census, *State Distribution of Public Employment in 1962,* G–GE62, No. 1, April, 1963, pp. 7–8.

[11] Los Angeles Police Department, *1960 Annual Report,* 1960, pp. 4–32.

vealed by the facts that 11.4 percent of the total number of employees of local governments are police employees and that 12.8 percent of the total local pay roll goes for police salaries. The figures for municipalities are considerably higher, reaching 14.8 and 15.9 percent respectively.

■ Fire Protection

Fire protection services of local governments include a number of important functions, the most colorful and best known being fire fighting. Probably the most important function of fire departments, however, is fire prevention by the correction of common hazards which result in fires and education of the citizenry in the careful use and control of fire. Closely related activities include keeping loss of life and property to a minimum in case of fire, investigating causes of fires, and salvaging operations. Activities of importance within the department include the installation and maintenance of a fire alarm system, repair and maintenance of equipment, and training of personnel.[12]

The magnitude of fire department activities can be shown in a number of ways. Fires took 11,700 lives in 1961 and resulted in a total loss of over one and a half billion dollars.[13] Over a million fires were reported by 2,777 communities of 2,500 or more population in 1961, resulting in a fire loss of $6.64 for every man, woman and child in the United States.[14] These great losses occur despite the fact that American communities have the finest fire fighting equipment in the world.

LOCAL ORGANIZATION

The volunteer fire department mentioned briefly at the start of this chapter is still the most common type of organization for small towns and rural areas. In 1950, there were more than 15,000 of these volunteer companies serving communities in the United States and Canada. In the larger of these communities, there is

[12] International City Managers' Association, *Municipal Fire Administration*, 5th ed., International City Managers' Association, 1950, p. 63.

[13] International City Managers' Association, *The Municipal Year Book, 1962*, International City Managers' Association, 1962, p. 383.

[14] National Board of Fire Underwriters, *Report of the Committee on Statistics and Origin of Losses*, New York, 1961, as reproduced in *Statistical Abstract of the United States*, 1962, p. 482.

commonly a skeleton force of paid firemen who provide a nucleus for the force of volunteers. A recent study of volunteer fire companies in Pennsylvania showed that there were over 1,700 active volunteer companies with about 250,000 members in that state. Two cities with populations of nearly 100,000 were among the communities relying primarily on the service of volunteer companies.[15]

As in the case of the fire company established by Benjamin Franklin, the volunteer fire company remains a social institution in many communities. The fire company in a Pennsylvania community in which the author lived for seven years had an annual Christmas party for the children of the township, an annual "corn boil" as a family picnic outing, frequent dances for members and friends, and made its hall available for such activities as wedding parties and social affairs of other community groups. Although this volunteer company was organized as an independent corporation, it had close relationships with the township governing board. This relationship was so cordial that the township actually purchased a new fire truck for the company and planned to write its cost off over a period of years through the annual contribution that the township granted the fire company "for services rendered."

While the popular stereotype of the volunteer fire company envisions it as a poorly organized, ineffective instrument for fighting fires, many operate with high efficiency. Such companies take an inordinate pride in their equipment and keep it bright and shining at all times. The volunteer fire company, however, is a development in small cities and towns or in unincorporated clusters of populations. Strictly rural areas still have little organized fire protection. A small number of counties have county fire departments with stations scattered throughout the county, and some townships pay volunteer fire companies for fire fighting services performed outside the boundaries of the immediate area served by the company. The four main plans for providing rural areas with fire protection call for (1) the establishment of a part-paid and/or volunteer department; (2) cooperating in forming a fire district; (3) cooperating in establishing a township or county fire department; and (4) negotiation of an agreement with the nearest governmental unit for fire protection services.[16]

[15] Harold F. Alderfer, *American Local Government and Administration,* Macmillan, 1956, pp. 529-30.

[16] International City Managers' Association, *Municipal Fire Administration,* International City Managers' Association, p. 70.

PUBLIC SERVICES

By the end of the nineteenth century, the volunteer fire company was being replaced by full-time, paid fire companies in larger cities. Now many cities between 5,000 and 10,000 have paid departments and most cities over 10,000 have such organizations. In 1961, the median number of fire department employees per 1,000 population ranged from 1.08 in cities between 10,000 and 25,000 to 1.59 in cities with populations between 100,000 and 250,000. Cities of over 500,000 had a median number of 1.50 firemen. Entrance median salaries ranged from $4,080 in small cities to $5,080 in cities over 500,000 and the median work week ranged from 70 hours in cities of 10,000 to 25,000 to 56 hours in cities of over 500,000.[17]

Fighting fires in cities is a technical and complex occupation. Large numbers of people, high buildings in close proximity to each other, and narrow streets cluttered with parked vehicles present formidable obstacles. However, fire fighting equipment is continually improving in effectiveness and in design. Table 19 indicates the number and variety of major fire fighting equipment in cities of over 25,000 in 1962.

Activities of the Los Angeles City Fire Department in 1959-1960 can serve as an illustration of these services in a large city. In that year, the department had a force of 3,100 firemen and 161 civilian employees, and over 23 million dollars were expended to pay

Table 19. *Fire Equipment in Cities over 25,000: 1962*

Population Group	Number of Cities	Pumpers Under 750 GPM	Pumpers of 750 GPM and over	Pumper Combinations	Service Ladder Trucks	Aerial Ladder Trucks
500,000 and over	20	7	1,401	15	32	556
250,000–500,000	30	75	667	23	27	221
100,000–250,000	77	65	915	24	42	267
50,000–100,000	156	115	963	94	46	273
25,000– 50,000	328	288	1,110	222	45	379
All Cities over 25,000	611	490	5,056	378	192	1,696

SOURCE: International City Managers' Association, *The Municipal Year Book, 1963*, Chicago, 1963, p. 380.

[17] International City Managers' Association, *The Municipal Year Book, 1962*, International City Managers' Association, 1962, pp. 388-9.

salaries, purchase equipment, and maintain its operations. The city had 94 engine houses, two fire boat stations, and one mountain patrol. During the year 38,745 incidents were reported of which 3,116 were false alarms. However, there were 56 fires each of which destroyed over $10,000 in property, 8,746 rescue ambulance calls, and 4,015 other rescue calls.[18]

FIRE PREVENTION

It is a truism that most fires could have been prevented with proper regulations and enforcement. It is also true that local governments have become more concerned with programs of fire prevention than they were in earlier years. An effective fire prevention program has three primary methods—inspection, enforcement, and education. The inspection program has a double purpose—to prevent fires and to familiarize firemen with the layout of buildings and the general area of their district. Inspections cover such items as rubbish burners, incinerators, fire doors, heating devices, chimneys, fire extinguishers, storage of combustible materials, etc.

Enforcement begins where inspection ends. If hazards are discovered, they should be reported and the property owner forced to correct or remove the potential hazard. One writer has described inspection as "our weak link in fire prevention. . . . The reason is that we do not follow-up and enforce the results of our inspections. It is not altogether the fault of the fire department. Public opinion in this country will not tolerate the arrest of citizens who endanger the lives and property of others by their carelessness, as has been the custom in European cities for decades."[19] A second aspect of enforcement relates to the granting of permits, licenses, and certificates of approval where hazards are involved or might develop, as in the case of use of dry-cleaning materials, licensing of motion picture operators, installation of oil burners, etc. In such cases, the adherence to prescribed standards, and inspection for compliance, often becomes a condition for the issuance and retention of licenses.

Fire prevention education, to be effective, is quite dependent on public cooperation. Many communities annually sponsor a fire prevention week during which special efforts are made to inform the public of safety regulations and the dangers from their misuse. Safety education should be a continuing operation, however, utiliz-

[18] Los Angeles Fire Department, *The Size-Up 1959-1960*, Annual Report, 1959–1960, pp. 26–29.
[19] Hodges, *op. cit.*, p. 504.

ing the public schools, the press, radio, t.v., posters and other means to educate the public. Other communities have clean-up campaigns which serve to remove potential fire hazards while informing the citizenry about their danger. In large cities, a trained public relations expert is often employed to spearhead the program of fire prevention education.

■ Police-Fire Integration

While police and fire services still have some essential differences, the recent strong emphasis on prevention has drawn the two departments closer together. In a number of cities a recognition of this development has resulted in the establishment of a single department of public safety. One form of integration is administrative only, and within a single department of public safety headed by a lay commissioner will be a bureau of police and a bureau of fire headed by professional careermen. A second type of integration recognizes that some duties are so similar that particular duties are integrated. A policeman walking the beat will also check on fire hazards and men on patrol function will be on guard against the outbreak of both an act of violence or a fire. In communities with this system, the patrol car will often be a patrol wagon equipped with a fire extinguisher and other basic fire fighting equipment. A third type of integration results in positions known as public safety officers—men who are trained to perform both police and fire fighting functions.

While the first and second kinds of integration exist in some large cities, the third has been limited to small communities—primarily those under 10,000 population. Among the advantages claimed by its proponents are that (1) it increases the supply of trained manpower available in emergency situations; (2) it provides full-time activity for the personnel; (3) it reduces overhead needs of equipment, personnel, and buildings; (4) it simplifies the keeping of safety records; (5) it simplifies the administrative organization of local government; and (6) it often results in more economical protective services for the community.[20]

Integration of public safety services is still the unusual rather

---

[20] For fuller accounts of integration in public safety programs, see Charles S. James, *op. cit.*, and his *Police and Fire Integration in the Small City,* Public Administration Service, 1955.

than the typical pattern of operation, even in small cities. However, integration seems to work well in those communities that have tried it and one writer believes that integrated departments present a design for the future. In his words:

It is a future that holds much promise, both in theory and as shown by the past experience of pioneering cities. It is also a future that will never become the present until people realize that the promise it holds is for better public safety service. If integration is held out as a device for cutting taxes, or a scheme for applying the industrial "speed-up" to police and fire administration, it can be reasonably argued that it is also a method of jeopardizing the public safety in the interests of economy and efficiency. The facts are that it is neither one of the former, and it follows that it then cannot be the latter.[21]

■ Air Pollution Control

Polluted air is an expensive by-product of the economic growth of America. For Americans in the nineteenth century, living in sooty cities was the price to pay if they hoped to get rich, for it was there that the nation's industrial plants were concentrated. Americans in the twentieth century, however, are not happy that this industrial might and its products—automobiles, freeways, skyscrapers, etc.—are filling their air with visible and invisible gases, smoke, and dust particles. Although there are no accurate records of the costs of polluted air, it has been estimated that the direct yearly economic costs for the nation as a whole are $7.5 billion.[22] In individual terms, it is estimated that air pollution now costs an average of at least $50 per year for each person in our nation to replace damaged goods, repair and repaint discolored surfaces, and launder and clean soiled clothes.[23]

At the request of President Eisenhower, the Department of Health, Education and Welfare set up an *ad hoc* Interdepartmental Committee on Community Air Pollution in 1954. This Committee framed a broad definition of air pollution as follows: "Community

[21] James, *Police and Fire Integration in the Small City,* p. 6.

[22] Luther L. Terry, "Poison in Your City's Air," *This Week Magazine,* (December 9, 1962), p. 18.

[23] Public Health Service, *Where We Stand on Smog Problem, What's Been Done, What's Ahead,* Washington, 1961, p. 20. Reprinted from *The Los Angeles Times,* Sunday, January 8, 1961.

air pollution is the presence in the ambient atmosphere of substances put there by the activities of man in concentrations sufficient to interfere directly or indirectly with his comfort, safety or health, or with the full use and enjoyment of his property. In general, it does not refer to the atmospheric pollution incident to employment in areas where workers are employed, nor is it concerned with airborne agents of communicable disease, nor with overt or covert acts of war."[24]

While the magnitude of the air pollution problem has increased greatly, it is actually an old problem to mankind. In England, coal smoke and fumes forced Queen Eleanor to move from Nottingham in 1257, and the first smoke abatement law was enacted there in 1273 under Edward I. The first known smoke abatement organization was formed by members of Parliament in 1306 in an effort to improve conditions of the air over London.[25] In the 1940s, the cities of St. Louis and Pittsburgh initiated clean-up campaigns and stringently reduced the smoke pollution resulting from the burning of solid fuels. In 1947, the now well-known efforts of Los Angeles to abate its smog problem were begun by the creation of an Air Pollution Control District following the passage of enabling legislation by the California legislature.

While the eye irritation resulting from air pollution is an unpleasant nuisance, the real concern is with the nature and extent of the relationship of polluted air to increase in chronic respiratory diseases, including asthma, bronchitis, emphysema, and lung cancer. In 1948, nearly 6,000 persons were made ill in Donora, Pennsylvania, as a result of a three-day period of fog, air inversion and excessive air pollution. Twenty deaths were attributed to that occurrence and follow-up studies were conducted pertaining to its effects on the health of others. During a heavy smog siege in Los Angeles in late August and early September in 1955, nearly 1,000 excess deaths occurred. The incidence of smog coincided with a period of unusually hot weather, and the latter is usually blamed for these excessive deaths. In both cities, however, the majority of the deaths and illnesses occurred among the elderly or persons with pre-existing heart or lung conditions which made them more susceptible to the irritants in the air that interfered with oxygen use.[26]

[24] Hazel Holly, *What's In the Air?* Public Affairs Pamphlet No. 275, 1958, p. 5.
[25] Public Health Service, *op. cit.*, p. 6.
[26] *Ibid.*, p. 13.

The necessity for cleaning up the air over our big cities is apparent from the following statement concerning man's relative needs for food, water, and air. "Man can live five weeks without food and five days without water. But he perishes after five minutes without air. Every day the average adult eats about 2¾ lb. of food and drinks 4½ lb. of water. But his lungs draw in and expire 30 lb. of air. Although oxygen requirements are the most critical of man's daily physical needs, he does less to control the purity of the air than he does to ensure the wholesomeness of his food and water."[27]

In addition to the effects of air pollution on humans, many plants are victimized by smog. The scope of this problem is apparent from the fact that photo chemical air pollution was known to exist in 1960 in 25 California counties, in 25 American states, and in seven nations on three continents. While there are no records concerning the economic losses in agriculture resulting from air pollution, a conservative estimate of the loss in leafy vegetables in California alone is about $8 million.[28]

The extent of our concern with air pollution problems is reflected by the number of projects and amount of money devoted to research in this field. In 1953, there were 110 air pollution agencies operating in the United States. By March, 1958, there were 297 such projects in operation. The first National Conference on Air Pollution met in Washington in November, 1958, bringing together leading scientists, industrialists and public officials. This meeting was heralded as a "significant milestone on the road toward cleaner air,"[29] and showed the concern of government at all levels in working cooperatively on this relatively recent but serious problem of major importance to all Americans. It also serves as a reminder that we have not yet solved a parallel problem that has been on the active agenda of governmental concern for a much longer time— the pollution of water supplies.

■ *Civil Defense*

The continuing crisis between the United States and the Soviet Union in the years following World War II and calls for individual

[27] *Ibid.*
[28] *Ibid.*, pp. 23–24.
[29] Holly, *op. cit.*, pp. 19–20.

and community action from the White House have motivated local governments to assume some responsibility for programs in the field of civil defense. Broadly conceived, civil defense can be defined as the protection of our home front by civilians against military attack or other disaster. In the mid-twentieth century, this means protection from the disasters which would occur during and following a nuclear attack by a foreign power.

Actually the concept of civil defense is not new. In our colonial communities, men, women and children united to save their community from fire in the event of an Indian attack. During the days of the Revolution, organizations of Minute Men were always on guard to meet challenges on the home front. But the magnitude of the problems of civil defense in a nuclear age dwarfs the problems faced in earlier years. According to a recent publication of the Office of Civil Defense:

A five-megaton nuclear burst at ground level would destroy most buildings two miles from the point of the explosion. Steel-framed buildings would be knocked sideways and great fires started. The destruction five miles away would be less severe, but fires and early fallout could be a significant hazard. At 10 miles, sturdy buildings would remain intact. At this distance fires probably would not be started by the fireball, but might be started by the blast-wave which could rupture gas lines and short-circuit wires. Flying glass would present a major danger, as would early fallout. At 50 miles from the bomb burst, all buildings would remain standing. The fading burst wave would take about five minutes to arrive, but would still shatter many windows. The greatest danger at this distance would be from early fallout which would begin arriving in some areas within three or four hours, depending upon weather conditions at the time.[30]

Because of the magnitude of potential hazards, civil defense is also an important citizen responsibility. The National Plan for Civil Defense and Defense Mobilization spells out this individual responsibility quite clearly. It states, "Civil defense and defense mobilization is the responsibility of every citizen. The individual must be capable of caring for himself in an emergency and contributing to the organized community survival effort. Similarly, the family unit

---

[30] Office of Civil Defense, *Fallout Protection, What to Know and Do About Nuclear Attack*, Washington, December, 1961, p. 9.

trains and prepares to solve its own emergency problems (including home preparedness) and to assist others in need."[31]

Community civil defense programs, like individual preparedness plans, are based ʌn the concepts of self-help and cooperative efforts. Each local goverᴜment is responsible for developing a plan of community shelters and a warning system to alert its citizens. Many communities across the nation have cooperative relationships with other near-by communities for their mutual benefit. State civil defense organizations exist, but these serve primarily as sources of leadership, advice, and coordination. Except in the time of extreme emergency, relationships of local civil defense officers is on a mutual aid, voluntary basis, but in such an emergency, authority over these local officers and local law enforcement officers would pass to the governor and the state civil defense director.

At least until the time of the Berlin crisis in the late summer of 1961 and the Cuban crisis the following year, civil defense activities in local communities were sporadic and inadequate. One responsible critic writing in 1958 stated bluntly that, "Most of the locally organized activities on 'civil defense' has been play acting in a dream world. Most of the energy used and the money spent has been completely wasted. Everybody knows this, but nobody has the political courage to stop the sham."[32] While what is to be done is spelled out neatly in civil defense manuals, the orderliness disappears in lifting the words from the printed page and implementing them. The result is too often complacent indifference or official confusion.

One key problem faced by every community is recruiting volunteers in sufficient numbers to fill the positions in its program of civil defense. In spite of citizen apathy, officials in some communities have rather effectively combined their civil defense activities with disaster plans to meet emergencies which might result from floods, tornadoes, serious fires, or unusually heavy snow fall.[33]

[31] Office of Civil and Defense Mobilization, *Individual and Family Preparedness,* Appendix 1, National Plan Appendix Series, Washington, December, 1960, p. 1. The President's temporary Commission on Intergovernmental Relations in its *Report* in 1955 viewed civil defense activity as primarily a concern for national government action. President Kennedy, too, seemed to feel it is more related to national defense problems than to local policing.

[32] Luther Gulick, "The Role of the State in Solution of Metropolitan Area Problems" in Stephen B. Sweeney and George S. Blair, *Metropolitan Analysis: Important Elements of Study and Action,* University of Pennsylvania Press, 1958, p. 177.

[33] Morton Kroll, "The Challenge of Disaster to Administration," *Public Administration Review, 19* (Summer, 1959), pp. 203–4; and R. H. Marden, "Disaster," *ibid., 20* (Spring, 1960), 100–4.

Many persons believe that the attitude of individual and community complacency can be overcome, and well-intended but misguided courses of action can be corrected only by a drastic overhaul of the entire civil defense program. Instead of giving pep talks from the sidelines to the activities of state and local governments, these critics see a need for federal program leadership and greatly expanded federal financial assistance to local communities. The need for stronger, central leadership was made clear by the results in one large metropolitan community at the height of the Cuban crisis in October, 1962. The civil defense director of the center city reminded citizens in a television statement that in the event of an enemy attack, all grocery stores would be closed for at least five days. The next two days following the broadcast of this statement witnessed mass purchasing of canned goods by the housewives of the city and its suburban communities.

While our best program of civil defense is the prevention of a nuclear attack, there are definite psychological values in community and individual efforts to ameliorate the dangers of the results of an enemy attack. In the words of a publication of the Office of Civil and Defense Mobilization, "We do not want a war. We do not know whether there will be a war. But we do know that forces hostile to us possess weapons that could destroy us if we were unready. These weapons create a new threat—radioactive fallout that can spread death anywhere. That is why we must prepare."[34]

■ Intergovernmental Cooperation

Because of the importance of the range of activities covered by the term public safety, there are aspects of this function which rightfully are performed by our national and state governments. The many national law enforcement agencies whose activities are of interest to and which render assistance to local agencies fall into three main categories. These are: (1) the Coast Guard, which has general criminal law enforcement powers within the limits of coastal waters and lake shore areas; (2) agencies with auxiliary police authority such as the Public Health Service and national park police units; and (3) regular civil police agencies such as the Federal Bureau of Investigation (which assists in the training of

---

[34] Office of Civil and Defense Mobilization, *The Family Fallout Shelter*, Washington, November, 1960, p. 19.

local police officers and often provide assistance in investigations), the T-men of the Secret Service Division of the Treasury Department, the Bureau of Narcotics, Post Office Inspectors, and the Immigration Border Control.[35]

The three major officers and agencies of state government most immediately concerned with law enforcement are the governor, the attorney general, and the state police. The governor is constitutionally charged with the responsibility of executing all civil and criminal laws of the state. The attorney general supervises local prosecuting attorneys in many states and, in cases of extreme importance, his office undertakes prosecution locally. While the state police system is usually charged primarily with enforcing highway traffic regulations, it typically serves as much more than a highway police force. The jurisdiction of state police extends to all parts of the state, but usually local police authorities are contacted before law enforcement functions are provided within incorporated communities. A number of state administrative agencies also render valuable service in the field of public safety through the enforcement of pertinent regulations. Among these would be certain operations of health departments, bank examiners, professional boards of licensing, and agricultural and insurance inspectors. Investigators attached to such state departments as liquor control and welfare also often supplement local police efforts.

In addition to assistance from national and state agencies, local governments negotiate a number of interjurisdictional agreements in the field of public safety. Many of these are formal arrangements to assist each other in police and fire department operations. A far greater number, however, are informal undertakings among local governments by which the police or firemen of neighboring jurisdictions will assist their counterparts when an emergency arises. Most fire departments have worked out what is known as "covering" arrangements so that equipment from the nearest fire station becomes on the alert when the equipment from another department is on call. Such arrangements assure that fire fighting equipment is always ready should a second fire break out in the same area. Cooperative relationships in the area of public safety often developed quite voluntarily because of a recognized need for assistance and cooperation in the important activities of protecting

[35] Smith, *op. cit.*, pp. 190-3.

the person and property of the citizenry. The successful operation of such agreements is to the credit of the men in uniform who negotiate and carry them out.

SUGGESTED READINGS

Books

Alderfer, Harold F., *American Local Government and Administration* (New York: Macmillan, 1956).

Center for the Study of Democratic Institutions, *The Police*, an interview by Donald McDonald with William H. Parker (New York: The Fund for the Republic, 1962).

Hodges, Henry G., *City Management: Theory and Practice of Municipal Administration* (New York: Crofts, 1939).

Holly, Hazel, *What's in the Air?* (New York: Public Affairs Pamphlet 275, 1958).

International City Managers' Association, *Municipal Fire Administration*, 5th ed. (Chicago: International City Managers' Association, 1950).

International City Managers' Association, *Municipal Police Administration*, 3rd ed. (Chicago: International City Managers' Association, 1950).

James, Charles S., *A Frontier of Municipal Safety* (Chicago: Public Administration Service, 1955).

James, Charles S., *Police and Fire Integration in the Small City* (Chicago: Public Administration Service, 1955).

Leonard, V. A., *Police Organization and Management* (Brooklyn: Foundation Press, 1951).

National Board of Fire Underwriters, *Standard Schedule for Grading Cities and Towns*, rev. ed. (New York: National Board of Fire Underwriters, 1942).

Phillips, J. C., *State and Local Government in America* (New York: American Book Co., 1954).

Sherwood, Frank P. and Markey, Beatrice, *The Mayor and the Fire Chief*, Inter-University Case No. 43 (University, Ala.: University of Alabama Press, 1959).

Smith, Bruce, *Police Systems in the United States*, rev. ed. (New York: Harper, 1949).

Wilson, O. W., *Police Administration* (New York: McGraw-Hill, 1950).

Articles

Annals of the American Academy of Political and Social Science, "New Goals in Police Management," Vol. 291 (January, 1954), entire issue.

Bendiner, Robert, "A Tale of Cops, Robbers, and the Visiting Professor," *The Reporter,* 23 (September 15, 1960), 33–36.

Held, Virginia P., "What Can We Do About 'J. D.'?" *The Reporter,* 21 (August 20, 1959), 12–18.

Kroll, Morton, "The Challenge of Disaster to Administration," *Public Administration Review,* 19 (Summer, 1959), 203–4.

Marder, R. H., "Disaster," *Public Administration Review,* 20 (Spring, 1960), 100–4.

Moses, Robert, "The Civil Defense Fiasco," *Harper's,* 215 (November, 1957), 29–34.

Purdom, Paul W., "Administration of Air Pollution Control in the United States," *Public Health Reports,* 72 (November, 1957), 957–61.

Terry, Luther L., "Poison in Your City's Air," *This Week Magazine,* (December 9, 1962), pp. 18–19.

Health and Welfare
Services

20

Increasing governmental concern with health and welfare problems reveals how social problems may become matters of public consideration and action. In earlier years, both health and welfare were regarded primarily as private responsibilities to be met by the individual, his family, his church, or by other private agencies. However, as the self-sufficient status of individuals was replaced by their social interdependence through industrialization and urbanization, governments have slowly assumed responsibility for seeking solutions to the many problems concerning the health and welfare needs of the citizenry. At first, these were primarily concerns of local government and were largely remedial—a local health organization was established to stop an epidemic or a welfare agency to aid needy children.[1] Now there are patterns of close cooperative relationships in both fields among all three levels of government.

Both public health and public welfare are broad terms without specific meaning which embrace a number of activities. Of the many services of local government which could be meaningfully included in this discussion, primary attention will be devoted to programs in

[1] W. G. Smillie, *Public Health Administration in the United States*, 2nd ed. Macmillan, 1940, p. 369.

public health, mental health, hospitals, public welfare categorical grants, and public housing.

■ Public Health

Although the importance of the contributions of our national and state governments in the field of public health are recognized, most health services rendered to the general public are performed by local organizations. The primary responsibility of local governments for public health administration was clearly recognized by a committee of the American Public Health Association in 1945 in its statement that "whatever may be the functions of the federal and state governments authorized by law to protect and promote the health of the people of the United States, it can be assumed now from the unanimity of professional opinion and the practical attitude of local government that the delivery of public health should continue to be, as has been the case in the past in this country, an important function of units of local government responsive intimately, and it may be said personally, to the needs of the families of each community . . ."[2]

While local health units exist in many forms, the main objectives of public health administration are essentially the same at all levels of and in all types of local government. Broadly conceived, public health may be defined as "the art and science of preventing disease, prolonging life and promoting physical and mental efficiency through organized community effort."[3] Public health administration is defined by the same author as "the application of public health principles and techniques for the benefit of the community, by official or unofficial organizations."[4] Typically, these services are provided through a department of city and county governments.

TYPES OF LOCAL ORGANIZATIONS

The Public Health Service classifies local health units into four types as follows:

[2] Haven Emerson and Martha Luginbuhl, *Local Health Units for the Nation,* The Commonwealth Fund, 1945, p. 1.
[3] Smillie, *op. cit.,* p. 3.
[4] *Ibid.*

PUBLIC SERVICES

1. Single county units which serve a single county and may or may not serve the city or cities therein, depending upon the existence of separate city health units.
2. City health departments which serve a single city. In three instances such departments serve a total of seven entire counties because of coterminous boundaries. These cities are New York (serving five counties), Philadelphia, and New Orleans.
3. Local health districts which serve two or more counties or other types of local governmental units. In such districts contiguous counties or municipalities have combined their resources and formally organized a single operating health unit with control vested in local authority and directed by one health officer or administrative head.
4. State health districts which are organized either for providing direct local services or for providing advisory and supervisory services to various types of local governmental units. In such districts, control is vested in the State.[5]

As of 1960, these four types of units embraced over 167 million people or 94.4 percent of our population. The 647 counties without organized local health services contain nearly 10 million people, or 5.6 percent of the population.

The map of the United States showing the distribution of the four types of local health organizations (Figure 21) reveals significant geographic differences. Single county units and local health districts prevail in southeastern and south central states, while independent city units are predominately located in the northeastern part of our country. Organized state districts are most common in north central and northeastern states. Lack of any local health organization is characteristic of the Rocky Mountain states, the Great Plains area, the southwest, and in three New England states. Vermont is the only state with no local health organizations, but in Montana, South Dakota and Wyoming 20 percent or less of the populations reside in areas organized for local health services.

SIZE AND EXPENDITURES OF LOCAL UNITS

While there is no uniform agreement as to the best size of a local health unit, there is unanimity that there is a minimum size below which an organization cannot be properly staffed and remain rela-

---

[5] Public Health Service, *Organization and Staff for Local Health Services*, P.H.S. Publication No. 682, Government Printing Office, 1961, p. 1.

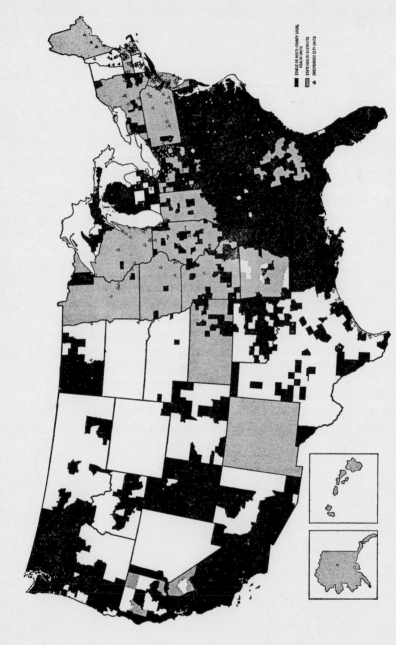

Figure 21. *Areas Organized for Local Health Services.* (U.S. Public Health Service, *Organization and Staffing for Local Health Services*, Washington, 1961, p. 8.)

SINGLE OR MULTI-COUNTY LOCAL HEALTH UNITS

STATE HEALTH DISTRICTS

INDEPENDENT CITY UNITS

tively economical in operation. The Committee on Local Health Units of the American Public Health Association recommends that a "community of 50,000 persons should be able generally . . . to employ the number and quality of persons necessary to assure basic and reasonably adequate local health services."[6] This same population base was advanced by Smillie,[7] while it was suggested in the *Municipal Year Book* in 1950 that a local health unit should serve at least 35,000 persons.[8] Of the local jurisdictions reporting in 1960, 47 percent exceeded the 50,000 population base, with 24 percent in the 50,000 to 100,000 size, 14 percent in the 100,000 to 250,000 grouping, and 9 percent in the class of 250,000 and over. Of the 53 percent with less than 50,000 population, 38 percent served populations of less than 35,000. There were 17 single county units each serving fewer than 5,000 persons and 189 units with populations between 5,000 and 15,000.[9]

In the fiscal year 1959, a total of $238 million was expended by the 2,425 health units reporting to the Public Health Service. Of this amount, 70 percent was derived from local sources, 24 percent from state funds, and 6 percent from federal funds. Expenditures by source of funds for the four types of local health organizations are shown in Figure 22. City health departments place greatest reliance on local funds and least on federal funds, while state health districts obtain the least amount from local resources and the most from state and federal funds.

Public health administrators have suggested that adequate local health services require an annual expenditure of from $2.00 to $3.00 per person. Average expenditures of local health units in 1959, however, were only $1.56 per capita, while the range varied from 34 cents per person served in Iowa to $3.72 in Alaska. In addition to Alaska, local health units in California, Hawaii, Maryland, and New York also spent over $2.00 per capita, while per capita expenditures in 11 states were between 50 cents and $1.00. Of the local organizations themselves, 37 percent had expenditures of less than $1.00 per person, 32 percent were between $1.00 and $1.50, 20 percent between $1.50 and $3.00, and only 11 percent reached $3.00 per capita.[10] By most standards, the recommended expendi-

[6] Emerson and Luginbuhl, *op. cit.*, p. 2.
[7] Smillie, *op. cit.*, p. 369.
[8] Estella F. Warner, "Local Public Health Units," *Municipal Year Book, 1950*, International City Managers' Association, 1950, p. 299.
[9] Public Health Service, *op. cit.*, p. 9.
[10] *Ibid.*, pp. 16–19.

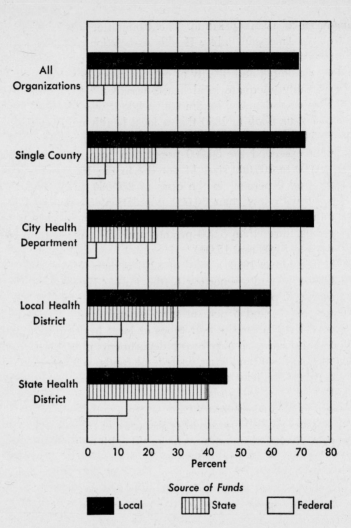

Figure 22. *Source of Funds of Local Health Organizations.* (U.S. Public Health Service, *Organization and Staffing for Local Health Service,* Washington, 1961, p. 18.)

ture of $3.00 per person would give a municipality an adequate health program, but full-time health service in rural areas present special problems. This same per capita expenditure would not result in an effective program in sparsely populated areas.

EMPLOYEES OF LOCAL UNITS

In 1960, the number of full-time employees of local health agencies totaled 44,007, including 533 nurses in voluntary agencies working full-time under contract for health departments. Each of 15 states had more than 1,000 full-time employees while each of seven states had fewer than 100 full-time employees in local health departments. The range varied from 6,338 in New York, in which 100 percent of its population is served by local units, to seven in Wyoming, where only 18.2 percent of the population is so covered. A breakdown of employees by type is shown in Table 20.

The number of employees per 100,000 population for all types of local health units was 26.3 in 1960. By types of units, the number was 34.7 per 100,000 in city health departments, 26.3 in local health districts, 25.9 in single county units, and 14.3 in state health districts. While the level of employees in 1960 showed a slight gain over that in 1958, personnel-population ratios were far below the level achieved in 1950, when the ratio was 31.3 as against the 26.3 a decade later. Comparable ratios for selected types of employees for 1950 and 1960 respectively are as follows: physician-population ratio dropped from 1.5 to 0.8; nurses from 10.4 to 8.6; and sanitation personnel from 6.5 to 5.5.[11]

Highest professional and technical personnel ratios to population served were found in the very small and the very large units— those under 5,000 and those over 500,000. Lowest ratios were found in districts serving between 15,000 and 35,000 persons. The Public Health Service report concludes with the important statement that, "the extent of public health protection which can be provided an increasing population is limited in a large proportion of the units by the absence of a team of workers adequate in number to meet the extensive demands of a modern public health program."[12]

LOCAL HEALTH SERVICES

Originally local health functions were primarily twofold—quarantine measures when communicable diseases were in the community, and the abatement of nuisances. Functions have expanded in recent years, however, with the new emphasis on services rather than on

[11] *Ibid.*, pp. 24–29.
[12] *Ibid.*, p. 56.

Table 20. *Public Health Personnel by Classification in Local Areas:*
January 1, 1960

Type of Personnel	Subtotal	Total
Medical Personnel		17,658
Public health physicians	1,402	
Public health dentists	309	
Dental hygienists	395	
Public health nurses	14,384	
Clinic nurses	647	
Medical social workers	228	
Psychiatric social workers	189	
Psychologists	104	
Laboratory Personnel		2,002
Laboratory technicians	1,489	
X-ray technicians	355	
Physical therapists	158	
Sanitation Personnel		9,236
Engineers	446	
Veterinarians	245	
Professional sanitarians	6,112	
Other	2,433	
Other Professional and Technical		1,218
Medical aides and assistants	807	
Technicians and therapists	288	
Practical nurses	123	
Administrative		11,414
Administrative management	509	
Fiscal and clerical	9,878	
Analysts and statisticians	217	
Public health investigators	393	
Health educators	281	
Nutritionists	136	
Maintenance, Custodial, and Service		1,839
All Others		640
		44,007

SOURCE: Public Health Service, *Organization and Staff for Local Health Services,* P.H.S. Publication No. 682, Government Printing Office, 1961, p. 58.

controls. Public health people and local government officials have generally agreed that local departments should provide at least six essential services. These are:

1. Collection and analysis of vital statistics, including the recording, tabulation, interpretation, and publication of the essential facts of births, deaths, and reportable diseases.

2. Communicable disease control, including tuberculosis, venereal diseases, malaria, and hookworm disease.
3. Community sanitation services, including supervision of milk and milk products, food processing, public eating places, and maintenance of sanitary conditions of employment.
4. Public health laboratory facilities and services for local physicians.
5. Maternal and child health services, including child hygiene and maternal care.
6. Public health education of the citizenry.[13]

A seventh basic function, the prevention and control of chronic diseases, has been recommended as an additional activity of local health units.[14] Additional functions for local units were forecast in a recent issue of the *American Journal of Health* which stated that, "accident prevention, the hygiene of housing, industrial hygiene, school health services, mental health, medical rehabilitation, and hospital and medical care administration are other areas of service and responsibility which have been incorporated into the programs of an increasing number of local health departments."[15]

While America's rural areas were once considered more healthful than were urban communities, the situation has changed substantially. With advances in preventive medicine and municipal sanitary engineering, cities have gained in healthfulness and are making more rapid progress in the prevention and treatment of disease than are rural communities. A report of the United States Department of Agriculture in 1945 pointed out some of the problems in rural health. It reported that three of every four rural families were without proper sanitary facilities and that the great majority of farm water supplies lacked sanitary pumps and adequate protection against surface contamination. One evidence of the inadequacy of rural health programs was shown by the fact that draftees from rural areas in World War II showed a higher rejection rate than the average for the nation as a whole.[16] The problem of adequate health services in rural areas is a dual one. First, there is the problem of getting physicians to locate their practice in small communities so that there is ample medical care

[13] Emerson and Luginbuhl, *op. cit.*, pp. 1-2.
[14] President's Commission on the Health Needs of the Nation, *America's Health Status, Needs and Resources: Building America's Health,* Government Printing Office, 1953, Vol. II, p. 79.
[15] *American Journal of Public Health,* "The Local Health Department—Services and Responsibilities," *41* (March, 1951), 303.
[16] Department of Agriculture, *Better Health for Rural America,* Government Printing Office, 1945, pp. 1-5.

available to private patients, and second, finding physicians who, either on a part- or full-time basis, can be utilized by public health authorities.

■ Mental Health

While the problem of mental health is primarily handled by state governments, there is growing participation in mental health programs by local communities. This increasing state-local cooperation is a move in the right direction, since the effectiveness of a program is more dependent on the adequacy and efficiency of community clinics than it is on the number and size of state hospitals.

The scope of state and local mental health programs, and the magnitude of mental problems are well known. It is estimated that one person in 10 in the United States suffers from some form of mental illness, and that an additional three percent of our population is handicapped by mental deficiencies of sufficient degree to require special training or commitment to an institution. In 1959, there were 616,384 patients in hospitals for mental diseases, and another 165,889 in institutions for mental defectives and epileptics.[17] More money is expended each year for mental health programs than for all other public health programs combined. The magnitude of the problem is further broadened by the significant relationship of mental diseases to such other social problems as crime, delinquency, suicide, alcoholism, narcotics addiction, and divorce rates.[18]

A two-year study of the mental health services in Los Angeles County completed in 1959 points up the magnitude of the mental health problem in that area.[19] Forty-seven community clinics were studied in the survey. In 1958, over 25,000 persons sought help from these clinics; nearly 11,000 were accepted for diagnosis and 6,897 were accepted for treatment. The waiting period for diagnosis often ran as long as six months after referral and the interim between diagnosis and treatment ranged from two months to two years. The professional staff of the 47 community clinics that year consisted of

[17] Public Health Service, *Patients in Mental Institutions,* Government Printing Office, 1960.
[18] National Committee Against Mental Illness, *What Are the Facts About Mental Illness?,* 1957.
[19] Welfare Planning Council Los Angeles Region, *Los Angeles County Surveys Its Mental Health Services,* 1960, 62 pp.

332 psychiatrists (36 of whom were full-time), 157 psychologists (37 full-time), and 121 psychiatric social workers (58 full-time).

According to the American Psychiatric Association, a clinic team of six professional persons—two psychiatrists, one psychologist, and three psychiatric social workers—is needed to serve a population of 150,000. Using these standards, the 47 community clinics could staff only 18 complete clinic teams—a number sufficient to serve less than half the county's population. Concerning the community clinics, the survey concluded, "Many of the community clinics are woefully understaffed and operate on subsistence budgets. Only four of them have budgets large enough to employ a complete full-time psychiatric team on an annual basis. Whether these clinics and their dedicated professional staffs would be using their resources more wisely by merging with other under-budgeted clinics is a question worthy of community consideration."[20]

This record of community mental health services is not a particularly bright one in our nation's biggest county, and in a state with one of the leading programs in mental health. In 1957, the California legislature enacted the Short-Doyle Act providing state financial aid for certain mental health services of community clinics, including out-patient services, in-patient hospital care, rehabilitation services, public education concerning mental illness, and consultation and counseling services. The commuity health program for Los Angeles County developed under this Act involved a budget of over one million dollars in 1959, with the state providing half of these funds.[21]

In all, the survey included 330 findings and 99 recommendations based upon them. Perhaps the conclusion of greatest potential impact stated simply, "What can you do about this? The least anyone can do is to be interested and informed. Community programs can't get far without public interest. Just by being interested and informed, you can make a contribution to the implementation of this survey. . . . It is a task that requires understanding, patience, perserverance, and follow-through. In short, it is a task worthy of any man or woman who aspires to contribute to the well-being of the community."[22]

[20] *Ibid.*, p. 25.
[21] *Ibid.*, p. 8.
[22] Dr. Wayne McMillen, "The Mental Health Needs of Los Angeles," in Digest of a Conference Jointly Sponsored by Town Hall and the Welfare Planning Council, Los Angeles Region, February, 1961, Town Hall, 1961, p. 9.

There is a great shortage of all types of specialists in the field of mental health. This problem is particularly acute since early diagnosis and treatment of mental illness can often eliminate the need for prolonged and custodial type care. Personnel shortages, however, often prevent this type of diagnostic and early treatment through community clinics. The availability of modern drugs and other treatments now allow persons with minor disorders to remain in their own communities while receiving treatment through "outpatient" facilities of state or community hospitals and clinics.

■ Hospitals

Ownership and operation of hospitals is an increasing but not a recent concern of local government. The Philadelphia General Hospital, dating from 1732, is our oldest such municipal institution and New York City's famed Bellevue, the largest municipal hospital, began only four years later. By 1960, there were 1,324 hospitals with a bed capacity of 201,000 owned and operated by local governments. Fifty-four of these institutions with a capacity of 6,000 beds began operations during that year.[23]

In larger cities and counties, the local health department is responsible for the management of the hospital. In smaller units, the hospital is more commonly managed by semi-autonomous hospital boards. Hospital financing follows these same general patterns, with large municipal hospitals treated as another governmental operation in budget planning, while such institutions in smaller communities are autonomous in their budget plans, with the local legislative body having no power of review. Hospitals in smaller communities are usually general-service institutions, while larger cities are more likely to operate special hospitals for patients of tuberculosis, contagious diseases, and mental disorders. New York City, for example, operates a total of 14 such hospitals and sanitoria.

Federal aid for the construction of needed hospitals has been available to communities since 1946. The program conducted by the Community Facilities Administration of the Housing and Home Finance Agency, discussed briefly in Chapter 5, has been a big

---

[23] These statistics are from American Hospital Association, *Hospitals*, Guide Issue, Chicago, as cited in *Statistical Abstract of the United States*, 1962, Table 93, p. 79.

boon in hospital construction and communities in all 50 states have benefited from it.

■ Public Welfare

Local governments in the United States have played an important role in providing public welfare services since the early years of our nation. The concept of public welfare held by English colonists was based on the Elizabethan Poor Law of 1601 which placed the responsibility for welfare activities on the individual, his family, and his local government. This basic law recognized and provided for three classes of indigent persons. These were: (1) those who were poor because of physical disability and required some type of permanent relief; (2) those who become needy as the result of injury or temporary illness and required temporary assistance; and (3) persons who were thriftless or vagrant and for whom certain penalties were imposed by law. The basic approach of colonial "poor" or "pauper" laws remained largely unchanged until the Great Depression of the late 1920s and 1930s required a fundamental change in public attitude toward welfare. This change was aptly phrased in one study as moving from one in which recipients of relief were "objects of disgrace and humiliation" to one in which the public has "come to realize that poverty, particularly in times of economic stress is unavoidable and that the individual who needs help should not be subjected to indignity and public disgrace because of circumstances beyond his control."[24]

Our modern and more charitable attitude toward the unfortunate has resulted in three important changes in our approach to welfare problems. First, welfare is a service in which all three levels of government cooperate in financing and administration. Second, greater emphasis is placed on ascertaining the causes of indigence and in rehabilitation of persons. And third, recent programs reveal an increased interest in preventive rather than remedial measures. New terminology in the welfare field reflects the changes in the public attitude. For instance, "pauper laws" are now "public assistance codes," "paupers" have become "needy persons," "poor relief"

[24] Tax Foundation, *Improving Public Assistance: Some Aspects of the Welfare Problem*, 1953, p. 6.

is now "public assistance," and "inmates" of institutions are now known as "patients" or "residents."

Public welfare is not a precise term and its meaning has changed in recent years as indicated above. Broadly conceived, public welfare might be defined as a "helping hand at public expense." This helping hand is now available to a number of groups such as our aging citizens, children, the blind, disabled and injured workers, and the unemployed. While many programs are not primarily programs of local government, they directly affect citizens living in communities across the nation. Thus, any discussion of public welfare programs would be inadequate without at least brief mention of the nature and scope of these federal-state programs.

PUBLIC ASSISTANCE PROGRAMS

There are two principal ways of classifying public assistance programs. One classification distinguishes between indoor and outdoor assistance. Indoor relief is used to describe the care and support provided persons within public institutions. Outdoor assistance, on the other hand, refers to the aid given recipients in their own or foster homes. In earlier years, indoor relief was the general pattern of supporting persons who were public charges, while outdoor relief was normal for those requiring only temporary help. Today, the tendency is to use outdoor relief in all cases except for the seriously ill and handicapped persons.

The second classification distinguishes between general and categorical assistance programs. General assistance is available to all persons whose support is a public responsibility and who do not qualify for categorical aid. The latter is limited to special classes or categories of needy groups such as dependent children, old-age citizens, and the blind. The general assistance program is administered and financed wholly by state and local governments, while the categorical programs are financed in part by federal aid.

General assistance programs are outdoor in nature and take one of two forms—food, clothing, shelter, medical supplies and other necessities, or money grants to purchase such necessities. These programs are an administrative responsibility of counties in most states although the township (or the town in New England) is charged with supplying this assistance in some states. According to Snider, "it seems unwise to administer outdoor assistance through any governmental unit smaller than the county. The average township is too small to maintain a welfare department with trained caseworkers and other personnel. Moreover, under township administration assistance standards are likely to vary considerably with the aid provided being adequate in some units and inadequate in others. Ordinarily, the townships with heavy case loads are the very ones which, because of low property valuations, are least able to support their poor from local taxes."[25]

Local welfare services vary widely from conmunity to community. In some places, work is required in return for local aid, and other areas provide assistance only when state aid is non-existent or too limited. A problem of increasing concern is how to adapt to prolonged technological unemployment which places many persons on these rolls for a long period. Should another serious business recession occur, it is probable that the national government would need to aid in financing this program just as it was necessary for it to begin support of categorical programs in the 1930s.

OLD-AGE SERVICES

According to the 1960 census, there are more than 17 million men and women who have passed their sixty-fifth birthdays. This group now comprises 9¼ percent of our total population. Some provision for the care of many of these persons must be made since their earning capacity declines rapidly because of our economic structure. There are now three programs primarily concerned with the problems of the aged.

The first of these is the Old Age and Survivors Insurance program enacted in 1935. Strictly speaking, this is not a public welfare program and it is financed and administered by the national government. Benefits received by recipients are based on contributions paid into the federal treasury by the recipient as a wage-earner and by his employers. The OASI program now covers a vast majority of employed persons and is a system of compulsory retirement insurance.

Recognizing that old-age insurance would not solve the problem of need for older citizens since large numbers of persons were beyond its immediate scope, a program of public assistance in the

---

[25] Clyde F. Snider, *Local Government in Rural America*, Appleton-Century-Crofts, 1957, p. 410.

form of pensions for the needy aged was also initiated in 1935. A statewide program is required which is financed by federal funds supplemented by state or state and local money according to a federally determined ratio. In some states, there is direct state administration through its own field offices, with no local financial participation; in other states, local governments share in both its administration and financing. Over two and one quarter million persons or approximately one-seventh of all persons over 65 received public assistance grants in 1961.

The third program is one of medical assistance for the aged. Enacted in 1960, this legislation established a cooperative federal-state medical care system. One phase of the program aids only persons now receiving public assistance pensions, and a second aids elderly persons not on assistance rolls but who need assistance to finance medical care. In 1961, over 72,000 persons in 17 states were recipients of such grants, which require the appropriation of state funds to supplement the federal grants.

A number of local communities have studied the needs of their older citizens in recent years and have attempted to develop programs of services and special agencies to assist their senior citizens. These include agencies to assist them in finding employment, recreation programs, reduced rates for riding public transit systems, and a wide variety of other programs and activities. As the number of elder citizens continues to increase, local services of special benefit to them can be expected to expand.

CHILDREN'S SERVICES

Federal, state, and local government services for children are a recognition that the very young, as well as the old, are in need of special consideration. For many years, it was common to care for dependent and neglected children in institutions maintained by the local community or by religious, social, or fraternal organizations. The old assumption that institutional life furnished a desirable environment for children has been vigorously challenged. In recent years, there has been a strong tendency to place dependent children in foster homes or to give financial assistance to mothers to care for dependent children in their own homes.

A dependent child, as defined in the Social Security Act, is a needy child who (1) is under the age of 18 years; (2) has been deprived of parental support or care by reason of the death, continued absence from the home, or physical or mental incapacity of the parent; and (3) is living with a parent or other relative in a place of residence maintained as a home. Under this act, federal funds are available to the states for financial assistance to mothers of such children, and administration is handled directly by the state or local governments. Aid to dependent children who need to be placed in foster homes, other than with near relatives, or in institutions is not ordinarily possible under the ADC program and is handled entirely by states and their local governments. In 1961, over 2¾ million children were receiving aid under this program.

The foster home arrangement for homeless children is a significant development in child welfare. Generally children are placed in homes with the understanding that they will be formally adopted, but many families assume the responsibility for caring for children in exchange for payment for their services. Proper placement and supervision after placement are essential features of an effective system, whether the placement results in adoption or care for the children for a specified period of time. Many visitors of foster homes are overworked and underpaid, and the supervision they can provide is often only nominal. But as long as the placement process is carefully planned, most foster home arrangements are superior to the orphanges of earlier years in which the children's life was highly regulated and too largely regimented.

AID FOR THE BLIND AND DISABLED

The Social Security Act also makes provision for federal participation in state programs of financial assistance to needy blind persons and to needy persons who are permanently and totally disabled. The standard of need required for applicants of assistance for the blind is similar to that for old-age assistance, but the blind are permitted to earn $50 per month without any reduction in their aid payments. In 1961, there were over 90,000 recipients of aid to the blind and 13,000 other recipients of state payments without federal participation in California, Missouri, and Pennsylvania.

The program of aid to the permanently and totally disabled was added to the categorical assistance programs of the Social Security Act as a result of 1950 amendments.[26] The amendments authorize

[26] This program of aid to the disabled is a form of relief for the needy, and it should not be confused with benefits available to the disabled who are covered by the insurance features of OASI.

aid to needy persons of over 18 years of age who are so disabled, but the definition of qualifying disability is left to the states. While these definitions vary among the states from harshly restrictive to liberal in coverage, they commonly permit assistance to persons who are prevented by disease or other disability from engaging in useful occupations. Common disabilities include heart disease, paralysis, arthritis, amputations, cancer, and tuberculosis. In 1961, such payments were received by nearly 400,000 recipients in 46 states. Only Alaska, Arizona, Indiana, and Nevada had failed to inaugurate federally approved programs for such assistance to disabled citizens.

WORKMEN'S COMPENSATION

Until the early years of the present century, employees had only the common law remedy to seek payment for injuries resulting from industrial accidents. This remedy was to sue the employer, a slow and expensive process, and one in which the employer had the benefit of the provisions of existing common law. Gradually, the concept that accidents were an inevitable aspect of modern industry and that industry should be responsible for medical treatment for injured employees and caring for their families was accepted by all the states.

While compensation laws and practices vary widely among the states, in general they provide for payments to injured or sick workers according to some established scale. In some states, the insurance system is administered entirely by the state, while in others an employer may use the state fund or insure through a private company, or even insure himself if he has sufficient resources. In cases of disagreement between the employer and employee, a referee decides the matter, with appeal to a state board provided if either side remains dissatisfied. In 1960, over one and one quarter million dollars in workmen's compensation awards were granted, with roughly one-third going for medical and hospitalization payments and the remainder in the form of payments to the employee or his survivors.

UNEMPLOYMENT COMPENSATION

The problem of welfare services is accentuated by the fact that a sizeable number of able-bodied adults are unable or unwilling to find employment. This condition exists in any society, whether it is an agricultural or industrial one and whether that society is enjoying a period of prosperity or a depression. In addition to the men and women who desire work but cannot find employment, the unemployed ranks also include some who are semi-professional vagrants and live off charity as a way of life and others who are only occasional workers.

The most far-reaching plan for solving our unemployment problem is the program of unemployment insurance which was a further feature of the Social Security Act of 1935. This act did not establish a federal system of compensation; it enables employers to take credit against a federal tax for amounts they pay a state. State collections are placed in an unemployment trust fund administered by the federal government, with the amounts credited to the individual states.

While the plans of the 50 states vary somewhat in their minor details, under all these plans any unemployed worker, covered by the law, may apply for compensation during periods of unemployment, unless his idleness is self-induced due to voluntary quitting or misconduct leading to dismissal. Benefits are not paid for a preliminary period, normally of two weeks, and do not extend beyond a specified number of weeks. Benefits are usually adjusted with reference to past earnings of the worker, except that there is a ceiling on the maximum weekly benefit. In 1961, the average payment period for unemployed workers was 14.7 weeks with an average weekly payment of $33.80. Over seven million workers received unemployment benefits that year totaling nearly three and one half billion dollars. Other unemployed citizens were also benefited by temporary state programs initiated in 1961.

■ *Intergovernmental Relations in Welfare*

The field of public welfare services is one calling for true partnership roles by the three levels of government. Generally, the principle of cooperative partnership seems to function smoothly, but causes of potential friction are numerous and sometimes they erupt into open controversy and direct conflict. While these controversies were largely between the state and the federal government in earlier years, much of the present conflict arises between the state and its local communities.

An interesting controversy concerning assistance programs arose in Newburgh, New York, in 1961. Concerned with rising welfare costs and declining assessments of property in slum areas, the city manager of Newburgh announced a 13-point program aimed to cut the city's welfare costs. Among other things, this program called for cutting off aid to unwed mothers who gave birth to additional illegitimate children; limiting aid to three months a year to all recipients except the aged, blind, and disabled; and requiring all able-bodied males on relief to earn their checks by working for the city. After a brief period of nationwide publicity, the Newburgh program was discarded since it established conditions beyond those in current New York state and federal legislation.[27]

Efforts of California counties to retain their role as "partners" in welfare administration are perhaps typical of the problem of state-local relations in this important field. The County Supervisors Association of California in 1957 adopted several principles relating to county home rule and intergovernmental undertakings. These were:

1. Areas where counties act primarily as agents of the state in performing a state service and do so with substantial state financing should be distinguished from areas of local or mixed state and local interest, so as to provide a basis for indicating where statewide standards and supervision may be justified.

2. Counties should be free to determine the scope and the extent of the governmental services each will render, subject to the recognized need for some uniformity in the standard of performance of services of national or statewide import.

3. In services of national or statewide import, the degree of uniformity required should be carefully determined in each case, with emphasis on the purpose of the individual requirement—to the end that uniformity will not be "uniformity for uniformity's sake," but in each case will serve a specific beneficial purpose and to the further end that the progress which can come only from the existence of a variety of administrative approaches and methods shall not be stifled.[28]

These principles of operating relationships among levels of government are clearly stated and have general applicability to a num-

[27] Meg Greenfield, "The 'Welfare Chiselers' of Newburgh, N.Y.," *The Reporter*, 25 (August 17, 1961), 37–40.

[28] William R. MacDougall, "Counsel Examines Welfare Administration and County Home Rule," *Newsletter of County Supervisors' Association of California*, 21 (December, 1962), p. 6.

ber of services shared by the three levels of governmental system. In large part, their philosophy parallels that of the principles enumerated by the President's Commission on Intergovernmental Relations in 1955. That Commission stated:

Precise divisions of governmental activities need always to be considered in the light of varied and shifting circumstances; they need also to be viewed in the light of principles rooted in our history. Assuming efficient and responsible government at all levels—National, State, and local—we would seek to divide our civic responsibilities so that we: Leave to private initiation all the functions that citizens can perform privately; use the level of government closest to the community for all public functions it can handle; utilize cooperative intergovernmental arrangements where appropriate to attain economical performance and popular approval; reserve National action for residual participation where State and local governments are not fully adequate, and for the continuing responsibilities that only the National Government can undertake.[29]

▪ Public Housing

The health and welfare of citizens is closely related to the homes in which they live. Studies of housing conditions in communities across the nation all disclose high public health and welfare costs in slum areas and in areas of inadequate housing. While the housing problem is particularly acute in many of our large cities, unsatisfactory conditions also exist in small cities and in rural areas. In 1960, there were 58 million housing units in the United States of which 74 percent were evaluated as sound, 7.8 percent as deteriorating, and 18.2 percent as dilapidated or lacking one or more plumbing facilities.[30]

Because of the general recognition that poor housing is a detriment to the community, local governments are empowered by state law to better housing conditions. They may regulate housing through building codes, sanitation laws, zoning ordinances, and housing codes. Laws pertaining directly to housing are now quite comprehensive and deal both with construction and maintenance. Principle construction provisions relate to requirements for light

[29] The Commission on Intergovernmental Relations, *A Report to the President for Transmittal to Congress,* Government Printing Office, 1955, pp. 5–6.
[30] *Statistical Abstract of the United States, 1962, Table 1072,* p. 759.

and ventilation, sanitation, and fire protection. Maintenance provisions of housing codes vary widely from community to community, but generally concern requirements of cubic feet of air space, the keeping of animals, and maintenance of such items as cellars, roofs, and fire escapes.

While this approach to housing problems is still vitally important, a new way of attacking the evils of poor housing began in 1937 with the passage of the Housing Act establishing the United States Housing Authority. Under this act and its subsequent amendments, the federal government stimulated action in the low-cost housing field by loans and grants and by actual operation of housing projects. Slum clearance programs were authorized by the Housing Act of 1949. Under this act, federal aid became available for tearing down old buildings in slum areas and building new housing on the cleared site. The Housing Act of 1954 extended further federal aid by authorizing urban renewal projects to prevent and eliminate urban decay. Details of this program were discussed in Chapter 5.

The extent of the low-rent housing program is evidenced by the growth of the number of units supervised by the Public Housing Administration. In 1950, there were 302,146 such units, but this total had risen to 624,094 by 1961. Of these, less than two thousand were federally owned, with the others locally owned. The program of low-rent public housing requires local initiative and action with federal approval and assistance. To qualify the community must first create a housing authority to administer the proposed project. This authority negotiates contracts with the Public Housing Administration for federal assistance to pay the difference between construction and operation costs and the anticipated collection from rentals. Rentals are usually quite low since tenants are limited to low-income families, the elderly, veterans, and families displaced by slum clearance projects.

The need for close and cooperative relations among the three levels of government in the field of housing has been aptly stated by one writer in these words: "Housing and urban-renewal programs demonstrate the interdependence of governments under a system of cooperative federalism. Municipalities acting alone cannot possibly provide an adequate housing policy for the nation. The resources and sanctions of state and national governments will also need to be invoked, and they will all have to be coordinated effectively if we are not to give in to unparalleled pressures for a

450   PUBLIC SERVICES

decline in housing standards."[31] Typically, local governments have great difficulty even in enforcing housing codes applicable to private housing and do not have resources to undertake major slum elimination or new construction projects.

■ Fair Employment Practices Commissions

Although their goals are only tangentially related to the fields of public health and welfare, the adoption of "fair employment practices" acts (FEPC laws) in 18 states and in a large number of cities reflect the acceptance of the principle that there should be no discrimination in employment. Such acts forbid employers to discriminate in hiring or firing employees on the basis of race, color, creed, or national origin. In seven states and some communities these laws also forbid discrimination on the basis of age. In coverage, such laws apply not only to employment in governmental agencies but also to private employment in business and industry and to labor union membership.

Enforcement of fair employment practices typically is accomplished through a plural-member commission. Most municipal commissions have only advisory and non-coercive powers, although some do have power to begin proceedings on their own initiative or on the basis of complaints lodged with them. In such communities, the commission, after investigation which might entail a public hearing, may issue an order directing compliance with the provisions of their ruling. Most commissions, however, avoid coercion in attempts to eliminate discrimination and depend upon education, conferences, social pressures, persuasion, and the threat of unfavorable publicity to obtain compliance with their directives. In most cases, even the formal hearing is not necessary since advice, suggestions, and the feared effects of adverse publicity are adequate.

The passage of these state and local laws reflect in part the influence of organized minorities in demanding equal employment rights. While most Americans would accept this in principle, many disagree as to the most effective methods for eliminating discrimination. Some would prefer programs of education to the establishment of fair employment practices commissions, but others feel that the basic principle of equal employment opportunities is too

[31] Charles R. Adrian, *Governing Urban America,* 2nd ed., McGraw-Hill, 1961, p. 456.

fundamental to put off any further. Certainly discrimination in employment, both public and private, is not uncommon. However, it is often difficult to prove and laws are easily violated.

Other communities which lack formal FEPC's have established intergroup committees to achieve many of the same goals. In some cities, these committees function effectively, but in others they are objected to on the basis that they violate the rights of employers to operate their businesses as they see fit or that they stir up more problems and antagonisms than they are able to alleviate. The march of social democracy in employment, however, appears to be on the move, and the political influence of active and astute minority groups will be increasingly effective.

SUGGESTED READINGS

Books

Banfield, E. C. and Grodzins, Morton, *Government and Housing in Metropolitan Areas* (New York: McGraw-Hill, 1958).

Commission on Intergovernmental Relations, *A Report to the President for Transmittal to Congress* (Washington: Government Printing Office, 1955).

Emerson, Haven and Luginbuhl, Martha, *Local Health Units for the Nation* (New York: The Commonwealth Fund, 1945).

Glasser, William, *Mental Health or Mental Illness?* (New York: Harper & Row, 1960).

Hiscock, Ira V., *Community Health Organization*, 4th ed. (New York: The Commonwealth Fund, 1950).

Meyerson, Martin and Banfield, E. C., *Politics, Planning and the Public Interest* (New York: Free Press, 1955).

President's Commission on the Health Needs of the Nation, *America's Health Status, Needs and Resources: Building America's Health* (Washington: Government Printing Office, Vol. II, 1953).

Public Health Service, *Organization and Staff for Local Health Services* (Washington: Government Printing Office, 1961).

Smillie, W. G., *Public Health Administration in the United States*, 2nd ed. (New York: Macmillan, 1940).

Tiboni, Emil A., *Philadelphia's Plan of Action for Housing and Neighborhood Improvement,* Philadelphia Department of Public Health, 1955.

White, R. Clyde, *Administration of Public Welfare*, 2nd ed. (New York: American Book Co., 1950).

Articles

American Journal of Public Health, "The Local Health Department—Services and Responsibilities," *41* (March, 1951), 302–7.

Barnes, M. E., "The County, the Logical Public Health Unit," *National Municipal Review,* 21 (August, 1932), 499–501.

Burroughs, Roy J., "Toward a Farm Housing Policy," *Land Economics,* 24 (February, 1948), 1–22.

Committee on Municipal Public Health Engineering, "Administration of Local Inspection Services," *American Journal of Public Health,* 45 (June, 1955), 799–806.

Hilliard, Raymond M., "The Emerging Function of Public Institutions in Our Social Security Structure," *Social Services Review,* 20 (December, 1946), 479–93.

Hovde, B. J., "The Local Housing Authority," *Public Administration Review,* 1 (Winter, 1941), 167–75.

Roemer, Milton I., "Rural Programs of Medical Care," *Annals of the American Academy of Political and Social Science,* 273 (January, 1951), 160–8.

Education and Recreation

21

In 1961, more than 16¾ billion dollars were expended by local governments to finance educational programs for over 40 million Americans. Public education is the largest operation of local governments, viewed in terms of capital investments, current operating expenditures, and number of employees. Viewed in terms of objectives, public education is also the most important and most vital service of local governments. Our system of democracy depends on the capacity of citizens to make informed, rational choices. The end of our educational programs is to equip citizens to participate in community affairs in an informed manner, and these programs for widespread education constitute the foundation of our free institutions.

The end of education, according to one writer, "presupposes that each individual be mentally, socially, and emotionally competent to the fullest possibility of his inborn capacities."[1] Political participation by citizens so equipped strengthens the institutions of a democratic society. Since it is essential that educational opportunities be available to all, the provision of school facilities logically

---

[1] Arthur B. Moehlman, *School Administration*, Houghton Mifflin, 1951, p. 11.

becomes a public service. Many private and sectarian educational institutions exist and have an important share in this great undertaking, but 85 percent of our students attend schools maintained at public expense and these will be the focus of the first part of this chapter. Subsequent sections will discuss public libraries and recreation programs and facilities.

■ Development of Public Education

Our modern educational system with its opportunities for free public education from kindergarten through college has been a logical development. However, widespread education beyond the elementary grades has been largely a product of the present century. In 1900, only 8 percent of high school aged boys and girls were actually enrolled in school; this is in sharp contrast to the 91.4 percent enrolled in 1961.

Since most of our early settlers were from England, it is only natural that our educational antecedents are also English. Early colonists, however, brought two philosophies of education to the new world. The philosophy adhering most closely to the traditions of England was followed in the southern colonies up through most of the nineteenth century. This concept called for the development of two divisions of education. One division from elementary grades through college was supported by private tuition and was intended for the children of families of the upper social classes. The other division was limited to elementary grades and was supported by public funds to educate the masses. One writer described this system as making no distinction "between putting a coat on a child's back, food into his stomach, and knowledge into his head."[2]

The second philosophy of education in the colonies flourished in Calvinistic New England where the belief was held that education was a collective responsibility and a right to be enjoyed equally by all. In 1647, the colonial legislature of Massachusetts required every town to establish free schools at which attendence was compulsory. This requirement gradually spread through New England and into the middle colonies to a lesser degree. The influence of this philosophy was apparent in the wording of the Northwest

[2] William A. Cook, *Federal and State School Administration*, Crowell, 1927, p. 35.

Ordinance adopted in 1787 under the Articles of Confederation. This act provided for a system of public schools in the western lands and stated further that, "Religion, morality, and knowledge being necessary to good government and the happiness of mankind, schools and the means of education shall forever be encouraged."

Although adopted only two years later, the Constitution of the United States does not mention education. The drafters of this document came from colonies with distinctive educational systems as indicated above and they were zealous guardians of the right of the states to develop their own patterns of education. Congress attempted to establish a Department of Education on a par with other executive departments as early as 1867, but unreceptivity on the part of the states soon relegated the department to the status of a bureau. The Office of Education was created for "the purpose of collecting such statistics and facts as shall show the condition and progress of education in the several States and Territories, and of diffusing such information respecting the organization and management of schools and school systems, and methods of teaching, as shall aid the people of the United States in the establishment and maintenance of efficient school systems, and otherwise promote the cause of education throughout the country." While education did achieve cabinet status in name in 1953 with the establishment of the Department of Health, Education, and Welfare, the agency in charge of education is only a bureau in that department.

While the principle of free, public education early won acceptance, implementation of the principle was not easily brought about. In addition to its being expensive, many persons objected to the practice of taxing one person to help pay the costs of educating the children of others. Others opposed the concept on a more philosophical ground—the common man did not need education and such efforts would only make him discontented. By 1850, however, all states except Arkansas had authorized the use of public tax monies for school purposes. High schools, or public academies as they were called, developed rapidly after the Civil War, but attendance did not become widespread until the early years of the present century.

Today, while the concept of free public education is accepted everywhere in the United States, there is considerable variety among public school systems. An interesting countertrend to the smaller number of public schools resulting from consolidation in recent years has been the rise in the number of private and church-supported schools. While the number of public elementary schools decreased from 247,581 in 1930 to 105,023 in 1960, the number of private elementary schools increased from 9,275 to 13,170 in the same period. During these same three decades, public elementary schools experienced a 16.2 percent increase in enrollment, compared to a 74.5 percent increase in private schools.[3] Oddly enough, the Calvinists who were leaders in the movement for public education systems in colonial times are now among those maintaining a number of parochial schools because of the almost complete secularization of the public schools.

■ Local Units of School Administration

While public education is a state function, it has been primarily a local responsibility. State constitutions and statutes set forth the general outline and objectives of public school systems, but local governments have been invested with authority to administer the schools. Thus, local governments construct and equip buildings, employ teachers and administrators, and control curriculum content within the general policy guides established by the state.

Four types of local governmental units are concerned with providing education. The most numerous are the school districts which are created only for school purposes and have a board with basic powers of control over their operations. As indicated in Chapter 12, such independent districts numbered 34,678 in 1961-1962 and were the sole or predominant unit responsible for operating public schools in 39 states and had partial responsibility in seven additional states. The county is employed to administer some or all schools in about two-thirds of the states. Relationships between county boards of education and county school superintendents and the county governing board vary from state to state, but typically the school officials are relatively free from control by the county board. Cities form independent school districts in most states. While the boundaries of the school district are often coterminous with those of the city, the school district is often completely independent, or largely free, of any municipal controls. Towns and townships also have school

[3] Bureau of the Census, *Statistical Abstract of the United States, 1962,* 1962, p. 408.

responsibilities. In New England, the towns serve both as the unit of general government and as the unit for school purposes. The same situation exists in regard to the township in all or part of six states. In 1962 there were 2,341 such "dependent" school systems which were operated by the state, by general purpose local units, or by agencies acting on behalf of groups of school districts.

Most states do not employ a single type of local government for the administration of its schools. In a number of states, all four units—the independent or special district, the county, the city, and the town or township—share in this important public undertaking. Whatever the types of units, there are two traditions which greatly influence our educational system. These are the tradition of local determination in educational matters and the tradition of independence of officials concerned with public schools from control by general governing bodies of local communities.

The general pattern of governance in school districts was discussed in previous chapters and will not be repeated at this time. One writer, commenting on the durability of our system, stated: "What the schools do may be altered, in kind or in degree; how they are run—the administrative and political structure of the typical American school system—will remain largely as it is today. Each community's stake in its own school system is so firmly grounded, and the general faith in local control is so deeply held, that only a cataclysmic upheaval would quickly change the general structural pattern."[4]

■ The Task of Public Schools

Public education in the 1960s faces enormous challenges. The nation's population has risen to over 183 million and is still climbing rapidly. While the trend in birth rates in the immediate future cannot be predicted with any certainty, all signs point to a further burgeoning of school populations. The sharp increase in school enrollments since 1950 and projections of enrollments to 1980 by five-year intervals are shown in Figure 23.

Coupled with the rising flood of school-age youth and the pressure it will place on our educational institutions in the next 20 years are a number of other social factors. One of these pertains

[4] Thomas H. Eliot, *Governing America, The Politics of a Free People,* State and Local Supplement, Dodd, Mead, 1961, p. 156.

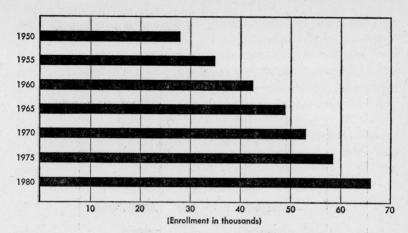

Figure 23. *Actual and Projected School Enrollments from Kindergarten Through High School: 1950–1980.* (U.S. Bureau of the Census, *Statistical Abstract of the United States, 1962,* Washington, 1962, p. 115.)

to the mobility of our society. It has been estimated that 20 percent of the people in the United States change their address each year. Such mobility results in severe strains on some school systems and drains on others. Another factor of mobility is the drift of population northward and westward to the great metropolitan centers, resulting in even greater strains on already overtaxed school resources.

In addition to the problem of numbers of students, our schools are faced with the problem of meeting the changing demands of society for their graduates. Organization in contemporary society depends upon an increasing range of skills and complexity of tasks. While the demand for better trained talent has been a continuing trend since the turn of the century, it is expected to accelerate in the years ahead. Thus the task of our school system is to educate an expanding number of students and to equip them with increasing skills to fill more demanding tasks within the labor force.

The difficulty of establishing meaningful population criteria for school districts was discussed in Chapter 12. However, a superficial analysis of school systems would appear to show too many students in a small number of schools and too few students in a large number of schools. The extremes show 26.3 percent of the students in 0.4 percent of the school systems, while 58 percent of the school systems educate only 3.4 percent of the student population. This development is likely to continue at least in the immediate future because of the mobility noted above.

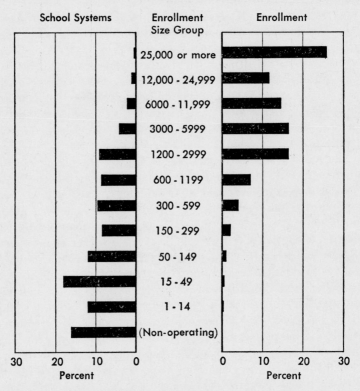

Figure 24. *Public School Systems and Public School Enrollment, by Enrollment Size of System: 1962 (pupils enrolled, October, 1961).* (U.S. Bureau of the Census, *Census of Governments, 1961,* Vol. I: *Governmental Organization,* Washington, 1962, p. 20.)

The question of how well our schools are doing their jobs is one which has been asked with increasing frequency in recent years. A sense of urgency about our schools began developing shortly after World War II, and it became a real concern after the successful launching of the first Sputnik by the Soviet Union in 1957. The question is an important one because of the magnitude of our public school system and the seriousness of the goals entrusted to

PUBLIC SERVICES

it. It is doubly important to ask ourselves this question about our schools in a period when respected authorities are making broad criticisms of their current performance.[5]

One study issued in December, 1959, by the Committee for Economic Development, did not attempt to minimize the seriousness of the problems, but it did emit a few rays of hope in a picture that has been often depicted in shades of doom and gloom. This report stated, "Gloomy predictions that the rising tide of enrollments would overwhelm our public schools began circulating a decade ago. Perhaps these predictions helped arouse us and thus to defeat themselves. They have not come true. We do not yet have the schools we should have or could afford. But neither have we allowed our schools to sink under the weight of big postwar enrollments. On the contrary, we have probably improved our schools somewhat. The record is encouraging."[6]

Specifically, the Committee reviewed the developments in our schools since 1947 and advanced six findings of considerable significance. First, not only more children but a higher proportion of children, are going to school today than before enrollments began to climb so rapidly. Second, the typical boy or girl probably goes to a better school than that of any previous time and schools provide more space per pupil. Third, the teaching staff of public schools has grown by 50 percent while enrollments increased 41 percent and the proportion of male teachers is the highest in a half century. Fourth, teachers have received more training, resulting in reduced use of teachers holding emergency certificates. Fifth, the relative income position of teachers has improved. And sixth, money to build classrooms, hire teachers and administrators, increase salaries and cover other necessary expenses tripled in the 11 years between 1947-1948 and 1958-1959; but most important, money was obtained to meet this rapid expenditure climb.[7]

[5] Among the most significant recent publications treating current and future problems of public education, see James Bryant Conant, *The Child, The Parent and the State,* Harvard University Press, 1959, and *The American High School Today,* McGraw-Hill, 1959; Myron Lieberman, *The Future of Public Education,* University of Chicago Press, 1960; Rockefeller Brothers Fund, Inc., *The Pursuit of Excellence, Education and the Future of America,* Doubleday, 1958; Committee for Economic Development, *Paying for Better Public Schools,* 1959; and John W. Gardner, *Excellence, Can We Be Equal and Excellent Too?* Harper & Row, 1961.

[6] Committee for Economic Development, *We Can Have Better Schools,* 1960, p. 4. This is a summary statement of their larger study cited above.

[7] *Ibid.,* pp. 4–7.

Of several specific kinds of positive action recommended, this Committee stressed that citizens working for better schools should improve their own effectiveness in their local communities. Better schools cannot be given—they must be created and paid for by the citizens. While citizen interest in schools may too often appear to rise and fall with the success of its competitive athletic teams, this is a most superficial index of community pride. Citizens in most communities are proud of their school buildings, their teachers and administrators, and the students who attend and graduate from the local schools.

Viewed in this light, the school in most communities is not just a school. It serves as a public forum for groups in the community and its grounds double as a recreation area. Teachers and administrators are also local citizens and they participate in other community affairs. The curriculum, in part, is influenced by the community and its content certainly has effects on the community in terms of knowledge and skills imparted.

A checklist of standards which most education experts and a number of citizen groups agree can test the quality of schools was printed in a recent issue of *Changing Times*.[8] Briefly stated, these standards relate to: (1) *attendance*—all youngsters should go to school for at least 12 years; (2) *scope*—school programs should be sufficiently diversified so that children of all types are helped to develop; (3) *curriculum*—elementary pupils should gain respect for learning and intellectual values and taught that people live, think and speak in different ways. Junior high and high school students should have academic, commercial, vocational, technical, and home-making courses available; (4) *teachers*—every teacher should have a liberal education and a knowledge of his subject field, and he should also be paid an adequate salary; (5) *staff size*—elementary classes should not exceed 25 students per teacher; secondary teachers should have no more than five periods involving a total of no more than 125 to 150 students; the school should also have a complement of specialists, consultants, supervisors, and administrators; (6) *school size*—an elementary school should have at least 250 to 300 students; a three-year high school at least 350; a four-year high school at least 500 students; (7) *buildings*—a construction program characterized by careful, long-range planning.

[8] *Changing Times,* "Your Money's Worth in Schools," (September, 1961), pp. 29-30.

The continuing controversy between educators and political scientists concerning the independent status of school districts was discussed briefly in Chapter 12. While teachers and school administrators often pride themselves that schools are "beyond" politics, the adjective public before public schools implies that they are very much in the mainstream of politics. This point was clearly made by Eliot when he wrote:

What is taught in the classroom, what is emphasized in the school, where the schools are to be located, and how they are to be paid for—these are the basic questions which, in theory, must be answered by the voters or their representatives on the school board, in the state legislature, and in Congress. They are therefore political questions. School systems cannot be considered usefully on the assumption that they operate in a kind of aseptic enclave, protected by high walls from the distempers of politics. Public schools are public businesses. Running them is a governmental and hence a political process.[9]

■ *The Teachers*

It is a truism that no educational system can be better than its teachers. It is also true that the popular public stereotype of school teachers is often not a very glamorous one. Movies and television programs often depict teachers as old maids or Ichabod Cranes, but there appears to be a discernible trend to present the school teacher in a more sympathetic and favorable light. While the teaching profession is made up of all types of people, a recent extensive nation-wide survey of 1,100,000 teachers resulted in composite pictures of the average female and male members of the profession.[10]

According to this study, the average woman teacher is 45.5 years old, married and the mother of one child. Actually, only 34.1 percent of women teachers have never married. She has taught an average of 15.4 years, including seven and one half years in the school system in which she is presently employed. Usually she is an elementary grade teacher with 30.8 students under her supervision. She is an active church member and participates in at least

[9] Eliot, *op. cit.*, p. 164.

[10] The following three paragraphs are based on the contents of a news story reporting on a survey conducted by the National Education Association in *The Philadelphia Inquirer*, April 3, 1957.

two other community organizations. Her annual salary of $3,932 represents 95.3 percent of her total income.

The typical male teacher is younger, less experienced, and higher paid. He is 35.4 years old, married, and is the father of one or two children. He has taught for eight years, over half the time in the school system of his present employment. Typically, he is a high school teacher and has 129.1 pupils in his classes. He, too, is an active church member and belongs to at least one other community organization. His annual salary is $4,374, representing 86 percent of his income which is supplemented by outside employment.

Comparatively speaking, the average woman teacher is less unhappy than her male counterpart about her chosen profession. Of the women teachers, 80.7 percent indicated they would elect to become teachers again if they were back in college. For men teachers, only 53.9 percent stated they would choose teaching if they were starting over, 29.5 percent said they would not, and 16.6 percent were undecided. Teachers of both sexes have voting records reflecting considerably higher participation than the performance of society as a whole. Male teachers reported a turnout of 84.8 percent in recent elections while 86.4 percent of the women teachers had voted in the most recent election.

Although this composite picture of teachers may dispel a few misconceptions about them, they do not erase the many problems concerning and affecting teachers. Prominent among these are problems concerning the supply of teachers at all levels, the quality of teachers, and both financial and social incentives of the teaching profession. Possibly the most harrowing problem, however, is largely an administrative one. As the Rockefeller study states, "Perhaps no profession has suffered such a general neglect of specialized talents as that of the teachers. Teachers at the pre-college level tend to be handled as interchangeable units in an educational assembly line. The best teacher and the poorest in a school may teach the same grade and subject, use the same textbook, handle the same number of students, get paid the same salaries, and rise in salary at the same speed to the same ceiling. Clearly, if the teaching profession is to be made more attractive, this will have to be changed."[11]

There have been determined and successful efforts in recent years to improve teacher salaries. While salary scales show a great di-

[11] Rockefeller Brothers Fund, Inc., *op. cit.*, p. 24.

versity among states, the common stereotype of the underpaid public school teacher is not a very accurate one today. Some public school teachers have admitted a preference for college teaching but felt they could not afford to make the financial sacrifice involved in making the change.

One writer has advanced the view that the acceptance of status as hirelings by teachers creates one of the chief obstacles to better schools.[12] Lieberman advocates that teachers regard themselves as professionals rather than as civil servants and that they establish a new national organization to become more effective as a group and as individuals through the development of standards of excellence, securing adequate salaries and improved working conditions, and reducing the harassment of local pressures. His overall program calls for federal support and would necessitate serious rethinking of our conventional system of local controls.

■ Financing Our Schools

It is commonplace to think of most of our problems in dollar and cents terms by stating that particular problems would not exist or continue if additional funds were available. While this solution is much too simple for many school problems, the matter of financing our schools is a major one indeed. As noted earlier, school expenditures tripled in the eleven years between 1947 and 1958, and some $16.75 billion were expended to finance educational programs in 1961. Since school enrollments will continue to rise in the years ahead, there is no question but that school expenditures will increase too. The Committee for Economic Development, a responsible organization of businessmen and educators, has estimated that the figure will rise to $21.1 billion by 1969-1970.[13]

In the early decades of the present century, the financial support of public schools was borne almost entirely by local governments. Gradually, the states assumed a partial responsibility, and since 1930 state assistance has increased rapidly. The comprehensive report on schools referred to above contained an excellent analysis of sources of public school revenues by states in 1958-1959. The methods of financing schools vary considerably among the states. As a whole,

[12] Lieberman, *op. cit.*
[13] Committee for Economic Development, *Paying for Better Schools,* 1959, p. 23.

public school systems obtained 56.8 percent of their revenues from local sources, 39.7 percent from the states and 3.5 percent from federal sources.[14] The proportion of revenues realized from local sources, however, ranged from as low as 14 percent in New Mexico to 90 percent in Nebraska, The range in state revenues was equally wide, varying from 5.2 percent in Nebraska to 80 percent in Delaware. Federal payments varied from one percent in New York to 18 percent in New Mexico.

A basic reason for increasing state financial aid to school districts is the great inequality of wealth among them and their limited tax resources. To determine the amount of state aid to each district, state legislatures typically adapt a formula based on one or more pertinent factors such as average daily attendance for the district's schools, the number of teachers, the assessed valuation of the taxable property in the district, or the number of school-age children living in the district. State aid formulas generally contain a flat grant per pupil plus provisions for equalization which amount to additional payments for those districts in which the combined local qualifying tax and the flat grants are deemed inadequate by state standards. The common purposes of such subsidies are to ease property tax burdens in local communities and to assure a minimum standard of educational services by giving larger grants to poorer districts than to more wealthy ones.

Federal aid for education has, up to now, been limited to special programs such as financing school lunches, helping areas where federal military or other installations bring an influx of students into the schools, etc. However, the continuing growth of school needs has prompted serious consideration and much hot debate over the need for and desirability of federal aid for education. Both proponents and opponents of federal aid appear to agree on two basic points. First, they agree that educational opportunities are unequal today in our many school districts and systems across the nation. Second, they agree that the federal government has no constitutional power to control or supervise our systems of elementary and secondary education. Beyond these two points, however, there is a very limited area of agreement.

Proponents of federal aid emphasize that the present mobility of our population makes education a matter of national concern; that

[14] *Ibid.*, p. 48.

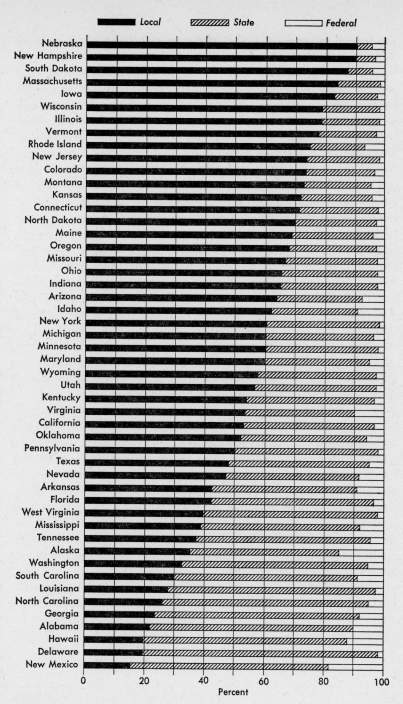

Figure 25. *Sources of School Revenues.* (Committee for Economic Development, *Paying for Better Schools*, New York, 1959, pp. 50-51.)

the federal government is the only agency that can effect an equitable distribution of educational opportunities; that numerous precedents of federal aid exist without the onus of controls in other service areas; and that the federal government is partly responsible for general education since the preservation of our democracy depends upon the existence of a high standard of education. Principal arguments of opponents include the points that the responsibility for education is reserved to the states; that education is better controlled to suit local needs by local and state authorities; that federal aid would further unbalance the budget and increase the national debt; and that such aid would increase the dangers of federal centralization and regimentation of our schools.[15]

Another line of reasoning in support of federal aid for education concerns the leadership of the national government in advancing the status of the American Negro. The bestowal of citizenship following the Civil War created problems in states with large Negro populations and created a responsibility for understanding and assistance on the federal government. This concern and responsibility was increased by the decision of the Supreme Court on May 17, 1954, in *Brown* v. *Board of Education of Topeka* (347 U.S. 483). This historic decision overruled the legal doctrine of "separate but equal" facilities established by the court in *Plessy* v. *Ferguson* (163 U.S. 537) in 1896. Recognizing the vast changes which would be required by this policy, the Court did not order prompt integration of schools but decreed that integration should proceed "with all deliberate speed," under the general supervision of the United States district courts in the various states. Though in the first eight years following the *Brown* v. *Topeka* decision the progress toward integration seemed to emphasize "deliberation" rather than "speed," delaying action and legislation by states seemed unlikely to succeed and could only delay school desegregation. To many thoughtful persons it seemed only logical that the federal government should assist states in meeting the financial problems involved in complying with this changed federal policy.

The need for some plan of federal aid is becoming more apparent as bond issues are more commonly defeated in local communities across the nation. These defeats seldom occur because the citizens

---

[15] For a fuller discussion of these and other arguments both for and against federal aid, see Charles A. Quattlebaum, *Federal Aid to Elementary and Secondary Education*, Public Administration Service, 1948, pp. i–ix.

feel that new schoolhouses are not needed; rather the voters reject the issues because they know the result will be an increase in property taxes. The fact that poorer states, judged on the basis of the proportion of tax revenues spent on education, are making a greater effort to support education than wealthier states is also gaining wider recognition and acceptance. A program of federal aid would be paid for by all the nation's taxpayers, including those in districts needing no new schools and able to finance educational programs without assistance.

Emotional reaction to the concept of federal aid ignores the fact that the principle of such aid has been a continuing one rather than a strikingly new and radical proposal. Aid to higher education has existed since the Land-Grant College Act of 1862 and was abetted by the National Defense Education Act of 1958. This Act declares as a matter of policy that "The national interest . . . requires that the Federal Government give assistance to education for programs which are important to our defense." This last phrase may be construed to mean whatever Congress may wish it to mean.[16] Thus, the issue of federal aid seems settled; the questions of how much federal aid and what specific kinds of federal aid remain. These will be answered differently by subsequent Congresses in response to or in rejection of specific proposals.

The ability of the people of our nation to support the needed expansion and improvements of our public schools is not seriously questioned. In a logical and highly persuasive argument in favor of federal aid for teachers salaries, Senator Joseph S. Clark of Pennsylvania concluded his statement with the following words:

> Mr. President, I close with the final if somewhat cynical figure that since 1948 the American people, through their State, local, and Federal tax system, have spent $78 billion for public elementary and secondary schools, while during the same period of time they have spent $151 billion for tobacco, alcoholic beverages, and cosmetics. Mr. President, I ask what kind of a country do we want to live in? Is it not about time we put our shoulders to the wheel and got America back on the spiritual and educational base it must be on if it is going to deserve the future which it has within its grasp?[17]

[16] Daniel P. Moynihan, "A Second Look at the School Panic," *The Reporter*, 20 (June 11, 1959), 14–19.

[17] Reprint of speech entitled "Federal Aid for Teachers Salaries" by Joseph S. Clark from Congressional Record, *Proceedings and Debates of the 86th Congress*, Second Session, February 3, 1960, p. 4.

■ Higher Education

A system of public colleges and universities seems a natural extension of our interest in making educational opportunities available for the many in our society. Our first state university was founded in Virginia, largely through the interest and efforts of Thomas Jefferson, and the Land-Grant College Act of 1862 was a great boon to public colleges and universities. These institutions, however, are state schools and as such are outside the scope of this study. There are a limited number of municipal colleges and a larger number of two-year, junior, or community colleges which are operated by counties, municipalities, or school districts.

The first municipal college in the United States was founded in Charleston, South Carolina, in 1770. This school changed from private to public hands in 1837, the same year that the University of Louisville was established. Our largest municipal college, the City University of New York, was founded in 1847, one year after the establishment of the University of Buffalo. In 1962, only 15 municipal colleges and universities were functioning in the United States,[18] but this number included such well known institutions as those in Akron, Cincinnati, and Toledo, Ohio; Wichita and Topeka (Washburn) Kansas; Omaha, Nebraska; and Houston, Texas, in addition to those mentioned above.

The public junior or community college movement is a more recent activity of both municipal and state governments. In 1920, there were only 10 publicly controlled junior colleges with a total enrollment of 2,940 students. Forty years later, the number had risen to 310 with a student population that had skyrocketed to over 348,000. In 1960 Minnesota had nine junior colleges which were totally supported by the students and the local communities in which they were located.

One of the continuing arguments in higher education centers around the question, Who should go to college? In a brilliant chapter on college and the alternatives for continuing education, John W. Gardner writes:

Because college has gained extraordinary prestige, we are tempted to assume that the only useful learning and growth comes from attending such an institution, listening to professors talk from platforms, and reproducing required information on occasions called examinations. . . .

[18] Bureau of the Census, *Census of Governments, 1962, Vol. I, Governmental Organization,* Washington, D. C., 1962, p. 9.

The more we allow the impression to get abroad that only the college man or woman is worthy of respect in our society, the more we contribute to a fatal confusion which works to the injury of all concerned. If we make the confusing assumption that college is the sole cradle of human dignity, need we be surprised that every citizen demands to be rocked in that cradle?[19]

■ Local Library Service

The public library is an important link in our system of public education. This was emphasized by a Committee of the American Library Association which stated in a 1943 report that "It (the public library) is basic to the education and continuous re-education of the American people as citizens, workers, and as civilized human beings. It plays a significant role in making democracy work by helping citizens to be enlightened participants in public affairs."[20] While the public library once was concerned almost exclusively with the distribution of books, the modern library also provides a wide variety of magazines and periodicals, newspapers, and recordings. Larger libraries also offer educational films, other audiovisual materials, and bookmobile service to outlying areas.

Public library service is usually an optional rather than a mandatory function of local governments; hence it is not a universal one, particularly in more rural areas. However, almost every city of 10,000 or more maintains a library, and a number of smaller towns and townships also provide this public facility. In addition, a number of school districts and counties maintain libraries or cooperate with adjoining units to provide regional library facilities, and there are some 350 libraries operated by special districts.

There are two principal patterns of organization for administration of local libraries which are common to both municipal and county governments. The first and most widely used one vests principal authority in a library board appointed by the governing board of the community's government or by its chief executive officer. The board determines policies and exercises general supervisory control over the library and typically selects a librarian to direct its day-to-day activities. The second does not utilize the library board but provides for the direct appointment of the

[19] Gardner, op. cit., pp. 80-82.
[20] Committee on Post-War Planning, Post-War Standards for Public Libraries, American Library Association, Chicago, 1943, p. 9.

librarian by the local governing board or the local executive officer. In addition, some communities use the public school library as a community library and have boards composed jointly of school board members and citizens appointed by some agency of the local governmental unit. A fourth pattern found in some cities is a city-county library established and administered jointly by the two units.

In addition to the services of city, county, and regional libraries, all states now maintain library extension agencies charged with promoting community library service. While the activities of such agencies varies widely, they typically encourage the establishment of local libraries, cooperate with them to improve personnel of local libraries, provide advice and assistance, promote expansion of local library coverage, and offer a book service through extension loans and traveling libraries.

The Library Services Act was passed by Congress in 1956 to stimulate development of public library service to rural areas. When the act was adopted, it was estimated that 26 million rural residents were without any library service and that another 50 million had access only to inadequate service. By the end of its five-year period, some four million citizens had libraries for the first time and 32 million were receiving improved services. The effectiveness of the program and the recognition that the job was still far from completed convinced Congress in 1960 to extend the act for an additional five years.[21]

The average current expenditure for all public libraries was only 72 cents per capita in 1950, a figure far below the standards advanced by the American Library Association. According to this Association, minimum library service in cities of 25,000 population or more would require an expenditure of $1.50 per capita, reasonably good service $2.25, and superior service $3.00 per capita. It is apparent that libraries, like so many other worthwhile civic endeavors, do not have sufficient resources to serve the community adequately.

■ *Public Recreation*

Recreation has been defined as "any form of leisure-time experience or activity in which an individual engages from choice

---

[21] Eleanor A. Ferguson, "Library Services and Legislation," *The Book of the States, 1962-63,* Council of State Governments, 1962, p. 331.

because of the enjoyment and satisfaction which it brings directly to him."[22] Thus, it is fitting to include recreation in a chapter dealing primarily with education because its chief value, as in the case of education, lies in its power to enrich the lives of individuals.

Recreation has been an important segment of life throughout most of recorded history. The athletic games of the Greeks, the circuses and public baths of the Romans, and the tournaments and hunts of the Middle Ages are all well-known as integral parts of life in those early years. The energies of early Americans were largely absorbed by their work but quilting bees and house warmings were social events of some significance in colonial times. Prior to 1900, however, leisure hours and recreation opportunities were greatly restricted and the modern recreation movement is one of the outgrowths of the period following World War I.

For too long a period, public recreation consisted of providing play areas for the young. The playground movement began with the opening of a sand garden in front of the Children's Mission in Boston in 1885. Four years later, a ten-acre tract along the Charles River in Boston was converted into a play area for boys and men, and a similar area was established for girls and women in 1891. A well-equipped playground was opened at Hull House in Chicago in 1892. In 1903, the South Park Playgrounds were opened under public auspices in New York and President Theodore Roosevelt heralded this as "the most notable civic achievement of any American city." The National Playground Association of America was established in 1906 and this agency, which later became the National Recreation Association, has done yeoman work to achieve public acceptance of local governmental support for recreation.

To provide recreation service in accordance with the criteria advanced by the International City Managers' Association, at least one acre of park and recreation space is needed for each 100 of the population.[23] The number and types of properties that this organization recommends for a city of 100,000 people are shown in Table 21. It should be noted that such services and facilities provide recreation opportunities for persons of all age groups rather than just for pre-school and school age children. A well-rounded recreation program offers year-round opportunities to spend free

---

[22] George D. Butler, *Introduction to Community Recreation,* McGraw-Hill, 1949, p. 8.
[23] International City Managers' Association, *Municipal Recreation Administration,* 2nd ed., 1945, pp. 73-79.

time profitably and enjoyably for all persons from toddlers to senior citizens.

Table 21. *Number and Types of Recreation Properties Recommended for a City of 100,000*

Type	Number	Average Size (in acres)	Total Area (in acres)
Neighborhood Playgrounds	20	5	100
Playfields	4	25	100
Playfields—Parks	2	40	80
Special Recreation Areas			
Athletic field	1	20	20
Golf course	1	120	120
Neighborhood Parks	6	15	90
Large Recreation Parks	2	120	240
Reservation	1	250	250
Total	37		1,000

SOURCE: International City Managers' Association, *Municipal Recreation Administration,* 2nd ed., 1945, p. 79.

While the discussion above emphasizes space requirements of a well-rounded recreation program, there are many other problems pertaining to this important service area. One concerns the financing of areas and programs. In 1961, only 2.3 percent of the direct expenditures of local government were expended for parks and recreation. In view of the public health and public welfare benefits which accrue from recreation programs, this seems a small investment which pays off handsomely. To others, however, the expenditure of public monies for such facilities as zoos, museums, golf courses or botanical gardens seem wrong since they never make use of such areas themselves.

Another problem concerns the use of free time, which is often equated with leisure. In a recent challenging study entitled *Of Time, Work and Leisure,* Sebastian de Grazia distinguishes sharply among the three elements in the title. In his words, "Time is a major element, since today's leisure is measured in units of time—hours, days, weeks. Work is included because today's time is considered free when not at grips with work. Work is the antonym of free time. But not of leisure. Leisure and free time live in two different worlds. . . . Leisure refers to a state of being, a condition of man, which few desire and fewer achieve."[24]

The close relationship between recreation and education was briefly noted earlier. To many persons, recreation is a form of education and is its own reason for being. The need for even closer cooperation between these two public activities becomes apparent when it is realized that the child has an amount of free time daily about equal to the time spent in school. "Yet," as one writer has commented, "we spend billions annually in highly refining the regimen for the hours in the classroom and devote almost nothing in most communities to the free hours. From the most expensive tuition in the world the youngster is dismissed without rapport into whatever happens to be his environment, however squalid it may be, however depraving."[25]

SUGGESTED READINGS

Books

Butler, George D., *Introduction to Community Recreation* (New York: McGraw-Hill, 1949).

Committee for Economic Development, *Paying for Better Public Schools* (New York, 1959).

Conant, James B., *The Child, The Parent, and the State* (Cambridge: Harvard University Press, 1959).

Conant, James B., *The American High School Today* (New York: McGraw-Hill, 1959).

Eliot, Thomas H., *Governing America, The Politics of a Free People,* State and Local Supplement (New York: Dodd, Mead, 1961).

Garceau, Oliver, *The Public Library in the Political Process* (New York: Columbia University Press, 1949).

International City Managers' Association, *Municipal Recreation Administration,* 2nd ed. (Chicago: International City Managers' Association, 1945).

Lieberman, Myron, *The Future of Public Education* (Chicago: University of Chicago Press, 1960).

Maslow, Will and Cohen, Richard, *School Segregation, Northern Style* (New York: Public Affairs Pamphlet 316, 1961).

[24] The Twentieth Century Fund, *Newsletter,* No. 45 (Fall, 1962), pp. 1–3.
[25] J. C. Charlesworth, "An Attitude Toward Recreation," *The Daily Pennsylvania,* May 4, 1959, p. 3.

Moehlman, Arthur B., *School Administration* (Boston: Houghton Mifflin, 1951).

Quattlebaum, Charles A., *Federal Aid to Elementary and Secondary Education* (Chicago: Public Administration Service, 1948).

Rockefeller Brothers Fund, Inc., *The Pursuit of Excellence, Education and the Future of America* (New York: Doubleday, 1958).

Thurston, Lee M. and Roe, William H., *State School Administration* (New York: Harper, 1957).

Articles

Barko, Naomi, "Dropouts to Nowhere," *The Reporter, 26* (March 29, 1959), 14–19.

Changing Times, "Your Money's Worth in Schools" (September, 1961), pp. 25–32.

Clark, Joseph S., "Federal Aid for Teachers Salaries," *Congressional Record*, February 3, 1960, reprint.

Freeman, Roger A., "State Aid and the Support of Our Public Schools," *State Government, 26* (October, 1953), 237–40, 252–3.

Malmberg, Margie S., "Books at Your Doorstep," *The County Officer, 15* (May, 1950), 10–13, 23–24.

Moynihan, Daniel P., "A Second Look at the School Panic," *The Reporter, 20* (June 11, 1959), 14–19.

Public Works and
Public Service
Enterprises

22

The two terms in the title of this chapter are both vague and without precise meaning. The public works department is usually one of the largest in city or county government in terms of expenditures, range of activities, and number of employees. The number and diversity of its activities are more elastic than those of any other department of local administration and vary considerably from jurisdiction to jurisdiction. One strand of unity among the activities of typical public works departments is their need for personnel trained in engineering. Public works activities have been defined as those "concerned with the installation, construction, operation, and maintenance of physical plant and equipment used to service the needs of the people of the community."[1] Activities which we will consider as public works undertakings include streets and highways, street lighting, traffic, parking lots, refuse collection and disposal, and public buildings and grounds.

Public service enterprises are more often referred to as public utilities. There is no single department in local government which

[1] Harold F. Alderfer, *American Local Government and Administration,* Macmillan, 1956, p. 546.

477

encompasses all of these activities, which are essentially business enterprises. If publicly owned, some may be operated by a line department, by an independent board or commission, or by a government corporation. Indeed a number of public utilities are not publicly owned and operated but are privately owned and managed by corporations, or by individual proprietors. The services which will be discussed as public service enterprises are water supply, sewage disposal, electricity, airports, and transportation, although this list is by no means exhaustive. One characteristic of such enterprises is that they are affected with more than the usual amount of public interest. Such undertakings as telephone, telegraph, natural gas, port facilities, toll bridges and roads, public markets, and slaughterhouses also qualify as utilities but will be excluded from the discussion that follows, even though they are occasionally operated by local governmental units.

■ Streets and Highways

Provision of ways for public travel has been a concern of local governments since colonial times. In the New England colonies "the physical features of the country were such as to render the construction and maintenance of highways an expensive and otherwise burdensome duty. Everywhere we find the towns each caring for their own roads and bridges; and for this purpose enacting by-laws, levying rates, and choosing surveyors."[2] The Connecticut legislature in 1643 required its towns to elect two surveyors empowered to impress persons and teams of horses into service to mend and repair highways, and similar legislation was enacted in the other New England colonies. The county was the important local unit for highways, as for other services, in southern colonies. In Virginia, for example, the responsibility for care of highways was imposed upon the county court. Surveyors were appointed for each of the precincts within the county.

Roads continued to be a function of local governments throughout the nineteenth century. Fairlie and Kneier write that "until nearly the end of the nineteenth century the building and care of

[2] George E. Howard, *Local Constitutional History of the United States*, Johns Hopkins University Studies in Historical and Political Science, Baltimore, 1889, Vol. I, p. 207.

roads in the United States was almost entirely carried on by local governments in counties, towns, and road districts. To a large extent road work (except in cities) was carried on by a labor tax, some of which was commuted by money payments, and little expert engineering construction was attempted."[3] In 1891, New Jersey provided the first state aid to local governments for highway purposes. A decade later, similar legislation had been enacted in eight states and by 1917 all states provided some aid to local governments for highways. The modern program of federal grants for highway purposes began with the passage of the Federal-Aid Road Act of 1916 allocating federal funds on the basis of area, population, and mileage of rural mail routes in each state.

Highway mileage in the United States in 1960 totaled 3,545,693 miles. Of this total, nearly 659,000 miles, or 18.3 percent, were under state control. Another 112,000 miles, mostly roads in national forests and on Indian reservations, were under federal control. The other 2,770,000 miles of roads, nearly 80 percent of the total, were under local control.[4] The total rural mileage is nearly eight times larger than the total municipal mileage.

The county is the most important unit for highway administration at the local level, controlling nearly half of the nation's total highway mileage. The governing board of the county has the general responsibility for locating, planning and financing county roads and bridges. The direct management of construction and maintenance is usually lodged in the office of a single administrative official known variously as the highway commissioner, superintendent, or engineer. However, in some counties the governing board itself supervises the details of road and bridge construction, maintenance, and repair.

The administrative organization for street and highways in city government is quite complex in comparison to that in county government. Most common in larger cities is a line department under the direction of a single director. A second common plan places the public works department under board or commission control. In small cities, supervision is commonly one of the functions of the city engineer.

Highways and streets may be classified a number of different

[3] John A. Fairlie and Charles M. Kneier, *County Government and Administration*, Century, New York, 1930, p. 351.
[4] Bureau of the Census, *Statistical Abstract of the United States, 1962*, Washington, D.C., 1962, pp. 551-2.

ways. A simple classification divides them into rural and urban categories. The federal government recognizes a threefold classification, identifying roads as components of the primary system, the secondary system, or urban streets. The primary system consists of a network of main highways selected by states for improvement with federal assistance. Secondary system roads are largely farm-to-market rural roads designated by the states and coordinated by the Bureau of Public Roads. Federal aid is also available for roads on the secondary program and for those urban streets that are extensions of the primary and secondary systems.[5]

The design and construction of a street or highway depends on a number of factors. Among the major considerations are what kind of traffic it will carry, how heavy its load will be, what its relationship to major arterial streets will be, and what types of land uses border the street. Many local streets and roads have surfaces of stone, gravel, cinder, and slag. The relative merits of the several types of surfacing materials are known to engineers who select a surface of concrete, asphalt, asphaltic concrete, macadam, stone blocks, wood blocks, or bricks depending on the use to be made of the particular street.

In addition to serving as travel ways from one point to another for pedestrians and vehicles, urban streets serve four other important functions. First, they provide access to abutting property by providing for pedestrian, vehicular, and utility access to the properties along them. Second, they serve as automobile storage space by providing for short-term, long-term, and overnight storage. Third, they serve as a provider of light and air for urban dwellers and buildings. And, fourth, they are a collector and carrier of storm drainage as an important element in the storm water run-off system.[6]

While the size and number of activities vary considerably, some appreciation of the magnitude of the problem can be gained from a closer look at the streets problem in Los Angeles County. In 1960, the County had a network, not counting the freeways which are under the State Department of Highways, extending some 16,000

[5] For a good report on the nature of our highways, see The President's Advisory Committee on a National Highway Program, *A Ten-Year National Highway Program, A Report to the President,* Washington, January, 1955.

[6] Associated Institutes of Government of Pennsylvania Universities, "Adequacy Ratings for Urban Streets," *Horizons for Modern Pennsylvania Local Government, 4* (February, 1957), p. 2.

miles. This mileage is greater than the road mileage in 42 of the 50 states, and, if laid end to end, the roads would reach nearly two-thirds of the way around the world. Of the 16,000 miles, the County Road Department takes care of 5,200 miles (4,200 in its own domain and another 1,000 miles in contract cities serviced by the County Department) while the remaining miles are inside cities and are maintained by them. County roads occupy land that have an estimated market value of somewhere near $500 million. However, if it were not for the presence of these roadways, the value of adjoining lands would be considerably less. The County Road Department spends in excess of $35 million a year and employs a force of 1,800 persons, about one-third of whom are engineers.[7]

Today there is a tripartite relationship among the three levels of government in highway administration—a pattern of cooperation which will likely be extended even further in the decades ahead. For instance, the Federal-Aid Highway Act of 1956 provides for a super network of 41,000 miles of two, four, six, and eight lane expressways. Known as the Interstate Highway System, these major highways will crisscross the nation, connecting 209 cities of over 50,000 population, 42 of the capitals of the 48 continental states, and wind through all 48 of these states. While these 41,000 miles represent only 1.2 percent of the nation's total road mileage, they are expected to carry about 20 percent of the total traffic.

The prevalence of state aid to local governments for streets and highways has been noted in earlier chapters. This aid takes two principal forms—a share of highway-user taxes, and grants-in-aid. The former is more important to local governments generally, but state grants continue to be of major importance to particular units from time to time.

Although streets and highways may appear to be a technical field where engineers would be expected to be in control, local governing bodies still commonly reserve to themselves formal approval of roadwork to be done. Local governments which perform their own construction and maintenance functions have a number of contracts to let and these are usually actively competed for by local business firms. In those units which do not have a formal merit system, there are a number of positions in this section of the public works department which can be filled by patronage appointments.

[7] "L. A. Spider Web of Streets Constantly in Need of Care," *Los Angeles Times,* September 11, 1960, Sec. F, pp. 1–2.

■ Street Lighting

Modern street lighting is considered to be an important element in both traffic and personal safety. But it was not always so. Early efforts to light city streets were often met with vehement citizen objections as a direct attempt to interfere with the Divine Plan. It was also feared that night lighting would tempt people to remain outdoors longer in the evening thus resulting in increased malaria and other health problems. A third objection advanced the argument that lighting would banish the normal fear of darkness and result in human depravity.

American cities, however, seemed more progressive than their European counterparts. The Common Council in New York in 1697 passed the following ordinance:

> It is Resolved *Nemine Contra Dicente* for the Regulating of the lights to be put out in the Darke time of the Moon within this city and for the case of the inhabitants that Every Seaventh house in the Severall Wards of this Citty doe Every Night in the Darke time of the Moon untill the twenty fifth day of March next cause a Lanthorne & Candle to be hung out on A Pole Every Night and that the Charge be defrayed in equal proportion by the Inhabitants of the Said Seaven houses Upon Penalty of Nine Pense for Every Default to be paid by the person whose turn itt is to put Out the Same. . . .[8]

A half century later, in 1753, New York's Common Council ordered the first public support of street lighting by providing two lamps in front and one in the rear of the City Hall. In 1826, the Council had over 100 more such lamps installed in the downtown area of New York City. During the nineteenth century, street lighting progressed rapidly as a number of new inventions were developed. Citizen street lighting was replaced by city contracts with local gas and coke companies, financed by a special lighting tax. Since street lighting assessments were difficult to collect, it became common practice to pay lighting costs from the general property tax revenues. Interestingly enough, a number of communities have reverted to the special assessment practice through the establishment of special purpose street lighting districts.

Modern street lighting serves three basic purposes. First, and most important, lighting promotes safety and convenience. Im-

---

[8] Henry G. Hodges, *Municipal Management, Theory and Practice of Municipal Administration*, Crofts, 1939, p. 561.

proved lighting systems have reduced traffic accident rates in a number of communities and have also served as a deterrent to crime. One of the slogans used by the Los Angeles County Sheriff's Department in its citizen education campaigns in recent years has been "Burn a light at night" to reduce crime. Second, lighting improves the appearance of streets and encourages their greater use by drivers and pedestrians alike. Third, adequate street lighting increases community street values. The close relationship between inadequate street lighting and accidents has been noted by the National Safety Council. In its words, "Traffic hazards and accident severity begin to increase at an alarming rate at sundown. The fatal accident rate per mile of travel is three times as high at night as during the day. Pedestrian accidents, primarily adults, constitute a relatively high proportion of night accidents in urban areas. Half the pedestrian deaths occur between 6 p.m. and midnight."[9]

The accomplishment of the purposes served by modern street lighting is a technical one. The determination of what type and intensity of illumination is necessary for the purposes to be served is now a science and there are technical specifications relating to height, spacing, intensity, and maintenance of street lighting.[10] Early complaints against efforts to illuminate streets have changed to criticisms of inadequate efforts. Although there has been substantial improvement in many cities, both large and small, most city streets still do not meet the standards recommended by experts.

■ Traffic Congestion

The oft-quoted description of the United States as a "nation on wheels" seems only too realistic and true to a driver caught in the five o'clock exodus of cars from a major urban center. Yet traffic problems are not new in urban life. The congestion problem in London in 1850 was described as a "stream of walkers, two, three and four miles long, converging on the city." As early as 1905, congested traffic at rush hours was considered to be the number one problem of large cities in the United States.[11]

[9] Quoted in Alderfer, op. cit., pp. 552–3.

[10] For a discussion of such standards, see American Public Works Association, Public Lighting Practice, Chicago, 1945, Chap. 13.

[11] Wilfred Owen, The Metropolitan Transportation Problem, Brookings Institution, 1956, p. 1.

While the problem of congestion is an old one, there is a distinct difference between the current problem and the one of old-style congestion mentioned above. In 1920, there were only 9.25 million motor vehicle registrations in the United States; by 1961, this number had increased more than eight times to 75,847,000. Traffic deaths in 1960 totaled 37,160, and over 4,500,000 persons were injured in motor vehicle accidents in 1961. The average speed of all vehicles, based on actual tests recorded on tangent sections of main rural highways during off-peak hours in 1961 was 52.5 miles per hour.[12] The ability to travel expeditiously and relatively free of danger is an economic necessity in modern life. In terms of the few statistics cited above, the first part of the goal has been achieved more successfully than the second.

Both continued population growth and the increasing concentration of people in large urban centers contribute to the traffic problem. An almost corollary factor is the increased number of motor vehicles and expanded vehicular movement. Commuter living results in increased traffic because of the travel patterns of persons to and from work. Daylight populations of our largest urban centers are often as high as 20 percent above official census counts, and smaller suburban communities with one or more large industrial employers often have daylight populations two or three times their actual resident populations. A third important factor relates to the physical characteristics of our streets, most of which were laid out before the coming of large numbers of automobiles and trucks. Street widths adequate for days of horse-and-buggy travel were not planned to carry either the types or volume of today's traffic.

In addition to these primary factors of urban congestion, there are a number of more immediate causes. As identified by Hodges, these include (1) dead-end and bottleneck streets; (2) steep grades and slippery surfaces; (3) concentrated business and amusement sections; (4) skyscraper office and department store buildings; (5) intermingling of fast and slow traffic; (6) intermingling of rail or tracked and free vehicles; (7) taxicab cruising; (8) auto parking; and (9) jaywalking.[13]

Despite the traffic engineering, street improvements, and large number of freeways and expressways built in recent years, most

[12] Statistics in this paragraph are from Bureau of the Census, *Statistical Abstract of the United States, 1962*, pp. 66, 69, 563, 565.

[13] Hodges, *op. cit.*, p. 451.

cities are not making real progress in meeting their traffic problems. The three "Es" of a traffic control program have been identified by Hodges as "Engineering, Enforcement, and Education."[14] Engineering, of course, is the technical and physical approach to the problem by attempting to eliminate or reduce the effect of the several immediate causes of congestion listed above. These efforts include the rounding of corners, increasing street width, use of traffic signals and other control devices, one-way streets, posting of speed limits, parking bans during rush hours, and a large number of other devices.

Enforcement of traffic regulations is largely the responsibility of the police and the courts. A growing percentage of the time of the average policeman is devoted to traffic problems, and police departments in large communities have traffic divisions with specialized officers and men whose primary concern is traffic regulation and enforcement. A noted traffic authority has stated that, "Training of the general uniformed forces in most of our city police departments today is such that it would be contrary to the public interest to place this added responsibility (traffic) in their hands. Enforcement quantity and quality would deteriorate rapidly. . . . we cannot hope that the much more complicated problems of traffic supervision can yet be turned over to the general uniformed forces with promise of good results. A relatively high degree of police traffic specialization is still required, and probably will be for many years."[15]

Traffic education is the capstone of a traffic control program since it recognizes that the most effective way to bring about improvement is to attack the problem at its source—the driver. In recent years, driver education courses have been offered in high schools across the nation and many schools also offer instruction in pedestrian and bicycle safety. The development of safe driving and safe walking habits is also a function of traffic police and other community organizations such as automobile clubs and citizen safety councils. Schools have been established for traffic violators in some communities with the final disposition of cases sometimes dependent upon the progress of the violator as reflected in his attitude and performance in class. A few judges have elected to pass out unusual sentences rather than imposing fines on traffic violators. Among the

14 *Ibid.*, p. 456.
15 Franklin M. Kreml, *Traffic Law Enforcement,* Traffic Institute, Northwestern University, 1952, pp. 15–16.

common sentences are to require the violator to spend a certain number of hours at the emergency ward of local hospitals to witness the admission of victims of traffic accidents, to pick up trash and debris along streets, to sweep streets, or to spend a designated number of hours reading to hospitalized victims of other traffic accidents. The problem of traffic education has been receiving increasing attention from schools, traffic police, and other community organizations.

■ Parking

The close relationship between parking and traffic congestion is an obvious one. Most of the vehicles overloading the streets at peak hours will also be in search of parking space when they arrive at their destinations. Streets were the primary parking facilities in most communities until recent years, when the number of available spaces became woefully inadequate for the growing number of vehicles. Parked vehicles also reduce the street space for moving vehicles, further adding to the traffic congestion.

Public streets are primarily dedicated to the movement of traffic rather than to the storage of automobiles. This point was clearly established in a decision of Lord Chief Justice Ellenborough in 1812 when he stated that "The King's Highway is not to be used as a stable yard." Despite the frequent repetition of this ancient decision, citizens were slow to realize that parking on public streets is a privilege, not a right, and, as such, it is subject to withdrawal by public authorities at any time.

The problem of inadequate parking facilities is a universal one common to business sections of small communities as well as to central business districts in large cities. In Boston, it has been estimated that one-third of the downtown buildings would have to be torn down if adequate parking space were to be provided for the patrons of the remaining structures. While the problem in Boston may be a bit extreme, in general the parking problem increases proportionately with the size of the city.

Parking facilities or the lack of them determine the shopping habits of many citizens. If customers cannot find parking places where they usually shop, they will soon seek other commercial centers where such facilities are available. Stores in central business districts have become acutely aware of the need for parking spaces as shopping centers in outlying areas have mushroomed in number and captured a sizeable portion of the customer's business. Curb parking, even if permitted in downtown areas, is inadequate, so means had to be developed to regulate curb parking to allow the use of the limited facilities where they existed by a larger number of customers and to establish off-street parking space.

Various means have been utilized to provide greater parking facilities. The parking meter, first installed in Oklahoma City in 1935, gained the favor of local officials in communities throughout the nation. Meters are now almost a universal feature along commercial streets in American cities of all sizes. In addition to regulating parking needs for short-term parkers, meters are a good source of revenue for cities, and income derived from them is often used to construct off-street parking facilities. Parking meters do not solve the parking problem; they provide for a more rapid turnover of parking spaces, but this meets only the needs of short-term parkers.

To meet the needs of all-day parkers, parking garages and parking lots have been constructed in large numbers in recent years. While many of these facilities are owned and operated by commercial firms, local governments in large numbers have entered the parking business. In 1960, three-fourths of the cities of 10,000 population or more had publicly owned parking lots. Such facilities are variously financed through general taxes, general obligation bonds, revenue bonds, parking meter receipts, or special assessments against benefiting property owners. In spite of the widespread efforts of both private and public agencies to ameliorate the parking problem, it remains serious in most large communities. Thus it seems likely that the efforts which have been generated to date will continue in the years ahead. To many public officials, the problem of supplying adequate parking facilities must seem to be incapable of solution with the number of cars increasing more rapidly than parking spaces can be made available.

■ Refuse Collection and Disposal

Refuse collection and disposal is another function usually performed by a division of the local public works department. However, in a number of communities the function is rendered by a private firm under contract with the local government. In other local governments, special districts have been established to provide these services. This is also a service area in which inter-local co-operation is common because of economics and the lack of suitable areas for disposal sites in some incorporated communities.

The refuse collection and disposal function consists of the pickup of wastes at households, business properties, and institutions, its transport to a disposal site, and its ultimate disposition so that nuisances are not created. Refuse, as the term is here used, includes garbage, rubbish, ashes, street refuse, industrial wastes, and dead animals. Although some communities provide for a combined refuse pickup, many others have three separate pickups, one each for garbage, rubbish, and ashes. Sanitation trucks are generally used for garbage collection in urban areas to reduce the health menace and are often used for rubbish and trash as well. As a general rule, collection pickups are on at least a once a week basis in residential areas and are often on a daily basis in commercial areas and at major institutions.

Disposal of refuse is accomplished by a variety of methods depending upon the soil and climatic conditions, availability of sites, and other circumstances. Incineration is one of the most common methods used for combined disposal. Under this method, refuse is transported to incinerators and destroyed in furnaces. Recent improvements in incinerator design and operation now make it possible to reduce the odors and eliminate the gases which were once a major problem of this method. A second popular method for combined disposal is known as the sanitary-fill method. Refuse is deposited in trenches or low areas and then covered with dirt. This method has the advantage of low cost, but its major drawback is the area required for disposal. It has been estimated that 8 to 10 acres are required for each 100,000 persons. This method is not a reasonable solution to many communities with no ready access to open space which could be used for this purpose.

There are a number of other disposal methods which are still in use. One of these is barging refuse out to sea, a method obviously limited to cities along shore lines. The open dump which has been condemned as both a health menace and a public nuisance is still used in some more rural areas. Landfill is a third method permitting combined disposal. This method is similar to sanitary-fill except that low areas rather than trenches are used. When the hole is filled, it is covered with dirt, usually scraped off an adjoining high area. Other methods for disposing of garbage include its feeding to hogs, garbage grinding in homes or in community grinders, reduction to retrieve the grease content of garbage, and fermentation. This method consists of placing garbage on large trays and applying heat to them to stimulate bacterial action. After a period of some 30 days, the garbage has dried to resemble humus and the liquids have drained off.

There are various arrangements for intermunicipal cooperation in refuse collection and disposal. Probably the most widely used method is the creation of a special district or authority which takes on the independence of a private corporation but enjoys the tax exemption of a governmental entity. Some counties assume the responsibility of collecting and disposing of refuse for the municipalities within it by establishing a countywide system. Smaller communities often enter into contractual arrangements with other communities for these services. Whether the cooperative arrangements are for disposal by incineration, land-fill or some other method, they enable the participating communities to solve a common problem through joint efforts resulting in reduced costs.[16]

■ Property Maintenance

If centralization of responsibility for property maintenance exists in a local government, it is commonly placed in a bureau of property maintenance within the department of public works. This division is responsible for the care and upkeep of public buildings and grounds including the city hall or county courthouse, police and fire stations, comfort stations, auditoriums, garages, and whatever other types of public property exist. Centralization of this responsibility should result in periodic inspections of all such properties, economies in operation, and yearlong employment schedules for employees. In some divisions, carpenters are employed to perform minor construction and repair jobs for the governmental unit.

Although auditoriums are not yet found in most cities, there seems to be a growing interest among cities in constructing and operating them. A study of 166 city auditoriums in 1950 found that

[16] Adapted from remarks in written statement of Elroy F. Spitzer, Engineering Editor, *The American City*, presented at University of Pennsylvania, April 16, 1959.

only 11 of them had been constructed before 1900 and that only one-third were privately owned and operated.[17] As a rule, auditoriums are handsome and spacious structures used for staging concerts, circuses, conventions and other public attractions. The Symons study reported that the cities with municipal auditoriums considered them excellent community facilities and aids to local business through the types of events they held and the conventions that were attracted to the city.

■ Public Service Enterprises

Public service enterprises or public utilities have been identified by one authority as "industries, properties, corporations, or other business concerns that furnish recognized public services through private forms of organization."[18] The concept that certain businesses were affected with a public interest was handed down in a decision of the United States Supreme Court in 1887 when it stated that property is "clothed with a public interest when used in a manner to make it of public consequence, and affect the community at large. When, therefore, one devotes his property to a use in which the public has an interest, he, in effect, grants to the public an interest in that use, and must submit to be controlled by the public for the common good, to the extent of the interest he has thus created."[19]

While the concept seems quite clear at first reading, it presents considerable difficulty when applied as a criterion to determine the extent of public interest of particular business enterprises. Obviously, some such as water or electricity are more important to the general public than are others. Bauer points out two distinguishing characteristics which identify the public nature of utilities. First, the services rendered are essential and virtually indispensable to modern business, industrial, and community life. Second, they are natural monopolies "in which competition is either physically or financially impossible, or publicly undesirable."[20] Early experience with competition in these service areas proved devastating to both consumer rates and services.

[17] Farrell G. H. Symons, *Municipal Auditoriums*, Public Administration Service, 1950.
[18] John Bauer, *Transforming Public Utility Regulations*, Harper, 1950, p. 3.
[19] *Munn* v. *Illinois*, 94 U.S. 113, 126 (1887).
[20] Bauer, *op. cit.*, p. 5.

PUBLIC SERVICES

There are several other characteristics usually associated with public utilities. They enjoy special privileges such as the power of eminent domain and the right to use public property. Utilities have unusually high capital investments and require continual additions of capital for expansion of their physical plants and equipment. Since the services of utility companies are affected with the public interest, they are subject to detailed public regulation even though they are under private ownership and management. Such regulation is designed to protect the interests of consumers, investors, and utility enterprisers alike, and is aimed to assure proper service at reasonable rates and financial stability.

The question of public versus private ownership of businesses affected with the public interest is one more often answered by emotion than reason or empirical study. As one writer has pointed out:

> Local politicians have coupled its affirmative answer with life, liberty, equality, and votes for themselves. The utility executives, giving free lectures at "institutes" financed by their own industries, have pointed out so many evil principles in municipal administration that one wonders how they dare drink from municipally owned and operated water systems. One orator is raising the rabble while the other is raising the rates and dividends, and neither contributes to the public service. The arguments of one are entirely positive, while the contributions of the other are entirely negative; when, added, they produce zero.[21]

While a number of advantages and disadvantages of public ownership have been advanced by proponents and opponents of municipal ownership respectively, existing data are insufficient either to prove or disprove most of these claims. By the careful selection of favorable statistics and considerations and de-emphasizing the unfavorable, strong cases can and are made by both sides. In reality, there can be no categorical answer either in favor of or in opposition to municipal ownership.

Both sides in the ownership controversy claim that their position tends to eliminate politics from the management of the utility. The inference, of course, is that politics is harmful; it may well be if policy is based on political rather than economic and technical considerations. On the other hand, the intrusion of political consideration may curtail irresponsible activities and the maximizing of profits at the expense of adequate service. In summary, there is

[21] Hodges, *op. cit.*, p. 588.

neither intrinsic good nor evil in public ownership, nor is public ownership the first step on the path to socialism. Individual cases must be decided on their merits, since public ownership has worked well in some communities and fared badly in others.

■ Water Supply

Water is the oldest of the public utilities because of the recognized close relationship of water to public health and the need for fire protection. Community pumps and springs were the first sources of water supply in colonial towns and these also served as community news centers. For fire purposes, river water was used, either passed directly from its source to the fire by hand-to-hand bucket brigades or from centrally located cisterns. America's first piped water supply was built in Boston in 1652. Water was brought in from neighboring springs through wooden pipes by gravity flow to a 12-feet square wooden reservoir tank from which people filled their water buckets. The first water supply system built to serve an entire town was built in Schaefferstown, Pennsylvania, about 1746. A farmer named Schaeffer piped a supply of water from a spring on his farm through pipes by gravity into large open troughs along the town's main street.

The first water works using mechanical engines to pump water uphill was built in 1764 in Bethlehem, Pennsylvania. The motive power was supplied by horse-operated treadmills. Among the other notable firsts in water supply in the United States was the construction of the first municipally owned waterworks in Winchester, Virginia, in 1799. Filters were first successfully installed in Poughkeepsie, New York, in 1872, and liquid chlorine was first applied to destroy disease-producing bacteria in 1912.[22]

The sources of all our water supplies are rivers, lakes, and underground reservoirs. Communities located along rivers or lakes often obtain their water supply from these sources, and a few coastal cities are beginning to use ocean water processed by desalting plants. Many communities depend upon underground sources such as wells and springs for their water supplies. Other communities are forced to bring water many miles from upland sources. Water

[22] American Water Works Association, *The Story of Water Supply*, New York, 1955, pp. 5–7.

PUBLIC SERVICES

for Los Angeles is carried 400 miles from the Colorado River through aqueducts as large as 16 feet in diameter.

To meet the overall needs of the average community, its water plant must supply 140 gallons of water per person per day. An average of 50 gallons per person goes for residential uses including drinking, cooking, laundering, bathing, flushing toilets, lawn or gardening watering, and other home uses. Another 50 gallons per person goes for industrial uses,[23] 20 gallons for commercial uses, and 10 gallons for public uses including fire fighting, street washing, swimming pools, public fountains, and water for public buildings. The other 10 gallons per day is a loss from leaks and breaks in underground pipes.[24]

Water supply is the most common of municipally owned utilities, with over 12,000 of the 16,000 water systems publicly owned. Water utilities are administered by independent water boards or commissions in some communities. Others are administered by boards of special districts and authorities with the facilities financed by the revenues received from the sale of water. In smaller communities, a committee of the local governing board often administers the water supply and supervises the engineer in charge of the plant operations. Some large cities have departments of water which function as important line departments. A fifth administrative arrangement occurs in communities where a popularly elected director of public works has water supply as one of his responsibilities.

One of the major political issues in the area of water supply in recent years has been the controversy over fluoridation. This involves adding controlled amounts of the chemical fluoride to water supplies as a means of reducing tooth decay. Although fluoridation has been opposed for a number of reasons including that it is "un-American," virtually all major health organizations, including the American Dental Association and the American Medical Association, have endorsed controlled fluoridation programs.[25] In many communities, citizens have taken the lead in bringing about fluoridation because its reduction of dental decay has been verified by

[23] It requires about 110 gallons of water to manufacture a pound of rayon, 300 gallons for a gallon of beer, 65,000 gallons for a ton of steel, and 600,000 gallons for a ton of synthetic rubber. See Council of State Governments, *State Administration of Water Resources*, Chicago, 1955, p. 5.

[24] American Water Works Association, *op. cit.*, p. 3.

[25] See B. Mausner and J. Mausner, "A Study of the Anti-scientific Attitude," *Scientific American, 192* (February, 1955), 35–39.

conclusive research findings of half a century. As of 1960, more than 42,000,000 Americans in 3,600 communities were drinking water with either natural or added fluoride, and the number can be expected to increase substantially in the years ahead. There are many perplexing problems in the field of water supply. The three of supply, administrative arrangement, and fluoridation have been mentioned briefly above. Another is the problem of rate charges for water use. The most common practice is to charge all classes of users on the basis of amount used. Another problem of charges concerns rates for residents and institutions outside the incorporated limits of the community. Charges outside the city vary from rates equal to three times as high as those within the city. Health considerations are the major technical problem, since chlorination and purification are usually essential processes to eliminate possible pollution.

The responsibility for providing an adequate and pure water supply is one shared by all three levels of government—local, state, and national. Because water resources do not follow local or state boundaries, higher levels of governmental authority must often be called upon to arbitrate both interlocal and interstate disputes.[26] According to Bernard Frank, "you could write the story of man's growth in terms of his epic concern with water."[27] Since man is so dependent upon water, its supply and conservation is one of the most important current domestic problems and one which will shape the patterns of future development in the United States.

■ Sewage Disposal

Sewage may be defined as a community's combined liquid wastes including those from residences, business establishments, and surface water. It is carried from its sources by a system of drains, sewers and pumps which make up the sewerage system to a disposal plant or other suitable disposal site. In some communities, a single sewerage system carries all three types of wastes—sanitary, industrial, and storm water. Other communities have separate storm

---

[26] See Albert Lepawsky, "Water Resources and American Federalism," *American Political Science Review*, 44 (September, 1950), 631–49; and N. D. Hunter, "Problems of the Colorado River as Reflected in Arizona Politics," *Western Political Quarterly*, 4 (December, 1951), 634–43.

[27] Bernard Frank, "The Story of Water as the Story of Man" in Alfred Stefferud (ed.), *Water*, Government Printing Office, 1955, p. 1.

sewerage systems for disposing of the waters from rains and melted snows. While a combined system offers the advantage of a single set of expensive sewerage installations, difficulties often arise at the treatment plant, in cleaning the system in dry periods, and there is some danger of backflow of contaminated water in times of heavy rainfall.

The first American city to install a system of sanitary sewers was Boston in 1823. In this period, it was common practice to dump the sewage into a nearby body of water. If a sufficient supply of moving water existed and if cities were sufficiently removed from each other, this method of disposal was safe. However, as populations and numbers of cities grew, it became necessary to treat sewage before disposal in most communities. There are several sewage treatment processes. The primary treatment removes the solids in suspension in the sewage, decomposes and then disposes of them by burning, by using them as fertilizer, or by some other means. Oxidation is a second process. This process utilizes bacteria to oxidize the organic material, either in solution or after it is removed from the tanks. The third method is known as sterilization or disinfection and it aims to kill the remaining germs. Chlorine is the germicide most commonly used for this purpose.[28]

Sewage disposal is an expensive operation and financing exclusively from property taxes is no longer as common as it once was. These costs in many communities are now increasingly borne by the householder and other users. Most communities assess the abutting property for sewer construction, charge fees for sewer connections, and levy special taxes for sewerage facilities. Two common bases are used to determine charges for householders. One is based on water consumption, with the bill normally a fixed percentage of the water rate. The second method is a flat rate charge on some unit such as front feet of the property, number of sewer connections, types of plumbing fixtures, number of persons in the household, or various combinations of these or other factors.

Nearly all urban communities own their own sewerage systems. The potential hazards to health in case of failure of the system are indeed fearful to contemplate and this may account in part for the almost universal recognition of sewage as a municipal function. Nearly half of sewage treatment plants are not publicly owned, however.

[28] International City Manager's Association, *Municipal Public Works Administration,* 3rd ed., 1946, pp. 145-80.

In recent years, there has been an increasing extent of state supervision over the activities of local governments in this important field. State concern has developed, in part, because of the tendency of a municipality to minimize costs to itself while ignoring the possible impact of its program on other communities. Stream pollution or the discharge of industrial wastes into water by an upstream community can place downstream communities at a considerable disadvantage. Problems also arise in rural areas where there is not always sufficiently careful policing of what happens to household and other wastes.

■ Electric Plants

Electric power is still a field dominated by commercial plants. Although there were 1,856 municipally owned electric utilities in 1960, they were generating only five percent of electric energy production in contrast to the almost 77 percent generated by privately owned companies. Only 802 of the municipally owned utilities had generating plants.[29] The other municipally owned facilities were distributing plants that purchased their supply from either privately or publicly owned facilities. Although most of the publicly owned systems are in smaller municipalities, some large cities own and operate their electric utilities in whole or in part. Among these are Seattle and Tacoma, Washington; Los Angeles, California; Cleveland, Ohio; Detroit, Michigan; and Jacksonville, Florida.

Since the great majority of publicly owned electric utilities are in smaller communities, the most common administrative arrangement is to place the utility directly under the control of the council or the chief executive officer who appoints the superintendent of the utility. Utility boards appointed by the council or chief executive are also common, and in a few communities members of the utility board are popularly elected.

■ Airports

Airports have been accepted as a municipal utility since the 1920s when local governments were authorized to construct, and

[29] Bureau of Census, *Statistical Abstract of the United States, 1962,* 1962, pp. 529–33.

usually to operate them. Local governments interested in airports have received two big boons since World War II. First, over 500 military airport facilities constructed during the war were turned over to cities, counties, and states for airport use. Second, the Federal Airport Act of 1946 called for the development of a "nationwide system of public airports" to meet present and future needs of civil aeronautics.[30] This Act provides aid for airport construction and expansion but makes no provision for aid in operation or maintenance, and these costs have proved burdensome in many communities since only about five percent of the airports operate at a profit.

Local airports, as most other utilities, are administered in a variety of methods. Some are directed by an airport manager appointed by the local governing board or chief executive officer. Others are managed by semiautonomous airport boards and commissions or by special districts. Various line departments including public works, public service, and utilities control airports in some communities, and the staff department of finance supervises their operations in some cities.

One of the major problems in providing airport facilties is the location of the airport itself. Most citizens do not want the airport near their homes for safety reasons, and the amount of space needed is often not available in or adjacent to the municipality. They are usually constructed some miles from the heart of the area served, resulting in an inconvenience to many users. Such distant locations in large cities are necessary, however, because of the noise generating from the increasing use of jet propelled planes. A second problem is financial and concerns the public subsidy that is usually necessary for their support. Other problems concern traffic congestion, noise, dirt, and the threat of accidents.

■ Public Transportation

The need for concern over the problems of mass transportation has been succinctly phrased by one writer in these words: "Every morning thousands—perhaps millions—of people travel from their

[30] Department of Commerce, *The National Airport Program*, Report of the Airport Panel of the Transportation Council on the Growth of the United States Airport System, Government Printing Office, 1954.

homes in the outskirts to their places of employment in the center of the city. Every evening they reverse the process. After the evening meal comes another hegira of suburban folk, on pleasure bent, and as the theaters and cafes close for the night there follows another exodus from the downtown section. At every hour of the day and night there is some crosstown travel."[31]

While large numbers of people have automobiles and could get along without public transportation if necessary, it remains a necessary utility to others. The numbers for whom it remains a vital necessity vary widely from community to community. A careful study in 1956 reported that 83 percent of center city travel in New York City was by mass transit, 66.8 percent in Chicago, 64.4 percent in Philadelphia, and 31 percent in Los Angeles.[32] Yet the story was the same in each of these cities—use of such facilities was declining.

Virtually all transit systems, whether publicly or privately owned, were losing money in 1960, with the Metropolitan Transit Authority in Los Angeles a notable exception.[33] The major cause for this decline was the switch to transportation by private automobile. Bauer explains this problem in these words: ". . . devolution of transit traffic and earning power has doubtless been due in part to the gradual shifts in community life. But it has been due chiefly to everyone's desire to own an automobile and to have the satisfaction of driving to and from work in his own or jointly in his neighbor's car. This is not only a matter of assumed riding convenience and advantage, but perhaps principally one of inferred prestige."[34]

Among the "pat" solutions to the economic problems of mass transit which are conspicuously absent are the demands that cities sell their systems to private companies and that private companies be taken over by public ownership. Experience in recent years in Chicago, Boston, and other cities have shown that operating losses remain although patterns of ownership change. The pattern of federal-local cooperation in airport construction holds some promise of a similar relationship in the construction of mass transit facilities. But, even should this come to pass, it is almost inevitable that there

---

[31] Austin F. MacDonald, *State and Local Government in the United States,* Crowell, 1955, p. 642.

[32] Owen, *op. cit.*

[33] In all fairness to the other mass transit systems, it should be noted that the network of bus lines in the Los Angeles area in no way parallels the elevated or subway systems in other large cities.

[34] John Bauer, "Municipal Utilities Developments in 1952," *Municipal Year Book, 1953,* International City Managers' Association, 1953, p. 355.

PUBLIC SERVICES

will have to be continued public subsidy for operating costs. The abandonment of public transportation is not a feasible solution, since no major city could handle either the street traffic or the parking problems that would result.

The problems created by a mass transit system, or the lack of one, are difficult ones indeed. Since movement of people between the central city and its suburbs is involved, the core city has a legitimate complaint in believing it should not bear all the costs. Thus, a number of metropolitan areas may seek to follow the recent action in the San Francisco area where voters approved a property tax increase to construct a mass transit system. Others may follow the lead of New York where a special tax on business is levied to help support its transit system which is recognized as a convenience to business. The relocation of business and industry in outlying areas has lessened the transportation problem in some areas but created new problems as a result of the loss of public and private investments in the central business district.

As with many other problems, solutions in the field of public transit must be tailored to the individual community. Where solutions are found, they will likely combine public subsidy, business support through special taxes, and continuing educational campaigns to encourage the use of transit facilities. Municipal bus drivers, for instance, may even adapt the Greyhound slogan and encourage persons to "take the city bus, and leave the driving to us."

SUGGESTED READINGS

Books

Adrian, Charles R., *Governing Urban America*, 2nd ed. (New York: McGraw-Hill, 1961).

Alderfer, Harold F., *American Local Government and Administration* (New York: Macmillan, 1956).

American Public Works Association, *Public Lighting Practice* (Chicago: American Public Works Association, 1945).

American Water Works Association, *The Story of Water Supply* (New York: American Water Works Association, 1955).

Bauer, John, *Transforming Public Utility Regulation* (New York: Harper, 1955).

Bauer, John and Costello, Peter, *Public Organization of Electric Power* (New York: Harper, 1947).

Committee for Economic Development, *Modernizing the Nation's Highways* (New York: Committee for Economic Development, 1956).

Hodges, Henry G., *Municipal Management: Theory and Practice of Municipal Administration* (New York: Crofts, 1939).

International City Managers' Association, *Municipal Public Works Administration*, 3rd ed. (Chicago: International City Managers' Association, 1946).

Kreml, Franklin M., *Traffic Law Enforcement* (Evanston: Traffic Institute, Northwestern University, 1952).

Ostrom, Vincent, *Water and Politics: A Study of Water Politics and Administration in the Development of Los Angeles* (Los Angeles: Haynes Foundation, 1951).

Owen, Wilfred, *The Metropolitan Transportation Problem* (Washington: Brookings Institution, 1956).

Articles

Burns, James M., "The Crazy Politics of Fluorine," *New Republic, 128* (July 13, 1953), 14–15.

Hunter, N. D., "Problems of the Colorado River as Reflected in Arizona Politics," *Western Political Quarterly, 4* (December, 1951), 634–43.

Lepawsky, Albert, "Water Resources and American Federalism," *American Political Science Review, 44* (September, 1950), 631–49.

Mausner, B. and Mausner, J., "A Study of the Anti-scientific Attitude," *Scientific American, 192* (February, 1955), 35–39.

Moynihan, Daniel P., "Epidemic on the Highways," *The Reporter, 20* (April 20, 1959), 16–22.

Moynihan, Daniel P., "New Roads and Urban Chaos," *The Reporter, 22* (April 14, 1960), 13–20.

Rivers, William J., "The Politics of Pollution," *The Reporter, 24* (March 30, 1961), 34–36.

Simpson, H. S., "Mass Transit Can be Saved," *Public Management, 35* (April, 1953), 77–81.

Stonier, C. E., "Metropolitan Traffic Crisis," *Traffic Quarterly, 11* (April, 1957), 214–31.

Planning and
Land-Use Controls

23

The four preceding chapters have been devoted to a discussion of the major service areas of local governments. Effective performance by the governmental unit in meeting problems in protective services, health and welfare, education and recreation, and public works and public service enterprises is greatly abetted if the policy-making officials of the community are aided by a planning department or commission. While planning does and should occupy an important place in any government program, local planning is a staff function, and, as such, is a means to an end. As identified by the Institute for Training in Municipal Administration, "The broad objective of city planning is to further the welfare of the people in the community by helping to create an increasingly better, more healthful, convenient, efficient, and attractive community."[1]

Local planning has been talked and written about so extensively in recent years that it may appear to be a concept with a clearly established meaning. Such, however, is not the case. One authority

[1] Institute for Training in Municipal Administration, *Local Planning Administration,* 2nd ed., International City Managers' Association, 1948, p. 8.

has defined local planning as "a science, an art, and a movement of policy concerned with the shaping and guiding of the physical growth and arrangement of towns in harmony with their social and economic needs."[2] Nearly two decades later, planning was defined as "the continuous and progressive application of research, prophecy, and value judgment to the felt needs of the municipality. It involves the coordination of the various programs within the city itself and between the city and affected political jurisdictions with the goal of making the city a good place to live today and a better place to live tomorrow."[3] A third definition of planning holds it to be "the conscious and deliberate guidance of thinking so as to create logical means for achieving agreed-upon goals. Planning always and inevitably sets priorities and calls for value judgments. Planning is a basic and fundamental approach or way of dealing with the human problems which beset us. Planning is a point of view, an attitude, an assumption that says it is possible for us to anticipate, predict, guide, and control our own destiny."[4] And, finally, to Donald Webster, planning "is essentially a process of understanding human needs and of influencing and shaping future public policy to serve those needs most effectively."[5]

While there may still be some controversy concerning the nature of planning, there is wide agreement that a background of professional preparation and experience is desirable for men and women who choose this career. The first American degrees in planning were awarded to two young men of the Harvard graduating class of 1929. Today, more than 25 leading universities have courses of study leading to advanced degrees in this field, and planners are now employed by city, county, state and federal governments as well as by industry and independent firms.

■ The Development of Local Planning

While local planning in the second half of the twentieth century is much broader in scope and more intricate and involved than it

[2] Thomas Adams, *Outline of Town and City Planning*, Russell Sage Foundation, 1935, p. 21.

[3] Alan P. Grimes, "What is City Planning?" in Charles M. Kneier and Guy Fox, *Readings in Municipal Government and Administration*, Rinehart, 1953, p. 435.

[4] Harleigh B. Trecker, *The Group Process in Administration*, rev. ed., Woman's Press, 1950, p. 232.

[5] Donald H. Webster, *Urban Planning and Municipal Public Policy*, Harper & Row, 1958, p. 4.

PUBLIC SERVICES

was in earlier periods, planning of some kind has existed throughout our nation's history. Notable examples of early planning were the checkerboard street system designed by William Penn for Philadelphia in 1682, and the combination of rectangular and radial streets around a central hub by L'Enfant for Washington, D. C., in 1791. In spite of deviations through the years, the important principles of the original plans of these two cities are still visible.

In a fascinating story of the changing forces that have dominated the American city, Tunnard and Reed wrote: "Americans and foreigners alike have been prone to describe our townscapes as haphazard, formless or the products of accident. Nothing could be farther from the truth. Although not often beautiful, each street or district of our towns and cities reflects from premeditation or planning on the part of an individual or a group, whether it be a homeowner, a banking institution, an individual corporation or a town government."[6]

Accepting the point that planning of a sort has existed since the early years of our nation, two events have been singled out as important stimuli to local planning. The first of these was Chicago's World Fair of 1893 which featured an orderly arrangement of monumental buildings, streets and parks. Men and women from all over the nation saw this site, publicized as the "City Beautiful," and were spurred to action by these words of Daniel Burnham: "Make no little plans; they have no magic to stir men's blood and probably themselves will not be realized. Make big plans; aim high in hope and work, remembering that a noble logical diagram once recorded will never die, but long after we are gone will be a living thing, asserting itself with ever growing insistency."[7] The idea of the city beautiful became a dominant one in communities across the nation, expressing itself in civic centers, civic buildings, parks, fountains and street planting.

The second stimulus was in 1909 when the first national conference on city planning was held in Washington. The economic rather than the aesthetic aspects of city planning were stressed at this meeting, as were the value of a comprehensive technical survey to the development of plans and the need for coordination in the treatment of related problems. As described by one writer, "This

[6] Christopher Tunnard and Henry G. Reed, *American Skyline, The Growth and Form of our Cities and Towns*, The New American Library, 1956, p. 1.
[7] Quoted in Harold F. Alderfer, *American Local Government and Administration*, Macmillan, 1956, p. 596.

conference was in many ways a confluence of the several urban reform movements. . . . It was, however, more the precursor than the true beginning of the organized planning movement."[8] One early consequence was the first meeting of the National Housing Association in 1911. This was followed by a period of intensive investigation and writing in the years immediately following. The American City Planning Institute was started in 1917 as a technical organization of the National Conference on City Planning, a movement given considerable encouragement by Herbert Hoover as Secretary of Commerce.

Planning activities in local communities were largely carried on by self-constituted committees of bankers, realtors and other businessmen, or similarly composed committees appointed by the local executive or governing board. Adrian points out that, "In typical American fashion, land-use decisions were, until recently, made by private businessmen, the realtors, land developers, and bankers in particular. . . . Planners were thus concerned with their profit-and-loss statements rather than with making Ackroyd City an attractive community with an imaginative physical design. It would be difficult to exaggerate the effect of their short-range concerns upon the face of urban America."[9]

The concept of local planning has broadened considerably since the Chicago Fair. Early planning was largely confined to cities and involved chiefly the layout of streets and location of major public facilities. The concept of comprehensive planning emerged in the 1920s, embracing the six elements of zoning, streets, transit, transportation (rail, water and air), public recreation, and civic appearance.[10] A decade later, the seven elements of community land planning were identified by Bassett as streets, parks, sites for public buildings, public reservations, zoning districts, routes for public utilities, and pierheads and bulkhead lines.[11] As Robert Walker observed in 1950, public planning should be "as broad as the scope of city government,"[12] and the planning concept has been expanded to include housing, slum clearance, location of business and industry,

[8] Robert A. Walker, *The Planning Function in Urban Government*, 2nd ed., University of Chicago Press, 1950, p. 11.
[9] Charles R. Adrian, *Governing Urban America*, 2nd ed., McGraw-Hill, 1961, pp. 457-8.
[10] Theodora K. Hubbard and Henry V. Hubbard, *Our Cities Today and Tomorrow*, Harvard University Press, 1929, p. 109.
[11] Edward M. Bassett, *The Master Plan*, Russell Sage Foundation, 1938.
[12] Walker, *op. cit.*, p. 10.

urban renewal, and redevelopment in our larger communities. But since the scope of government is still relatively narrow in more sparsely populated rural communities, planning, if it exists at all as a governmental function, is still narrowly conceived and implemented. Enlightened rural communities, however, will often have some form of zoning ordinance designed to prevent some of the adverse consequences of unplanned land use.

■ Local Planning Commissions

The first permanent planning commission as a municipal agency was established in Hartford, Connecticut, in 1907. This pattern of organization has been followed almost universally since that time as evidenced by the existence of official planning commissions in over 90 percent of American cities of 10,000 or more population in 1960. A few communities have entrusted the planning function to a department under a full-time professional director responsible to the chief executive officer. The relative merits of a staff agency versus an independent commission for planning will be discussed following a description of the organization and functions of the typical local planning commission.

The official local planning agency in most local governments is a plural-member commission which carries on planning activities of a community-wide nature, and coordinates the plans of governmental departments and agencies.[13] The organization of the planning commission varies considerably among local governments. Its typical size is five or seven members, but it may have as many as 50. The members may be *ex officio*, that is composed of designated public officials, citizen appointees serving without pay, or a combination of *ex officio* and citizen appointees. In most communities, the power to appoint citizen members lies in the local executive officer. In some, however, planning is viewed as a legislative rather than as a staff responsibility, and citizen members are appointed by the local governing body.

Powers and duties of city and county planning commissions also vary greatly. In general, their responsibilities parallel those suggested for such an agency in the Model County Charter. It pro-

[13] See Harold V. Miller, *Mr. Planning Commissioner*, Public Administration Service, 1954.

posed that the commission (1) report its recommendations and advice to the county board on all proposals submitted to it, and on such other matters pertaining to planning as the commission desires or the board requests; (2) formulate and develop planning proposals for submission to the board whenever requested to do so by the board or upon its own motion; (3) keep informed on all matters pertaining to planning and hold hearings concerning such matters whenever necessary; (4) promote public interest in and understanding of the county plans and related matters; and (5) perform such other advisory functions and duties and exercise such other powers as the board may establish.[14]

Recognizing that planning commissions assisted by professional staffs are often well equipped to serve additional functions, Martin Meyerson has suggested that they be given expanding responsibilities. Labeling these proposed additions as "middle-ground community planning functions," he believes they would bring planning and policy closer together in the community. These suggested new functions are those of (1) a central intelligence function to facilitate market operations for housing, commerce, industry, and other community activities through the regular issuance of market analyses; (2) a pulse-taking function to alert the community through periodic reports to danger signs in such areas as blight formation, economic changes, population movements and other shifts; (3) a policy-clarification function to help frame and regularly revise development objectives of local government; (4) a detailed development plan function to phase specific programs—both public and private—as part of a comprehensive course of action covering a period of time of up to 10 years; and (5) a feed-back review function to analyze carefully the consequences of programs and activities as a guide to future action.[15]

The most important task of local planning commissions is to prepare a comprehensive or master plan to serve as a blueprint for the future development of the community. Upon approval by the local governing board this plan becomes "official." According to Bassett, the master plan is "nothing more than the easily changed instrumentality which will show a commission from day to day the

---

[14] National Municipal League, *Model County Charter*, Art. VI, Sec. 6.04, 1956, p. 36.

[15] Martin Meyerson, "How to Bring Planning and Policy Together" in Edward C. Banfield (ed.), *Urban Government, A Reader in Administration and Politics*, Free Press, 1961, p. 491.

progress it has made."[16] The zoning plan for the community is also prepared by the planning commission for approval by the governing board, but this function will be discussed in the latter part of this chapter.

The effectiveness of the advisory powers of the commission are in large part dependent on its relationship with the local governing board. Enabling legislation in some states specifies that the local executive officer and governing board may seek the advice of the planning commission if they see fit to do so, implying that they may act without consulting the commission if they choose to do so. In other states, it is mandatory that the advice of the planning commission be sought before action—but the advice need not be followed by the local board or executive officer. In some cases, the planning commission has real authority since the local governing board is not only required to seek its advice, but is also required to follow its recommendation unless it votes by a three-fifths or greater majority vote not to do so.

In general, planning implies something to be done in the future. It seeks to correct or minimize the effects of past mistakes and to avoid them in the future if possible. As such, it is a sizeable undertaking involving an array of professional skills and commitment of time that the commission members are unable to contribute. Thus, in most communities of 25,000 or larger there is a full-time director and planning staff in addition to the planning commission. A full-time resident director and staff usually means that planning is a continuing rather than a periodic process, and this is highly desirable and needed in most communities. When the community is too small or feels it cannot afford a permanent staff, outside specialists are often consulted to assist the planning commission on a contractual or per diem basis. The resident planner usually becomes a major adviser to the policy innovator for the executive officer or governing board to which he is responsible. He also has advantages in seeking and securing public support for the plans he and the commission propose. Too often the work of the consultant is placed on the shelf to collect dust because he is not present to defend and conduct a sales campaign to translate the plan into reality.

The planning director is selected in various ways. He is usually an appointee of the local executive officer or local governing board.

[16] Bassett, *op. cit.*, p. 5.

In communities with the council-manager form, he is usually appointed by the manager, while he is appointed by the commission in commission-governed communities. In some communities, he is appointed by the planning commission itself, and in others the functions of planning officer are assumed by some other local official such as the manager, mayor, engineer, or director of public works.

Reverting again to the proposals of the Model County Charter, it is recommended that the director of planning be appointed by the county manager with the approval of the county board. His recommended powers and duties are to (1) serve as the chief planning officer and regular technical adviser of the manager and board on all planning and related matters, and to direct the activities of the planning staff; (2) coordinate the planning and related activities of the county with similar activities of the municipalities within the county, confer with and advise officials and agencies of such municipalities on planning matters, and cooperate with state, regional and other local planning agencies; (3) maintain an up-to-date file of municipal plans, zoning ordinances, official maps, building codes and subdivision regulations, and amendments to any of them, of municipalities within the county; (4) supply technical planning services to any municipality of the county upon agreement between the affected governing boards; (5) assist the county manager in preparation of the capital program; and (6) perform such other duties and exercise such other powers as the manager or board may establish.[17]

The issue of planning commission versus planning department mentioned earlier is not easily resolved. There is a sharp divergence of opinion on this point, with planners generally preferring the commission arrangement and political scientists and generalist administrators advocating the department of planning. Two classic statements of these positions were presented at the Philadelphia Planning Conference in 1941. Speaking for the administrative school of thought, Donald C. Stone stated:

Perhaps one of the reasons why city planning has not had more influence on community development grows out of its frequent creation as a supergovernmental body which serves as a check upon the responsible city officials rather than as an administrative aid to them. If tangible results are to be secured from planning work, it must be tied into the regu-

[17] National Municipal League, *op. cit.*, Art. VI, Sec. 6.05, p. 37.

PUBLIC SERVICES

lar operating divisions of the city. The submission of peerless proposals and pretty pictures to the city council or chief executive is not enough. The budget, public works, recreation, parks, and other departments must be tied in all along the line, so that proposals are not the planning commission's proposals but rather the city government proposals.[18]

John Nolen, Jr., then serving as Director of Planning, National Capitol Park and Planning Commission, presented the planner's view. In his words:

Planning is the prerogative of the whole community and not that of an individual alone, whether he be appointed administrative official, an elective official, or even a legislator elected for a brief term of office. This fact, more perhaps than the desire to make the planning board independent of politics, was what gave rise to the original planning commission as the desirable form of organization for planning. Nothing that has happened or will happen, so long as our form of government is democratic, will change that reason.[19]

For the reasons advanced by Nolen, the planning commission is preferred over a department of planning in most local communities. However, the question is not purely an academic one. Most state planning agencies have a single director who is appointed by and is responsible to the governor, and it is probable that this administrative arrangement will become more common in local governments in the future. At the conference referred to above, Russell V. Black, a planner, believed this so-called "stream-lined" approach to planning could work when two conditions existed. These were, first, the presence of an unusually competent planning director, and second, the presence of an intelligent and sympathetic administrative body.[20] It is probable that these two conditions now exist in many of our local governments. Certainly planners are better equipped for their positions than they were when engineering and landscape architecture were the core subjects in their training. A sympathetic board is also more commonplace as the skills of the planner have become an indispensable aid to local officials who are concerned with the defects of their communities and attempt to overcome them.

[18] Summary of a session of the planning conference appearing in *The Planners' Journal*, 7 (April-June, 1941), 10-13, reproduced in Kneier and Fox, *op. cit.*, pp. 439-40.
[19] *Ibid.*, p. 441.
[20] *Ibid.*, p. 442.

■ The Comprehensive Plan

As mentioned above, one of the major functions of a local planning commission is to prepare a comprehensive plan to project the future development of the community. Planning must be based upon facts which can be collected and made known, and the collection and assembling of information is the first stage in the development of a comprehensive plan. At this stage, the planning commission usually relies heavily upon professional help. The principal sources of the planning data needed are the community records which provide such information as population, school population, existing land-use patterns, tax rates, bonded indebtedness, capacity of utilities, subdivision regulations, housing, parks, etc. After the data are assembled, they will be used in various ways. Base maps will be prepared showing such things as existing land-use patterns, population densities, age of population, racial composition, and other characteristics of the community and its citizenry.

The second stage of work on the comprehensive plan consists of careful study of the existing patterns within the community. From this study, judgments must be made concerning the adequacy of certain patterns, needed projections in certain areas, and the allocation of space for various types of land use. Economic forces are usually given considerable weight since most communities have an economic reason for their existence. Future plans are intricately related to projected populations which, in turn, are closely dependent on what happens to the community's industrial and commercial growth.

The third stage in the development of the community plan involves the actual preparation of the blueprint for development. This will show recommended uses of private land and the proposed location of all necessary and desirable public facilities. In most communities, the plan as it finally emerges will be a compromise between the recommendations of the professional staff, the sober judgments of the members of the planning commission, and the demands of various interests within the community.

The plan, when completed, will usually consist of a series of maps supplemented by a descriptive report outlining and explaining the principal reasons for the plan and its component elements. In many communities, the comprehensive plan is given the force of law upon its approval by the governing body. It is a flexible "law," however, since before some of its proposals can be realized community conditions will change, requiring modifications in the plan.

Thus, the development of the comprehensive plan, like planning itself, is a continuing process. The plan must be subject to change but changes should be approved only after the same careful study that went into the preparation of the plan itself. Because of the recognized need for flexibility, many communities never adopt the comprehensive plan formally as a single document but the governing board adopts its various features when they can be implemented. This method has the advantage of not requiring formal action of the governing board if any changes must be made subsequent to its adoption.

It is obvious that the comprehensive plan cannot remake most communities—it can only make adjustments. The existing situation of the community must be accepted and changes can be made only slowly and against community inertia and the resistance of vested interests. But changes can be made, as evidenced by the many communities which have slowly transformed themselves into more desirable places for residents, commercial enterprises, and industries through harmonious development of public and private land uses.

To implement the community plan, most local governments are forced to acquire considerable amounts of land for public uses. Use of foresight through planning and proper legal devices can save the community considerable sums of money. Some property is acquired by outright gift, but such gifts come infrequently and often do not occur at the time of most need. Other property is obtained through dedication or the giving of property for a specified use. A common source of dedicated property comes in subdivision development. The developer is normally required to lay out strips of land for street purposes and may be required to set aside land for park or school use. Such lands are then given to the community for the stated public use.

Most of the land which the local government requires for public use, however, is acquired through purchase. Normally, the community and the owner of the land can agree on a reasonable purchase price for his property. When agreement cannot be reached, the local government has the power of eminent domain under which it can take property for a public use upon payment of fair compensation. The proceedings can be settled in court if the landowner refuses to sell or demands an unreasonable price. It is obvious that the use of eminent domain before the construction of private buildings on the needed property is less costly to the community than its exercise subsequent to such construction.

■ Regional Planning

While considerable progress has been made in local planning, there is a growing awareness of the limitations of planning on small-area basis. This limitation is especially obvious in metropolitan areas where to most people the physical division between local governments means only the inevitable sign reading "city limits." However, even for a community separated from others, regional planning is logical and beneficial. Such a community is usually a center of an economic area and the system of streets and highways leading to and from it require coordination beyond its own boundaries.

In addition to highways, planning for the location of parks and recreation facilities, utilities, industrial areas, and a number of other urban matters is more logically approached on a regional rather than on an individual community basis. To fill the gap between the need for regional planning and its political practicality, a number of cooperative planning commissions, groups and agencies have been established in recent years. In some states, such joint planning efforts are encouraged through the passage of enabling legislation. In other communities, such agencies are private and unofficial and may be composed primarily of businessmen. When such agencies are public, they are usually composed of representatives of the local governments in the region.

Metropolitan or regional planning has been variously defined. According to one authority:

Metropolitan planning is properly a process for designing the spatial arrangements of activity-engaged populations within metropolitan space and, in turn, for making rational decisions that will lead development in the direction of the design-goal. These spatial goals must of course reflect, and in turn help to attain, certain higher-order, nonspatial goals concerned with the qualities of urban life that are sought. A metropolitan plan reflects these goals, but it is a plan for the spatial organization of the metropolitan area's people and activities. This is to say, it is a plan for the qualities of "cityness" that are sought in the long-range future.[21]

The major functions of metropolitan planning according to Webber are to help communities within the area (1) identify their many competing wants; (2) understand the compatibilities and the incompatibilities among these wants and between these wants and resources; (3) identify and then examine the alternative, internally consistent sets of goals that fall within the range of choice; (4) gain agreement upon one internally consistent set of long-, middle-, and short-range goals for the qualities of living and working environments; and (5) develop courses of action whereby the community's resources can be rationally and economically allocated to best achieve the deliberately selected goals.[22]

While some progress has been made in regional planning, such joint or cooperative agencies usually have only advisory powers. Their recommendations are followed only if they are acceptable to and approved by the participating local governments. Too often, of course, one or more of the member communities are unwilling to accept the recommended plans and they are never carried out. While noting the American preference to plan on a small-area basis, one planner has commented that "if piecemeal planning is to be the rule, it is evident that the pieces are getting bigger and that a larger variety of factors are being taken into accord than ever before."[23]

■ Land-Use Controls

The police power of local governments permits them to regulate and limit the use of private property when it is necessary for the "public health, safety, welfare, or morals" of the community. The use of this power does not require compensation to property owners since their property is not taken for public use as in the exercise of eminent domain. Thus, the police power of the community is

[21] Remarks of Melvin M. Webber, Department of City and Regional Planning, University of California, Berkeley, as reported in Stanley Scott (ed.), *Metropolitan Area Problems*, Report of the Pacific Coast Conference on Metropolitan Problems, University of California, Berkeley, 1960, p. 134.

[22] *Ibid.*, pp. 152–3.

[23] Richard L. Meier, "Systems and Principles for Metropolitan Planning," *Centennial Review, 3* (Winter, 1959), 79–94.

the means by which private property use is controlled in local planning. Three primary means of such controls are zoning regulations, subdivision regulations, and building codes.

BUILDING CODES

Briefly defined, a building code is a legislative set of principles for administrative guidance in regulating original construction and improvements. The code provides for minimum standards of building construction and condition and for human occupancy, and concerns such factors as lighting, ventilation, heating, sanitation, plumbing, electrical work, types of building materials, fire prevention, and protection. While smaller cities may have a single code setting standards in each of these areas, larger cities usually publish sections of their building codes as separate documents. For instance, the sanitary code in a large community might well run to several hundred pages in length. It would cover a variety of commercial businesses such as bakeries, barbershops, drugstores; hospitals; hotels; and it would also regulate noises, nuisances, and morals.

Building codes are not a recent development in most cities. They have been utilized for enforcement of subdivision and zoning regulations and to attain desired housing standards by requiring permits to build, renovate, or install equipment. Building codes in some communities seem excessively restrictive and require materials of a quality beyond what is reasonably adequate, resulting in high building costs. More often, such codes lag somewhat behind in the times. In communities with outdated codes, they permit construction of substandard housing and/or the conversion of old homes into apartments which are inadequate for accepted standards of human living. Other codes fail to allow modern building techniques because they are not kept up to date.

In addition to the requirement of the building permit, most building codes provide for inspection of the premises to determine whether or not standards are being met. According to Webster, the building inspector "can destroy the effectiveness of the code by overlooking violations or permitting exceptions to the regulations. The integrity of such officer is, therefore, most essential."[24] The serious effects of inadequate building codes and ineffective enforce-

[24] Webster, *op. cit.*, p. 424.

ment procedures are ameliorated to some extent for the individual home purchaser by regulations established by the Federal Housing Authority for housing in which financing is insured by this agency. However, as more local governments recognize that the reputation, as well as the physical appearance, of their communities depend in large part on the provisions and enforcement of their building codes, we can expect stricter codes and more careful enforcement.

SUBDIVISION REGULATIONS

The necessity for control over subdivision development if the community plan is to be realized is now obvious. However, this need was learned from bitter experience in too many communities. The tremendous expansion into the countryside around almost every sizable city has resulted in the parceling of the once open land into lots for homes. Much of the expansion was unplanned and un-regulated because of the profit motive of real estate and other private interests. In some cases, developers did not even provide such necessities as streets, water supply, or adequate sewerage fa-cilities. Homeowners in such subdivisions found themselves unable to finance the necessary improvements on these properties. The ad-justments often proved costly and inconvenient to the community and citizens of the subdivision alike.

With subdivision control, communities can prevent the develop-ment of land without provision for necessary services. The laying out of subdivisions is regulated through the power of the local government to withhold the privilege of recording plats that do not meet required standards or do not have official approval. If the plat is not recorded, lots within it are sometimes more difficult to sell. They cannot be sold by lot number but only by "metes and bounds" descriptions of their boundary lines. Since the danger of future title disputes may be greater than with recorded plats, such unapproved and unrecorded homesteads may be less attractive to would-be purchasers.

State enabling acts granting local governments the right to regu-late land subdivisions generally give this power directly to local planning boards or permit local governing bodies to delegate this function to them. The conditions which the planning commission re-quires before granting approval to have the plat recorded are those which will prevent the property from becoming a liability to the community and purchaser alike. In general, the layout and width of streets, length and depth of blocks, width and depth of lots, provision for open space, and the provision of water and sewerage are the conditions checked.[25]

The typical procedure begins with the filing by the subdivider of a preliminary plan for his proposed development with the local planning commission. Normally, the subdivider will have obtained a copy of the platting regulations of the community before he submits his proposal. The planning agency reviews the plans and they are also checked by other city officials for compliance with pertinent regulations. Then abutting property owners are given an opportunity to discuss the development at hearings held by the planning commission. At this point, the subdivider is given preliminary approval and the proper permits are issued by the building officers when he is ready to begin construction.

In many communities, acceptance of subdivisions is a county function. The board which has this power of approval may be limited by law to accepting only those subdivision plans which meet prescribed standards and the specific approval of the planning authority, where one exists. This approval is a rough equivalent to a building permit. Problems occasionally arise when the subdivision is outside a municipality and in the eyes of the municipality, county controls are inadequate. Some states have granted cities extraterritorial powers over subdivisions built within adjacent areas with the extent of this grant commonly ranging from three to seven miles.

ZONING

Zoning is a form of governmental regulation providing for the orderly social and economic development of a community. According to Alderfer, zoning is "the division of the community into districts for the purpose of regulating the use of the land and buildings in each district in accordance with the desired character of the district, for the purpose of regulating the height and bulk of

[25] For more extensive readings on subdivision control, see H. W. Lautner, *Subdivision Regulations*, Public Administration Service, 1941; P. H. Cornick, *Premature Subdivision and Its Consequences*, Institute of Public Administration, Columbia University, 1938; Institute for Training in Municipal Administration, *op. cit.*, Chap. XII; and National Housing Agency, *A Check List for the Review of Local Subdivision Controls*, Government Printing Office, 1947.

buildings, the proportion of the lot that can be covered by them, and the density of population."[26] The close relation of zoning to planning was noted by the Metropolitan Housing Council of Chicago in these words, "In discussing problems of zoning, it is essential not to lose sight of the fact that zoning is not an end in itself, but a means of arriving at a systematic and economical pattern of land use as a part of planning for the entire city."[27]

Although there are early examples of the use of restricted zones in American communities, there was little progress in zoning until the enactment of a New York City ordinance in 1916. It was feared that the construction of a new transit system might further intensify the congestion it was intended to relieve, and committees studied the practicality of regulating the height and area and the use of buildings under the police power of the state.[28] Now zoning is one of the major means by which private land use is integrated into the overall community plan.[29]

To ensure the efficient use of land and achieve the goals of the comprehensive plan, the community is normally divided into subcategories of residential, commercial, and industrial zones. Residential districts may include zones for single-family residences, two-family residences, four-family residences, and multi-family or apartment residences. Commercial districts are of two types—the central business district and neighborhood shopping centers. Typical divisions for industrial zones are those for light industry, heavy industry, and unrestricted districts. Most communities do not permit a lower use in a zoning district, but will permit a higher use in a lower zoned area. For instance, no plural family residences would be allowed in an area zoned for single-family homes, but the latter would be permitted in areas zoned for plural-family residences.

Zoning on the basis of use is one of the principle types of land-use regulations. A second type restricts the height of buildings in relation to the width of the street, size of side yards, and the use to which the area is put. The single-family residential districts are

[26] Alderfer, *op. cit.*, p. 608.

[27] Metropolitan Housing Council, *Zoning and Zoning Administration in Chicago*, 1938, p. 15.

[28] Edward M. Bassett, *Zoning*, Russell Sage Foundation, 1936, pp. 23–26.

[29] The validity of use of police power for zoning was upheld by the United States Supreme Court in 1926 in *Village of Euclid* v. *Ambler Realty Co.*, 272 U.S. 365. The Court held, however, that the reasonableness of a particular zoning ordinance is always open to question.

the most restricted zones in terms of height. Height limitations are sometimes expressed in terms of stories or in maximum number of feet. Apartment house and commercial zones usually have the least restrictive height limitations.

A third type of zoning restriction limits the amount of the lot area than can be occupied with the amount varying by type of district. This requirement specifies the building line as a prescribed number of feet back from both the front and rear of the lot as well as from its side lines. Area regulations also include such factors as maximum permitted density of population, the percentage of the lot that may be built upon, the minimum size of courts, and provision of garage and parking areas.

THE ZONING ORDINANCE

The zoning ordinance, of course, includes regulations other than those pertaining to land-use restrictions. A good zoning ordinance can be prepared only after careful and painstaking study and cannot be lifted from sections of laws of other communities. The ordinance is usually complemented by the preparation of a zoning map marking out the lines of the several types of use districts. In addition to protecting property values, the zoning ordinance can also ensure the accessibility to all property and the availability of adequate light and air to protect public health and minimize fire hazards.

Following its adoption, the zoning ordinance is enforced by the building commissioner, engineer, manager, or other local official responsible for issuing building permits. Appeals against the administration of the ordinance are taken to the planning commission or to the board of zoning appeals or adjustment. The three major functions of the appeal agency are (1) to hear appeals alleging error of the administrative officer in enforcing the ordinance; (2) to pass on exceptional cases as required in the basic ordinance; and (3) to grant departures or variations from the strict letter of the law if enforcement would cause a needless hardship.

Members of the board of zoning appeals are usually appointed by the local executive officer with the approval of the local governing body, but as mentioned above the planning commission serves *ex officio* as the zoning board in some communities. The principal device for the implementation of the community plan is lost unless the zoning board exercises its authority free from favoritism and undue political pressures. The possible application of politics to zoning was clearly stated by a chief engineer of the Chicago Planning Commission in these words: "The administration of the zoning ordinance is an almost continuous matter of fighting favors. A strong buffer committee is greatly needed. No variance of any consequence would ever get by without political backing."[30] This statement is perhaps too strong, since there may be carefully considered reasons for granting variances. For example, the possible loss of an industry may result in the approval of a variance on the theory that the gain to the community outweighs the loss in value of adjacent properties.

NON-CONFORMING USES

While courts have sustained retroactive exclusion of nuisances from certain types of zoned districts, it is not probable that exclusion of non-nuisance uses would be upheld. The usual plan in communities is to allow for non-conforming uses—a term applied to uses contrary to the zoning ordinance which were established prior to the enactment of the zoning law itself. Examples of such uses are the existence of a corner filling station in a residential district or a fraternity house in a district zoned for single-family residences.

The generally accepted method for handling the problem of non-conforming uses is to allow such use to be continued subject to certain limitations. The usual restrictions include prohibitions against enlargement of the non-conforming use, repair of structure up to a stated percentage of its value if it is destroyed or damaged, and renewal of non-conforming use after discontinuance for a stated period of time. While it was anticipated that non-conforming uses would gradually die out and remove the problem, experience has not been too satisfactory in this regard. In some communities, quite the reverse has actually occurred through the granting of use variances which permit the establishment of new non-conforming uses. According to Walker, "The problem of city planning is no longer primarily one of guiding growth; it is a matter of replanning

[30] Hugh E. Young, "Need for and Some Practical Methods of Rezoning Urban Areas," address before City Planning Division, American Society of Civil Engineers, New York City, January 21, 1937, p. 4.

areas already built up."[31] He views the gradual elimination of non-conforming uses as the "logical next step."

A relatively recent approach to the problem of eliminating such uses is to establish a policy for their abandonment over variable periods of time. This allows the private detriment to be amortized over a period of time resulting in less hardship on the property owner. For example, the period of amortization for a "five-and-dime variety" store in a residential district might well be relatively short, since such stores anticipate a fairly rapid turnover of merchandise. On the other hand, the amortization period might be considerably longer for other types of commercial uses which experience slower rates of merchandise turnover. The period of amortization might well also relate to the nature of the structure housing the non-conforming use. The period of time could be considerably shorter for a non-conforming commercial use in a residential building—say a dental office or beauty salon in rooms of a private home—than for a similar use in a building constructed for that purpose.[32]

There is reason to believe that amortization policies hold real promise for the future elimination of non-conforming uses. One clear statement of this view holds that, "Amortization of non-conforming uses is fair. The useful life of the building or use to which the premises are devoted is determined and the owner has that length of time to conform. The loss he suffers, if any, is spread out over a period of years, and he further enjoys a monopolistic position by virtue of the zoning ordinance as long as he remains."[33]

Houston, Texas, is the only major city in the United States that does not have a zoning ordinance. At the present time, there are still no laws in Houston preventing the owner of a large house from converting it into several apartments in a neighborhood with only single-family residences. Similarly, a filling station could be located on the corner lot of a residential neighborhood and a barber could open a shop in his home, complete with the traditional whirling barbershop sign near the front door. Interestingly enough, Houston has seven small suburban communities that incorporated, at least in part, so they could adopt and enforce zoning ordinances within their own areas.

---

[31] Walker, op. cit., p. 103.

[32] See University of Chicago Law Review, "Amortization of Property Uses Not Conforming to Zoning Regulations," 9 (1942), 477; and Virginia Law Review, "Elimination of Non-conforming Use," 35 (1949), 348.

[33] Virginia Law Review, loc. cit.

As an exercise of the police power, zoning should be used to further the general welfare of the community. When used properly, it can remedy some of the mistakes of the past as well as control private land use in the interest of the community. Attempts have been made in some local governments, however, to obtain ends through zoning which are not compatible with a proper exercise of the police power. One misuse of zoning is to exclude undesirable but necessary uses from the community. Garbage disposal plants, sewage disposal plants, laundries and dry-cleaning establishments may have disagreeable effects on abutting properties, but they are essential services in most urban areas.

A more serious misuse of zoning occurred in communities which once attempted to achieve racial segregation through the exercise of police power. The technique used was to establish certain residential zones within which certain racial groups would be forbidden to settle. Ordinances to this effect have been held an unconstitutional limitation upon property rights under the Fourteenth Amendment and as an unreasonable exercise of the police power.[34] Attempts by subdividers to place restrictive covenants in deeds whereby the purchaser would agree never to sell certain racial groups have been fairly inoperative since 1948. In that year, the Supreme Court held that such agreements are not enforceable in state courts when the parties to the transaction are willing buyers and sellers.[35]

In addition to racial zoning, some communities have been overly enthusiastic in their efforts to protect property owners from depreciation of the value of their homes by the construction of "cheaper" houses in the immediate neighborhood. Such efforts are sometimes known as "snob" zoning, and their protective regulations have imposed minimum building costs, minimum floor area or cubic content of homes, and minimum lot sizes. Zoning on the basis of cost has not received court approval and courts are in disagreement as to the legality of minimum floor area and lot size restrictions. The general test that the court imposes is the reason-

[34] *Buchanan* v. *Warley*, 245 U.S. 60 (1917) and *Harmon* v. *Tyler*, 273 U.S. 668 (1927). Zoning specifications on these scores should not be confused with "covenants running with the land" that are written into the deeds by property owners whose land is converted from rural acreage to city lots.
[35] *Shelley* v. *Kraemer*, 334 U.S. 1 (1948).

ableness of such restrictions in relation to health, safety, and general welfare. As long as the minimum requirements in measures of floor size and lot size are reasonable, courts will probably be more responsive in approving them.

A further question on which courts have not agreed relates to restrictions on the use of property on aesthetic grounds. The Supreme Court indicated qualified approval of the use of police power for aesthetic reasons in a 1954 decision by stating, "The concept of the public welfare is broad and inclusive. The values it represents are spiritual as well as physical, aesthetic as well as monetary. It is within the power of the legislature to determine that the community should be beautiful as well as healthy, spacious as well as clean, well-balanced as well as carefully patrolled."[36]

The possible undesired aspects of extending aesthetic zoning, however, have been pointed out by Mackesey. In his words:

> The extension of zoning powers so that provisions for control over the appearance of buildings may be written into the ordinance cannot be recommended unreservedly in this country. What is needed is an expansion of the powers of zoning so that the protection of spots of scenic interest and beauty and of historic significance may be accomplished under the police power on the basis of promotion of the public welfare, without resort to the usual subterfuge of trying to find some justification on the grounds of promotion of health, safety, and morals. The improvement of architecture can perhaps best be brought about by education and cooperation rather than by ordinance. . . .[37]

REGIONAL ZONING

In zoning, as in planning, there has been considerable progress in individual communities and a growing awareness of the desirability of zoning on a larger areal basis. The need is especially great in metropolitan areas. The desirability of the regional approach in industrial zoning has been stated in one study as, "the economy of the metropolitan area represents a sum of interrelated parts, so the best results in industrial zoning can be achieved when undertaken on a metropolitan basis. The zoning plan should extend across corporate limits whether by extraterritorial powers available

---

[36] *Berman* v. *Parker,* 348 U.S. 26 (1954).
[37] Thomas W. Mackesey, "Aesthetics and Zoning," *The Planners' Journal,* 5 (October–December, 1939), 98.

to the municipalities or by close coordination between municipalities or other political subdivisions."[38]

The political practicality of zoning beyond the confines of a single community received a considerable assist in a 1954 decision of the Supreme Court of New Jersey. This court held that the view that the responsibility of a municipality halted at the boundary lines "cannot be tolerated where as here the area is built up and one cannot tell when one is passing from one borough to another. . . . At the very least Dumont owes a duty to hear any residents and taxpayers of adjoining municipalities who may be adversely affected by proposed zoning changes and to give as much consideration to their rights as they would to those of residents and taxpayers of Dumont. To do less would be to make a fetish out of invisible boundary lines and a mockery of the principles of zoning."[39] The implementation of the obvious need for inter-local cooperation, however, is difficult to achieve.

SUGGESTED READINGS

Books

Bassett, Edward M., *The Master Plan* (New York: Russell Sage Foundation, 1938).

Black, Russell V., *Planning for the Small American City* (Chicago: Public Administrative Service, 1944).

Caplow, Theodore (ed.), *City Planning: A Selection of Readings in its Theory and Practice* (Minneapolis: Burgess, 1950).

Institute for Training in Municipal Administration, *Local Planning Administration*, 2nd ed. (Chicago: International City Managers' Association, 1948).

Lautner, H. W., *Subdivision Regulations* (Chicago: Public Administration Service, 1941).

Miller, Harold V., *Mr. Planning Commissioner* (Chicago: Public Administration Service, 1954).

National Housing Agency, *A Check List for the Review of Local Subdivision Controls* (Washington: Government Printing Office, 1947).

Perloff, Harvey S. (ed.), *Planning and the Urban Community* (Pittsburgh: University of Pittsburgh Press, 1961).

[38] National Industrial Zoning Committee, *Principles of Industrial Zoning*, 1951, as cited in Charles M. Kneier, *City Government in the United States*, 3rd ed., Harper, 1957, p. 580.

[39] *Borough of Cresskill* v. *Borough of Dumont*, 15 N. J. 247, 104 A. 2nd 445 (1954).

Tunnard, Christopher and Reed, Henry G., *American Skyline, The Growth and Form of Our Cities and Towns* (New York: The New American Library, 1956).

Walker, Robert A., *The Planning Function in Urban Government,* 2nd ed. (Chicago: University of Chicago Press, 1950).

Webster, Donald H., *Urban Planning and Municipal Public Policy* (New York: Harper, 1958).

Yokley, E. C., *Zoning Law and Practice,* 2nd ed. (Charlottesville, Va.: Michie Co., 1953).

Articles

Clay, Grady, "Needed: Critics of City Planning," *Urban Renewal, A Nieman Seminar,* Supplement to Nieman Reports (October, 1960), pp. 12–16.

"Flexible Zoning Controls," *Horizons for Modern Pennsylvania Governments,* 7 (June, 1960), 1–2, 4.

Mackesey, Thomas W., "Aesthetics and Zoning," *The Planners' Journal,* 5 (October–December, 1939), 95–98.

Meier, Richard L., "Systems and Principles for Metropolitan Planning," *Centennial Review,* 3 (Winter, 1959), 79–94.

Meyerson, Martin, "How to Bring Planning and Policy Together" in Edward C. Banfield (ed.), *Urban Government, A Reader in Administration and Politics* (New York: Free Press, 1961), pp. 488–97.

"Amortization of Property Uses Not Conforming to Zoning Regulations," *University of Chicago Law Review,* 9 (1942), 477.

Whyte, William H., Jr., "A Plan to Save Vanishing U. S. Countryside," *Life,* 47 (August 17, 1959), 88–102.

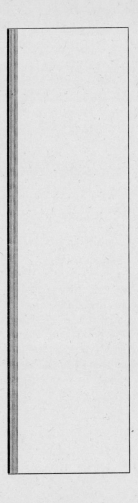

METROPOLITAN AREAS

Seven

Rise and Growth of
Metropolitan Areas

24

The continuing urbanization of American society was noted in Chapter 10 as one of the most significant and spectacular population trends of our history. In the period of 170 years stretching from 1790 to 1960, we have grown from a nation with only 5.1 percent of its population living in urban communities to one with 69.9 percent classified as urban residents.

Americans seemed hesitant to recognize and accept the fact that their nation had changed from a rural to an urban one. According to one author, "It took a host of things to convince Americans that they were to be a nation of urbanites. One of these was that wherever they went, the city caught up with them: Farmland became exurbia; exurbia became suburbia; and suburbia became part of the metropolitan area. Another factor was the imperialism of urban culture. . . ."[1]

Most of the change, as Ylvisaker sees it, was accomplished by a single statistic repeated time and time again in the period between 1955 and 1960. This statistic, the origin of which is obscure and

[1] Paul N. Ylvisaker, "Innovation and Evolution: Bridge to the Future of Metropolis," *The Annals of the American Academy of Political and Social Science,* *314* (November, 1957), 156.

which was probably compiled by some anonymous census tabulator merely doing his duty, was that some 60 million would be added to the American population in the next 20 years and that almost all of them would live in and around the major cities. Thus, to Ylvisaker, "A shot fired at Lexington convinced a band of villagers that they were to be a great nation. Some bombs at Pearl Harbor brought that nation face to face with its destiny as a great power. A statistic awoke that power to the fact that it had become a nation of great cities."[2]

While the statistic cited above may have convinced us, it could hardly have awakened us to the fact of our increasing urban character. America has experienced three great changes in its living patterns within the span of the last century. The shift from a predominately rural to an urban society was accomplished by 1930, when 56 percent of our population lived in urban communities. Since 1930, the second change, a shift from an urban to a metropolitan society has occurred. In 1930, 49.7 percent of us resided in metropolitan areas while the percentage had risen to 62.9 percent by 1960. The trend of growth in metropolitan areas since 1900 is shown in Figure 26.

The third shift has been occurring since 1940. This change is recasting us as a suburban rather than a metropolitan society. In 1940, 38.2 percent of the population of metropolitan areas lived outside the central cities. But in the decade from 1940 to 1950, the rate of population growth in the suburban communities was nearly two and a half times as large as the rate of center city growth. Between 1950 and 1960, the suburban ring experienced an increase of 48.6 percent in contrast to a 10.7 percent growth for center cities. Territory added to center cities by annexation actually accounted for most of their population growth. Such annexations added 5.6 of the 6.4 million increase experienced by the core cities.[3] Thus, by 1960, the suburban ring contained nearly half, 48.9 percent, of metropolitan area population. One careful estimate projects that to a little over 57 percent by 1975.[4]

According to Adrian, "The postwar rush to the suburbs ranks in American history with the move across the Appalachians, and the

[2] *Ibid.*, pp. 156–7.

[3] Advisory Commission on Intergovernmental Relations, *Governmental Structure, Organization, and Planning in Metropolitan Areas*, Government Printing Office, 1961, p. 6.

[4] Committee for Economic Development, *Guiding Metropolitan Growth*, 1960, p. 47.

METROPOLITAN AREAS

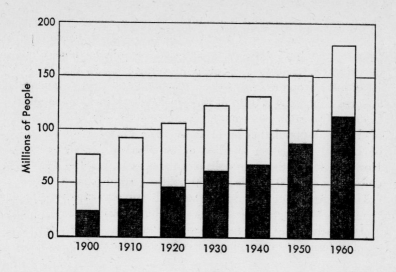

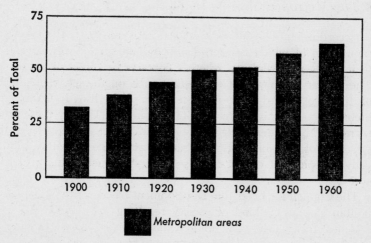

Metropolitan areas

Figure 26. *Population Growth in the United States and in Metro-politan Areas: 1900–1960.* (Figures for 1900–1950: Committee for Economic Development, *Guiding Metropolitan Growth*, New York, August, 1960, p. 46; 1960: U.S. Bureau of the Census, *Statistical Abstract of the United States, 1963*, Washington, 1963, pp. 9, 13.)

later migrations to Oregon, Utah, and California, as one of the great mass migrations of a historically restless people."[5] Actually the

[5] Charles R. Adrian, *State and Local Governments, A Study in the Political Process*, McGraw-Hill, 1960, p. 234.

movement of persons to the suburbs is not a recent phenomenon. Philadelphia was the first American city to have a pattern of independent suburban communities. Instead of Philadelphia growing as expected, clusters of population formed along the Delaware River just beyond the established limits of the city. Four contiguous suburbs containing a third of the population of the area existed by 1790, and six suburban communities contained some three-sevenths of the area's population by 1810. By 1850, Philadelphia was a city of 121,000 population huddled in an area of two square miles. However, it was the metropolis of an area of some 140 square miles embracing 422,000 people and 30 political subdivisions.[6]

These few statistical highlights indicate the rapidly growing significance of metropolitan areas on the American scene. It now appears advisable to define metropolitan areas before discussing them in terms of geographical distribution, size, and type.

▣ The Metropolitan Area Defined

According to Hawley, a community is an "area, the resident population of which is interrelated and integrated with reference to its daily requirements, whether contacts be direct or indirect."[7] The primary emphasis of this definition is on the interdependence of the people and their institutions in daily life. In effect, the metropolitan area is a new type of community. Usually these areas surround an old and congested city and are characterized by the existence of a number of suburban governments which are politically independent of but have social and economic ties with the core city.

The Council for Economic Development has described the metropolitan area as "a kind of society resulting from higher average incomes, the development of new tastes in living standards, and technological means for releasing people from the old patterns. . . . Its boundaries often are hard to define. In some instances they change and expand frequently. The area ignores old geographic boundaries, jumping over and around rivers and land masses. It

[6] Stephen B. Sweeney and George S. Blair (eds.), *Metropolitan Analysis, Important Elements of Study and Action*, University of Pennsylvania Press, 1958, pp. 81–82.

[7] Amos Hawley, *Human Ecology: A Theory of Community Structure*, Ronald, 1950, pp. 257–8.

ignores the political lines of districts, villages, towns, cities, counties and states."[8]

While there are many colorful descriptive definitions of a metropolitan area, a meaningful operational definition is more difficult to come by. The one most common today is the one established by the United States Bureau of the Budget and followed by the Bureau of the Census in its compilation of data. More fully, these areas are known as "standard metropolitan statistical areas," and such an area is defined as "a county or group of contiguous counties which contain at least one city of 50,000 inhabitants or more or 'twin cities' with a combined population of at least 50,000. In addition to the county or counties containing such a city or cities, contiguous counties are included in an SMSA, if according to certain criteria, they are essentially metropolitan in character and are socially and economically integrated with the central city."[9]

The criteria of metropolitan character, referred to above, relate primarily to the attributes of the county as a place of work or as a home for its non-agricultural workers. Specifically, the criteria are:

3. At least 75% of the labor force of the county must be in the non-agricultural labor force.
4. In addition to criterion 3, the county must meet at least one of the following conditions:
    (a) It must have 50% or more of its population living in contiguous minor civil divisions with a density of at least 150 persons per square mile, in an unbroken chain of minor civil divisions with such density radiating from a central city in the area.
    (b) The number of nonagricultural workers employed in the county must equal at least 10% of the number of nonagricultural workers employed in the county containing the largest city in the area, or be the place of employment of 10,000 nonagricultural workers.
    (c) The nonagricultural labor force living in the county must equal at least 10% of the number of the nonagricultural labor force living in the county containing the largest city in the area, or be the place of residence of a nonagricultural labor force of 10,000.
5. In New England . . . towns and cities are the units used in defining standard metropolitan statistical areas. In New England, because

[8] Council for Economic Development, op. cit., p. 13.
[9] Bureau of the Census, "Population of Standard Metropolitan Statistical Areas: 1960 and 1950," PC(SI)-1, April, 1961, p. 4.

smaller units are used and more restricted areas result, a population density criterion of at least 100 persons per square mile is used as the measure of metropolitan character.

6. A county is regarded as integrated with the county or counties containing the central cities of the area if either of the following criteria is met:

    (a) If 15% of the workers living in the county work in the county or counties containing central cities of the area, or

    (b) If 25% of those working in the county live in the county or counties containing central cities of the area.

Only where data for criteria 6(a) and 6(b) are not conclusive are other related types of information used as necessary. This information includes such items as average telephone calls per subscriber per month from the county to the county containing central cities of the area; per cent of the population in the county located in the central city telephone exchange area; newspaper circulation reports prepared by the Audit Bureau of Circulation; analysis of charge accounts in retail stores of central cities to determine the extent of their use by residents of the contiguous county; delivery service practices of retail stores in central cities; official traffic counts; the extent of public transportation facilities in operation between central cities and communities in the contiguous county; and the extent to which local planning groups and other civic organizations operate jointly.[10]

In 1950, 168 urban communities met these criteria and were designated as standard metropolitan statistical areas, while 212 such areas were recognized in 1960. The name of the metropolitan area is that of its principal and largest city. However, up to two additional city names may appear in the area title if they have a population of at least 250,000 inhabitants, or if they have a population of at least one-third of that of the largest city and a minimum population of 25,000. In addition to city names, the name of the state or states included in the area are also included as a part of the official name of the standard metropolitan statistical area.[11]

The reader burdened with these statistics can readily appreciate that tools used by the Bureau of the Census, and found useful for its purposes, may seem to others to obscure the proportions of the metropolitan problem by tendering 212 subjects of such varying size for analysis. Many writers tend to segregate a relatively few

[10] *Ibid.*

[11] For the sake of brevity, standard metropolitan statistical areas will hereafter be referred to more simply as SMSAs or as metropolitan areas.

METROPOLITAN AREAS

of the metropolitan areas—those in which the problems of local government in a densely populated community are most complex—for their concern and analysis. The sections which follow will approach metropolitan areas from a number of variant bases of analysis in an attempt to show what they are in a true sense by looking at them in terms of geographical distribution, population size, and areal composition.

■ Distribution of Metropolitan Areas

The 212 SMSAs recognized in 1960 are distributed in an irregular geographical pattern among 46 of the 50 American states, with only Alaska, Idaho, Vermont and Wyoming having none. Their geographical location is depicted in Figure 27 which reveals a heavy concentration along the Atlantic seaboard from Haverhill, north of Boston, to Norfolk, Virginia. This eastern seaboard region has been described as one continuing metropolitan community with the descriptive title of "megalopolis."[12]

Texas with 21 has the largest number of metropolitan areas but each of the five states of California, Massachusetts, Michigan, Ohio, and Pennsylvania has 10 or more. On the other hand, Delaware, Hawaii, Maryland, Mississippi, New Hampshire, North Dakota, Rhode Island, and South Dakota have only one apiece. The District of Columbia is also listed in this table since Washington, our capital city, meets the criteria to qualify as an SMSA.

In Figure 28 the states are shown in terms of the proportion of all their inhabitants who lived within metropolitan areas in 1960. California was the most "metropolitan" of our states, with 86.5 percent of its people residing in its 10 SMSAs. In 10 states, at least three of every four citizens resided in metropolitan areas, and in 16 others at least half did so. In general, states with one or two SMSAs are at the lower end of the table, but Hawaii and Delaware are important exceptions. Over 79 and nearly 70 percent of their total populations reside in the Honolulu and Wilmington metropolitan areas respectively. On the other hand, North Carolina has six metropolitan areas but a little under 25 percent of its total population resides in them.

[12] Jean Gottmann, *Megalopolis: The Urbanized Northeastern Seaboard of the United States,* Twentieth Century Fund, 1961.

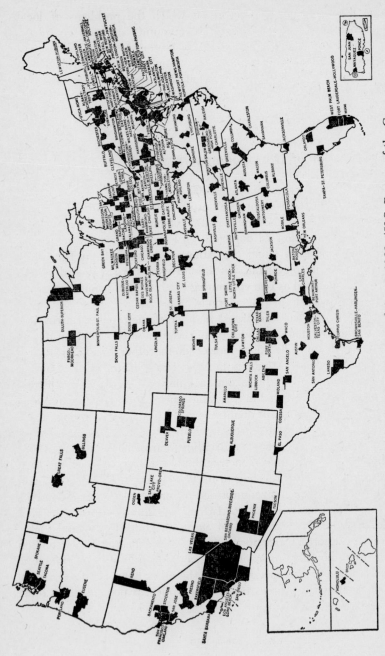

Figure 27. *Standard Metropolitan Statistical Areas: 1960.* (U.S. Bureau of the Census, *Population 1960, U.S. Summary, Washington, 1960, p. S-6.)

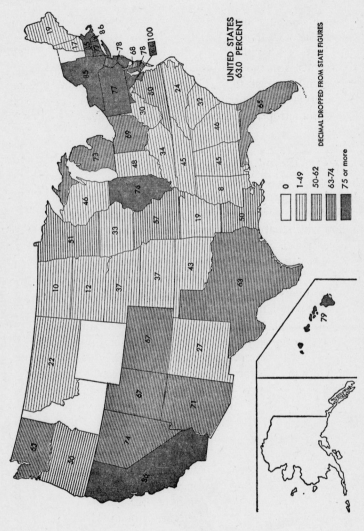

Figure 28. *Percent of State Inhabitants in Metropolitan Areas: 1960.* (U.S. Bureau of the Census, *Population 1960, U.S. Summary*, Washington, 1960, p. S-29.)

Another view of the metropolitan character of our nation can be shown by a regional analysis. In three of the four broad geographic regions of the United States, 60 percent or more of the total population is found within metropolitan areas. Only in the southern region are more people found outside than within the SMSAs, but even here the spread is narrowing rapidly and was only 2.1 million in a total regional population of nearly 55 million in 1960. The metropolitan areas in the South had a 36.2 percent increase in the last decade, in contrast to a 2.7 percent increase outside these areas. Population increase outside metropolitan areas exceeded the growth within metropolitan areas only in the Northeast region.

■ Size of Metropolitan Areas

Among the 212 metropolitan areas, there is a tremendous range in size. As the two extremes, New York has a population of over 10.5 million while that of Meriden, Connecticut, is less than 52,000. In 1960 twenty-four SMSAs had populations exceeding one million, while 22 areas were under 100,000. Slightly more than half—109 of the 212 areas—have populations between 100,000 and 300,000.

Table 22 presents comparative information on the 24 largest areas including their population increase in the past decade, and the rates of population change in both core cities and suburban areas.

While all of the areas showed an increase in total population, the rate of growth varied from 85.5 percent in San Diego to 7.4 percent in Boston. Only nine of the 24 core cities experienced a population increase between 1950 and 1960, and, except for Los Angeles, these were the smaller of these large SMSAs. The population of the core city in 15 metropolitan areas actually decreased in the past decade with Boston and St. Louis losing one of every eight citizens. Suburban rings around each of the 24 core cities showed sizable gains with eight increasing over 70 percent. Suburban gains were smaller than core city gains only in Houston, Dallas and Atlanta.

The population of all but eight of the 212 SMSAs increased in the past decade. Increases in both core city and suburban ring populations occurred in 128 metropolitan areas. In 24 areas, the total population and the population of the core city increased, but the population of the suburban ring decreased. In most cases, the suburban decrease resulted from annexation of territory to the

METROPOLITAN AREAS

Table 22. *Comparative Population Data for Twenty-four SMSAs*

Metropolitan Area	Total Population	Percent Increase 1950–1960	Core City Change	Suburban Change
New York	10,694,633	11.9	— 1.4	75.0
Los Angeles	6,742,696	54.4	27.1	82.6
Chicago	6,220,913	20.1	— 1.9	71.5
Philadelphia	4,343,897	18.3	— 3.3	46.3
Detroit	3,762,360	24.7	— 9.7	79.3
San Francisco	2,783,359	24.2	— 4.5	55.0
Boston	2,589,301	7.4	—13.0	17.6
Pittsburgh	2,405,435	8.7	—10.7	17.2
St. Louis	2,060,103	19.8	—12.5	51.9
Washington	2,001,897	36.7	— 4.8	87.0
Cleveland	1,796,595	22.6	— 4.2	67.2
Baltimore	1,727,023	22.9	— 1.1	72.9
Newark	1,689,420	15.0	— 7.6	24.7
Minneapolis–St. Paul	1,482,030	28.8	— 4.4	115.7
Buffalo	1,306,957	20.0	— 8.2	52.1
Houston	1,243,158	54.1	57.4	44.8
Milwaukee	1,194,290	24.8	16.3	41.7
Paterson–Clifton–Passaic	1,186,873	35.5	6.9	47.6
Seattle	1,107,213	31.1	19.1	45.9
Dallas	1,083,601	45.7	56.4	30.7
Cincinnati	1,071,624	18.5	— 0.3	42.1
Kansas City	1,039,493	27.6	4.1	57.6
San Diego	1,033,011	85.5	71.4	106.7
Atlanta	1,017,188	39.9	47.1	33.9

SOURCE: Bureau of the Census, *Statistical Abstract of the United States, 1962,* Washington, D.C., 1962, Table 10, pp. 13–18.

center city. Fifty-two areas had increases in both total and suburban population but decreasing core city populations. The eight SMSAs which had smaller populations in 1960 than in 1950 showed three patterns of population loss. In five areas—Jersey City, New Jersey, Wheeling, West Virginia, and Johnstown, Scranton, and Wilkes-Barre, Pennsylvania—both the core city and suburban areas had population decreases. In Altoona, Pennsylvania, the suburban gain was not large enough to overcome the population loss of the core city, while in St. Joseph, Missouri, and Texarkana, Texas, the loss of population in the suburban ring communities was greater than the population increase of those core cities.

RISE AND GROWTH OF METROPOLITAN AREAS   537

■ Types of Metropolitan Areas

In addition to grouping metropolitan areas into classes according to their population, they can be meaningfully classified in terms of their geographical limits. A metropolitan area containing the territory of a single county is an intra-county area, while an area embracing two counties would be a bi-county area. If the metropolitan area extends over three or more counties, it can be classified as a multi-county area.

Most metropolitan areas—133 of the 212, or nearly 63 percent—are intra-county areas. The other 79 areas are divided almost evenly into bi-county and multi-county classes, with 39 or 18.4 percent in the former and 40 or 18.9 percent in the latter. Of the 40 multi-county areas, 22 are comprised of three counties, while five each contain four, five, and six counties respectively. One is a seven-county area, and two have eight counties.

Since counties vary so widely in terms of size, a metropolitan area with two or more counties does not necessarily mean that it is larger than an intra-county area. The largest SMSA in terms of square miles is a bi-county area—San Bernardino-Riverside-Ontario Metropolitan Area in California. This area extends over an area of 27,308 square miles. Boston, on the other hand, extends over an area of only 968 square miles. Phoenix, Arizona, and Bakersfield, California, both intra-county SMSAs, embrace 9,226 and 8,152 square miles respectively. The real political significance of bi-county or multi-county areas is that their territory does not lie within the limits of any one political unit of government. The importance of this fact will be discussed in some detail in the following chapter.

A sizable number of bi-county and multi-county areas have a further characteristic—they are also interstate metropolitan areas. The 26 interstate areas include seven of the 24 SMSAs of over 1,000,000 population, three of the 29 between 500,000 and 1,000,000, seven of the 48 areas between 250,000 and 500,000, eight of the 89 between 100,000 and 250,000, and only one of the 22 areas under 100,000 in population. All but two of the 26 interstate areas are bi-state in character. However, the Washington SMSA includes territory in Maryland and Virginia in addition to the District of Columbia, and the Huntington-Ashland area includes territory in West Virginia, Kentucky, and Ohio.

METROPOLITAN AREAS

Table 23. *Interstate Metropolitan Areas*

Metropolitan Area	Population in 1960	States Included in Metropolitan Area	Number of Counties
Allentown–Bethlehem–Easton	492,168	Pa., N. J.	3
Augusta	216,639	Ga., S. C.	2
Chattanooga	283,169	Tenn., Ga.	2
Cincinnati	1,071,624	Ohio, Ky.	3
Columbus	217,985	Ga., Ala.	3
Davenport–Rock Island–Moline	270,058	Iowa, Ill.	2
Duluth–Superior	276,596	Minn., Wis.	2
Evansville	199,313	Ind., Ky.	2
Fall River	138,156	Mass., R. I.	2
Fargo–Moorhead	106,027	N. Dak., Minn.	2
Huntington–Ashland	254,780	W. Va., Ky., Ohio	4
Kansas City	1,039,493	Mo., Kans.	4
Lawrence–Haverhill	187,601	Mass., N. H.	2
Louisville	725,139	Ky., Ind.	3
Omaha	457,873	Nebr., Iowa	3
Philadelphia	4,342,897	Pa., N. J.	8
Portland	821,897	Oreg., Wash.	3
Providence–Pawtucket	816,148	R. I., Mass.	8
St. Louis	2,060,103	Mo., Ill.	5
Steubenville–Weirton	167,756	Ohio, W. Va.	3
Texarkana	91,657	Texas, Ark.	2
Washington, D.C.	2,001,897	D.C., Md., Va.	6
Wheeling	190,342	W. Va., Ohio	3
Wilmington	366,157	Del., N. J.	2
Chicago–Northwestern Indiana	6,794,461	Ill., Ind.	8[a]
New York–Northeastern N. J.	14,759,429	N. Y., N. J.	13[b]

[a] This is a standard consolidated area and consists of the Chicago and Gary-Hammond–East Chicago SMSAs.
[b] This is a standard consolidated area and consists of the New York, Newark, Jersey City, Paterson-Clifton-Passaic SMSAs and Middlesex and Somerset Counties.
Source: Bureau of the Budget, *Standard Metropolitan Statistical Areas*, Government Printing Office, 1961, pp. 6–40.

Four other metropolitan areas are actually international urban communities. These are El Paso, Texas, and San Diego, California, both of which are met by urban communities of Mexico; and Buffalo and Detroit, which border on Canadian urban communities. In addition, eight other metropolitan areas bordering on the Great Lakes face problems of international significance in such service areas as water supply and water pollution.

■ The Concept of Urban Regions

The map showing the geographical distribution of the SMSAs also reveals that a number of separately identified metropolitan areas now adjoin each other, forming metropolitan clusters. In such clusters, the historic concept of a metropolitan area as a core city surrounded by suburbs becomes inadequate; it does not describe existing conditions and cannot be utilized as a basis for solving governmental problems. The term "urban region," defined as an area in which two or more standard metropolitan statistical areas adjoin, was developed to identify these metropolitan clusters.[13]

Based on 1950 census data, Chute identified 19 urban regions scattered from coast to coast and from border to border. He described such a region further as "an area so densely settled by people living in municipalities, either now or potentially so in the near future, that they live under urban conditions, and many of their important urban needs are interrelated. In some cases the territory lying between the central cities of two adjacent metropolitan areas is completely built up and the result is really one city, although divided by law into many cities."[14]

Writing three years later on the continuing trend toward metropolitanization in the United States, Jerome Pickard defined four kinds of urban communities.[15] These were: (1) a metropolitan area which is an urban area including one or more adjacent or nearby cities having a total population of 100,000 or more; (2) a major metropolitan area which is one having a total population of 250,000 or more; (3) a region which is a geographical area determined by the factors of size, spacing, and growth rates of the metropolitan areas included within it; and (4) a metropolitan region which is a region with an overall average population density of at least 100 persons per square mile and with at least 50 percent of the total population residing in major metropolitan areas.

Pickard identifies three metropolitan regions and six regions within our nation. The Atlantic Metropolitan Region extends from Portland, Maine, to Norfolk, Virginia, and westward 175 miles from the Atlantic Ocean. It embraces 32 metropolitan areas as they were

---

[13] Charlton F. Chute, "Today's Urban Regions," *National Municipal Review, 45* (June and July, 1956), 274–80, 334–9.

[14] *Ibid.*, p. 276.

[15] Jerome P. Pickard, *Metropolitanization of the United States*, Urban Land Institute, Research Monograph 2, 1959, p. 12.

METROPOLITAN AREAS

identified in 1950. The Great Lakes-Midwest Metropolitan Region extends from the St. Lawrence Valley in northern New York westward to Davenport and St. Louis and southward to Cincinnati and Louisville. It embraces 36 metropolitan areas. The California Metropolitan Region embraces the central and southern portions of California and includes nine metropolitan areas. Pickard also distinguished the "metropolitan region of the United States" as the large region in the northeastern quarter of the United States embracing the Atlantic Metropolitan and the Great Lakes-Midwest Metropolitan regions. The titles of the six regions are fairly descriptive of the areas included within them. These were the Southeast, Floridian, Mid-Southwest, Mid-West, West, and Southwest Regions.

Recognizing the probable continuing urban growth in our nation, Meyerson and Terrett wrote in 1957 that:

Each year more American communities grow to metropolitan size. As their populations increase and their activities expand beyond one political jurisdiction into one or more others, they assume many of the attributes of a crazy quilt. Like the quilt itself, they are both haphazard and planned. Every metropolis is characteristically a practical patchwork of income, race, and age; of private and public ownership; of the new and the old; of identical and of mixed land uses; of households, firms, and institutions whose interests converge, diverge, conflict with, and complement each other. . . . All of these competitions draw together, just as the patches do in the quilt, and provide a perceptible fabric. Compromises, conflicts, congruities, incongruities, agreements, and disagreements in behavior and interest come together in that colorful make-do, the metropolis.[16]

Being neither Cassandra-like in predicting a dire future nor Pollyannish in predicting a rosy one, these writers conclude:

We reject the pessimistic view that metropolis is all dissatisfaction, the overly optimistic view that metropolis will automatically grow bigger and better, and the manipulative view that the expert alone, with his laudably growing competence, should control most of the behavior choices which shape metropolis. Rather, what we have in mind is that just as the citizens of this country have repeatedly succeeded together in spite of many a stupidity or peculation along the way, so they will see their own interest in meeting the challenge of Metropolis in Ferment, too, and will devise a hundred ways of meeting it for every form it takes. We are

[16] Martin Meyerson and Barbara Terrett, "Metropolis Lost, Metropolis Regained," *Annals of the American Academy of Political and Social Science, 314* (November, 1957), 1.

not sure that Metropolis, like Paradise, is lost; but if it is, then, like Paradise, it can be regained.[17]

SUGGESTED READINGS

Books

Advisory Commission on Intergovernmental Relations, *Governmental Structure, Organization, and Planning in Metropolitan Areas* (Washington: Government Printing Office, 1961).

Anderson, Nels, *The Urban Community: A World Perspective* (New York: Holt, Rinehart and Winston, 1959).

Bogue, Donald J., *The Structure of the Metropolitan Community: A Study of Dominance and Subdominance* (Ann Arbor: University of Michigan Press, 1949).

Bureau of the Budget, *Standard Metropolitan Statistical Areas* (Washington: Government Printing Office, 1961).

Bureau of the Census, *Population of Standard Metropolitan Statistical Areas: 1960 and 1950*, PC (SI)–1 (Washington: Government Printing Office, 1961).

Committee for Economic Development, *Guiding Metropolitan Growth* (New York: Committee for Economic Development, 1960).

Fortune Magazine, *The Exploding Metropolis* (New York: Doubleday, 1958).

Gottmann, Jean, *Megalopolis: The Urbanized Northeastern Seaboard of the United States* (New York: Twentieth Century Fund, 1961).

Hawley, Amos, *Human Ecology: A Theory of Community Structure* (New York: Ronald, 1950).

Hawley, Amos, *The Changing Shape of Metropolitan America* (New York: Free Press, 1956).

Hoover, Edgar and Vernon, Raymond, *Anatomy of a Metropolis* (Cambridge: Harvard University Press, 1960).

Pickard, Jerome P., *Metropolitanization of the United States* (Washington: Urban Land Institute, 1959).

Self, Peter, *Cities in Flood: The Problems of Urban Growth* (London: Faber and Faber, 1957).

Sweeney, Stephen B. and Blair, George S. (eds.), *Metropolitan Analysis: Important Elements of Study and Action* (Philadelphia: University of Pennsylvania Press, 1958).

Articles

Bogue, Donald J., "Urbanism in the United States, 1950," *American Journal of Sociology*, 60 (March, 1955), 471–86.

[17] *Ibid.*, p. 9.

Chute, Charlton F., "Today's Urban Regions," *National Municipal Review*, 45 (June and July, 1956), 274–80, 334–9.

Hauser, Philip M., "The Changing Population Pattern of the Modern City," in Paul K. Hatt and Albert J. Reiss, Jr. (eds.), *Cities and Society*, rev. ed. (New York: Free Press, 1957), pp. 157–74.

Meyerson, Martin and Terrett, Barbara, "Metropolis Lost, Metropolis Regained," *The Annals of the American Academy of Political and Social Science*, 314 (November, 1957), 1–9.

Reiss, Albert J., Jr., "The Community and the Corporate Area," *University of Pennsylvania Law Review*, 105 (February, 1957), 443–63.

Ylvisaker, Paul N., "Innovation and Evolution: Bridge to the Future of Metropolis," *The Annals of the American Academy of Political and Social Science*, 314 (November, 1957), 156–64.

Problems of
Metropolitan Areas

25

That we have become a nation of great cities was noted in the last chapter. Acceptance of the statistic that most of the 60 million persons to be added to the population in the next 20 years would live in and around our major cities has prompted an increased awareness of the problems of these large population clusters and expanded efforts to do something about these problems. The term "metropolitan problem" has become a familiar one as students and practitioners of government, club speakers, researchers and writers, leagues of women voters, and other study groups have expressed a new concern with existing problems and others that are certain to develop.

The term "metropolitian problem" has been variously defined, however, although there is general agreement that one exists. To Luther Gulick, the metropolitan problem "is millions of human beings who want to do something effective to solve the rising difficulties they are experiencing from the new pattern of urban settlement, but who do not have the clear ideas, the teamwork machinery, or the leadership with which to proceed."[1] A similar

[1] Luther H. Gulick, *The Metropolitan Problem and American Ideas,* Knopf, 1962, p. 163.

definition was advanced by Coleman Woodbury a few years earlier when he wrote that the metropolitan problem is "the inability of metropolitan residents to reach any substantial degree of consensus as to what should be done in the public interest, about the generally recognized issues of their common life—government organization, finance, blight and redevelopment, schools, race relations, land use control, and so on."[2]

To others, the metropolitan problem lies in the multiplicity of units within the metropolitan area and the absence of any governing agency with regional authority. Scott Greer notes that the metropolitan community reflects a social and economic unity which "is not reflected in government. The problems created by contiguity and mutual dependence are not allocated to any government which includes all of those affected and affecting others."[3] The governmental dichotomy of the metropolis and fragmentation of suburbia results, as Greer sees it, in a "schizoid polity" with serious consequences for both the political and governmental processes. The political significance of the fragmented pattern of local government in the metropolitan area will be discussed in a later section in this chapter.

Another view equates the metropolitan problem to the service needs of the central city and its suburbs. The Committee for Economic Development lists as the major problems of central cities those of handling a daylight population in excess of the residential population, building expressways and providing parking space, adapting newcomers to the urban environment, and halting the spread of blight and obsolescence. Suburban communities, on the other hand, feel the brunt of demands for new schools, water systems, sewage disposal plants, fire stations, streets and utility lines. Other essential services become areawide problems because the "size and geographic extent of the capital investment, the economic forces at work, the nature of the physical environment, or the claims for use by the residents of the area make it almost impossible for communities to provide services or meet these needs separately. Among these are the provision of areawide transportation systems, the control of air and water pollution, the reservation of open land for outdoor recreation, broad land-use planning, a fair

---

[2] Coleman Woodbury, "Great Cities, Great Problems, Great Possibilities," *Public Administration Review, 18* (Autumn, 1958), 339.

[3] Scott Greer, *Governing the Metropolis,* Wiley, 1962, p. 56.

distribution of tax resources, and the stimulation of growth in the economy of the area."[4]

The pluralistic nature of the problem has been pointed out by two authorities. To Victor Jones, the problem results from "the need for servicing a large population scattered under the jurisdiction of many units of local government, most of which are crippled by limited powers over a restricted area, by inadequate tax resources, and by such consequences of premature subdivision as heavy indebtedness and extensive tax arrears."[5] In a report prepared for the Council of State Governments, John Bollens describes the metropolitan problem in these words: "The basis of the problem is the absence of general local governmental organizations broad enough to cope with metropolitan matters. There is a lack of areawide governmental jurisdictions that can effectively provide and finance services, that can plan and regulate and that are constituted to facilitate adequate accountability to the metropolitan public for their actions."[6]

A few writers have attempted broader definitions. Coke states, "a problem is metropolitan if all of the following conditions are satisfied: (1) if the problem is urban in character, (2) if it transcends the boundaries of a single political subdivision, and (3) if it is thought to be an appropriate subject for community decision-making."[7] The second aspect of this definition emphasizes that the involvement of more than one unit of local government is an essential characteristic of a metropolitan problem and that it is this factor rather than sheer size which so identifies a problem.

The centripetal movement of people to metropolitan areas and the internal centrifugal movement of population and industry to the area's outlying communities result in both problems which are areawide and in problems peculiar to each of its two major parts. While most of the specific problems discussed below are areawide in scope, they may have quite opposite effects in the core city and the suburbs.

[4] Committee for Economic Development, *Guiding Metropolitan Growth,* New York, 1960, pp. 21–22.

[5] Victor Jones, *Metropolitan Government,* University of Chicago Press, 1942, p. 24.

[6] The Council of State Governments, *The States and the Metropolitan Problem,* Chicago, 1956, p. 17.

[7] James G. Coke, "The Objectives of Metropolitan Study" in Stephen B. Sweeney and George S. Blair (eds.), *Metropolitan Analysis: Important Elements of Study and Action,* University of Pennsylvania Press, 1958, p. 21.

■ Inadequate Government Structure

The close relationship between the governmental pattern and the metropolitan problem has been noted by almost every observer. The problem is actually a dual one which Gulick identifies as a governmental vacuum on the one hand and a fractionalization of assigned duties on the other.[8] The governmental vacuum exists because there is no governmental body with authority to cope with the major problems which affect the whole area. The fractionalization of duties occurs because each of the local units has quite limited jurisdiction. Thus, while all of the metropolitan community is under some form of governmental control, there is no single governmental unit which can exercise any degree of control over the whole—except when the metropolitan community is contained within the limits of a single county.

The pattern of local government in metropolitan areas is almost unbelievably complex. The 212 metropolitan areas recognized in 1962 contained a total of 18,442 separate governmental units—an average of 87 units per SMSA. The average number of units, however, is deceiving in some specific areas. For example, the New York-northeastern New Jersey metropolitan community contained 1,112 local governments and the Chicago-northwestern Indiana area had 1,170. A comparison of numbers and types of local governments in metropolitan areas in 1957 and 1962 is shown in Figure 29, while Figure 30 shows the distribution of local governments in metropolitan areas in terms of their populations.

The problem of the number of closely compacted municipalities is vividly described in the following statement concerning the path of a state police car along a major thoroughfare in the Philadelphia area:

Leaving Philadelphia, the driver moves between Yeadon on the left and Upper Darby on the right. He then drives through a short stretch of Upper Darby. Minutes later, he finds East Lansdowne on the right, Upper Darby on the left. He then enters Lansdowne and drives through it to Clifton Heights.

The car leaves Clifton Heights and goes through another little piece of Upper Darby. The driver then enters Springfield. In a minute or two of driving, there's a hunk of Morton on the left. Then it's all Springfield

---

[8] Luther Gulick, *Metro: Changing Problems and Lines of Attack,* Governmental Affairs Institute, 1957.

Number
20,000

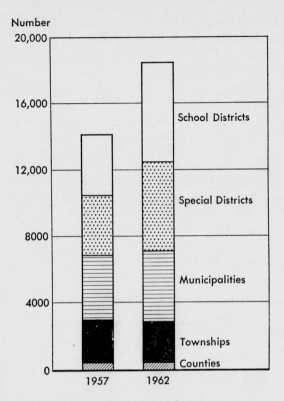

Figure 29. *Number of Local Governments in Standard Metropolitan Statistical Areas, by Type: 1957 and 1962 (with the 212 SMSAs as defined in 1962).* (U.S. Bureau of the Census, *Census of Governments, 1962,* Vol. I: *Governmental Organization,* Washington, 1962, p. 24.)

again. Minutes later, Swarthmore's on the left. The driver ends in Media after a stretch of Nether Providence.

By the time the driver reaches Media—a distance of eight miles—he's been through seven boroughs and three townships.[9]

The substitution of other community names for those in the Philadelphia area would make the above description equally applicable in many of our large metropolitan areas.

[9] James M. Perry, "Many Suburbanites Don't Get Adequate Police Protection," *The Sunday Bulletin,* Philadelphia, February 16, 1958.

The confusion resulting from mere numbers is additionally confusing because of the frequent territorial overlapping of these units. A school district, though independent, often has boundaries which are coterminous with those of a general purpose local governmental unit, and the same is true of other special districts. In fact, several types of special districts may serve all or portions of the area of a unit of local government. A further layer of government may exist in those states in which a township can overlie a municipal area or in which every foot of soil is incorporated into some type of municipality.

An interesting but somewhat atypical complex exists in Park Forest, Illinois, a suburb of Chicago. Banfield and Grodzins discovered in a 1956 study that the people of Park Forest were directly

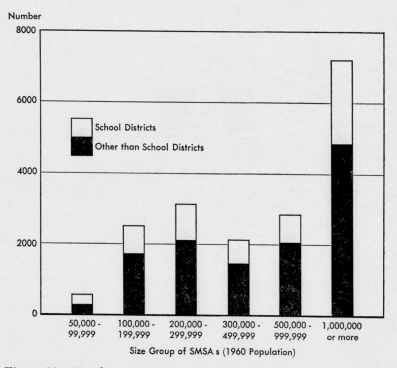

Figure 30. *Number of Local Governments in Standard Metropolitan Statistical Areas, by Population Size of Area: 1962.* (U.S. Bureau of the Census, *Census of Governments, 1962,* Vol. I: *Governmental Organization,* Washington, 1962, p. 24.)

concerned with the governments of two counties, three townships, four school districts, a forest preserve district, and a mosquito abatement district, all in addition to their own village.[10]

While few modern writers would consider the problem of illogical boundaries and inadequate governmental areas as the source of all metropolitan problems, they are recognized as an important element. One recent survey points out four ways in which the boundary-jurisdictional problem is important. These are:

1. Inadequate governmental areas mean that there is no agency large enough to cope with needs affecting the whole of a metropolitan community.
2. The small areas of many local units sometimes cause inefficiency and often greatly aggravate the problem of financing public services.
3. In the suburban portions of metropolitan areas, the absence of municipal government has often meant inadequate zoning and other controls, as well as substandard public services.
4. The tangle of governments found in most metropolitan areas has been a real barrier to the public understanding and participation which insures effective democratic control.[11]

As noted earlier, Scott Greer refers to the governmental pattern in metropolitan areas as the "schizoid polity." He sees two serious consequences for the total community as a result of its fragmented pattern of governance.

First of all, the political processes are in no sense those of a unified metropolitan community. They are limited by the forces in play in each of the various subparts of the area, though the consequences of these forces may be very general. Furthermore, this fragmented polity confronts problems that are areawide in their origins, affecting all parts of the metropolitan area; they are problems which seem, logically and technically, to demand an areawide governmental response. Such a response, however, is difficult to imagine in an urban complex made up of a hundred or a thousand separate governmental jurisdictions.[12]

The specific problems concern the provision of necessary and essential services, the creation of an acceptable equity between costs and benefits, and the formation and acceptance of a consensus as to

[10] Edward C. Banfield and Morton Grodzins, *Government and Housing in Metropolitan Areas*, McGraw-Hill, 1958, p. 18.
[11] Government Affairs Foundation, *Metropolitan Surveys: A Digest*, 1959, pp. 5-6.
[12] Greer, *op. cit.*, pp. 107-8.

what kind of a community can be planned for and achieved in the future. Each of these specific problems will be discussed below.

■ Service and Regulatory Inadequacies

Greer's statement leads naturally into the problems of providing services and effective regulatory measures within the metropolitan community. Service failure is regarded by Gulick as one of the shortcomings of contemporary governments in metropolitan areas. He notes that when the things that are wrong in America today are identified and located on a map we find that most of our current headaches arise out of spreading urban concentrations in metropolitan areas. Among these "headaches," he identifies the following: "slums; congestion; obsolete buildings and factories; juvenile and other crime; rackets; crowded schools; reduced standards of educational quality; deteriorating transportation with rising costs; increasing water and air pollution; traffic congestion and accidents; chronic unemployment; reduced individual and social responsibility; segregation and handicaps for minority groups; ugly and insulting 'developments'; silly and extravagant mass 'consumerism'; the needless destruction of natural values; and the deterioration of cultural standards and resources."[13]

The deficiencies in these areas and in such service areas as water, transportation, sewage, health, protective services, and recreation are numerous because each of the governmental units concerned operates in only limited portions of the whole area. The result is that the services and standards of regulation are uneven and vary widely; frequently services and actions are uncoordinated, inadequate, uneconomic, and ill-fitted to accomplish their intended purposes.

One of the major problems of central cities is the burden of handling daytime populations greater than their residential populations. The location of commuter lines and condition of commuter facilities are often not such to encourage their wide use. Commuting workers then turn to private cars, resulting in traffic congestion, parking problems, and the need for additional expressways.

Central cities also carry a major share of the responsibility for

[13] Gulick, *The Metropolitan Problem and American Ideas*, p. 10.

caring for low-income migrants from outside the area. In helping such new arrivals adapt to an urban environment, core city expenditures for social welfare services, health, and public housing are normally considerably higher per capita than are such expenditures in suburban communities.

The dual problem of "flight and blight" also affects core cities more than suburban areas. "Flight" refers to the outside movement of higher- and middle-income families from the city to a suburb, and "blight" is a term describing the spreading obsolescence of both public and private facilities within the core city. Such deterioration in old sections affects all property, whether it is residential, commercial, or industrial. Effective programs to check the conditions resulting from blight and obsolescence are tremendously expensive and involved undertakings.

Service needs in older suburban communities may largely parallel those of the center city. More typically, however, needs of suburbia demand expansion of existing services or the provision of additional ones rather than rebuilding and replacing older facilities. Capital expenditures may run substantially higher in rapidly growing suburban communities than in core cities. This problem can be solved by intelligent planning to meet current and future community needs, rather than planning to correct past bad judgments as is often true in the core city.

In addition to needs peculiar to core cities and suburban communities, there are others that are common to the whole area. A smoke abatement program in outlying communities is of little value on the days when the wind blows in smoke from the central city unless the central city has a similar program. A system of highways and traffic feeder streets is a matter of areawide concern. As a third example, germs of communicable diseases do not stop spreading in the middle of a street which happens to mark the end of one governmental unit and the beginning of another.

Attempts to achieve some sort of service integration has been particularly necessary in the field of protective services. The revolutionary improvements in transportation and communication have been utilized by criminal elements to expand their operations, and police cooperation is urgently needed to enable local police forces to combat modern crime effectively. An often-quoted reference to conditions in the Chicago area in the early 1930s underscores the primary reason why jurisdictional sanctity has been partially alleviated in the field of police services. In a study published in 1933, Merriam, Parratt, and Lepawsky found that:

Within twenty miles of Chicago there are some 75 independent jurisdictions, all wedged against another. Where a crime is committed in Chicago and the malefactors are making for the country, the Chicago police department may notify five or often ten police departments to be on the watch. Radio has helped to minimize the time spent, but even now only a small minority of the surrounding towns are in communication. The perpetration of one bank robbery necessitated twenty minutes of telephoning to advise the proper towns along the route taken by the bandits. Later it was found that they had broken through the cordon before the calls could be taken and acted upon, and by the time half a dozen police departments were on the lookout, the bandits' car was speeding along, a dozen miles from the searchers.[14]

As in the case of police protection, the need for interjurisdictional cooperation is self-evident in a number of other areas. Bruce Smith, a recognized authority in the field of police administration, has aptly described this decentralization in this important function in the following words: "There is therefore no such thing in the United States as a police system, nor even a set of police systems within any reasonably accurate sense of the term. Our so-called systems are mere collections of police units having some similarity of authority, organization, or jurisdiction; but they lack any systematic relationship to each other."[15]

Labeling the provision of services as the "housekeeping problems" of the metropolitan area, Greer concludes:

The metropolitan household is in many respects one; but its housekeeping is organized in dozens or hundreds of families, each indifferent to (if not hostile to) the neighbors. Thus the central city is perennially in need of close coordination of its services with those of the suburbs. . . . The suburbs also run into augmented problems as a result of their fragmentations. They suffer the consequences of spatial congruity and resulting interdependence. . . . In short, the housekeeping problems of the individual governments, suburban as well as central city, are greatly increased by the political fragmentation of metropolitan areas.[16]

---

[14] Charles E. Merriam, Spencer D. Parratt, and Albert Lepawsky, *The Government of the Metropolitan Region of Chicago*, University of Chicago Press, 1933, pp. 88–89.

[15] Bruce Smith, *Police Systems in the United States*, rev. ed., Harper, 1949, p. 22.

[16] Greer, *op. cit.*, pp. 113–4.

■ Financial Inequalities

The inadequacies discussed above result largely from financial inequalities and weaknesses within the metropolitian area. The problems generated by the twin phenomena of flight and blight are not diffcult to visualize, particularly within the core city. As high- and middle-income families move outward to the suburbs, retail stores also leave the center city or establish branch stores. In time, retailers are joined by wholesalers, further deflating the tax base of the core city. The migration of lower-income families to the core city increases the demand for public services at the time the property base for supporting them is dwindling.

Lyle Fitch suggests that financial problems in metropolitan areas arise primarily from the lack of adequate fiscal machinery rather than from lack of capacity. He identifies the three major deficiencies of metropolitan fiscal machinery as: (1) a revenue-producing machinery which is generally inadequate for the task of financing local government functions both locally and communitywide; (2) the difficulty in relating benefits to costs at the local level when activities extend across boundary lines of local governmental units; and (3) the discrepancies in the capacities of local governments to provide needed services. He describes the following condition as a financial "fact of life" in the modern metropolitan community: ". . . a family may reside in one jurisdiction, earn its living in one or more others, send the children to school in another, and shop and seek recreation in still others. But to a considerable extent, the American local financial system still reflects the presumption that these various activities are concentrated in one governmental jurisdiction."[17]

The problem of fiscal inequity is similarly summarized by Bollens in these words: "There are wide variances in different sections of metropolitan areas between service needs and financial resources. The policy of providing city-wide services on the basis of need rather than the fiscal resources of each block, precinct or ward, is not extended in the great majority of instances to metropolitan areas. Instead, the individual governmental unit relies upon a small amount of territory for its local financial resources. Thus some units

[17] Lyle C. Fitch, "Metropolitan Financial Problems," *The Annals of the American Academy of Political and Social Science, 314* (November, 1957), 67.

are wealthy but have relatively few needs; others are extremely poor and have extensive needs."[18]

Generally speaking, the problem of financial equity in metropolitan areas increases in direct relation to the number of independent governments within the area. For three reasons these problems are particularly severe with respect to services financed through the local property tax, which remains the time-honored major source of local revenue. They result from the relatively small taxing areas, the uneven distribution of valuable industrial properties, and the low correlation in many instances between the location of a citizen's home and his consumption of governmental services.

An example of these problems exists in the Los Angeles metropolitan area between the core city and the suburban city of Vernon. Los Angeles has a population 10,000 times that of Vernon, but an assessed valuation only 20 times greater. Thus, the property tax base in Los Angeles is $1,600 per person, compared to a tax base of one million dollars per person in Vernon.[19] This is not an isolated case. In a study of the New York region in 1955, Wood discovered that the per capita total public expenditures in the highest cost jurisdiction was over 700 times greater than in the lowest and that the highest per capita current operating expenditure was 85 times larger than the lowest. These findings prompted him to write: "The dark corners and trouble spots of each metropolitan area raise the obvious issue of equity—of why members of a labor force working within a single economic system receive different public services and pay different tax bills because of their residential location."[20]

The heart of the problem of financial inequities within the metropolitan community is stated by Wood in these words:

Throughout this century, people have debated the question of whether or not the American political system could countenance an unbridled laissez-faire economy—whether it did not have to intervene by selective measures to redress the balance of competition, at times to preserve it, and at times to guide it. But in the modern metropolitan region, the question is reversed. The issue is whether or not a modern economic system, requiring positive stimulation and selective aid and

[18] The Council of State Governments, op. cit., p. 20.
[19] Frank P. Sherwood, "Some Major Problems of Metropolitan Areas," in The Governor's Commission on Metropolitan Area Problems, Metropolitan California, 1961, p. 18.
[20] Robert C. Wood, Metropolis Against Itself, Committee for Economic Development, 1959, pp. 23–25.

direction by public authority, can tolerate an unbridled laissez-faire profusion of governments which systematically avoid any responsibility for these matters.[21]

Various devices to limit the severity of metropolitan fiscal problems have been advanced. These include such proposals as wider use of local income taxes to enable core cities to derive some revenue from non-residents who earn income in the city, improved bases for assessing charges for services rendered by one governmental unit for another, a tax on urban motorists for the privilege of using city streets, heavier reliance upon grants and shared revenues from state governments, and the use of areawide property tax levies to finance certain governmental functions. Concerning the effectiveness of these and other proposals, the Advisory Commission on Intergovernmental Relations warns that "Each of these approaches will no doubt be found helpful in some situations, though each has its problems or limitations. Even altogether, however, they cannot be expected to solve the problem of inequitable financing in metropolitan areas having a highly fragmented pattern of local government."[22]

■ Social, Ethnic and Racial Problems

While the extent of social problems may be difficult to calculate in any particular metropolitan area, the human eye finds ready evidence of their existence. Juvenile delinquency, family disorganization, racial tension, mental illness, alcoholism, slums, and ethnic unrest are in evidence in sections of the metropolitan community.

One sociologist has defined social problems as the recurring events that involve sizable groups of people, that cause distress to persons directly involved or to the larger society, and that are believed to be subject to amelioration or prevention through a change in the whole or in some part of society.[23] Social problems appear to exist if one or more of the following situations occur:

[21] *Ibid.*, p. 44.
[22] Advisory Commission on Intergovernmental Relations, *Governmental Structure, Organization, and Planning in Metropolitan Areas*, Government Printing Office, 1961, p. 16.
[23] Lee N. Robins, "Social Problems Associated with Urban Minorities" in Werner Z. Hirsch (ed.), *Urban Life and Form*, Holt, Rinehart and Winston, 1963, p. 201.

1. There are relatively widespread violations of the majority's norms. Crime, divorce, public drunkenness, and wife desertion are examples of behavior that fit this category.

2. There is a significant deviation from what is generally accepted as an attainable level of health. Physical and mental health problems that are considered either to result from man-controlled causes (for example, venereal disease and occupational diseases) or to be receiving less than the optimal treatment or prevention considering the current level of medical knowledge are included here.

3. Solvent segments of society are called upon to meet costs of care for other parts of society that are preferably met by the persons receiving the care. Payment, through taxes or gifts to private agencies, of unemployment benefits, welfare subsidies, or hospitalization would be included here.

4. Society is failing to provide for the fulfillment of the vocational, intellectual, and social potential of its members. We would classify here failure to complete education commensurate with natural endowment and widespread subjective feelings of worthlessness, boredom, or isolation.[24]

These four classifications of social problems have higher rates of occurrence in minority or disadvantaged groups than in the dominant majority. Among the explanations for this condition are: differences in cultural traditions, readjustments consequent to industrialization, psychological damage resulting from prejudice, frustrations of individuals of low socioeconomic status who accept the achievement goals of the majority without having traits, education and assets required to achieve them, and adjustments necessary because of moving from rural to urban areas. The following quotation states in picturesque words some of the social problems resulting from the great migration of people to our metropolitan areas: ". . . illiterate white hillbillies, underprivileged Southern Negroes, and poorly educated Puerto Ricans constitute problems in their native environments. But when transferred to the metropolis their behavior has even more serious ramifications for far more people. And providing adequate basic facilities, such as housing and schools, for such groups is vastly more expensive in Manhattan than in rural Mississippi or Puerto Rico."[25]

Greer identifies the city as a problem of social order. In his words, "The city is a maze, a social zoo, a mass of heterogeneous

[24] *Ibid.*, pp. 201–2.
[25] Roscoe C. Martin and Douglas Price, *The Metropolis and Its Problems*, Maxwell Graduate School of Citizenship and Public Affairs, 1960, p. 34.

social types. They come from the four corners of the earth. Much of their behavior is completely beyond the understanding of any one actor, and they are related in a thousand different ways. Their city teems with conflict and hums with tension . . ."[26] He cautions, however, that impatience with the existing order and hopes for a better one should not blind us to the magnitude of our past achievements.

That much remains to be done goes without serious debate. As one writer points out, ". . . metrogovernment will have to work at improving the adjustment of the in-migrant groups to urban life. It is not enough to turn over the heartland of the metropolis to the untutored use of successive generations of urban newcomers. Whether at the source of the migrant streams, or at the urban delta onto which they spill, or both—a program of habilitation must be developed."[27]

■ Political Leadership Needs

The problem of the inadequacy or even total absence of area-wide political leadership in metropolitan communities has been aptly stated by Greer. In his words, "The mayors of our great cities, symbols and symbolic leaders of the metropolitan community, reign but do not rule. They are brokers, conciliators, who reconcile the people to what they get from their government. They legitimatize the *fait accompli* on the rare occasions when the necessary resources for action result from transitory coalitions among the major contending organizations. For the rest, they preside over routine caretaker governments."[28]

One big reason for the absence of areawide leadership is the fact that no elective public officials have the whole metropolitan community as their constituency. Gulick notes that "Men generally win elections by appealing to local patriotism and narrow parochialism. Even where co-operation is preached, the home town is not expected to make any sacrifices to pay more taxes. No one gets elected in jurisdiction A by appealing courageously to the people of B, C,

[26] Greer, *op. cit.*, pp. 36–37.
[27] Paul Ylvisaker, "Metropolitan Government—for What?" in Stanley Scott (ed.), *Metropolitan Area Problems*, Bureau of Public Administration and University Extension, University of California, Berkeley, 1960, p. 67.
[28] Greer, *op. cit.*, p. 80.

or D."[29] Political leaders within the several local governments of a metropolitan area are generally debarred from exercising leadership beyond the boundaries of their own jurisdictions, for both political and psychological reasons. Supporters of a leader must have a basic feeling of identity with him if he is to be effective. Gulick also advances two other characteristics of metropolitan leadership. First, most geographic constituencies create political leadership in their own geographic image. Second, effective and conspicuous political leadership seldom arises except on the foundation of a political constituency already in existence.[30]

These characteristics concerning political leadership in the metropolitan community help explain the almost universal failure of plans for the creation of a new political entity for metropolitan government. Most existing local political leadership is either opposed to a change or largely "disqualified" from influence if it does favor change. The proposed new constituency cannot produce its own acceptable leadership until it is established as a constituency. One writer has stated, "In the sheerest Aristotelian terms the search for metropolitan government is the search for a potential metropolitan governing class, the institutions through which it can function and a set of ideal goals which it can embody and which will render its leadership legitimate in the eyes of the people."[31]

While this is a pessimistic outlook for the possibility of significant governmental change, Gulick points out that there are known methods of creating a new political constituency. These normally include the following steps:

1. Lay out the geographic boundaries of the proposed new constituency with relevance to the administrative and political functions involved.
2. Define the specific work to be done by the constituency and the major powers to be granted.
3. Specify the officers who will exercise these powers and administer these duties, and the method of their selection by the constituency.[32]

To achieve the goal of a metropolitan leadership and constituency, he advocates the creation of a "Metropolitan Council" as a

---

[29] Gulick, *Metro: Changing Problems and Lines of Attack*, p. 16.

[30] Gulick, *The Metropolitan Problem and American Ideas*, p. 97.

[31] Norton Long, "Recent Theories and Problems of Local Government," a paper presented at American Political Science Association meeting, Washington, D. C., September 6, 1956.

[32] Gulick, *The Metropolitan Problem and American Ideas*, p. 161.

wide-reaching, sub-legislative body. Members of the council would be elected directly by the voters, and the council would stand between the state and the existing local governments. Its primary function would be to provide the coordination that is now conspicuously lacking. Thus, without destroying existing local governments, the council would give the metropolitan area an official organization through which the governments could get together, debate problems, make up their minds, and move toward unified action. In Gulick's words, "No one should think that the proposed Metropolitan Council would be a 'dictatorial body' riding roughshod over the present local governments. The Council would be a representative and democratic body always held accountable by the voters and would include ex officio officials drawn directly from the underlying local governments. It would have only defined powers."[33]

In a more optimistic prognosis, Norton Long reminds us that, "Only relatively small elites need to be highly motivated with the vision of what the resources of a modern metropolitan area could be made to produce in the way of a challenging, significant theater of action. Revolutions, as we know, are characteristically made by minorities."[34] Long recognizes the need for active leaders among the metropolitan citizenry as a real one, deserving of careful study. He suggests that such leadership might be more effective when its vision reaches beyond the efficiency and economy theme of most metropolitan reform movements. He states:

Democracy itself is a highly aristocratic form of government depending on self-selected natural aristocracies for manning its table of civic organizations. Most of the most ardent enthusiasts for metropolitan integration campaign under the banner of fixing the plumbing and relieving the traffic jam with just a flourish of Chamber of Commerce boosterism. There are signs that some, at least, are willing to claim for themselves and the metropolis they struggle to create a more inspiring vision. If the bulk of the country is to live in a few huge metropolitan areas we need give some thought as to how those political habitations can be provided some spiritual warmth and light for we desperately need to motivate natural and even artificial aristocracies to leaven what may become mere massive demographic lumps.[35]

[33] Gulick, *Metro: Changing Problems and Lines of Attack*, p. 28.
[34] Norton E. Long, *The Polity*, Rand McNally, 1962, p. 214.
[35] *Ibid.*

METROPOLITAN AREAS

■ Deficiencies in Citizen Control

Citizen apathy is a problem in almost all communities, but it is perhaps most observable in metropolitan areas. For one reason, the concept of the metropolis is abstract and quite difficult to deal with in concrete terms or to make meaningful to the average citizen. Second, the scattering of public authority and responsibility confronts the voter with a large number of issues and personalities on which he is to form a judgment. Bollens describes deficiences in citizen control in these colorful terms: "The pattern of many governments functioning in portions of metropolitan areas resembles a circus containing far more than the usual three rings. Public confusion, disinterest and cynicism mount because the time needed to watch over and control so many independent governmental operations is so large."[36]

A third reason for public apathy is the wide use of special districts and the employment of technically professionally trained men to administer them. One writer has pinpointed this problem by stating that it is "increasingly difficult for the citizens' elected agents to stay 'on top' of the highly trained experts whom it is their duty to keep in line as servants, not masters, of the people. . . . The citizen votes on a horizontal basis, but an increasing number of governmental policies and programs is being determined by functional specialists organized on a vertical basis and remote from popular control."[37] "Horizontal" in this sense relates to the voter's continuing allegiance to specific local governmental units, while "vertical" describes the transfer of services from general-purpose governments to special-purpose districts on an areal basis, encompassing more than one governmental unit.

Expressed in terms of desirable principles, the governmental machinery within the metropolitan area should be so organized that (1) political decisions are made through processes in which all citizens can share; (2) political decisions are made by an informed citizenry through discussion and vote; and (3) political decisions are made so that the process of public education is a continuing phenomenon. The realization of these goals is an undertaking of great difficulty, but one deserving of careful consideration and concentrated effort.

[36] The Council of State Governments, *op. cit.*, p. 21.
[37] Joseph McLean, "Threat to Responsible Rule," *National Municipal Review*, 40 (September, 1951), 412.

Their achievement could solve a major problem of metropolitan communities, for as Charles Adrian has pointed out:

Our biggest problem in the end—given America's commitment to democracy—may be that of preventing the ordinary metropolitanite from developing a sense of alienation from the local political process. If our goal is to preserve the institutions of democracy, the burden of proof is on those who would take away the little governments (or give them nothing to decide, which amounts to the same thing). For all their faults, little governments almost certainly, in comparison with all other governments, maximize the ordinary citizen's sense of participation —and they do continue to muddle through.[38]

SUGGESTED READINGS

Books

Banfield, Edward C. and Grodzins, Morton, *Government and Housing in Metropolitan Areas* (New York: McGraw-Hill, 1958).

Committee for Economic Development, *Guiding Metropolitan Growth* (New York: Committee for Economic Development, 1960).

Council of State Governments, *The States and the Metropolitan Problem* (Chicago: Council of State Governments, 1954).

Dinerman, Beatrice, Clayton, Ross, and Yerby, Richard D., *Metropolitan Services, Studies of Allocation in a Federated Organization* (Los Angeles: Bureau of Governmental Research, University of California, 1961).

Governor's Commission on Metropolitan Area Problems, *Metropolitan California* (Sacramento: 1961).

Greer, Scott, *Governing the Metropolis* (New York: Wiley, 1962).

Gulick, Luther H., *The Metropolitan Problem and American Ideas* (New York: Knopf, 1962).

Gulick, Luther H., *Metro: Changing Problems and Lines of Attack* (Washington: Governmental Affairs Institute, 1957).

Hirsch, Werner Z. (ed.), *Urban Life and Form* (New York: Holt, Rinehart & Winston, 1963).

Jones, Victor, *Metropolitan Government* (Chicago: University of Chicago Press, 1942).

Long, Norton E., *The Polity* (Chicago: Rand McNally, 1962).

Martin, Roscoe C. and Price, Douglas, *The Metropolis and Its Problems* (Syracuse: Maxwell Graduate School of Citizenship and Public Affairs, 1960).

[38] Charles R. Adrian, "Metropology: Folklore and Field Research," *Public Administration Review*, 21 (Summer, 1961), 157.

Owen, Wilfred, *The Metropolitan Transportation Problem* (Washington: Brookings Institution, 1956).

Scott, Stanley (ed.), *Metropolitan Area Problems* (Berkeley: Bureau of Public Administration and University Extension, University of California, 1960).

Wood, Robert C., *Metropolis Against Itself* (New York: Committee for Economic Development, 1959).

Wood, Robert C., *Suburbia, Its People and Their Politics* (Boston: Houghton Mifflin, 1959).

Woodbury, Coleman (ed.), *The Future of Cities and Urban Redevelopment* (Chicago: University of Chicago Press, 1953).

Articles

Adrian, Charles R., "Metropology: Folklore and Field Research," *Public Administration Review, 21* (Summer, 1961), 148–57.

Fitch, Lyle C., "Metropolitan Financial Problems," *The Annals of the American Academy of Political and Social Science, 314* (November, 1957), 66–73.

Greer, Scott, "The Social Structure and Political Process of Suburbia," *American Sociological Review, 25* (August, 1960), 514–26.

Hawley, Amos, "The Incorporation Trend in Metropolitan Areas, 1900–1950," *Journal of the American Institute of Planners, 25* (February, 1950), 41–46.

Long, Norton E., "Recent Theories and Problems of Local Government," paper presented at American Political Science Association meeting, Washington, September 6, 1956.

McLean, Joseph, "Threat to Responsible Rule," *National Municipal Review, 40* (September, 1951), 412–7.

Moak, Lennox L., "Some Practical Obstacles in Modifying Governmental Structure to Meet Metropolitan Problems," *University of Pennsylvania Law Review, 105* (February, 1957), 603–16.

Scott, Stanley, "Metropolitan Area Problems: What Are They?" *Public Affairs Report, 1* (October, 1960), 1–4.

Woodbury, Coleman, "Great Cities, Great Problems, Great Possibilities," *Public Administration Review, 18* (Autumn, 1958), 332–40.

Zimmer, Basil G. and Hawley, Amos, "Local Government as Viewed by Fringe Residents," *Rural Sociology, 23* (December, 1958), 363–70.

Governmental Patterns
in Metropolitan Areas

26

The present pattern of government in metropolitan areas has been variously described as "a crazy-quilt pattern," "a governmental maze," "a governmental hodge-podge," and "a Topsy-like arrangement—one which has just 'growed' without planning and forethought." Just as there is similarity in metaphorical descriptions, there is near unanimity of opinion that the division of authority and responsibility among a large number of independent political units is a major factor in the complexity of metropolitan problems. This complex maze is worthy of more careful examination, since its structure and operation affects the daily lives of nearly two out of every three Americans.

Contrary to the national trend which showed a decrease in the total number of local units in the last five years, the number of local governments in the SMSAs increased by 3 percent since 1957. Municipal incorporations increased by 8 percent in metropolitan areas, compared to a nationwide increase of 4.5 percent. The number of school districts in metropolitan areas, on the other hand, decreased by 20 percent since 1957, in contrast to the 31 percent decrease in the nation as a whole. A reclassification of special districts makes it difficult to compare the relative numbers of these units existing in SMSAs in 1957 and 1962, but it is most probable that a higher number of these units have been created within the metropolitan areas than in our less urban and rural areas. As has been noted, these figures indicate that "metropolitan areas are leading the nation in municipal incorporations and establishment of special districts, and lagging in reduction of school districts."[1]

■ Governmental Trends in Metropolitan Areas

The introductory paragraphs may seem to indicate that the pattern of local governments in metropolitan areas is becoming more complex and that the only discernible trend is one toward a more complicated system of local governments. In terms of numbers of units, as noted above, this development appears to be a most probable one. However, along with the trends of continuing incorporation of new municipalities and increasing use of special districts, at least two other movements can be identified. One is the creation of metropolitan associations of local governments, and the second is the increased interest of the federal and of many state governments in metropolitan problems.[2]

Concerning the trend toward associations of local governments, Jones states "The 1960's may well be known as the decade of metropolitan cooperation through the association of local governments."[3] Four such associations were created in 1961—in the San Francisco Bay Area, Philadelphia, Baltimore, and Ithaca—to join five other voluntary associations already in existence. The earlier ones, in the order of their establishment, were the Detroit Area Supervisors Inter-County Committee organized in 1954; the New York Metropolitan Region Council in 1956; the Washington (D. C.) Metropolitan Regional Conference in 1957; and the Salem (Oregon) Intergovernmental Cooperation Council in 1958. The major attractive features of such associations, according to Jones, are fourfold. "In the first place, local officials can take full credit for voluntarily associating without any legal compulsion, to 'meet the problems of overcoming the geographical fragmentation of our

---

[1] Norman Beckman and Marjorie Cahn Brazer, "Governments Galore," *National Civic Review, 52* (March, 1963), 137.

[2] Victor Jones, "Associations of Local Governments: Patterns for Metropolitan Cooperation," *Public Affairs Report, 3* (April, 1962), 1-5.

[3] *Ibid.,* p. 1.

urban regions.' Secondly, such an association is said to make un-necessary the creation or imposition of a 'super-government' for the metropolis. Furthermore, it recognizes the local sovereignty of each county and each municipality in the metropolitan area. And, finally, it provides an instrument for common defense against local or state attacks on local sovereignties."[4]

Jones recognizes that the emergence of voluntary associations of local governments is at present an ineffectual alternative to the establishment of additional special districts. However, he also views the rise of these associations as the most promising development in our American federal system, for four reasons. First, their creation demonstrates as awareness on the part of local elected officials of the areawide implications of some of their own problems, needs and activities. Second, the forum provided by the association establishes a means for discussing important matters. Third, the association can serve as an equal partner in discussions with federal and state agencies. And, fourth, the association "appears to be a necessary and viable first stage of the 'emergent federalism' of metropolitan communities."[5]

The increasing interest of our federal government and of many of our state governments in the problems of metropolitan areas scarcely needs further documentation. Chapters 4 and 5 on relations of local governments to states and to the federal government noted their increasing concern with urban problems. In recent years, all three levels of government have given attention to the desirability for and the means of maintaining strong and responsible local governments in metropolitan areas. The attempts to establish a Department of Urban Affairs, though unsuccessful, are well known. Also at the federal level, the Advisory Commission on Intergovernmental Relations has studied and prepared an excellent report on metropolitan problems.[6]

Gulick believes that any effective program of action must recognize that all three levels of government must take a hand in dealing with our rising metropolitan problems. In his words, "What we now need from the federal government is an honest recognition that there is nothing to be ashamed of when the national govern-

[4] *Ibid.*
[5] *Ibid.*, pp. 4–5.
[6] Advisory Commission on Intergovernmental Relations, *Governmental Structure, Organization and Planning in Metropolitan Areas,* Government Printing Office, 1961.

ment does something for urban populations to help solve their nationwide metropolitan problems. Next we need from the federal government a decent coordination at the top among the many federal programs which have an impact on metropolitan affairs."[7]

In a careful study of state responsibilities for obtaining appropriate organization and development in metropolitan areas, John Bollens suggested a five-point program for state action. The basic and clearly related steps were:

1. Establish legal authorizations for the creation of general metropolitan units that can be adequate in functions, financing ability, and structure. These units may be one or more of three types: multi-purpose metropolitan district, federation, and urban county.
2. Determine which method is preferable for putting the selected type or types of unit into effect: legislative action, local voter decision, or administrative or judicial determination.
3. Provide suitable legal provisions relating to two supplementary procedures: annexation and inter-local agreements.
4. Appraise the adequacy of local governments in terms of area, financial ability, administrative organization, administrative methods, and amount of discretion in the exercise of powers. Make necessary changes in accordance with the results of the appraisal.
5. Create or adapt an agency (1) to aid in determining the present and changing needs of metropolitan and non-metropolitan areas in the state and (2) to analyze the effects in such areas of current and contemplated policies of national state and local governments and major private organizations.[8]

Even with these basic changes of attitude and approach at the federal and state levels, however, there remains a significant role for the local governments within metropolitan areas. Gulick sees four kinds of governmental duties handled by local governments. These are: (1) the normal run of traditional local activities assigned to local governments by the state. These include aspects of law and order, public safety, parks and recreation, education, health and welfare, various utilities, streets, etc.; (2) continuing participation in functions or responsibilities which are transferred to a wider jurisdiction, since the action basis is broadened rather than taken away; (3) the development of a comprehensive general program and plan

[7] Luther H. Gulick, *The Metropolitan Problem and American Ideas*, Knopf, 1962, p. 133.
[8] The Council of State Governments, *The States and the Metropolitan Problem*, Council of State Governments, 1956, p. 128.

for areawide progress and guidance through broad community agreement as to where the area expects and is determined to go; and (4) grass-roots coordination of federal, state, and local programs.[9]

■ Approaches to Governing the Metropolis

The problem of metropolitan government stems largely from the contradiction between the underlying unity of a metropolitan area and its fragmented governmental structure. A web of inter-relationships creates a community of interest that is fractionalized among a number of separate governmental units. To meet this problem, a number of approaches are being tried. Some involve few or no changes in the structure of government within the area, while others do call for fundamental changes in the jurisdiction, structure and functions of existing units. Devices in the first category are interjurisdictional agreements, annexation, single-purpose special districts, functional transfers, metropolitan planning, and extension of administration by state and federal governments. Five approaches involving government changes are city-county consolidation, city-county separation, multi-purpose special districts, metropolitan counties, and federation.

INTERJURISDICTIONAL AGREEMENTS

Interjurisdictional agreements are here defined to include both formal or written compacts and informal or clearly understood unwritten compacts by which two or more governmental units voluntarily attempt to solve a mutual problem. As a cooperative device, the interjurisdictional agreement has five characteristics which account in large part for their popularity. The device permits (1) joint action by the participating governmental units on problems of common concern, (2) usually at financial savings, and (3) normally the problem is met more efficiently than it could be through separate efforts. In addition, the device maintains the corporate identity of the participating units, and it permits their elected officials to retain a degree of control over and responsibility for the functions which are provided cooperatively.

[9] Gulick, *op. cit.*, pp. 139-44.

A recent study of interjurisdictional agreements in the Philadelphia area reported 693 such agreements, in which 887 local units were participants. The largest number of agreements existed in service areas—police and fire protection, public education, sewage disposal, etc.[10] Although cooperative action through interjurisdictional agreement seemed widely accepted in the five-county area around Pennsylvania, the writer concluded "it is difficult to point out even a single service area in which a problem has been solved although there are numerous instances in which a problem has been met for the present. This may appear to be a fine point of distinction, but it is a very real one. The interjurisdictional agreement device at its best can be only a stop-gap arrangement to meet a current problem and it can only ameliorate—not solve the problem."[11]

ANNEXATION

Annexation means the addition of new territory to an established governmental unit—to the core city in metropolitan areas. At first glance, this method seems the most obvious one to be adopted, but it has become increasingly unsatisfactory and holds little promise for the future. The basic reason for its decline is the requirement in most states that areas can be annexed only upon approval by the voters in the unincorporated areas affected as well as in the annexing city. Thus, except in a few states, notably Virginia, Texas, and Missouri, constitutional or statutory provisions make the annexation of incorporated municipalities almost impossible and the annexation of unincorporated territory most difficult.

While annexation may still be desirable in a number of instances, it was never a permanent solution to the problem of fringe settlements around a city. Population growth outran annexations in almost every community. A second problem is that most state laws prohibit annexations across county lines, and annexations across state boundaries are impossible. Yet modern urban developments certainly flow over into areas of adjoining counties and states. A

[10] George S. Blair, *Interjurisdictional Agreements in Southeastern Pennsylvania*, Fels Institute of Local and State Government, University of Pennsylvania, 1960.

[11] *Ibid.*, p. 124. Also see Guthrie S. Birkhead, Jr., *Inter-local Cooperation in New York State*, Department of Audit and Control, 1958, and Matthew Holden, Jr., *Inter-Governmental Agreements in the Cleveland Metropolitan Area*, staff report to Study Group on Governmental Organization, 1958.

third factor is the increasing tendency of territories in and around center cities to incorporate as separate municipal entities.

Writing in 1942, Victor Jones proved a good prophet. He wrote, "There is less hope today that this device (annexation) will bring any large part of the metropolitan population under what might be called a 'metropolitan government' than there was before technological developments had facilitated the flow of population from the city to the suburbs, before suburban pressure groups had written cumbersome procedures into statutes and constitutions, and before the development of alternative schemes of integration that arouse less opposition on the part of people who live outside the central cities."[12]

SPECIAL DISTRICTS

Since special districts were discussed in an earlier chapter, they will be considered only briefly here. However, their importance in metropolitan areas is attested to by their continuing growth in numbers. As designated by the Bureau of the Census, there were 12,340 non-school special districts in 1952, 14,424 in 1957, and 18,323 in 1962. While nearly 1,700 of the districts recognized in 1962 as special districts were regarded as dependent agencies rather than independent agencies prior to that enumeration, the growth of special districts has been a continuing and important trend.[13]

According to Jones, the growth of special districts reflects the immediateness of their advantages and the dimness of their disadvantages. Their four advantages over other forms of metropolitan organization are: (1) their creation does not do away with the corporate identity of any of the existing units of local government; (2) they can cross county and state boundary lines; (3) they may circumvent constitutional and statutory limitations on debt and tax capacities of local units and enable the financing of needed capital improvements; and (4) they are easily established in most

[12] Victor Jones, *Metropolitan Government,* University of Chicago Press, 1942, p. 129. For additional information on annexation, see Council of State Governments, *op. cit.,* pp. 25-52; A. O. Spain, "Politics of Recent Municipal Annexations in Texas," *Southwestern Social Science Quarterly, 30* (June, 1949), 18-28; and Chester W. Bain, "Annexation: Virginia's Not-so-judicial System," *Public Administration Review, 15* (Autumn, 1955), 251-62.

[13] Bureau of the Census, *Governmental Units in 1962,* GC-P6, 1962 Census of Governments, December 6, 1962, pp. 1-2.

states. Their major disadvantage lies in the cumulative effect of their use. As Jones sees it, "One special district may be of no import, but ultimately their use will lead to functional disintegration. This is a problem of politics, of control, as well as of administration and will force us to reorder our values or start all over again to build a community from functional fragments."[14]

Words of equal censure have been written by John Bollens, the most thorough student of special districts in the United States. In his words, "As presently used, the district approach lacks sufficient comprehensiveness to deal with the general metropolitan problem. Its limited functional nature leads us to further proliferation of governmental units, to more widespread citizen confusion and to inadequate popular control of the governmental system. . . . they may tend to lull local residents into a false sense of satisfaction that the total metropolitan problem, which consists of many deficiencies, has been solved."[15] It should be noted, however, that most special districts are single-purpose and have a limited functional responsibility. The use of multi-purpose districts, discussed below, might yield a different analysis of the potential of this device.

METROPOLITAN PLANNING

In order to fill the gap between the need for metropolitan planning and its political practicality, a number of metropolitan planning commissions have been established in recent years. While it is sometimes stated that metropolitan planning would make formal metropolitan government unnecessary, one writer notes that "these claims are not false but exaggerated."[16] While planning is necessary for effective legislative and administrative action on metropolitan problems, it is not a reasonable substitute if no machinery for implementing its recommendations exists.

Regional planning commissions are now operating in a number of metropolitan areas including Washington, D. C., Little Rock, the Minneapolis–St. Paul area, Cleveland, Toledo, Chicago, and Atlanta. One of the more comprehensive regional planning agencies is the

---

[14] Victor Jones, "The Organization of a Metropolitan Region," *University of Pennsylvania Law Review, 105* (February, 1957), 545.

[15] Council of State Governments, *op. cit.,* p. 122. The basic reference on special districts is John C. Bollens, *Special District Governments in the United States,* University of California Press, 1957.

[16] Jones, "The Organization of a Metropolitan Region," *op. cit.,* p. 546.

Detroit Metropolitan Area Regional Planning Commission, a statutory body created in 1947 to serve both immediate and long-range planning objectives. The area initially served by the Commission included Wayne, Oakland, and Macomb Counties and three townships in Washtenaw County. The Commission consists of 23 public officials selected from participating governmental units and an equal number of citizens representing important civic, social, and economic fields. All members are appointed by the governor for overlapping terms of three years, and in practice, members have been reappointed.

The Commission has purely advisory powers, but it is granted access to studies and records of governmental agencies. It has obtained and maintained stature by the quality of its work, and it influences the policies of other agencies. In part, this has been a result of the philosophy of the Commission which has been to work closely with the agencies and people of the region. The Commission acts as advisor to both the Wayne County Zoning and Coordinating Committee and the Detroit Area Industrial Dispersion Committee.

The subordinate structure of the Commission is an important contribution to a workable organization for regional planning. Two types of groups are used. The first consists of advisory committees representing interest either in a specific problem or in self-contained segments of a problem. The second is the development area council as a means of making contact with the units of government in the region and of overcoming the problem of the corporate boundary. The region has been divided into 19 development areas on the basis of the forces affecting the growth of each. Area councils within the areas assemble data concerning land use, economic base, and population. The Commission has completed a number of significant studies and the area it serves has now been expanded to include five counties.[17]

FUNCTIONAL TRANSFERS

Transfer of functions is a mild approach to the metropolitan problem, and yet it can be reasonably effective in one-county

[17] For a fuller explanation of the area council plan, see: T. L. Blakeman and R. D. Carpenter, "Why Development Area Councils?" *The American City,* 27 (August, 1952), 102–3; and T. L. Blakeman, "Detroit's Regional Plan," *National Municipal Review, 44* (October, 1955), 466–70.

METROPOLITAN AREAS

metropolitan areas. This approach involves reallocation of a service or services by transferring them from municipalities to the county or from the county to the municipalities. One of the most significant reassignments of local functions occurred between Atlanta and Fulton County, Georgia, in 1952, following the preparation of a Plan of Improvement to eliminate overlapping and duplication.

The Plan of Improvement contained four major types of provisions. One resulted in the annexation of 82 square miles to Atlanta. A second established a procedure for future annexations to the city by judicial determination. A third was the reallocation of functions between the city and county. And the fourth virtually excluded the county government from further performance of municipal functions.

Under the reassignment of functions, the following services were to be provided by Atlanta for the area: fire and police protection, inspections, garbage collection, parks and recreation, airports, water, sewers, library, auditorium, and traffic engineering. The county assumed the functions of public health, public welfare services, courts, and surveying. Both city and county provide public education, road and street maintenance and construction, planning and zoning, and law enforcement. The Georgia state legislature appropriated money to pay for an appraisal of all property in the county, resulting in the merger of the city and county offices of tax assessment and collection.[18]

DIRECT ACTION BY HIGHER LEVELS

The shifting of power from a lower level of government to a higher level has been a subject of much concern in the past few decades. While the weight of expressed opinion seems to be against this trend, the movement itself is unmistakable. As even larger percentages of the American populace become concentrated in metropolitan areas, we can expect both the state and federal governments to become more directly involved in a number of service problems including those of water, transportation, air pollution, water pollution, and health.

Recognizing this probable increasing role of higher levels of

[18] For a fuller account of the Atlanta-Fulton County story, see M. C. Hughes, "Annexation and Reallocation of Functions," *Public Management, 34* (February, 1952), 26–30.

government in concern for metropolitan problems, Gulick calls for the working out of appropriate assignments of the three "extensions" of government under the principle of intergovernmental cooperation. He states, "In the process of assignment we will deal with 'aspects' of functions, not with the allocation of whole functions. We will look at highways, at water supply and sewers, at pollution control, at education, at crime control, at planning and zoning, and at every other service and governmental activity, and decide what 'aspects' of these functions shall be done by the federal government, what by the state, and what by the local constituency."[19]

While there is no metropolitan area in which there has been extensive integration through action by higher levels (with the obvious exception of Washington, D. C.), there are a number of specific examples of state and federal influence and leadership. Federal programs now encourage regional planning for such programs as housing, urban renewal and redevelopment, and highways. Most federal grant-in-aids are funneled through the county government, thus strengthening it as the administrative unit of local government in metropolitan areas. A number of these grants were discussed in Chapter 5. Examples of state assumption of services previously exercised by local governments are more numerous. While the specific services assumed vary among the states, they include such services as welfare, highways, health and hospitals.

CITY-COUNTY CONSOLIDATION

City-county consolidation, as the term implies, consists of a partial or complete merger of the area and government of a county with that of the city or cities lying within it. Theoretically, this seems a reasonable approach to governmental integration in one-county metropolitan areas. But despite the fact that it is widely advocated, city-county consolidation has been adopted in only a few instances, and five of the seven consolidations are not of recent origin.

Of the five consolidations that occurred prior to the last half-century, three, in the order of their occurrence, were in the City and Parish of New Orleans in 1805, Boston and Suffolk County in 1821, and the City and County of Philadelphia in 1854. Through a series of consolidations, New York City was extended to encompass the five counties of New York, Kings, Richmond, Queens, and

[19] Gulick, *The Metropolitan Problem and American Ideas*, p. 130.

Bronx. These consolidations occurred between 1730 and 1912, with the 1898 consolidation the best known and the one involving the largest amount of territory. The fifth early consolidation occurred in 1907 when the City and County of Honolulu were joined.

City-county consolidation seemed an approach of the past until 1947 when a consolidation charter was adopted by the voters of the City of Baton Rouge and East Baton Rouge Parish by the narrow margin of 307 votes. The legal identities of the two units were retained, but their governments were interlocked in several ways. The city councilmen of Baton Rouge constitute a majority of the members of the parish council. A mayor-president, elected on a parishwide basis, presides over both councils and serves as the chief administrator of both governments. He appoints a number of administrative officials who serve both the city and the parish.

The parish was divided for taxation and service purposes into an urban area, two industrial areas, and a rural area. This was done to provide tax rate differentials among the types of areas as well as for establishing differing service levels. The boundaries of the City of Baton Rouge were extended to the limits of the urban area, thus increasing its territory from 6.5 to 30 square miles. Procedures were established for further annexations to the city and for the creation of additional industrial areas. A town and a village, which are the only other incorporated places in this metropolitan area, were largely unaffected by the plan. The charter, however, prohibits incorporation in the parish of additional cities, towns or villages.[20]

A second modern city-county consolidation occurred in June, 1962, when the voters of Nashville and Davidson County, Tennessee, gave consolidated government a clean-cut victory. Under the terms of the charter, the new government was to begin operations in the spring of 1963. However, the transition necessary to effect the consolidation began almost immediately. The city and county school boards were merged on July 1, 1962, and a single tax assessment program became effective September 1 of that year. The first mayor of the metropolitan government was elected in November, 1962, with C. Beverly Briley, a county judge who led the campaign for the consolidation movement, chosen for the new office. While it is

[20] See J. M. Stoker, *Our City-Parish Government: A Thumbnail Sketch,* Baton Rouge Junior Chamber of Commerce, 1954; T. H. Reed, "Progress in Metropolitan Integration," *Public Administration Review,* 9 (Winter, 1949), 1–10; and R. G. Kean, "Consolidation that Works," *National Municipal Review, 45* (November, 1956), 478–85.

still too early to know how this consolidation will work, its successful initiation probably means that renewed efforts will be waged to achieve similar consolidation between Knoxville and Knox County and between Memphis and Shelby County, also in Tennessee.[21]

In an appraisal of the merits of city-county consolidation, Bollens states, "The greatest merit of the city-county consolidation approach lies in providing a unified, coordinated program of service, development and control over an area larger than that previously served exclusively by one general local government. It eliminates duplication of certain services formerly provided by both city and county governments, and consequently it is financially attractive, particularly when municipalities occupy most of the territory that is consolidated."[22]

CITY-COUNTY SEPARATION

City-county separation involves the detachment of a city, sometimes after territorial enlargement, from the rest of the county, with the new city government performing both municipal and county functions within its territory. Current city-counties, which resulted from such separation movements, exist in Baltimore, Denver, St. Louis, and San Francisco, and in a number of Virginia cities. In Virginia, city-county separation occurs through an automatic legal process, while in the other four cities it resulted from local sponsorship.

It is interesting to note that none of the major city-county separations is of recent origin. The operative dates of separation are Baltimore in 1851, San Francisco in 1856, St. Louis in 1876, and Denver in 1902. The fact that there have been no additional separations, outside of Virginia, for 60 years attests to some of the shortcomings of this method. For one thing, city-county separation traps the city within the territorial confines established at the time of separation, and it cannot grow as the area around it becomes urbanized and dependent upon it. Second, this device removes the richest source of income from the parent county and the remains of the county may be such that economical and efficient government is difficult to maintain. Third, the city is often removed from a position of influence in the area and another governmental unit

[21] Daniel R. Grant, "Merger Approved in Nashville Area," *National Civic Review*, 51 (September, 1962), 449-50; and *Metropolitan Area Problems*, "Metro Victory in Tennessee," 5 (July–August, 1962), 1, 5.
[22] Council of State Governments, *op. cit.*, p. 74.

has been created. Bollens appraises city-county separation as "a step backward from attainment of a governmental jurisdiction of metropolitan scope. It cannot be regarded as a generally effective approach to the metropolitan problem."[23]

City-county separation in Virginia differs appreciably from the four cases mentioned above. Separation of the city is an automatic process, applicable to cities of at least 5,000. Cities of 10,000 or more are completely separated from the county and perform all the functions of both city and county governments within their boundaries. Cities of 5,000 which separate from the county are equally independent except for sharing the circuit court of the county. In 1962, there were 33 such city-counties in Virginia.

MULTI-PURPOSE METROPOLITAN DISTRICTS

The multi-purpose metropolitan district is a method to ameliorate metropolitan problems, combining the advantages of the special district and broadening the purposes it serves and the services it can render. Thus, it meets, at least in part, the problem of the limited functional nature of single-purpose districts. However in undertaking to solve a few critical problems, such multi-purpose districts tend to divert interest away from more thorough efforts at reorganization.

The Boston experience with special districts is an interesting one. The Metropolitan District Commission in the Boston area is an outgrowth of three separate commissions—the Metropolitan Sewer Commission, the Metropolitan Water Board, and the Metropolitan Parks Commission. The Water and Sewer Commissions were merged in 1901 and this body was merged with the Parks Commission in 1919. This Commission is an agency of the Commonwealth of Massachusetts rather than a direct instrument of the local governments it serves. Its five commissioners are appointed by the governor and the expenditures of the Commission are included in the annual Commonwealth budget established by the state legislature. However, most of the amounts spent by the Commission are later recovered by a levy on participating units.

In one capacity or another, the Metropolitan District Commission serves Boston and 44 suburban communities. Thirty-eight cities and towns subscribe to its park services, 34 subscribe to the sewer system service, and 24 subscribe for water services. Boston is in-

[23] *Ibid.*, p. 85.

cluded in each. The Commission serves as a "wholesaler" to the participating governments in the service areas of water and sewers. It procures and sells water to the local units, which in turn sell it to their residents in locally owned and operated distribution systems. Collection of sewage is similar in that the local units pump it to the district which collects, treats and disposes of it. The district owns more than 11,380 square miles of parks with some 120 miles of streets and roads under its control. A Metropolitan District Police force of almost 400 men was organized to serve the several departments of the Commission, with duties ranging from protection of a water supply reservoir to pulling would-be suicides from rivers.

The Boston Commission seems to have carried out its three basic functions satisfactorily and with reasonable honesty and efficiency. However, the areas served by the Commission are not large enough to include all the area which should be included for effective planning and programming of the three services. Newer metropolitan functions have not been assigned to the Commission but have been placed in other agencies such as the Metropolitan Transit Authority, which now operates in 14 cities and towns, and the Port Authority Agency.[24]

In its recent report, the Governor's Commission on Metropolitan Area Problems in California recommended the establishment of a multi-purpose special district in each of the state's 10 metropolitan areas. The districts would be responsible for regional planning and at least one additional function from a list of such functions as air pollution control, water supply, sewage disposal and drainage, transportation, parks and parkways, law enforcement, fire protection, urban renewal, or civil defense.[25] While the recommendation has not yet been implemented, and may never be in California, the report probably accurately depicts a growing importance of multi-purpose special districts as a solution to metropolitan area problems.

METROPOLITAN COUNTY PLAN

Since a little over three-fifths of the metropolitan areas are contained within a single county, well-organized and well-governed county governments have real possibilities as the best units to

[24] For a fuller discussion, see Charles R. Cherrington, "Metropolitan Special Districts: The Boston Metropolitan District Commission," in Stephen B. Sweeney and George S. Blair (eds.), *Metropolitan Analysis: Important Elements of Study and Scope*, University of Pennsylvania Press, 1958, pp. 127–42.

[25] Governor's Commission on Metropolitan Area Problems, *Meeting Metropolitan Problems*, Sacramento, December, 1960.

achieve metropolitan integration. Because of the general poor reputation of county government in America and the decentralized structure of county government, two basic reforms are needed to convert the county into an effective metropolitan unit. First, the structure of government should be modernized to provide for a chief executive officer. Second, counties must be given powers to perform urban-type services.

There have been numerous proposals and some actions in recent years to establish urban counties. In 1947, voters in Erie County (Buffalo), New York, approved several measures aimed at making the county an instrument of urban government. Similarly, Milwaukee County has assumed a number of functions in recent years qualifying it as an urban county. Voters in Dade County, Florida, in 1956, approved a plan creating an urban county. Because of the federated nature of the plan for composing the governing board, this plan will be discussed in the section on federation which follows. More modern charters have also been adopted in St. Louis and Baltimore Counties creating these suburban counties, which adjoin but are not part of the cities with the same names, as modified urban counties.

The most extensive urban county development has occurred in California which has granted four important authorizations to county governments. In 1911, counties were authorized to adopt home rule charters; counties were authorized to undertake municipal functions in 1913; in 1921, counties and cities were permitted to contract with other governmental jurisdictions to provide services; and in 1953, the county service area law was enacted providing a method for people in unincorporated urban areas to receive and pay for county services.

The development of the urban county in California is epitomized by the expansion of services rendered by Los Angeles County. This county acts as a county coordinator by five principal means. These are: (1) performing certain services directly on a countywide basis, (2) directing activities of certain special districts that have countywide significance, (3) performing functions transferred to it by other local governments, (4) performing municipal services for cities on the basis of contracts, and (5) exercising leadership influence because of its size and the recognized qualities of its administration.[26]

[26] Winston Crouch, "Expanding the Role of the Urban County: The Los Angeles Experiment," in Sweeney and Blair, *op. cit.*, pp. 107-8.

One of the first and best known examples of county service to cities in Los Angeles County is the contractual arrangement for the assessment and collection of taxes. All but three or four of the 74 incorporated municipalities utilized this county service in 1962. Other examples among the more than 500 different services performed by the county for one or more municipalities include health administration, personnel administration, enforcement of industrial waste ordinances, issuance of building permits, election administration, fire protection, law enforcement, library services, parks, planning and zoning, sewer construction and maintenance, and street lighting.

Services provided to cities by Los Angeles County are usually arranged for in one of two ways—through contracts or through county service area districts. Contractual arrangements must be approved by the city and county and include one or more of four financial arrangements. These are through direct citizen payment for services, maximum rates established by state law, a cost per unit of service basis, or an annual rate basis. Services provided through county service areas are financed by a special tax levy on the residents of the specific area receiving those services. Control of the types and levels of service is determined by the local community and all contractual agreements are entered into voluntarily.

The logical development of the county contract program reached fulfillment in 1954 in the so-called "Lakewood Plan," named for the city of Lakewood. As a newly incorporated city, Lakewood negotiated a master contract with the county for all its administrative services. The local officials of Lakewood serve largely as negotiators with the county government and as liaison agents with the various county departments to arrange for services requested by the local council. Crouch describes this arrangement as "coordination of consumer demand—a new dimension perhaps in city government."[27] More recently incorporated cities have tended to follow the Lakewood pattern and contract for a large number of services from the county.

The contractual pattern as provided by Los Angeles County has been both highly praised and sharply criticized. A recent statement by the mayor of Lakewood concerning the system is worth quoting. In his words,

[27] *Ibid.*, p. 114.

The advantages of the contractual system are that it permits a city to retain home rule, acquire municipal services without any needless duplication of costs, and at the same time preserve the right to specify the level and the performance of services. The only disadvantage which can be ascribed to this system is that the county or the agency may unfairly charge a contracting city for the services. However, by means of negotiation and conferences, this is a remote possibility. Furthermore, the city retains the right to terminate contracts at appropriate intervals. This permits developing other arrangements, perhaps with other agencies, to perform the equivalent services at fairly reasonable costs.[28]

FEDERATION

The basic element of federated forms of metropolitan government is the division of functions between a newly established metropolitan government agency and the existing local governments. The metropolitan governing body consists of representatives of the local units who are either elected to serve on the metropolitan board or serve on it in an *ex officio* capacity because of their positions in their home communities. While this device has been much heralded as the most promising device for metropolitan integration, there have been few serious efforts and only three successful ones to implement it.[29]

A plan for a federated metropolitan government in Toronto was prepared after extensive hearings by the Ontario Municipal Board. Becoming operative on January 1, 1954, the action established the Municipality of Metropolitan Toronto, an areawide unit of government overlying the territory of 13 municipalities. The city of Toronto and 12 suburban municipalities were continued in existence and were assigned all functions not allocated to the metropolitan unit. The governing body is a 25-member board, 12 of whom are from Toronto, 12 from the smaller municipalities, and a chairman chosen by the other members. All members, except the chairman, serve because of the nature of the local offices they hold.

Major powers assigned to the metropolitan government include areawide aspects of water supply, sewage disposal, arterial high-

[28] Angelo M. Iacaboni, "Statement," in The Governor's Commission on Metropolitan Area Problems, *Metropolitan California*, p. 56.

[29] In 1960, the Metropolitan Corporation of Greater Winnipeg was created by the Manitoba Provincial legislature. This federation is similar to the one established earlier in Toronto.

ways, certain health and welfare services, housing and redevelopment, metropolitan parks, and overall planning. The metropolitan council was also given complete charge of assessment and was to establish a uniform basis of assessment for the area. Important functions reserved to the local municipalities are fire protection, most public health services, direct public relief, libraries, and building regulation. Law enforcement, initially allotted to the local municipalities, was transferred to the metropolitan government in 1957. In the functional fields in which it operates, the metropolitan government serves as a wholesaler supplying services to the constituent municipalities which in turn sell the services to their citizens.

Federation was implemented in the Toronto area without having to satisfy two requirements, one or both of which have proved to be insurmountable obstacles to most attempts at federation in the United States. Neither constitutional authorization nor local voter consent was necessary, since the plan was submitted to the provincial legislature by the Ontario Municipal Board, a quasi-judicial body with wide jurisdiction over municipal affairs.[30]

The Dade County (Florida) metropolitan government is not a federation strictly speaking since it combines features of the urban county with those of a federation. Voters adopted a locally prepared home rule charter on May 21, 1957, redistributing functions between the strengthened county and its 26 municipalities. The charter set up the legislative and governing body of the county as a Board of Commissioners of undetermined size. Five members were to be chosen by countywide vote from districts, five from and by districts, and each city of 60,000 or more was authorized to elect one member to the board. As of 1963, the three cities of Miami, Miami Beach, and Hialeah qualified for their own representatives, making the board of commissioners a body of 13 members.

The charter abolished all previously independently elected county

[30] For a fuller account of the Toronto experiment with federation, see Frederick G. Gardiner, "Metropolitan Federation: Toronto's Experiment" in Sweeney and Blair, *op. cit.*, pp. 148-164; Council of State Governments, *op. cit.*, pp. 86-104; Winston Crouch, "Federated Local Government: One Approach to Metropolitan Organization," in The Governor's Commission on Metropolitan Area Problems, *op. cit.*, pp. 97-104; Winston Crouch, "Metropolitan Government in Toronto," *Public Administration Review, 14* (Spring, 1954), 85-95; James B. Milner, "The Metropolitan Toronto Plan," *University of Pennsylvania Law Review, 105* (February, 1957), 570-87; and John G. Grumm, *Metropolitan Area Government: The Toronto Experiment,* Governmental Research Center, University of Kansas, 1959.

officers except the school board, the school superintendent, and court officials. The county board was authorized to appoint a county manager and a county attorney. The manager, who heads the administrative organization of the county government, determines the selection of key administrative officers. County departments have been reduced from 35 to 17 under the new charter.

Among the functions assigned to the metropolitan government are mass transit, major streets and highways, planning, water and sewer systems, port facilities, the major parks and public beaches, hospitals, welfare services, assessment and collection of taxes, flood control, and water conservation. Additional functions may be transferred to the county from time to time with traffic engineering and penal functions already so transferred. The county commission is also responsible for performing the traditional rural functions in rural portions of the county. In addition, the county government is responsible for setting minimum standards for the services performed by the municipalities. If the standards are not met, the county may take over and perform the services in the non-complying municipalities.

In spite of the broad powers of the county board, it is the clear intention of the charter to preserve a large measure of local authority. Cities retain purely local aspects of the functions enumerated above as well as responsibility for providing police, fire, health, and other basic services. In addition, the charter specifically states that the municipalities retain local authority to conduct their own affairs and may raise the standards of zoning and service levels above those established by the county board within their own area.[31]

In its first years of corporate existence, the Dade County metro plan has met frequent opposition. The severest test came in October, 1961, when a package of over 40 amendments, which in effect would have revoked most of the metro charter, was defeated in a bitterly fought election. Some of its critics feel that the new government has assumed too much authority at the expense of the cities, while others feel it has moved with disappointing slowness in vital service areas. The dual nature of this criticism probably points to continu-

[31] For additional information on federation in Miami, see Public Administration Service, *The Government of Metropolitan Miami*, 1954 ; Gustave Serino, *Miami's Metropolitan Experiment*, Public Administration Clearing Service, University of Florida, 1958 ; Harry Toulmin, "First Metropolitan Government Created," *Public Management*, 39 (July, 1957), 151-3 ; and Crouch, "Federated Local Government: One Approach to Metropolitan Organization," *op. cit.*

ing controversy around the Dade County metropolitan government in the years ahead.

Appraising the merits of metropolitan federation, Bollens states:

Broad flexibility is a great potential merit of federation that is absent in certain other metropolitan reorganization approaches. Usually it is within the power of the local framers of a federation charter to include in the document a method of local initiation and approval of amendments. As conditions and attitudes change, the amending procedure can be used to reallocate functions between the metropolitan and local levels or to reconstitute the membership of the metropolitan governing body. It may be possible in some instances to specify in the locally formulated charter a simpler voting procedure for amending than that required in the constitutional authorization to adopt the plan initially. Territorial expansion of the federated area, however, usually must be preceded by altering the state constitution, and, less often, by passage of a state law.[32]

■ An Evaluation of Approaches

It is possible to evaluate the alternate approaches to the problem of metropolitan government in a number of ways. One of the most fruitful methods is to measure the approach in terms of the objectives sought in governmental reorganization. One statement of such objectives holds that metropolitan government should be so organized that it

1. Is easily adaptable to current and future problems that arise from changes in social organization, technology, and public attitudes.
2. Is capable of making long-range plans for the area and of implementing areawide policy.
3. Provides for reasonable citizen control and participation.
4. Maintains a system of strong local governments.
5. Provides an adequate level of urban public services, of acceptable quality, at reasonable unit costs, and without overlapping and duplication of services.
6. Distributes tax burdens fairly among all classes of citizens.
7. Receives adequate consideration by state and federal administrative agencies.
8. Provides an orderly means for the attainment of commonly agreed

---

[32] Council of State Governments, *op. cit.*, p. 104.

upon objectives and for the reconciliation or adjudication of conflicting interests.[33]

In view of these criteria, federation currently seems the most promising of the several approaches discussed. It provides for a two-layer system of government, with the metropolitan agency composed of representatives chosen by the citizens of the several community units. However, metropolitan areas continue to provide new frontiers for new solutions, and it is probable that a number of new ways will be devised in the years ahead.

SUGGESTED READINGS

Books

Blair, George S., *Interjurisdictional Agreements in Southeastern Pennsylvania* (Philadelphia: Fels Institute, University of Pennsylvania, 1960).

Bollens, John C., *Special District Governments in the United States* (Los Angeles: University of California Press, 1957).

California Governor's Commission on Metropolitan Area Problems, *Metropolitan California* (Sacramento: 1960).

Council of State Governments, *The States and the Metropolitan Problem* (Chicago: Council of State Governments, 1956).

Grumm, John G., *Metropolitan Area Government: The Toronto Experiment* (Lawrence: Governmental Research Center, University of Kansas, 1959).

Gulick, Luther H., *The Metropolitan Problem and American Ideas* (New York: Knopf, 1962).

Jones, Victor, *Metropolitan Government* (Chicago: University of Chicago Press, 1942).

Maddox, Russell W., *Extraterritorial Powers of Municipalities in the United States* (Corvallis: Oregon State College Press, 1955).

Serino, Gustave, *Miami's Metropolitan Experiment* (Gainesville: Public Administration Clearing Service, University of Florida, 1958).

Stoker, J. M., *Our City-Parish Government: A Thumbnail Sketch* (Baton Rouge: Junior Chamber of Commerce, 1954).

Sweeney, Stephen B. and Blair, George S. (eds.), *Metropolitan Analysis: Important Elements of Study and Action* (Philadelphia: University of Pennsylvania Press, 1958).

Tableman, Betty, *Governmental Organization in Metropolitan Areas* (Ann Arbor: University of Michigan Press, 1951).

[33] Sweeney and Blair, *op. cit.,* p. 80.

Articles

Bain, Chester W., "Annexation: Virginia's Not-so-judicial System," *Public Administration Review, 15* (Autumn, 1955), 251–62.

Blakeman, T. L., "Detroit's Regional Plan," *National Municipal Review, 44* (October, 1955), 466–70.

Bromage, A. W., "Political Representation in Metropolitan Areas," *American Political Science Review, 52* (June, 1958), 406–18.

Crouch, Winston, "Metropolitan Government in Toronto," *Public Administration Review, 14* (Spring, 1954), 85–95.

Gulick, Luther H., "Metropolitan Organization," *Annals of the American Academy of Political and Social Science, 314* (November, 1957), 57–65.

Hughes, M. C., "Annexation and Reallocation of Functions," *Public Management, 34* (February, 1952), 26–30.

Jones, Victor, "Associations of Local Governments: Patterns for Metropolitan Cooperation," *Public Affairs Reports, 2* (April, 1962), 1–5.

Jones, Victor, "The Organization of a Metropolitan Region," *University of Pennsylvania Law Review, 105* (February, 1957), 538–52.

Scott, Stanley and Corzine, John, "Special Districts in the San Francisco Bay Area: An Excess of Home Rule?" *Public Affairs Report, 3* (October, 1962), 1–2.

Toulmin, Harry, "First Metropolitan Government Created," *Public Management, 39* (July, 1957), 151–3.

Wood, Robert C., "A Division of Powers in Metropolitan Areas," paper presented at annual meeting of American Political Science Association, Washington, September 6, 1956.

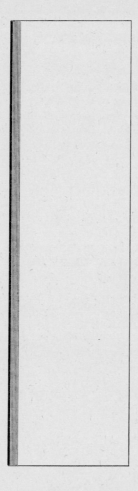

A LOOK AHEAD

Eight

The Prospect of
Local Government

27

From the discussion in the preceding chapters, it is clear that the performance of local government seldom achieves the promise expected by its most ardent supporters. On the other hand, its performance has far exceeded that envisioned by the prophets of doom who have predicted its demise. The rather paradoxical position of local government in the second half of the twentieth century was pointed out in Chapter 1. Although the services rendered are increasingly important, citizen attention is centered on the problems and performance of higher levels of government.

This chapter will focus on the role of local governments in the foreseeable future without attempting to get science-fictiony. Barring unexpected developments, that role will continue to be an important one, for local governments do provide services and make policies that shape the communities in which Americans live, work, and play. While these policies were largely limited to housekeeping functions in the past, local governments are now called upon to determine and achieve goals of social policy. This larger role envisions their continuing and increasingly successful struggle to ameliorate the effects of certain dilemmas resulting from conflicts between theory and practice. Roscoe Martin has described these efforts as the "permanent preoccupation of a democracy which is always striving but never quite achieving."[1]

■ Rural-Urban Values

The transformation of our nation from a rural-agrarian to an urban-industrial one has been sufficiently documented in previous chapters. However, the romanticized myth of small, responsive, democratic communities as the backbone of our governmental system remains almost intact. While the trends of urbanization and suburbanization of our population are certain to continue in the foreseeable future, the agrarian myth is almost as certain to persist.

The general shibboleths surrounding rural government and democracy cast considerable doubt about big units of local government. In summary form, these charges assess big government as being (1) more impersonal and less human, (2) less subject to popular control, (3) more subject to political control, (4) more out of touch with local conditions, (5) less flexible, (6) more bureaucratic, and, as a result, (7) less democratic than rural grass-roots government.[2] Martin allows that there is much that is virtuous in local rural government, but that a careful reappraisal must assess its performance at least one step this side of perfection. Recent assessments of big city governments, on the other hand, stress the transformation which has made them among the most skillfully managed American corporations.[3]

Martin concludes that the conditions of government in rural America are less hospitable to a favorable climate for democracy than is true in more urban areas. He describes rural government as "too picayune, too narrow in outlook, too limited in horizon, too self-centered in interests, to challenge the imagination or to enlist the support of the voter."[4]

Thus both rural and large urban governments have similar problems in challenging and enlisting citizen support. In many rural

---

[1] Roscoe C. Martin, *Grass Roots*, University of Alabama Press, 1957, p. 79.

[2] *Ibid.*, p. 69.

[3] See for example Seymour Freedgood, "New Strength in City Hall," in Fortune Magazine (ed.), *The Exploding Metropolis*, Doubleday, 1958, p. 62 ; and Wallace Sayre and Herbert Kaufman, *Governing New York City*, Russell Sage Foundation, 1960.

[4] Martin, *op. cit.*, pp. 91-92.

A LOOK AHEAD

units, the problem exists because of small size, and it exists in our larger urban areas because the citizenry is so large that it is difficult to reach and enlist the support of all the groups within it. Its solution is particularly important since population projections envision a population of about 260 million persons within the United States by 1980. Of this number, approximately three-fourths—more than 190 million—will be living within metropolitan areas.

Unless current trends are altered, population within metropolitan areas will continue to be distributed somewhat along economic and racial lines. According to William H. Whyte, "the city is becoming a place of extremes—a place for the very rich, or the very poor, or the slightly odd. Here and there, in pleasant tree-shaded neighborhoods, there are still islands of middle-class stability, but for young couples on the way up—most young couples at any rate—these are neighborhoods of the past. They are often the last stand of an ethnic group, and the people in them are getting old."[5]

The racial composition of population growth in our 10 largest cities in the past decade is shown in Table 24 and Figure 31. Only two of these cities—Los Angeles and Houston—had an increasing white population during the past decade, while Washington showed a net loss of one of every three white citizens and St. Louis and Baltimore each lost approximately one-fourth of their white citizenry. All 10 cities, on the other hand, showed increases of 40 percent or more in their non-white populations. Los Angeles had the greatest increase—slightly over 97 percent, but increases of 60 percent or greater occurred in four other cities. As of 1960, the non-white population comprised nearly 55 percent of the citizenry of our nation's capital, 35 percent in Baltimore, and approximately one-fourth or more in six of the other eight largest cities.

To some persons, Thomas Jefferson's words, penned in his *Notes on Virginia* in 1782, still reflect life in big cities. He stated, "The mobs of great cities add just so much to the support of pure government, as sores do to the strength of the human body." Today, there is no question but that rural America remains important, but no one can seriously doubt that our culture and politics are dominated by our urban communities. The small communities which once produced the leadership for our states and nation now face serious problems of their own, just as do the large urban centers. Thus,

[5] William H. Whyte, Jr., "Introduction," in Fortune Magazine, *op. cit.,* pp. viii–ix.

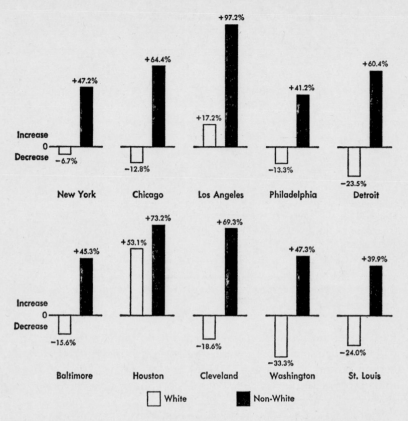

Figure 31. *Percent Change in Population, White and Non-White, in the Ten Largest Cities: 1950–1960.* (Advisory Commission on Intergovernmental Relations, *Government Structure, Organization, and Planning in Metropolitan Areas*, Washington, Government Printing Office, 1961, p. 7.)

the basic problems differ more in degree than in kind as local government strives to become a positive force in achieving richer, fuller lives for its citizens.

■ *Too Many, Too Little*

As noted in Chapter 3, the Commission on Intergovernmental Relations coined the illuminating phrase "too many local governments, not enough local government." The existence of over 91,000

Table 24. *Racial Composition and Growth Rate, 1950–1960, in Our Ten Largest Cities*

City	Total Population 1960	Non-white as a Percent of Total Population 1960	1950
New York	7,781,984	14.7	9.8
Chicago	3,350,404	23.6	14.1
Los Angeles	2,479,015	16.8	10.7
Philadelphia	2,002,512	26.7	18.3
Detroit	1,670,144	29.2	16.4
Baltimore	939,024	35.0	23.8
Houston	938,219	23.2	21.1
Cleveland	876,050	28.9	12.3
Washington	763,956	54.8	35.4
St. Louis	750,026	28.8	18.0

SOURCE: Advisory Commission on Intergovernmental Relations, *Governmental Structure, Organization, and Planning in Metropolitan Areas,* Government Printing Office, 1961, p. 7.

local governmental units would seem to substantiate the first part of the indictment. The combination of state hesitation to grant certain powers to local communities and the failure of many local units to exercise powers they have been granted gives credence to the second part, also.

The superstructure of local government in the United States is indeed a complicated one. The typical citizen lives under several layers of local government including, in most cases, a county, a municipality, a school district, and one or more special districts. This patchwork pattern is both uneconomical and confusing to the citizen who tries to perform his civic responsibilities of maintaining an interest in and participating in the affairs of his community.

There have been many prescriptions for simplifying the structure of local government. Of these, only one—the move for consolidation of small school districts—has achieved acceptance. Because of this success, many students of local government are now more optimistic concerning the consolidation of other local governmental jurisdictions in the years ahead.

Consolidation of counties has been widely advocated as a desirable step in local reorganization, and many states have constitutional or statutory provisions authorizing the voluntary consolidation of con-

THE PROSPECT OF LOCAL GOVERNMENT   593

tiguous counties. The progress of voluntary county consolidation, however, has been extremely slow. Since the beginning of the present century, there have been only two consolidations, and neither involved only rural counties.[6]

While the movement toward school district consolidation has been proceeding for the past three decades, it can be expected to continue at least for another decade or two. In 1962, 15 states each still had over 1,000 school districts,[7] but the consolidation movement is now progressing rapidly in these states. The sharp decline in school districts will probably not continue much beyond the next 10 to 15 years, however. Thirteen states reported slight increases in school districts in the five-year period between 1957 and 1962.

One other area in which consolidation of local governmental units is urged pertains to city-county consolidation in one-county metropolitan areas. The slow progress in this area was noted in the previous chapter, and needs no elaboration at this point. However, it seems reasonable to predict that there will be a limited but increasing number of such consolidations in the coming years as solutions are sought for the governmental problems of our urban areas.

A more promising development in the field of local government is the growing use of functional consolidation. This device involves the cooperation of two or more local governmental units in the performance of a common service. While it has no effect on the number of local governments, it does do away with some duplication, waste and inefficiency in the provision of certain services. Functional consolidations, in the form of interjurisdictional agreements, are in wide use in metropolitan areas, and offer promise for more cooperative relations among rural governments as well.

One other unit of local government figures prominently in most proposals for changing our local governmental structure. There has been widespread advocacy for the abolition of the rural township as it exists in 16 states. The tradition of the township is strong, and such a change will take a number of years to effect. However, evidence points to the transfer of most township functions to other units of local government if not to actual dissolution.

[6] In 1919, James County, Tennessee, consolidated with Hamilton (Chattanooga) County and in 1932 the counties of Campbell and Milton, Georgia, were merged with Fulton (Atlanta) County.

[7] School district figures are from Bureau of the Census, *Governmental Units in 1962*, GC-P6, December, 1962, p. 9.

594

A LOOK AHEAD

be plagued with the problem of generalist versus specialist programs of study. There are important roles for both generalist and
specialist in the conduct of local affairs, and the generalists, except
for the elected executives and legislators, will probably increasingly
rise to policy positions after exercising administrative specialist
functions. Thus, as a recent study of education for careers in the
public service concluded, the educational programs of schools have
a dual responsibility. First, they should prepare students for the
exercise of leadership functions and for the assumption of responsibilities as they rise on the rungs of the career ladder; and, second,
they should equip graduates with the basic knowledge and skills
necessary to enable them to begin and develop in the career
service.[12]

■ An Informed Citizenry

General consensus among students of local government in the
United States holds that there are three principal requisites for good
government. The first two—good structure and honest and competent personnel—have been discussed in the preceding two sections.
The third requisite is an informed, interested and active citizenry,
our concern in this section. Actually, there is a close relationship
among these three conditions. If the third is present, the first two
are likely to exist also. If the citizenry is not active and informed,
the first two conditions can deteriorate to a degree that the community is not well governed.

The problem of citizen apathy and inertia has been discussed in
Chapter 8. No community is faced with complete citizen indifference since some persons are always concerned with government
and its activities, particularly as it relates to their interests. The
greater the citizen abdication of responsibilities, the greater the
influence over the many that can be exercised by the few. If the
theory of the citizen's role in local government were faithfully
carried out in practice, as Wood points out, it would "demand so
much of his time, so great a communion with his neighbors, so high
a competence in public affairs, as to be nearly all-consuming."[13]

There is, however, a middle ground between stark indifference

[12] Stephen B. Sweeney and Thomas J. Davy, *Education for Administrative Careers in Government Service,* University of Pennsylvania Press, 1958, p. 52.

[13] Robert C. Wood, *Suburbia, Its People and Their Politics,* Houghton Mifflin,
1958, p. 97.

and inaction on the one hand, and constant participation and concern on the other. The prepositional trilogy of government "of, by, and for" the people advocated by Lincoln is still of significant value in our local communities. The first condition above—indifference and inaction—represents government "for" the people at its extreme just as the second—constant participation and concern—represents the "by" the people theme. There remains the third preposition—of the people—which is the basis for the middle ground concept mentioned above. This implies that the citizens select persons to act for them and to represent them for a definite term of office. Then these agents are either re-elected for another term or replaced by other persons who are the choice of a majority of the citizens voting in that election. This is the essence of representative democracy in which the people retain the power of direction through delegated authority.

To many thoughtful students of local government, one of our most serious problems concerns the alienation of the citizen from the local political process. In part, this estrangement results from the appeal of national and international problems and concerns. A second, and probably more serious, reason is because of commuting citizens—those who reside in one governmental unit and work in another. These daylight citizens cannot participate in the affairs of the community where they work because they are not citizens and the affairs of their dormitory communities seem to be operating satisfactorily and hence they do not participate there either. As a result, they become alienated from the local political and governmental process and become consumers rather than stockholders in their local governments.

Although a more active citizenry is a desirable community goal, there is some evidence to support the belief that what in part appears to be citizen apathy and inertia is really citizen satisfaction. When community crises occur, electorates do become aroused to meet the situations which require community decision. Some persons now support the "crisis" policy of active citizen participation as a proper functioning of the local electorate. While meeting crises satisfactorily is to be commended, preventive rather than corrective community action is even more laudable. Such action spares the community the divisive effects which often accompany crises and the necessity for patching over the misunderstandings inevitably accompanying them.

A LOOK AHEAD

Most listings of current problems of local government are statements of service needs and lags. While there are many financial and administrative problems involved in providing new and extended services to citizens, the more basic problem has been identified as that of "cultivating more enlightened civic leadership and more understanding support for such leadership."[14] These same authors issue a stirring appeal for a more active citizenry by stating:

> If the ordinary citizen would simply raise his sights to what his city, his county, his school district, and his state could be if everyone cared just a little more about the common good—and would then bestir himself a bit toward the fulfillment of that vision—there is hardly any limit to what could be accomplished. There would be disappointments and defeats, but the effort would also bring rich rewards, for the toil and danger of an active citizenship are compensated by the fun and satisfaction it affords. Pasteur was right: democracy flourishes when every man contributes his best to the community. But the citizen flourishes, too.[15]

■ *Relations with Higher Levels*

Democratic local government in a federal system faces two perplexing problems. These concern the distribution of powers and functions among the governmental levels and the pattern of representation for comprising legislative bodies at higher levels. Both of these problems are of great importance to local governments, and vitally affect the future of our miniature republics.

The substitution of the concept of a "marble-cake" federalism to replace the outmoded view of a three-tier layer-cake in describing our federal system was discussed in Chapter 5. This newer approach is a more realistic one recognizing that aspects of functions rather than functions themselves are assigned to the three governmental levels. There is increasing intergovernmental activity in service areas once considered responsibilities of local governments and private agencies, and local governments are encouraged to undertake new programs of services and activities with financial assistance from higher levels. As the budgets and activities of local

---

[14] Henry A. Turner and John A. Vieg, *The Government and Politics of California*, McGraw-Hill, 1960, p. 266.

[15] *Ibid.*, pp. 266–7.

governments continue to grow, only the most pessimistic observers of our governmental scene continue to predict their demise.

However, there is some concern over the role that local governmental units will assume in the future. Some persons view local governments only as administrative units to carry out the policies and programs of their creating state government. Others see the policy role of local governments as an expanding one making them even stronger political communities. In all probability, both roles will be maintained in the years ahead. In those areas where the state enacts social policy, the local community will administer these within its boundaries. There will be other areas of social policy, however, where the state will not act and where the local community will be called upon to initiate, enact, and enforce policy. In addition, local communities will play an increasing role in shaping those policies which are enacted by the state.

The second problem—the pattern of representation of local governments in state legislatures—remains a thorny one. In general, the pattern has been one of under-representation of urban areas to the advantage of less populated units. An excellent summary of this condition was stated in an *amicus* brief by the National Institute of Municipal Law Officers before the Supreme Court in the historic case, *Baker* v. *Carr*, in 1962. This brief stated in part:

Regardless of the fact that in the last two decades the United States has become a predominantly urban country where well over two-thirds of the population now lives in cities or suburbs, political representation in the majority of state legislatures is 50 or more years behind the times. Apportionments made when the greater part of the population was located in rural communities are still determining and undermining our election.

As a consequence, the municipality of 1960 is forced to function in a horse and buggy environment where there is little political recognition of the heavy demands of an urban population. These demands will become even greater by 1970 when some 150 million people will be living in urban areas. . . .

Since World War II, the explosion of city and suburban population has created intense local problems in education, transportation, and housing. Adequate handling of these problems has not been possible to a large extent, due chiefly to the political weakness of municipalities. This situation is directly attributable to considerable under-representation of cities in the legislatures of most states.[16]

[16] *Baker* v. *Carr*, U.S. 186, 249 (1962), Prelim. Print.

As a result of this Supreme Court decision that allegations of denial of equal protection present a justifiable case under the Fourteenth Amendment, suits of citizens concerning patterns of apportionment have been filed in about three-fourths of the states. In a second important case decided in 1963, the Supreme Court took another major step to end discrimination of urban residents at the ballot box. By a vote of eight to one, it struck down the county unit system in Georgia which operated to give voters of rural counties extra weight in choosing statewide officers.[17] One statement in the language of the majority opinion written by Justice William O. Douglas seemed particularly significant. He wrote, "The conception of political equality from the Declaration of Independence, to Lincoln's Gettysburg Address, to the 15th, 17th and 19th Amendments can mean only one thing—one person, one vote."

While this view has been advanced as the proper basis of representation by leading statesmen and scholars, it has never prevailed widely in practice.[18] In Justice Frankfurter's dissent in *Baker* v. *Carr*, he stated that, "It (political equality) was not the English system, it was not the colonial system, it was not the system chosen for the national government by the Constitution, it was not the system exclusively or even predominantly practiced by the States at the time of adoption of the Fourteenth Amendment, it is not predominantly practiced by the states today."[19] However, it promises to become more of a reality in the future as reapportionment efforts are being undertaken in a number of states and law suits are pending judicial decision in a number of others.

Another almost certain result of the decisions of the Supreme Court in the two cases mentioned above is the encouragement of citizen suits against malportionment in the size of districts comprising local legislative bodies. Indeed, such suits have already been initiated in some states concerning county supervisoral districts. The outcome can never be full equality because of a number of factors, and modest departure from per capita equality can be tolerated. Present conditions in a number of communities, however, would hardly qualify as "modest departures." Discrepancies of nearly 50 to one between the most populous and least populous

[17] *Gray* v. *Sanders*, 9 L ed 2d 821, 830–1.
[18] See, for example, Belle Zeller (ed.), *American State Legislatures*, Crowell, 1954; and Twentieth Century Fund, *One Man—One Vote, A Statement of Basic Principles of Legislative Apportionment*, New York, 1962.
[19] *Baker* v. *Carr*, 369 U.S. 186, 301 (1962).

districts exist in some counties and distorted ratios also exist in a number of cities. If metropolitan government becomes a wider reality, it is highly probable that problems just as acute as those pertaining to proper representation in state legislatures would develop in these communities between the claimants for representation plans based on population and those supporting representation based on existing local units.

■ Provision of Adequate Services

As noted in Chapter 25, the failure to provide adequate services has been described by Gulick as the most obvious governmental failure in our big urban regions. Discussing the inadequacy of various remedial measures which have been attempted, Gulick concludes that "Many of the heralded 'solutions' have only made matters worse. In fact, conditions are generally deteriorating, and deteriorating fast, even with respect to the services where dramatic 'solutions' have been adopted. Traffic, slums, commuter services, schools, water supplies, water and air pollution, urban crime, noise and dirt—one has only to mention these to recognize the facts."[20]

The need for more adequate services in rural and smaller urban communities has also been noted in the chapters on public services. Thus, the problem of providing the necessary and essential services under existing financial limits is a common one to most of our governmental units. The hub of this problem has been aptly stated by one writer in these words: "The difficulty of pricing public goods results because consumer-voter-taxpayers do not reveal their preferences. If they were to make known their true demand for public goods, the proper quantity and quality could be produced and the appropriate benefit tax levied. In the absence of preference information, the rational consumer of public goods will tend to understate his demand, hoping to benefit without paying or by paying as little as possible."[21] He concludes, "Citizens can always vote for changes in services and taxes but the method is slow and produces incomplete results. As a further alternative, residents can

[20] Luther H. Gulick, *The Metropolitan Problem and American Ideas*, Knopf, 1962, p. 3.
[21] Werner Z. Hirsch, "Urban Government Services and Their Financing" in Hirsch (ed.), *Urban Life and Form*, Holt, Rinehart & Winston, 1963, p. 134.

move into another community but generally such extreme action is only taken if large scale incentives are offered by a rival area."[22]

While it is not feasible to take up major service needs and discuss the problems they present and the difficulties inherent in ameliorating them individually, it seems most likely that heavy service demands will continue in our local communities. It is also highly probable that citizens will increasingly turn to their local governments for help in meeting these needs and will come to depend more upon government for such services. As this occurs, local governments will be forced to work cooperatively to an extent which far exceeds current intergovernmental arrangements. Working together to solve mutual concerns and meet common needs could conceivably pave the way for a new breakthrough in cooperative relations among local governments and serve as a testing ground for and a means to produce more effective local leadership both in metropolitan areas and in less urban and rural communities.

■ Concluding Statement

Great changes have taken place in American local government since the beginning of the present century. The "shame of the cities" era of local government, with its graft, corruption and inefficiency has been replaced by honest, competent administration in most local governments. The limited role of government in earlier years has been replaced by positive actions to advance and improve the amenities of community life. The tools and techniques needed to improve local governments are known and are receiving increasing adoption and use.

Any attempt to prophesy the future course of American local government in detail would require a non-existent crystal ball. However, a general prediction can be ventured with a considerable degree of confidence. Barring unforeseen developments, it seems reasonable to predict that the future of American local governments is a bright one. They have made great strides in satisfying citizen demands and in providing a satisfying environment within local communities. Even more important, their record is one of continuing improvement—one deserving of citizen support and understanding in the years ahead.

[22] *Ibid.*, p. 135.

SUGGESTED READINGS

Books

Advisory Commission on Local Government, *Local Government, A Report to the Commission on Intergovernmental Relations* (Washington: Government Printing Office, 1955).

Anderson, William, *The Units of Government in the United States* (Chicago: Public Administration Service, 1945, 1949).

Carpenter, William S., *Problems in Service Levels: The Readjustment of Services and Areas in Local Government* (Princeton: Princeton University Press, 1940).

Drucker, Peter F., *America's Next Twenty Years* (New York: Harper, 1957).

Gardner, John W., *Excellence, Can We Be Equal and Excellent Too?* (New York: Harper & Row, 1961).

Gulick, Luther, *The Metropolitan Problem and American Ideas* (New York: Knopf, 1962).

Maass, Arthur (ed.), *Area and Power, A Theory of Local Government* (New York: Free Press, 1959).

Martin, Roscoe C., *Grass Roots* (University, Ala.: University of Alabama Press, 1957).

Thorson, Thomas L., *The Logic of Democracy* (New York: Holt, Rinehart & Winston, 1962).

Tussman, Joseph, *Obligation and the Body Politic* (New York: Oxford University Press, 1960).

Articles

Bailey, Stephen K., "Leadership in Local Government," *Yale Review,* 45 (Summer, 1956), 563–73.

Blair, George S., "A New Look at the 'Dark Continent' of American Politics," *The County Officer,* 19 (September, 1954), 182–6, 194.

Cassella, William N., "County Government in Transition," *Public Administration Review,* 16 (Summer, 1956), 223–31.

Havard, W. C. and Diamant, Alfred, "The Need for Local Government Reform in the United States," *Western Political Quarterly,* 9 (December, 1956), 967–95.

Herson, Lawrence J. R., "The Lost World of Municipal Government," *American Political Science Review,* 51 (June, 1957), 330–44.

Long, Norton E., "Aristotle and the Study of Local Government," paper presented at American Political Science Association, Boulder, Colorado, September 8, 1955.

INDEXES

Index of Names

Adams, Thomas, 502
Adrian, Charles R., 138–139, 216, 220–221, 309–310, 341–342, 351, 382, 450–451, 504, 528–529, 562
Alderfer, Harold F., 289, 386, 477, 516–517
Alexander, John W., 231
Ames, John H., 339–340
Anderson, William, 12, 44, 57–58, 83
Aristotle, 52–53
Asseff, Emmett, 255, 259

Bailey, Stephen K., 15–16, 294, 595–596
Banfield, Edward C., 133–134, 300–301, 549–550
Bassett, Edward M., 504, 506–507
Bauer, John, 490, 498
Beard, Charles A., 132, 139, 158
Bensman, Joseph, 235–236, 270–271
Benson, George C. S., 97
Bent, Frederick T., 292–293
Berger, Morroe, 231
Blair, George S., 569, 585
Bollens, John C., 244, 254–255, 258, 546, 554–555, 561, 567, 571, 576–577, 584
Bowman, Emma L., 373
Bromage, Arthur W., 271–272, 286–287, 331–332, 342
Brown, William H., Jr., 373
Bryce, James, 9
Buck, A. E., Jr., 364
Buehler, Alfred, 381
Burnham, Daniel, 503
Butler, George D., 472–473

Cardozo, Benjamin, 62
Carpenter, William S., 43
Chamberlain, Lawrence H., 164
Charlesworth, James C., 369, 475
Cherrington, Charles R., 578
Childs, Richard S., 151, 212–213
Chute, Charlton F., 540
Clark, Joseph S., 469
Coke, James G., 546
Cook, William A., 455
Coolidge, Calvin, 83
Connery, Robert F., 96
Contalonia, G. T., 247

Crouch, Winston W., 579

Dahl, Robert, 121
Davy, Thomas J., 293–294
Dillon, John, 61

Ebel, Alice L., 286
Eliot, Thomas H., 246, 458, 463
Emerson, Haven, 430, 433, 436–437
Eulau, Heinz, 269–270

Fairlie, John A., 478–479
Fitch, Lyle C., 554
Forbes, Russell, 371
Ford, John A., 166
Fordham, Jefferson, 76
Frank, Bernard, 490
Franklin, Benjamin, 406
Freedgood, Seymour, 133, 302–303, 305–306

Gardner, John W., 470–471
Gaus, John M., 338
Gilbert, Charles E., 373
Grace, A. G., 250
Graves, W. Brooke, 363
Grazia, Sebastian de, 474–475
Greer, Scott, 545, 550, 553
Grimes, Alan P., 502
Grodzins, Morton, 85, 549–550
Gulick, Luther H., 132–133, 198, 292, 544, 547, 551, 557–560, 566–568, 574, 602

Hallett, George H., Jr., 276
Harrell, C. A., 307–308
Harris, Joseph S., 149
Hawley, Amos, 530
Hillhouse, A. M., 398–399
Hirsch, Werner Z., 602–603
Hodges, Henry G., 406, 418, 484, 491
Hollingsworth, Frank, 323
Holly, Hazel, 420–421
Holmes, Oliver W., 314
Hosmer, James K., 24
Howard, George E., 478
Hyneman, Charles S., 28, 106

Iacaboni, Angelo M., 581

Jackson, Andrew, 350
James, Charles S., 419–420
Jefferson, Thomas, 198, 591

Jones, Victor, 546, 565–566, 570–571

Kaplan, H. Eliot, 347
Kaufman, Herbert, 279
Kefauver, Estes, 97
Kendrick, W. Slade, 389
Kennedy, John F., 83–84
Kent, Frank R., 126–127
Kinnard, William N., 300
Kneier, Charles M., 143, 478–479
Kreml, Franklin M., 485

Lancaster, Lane W., 241
La Palombara, J. G., 158
Lasswell, Harold, 104
Leach, Richard H., 96
Lepawsky, Albert, 335, 553
Lieberman, Myron, 465
Long, Norton E., 559–560
Luginbuhl, Martha, 430, 433, 436–437

MacDonald, Austin F., 497–498
MacDougall, William R., 448
McGeary, M. Nelson, 287
MacIver, Robert, 7
Mackesey, Thomas W., 521
McKinley, John R., 387–388
McLean, Joseph E., 561
McMillan, T. E., 75
McMillen, Wayne, 439
MacMillin, F. N., 271
McQuillin, Eugene, 65, 72
Martin, Roscoe C., 134, 259, 298, 557, 590, 595
Meier, Richard L., 513
Merriam, Charles E., 553
Meyerson, Martin, 133–134, 300–301, 506, 541–542
Mill, John Stuart, 53, 75, 268–269
Millett, John D., 368
Mills, C. Wright, 105
Millspaugh, Arthur, 12
Moak, Lennox L., 373
Moe, G. A., 250
Moehlman, Arthur B., 454
Morgan, Arthur E., 11
Moynihan, Daniel P., 469
Munro, William B., 119–120, 153

Nolen, John, Jr., 509

O'Rourke, Lawrence, 119

Parker, W. H., 409–410
Parkinson, C. Northcote, 389
Parratt, Spencer D., 553
Perry, James M., 547–548
Peterson, Elmer, 198
Phillips, J. C., 410
Pickard, Jerome P., 540–541
Plato, 52
Pope, Herman G., 340
Porter, Kirk H., 144, 281
Price, Douglas, 557
Price, H. D., 119

Reed, Henry G., 503
Ridley, Clarence E., 307, 344
Riordon, W. L., 161
Robbins, L. H., 224
Robins, Lee N., 556–557
Rossiter, Clinton, 126
Rowe, L. S., 198

Sayre, Wallace S., 211–212, 279
Scott, Stanley, 256–257
Sherwood, Frank P., 555
Simon, Herbert A., 344
Sly, John F., 232
Smillie, W. G., 430
Smith, Adam, 382
Smith, Bruce, 410–411
Smith, Chester H., 320
Smith, T. V., 265
Snider, Clyde F., 241, 297, 442–443
Stone, Donald C., 508–509
Strayer, Paul J., 389
Sweeney, Stephen B., 585

Tead, Orway, 292, 294
Terrett, Barbara, 541–542
Tocqueville, Alexis de, 9
Trecker, Harleigh B., 502
Truman, Harry S, 125
Tunnard, Christopher, 503
Turner, Henry A., 204, 599

Vanderbilt, Arthur T., 327–329
Vidich, Arthur J., 235–236, 270–271
Vieg, John A., 204, 599

Waldo, Dwight, 332–333, 339
Walker, Robert A., 503–504, 519–520
Wallace, Schuyler, 74
Warner, Kenneth O., 346
Webber, Melvin M., 512–513
Webster, Donald H., 502, 514
Weiford, D. G., 307–308
Wells, Roger H., 227
Wendell, Mitchell, 98
White, Leonard D., 355
Whitlock, Brand, 137, 152
Whyte, William H., Jr., 591
Williams, Oliver P., 139
Willoughby, W. F., 314–315
Wilson, O. W., 413
Wilson, Woodrow, 134, 351
Wood, Robert C., 140, 168–169, 555–
    556, 597
Woodbury, Coleman, 545

Ylvisaker, Paul N., 294–295, 527–528,
    558

Zimmerman, F. L., 98

Index of Subjects

INDEX OF SUBJECTS

Eminent domain, 571
Employment, local, 14–15, 345–351
Executive, forms of local, 296–309
  appointed, 306–310
  divided, 296–298
  strong, 302–306
  weak, 298–302
Executive, local, 290–310
  defined, 292–296
  responsibilities of, 293–294
Executive function, 292–296
Executive officers, 309–310
Expenditures, local, 389–394
  classification of, 390–391
  growth of, 389–390
  mandatory, 393–394
  patterns of, 391–392
Extraterritorial powers, 516

Fair Employment Practices Commissions, 451–452
Federal aid programs, for highways, 91–92
  for hospitals, 92–93, 440–441
  urban planning assistance, 90–91
  urban renewal, 88–89
Federal-local relations, 83–99
  agency of local government, 93–96
  future of, 96–99
  pre-1932, 82–84
  post-1932, 84–99
  programmatic grants, 87–93
Federation, in metropolitan government, 581–582
Fees, as revenue source, 384
Fee-spliting, 321
Felonies, 317
Finance committee, in town government, 229–230
Finances, local, 376–399
  debt administration, 394–399
  expenditures, 389–394
  intergovernmental grants, 386–388
  non-tax revenues, 384–385
  patterns of revenues, 377–379, 388–389
  revenue sources, 379–384
  special assessments, 385–386
Financial planning, 372–374
Financial reporting, 369–370
Fire protection, 415–420
Fiscal management, 355–359
  centralized, 356

Fiscal management (*Continued*)
  decentralized, 359
  officers, 356–358
Fluoridation of water, 493–494
Forms of local government, *see* under specific types
Functional consolidation, 594
Funds, custody of, 365–366

Garbage disposal, 487–489
Governmental character, criterion of, 43–44
Governmental simplification, proposals for, 56–58
Governmental units, criteria of, 42–44; autonomy, 42–43; entity existence, 43; governmental character, 43–44
  types and number, 44–50; cities, 48–49; counties, 45–48; school districts, 50–51; special districts, 50–51; towns and townships, 49–50
Grand jury, 325
Grants-in-aid, federal, 87–93
  state, 386–388
Gray v. *Sanders*, 601

Habeas corpus, writ of, 316
Hare System, 275–276
Health, public, 430–441
  defined, 430
  hospitals, 440–441
  intergovernmental relations in, 433
  as local function, 430
  mental health, 438–440
  organization, 430–431
  services, 435–438
Hearings, public, 168
Highways and streets, 478–481
  administrative organization, 479
  classification, 479–480
  functions of, 480
  intergovernmental relations in, 481
  mileage, 479
Home demonstration agent, 177, 190
Home rule, 66–68
  meaning of, 66
  procedures for adopting charters, 67–68
  types of, 67
Hospitals, 440–441
Housing, public, 449–451

Housing and Home Finance Agency,
85–86, 88, 440
Hundreds, in colonies, 28, 35
in England, 19, 21

Income taxes, local, 382–383
Incorporation procedures, 202–204
Indebtedness, *see* Debt administration
Information for citizens, 165–169
Informed citizenry, 597–599
Inherent right of local government,
theory of, 61–62
Initiative, 154–155, 158–159
appraisal, 158–159
direct, 154
indirect, 154–155
Injunction, 316
Interest groups, 161–165
checks on, 164
criticisms of, 163–164
functions, 163
techniques, 163
Intergovernmental relations, *see* under
specific service fields
Intergovernmental revenues, 386–388
Interlocal relations, 78–80
International City Managers' Association, 219, 295, 364, 473–474, 501

Jacksonian democracy, 114
Judicial controls, 75–76
Judicial process, 312–329
court organization, 318–325
due process of law, 326–328
role of courts, 313–316
types of cases, 316–318
Judicial review, 76–77
Judicial systems, *see* Courts
Jury, grand, 325
Jury, trial, 323–325
Justice, concept of, 312
Justice of peace courts, 319–322
Juvenile delinquency, 413

Lakewood plan, 580–581
Land-use controls, 513–524
building codes, 514–515
subdivision regulations, 515–516
zoning, 516–524
Law enforcement, and intergovernmental relations, 425–427
and local officers, 410–415

Law, types of, 315
Leadership in local government, 595–597
Legislative control, 71–73
Legislative process, 265–269
functions, 266–269
local bodies, 266
Legislators, local, 269–276
functions, 271
roles, 269–270
selection, 272–276; at-large election, 272–274; combination plan, 274–275; limited voting, 275–276; ward election, 274
traits, 271–272
Liability, tort, 317
Library service, 471–472
Library Services Act, 472
Line agency, defined, 334
Literacy, as voting qualification, 112–113
Local government, county system, 26–31
county-township system, 26–31
criterion of power, 54–55
criterion of size, 52–54
defined, 42
English roots, 18–21
future of, 603–604
importance of, 13–17
proposals for simplification, 56–58
territorial plan, 36–38
town system, 21–26
values of, 8–13
Los Angeles, citizen commissions in, 338
fire protection in, 417–418
mental health in, 438–439
police protection in, 413–414
recall in, 153
streets and highways, 480–481
transit in, 498
as urban county, 580–581
voting splits in, 287

Manager, *see* Council-manager plan
Mandamus, writ of, 76, 316
Marble-cake federalism, 85
Master plan, 506, 510–512
Mayor, powers of, 304–305
selection of, 304–305
term of, 303–304
veto by, 305

Mayor-council form, 206–212
  strong mayor, 208–210
  strong mayor with CAO, 210–212
  weak mayor, 206–208
Mental health, 438–440
Merit system, 346–347
Metes-and-bounds, in land description, 515
Metropolitan areas, definition, 51, 530–532
  geographic distribution, 533–536
  number of, 51–52, 532
  population of, 590–592
  size, 536–537
  types of, 538–539; bi-county, 538; international, 539; interstate, 538–539; intra-county, 538; multi-county, 538
Metropolitan government, evaluation, 584–585
  principles of, 561–562
  state responsibility, 567
  trends in, 565–568
Metropolitan governmental patterns, 564–585
  annexation, 569–570
  association of local governments, 565–566
  city-county consolidation, 574–576
  city-county separation, 576–577
  direct action by higher levels, 573–574
  federation, 581–584
  functional transfer, 572–573
  interjurisdictional agreements, 568–569
  metropolitan planning, 571–572
  multi-purpose special districts, 577–578
  single-purpose special districts, 570–571
  urban county, 578–581
Metropolitan problems, 544–562
  deficiencies in citizen control, 561–562
  defined, 544–546
  financial inequalities, 554–556
  inadequate government structure, 547–551
  political leadership needs, 558–560
  service and regulatory inadequacies, 551–553
  social, ethnic and racial, 556–558

Minority groups, 117–119, 556–558
Misdemeanor, 317–318
Model County Charter, 506, 508
Model State Constitution, 109
Municipal authorities, 254
Municipal corporations, 60–64
Municipal Finance Officers Association, 362, 364, 371
Municipal ordinances, 281–284
Munn v. *Illinois,* 490

National Commission on School Reorganization, 53
National federalism, 99
National Institute of Municipal Law Officers, 600
National Municipal League, 275
National Resources Committee, 82–83
National Safety Council, 482
Newburgh, New York, 448
New Deal, and local government, 84–85
Newspapers and community, 165–166
Nomination, methods of, 140–145
  caucus, 140–141
  convention, 141
  direct primary, 142–144
  non-partisan primary, 143
  petition, 141–142
  preferential voting, 142
  self-announcement, 140
Non-conforming uses, 519–520
Non-partisan elections, 136–140
Non-property taxes, 382–384
Non-voting, 119–121
Northwest Ordinance, 6, 36–38, 455–456

Office consolidation, 191
Old-age assistance, 443–444
Old Age and Survivors Insurance, 443–444
Open meetings, 160–161
Optional charters, 68–69, 176
Ordinances, 281–284

Parish, in colonies, 27–28
  in England, 19–20
  in Louisiana, 45, 173
Parking, 486–487
  meters, 487
  types of needs, 487
Parks, 473–474

Format by Faith Nelson
Set in Linotype Caledonia
Composed, printed and bound by The Haddon Craftsmen, Inc.
HARPER & ROW, PUBLISHERS, INCORPORATED

Format by Faith Nelson
Set in Linotype Caledonia
Composed, printed and bound by The Haddon Craftsmen, Inc.
HARPER & ROW, PUBLISHERS, INCORPORATED

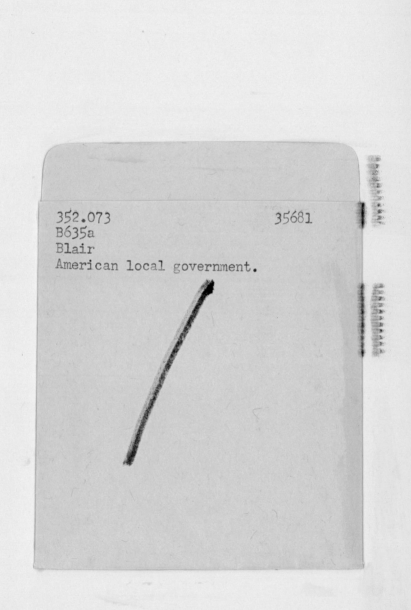

QUALIFICATIONS FOR VOTING

State	Minimum Age	U.S. Citizen	RESIDENCE IN State	County	District	Literacy Test	Poll Tax
Alabama	21	Yes	2 yrs.	1 yr.	3 mo.	—	Yes
Alaska	19	Yes	1 yr.		30 da.	English	—
Arizona	21	Yes	1 yr.	30 da.	30 da.	Yes	—
Arkansas	21	Yes	12 mo.	6 mo.	1 mo.	—	Yes
California	21	90 da.	1 yr.	90 da. (d)	54 da.	Yes	—
Colorado	21	Yes	1 yr.	90 da.	15 da.	—	—
Connecticut	21	Yes	1 yr.	—	6 mo.	Yes	—
Delaware	21	Yes	1 yr.	3 mo.	30 da.	Yes	—
Florida	21	Yes	1 yr.	6 mo.	—	—	—
Georgia	18	Yes	1 yr.	6 mo.	—	Yes	—
Hawaii	20	Yes	1 yr.	—	3 mo.	Yes	—
Idaho	21	Yes	6 mo.	30 da.	—	—	—
Illinois	21	Yes	1 yr.	90 da.	30 da.	—	—
Indiana	21	Yes	6 mo.	60 da. (b)	30 da.	—	—
Iowa	21	Yes	6 mo.	60 da.	10 da.	—	—
Kansas	21	Yes	6 mo.	30 da. (b)	30 da.	—	—
Kentucky	18	Yes	1 yr.	6 mo.	60 da.	—	—
Louisiana	21	Yes	1 yr.	1 yr.	3 mo.	Yes	—
Maine	21	Yes	6 mo.	3 mo.	3 mo.	Yes	—
Maryland	21	Yes	1 yr.	6 mo.	6 mo.	—	—
Massachusetts	21	Yes	1 yr.	—	6 mo. (c)	Yes	—
Michigan	21	Yes	6 mo.	—	30 da.	—	—
Minnesota	21	90 da.	6 mo.	—	—	—	—
Mississippi	21	Yes	2 yrs.	—	1 yr.	Yes	Yes
Missouri	21	Yes	1 yr. (d)	60 da.	60 da.	—	—
Montana	21	Yes	1 yr.	30 da.	—	—	—
Nebraska	21	Yes	6 mo.	40 da.	10 da.	—	—
Nevada	21	Yes	6 mo.	30 da.	10 da.	—	—
New Hampshire	21	Yes	6 mo.	—	6 mo.	Yes	—
New Jersey	21	Yes	6 mo.	60 da.	—	—	—
New Mexico	21	Yes	12 mo.	90 da.	30 da.	—	—
New York	21	90 da.	1 yr.	4 mo.	30 da.	Yes	—
North Carolina	21	Yes	1 yr.	—	30 da.	Yes	—
North Dakota	21	Yes	1 yr.	90 da.	30 da.	—	—
Ohio	21	Yes	1 yr. (d)	40 da.	40 da.	—	—
Oklahoma	21	Yes	1 yr.	6 mo.	30 da.	—	—
Oregon	21	Yes	6 mo. (d)	—	30 da.	Yes	—
Pennsylvania	21	Yes	1 yr.	—	60 da.	—	—
Rhode Island	21	Yes	1 yr.	—	6 mo.	—	—
South Carolina	21	Yes	2 yrs.	1 yr.	4 mo.	(e)	—
South Dakota	21	Yes	1 yr.	90 da.	30 da.	—	—
Tennessee	21	Yes	12 mo.	3 mo.	—	—	—
Texas	21	Yes	1 yr.	6 mo.	6 mo.	—	Yes
Utah	21	90 da.	1 yr.	4 mo.	60 da.	—	—
Vermont	21	Yes	1 yr.	—	3 mo. (b)	—	—
Virginia	21	Yes	1 yr.	6 mo.	30 da.	Yes	(f)
Washington	21	Yes	1 yr.	90 da.	30 da.	Yes	—
West Virginia	21	Yes	1 yr.	60 da.	—	—	—
Wisconsin	21	Yes	1 yr.	—	10 da.	—	—
Wyoming	21	Yes	1 yr.	60 da.	10 da.	Yes	—

(a) All states which have permanent registration, except Alabama, Delaware, Florida, Maine, Mississippi, Nebraska, New Hampshire, and South Dakota make it subject to cancellation for failure to vote at certain specified intervals.

(b) Township.

(c) In city or town.

(d) When voting for Presidential and Vice Presidential electors, a shorter period is required.

(e) Ownership of property is an alternative to literacy.

(f) Must owe no past due taxes.